The RIVERSIDE READER

The RIVERSIDE READER

FOURTH EDITION

Joseph F. Trimmer
Ball State University

Maxine Hairston
University of Texas at Austin

Houghton Mifflin Company Boston Toronto
Dallas Geneva, Illinois Palo Alto Princeton, New Jersey

Senior Sponsoring Editor: Dean Johnson
Associate Project Editor: Danielle Carbonneau
Design/Production Coordinator: Renée LeVerrier
Senior Manufacturing Coordinator: Marie Barnes
Marketing Manager: George Kane

Cover design by Perennial Design. Cover Image: The Image Bank/Daniel Weinberg.

Acknowledgments: Copyrights and Acknowledgments appear on pages 665–668, which constitute a continuation of the copyright page.

Printed in the U.S.A.

Library of Congress Catalogue Card Number: 92-72402

ISBN: 0-395-61962-9

123456789 = CW = 96 95 94 93 92

CONTENTS

of sending lawbreakers to prison for long terms, exposing cultural smugness and ignorance behind these value judgments.

DAVID HAGE et al. *Hidden Monopolies* 607

A group of investigative reporters documents how monopolies, often aided by government regulations, raise prices for millions of American consumers.

BARBARA EHRENREICH *Marginal Men* 618

A social critic uses case histories to exemplify her concept of "marginal men," young suburban males she sees as increasingly likely to become criminals because they have acquired expensive tastes but not the means to afford them.

LUCY KAVALER *Of Riot, Murder, and the Heat of Passion* 624

A scientist cites case studies, anecdotes, statistics, and folklore to document her conclusion that people everywhere tend to react to high temperatures with more violent and uncontrolled behavior.

DIANE JOHNSON *Rape* 637

Examining the social and psychological complexities of rape, this novelist concludes that effective solutions for this crime will have to come primarily from women.

FRANK O'CONNOR *Guests of the Nation* 650

This story, set in twentieth-century Ireland, dramatizes the tragic choices that ordinary men are forced to make when they are drawn into the vicious and seemingly endless conflict between the Irish rebels and the British Army.

Index 669

ALTERNATE THEMATIC TABLE OF CONTENTS

The Other

The Woman's Perspective

The Family

Heroes

Teaching and Learning

Leisure and the Arts

Science and Technology

Business and Ethics

PREFACE

The fourth edition of *The Riverside Reader,* like its predecessors, presents essays by acknowledged masters of prose style, including George Orwell, Flannery O'Connor, Maya Angelou, and Russell Baker, along with many new voices, such as Mike Rose, Le Ly Hayslip, Lars Eighner, and Deborah Tannen. More than half of the selections are new to this edition. As always, introductions, readings, study questions, and writing assignments are arranged in a simple, clear, and cogent design.

FEATURES OF THE FOURTH EDITION

At the center of *The Riverside Reader* is our desire to assist students in their reading and writing by helping them to understand the interaction between these two processes.

- □ The **connection between the reading and writing processes** is highlighted in the general introduction. The familiar terminology of *purpose, audience,* and *strategy* provides a framework for the introduction and for subsequent study questions and writing assignments.

- A **new annotated essay** appears in the general introduction—"Execution" by Anna Quindlen. The annotations illustrate how a reader responds to her reading by writing.
- In each section introduction, an **annotated paragraph,** such as the excerpt from Maxine Hong Kingston's "A Song for a Barbarian Reed Pipe," concisely demonstrates reading and writing strategies at work.
- This edition contains **twenty-six new selections,** among them Tom and Ray Magliozzi's "Inside the Engine," Rose del Castillo Guilbault's "Americanization Is Tough on 'Macho'," and Alice Stewart Trillin's "Of Dragons and Garden Peas." The complete collection, which includes popular essays from previous editions, provides a variety of readings to engage the interest of all students.
- **The selections in the Persuasion and Argument section are paired** to present different perspectives on issues of race, animal rights, business ethics, and the economy. This feature reflects our continuing emphasis on analytical and interpretive reading and writing.
- A **short story** concludes each section to provide an interesting perspective on a particular writing strategy and to give students opportunities to broaden their reading skills. New to this edition are W. D. Wetherell's "The Bass, the River, and Sheila Mant," Paule Marshall's "To Da-duh, In Memoriam," and Frank O'Connor's "Guests of the Nation."
- **Study questions and writing assignments** throughout the text have been extensively revised.
- A thematically organized final section, **Resources for Writing,** focuses on the subject of crime and includes seven essays, each exemplifying one rhetorical mode, and one short story. The writing assignments following each reading encourage students to use what they already know to *respond, analyze,* and *argue* about the essays.

THE RIVERSIDE READER TRADITION

The first seven sections in this reader are arranged in a sequence that is familiar to most writing teachers. Beginning with narration and description, moving through the five expository patterns, and ending with persuasion and argument, these sections group readings according to traditional writing strategies.

Each of the sections begins with a simple, direct introduction previewing that writing strategy and helping the student become an active reader of that type of writing. The introduction to each selection (headnote) contains basic biographical information about the author. Together, this introductory material focuses on four questions about the writing situation: *Who* is writing? What is the writer's *purpose? Whom* is the writer addressing? *How* does the writer accomplish his or her purpose?

The readings within each section have been chosen to illustrate what the section introductions say they illustrate: there are no strange hybrids or confusing models. Within each section, the selections are arranged in ascending order of length and complexity; that is, the readings at the beginning are generally shorter and simpler; those near the end are longer and more complicated. *The Riverside Reader* contains writing by the best traditional and contemporary authors.

The study questions placed at the end of each selection are organized according to a consistent pattern. The questions ask students to respond to their reading, to apply the information presented in the section introductions, and to extend and sharpen their thinking about each essay.

The ultimate purpose of *The Riverside Reader* is to produce writing. For that reason, the writing assignments in this book are presented as the culminating activity of each section. Six assignments at the end of each section ask students to write essays that cover a range of writing tasks from personal response to analysis and argument.

For those instructors who prefer to organize their courses

in terms of themes or issues, an alternate thematic table of contents follows the annotated table of contents.

Instructor's Guide

The new Instructor's Resource Manual by Rai Peterson of Ball State University is available to any instructor using *The Riverside Reader.* The Manual includes extensive rhetorical analysis of each essay and story, reading quizzes, and vocabulary lists. The Manual also includes advice on teaching the reading and writing strategies.

ACKNOWLEDGMENTS

We are grateful to the following writing instructors who have shared with us their responses to *The Riverside Reader* for this revision:

Elaine Bobrove, Camden County College, NJ
Linda Daigle, Houston Community College, TX
Barbara Huval, Lamar University–Port Arthur, TX
Charles Piltch, John Jay Community College of Criminal Justice, NY
Donna Schouman, Macomb Community College, MI
Janet Streepy, Indiana University Southeast
Robin Visel, Furman University, SC

Special thanks go to Karen Taylor for her help in manuscript preparation. And of course, our debt to our students is ongoing.

INTRODUCTION

As a college student, you are necessarily a reader and a writer. Not that either role is new to you—certainly you were a reader and a writer before you started college, and you read and write outside of college. In college, however, you're in a different kind of reading and writing environment: the stakes are higher and you often have to work under pressure. You have to read a broad variety of material, some of it difficult and unfamiliar, and write more demanding kinds of assignments, many of them about or in response to your reading. Your success in college depends, in part, on how well you can read and write and how well you can connect these two processes. Why is the connection important? Because the processes interact closely: as you become a more skillful and knowledgeable reader, you will also become a better writer. In turn, as you become a more competent writer, you will become a more skilled reader.

BECOMING A READER WHO WRITES

The first time you read one of the essays or short stories in this book, try to go with the flow of the words, moving along in the direction the author wants to take you. Enjoy what you're reading just because it's entertaining or because you're learning something. Unless you get really lost and have to backtrack to find the idea, don't stop very often to analyze or criticize what you're reading. Instead, try to absorb the author's main points as you go, occasionally speculating about what may be coming up ahead, and try to come out with an overall dominant impression of the tone and feeling of the essay or story and the impact it makes on you. At this stage underline or write in the margins sparingly, if at all.

When you've finished your first reading, stop to reflect briefly, then take a look at the comment or questions that come after each selection. They are designed to start you thinking about your responses to your reading and about how you might use those responses. Then go back to the selection for the second reading that is virtually always necessary for serious material if you want to understand and respond to it.

The Second Reading

When you read the piece for the second time, you need to read more aggressively and alertly. Don't just think analytically about your reactions, but reflect on why you have those reactions and how the author provoked them. Now is the time to start moving back and forth between the roles of reader and writer, *interacting* with the piece of writing—looking for high points and weak spots, making associations, and asking questions. Get your pencil ready to start jotting notes in the margin.

Begin an imaginary conversation with the author. Ask,

"What is your *purpose* here? What are you trying to do?" Then ask, "Who is your *audience*? Who are you writing for?" and "Why are you organizing your material this way? What is your *strategy*?" If you keep these questions in mind during your second reading, you'll begin to get a sense of the writer behind the print who had something to say and had to work at getting it across to his or her readers.

Interacting with a piece of writing includes responding to the content of what you're reading. Don't accept passively what an author says. Instead, ask questions, argue, comment, and match your experience and what you know against what the writer is telling you. You might say, "Yes, that's how I'd react too," or "Oh, no, I don't agree with that," or "Well, maybe so, but what's your evidence?" Such comments and questions can help you work out what the essay or story means *for you*. The phrase "for you" is important here because a piece of writing never means precisely the same thing for every reader. Nor should it. You are not an empty mold into which a writer can pour meaning. Instead, you are a unique reader who brings unique experiences and attitudes with you, and you shape your own meaning by joining what you know and feel with what the writer tells you. You put together your own interpretation when you read someone else's writing, just as you put together an interpretation of events when you write something yourself.

For example, as you read you may be comparing the author's account of something that happened to her—perhaps an encounter with stereotyping or sex discrimination—with a similar experience of yours and thinking about how differently you reacted. Or in reading another essay you may disagree with the author's analysis of an American political problem and decide you'd like to refute him in your next paper. As you respond, write it down—if you don't, you may forget.

Notes and Questions in the Margins

Interact with what you read by underlining and writing as you read: put notes, summaries, and questions in the margins of your book (or on a separate piece of paper if you have to). With serious material, this kind of writing is a crucial part of the reading process. It helps you to engage with the material you're reading: summarize it for recall, organize it by noting and numbering main points, and question anything you don't understand. It also helps you sort through the writer's ideas, looking for material that may generate resources for your own writing.

Most readers who frequently encounter difficult reading in the course of their work and must master its content underline and write in the margins almost routinely. They're active and interactive readers, so much so that if they don't own a book they need to read and master, they will either buy it or photocopy from it so they can read with a pencil in hand. At the end of this introduction, we have included a short annotated essay that shows how one reader used this method to interact with a piece of writing.

We believe that trying this method and using the guideline questions on pages 10–11 will help you become a good reader who enjoys college reading and knows how to use it effectively in college writing.

BECOMING A WRITER WHO READS

When you write college essays, you need to work at moving between the roles of reader and writer. As you write, you have to be aware of interacting with various readers.

The Self as Reader

The first reader is that writer's other half, the self as reader—in other words, you. To be a good writer, you have to read as you write, continually spiraling back to read what you have written, then writing again because of what you have read. You write in response to your own reading. You're inventing as you go. When you get to the revision stage, you *rewrite* because you realize, as a reader, that things didn't come out quite right. And when you get to the final editing stage, you proofread and polish because you are acting as that most critical of all readers, the editor.

Other Readers

As you write, you need to be conscious of the other people who will read what you've written. In at least one corner of your mind, remember those readers and ask yourself, "What do I want to achieve with this audience? What is my *purpose?* How do I want them to respond?" Ask also, "What kind of *audience* am I writing for?" And finally, ask yourself, "How should I write? What *strategies* can I use to get my ideas across? What is my audience likely to respond to?" After you have written your first draft, it's particularly important that you stand back from it and imagine yourself as part of that audience. Anticipate how an outside reader might respond and what questions he or she might have.

Keeping up the relationship between your two roles, as reader and writer, may seem complicated for a while, but it gets easier as you read and write more. Gradually you will recognize the interaction between the two processes.

READING TO BECOME MORE AWARE ABOUT THE WRITING PROCESS

When you become a critical reader, the writer in you reacts to what you're reading—commenting, arguing, making marginal comments, and jotting down notes as you think ahead about your own writing. But as you read and react you can also sharpen your own writing skills if you take playing the role of writer even farther and think about the *writing process* in the essay you're reading. Try to see what's going on beneath the surface of the words, get behind them into the writer's mind, and watch him or her at work. You can't really do that, of course, but by asking certain questions you can do a kind of simulation exercise that can give you some understanding of the writer's thinking process.

Purpose

For example, we know that most writers have goals when they write, certain things they want to accomplish in their writing. So ask yourself,

Why is the author writing? What is his or her purpose? Think about what motivated the author to write that particular piece. What did he or she want to achieve and why? Does the writer tell the readers the purpose or expect them to figure it out for themselves? Until you have some insight into an author's purpose, you can't really judge how successful the piece is.

Audience

We also know that most writers—especially professionals—write for a definite audience and tailor their writing to meet that audience's needs and expectations. So the next question you ask is,

For whom is the writer writing? Who is the audience? Speculate about who the author is writing for. Why would the writer have chosen that audience and what would he or she need to know about those readers before starting to write? Again, it's difficult to judge how successful any writing is unless you know who the intended readers are and what they're like.

Strategy

Finally, writers can improve their own writing by noticing how skilled writers work, how they go about appealing to their readers, and how they use language to achieve the effects they want. So the third question is,

How does the author work? What are his or her strategies? Analyzing strategies requires that you pay attention to a number of elements in writing—organization, examples, metaphor and analogies, vivid descriptions, and so on. Read-

ing a well-crafted essay is like watching a well-made movie on two levels: on one level you enjoy the drama itself, and on another level you admire the talent and skill of artists at work. In both cases, you're learning by watching a good professional at work.

Do we guarantee that close analysis of another person's writing will make you a better writer? No, of course we don't. But we do believe that learning to read responsively, critically, and analytically will give you insights into the craft of writing and make it a less intimidating and more manageable process. What professional writers do isn't mysterious or magical, although it can dazzle and impress. They're people who are good at their craft, a craft that can be at least partially analyzed and understood. They succeed at that craft mainly because they're observant, disciplined, sensitive people who pay attention to what goes on around them and who read widely and love language. Most important, they succeed because they use their skill to communicate their experiences and ideas to readers for a purpose.

READING TO LEARN ABOUT WRITING STRATEGIES

In *The Riverside Reader,* you will find essays and short stories that comment on events and concerns that affect all our lives—the environment, health and medicine, our country's changing demographics, and women's roles, to name just a few. The essays connect to other strands in your college education and are as pertinent in a sociology, government, or women's studies course as they are in your college writing course. The short stories expand and enrich your understanding of these essays by demonstrating how the thinking processes that shape nonfiction also connect with the worlds of fiction. All these readings will touch on matters that affect your personal life or your jobs. The last section of this book, Resources for Writing, is devoted exclusively to issues that concern the subject of crime.

Common Writing Strategies

In *The Riverside Reader,* the essays are arranged according to common patterns of organization that have been serving writers well for centuries: *narration and description, process, comparison and contrast, division and classification, definition, cause and effect,* and *persuasion and argument.* These patterns can serve as *strategies* for the development of ideas in writing. Study how professional writers use these traditional strategies in their writing. If you know from your reading how these strategies are used, you will be able to choose one that fits your writing situation. For example, if you notice how Maya Angelou uses narrative to dramatize racial stereotyping, you may see how you can relate an incident from your life to illustrate a point. If you are convinced by Gloria Steinem's analysis of why many college women seem indifferent to the women's movement, you may see the potential for using a similar cause-and-effect strategy in a sociology or anthropology paper. Not that you have to limit yourself to a single strategy for the entire paper—certainly professional writers don't. They mix strategies as they need them, perhaps using narrative to get started, comparison and contrast to highlight differences between two cultures, and cause and effect to argue for a certain course of action. Often, however, they structure a piece of writing around one central pattern, and for *The Riverside Reader* we have chosen essays with one dominant strategy so that you can see particularly strong examples of such strategies in action.

Strategies for Your Writing

You can also use the traditional strategies to generate resources and then transform them into writing. Suppose you are trying to get started writing an essay on the first impressionist painters for a humanities course. One way to start thinking would be to *define* the impressionist school of painting. Another would be to explore what *caused* the rise of impressionism in the nineteenth century—what were the artists in the movement reacting to? Another potentially rich approach would be to *compare* these painters to other painters of the time. You could also *describe* an important early impressionist painting or relate a *narrative* about one of the early painters. Each of the strategies provides a kind of special lens for viewing your topic, a different way of looking at it so that you can see its possibilities. When you become aware of how these "lenses" work—how each one helps you see and shape your subject—you can select one strategy or combine two or three to draft and revise your essay. That is the procedure you can follow in Resources for Writing. Each selection in that section uses one of the common writing strategies to explore a different aspect of crime. As you read these selections, recalling what you know about crime, you can expand and shift your perspective on the subject, uncovering all sorts of resources to develop in your writing.

USING *THE RIVERSIDE READER*

The Riverside Reader will help you become an active, critical reader and an effective writer. At the start of every section, you will find an introduction that previews strategy, gives you clues about what to look for as you read, and demonstrates how the strategy works in a paragraph. You will also find headnotes before each essay and short story that tell you about the author's background and credentials and about how and where the selection originated. After each essay and short story, you will find study questions or commentary to help you, as you reread a selection, connect your reading to the author's writing process. At the end of each section, you will find writing assignments that give you opportunities to respond to your reading using your own experiences and knowledge.

On the following pages, you will find a set of questions headed Guidelines for Reading an Essay. They will help you to preview an essay, to read it critically and respond to it fully, and to see it from a writer's point of view. After the Guidelines, you will find a Sample Analysis of an essay that shows how a reader might critically read, annotate, and respond to an essay.

Guidelines for Reading an Essay

I. WHAT IS YOUR RESPONSE TO THE ESSAY?

a. What questions do you have for the author?
b. What did you find in the essay that surprised, annoyed, or puzzled you?
c. At what places were you reminded of some experience you have had or heard about or of something else you have read about? What were those experiences?
d. How did you react to the essay? Does your own experience reinforce or contradict the essay?

II. WHAT IS THE WRITER'S PURPOSE?

a. What goal or purpose do you think the author had for writing? To what extent did he or she achieve it?
b. What features or clues did you find in the essay that revealed the author's purpose?
c. How do you respond to the author's purpose?
d. What kind of essay would you write if you had a similar purpose? Why?

III. WHO IS THE WRITER'S AUDIENCE?

a. How would you describe the audience you think the writer had in mind?
b. What clues in the essay help you identify the audience?
c. What would that audience expect when starting to read this essay? What questions might the audience have for the writer?
d. To what extent do you think you are like the original audience for this essay? How does that similarity or lack of it affect your response?

IV. WHAT STRATEGIES DOES THE WRITER USE?

a. How does the writer catch and hold the reader's attention?
b. What patterns do you see frequently in the essay? What is the main pattern?
c. What special strategies—analogy, figurative language, narrative, vivid description, for example—do you notice in the essay? What do you think the writer does particularly well?
d. To what extent do you think the writer's strategies work? How satisfying do you find the essay? Why?

Sample Analysis of an Essay

ANNA QUINDLEN

Anna Quindlen was born in Philadelphia, Pennsylvania, in 1952 and was educated at Barnard College. She began reporting for the New York *Post* and then *The New York Times,* covering city hall and "some of the worst back alleys in New York City." Her first column, "About New York," covered the same beat, but her next column, "Life in the Thirties," featured personal reflections and reminiscences. The best of these columns is collected in her book *Living Out Loud* (1988). Quindlen published her first novel, *Object Lessons,* to wide acclaim, and her current *New York Times* column, "Public and Private," won the Pulitzer Prize for commentary in 1992. In "Execution," reprinted from *Living Out Loud,* Quindlen introduces a personal perspective into the usually abstract arguments about capital punishment.

In the essay, Quindlen demonstrates her special ability to bring human drama to questions about broad social policy and make readers see how those questions affect their own lives. In the first paragraph, she describes the victims of Ted Bundy, a serial killer who has been condemned to death, and identifies with them: "I knew if I had been in the wrong place at the wrong time I would have been a goner." Tailoring her appeal to people who support the death penalty, she says, "[Ted Bundy] and the death penalty seemed made for each other." She goes on to admit that even though intellectually and ethically she's against capital punishment, her gut reaction tells her that if it were her daughter Bundy had killed, she'd cheerfully murder him herself. Here, and later when she mentions the parents of a six-year-old boy whose killer decapitated him, she knows she is touching her readers' basic emotions. She goes on to theorize that the real appeal of the death penalty is retribution: we want to hurt people who've hurt other people.

In the rest of her essay, however, she makes her argument against the death penalty by saying that it's really not possible for individuals to retaliate against killers for what they've done, no matter how horrible their crimes. She points out that we live in a society that doesn't allow such violence, and she suggests that we wouldn't really want to live in any other kind. Therefore, since we can't get what we want emotionally from the death penalty, there's no point to it. She dismisses the claim that capital punishment deters criminals, and she disposes of another argument often made for it—that too often criminals who are convicted and sentenced are later released and kill again—by saying killers could get life sentences without parole. She doesn't mention a traditional argument against the death penalty: that sometimes the courts have been wrong and innocent people are put to death.

Comments in the left margin summarize Quindlen's main points and note her strategies; in the right margin, the reader notes her responses to Quindlen's ideas and jots down questions she thinks the essay raises. This process of annotating and responding has generated several ideas that one might write about. Some of those are given after the essay.

Execution

Q. identifies with Bundy's victims—could have been her

Feels vulnerable—B.'s crimes seem to justify death penalty

Q. immediately makes issue personal

Ted Bundy and I go back a long way, to a time when there was a series of unsolved murders in Washington State known only as the Ted murders. Like a lot of reporters, I'm something of a crime buff. But the Washington Ted murders—and the ones that followed in Utah, Colorado, and finally in Florida, where Ted Bundy was convicted and sentenced to die—fascinated me because I could see myself as one of the victims. I looked at the studio photographs of young women with long hair, pierced ears, easy smiles, and I read the descriptions: polite, friendly, quick to help, eager to please. I thought about being approached by a handsome young man asking for help, and I knew if I had been in the wrong place at the wrong time I would have been a goner. By the time Ted finished up in Florida, law enforcement authorities suspected he had murdered dozens of young women. He and the death penalty seemed made for each other.

But morally and intellectually opposed to death penalty

The death penalty and I, on the other hand, seem to have nothing in common. But Ted Bundy has made me think about it all over again, now that the outlines of my sixties liberalism have been filled in with a decade as a reporter covering some of the worst back alleys in New York City and three years as a mother who, like most, would lay down her life for her kids. Simply put, I am opposed to the death penalty. I would tell that to any judge or lawyer undertaking the *voir dire* of jury candidates in a state in which the death penalty can be imposed. That is why I would be excused from such a jury. In a rational, completely cerebral way, I think the killing of one human being as punishment for the killing of another makes no sense and is inherently immoral.

Contrasts intellectual reasons with visceral reaction

Knows she really thinks Bundy should die—admits gut reaction.

But whenever my response to an important subject is rational and completely cerebral, I know there is something wrong with it—and so it is here. I have always been governed by my gut, and my gut says I am hypothetical about the death penalty. That is, I do not in theory think that Ted Bundy, or others like him, should be put to death. But if my daughter had been the one clubbed to death as she slept in a Tallahassee sorority house, and if the bite mark left in her buttocks had been one of the prime pieces of evidence against the young man charged with her murder, I would with the greatest pleasure kill him myself.

Brutal detail

Talking to people who believe in eye-for-an-eye code

Problem with emotional response—it's revenge

Not a deterrent

The State of Florida will not permit the parents of Bundy's victims to do that, and, in a way, that is the problem with an emotional response to capital punishment. The only reason for a death penalty is to exact retribution. Is there anyone who really thinks that it is a deterrent, that there are considerable numbers of criminals out there who think twice about committing crimes because of the sentence involved? The ones I have met in my professional duties have either sneered at the justice system, where they can exchange one charge for another with more ease than they could return a shirt to a clothing store, or they have simply believed that it is the other guy who will get caught, get convicted, get the stiffest sentence. Of course, the death penalty would act as a deterrent by eliminating recidivism, but then so would life without parole, albeit at greater taxpayer expense.

Wants murderers to suffer as victims did—not possible

I don't believe deterrence is what most proponents seek from the death penalty anyhow. Our most profound emotional response is to want criminals to suffer as their victims did. When a man is accused of throwing a child from a high-rise terrace, my emotional—some might say hysterical—response is that he should be

Is this really why people want death penalty? Simplistic interpretation

given an opportunity to see how endless the seconds are from the thirty-first story to the ground. In a civilized society that will never happen. And so what many people want from the death penalty, they will never get.

Death is death, you may say, and you would be right. But anyone who has seen someone die suddenly of a heart attack and someone else slip slowly into the clutches of cancer knows that there are gradations of dying.

More gory details

I watched a television reenactment one night of an execution by lethal injection. It was well done; it was horrible. The methodical approach, people standing around the gurney waiting, made it more awful. One moment there was a man in a prone position; the next moment that man was gone. On another night I watched a television movie about a little boy named Adam Walsh, who disappeared from a shopping center in Florida. There was a reenactment of Adam's parents coming to New York, where they appeared on morning talk shows begging for their son's return, and in their hotel room, where they received a call from the police saying that Adam had just been found: not all of Adam, actually, just his severed head, discovered in the waters of a Florida canal. There is nothing anyone could do that is bad enough for an adult who took a six-year-old boy away from his parents, perhaps tortured, then murdered him and cut off his head. Nothing at all. Lethal injection? The electric chair? Bah.

Concludes death penalty is wrong—makes killers of us but is not really retribution

And so I come back to the position that the death penalty is wrong, not only because it consists of stooping to the level of the killers, but also because it is not what it seems. Just before one of Ted Bundy's execution dates was postponed pending further appeals, the father of his last known victim, a twelve-year-old girl, said what almost every father in his situation must feel. "I wish they'd bring him back to Lake City,"

Is she suggesting death penalty would be OK if it hurt enough? Confusing said Tom Leach of the town where Kimberly Leach lived and died, "and let us all have at him." But the death penalty does not let us all have at him in the way Mr. Leach seems to mean. What he wants is for something as horrifying as what happened to his child to happen to Ted Bundy. And that is impossible.

Possible Writing Topics

1. Read about ways criminals in Europe used to be killed in public executions not too long ago—drawn and quartered, torn to pieces by horses, etc.—and consider what the rationale was for those kinds of punishment. Did authorities consider such punishment a deterrent? If they did, did the deterrent work? If not, what was their excuse? What factors put a stop to such spectacles?
2. Current theories about child rearing hold that severe punishments such as whipping or hurting children do more to make them violent adults than do to change inappropriate behavior. What arguments can be made for and against drawing correlations between this theory and a government killing people?
3. Most Western European societies no longer have the death penalty. Investigate to determine what the results have been in those countries. Are there more or fewer of what we call capital offenses in those societies than there are in the United States? What could we learn from those countries?

NARRATION AND DESCRIPTION

The writer who *narrates* tells a story to make a point. The writer who *describes* evokes the senses to create a picture. Although you can use either form by itself, you will probably discover that they work best in combination if you want to write a detailed account of some memorable experience—your first trip alone, a last-minute political victory, a picnic in some special place. When you want to explain what happened, you will need to tell the story in some kind of chronological order, putting the most important events—I took the wrong turn, she made the right speech, we picked the perfect spot—in the most prominent position. When you want to give the texture of the experience, you will need to select words and images that help your readers see, hear, and feel what happened—the road snaked to a dead end, the crowd thundered into applause, the sunshine softened our scowls. When you show and tell in this way, you can help your readers see the meaning of the experience you want to convey.

PURPOSE

You can use narration and description for three purposes. Most simply, you can use them to introduce or illustrate a complicated subject. You might begin an analysis of the energy crisis, for example, by telling a personal anecdote that dramatizes wastefulness. Or you might conclude an argument for gun control by giving a graphic description of a shooting incident. In each case, you are using a few sentences or a detailed description to support some other strategy such as causal analysis or argument.

Writers use narration and description most often not as isolated examples but as their primary method when they are analyzing an issue or theme. For example, you might spend a whole essay telling how you came to a new awareness of patriotism because of your experience in a foreign country. Even though your personal experience would be the center of the essay, your narrative purpose (what happened) and your descriptive purpose (what it felt like) might be linked to other purposes. You might want to *explain* what caused your new awareness (why it happened) or to *argue* that everyone needs such awareness (why everyone should reach the same conclusion you did).

The writers who use narration and description most often are those who write autobiography, history, and fiction. If you choose to write in any of these forms, your purpose will be not so much to introduce an example or tell about an experience as to throw light on your subject. You may explain why events happened as they did or argue that such events should never happen again, but you may choose to suggest your ideas subtly through telling a story or giving a description rather than stating them as direct assertions. Your primary purpose is to report the actions and describe the feelings of people entangled in the complex web of circumstance.

AUDIENCE

As you think about writing an essay using narration and description, consider how much you will need to tell your readers and how much you will need to show them. If you are writing from personal experience, few readers will know the story before you tell it. They may know similar stories or have had similar experiences, but they do not know your story. Because you can tell your story in so many different ways—adding or deleting material to fit the occasion—you need to decide how much information your readers will need. Do they need to know every detail of your story, only brief summaries of certain parts, or some mixture of detail and summary?

In order to decide what details you should provide, you need to think about how much your readers know and what they are going to expect. If your subject is unusual (a trip to a volcano), your readers will need a lot of information, much of it technical, to understand the novel experience you are going to tell. They will expect an efficient, matter-of-fact description of volcanoes but also want you to give them some sense of how it feels to see one erupting. If your subject is familiar to most people (your experience with lawn sprinklers), your readers will need few technical details to understand your subject. But they will expect you to give them new images and insights that create a fresh vision of your subject—for example, portraying lawn sprinklers as the languid pulse of summer.

STRATEGIES

The writers in this section demonstrate that you need to use certain strategies to write a successful narrative and descriptive essay. For openers, you must recognize that an experience and an essay about that experience are not the same thing. When you have any experience, no matter how long it lasts, your memory of that experience is going to be disorganized and poorly defined, but the essay you write about that experience must have a purpose and be sharply focused. When you want to transform your experience into an essay, start by locating the central **conflict**. It may be (1) between the writer and himself, or herself, as when George Orwell finds himself in a quandary about whether to shoot the elephant; (2) between the writer and others, as when Maya Angelou responds to Mrs. Cullinan and her friends, or (3) between the writer and the environment, as when N. Scott Momaday tries to come to terms with the landscape of the Kiowa culture.

Once you have identified the conflict, arrange the action so that your readers know how the conflict started, how it developed, and how it was resolved. This coherent sequence of events is called a **plot**. Sometimes you may want to create a plot that sticks to a simple chronological pattern. In Le Ly Hayslip's "Playing Stupid," she simply begins at the beginning and describes events as they occur. At other times, you may want to start your essay in the middle or even near the end of the event you're describing. N. Scott Momaday begins near the end, with the death of his grandmother, and works his way back to the beginning as he searches for his ancestral roots. Each author chooses a pattern according to his or her purpose; Hayslip wants to describe the immediate causes of an event in the present, while Momaday wants to look for the ultimate causes of an event in the past.

When you figure out what the beginning, middle, and end of your plot should be, you can establish how each event in those sections should be paced. **Pace** is the speed at which the writer recounts events. Sometimes you can narrate events quickly by omitting details, compressing time, and summarizing experience. For example, N. Scott Momaday summarizes the history of the Kiowa people in two paragraphs. At other times you must pace events more slowly and carefully because they are vital to your purpose. You will need to include every detail, expand on time, and present the situation as a fully realized scene rather than in summary form. Momaday creates such a scene when he describes his last vision of his grandmother.

You can make your scenes and summaries effective by your careful **selection of details**. Just adding more details doesn't satisfy this requirement. You must select those special details that satisfy the needs of your readers and further your purpose in the essay. For example, sometimes you will need to give *objective* or technical details to help your readers understand your subject. Mike Rose provides this kind of detail when he describes the curriculum of vocational education. At other times you will want to give *subjective* or impressionistic details to appeal to your readers' senses. Orwell provides much of this sort of detail as he tries to recreate his physical and psychological response to shooting the elephant. Finally, you may want to present your details so they form a *figurative image* or create a *dominant impression*. Hayslip uses both of these strategies: the first when she refers to the American helicopters as "dragonflies," for example, and the second when she describes the pattern of nightly beatings and daily interrogations.

In order to identify the conflict, organize the plot, vary the pace, and select details for your essay, you need to determine your **point of view**. Simply stated, point of view refers to the person and position of the narrator (point) and the attitude toward the experience being presented (view). You choose your *person* by deciding whether you want to tell your story as "I" saw it (as in Maya Angelou's story about her confrontation with Mrs. Cullinan), or as "he" or "she" saw it (as in N. Scott Momaday's account of his grandmother's last days); or as "you" might see it (as in Rose's attempt to portray how academic work looks to "remedial" students).

Your *position* refers to how close you are to the action in time and space. You may be involved in the action or view it from the position of an observer, or you may tell about the events as they are happening or many years after they have taken place. For example, George Orwell, the young police officer, is the chief actor in his narrative, but George Orwell, the author, still wonders, years after the event, why he shot the elephant. You create your attitude—how you view the events you intend to present and interpret—by the person and position you choose for writing your essay. The attitudes of the narrators in the following essays might be characterized as angry (Angelou), perplexed (Rose), nostalgic (Momaday), cunning (Hayslip), and ambivalent (Orwell).

Using Narration and Description in a Paragraph

MAXINE HONG KINGSTON
from "A Song for a Barbarian Reed Pipe"

Sets up conflict

Not all of the children who were silent at American school found a voice at Chinese school. One new teacher said each of us had to get up and recite in front of the class, who was to listen. My sister and I had memorized the lesson perfectly. We said it to each other at home, one chanting, one listening. The teacher called on my sister to recite first. It was the first time a teacher had called on the second-born to go first.

Conflict

Slows pace; heightens suspense

My sister was scared. She glanced at me and looked away; I looked down at my desk. I hoped that she could do it because if she could, then I would have to. She opened her mouth and a voice came out that wasn't a whisper, but it wasn't a proper voice either. I hoped that she would not cry, fear breaking up her voice like twigs underfoot.

Appeals to sense

She sounded as if she were trying to sing though weeping and strangling. She did not pause or stop to end the embarrassment. She kept going until she said the last word, and then she sat down. When it was my turn, the same voice came out, a crippled animal running on broken legs. You could hear splinters in

Creates new image

Confirms point of view

my voice, bones rubbing jagged against one another. I was loud, though. I was glad I didn't whisper.

Comment This paragraph, taken from the final section of *The Woman Warrior,* recounts an embarrassing scene involving two Chinese sisters. Kingston describes how she and her sister prepare for the expected recitation. The conflict occurs when the teacher calls on the second-born sister first—a breach of Chinese etiquette. By describing how she looks down at her desk, Kingston slows the pace and heightens the anxiety of the situation. She then selects details and images to evoke the sound of her sister's and then her own voice as they complete the lesson.

MAYA ANGELOU

Maya Angelou (given name, Marguerita Johnson) was born in St. Louis, Missouri, in 1928 and spent her early years in California and Arkansas. A woman of varied accomplishments, she is a novelist, poet, playwright, stage and screen performer, composer, and singer. She is perhaps best known for her autobiographical novels: *I Know Why the Caged Bird Sings* (1970), *Gather Together in My Name* (1974), *Singin' and Swingin' and Gettin' Merry Like Christmas* (1976), *Heart of a Woman* (1981), and *All God's Children Need Traveling Shoes* (1986). Angelou's volumes of poetry are equally well respected—they include *Oh Pray My Wings Are Gonna Fit Me Well* (1975) and *And Still I Rise* (1978), and *I Shall Not Be Moved* (1990). In the following selection from *I Know Why the Caged Bird Sings,* Angelou recounts how she maintained her identity in a world of prejudice.

My Name Is Margaret

Recently a white woman from Texas, who would quickly describe herself as a liberal, asked me about my hometown. When I told her that in Stamps my grandmother had owned the only Negro general merchandise store since the turn of the century, she exclaimed, "Why, you were a debutante." Ridiculous and even ludicrous. But Negro girls in small Southern towns, whether poverty-stricken or just munching along on a few of life's necessities, were given as extensive and irrelevant preparations for adulthood as rich white girls shown in magazines. Admittedly the training was not the same. While white girls learned to waltz and sit gracefully with a tea cup balanced on their knees, we were lagging behind, learning the mid-Victorian values with very little 1 money to indulge them. (Come and see Edna Lomax spending the money she made picking cotton on five balls of ecru tatting thread. Her fingers are bound to snag the work and she'll have to repeat the stitches time and time again. But she knows that when she buys the thread.)

We were required to embroider and I had trunkfuls of 2
colorful dishtowels, pillowcases, runners and handkerchiefs to my credit. I mastered the art of crocheting and tatting, and there was a lifetime's supply of dainty doilies that would never be used in sacheted dresser drawers. It went without saying that all girls could iron and wash, but the finer touches around the home, like setting a table with real silver, baking roasts and cooking vegetables without meat, had to be learned elsewhere. Usually at the source of those habits. During my tenth year, a white woman's kitchen became my finishing school.

Mrs. Viola Cullinan was a plump woman who lived in a 3
three-bedroom house somewhere behind the post office. She was singularly unattractive until she smiled, and then the lines around her eyes and mouth which made her look perpetually dirty disappeared, and her face looked like the mask of an impish elf. She usually rested her smile until late afternoon when her women friends dropped in and Miss Glory, the cook, served them cold drinks on the closed-in porch.

The exactness of her house was inhuman. This glass went 4
here and only here. That cup had its place and it was an act of impudent rebellion to place it anywhere else. At twelve o'clock the table was set. At 12:15 Mrs. Cullinan sat down to dinner (whether her husband had arrived or not). At 12:16 Miss Glory brought out the food.

It took me a week to learn the difference between a salad 5
plate, a bread plate and a dessert plate.

Mrs. Cullinan kept up the tradition of her wealthy parents. 6
She was from Virginia. Miss Glory, who was a descendant of slaves that had worked for the Cullinans, told me her history. She had married beneath her (according to Miss Glory). Her husband's family hadn't had their money very long and what they had "didn't 'mount to much."

As ugly as she was, I thought privately, she was lucky to 7

get a husband above or beneath her station. But Miss Glory wouldn't let me say a thing against her mistress. She was very patient with me, however, over the housework. She explained the dishware, silverware and servants' bells. The large round bowl in which soup was served wasn't a soup bowl, it was a tureen. There were goblets, sherbet glasses, ice-cream glasses, wine glasses, green glass coffee cups with matching saucers, and water glasses. I had a glass to drink from, and it sat with Miss Glory's on a separate shelf from the others. Soup spoons, gravy boat, butter knives, salad forks and carving platter were additions to my vocabulary and in fact almost represented a new language. I was fascinated with the novelty, with the fluttering Mrs. Cullinan and her Alice-in-Wonderland house.

Her husband remains, in my memory, undefined. I lumped him with all the other white men that I had ever seen and tried not to see. 8

On our way home one evening, Miss Glory told me that Mrs. Cullinan couldn't have children. She said that she was too delicate-boned. It was hard to imagine bones at all under those layers of fat. Miss Glory went on to say that the doctor had taken out all her lady organs. I reasoned that a pig's organs included the lungs, heart and liver, so if Mrs. Cullinan was walking around without those essentials, it explained why she drank alcohol out of unmarked bottles. She was keeping herself embalmed. 9

When I spoke to Bailey about it, he agreed that I was right, but he also informed me that Mr. Cullinan had two daughters by a colored lady and that I knew them very well. He added that the girls were the spitting image of their father. I was unable to remember what he looked like, although I had just left him a few hours before, but I thought of the Coleman girls. They were very light-skinned and certainly didn't look very much like their mother (no one ever mentioned Mr. Coleman). 10

My pity for Mrs. Cullinan preceded me the next morning like the Cheshire cat's smile. Those girls, who could have been her daughters, were beautiful. They didn't have to 11 straighten their hair. Even when they were caught in the rain, their braids still hung down straight like tamed snakes. Their mouths were pouty little cupid's bows. Mrs. Cullinan didn't know what she missed. Or maybe she did. Poor Mrs. Cullinan.

For weeks after, I arrived early, left late and tried very 12
hard to make up for her barrenness. If she had had her own children, she wouldn't have had to ask me to run a thousand errands from her back door to the back door of her friends. Poor old Mrs. Cullinan.

Then one evening Miss Glory told me to serve the ladies 13
on the porch. After I set the tray down and turned toward the kitchen, one of the women asked, "What's your name, girl?" It was the speckled-faced one. Mrs. Cullinan said, "She doesn't talk much. Her name's Margaret."

"Is she dumb?" 14

"No. As I understand it, she can talk when she wants to 15
but she's usually quiet as a little mouse. Aren't you, Margaret?"

I smiled at her. Poor thing. No organs and couldn't even 16
pronounce my name correctly.

"She's a sweet little thing, though." 17

"Well, that may be, but the name's too long. I'd never 18
bother myself. I'd call her Mary if I was you."

I fumed into the kitchen. That horrible woman would 19
never have the chance to call me Mary because if I was starving I'd never work for her. I decided I wouldn't pee on her if her heart was on fire. Giggles drifted in off the porch and into Miss Glory's pots. I wondered what they could be laughing about.

Whitefolks were so strange. Could they be talking about 20
me? Everybody knew that they stuck together better than the Negroes did. It was possible that Mrs. Cullinan had friends in St. Louis who heard about a girl from Stamps being in court and wrote to tell her. Maybe she knew about Mr. Freeman.

My lunch was in my mouth a second time and I went 21
outside and relieved myself on the bed of four-o'clocks. Miss

Glory thought I might be coming down with something and told me to go on home, that Momma would give me some herb tea, and she'd explain to her mistress.

I realized how foolish I was being before I reached the pond. Of course Mrs. Cullinan didn't know. Otherwise she wouldn't have given me two nice dresses that Momma cut down, and she certainly wouldn't have called me a "sweet little thing." My stomach felt fine, and I didn't mention anything to Momma. 22

That evening I decided to write a poem on being white, fat, old and without children. It was going to be a tragic ballad. I would have to watch her carefully to capture the essence of her loneliness and pain. 23

The very next day, she called me by the wrong name. Miss Glory and I were washing up the lunch dishes when Mrs. Cullinan came to the doorway. "Mary?" 24

Miss Glory asked, "Who?" 25

Mrs. Cullinan, sagging a little, knew and I knew. "I want Mary to go down to Mrs. Randall's and take her some soup. She's not been feeling well for a few days." 26

Miss Glory's face was a wonder to see. "You mean Margaret, ma'am. Her name's Margaret." 27

"That's too long. She's Mary from now on. Heat that soup from last night and put it in the china tureen and, Mary, I want you to carry it carefully." 28

Every person I knew had a hellish horror of being "called out of his name." It was a dangerous practice to call a Negro anything that could be loosely construed as insulting because of the centuries of their having been called niggers, jigs, dinges, blackbirds, crows, boots and spooks. 29

Miss Glory had a fleeting second of feeling sorry for me. Then as she handed me the hot tureen she said, "Don't mind, don't pay that no mind. Sticks and stones may break your bones, but words . . . You know, I been working for her for twenty years." 30

She held the back door open for me. "Twenty years. I wasn't much older than you. My name used to be Hallelujah. That's what Ma named me, but my mistress give me 'Glory,' and it stuck. I likes it better too." 31

I was in the little path that ran behind the houses when Miss Glory shouted, "It's shorter too." 32

For a few seconds it was a tossup over whether I would laugh (imagine being named Hallelujah) or cry (imagine letting some white woman rename you for her convenience). My anger saved me from either outburst. I had to quit the job, but the problem was going to be how to do it. Momma wouldn't allow me to quit for just any reason. 33

"She's a peach. That woman is a real peach." Mrs. Randall's maid was talking as she took the soup from me, and I wondered what her name used to be and what she answered to now. 34

For a week I looked into Mrs. Cullinan's face as she called me Mary. She ignored my coming late and leaving early. Miss Glory was a little annoyed because I had begun to leave egg yolk on the dishes and wasn't putting much heart in polishing the silver. I hoped that she would complain to our boss, but she didn't. 35

Then Bailey solved my dilemma. He had me describe the contents of the cupboard and the particular plates she liked best. Her favorite piece was a casserole shaped like a fish and the green glass coffee cups. I kept his instructions in mind, so on the next day when Miss Glory was hanging out clothes and I had again been told to serve the old biddies on the porch, I dropped the empty serving tray. When I heard Mrs. Cullinan scream, "Mary!" I picked up the casserole and two of the green glass cups in readiness. As she rounded the kitchen door I let them fall on the tiled floor. 36

I could never absolutely describe to Bailey what happened next, because each time I got to the part where she fell on the floor and screwed up her ugly face to cry, we burst out laughing. She actually wobbled around on the floor and picked up shards of the cups and cried, "Oh, Momma. Oh, dear Gawd. It's Momma's china from Virginia. Oh, Momma, I sorry." 37

Miss Glory came running in from the yard and the women from the porch crowded around. Miss Glory was almost as broken up as her mistress. "You mean to say she broke our Virginia dishes? What we gone do?" 38

Miss Cullinan cried louder, "That clumsy nigger. Clumsy little black nigger." 39

Old speckled-face leaned down and asked, "Who did it, Viola? Was it Mary? Who did it?" 40

Everything was happening so fast I can't remember whether her action preceded her words, but I know that Mrs. Cullinan said, "Her name's Margaret, goddamn it, her name's Margaret." And she threw a wedge of the broken plate at me. It could have been the hysteria which put her aim off, but the flying crockery caught Miss Glory right over the ear and she started screaming. 41

I left the front door wide open so all the neighbors could hear. 42

Mrs. Cullinan was right about one thing. My name wasn't Mary. 43

For Study and Discussion

QUESTIONS FOR RESPONSE

1. In what ways do you identify with your name? How do you feel when someone mispronounces, changes, or forgets it?
2. What questions do you have about some of the unresolved issues in the narration? For example, what do you think will happen when Margaret loses her job?

QUESTIONS ABOUT PURPOSE

1. In what sense does Mrs. Cullinan's kitchen serve as Angelou's "finishing school"? What is she supposed to learn there? What does she learn?
2. How does Angelou's description of Mrs. Cullinan's house as *exact* and *inhuman* support her purpose in recounting the events that take place there?

QUESTIONS ABOUT AUDIENCE

1. How does Angelou's comment about the liberal woman from Texas identify the immediate audience for her essay?
2. What assumptions does Angelou make about her other readers when she comments on the laughter of the white women on the porch?

QUESTIONS ABOUT STRATEGIES

1. How does Angelou use the three discussions of her name to organize her narrative? How does she pace the third discussion to provide an effective resolution for her essay?
2. How does Angelou's intention to write a poem about Mrs. Cullinan establish her initial attitude toward her employer? What changes her attitude toward Mrs. Cullinan's "loneliness and pain"?

QUESTIONS FOR DISCUSSION

1. How did you feel about Glory's and Bailey's reactions to the destruction of the fish-shaped casserole? Explain their strengths and weaknesses as a teacher or adviser.
2. Angelou admits that poor black girls in small southern towns and rich white girls in magazines do not receive the same training. What evidence in the essay suggests that both girls were given "extensive and irrelevant preparation for adulthood"?

MIKE ROSE

Mike Rose was born in 1944 in Altoona, Pennsylvania, and was educated at Loyola College at Los Angeles, University of Southern California, and the University of California, Los Angeles. He has taught elementary students in the Teacher's Corps, adult writers in UCLA's extension program for Vietnam veterans, and basic writers in UCLA's writing program. He has published articles on writer's anxiety, theories of cognition, and assessment in academic journals such as *College English, College Composition and Communication,* and *Written Communication.* In 1989, Rose published *Lives on the Boundary: The Struggles and Achievements of America's Underprepared,* an extraordinary fusion of autobiography, case study, and cultural criticism. In "I Just Wanna Be Average," reprinted from *Lives on the Boundary,* Rose describes the drudgery and despair he experienced when his school mistakenly assigned him to a vocational education program.

I Just Wanna Be Average

It took two buses to get to Our Lady of Mercy. The first started deep in South Los Angeles and caught me at midpoint. The second drifted through neighborhoods with trees, parks, big lawns, and lots of flowers. The rides were long but were livened up by a group of South L.A. veterans whose parents also thought that Hope had set up shop in the west end of the county. There was Christy Biggars, who, at sixteen, was dealing and was, according to rumor, a pimp as well. There were Bill Cobb and Johnny Gonzales, grease-pencil artists extraordinaire, who left Nembutal-enhanced swirls of "Cobb" and "Johnny" on the corrugated walls of 1 the bus. And then there was Tyrrell Wilson. Tyrrell was the coolest kid I knew. He ran the dozens like a metric halfback, laid down a rap that outrhymed and outpointed Cobb, whose rap was good but not great—the curse of a moderately soulful kid trapped in white skin. But it was Cobb who would sneak a radio onto the bus, and thus underwrote his patter with Little Richard, Fats Domino, Chuck Berry, the Coasters, and Ernie K. Doe's mother-in-law, an awful woman who was "sent from down below." And so it was that Christy and Cobb and Johnny G. and Tyrrell and I and assorted others picked up along the way passed our days in the back of the bus, a funny mix brought together by geography and parental desire.

Entrance to school brings with it forms and releases and assessments. Mercy relied on a series of tests, mostly the Stanford-Binet, for placement, and somehow the results of my tests got confused with those of another student named Rose. The other Rose apparently didn't do very well, for I was placed in the vocational track, a euphemism for the bottom level. Neither I nor my parents realized what this meant. We had no sense that Business Math, Typing, and English-Level D were dead ends. The current spate of reports on the schools criticizes parents for not involving themselves in the education of their children. But how would someone like Tommy Rose, with his two years of Italian schooling, know what to ask? And what sort of pressure could an exhausted waitress apply? The error went undetected, and I remained in the vocational track for two years. What a place. 2

My homeroom was supervised by Brother Dill, a troubled and unstable man who also taught freshman English. When his class drifted away from him, which was often, his voice would rise in paranoid accusations, and occasionally he would lose control and shake or smack us. I hadn't been there two months when one of his brisk, face-turning slaps had my glasses sliding down the aisle. Physical education was also pretty harsh. Our teacher was a stubby ex-lineman who had played old-time pro ball in the Midwest. He routinely had us grabbing our ankles to receive his stinging 3 paddle across our butts. He did that, he said, to make men of us. "Rose," he bellowed on our first encounter; me standing geeky in line in my baggy shorts. "'Rose'? What the hell kind of name is that?"

4 "Italian, sir," I squeaked.

5 "Italian! Ho. Rose, do you know the sound a bag of shit makes when it hits the wall?"

6 "No, sir."

7 "Wop!"

8 Sophomore English was taught by Mr. Mitropetros. He was a large, bejeweled man who managed the parking lot at the Shrine Auditorium. He would crow and preen and list for us the stars he'd brushed against. We'd ask questions and glance knowingly and snicker, and all that fueled the poor guy to brag some more. Parking cars was his night job. He had little training in English, so his lesson plan for his day work had us reading the district's required text, *Julius Caesar,* aloud for the semester. We'd finish the play way before the twenty weeks was up, so he'd have us switch parts again and again and start again: Dave Snyder, the fastest guy at Mercy, muscling through Caesar to the breathless squeals of Calpurnia, as interpreted by Steve Fusco, a surfer who owned the school's most envied paneled wagon. Week ten and Dave and Steve would take on new roles, as would we all, and render a water-logged Cassius and a Brutus that are beyond my powers of description.

9 Spanish I—taken in the second year—fell into the hands of a new recruit. Mr. Montez was a tiny man, slight, five foot six at the most, soft-spoken and delicate. Spanish was a particularly rowdy class, and Mr. Montez was as prepared for it as a doily maker at a hammer throw. He would tap his pencil to a room in which Steve Fusco was propelling spitballs from his heavy lips, in which Mike Dweetz was taunting Billy Hawk, a half-Indian, half-Spanish, reed-thin, quietly explosive boy. The vocational track at Our Lady of Mercy mixed kids traveling in from South L.A. with South Bay surfers and a few Slavs and Chicanos from the harbors of San Pedro. This was a dangerous miscellany: surfers and

hodads and South-Central blacks all ablaze to the metronomic tapping of Hector Montez's pencil.

One day Billy lost it. Out of the corner of my eye I saw 10
him strike out with his right arm and catch Dweetz across the neck. Quick as a spasm, Dweetz was out of his seat, scattering desks, cracking Billy on the side of the head, right behind the eye. Snyder and Fusco and others broke it up, but the room felt hot and close and naked. Mr. Montez's tenuous authority was finally ripped to shreds, and I think everyone felt a little strange about that. The charade was over, and when it came down to it, I don't think any of the kids really wanted it to end this way. They had pushed and pushed and bullied their way into a freedom that both scared and embarrassed them.

Students will float to the mark you set. I and the others 11
in the vocational classes were bobbing in pretty shallow water. Vocational education has aimed at increasing the economic opportunities of students who do not do well in our schools. Some serious programs succeed in doing that, and through exceptional teachers—like Mr. Gross in *Horace's Compromise*—students learn to develop hypotheses and troubleshoot, reason through a problem, and communicate effectively—the true job skills. The vocational track, however, is most often a place for those who are just not making it, a dumping ground for the disaffected. There were a few teachers who worked hard at education; young Brother Slattery, for example, combined a stern voice with weekly quizzes to try to pass along to us a skeletal outline of world history. But mostly the teachers had no idea of how to engage the imaginations of us kids who were scuttling along at the bottom of the pond.

And the teachers would have needed some inventiveness, 12
for none of us was groomed for the classroom. It wasn't just that I didn't know things—didn't know how to simplify algebraic fractions, couldn't identify different kinds of clauses, bungled Spanish translations—but that I had developed various faulty and inadequate ways of doing algebra and making

sense of Spanish. Worse yet, the years of defensive tuning out in elementary school had given me a way to escape quickly while seeming at least half alert. During my time in Voc. Ed., I developed further into a mediocre student and a somnambulant problem solver, and that affected the subjects I did have the wherewithal to handle: I detested Shakespeare; I got bored with history. My attention flitted here and there. I fooled around in class and read my books indifferently—the intellectual equivalent of playing with your food. I did what I had to do to get by, and I did it with half a mind.

But I did learn things about people and eventually came into my own socially. I liked the guys in Voc. Ed. Growing up where I did, I understood and admired physical prowess, and there was an abundance of muscle here. There was Dave Snyder, a sprinter and halfback of true quality. Dave's ability and his quick wit gave him a natural appeal, and he was welcome in any clique, though he always kept a little independent. He enjoyed acting the fool and could care less about studies, but he possessed a certain maturity and never caused the faculty much trouble. It was a testament to his independence that he included me among his friends—I eventually went out for track, but I was no jock. Owing to the Latin alphabet and a dearth of *R*s and *S*s, Snyder sat behind Rose, and we started exchanging one-liners and became friends. 13

There was Ted Richard, a much-touted Little League pitcher. He was chunky and had a baby face and came to Our Lady of Mercy as a seasoned street fighter. Ted was quick to laugh and he had a loud, jolly laugh, but when he got angry he'd smile a little smile, the kind that simply raises the corner of the mouth a quarter of an inch. For those who knew, it was an eerie signal. Those who didn't found themselves in big trouble, for Ted was very quick. He loved to carry on what we would come to call philosophical discussions: What is courage? Does God exist? He also loved words, enjoyed picking up big ones like *salubrious* and *equivocal* and using them in our conversations—laughing at himself as the word hit a chuckhole rolling off his tongue. Ted 14 didn't do all that well in school—baseball and parties and testing the courage he'd speculated about took up his time. His textbooks were *Argosy* and *Field and Stream,* whatever newspapers he'd find on the bus stop—from *The Daily Worker* to pornography—conversations with uncles or hobos or businessmen he'd meet in a coffee shop, *The Old Man and the Sea.* With hindsight, I can see that Ted was developing into one of those rough-hewn intellectuals whose sources are a mix of the learned and the apocryphal, whose discussions are both assured and sad.

And then there was Ken Harvey. Ken was good-looking 15
in a puffy way and had a full and oily ducktail and was a car enthusiast . . . a hodad. One day in religion class, he said the sentence that turned out to be one of the most memorable of the hundreds of thousands I heard in those Voc. Ed. years. We were talking about the parable of the talents, about achievement, working hard, doing the best you can do, blah-blah-blah, when the teacher called on the restive Ken Harvey for an opinion. Ken thought about it, but just for a second, and said (with studied, minimal affect), "I just wanna be average." That woke me up. Average?! Who wants to be average? Then the athletes chimed in with the clichés that make you want to laryngectomize them, and the exchange became a platitudinous melee. At the time, I thought Ken's assertion was stupid, and I wrote him off. But his sentence has stayed with me all these years, and I think I am finally coming to understand it.

Ken Harvey was gasping for air. School can be a tremen- 16
dously disorienting place. No matter how bad the school, you're going to encounter notions that don't fit with the assumptions and beliefs that you grew up with—maybe you'll hear these dissonant notions from teachers, maybe from the other students, and maybe you'll read them. You'll also be thrown in with all kinds of kids from all kinds of backgrounds, and that can be unsettling—this is especially true in places of rich ethnic and linguistic mix, like the L.A. basin. You'll see a handful of students far excel you in courses that sound exotic and that are only in the curriculum of the

elite: French, physics, trigonometry. And all this is happening while you're trying to shape an identity, your body is changing, and your emotions are running wild. If you're a working-class kid in the vocational track, the options you'll have to deal with this will be constrained in certain ways: You're defined by your school as "slow"; you're placed in a curriculum that isn't designed to liberate you but to occupy you, or, if you're lucky, train you, though the training is for work the society does not esteem; other students are picking up the cues from your school and your curriculum and interacting with you in particular ways. If you're a kid like Ted Richard, you turn your back on all this and let your mind roam where it may. But youngsters like Ted are rare. What Ken and so many others do is protect themselves from such suffocating madness by taking on with a vengeance the identity implied in the vocational track. Reject the confusion and frustration by openly defining yourself as the Common Joe. Champion the average. Rely on your own good sense. Fuck this bullshit. Bullshit, of course, is everything you—and the others—fear is beyond you: books, essays, tests, academic scrambling, complexity, scientific reasoning, philosophical inquiry.

The tragedy is that you have to twist the knife in your own gray matter to make this defense work. You'll have to shut down, have to reject intellectual stimuli or diffuse them with sarcasm, have to cultivate stupidity, have to convert boredom from a malady into a way of confronting the world. Keep your vocabulary simple, act stoned when you're not or act more stoned than you are, flaunt ignorance, materialize your dreams. It is a powerful and effective defense—it neutralizes the insult and the frustration of being a vocational kid and, when perfected, it drives teachers up the wall, a delightful secondary effect. But like all strong magic, it exacts a price. 17

My own deliverance from the Voc. Ed. world began with sophomore biology. Every student, college prep to vocational, had to take biology, and unlike the other courses, the 18 same person taught all sections. When teaching the vocational group, Brother Clint probably slowed down a bit or omitted a little of the fundamental biochemistry, but he used the same book and more or less the same syllabus across the board. If one class got tough, he could get tougher. He was young and powerful and very handsome, and looks and physical strength were high currency. No one gave him any trouble.

I was pretty bad at the dissecting table, but the lectures and the textbook were interesting: plastic overlays that, with each turned page, peeled away skin, then veins and muscle, then organs, down to the very bones that Brother Clint, pointer in hand, would tap out on our hanging skeleton. Dave Snyder was in big trouble, for the study of life—versus the living of it—was sticking in his craw. We worked out a code for our multiple-choice exams. He'd poke me in the back: once for the answer under *A,* twice for *B,* and so on; and when he'd hit the right one, I'd look up to the ceiling as though I were lost in thought. Poke: cytoplasm. Poke, poke: methane. Poke, poke, poke: William Harvey. Poke, poke, poke, poke: islets of Langerhans. This didn't work out perfectly, but Dave passed the course, and I mastered the dreamy look of a guy on a record jacket. And something else happened. Brother Clint puzzled over this Voc. Ed. kid who was racking up 98s and 99s on his tests. He checked the school's records and discovered the error. He recommended that I begin my junior year in the College Prep program. According to all I've read since, such a shift, as one report put it, is virtually impossible. Kids at that level rarely cross tracks. The telling thing is how chancy both my placement into and exit from Voc. Ed. was; neither I nor my parents had anything to do with it. I lived in one world during spring semester, and when I came back to school in the fall, I was living in another. 19

Switching to College Prep was a mixed blessing. I was an erratic student. I was undisciplined. And I hadn't caught onto the rules of the game: Why work hard in a class that didn't grab my fancy? I was also hopelessly behind in math. 20

Chemistry was hard; toying with my chemistry set years before hadn't prepared me for the chemist's equations. Fortunately, the priest who taught both chemistry and second-year algebra was also the school's athletic director. Membership on the track team covered me; I knew I wouldn't get lower than a C. U.S. history was taught pretty well, and I did okay. But civics was taken over by a football coach who had trouble reading the textbook aloud—and reading aloud was the centerpiece of his pedagogy. College Prep at Mercy was certainly an improvement over the vocational program—at least it carried some status—but the social science curriculum was weak, and the mathematics and physical sciences were simply beyond me. I had a miserable quantitative background and ended up copying some assignments and finessing the rest as best I could. Let me try to explain how it feels to see again and again material you should once have learned but didn't.

You are given a problem. It requires you to simplify algebraic fractions or to multiply expressions containing square roots. You know this is pretty basic material because you've seen it for years. Once a teacher took some time with you, and you learned how to carry out these operations. Simple versions, anyway. But that was a year or two or more in the past, and these are more complex versions, and now you're not sure. And this, you keep telling yourself, is ninth- or even eighth-grade stuff. 21

Next it's a word problem. This is also old hat. The basic elements are as familiar as story characters: trains speeding so many miles per hour or shadows of buildings angling so many degrees. Maybe you know enough, have sat through enough explanations, to be able to begin setting up the problem: "If one train is going this fast . . ." or "This shadow is really one line of a triangle. . . ." Then: "Let's see . . ." "How did Jones do this?" "Hmmmm." "No." "No, that won't work." Your attention wavers. You wonder about other things: a football game, a dance, that cute new checker at the market. You try to focus on the problem again. You scribble on paper for a while, but the tension wins out and 22 your attention flits elsewhere. You crumple the paper and begin daydreaming to ease the frustration.

The particulars will vary, but in essence this is what a number of students go through, especially those in so-called remedial classes. They open their textbooks and see once again the familiar and impenetrable formulas and diagrams and terms that have stumped them for years. There is no excitement here. *No* excitement. Regardless of what the teacher says, this is not a new challenge. There is, rather, embarrassment and frustration and, not surprisingly, some anger in being reminded once again of long-standing inadequacies. No wonder so many students finally attribute their difficulties to something inborn, organic: "That part of my brain just doesn't work." Given the troubling histories many of these students have, it's miraculous that any of them can lift the shroud of hopelessness sufficiently to make deliverance from these classes possible. 23

For Study and Discussion

QUESTIONS FOR RESPONSE

1. What kind of strategies do you use for "tuning out" when you fear academic subjects are "beyond you"?
2. In what ways were your high school teachers similar to those who taught Rose in the vocational track? What techniques did your best teachers use to engage your imagination?

QUESTIONS ABOUT PURPOSE

1. In what ways does the phrase "I just wanna be average" explain Rose's purpose in describing the vocational track as the "dumping ground for the disaffected"?
2. Why does Rose think his deliverance into the college prep program was a "mixed blessing"?

QUESTIONS ABOUT AUDIENCE

1. Who is the primary audience for Rose's narrative—students, parents, teachers, or educational administrators? Explain your answer.
2. What assumptions does Rose make about his audience when he identifies "you" as someone struggling with a "word problem"?

QUESTIONS ABOUT STRATEGIES

1. How does Rose's summary descriptions of the other students in the vocational track suggest that some of them could be "delivered" into college prep?
2. How does Rose use point of view to demonstrate what it *feels* like to be a remedial student?

QUESTIONS FOR DISCUSSION

1. What does this essay suggest about the kind of teachers who *should* be assigned to remedial classes?
2. To what extent do you agree with Rose's assertion that "students will float to the mark you set"? What mark did your parents and teachers set for you? What mark was set for your high school classmates who didn't attend college?

N. SCOTT MOMADAY

N. Scott Momaday, a Kiowa, was born in Lawton, Oklahoma, in 1934 and was educated at the University of New Mexico and Stanford University. Although he has taught English and comparative literature at several universities, his vital interests are Native American art, history, and literature. His books include *House Made of Dawn* (1968), winner of the Pulitzer Prize for fiction, and *The Ancient Child* (1989); two collections of poetry, *Angle of Geese and Other Poems* (1974) and *The Gourd Dancer* (1976); and two memoirs, *The Way to Rainy Mountain* (1969) and *The Names: A Memoir* (1976). In this excerpt from *The Way to Rainy Mountain,* Momaday evokes the landscapes, the legends, and the people that created the Kiowa culture.

The Way to Rainy Mountain

A single knoll rises out of the plain in Oklahoma, north and west of the Wichita Range. For my people, the Kiowas, it is an old landmark, and they gave it the name Rainy Mountain. The hardest weather in the world is there. Winter brings blizzards, hot tornadic winds arise in the spring, and in summer the prairie is an anvil's edge. The grass turns brittle and brown, and it cracks beneath your feet. There are green belts along the rivers and creeks, linear groves of hickory and pecan, willow and witch hazel. At a distance in July or August the steaming foliage seems almost to writhe in fire. Great green and yellow grasshoppers are everywhere in the tall grass, popping up like corn to sting the flesh, and tortoises crawl about on the red earth, going nowhere in the plenty of time. Loneliness is an aspect of the land. All things 1 in the plain are isolate; there is no confusion of objects in the eye, but *one* hill or *one* tree or *one* man. To look upon that landscape in the early morning, with the sun at your back, is to lose the sense of proportion. Your imagination comes to life, and this, you think, is where Creation was begun.

I returned to Rainy Mountain in July. My grandmother had died in the spring, and I wanted to be at her grave. She had lived to be very old and at last infirm. Her only living daughter was with her when she died, and I was told that in death her face was that of a child. 2

I like to think of her as a child. When she was born, the Kiowas were living the last great moment of their history. For more than a hundred years they had controlled the open range from the Smoky Hill River to the Red, from the headwaters of the Canadian to the fork of the Arkansas and Cimarron. In alliance with the Comanches, they had ruled the whole of the southern Plains. War was their sacred business, and they were among the finest horsemen the world has ever known. But warfare for the Kiowas was preeminently a matter of disposition rather than of survival, and they never understood the grim, unrelenting advance of the U.S. Cavalry. When at last, divided and ill-provisioned, they were driven onto the Staked Plains in the cold rains of autumn, they fell into panic. In Palo Duro Canyon they abandoned their crucial stores to pillage and had nothing then but their lives. In order to save themselves, they surrendered to the soldiers at Fort Sill and were imprisoned in the old stone corral that now stands as a military museum. My grandmother was spared the humiliation of those high gray walls by eight or ten years, but she must have known from birth the affliction of defeat, the dark brooding of old warriors. 3

Her name was Aho, and she belonged to the last culture to evolve in North America. Her forebears came down from the high country in western Montana nearly three centuries ago. They were a mountain people, a mysterious tribe of hunters whose language has never been positively classified 4 in any major group. In the late seventeenth century they began a long migration to the south and east. It was a journey toward the dawn, and it led to a golden age. Along the way the Kiowas were befriended by the Crows, who gave them the culture and religion of the Plains. They acquired horses, and their ancient nomadic spirit was suddenly free of the ground. They acquired Tai-me, the sacred Sun Dance doll, from that moment the object and symbol of their worship, and so shared in the divinity of the sun. Not least, they acquired the sense of destiny, therefore courage and pride. When they entered upon the southern Plains they had been transformed. No longer were they slaves to the simple necessity of survival; they were a lordly and dangerous society of fighters and thieves, hunters and priests of the sun. According to their origin myth, they entered the world through a hollow log. From one point of view, their migration was the fruit of an old prophecy, for indeed they emerged from a sunless world.

Although my grandmother lived out her long life in the 5
shadow of Rainy Mountain, the immense landscape of the continental interior lay like memory in her blood. She could tell of the Crows, whom she had never seen, and of the Black Hills, where she had never been. I wanted to see in reality what she had seen more perfectly in the mind's eye, and traveled fifteen hundred miles to begin my pilgrimage.

Yellowstone, it seemed to me, was the top of the world, 6
a region of deep lakes and dark timber, canyons and waterfalls. But, beautiful as it is, one might have the sense of confinement there. The skyline in all directions is close at hand, the high wall of the woods and deep cleavages of shade. There is a perfect freedom in the mountains, but it belongs to the eagle and the elk, the badger and the bear. The Kiowas reckoned their stature by the distance they could see, and they were bent and blind in the wilderness.

Descending eastward, the highland meadows are a stair- 7
way to the plain. In July the inland slope of the Rockies is luxuriant with flax and the buckwheat, stonecrop and larkspur. The earth unfolds and the limit of the land recedes.

Clusters of trees, and animals grazing far in the distance, cause the vision to reach away and wonder to build upon the mind. The sun follows a longer course in the day, and the sky is immense beyond all comparison. The great billowing clouds that sail upon it are shadows that move upon the grain like water, dividing light. Farther down, in the land of the Crows and Blackfeet, the plain is yellow. Sweet clover takes hold of the hills and bends upon itself to cover and seal the soil. There the Kiowas paused on their way; they had come to the place where they must change their lives. The sun is at home on the plains. Precisely there does it have the certain character of a god. When the Kiowas came to the land of the Crows, they could see the dark lees of the hills at dawn across the Bighorn River, the profusion of light on the grain shelves, the oldest deity ranging after the solstices. Not yet would they veer southward to the caldron of the land that lay below; they must wean their blood from the northern winter and hold the mountains a while longer in their view. They bore Tai-me in procession to the east.

A dark mist lay over the Black Hills, and the land was like 8
iron. At the top of a ridge I caught sight of Devil's Tower upthrust against the gray sky as if in the birth of time the core of the earth had broken through its crust and the motion of the world was begun. There are things in nature that engender an awful quiet in the heart of man; Devil's Tower is one of them. Two centuries ago, because they could not do otherwise, the Kiowas made a legend at the base of the rock. My grandmother said:

Eight children were there at play, seven sisters and their brother. Suddenly the boy was struck dumb; he trembled and began to run upon his hands and feet. His fingers became claws, and his body was covered with fur. Directly there was a bear where the boy had been. The sisters were terrified; they ran, and the bear after them. They came to the stump of a great tree, and the tree spoke to them. It bade them climb upon it, and as they did so it began to rise into the air. The bear came to kill them, but they were just beyond its reach. It reared against the tree and scored the bark all around with its claws. The seven sisters were borne into the sky, and they became the stars of the Big Dipper.

From that moment, and so long as the legend lives, the Kiowas have kinsmen in the night sky. Whatever they were in the mountains, they could be no more. However tenuous their well-being, however much they had suffered and would suffer again, they had found a way out of the wilderness.

My grandmother had a reverence for the sun, a holy regard 9
that now is all but gone out of mankind. There was a wariness in her, and an ancient awe. She was a Christian in her later years, but she had come a long way about, and she never forgot her birthright. As a child she had been to the Sun Dances; she had taken part in those annual rites, and by them she had learned the restoration of her people in the presence of Tai-me. She was about seven when the last Kiowa Sun Dance was held in 1887 on the Washita River above Rainy Mountain Creek. The buffalo were gone. In order to consummate the ancient sacrifice—to impale the head of a buffalo bull upon the medicine tree—a delegation of old men journeyed into Texas, there to beg and barter for an animal from the Goodnight herd. She was ten when the Kiowas came together for the last time as a living Sun Dance culture. They could find no buffalo; they had to hang an old hide from the sacred tree. Before the dance could begin, a company of soldiers rode out from Fort Sill under orders to disperse the tribe. Forbidden without cause the essential act of their faith, having seen the wild herds slaughtered and left to rot upon the ground, the Kiowas backed away forever from the medicine tree. That was July 20, 1890, at the great bend of the Washita. My grandmother was there. Without bitterness, and for as long as she lived, she bore a vision of deicide.

Now that I can have her only in memory, I see my grand- 10
mother in the several postures that were peculiar to her: standing at the wood stove on a winter morning and turning meat in a great iron skillet; sitting at the south window, bent above her beadwork, and afterwards, when her vision failed, looking down for a long time into the fold of her hands; going out upon a cane, very slowly as she did when the weight of age came upon her; praying. I remember her most often at prayer. She made long, rambling prayers out of

suffering and hope, having seen many things. I was never sure that I had the right to hear, so exclusive were they of all mere custom and company. The last time I saw her she prayed standing by the side of her bed at night, naked to the waist, the light of a kerosene lamp moving upon her dark skin. Her long, black hair, always drawn and braided in the day, lay upon her shoulders and against her breasts like a shawl. I do not speak Kiowa, and I never understood her prayers, but there was something inherently sad in the sound, some merest hesitation upon the syllables of sorrow. She began in a high and descending pitch, exhausting her breath to silence; then again and again—and always the same intensity of effort, of something that is, and is not, like urgency in the human voice. Transported so in the dancing light among the shadows of her room, she seemed beyond the reach of time. But that was illusion; I think I knew then that I should not see her again.

For Study and Discussion

QUESTIONS FOR RESPONSE

1. How has American history (and movies) influenced your attitudes toward Native Americans and their culture?
2. In what ways does Momaday's essay correct or enrich your conception of various Native American cultures?

QUESTIONS ABOUT PURPOSE

1. How does Momaday's title provide an explanation of his purpose? How do paragraphs 2 and 5 clarify that purpose?
2. What is the purpose of Momaday's detailed description in paragraph 1? How does he use the concluding sentence to connect this description to the larger issues of his essay?

QUESTIONS ABOUT AUDIENCE

1. What audience does Momaday presume he is addressing throughout the essay? How do you know?
2. Why is the historical information (for example, paragraph 9) necessary for that audience?

QUESTIONS ABOUT STRATEGIES

1. How does Momaday arrange the events in his narrative to distinguish between the Kiowas and his own journey to the continental interior?
2. Momaday remembers his grandmother in several significant poses. What does each one of these "pictures" tell us about her?

QUESTIONS FOR DISCUSSION

1. How does the Kiowas' belief that they could measure "their stature by the distance they could see" explain their history?
2. What does this essay reveal about the importance of oral traditions? What significance does Momaday attach to the fact that he does not speak Kiowa?

LE LY HAYSLIP

Le Ly Hayslip was born in 1949 in Ky La, now called Xa Hoa Qui, a small village near Da Nang in central Vietnam. During most of her childhood, she fought for the Viet Cong against the Americans and South Vietnamese. At the age of fifteen, she was accused of treason and condemned to die. Her father petitioned the Viet Cong and she was pardoned and exiled to Saigon, where she and her mother worked as house servants. Eventually she returned to Da Nang, working first in the black market and then in an American hospital. In 1970, she married an American civilian contractor from San Diego and moved to southern California. In 1986, she returned to Vietnam, in search of her family and her past. With the help of co-author Jay Wurts, Hayslip recounts her coming of age in Vietnam and her trip back to her homeland in *When Heaven and Earth Changed Places: A Vietnamese Woman's Journey from War to Peace* (1989). Hayslip is currently completing a second book, *At Home in the Land of the Enemy.* In "Playing Stupid," reprinted from her first book, Hayslip reveals the many "disguises" she had to adopt to survive in her war-torn country.

Playing Stupid

When the Viet Cong could not be found (they spent most of their time, after all, hiding in caverns underground with entrances hidden by cookstoves, bushes, false floors, or even underwater by flowing rivers themselves), the Republican soldiers took out their frustration on us: arresting nearby farmers and beating or shooting them on the spot, or carting anyone who looked suspicious off to jail. As these actions 1 drove even more villagers to the Viet Cong cause, more and more of our houses were modified for Viet Cong use. The cadremen told us that each family must have a place in which liberation troops could hide, so my father dug an underground tunnel beneath our heavy cookpot which could house half a dozen fighters. While my father and other villagers worked on their tunnels, we children were taken to a clearing beyond the village graveyard, on the threshold of the swamp, where we were taught revolutionary songs. One of the first we learned was in praise of Uncle Ho—Ho Chi Minh—who, we were told, awaited news of our heroism like a kindly grandfather:

The full moon shines on our land,
So that we can sing and dance
And make wishes for Uncle Ho.
Uncle Ho—we wish you a long life!
We wish you a long beard that we can stroke
While you hold us in your arms
And tell us how much you love us and our country!

We were also taught what we were expected to do for our 2
village, our families, and the revolution. If we were killed, we were told we would live on in history. We learned that, like the French, men of another race called *Americans* wanted to enslave us. "Their allies are the traitorous Republicans of Ngo Dinh Diem!" the Viet Cong shouted. "Just as our fathers fought against the French and their colonial administrators, so must we now fight against these new invaders and their running dogs!" We learned that cheating, stealing from, and lying to Republican soldiers and their allies were not crimes, and that failing to do these things, if the situation demanded it, was treason of the highest sort. Girls were shown the pattern of the Viet Cong flag—half blue (for the North—the direction of peace), half red (for the bloody South), with a yellow star (for the union of yellow-skinned people) in between—and told to sew as many as they could for use in demonstrations or whenever one was asked for by a fighter. Even when the hated Republicans were in our

village and our flag could not be displayed, we were to fly it proudly in our hearts. We then sang songs to celebrate those brothers and fathers that went north to Hanoi in 1954. I sang loudly and thought of Bon Nghe and knew he would be proud.

Although it was nearly dawn when I got home from the first meeting, my parents were still awake. They asked what I'd been doing and I told them proudly that I was now part of the "political cadre"—although I had no idea what that meant. I told them we were to keep an eye on our neighbors and make sure the liberation leaders knew if anyone spoke to the hated Republicans. I told my mother to rejoice, that when her son—my beloved brother Bon—came back from Hanoi, he would be a leader in the South, just as the leaders of our own cadre had been trained in Hanoi and now were helping our village gain victory over the invaders. 3

Although my mother was not sure that my involvement with the cadre was a good idea, she seemed happy that through them, somehow, Bon's return might be hastened. My father, however, looked at me with an expression I had never seen before and said nothing. Although Ky La's first big battle had yet to be fought, it was as if he had seen, in my shining, excited, determined little face, the first casualty of our new war. 4

It was a hot afternoon and I was tending our water buffalo in the fields, prodding it left and right with a bamboo stick and daydreaming when the motor noise began. The sound of trucks and jeeps was now so familiar in Ky La, especially during the day, that nobody paid any attention to it except as a reminder to keep to his own business and make sure that business was as far as possible from the Republicans'. 5

But this motor noise was different. Like a tiger growling in a cave, the hollow noise became a roar and our buffalo grunted and trotted without prodding toward the trees. Steadily, the roar increased and I looked into the sun to see two helicopters, whining and flapping like furious birds, settle out of the sky toward me. The wind whipped my 6 clothes and snatched the sun hat from my head. Even the ankle-deep water itself retreated before the down blast of their terrible beating wings. What could a puny girl do but fall down on her knees and hold fast to mother earth?

To my surprise, I did not die. Almost as quickly as it arrived, the roar spun down and the dying blast of wind and water gave back the heat of day. As I raised my eyes, the dull green door on the side of the ship slid open and the most splendid man I had ever seen stepped out onto the marshy ground. 7

He was a giant, even bigger than the Moroccans who occasionally still haunted my dreams, but crispy clean in starched fatigues with a yellow scarf tucked into his shirt and a golden patch upon his shoulder. The black boots into which his battle pants were bloused shone bright as a beetle's shell. 8

Still cowering, I watched his brawny, blond-haired hands raise binoculars to his eyes. He scanned the tree line around Ky La, ignoring me completely, and chewed the lip below his scrubby mustache. In a husky voice, he said something in his queer language to another fair-skinned soldier inside the door, then dropped the field glasses to his chest and climbed back inside his machine. 9

Instantly, the flap-flap-flap and siren howl increased and the typhoon rose again. As if plucked by the hand of god, the enormous green machine tiptoed on its skids and swooped away, climbing steadily toward the treetops, the second craft behind it. In seconds even the hollow growl was gone, replaced by my father's voice. 10

"Bay Ly—are you all right?" 11

I looked up at him from my knees. My face must have revealed my wonder because his expression of anguish turned quickly to relief—and then to anger. 12

"The *may bay chuong-chuong*—the dragonflies—weren't they wonderful!" I blurted out what was in my heart. 13

My father cupped my face roughly and cleared the wet hair from my eyes. "Wonderful? Hah! They were *Americans!* You risked your life hanging around here while they landed. 14

Even our buffalo has more sense than you!" He raised me to my feet. My legs were still wobbly with excitement.

"But didn't you see them, Father?" 15

"Yes—I saw them. So did everyone else. So did the Viet 16 Cong. Now go catch your ox and take him home. It's almost lunchtime."

Only when I retrieved my hat and stick and began spat- 17 tering across the field to the trees did I notice that other people were staring in my direction. At supper that evening, my father had not only lost his anger, he actually seemed pleased.

"Father—why are you smiling?" my mother snapped. 18 "Your daughter was almost killed today by Americans. The propellers could have chewed her up and spat her all the way to Danang. What's wrong with you?"

My father put down his bowl. Little rice grains stuck to 19 his chin. "I'm smiling because I'm told we have a brave woman warrior in our house—although she'd better be more careful if she wants to be around for New Year's, eh?" He mussed the stringy black hair on my head.

"What are you talking about?" my mother asked. 20

"Oh, haven't you heard the news? It's the talk of Ky La: 21 How little Bay Ly stood her ground against the enemy's *may bay chuong-chuong cua My huy*. She didn't budge an inch!"

"That's what the neighbors are saying?" My mother 22 couldn't believe that her lazy, absentminded daughter could have done anything so grand.

I didn't have the heart to tell them it was awe, not courage, 23 that nailed my feet to the ground when the Americans landed. In time, we all would learn the wisdom of standing still at the approach of Americans—the way one learns to stand still in the face of an angry dog. Before long, any Vietnamese who ran from American gunships would be considered Viet Cong and shot down for the crime of fear.

Although Americans had been in the village before and 24 now came more frequently to Ky La, we children never got used to them. Because they had blue eyes and always wore sunglasses, a few of us thought they were blind. We called them *mat meo*—cat eyes—and "long nose" to their backs and repeated every wild story we heard about them. Because the Viet Cong, when they captured them, always removed the Americans' boots (making escape too painful for their soft, citified feet), we thought we could immobilize the Americans by stealing both their sunglasses and their shoes. How can a soldier fight, we reasoned, if he's not only blind but lame?

Still, the arrival of the Americans in ever-increasing num- 25
bers meant the new war had expanded beyond anyone's wildest dreams. A period of great danger—one we couldn't imagine at the time—was about to begin.

The Viet Cong, too, sensed this grave development and 26
stepped up their activities. In our midnight meetings, which were now held more often, they told us how to act when the Americans and their Republican "lap dogs" were around.

"What will you do when the enemy sleeps in your house?" 27
the cadre leader asked.

"Steal his weapons!" we answered in chorus. "Steal his 28
medicine! Steal his food!"

"And what will you do with what you steal?" 29

"Give it to you!" The village children laughed happily and 30
applauded our own correct answers. Whenever we turned something in to the Viet Cong—even something as small as a mess kit or pocketknife—we were rewarded like heroes. Handmade medals were pinned to our shirts and our names were entered on the Blackboard of Honor.

My name quickly rose on the list because the Republicans 31
in our house were so careless. We lived on a rise of ground near the fields and swamps and because it was easy to see in all directions, the soldiers there would relax. A few of us stole firearms—automatic rifles and pistols—but the Viet Cong seldom used them because the ammunition was different from the kind they received from the North. What they really wanted were hand grenades and first aid kits—things any fighter could use—things that were in perilously short supply. Once, I stole a hand grenade and hid it in a rice container that also held *man cau* fruit, which looks just like pineapples. My father discovered it by chance and his

mouth fell open when one "fruit" he grabbed weighed so much more than the others. He buried it in a secret place and lectured me sternly about taking such chances, but I didn't care and promptly stole another one as soon as I had the chance. We kids used to laugh when a careless Republican got chewed out by his superior for losing such equipment. The fact that those things might lead to new deaths on both sides, including women and children in our own village, never occurred to us. For us, the new war was a game for earning medals and an honored place on lists—ideas we had been taught to honor for years in the government's own school.

Of course, every once in a while, one of us would get 32
caught. If the stolen thing was a bit of food or clothing, the soldiers would just box our ears and take it back. But if it was a weapon or a piece of expensive equipment, the child would be arrested and taken away, to be tortured if she did not tell the soldiers what she knew about the Viet Cong. One friend of mine—a girl named Thi, whose parents "went north" when the war began—was about two years older than I was and very clever. Because she lived with her grandmother and there were no men around, the Republicans often used her house as a base and were very careless with their gear. One afternoon, she stole not only several hand grenades, but a large Republican machine gun. Unfortunately for her, she was caught when the soldiers found her struggling with a box of heavy ammunition and was spirited out of town in the officer's jeep. The Republicans never publicized these arrests because they were ashamed to admit that so many peasants in our village were against them. It was easier for the suspect to "just disappear," like the wayward equipment itself.

The cadre leaders were very clear about how we were 33
supposed to act if we were threatened with capture. Because we knew where many secret tunnels were hidden, we were told to hide in them until the Viet Cong could help us. If they could not, we were expected to commit suicide—using, if need be, the weapon or explosives we had just stolen. Our

deaths would mean nothing if they came after torture; only by dying in battle or by our own little hands would we be immortalized as heroes. This had been programmed into us by the Viet Cong and our own ancient, heroic legends, so we never questioned it for an instant. We didn't realize the Viet Cong were more concerned about terrified children giving away their secrets than guaranteeing our places in history. Loyalty was something the Viet Cong always worried about—more than battles or American bombs—and I would one day find out just how dangerous these worries could make them.

Eventually, the children my age and older went to fight 34
for the Viet Cong. As you would expect, few parents approved of this, even the ones who hated the Republicans and Americans the most. Many parents, including my own, begged to have their children excused but few exceptions were made. Fortunately, because I was my parents' last daughter (my brother Sau Ban, by this time, was away in Saigon working with the youth construction brigade), and because my father had worked so diligently to build bunkers and tunnels for the Viet Cong in our village, and because my eldest brother Bon Nghe had gone to Hanoi, and because I had already proved my loyalty and steadfastness on other occasions—including the arrival of the American helicopters—I was allowed to remain at home and perform other duties. In a solemn ceremony, I was inducted into the secret self-defense force and told I would be responsible for warning the Viet Cong about enemy movements in my village. After a battle, I was to help the nurses tend our wounded and report on enemy casualties. Although I was disappointed that I could not join my friends in combat, I was proud to be doing a job so similar to that of brother Bon Nghe.

My main assignment was to keep an eye on the stretch of 35
jungle that ran between Ky La and the neighboring village. As usual, my father played an important role in keeping me safe and alive. He would stand on the high ground behind our house—the same ground on which he had first instructed me about my duty to Vietnam—and relay my signal to the

Viet Cong sentinels at the far edge of the forest. If Republicans or Americans were inside the village, he would take off his hat and fan himself three times. If the enemy was approaching the village, he would fan himself twice. If the coast was clear, and no enemy troops were around, he would fan himself once. This system, my father told me, had been used by the Viet Minh and was very effective. It allowed me to stay near the village where I would be safer and less suspect, and permitted the adult, my father in this case, to take most of the risk by giving the signal himself. If the system went wrong and some Viet Cong were killed, he assured me that his, not mine, would be the next body found on the road to Danang. Similarly, if the Republicans figured out the signals, he would also be killed—but only after being tortured for information. Although I was still blinded by my young girl's vision of glory, I began to see dimly what a terrible spot the war had put him in. For me and most other children, the new war was still an exciting game. For my father, it was a daily gamble for life itself.

As the war around Ky La dragged on, the Viet Cong established regular tasks for the villagers. One week, our family would cook rations for them—although the Viet Cong never asked for anything special and refused to take food if it meant we would have nothing ourselves. The next week, it might be our duty to sew clothes: to repair old uniforms or make new ones—sometimes with the parachute silk taken from captured fliers or from the wreckage of an American plane. As standing orders, young girls like me were supposed to make friends with the Republicans and steal their toothpaste, cigarettes, and other sundries that were welcomed in the jungle. To make sure these false friendships didn't blossom into real ones, we were reminded during our midnight meetings of the differences between our liberation soldiers and the Republicans and Americans who fought them. 36

"The imperialists and their running dogs," the cadre leader said, shaking his fist in the air and showering spit on those nearest him, "have aircraft and bombs and long-range artil- 37 lery and ten men for every one of ours. We have only rags and rifles and those supplies we carry on our backs. When the Republicans and Americans come to your village, they trample your crops, burn your houses, and kill your relatives just for getting in the way. We respect your homes and the shrines of your ancestors and execute only those who are traitors to our cause. President Diem gives you foreign invaders while Ho Chi Minh promises you a free Vietnam. The Republicans fight for pay, like mercenaries, while we fight only for your independence."

38 As much as we disliked the wartime dangers, we could not argue with what the leader said. For every American who yielded the right of way to us on the road, many more bullied us like cattle. For every Republican whose politeness reminded us of our sons and brothers, there were others who acted like pirates. Whenever it was safe to do so, we organized demonstrations and walked from village to village in our area, waving the Viet Cong flag and shouting slogans to our neighbors. We cursed the "Republican lap dogs" and told the safely distant Americans to get out of our country. It was helpless rage that drove us, but it made us feel better and seemed to even the odds, if only in our hearts. Unfortunately, on one occasion, those terrible odds—and the awful reality of the war—finally caught up with me.

39 It was during one of these demonstrations, on a hot windless night, that a Viet Cong runner came up and told us the Republicans were about to bombard the area. Everyone ran to the roadside trenches and the Viet Cong themselves disappeared into the jungle.

40 At first, the shells hit far away, then the explosions came toward us. Flares drifting down on parachutes lit up the sky and threw eerie, wavering shadows across my trench. The bombardment seemed to go on for hours, and as I lay alone in my hiding place, flinching with each explosion, I began to worry about my family. I had a terrifying vision of my house and parents coming apart as they rose high on a ball of flame. I had a powerful urge to run home, but somehow I overcame it. Leaving the trench before the shelling stopped

would have been suicide—even silly young farm girls knew that.

When the explosions stopped, I stretched out from my embryonic coil and poked my head out of the trench. The night air smelled terrible—like burning tires—and splintered trees and rocks lay all over the road. From the direction of Ky La, a big force of Republicans were coming up the road, rousting civilians from the trenches. It was illegal to be outside after dark, even in your own village. To be away from your local area on top of that was all but a confession of being a Viet Cong. 41

I lay in my burrow and tried to decide what to do. All I could think of was our two neighbors, sisters named Tram and Phat, whose two brothers had gone to Hanoi while a third had stayed in Ky La. The Ky La brother was arrested and tortured by Republicans because of his connections to the North. When he was released, the first thing he did was kiss his family good-bye and slash his wrists. This so shocked and angered the sisters that they became staunch supporters of the Viet Cong. When the Republicans came back to arrest them, the sisters let it be known they were hiding in their family bunker, too afraid to come out. The soldiers, of course, went in after them. When they crawled inside the bunker, they saw the sisters sitting together, calm as can be, each holding a grenade without its pin. Their small hands were clasped around the safety handle, ready to release it should either of them be bothered. The soldiers, fearing to shoot them and thus set off the grenades, scrambled to get out. But the sisters released the grenades anyway and perished with three of their enemies. The next day, their mother buried what was left of her daughters beside her son and went to work in the fields. The Republicans followed her and, fearing to get too close to the last member of such a dangerous, desperate family, shot her down from behind the dikes. 42

I did not have a weapon, but it would be easy enough to goad the soldiers into shooting me, or, for that matter, to grab the barrel of one rifle and pull it against my chest. Still, 43

I did not want my own mother to die because of my heroism or bad luck. Over and over in my head I repeated her advice for just this situation: *If you're too smart or too dumb, you'll die—so play stupid, eh? That shouldn't be too hard for a silly girl who lets herself get caught! Act like you don't know anything because you are young and stupid. That goes for either side, no matter's who's asking the questions. Play stupid, eh? Stupid, stupid child!*

When the soldiers finally lifted me from the trench, muttering and covered with dirt, they must have thought I was simpleminded or shell-shocked by the explosions. Instead of questioning me or beating me or shooting me on the spot, as they had done with some others, they tied my hands behind my back and pushed me into a truck with other people from the parade and drove us all to the nearest jail. 44

From the truck we were led to a room with no furniture and told to wait silently. One by one, the guards took people to another room for interrogation. I was the fifth or sixth to be taken, and until that time, no one before me had come back. Because I hadn't heard shots, I was foolish enough to think they had been released. 45

When my turn came, the guards hustled me down a corridor to a windowless cell with a single electric light bulb hanging from the ceiling. A young Vietnamese soldier with many stripes and decorations made me squat in the middle of the floor and began to ask simple questions like "What is your name? Where are you from? Who is in your family?" and, most importantly, "What were you doing so far from your home in the middle of the night?" I answered each question like a terrified little girl, which, as my mother had promised, was not difficult. I said I sneaked away from home to follow what sounded like a feast-day parade. The people in the parade said we were going down the road to see a play. I told the soldier I was always getting into trouble like this and asked him to please not tell my parents because my father would whip me and my mother would— 46

The soldier's blow stopped my clever story and almost knocked me out. The next thing I remember I was being 47 jerked up by my hair with my face pointed up at the light bulb. The interrogator asked again, in a rougher voice, what I had been doing away from my village. Sobbing, I answered again that I had heard a parade and followed it to see a play. I didn't mean any harm to anyone. I only wanted to see the play and have fun—

The guard behind me lifted me by my hair and I yelped and he kicked the small of my back—once, twice, three times—with his heavy boots. I now screamed as loud as I could—no acting!—but he kept me dangling and kicked me some more, my scalp and back on fire. Each time I tried to support myself, the soldier kicked my legs out from under me, so the more I struggled the worse it hurt. Finally I went limp and the guard dumped me on the floor. The interrogator screamed his questions again, but I could only cry hysterically. He hit me a few more times, then pulled me up by my tied hands and shoved me out the door. The guard took me down the hall and into a big room that had been divided by bamboo bars into a dozen tiny cages. They thrust me into one of them—a space not big enough for even a small girl like me to stand up or stretch out in—and padlocked the door. 48

For a long time I simply lay sobbing on the cage's bamboo floor. My tears stung the welts rising on my face and my back was beginning to throb. With my hands still tied behind me, I rolled upright against the bars. The room smelled like a sewer and when I focused my eyes I saw that a single drain at its center was used as the toilet for the cages. At once I recognized some people from the demonstration, although nobody was from my village. What we all had in common, though, was the badge of interrogation: purple eyes, puffed foreheads, mouths and noses caked with blood, teeth chipped or missing behind split lips and broken jaws. Like the interrogation cell, the dingy room had but a single unblinking light bulb from which even closed eyes offered no relief. 49

I began to feel desperate pain now in my lower back and bladder. Afraid I would wet my pants, I hiked down my trousers and relieved myself shamelessly on the floor. I 50 watched the stream of frothy liquid tinged with red meander down the drain and I almost fainted. I had never seen blood in my urine before, and assumed it meant I was dying. Still, the painful river inside me flowed on, blood or no blood, and my little girl's bottom sank to the bars and I sat there shivering, peeing, and crying—careless of anyone—wanting only my mother and my bed and an end to this terrible nightmare.

After crying myself out, I went to sleep. The next thing I 51
knew the door of my cage banged open and strong hands dragged me by the ankles toward the door. I was put on my feet and shoved down the hall toward the interrogation cell, which, just by my seeing its door, almost made me vomit. By the hazy light at the end of the hall I knew that the sun had come up—perhaps to mock my misery—on a beautiful summer day.

Inside the airless cell, however, everything was midnight— 52
except for the harsh, unsleeping bulb. But a different, older soldier greeted me now and, to my astonishment, he ordered the guard to untie me. My little joints popped as I stretched out my arms and rubbed the welts on my wrists.

"Con an com chua?" (Have you eaten?), the soldier asked 53
politely.

I didn't know how to answer. The question might have 54
been what it seemed—a jailer's inquiry about the status of an inmate. But the question was also the formal greeting made between peasants from the earliest mists of time in a land where food was always scarce. I chose the most traditional, politest answer possible.

"Da con an com roi" (I have already eaten, thank you), and 55
cast my eyes down at the filthy floor. It seemed to satisfy him, although he said nothing more about my breakfast.

"Sergeant Hoa tells me you were most uncooperative last 56
night." The soldier circled me slowly, inspecting my wounds, gauging, perhaps, which weeping cut or puffy bruise would render pain—and therefore answers—most quickly. He paused, as if expecting me to dispute Sergeant Hoa, then said, "Anyway, all that's in the past. Others have told us

everything we want to know about last night. All you need do is confirm a few details, then we can get you cleaned up and back to your family—perhaps in time for lunch, eh? You'd like that, wouldn't you, Le Ly?"

My heart leaped at the sound of my name spoken kindly on this strange man's lips—as well as at the prospect of seeing my family. As my surprised and hopeful face looked up, I saw he was reading a piece of paper—perhaps Sergeant Hoa's report from the night before. Possibly, it contained a good deal more. 57

"Yes, I would like to go home," I said meekly. 58

"Good. Well now, Le Ly, let's talk a moment about the Viet Cong hiding places around Binh Ky. We know about their tunnels beneath the haystacks and their rooms behind the artillery shelter south of the village—" He trailed off, hoping, perhaps, that I would add some other places to his list. "By the way, why *were* you in the trenches last night?" 59

"I jumped in to escape the explosions." 60

"Of course. And why were you outside at all?" 61

"I woke up and saw a parade pass our house. I joined it without waking my parents and was told we were going to see a play. We were almost to the playhouse when the explosions began. I got scared and jumped in a trench. I was too afraid to go home because I thought my parents would spank me." 62

"I see. And what was the play about?" 63

I was quiet a moment, then said, "I don't know. I didn't see it." 64

"Just so. And who was to be in the play?" 65

"I—I don't know that either." 66

"Tell me, Le Ly, do you know this song? 67

We are so cheerful and happy,
We act and sing and dance,
Vietnam's stage is in sunlight,
Because Uncle Ho fills us with joy.

"I know that song," I replied, "but you sang the wrong words. The song I know goes: 68

We are so cheerful and happy,
We act and sing and dance,
Vietnam's stage is in sunlight,
Because Ngo Dinh Diem fills us with joy.

69 My little girl's voice, choked with fear and bruises, must have sounded funny because the soldiers in the room laughed loudly. Perhaps I was the first peasant girl they'd met whose father knew two versions of every political song.

70 "Do the Viet Cong ever come to your village, Le Ly?"

71 "Yes."

72 "And what do they look like?"

73 "They look like you—except they wear black uniforms."

74 The soldier lit a cigarette. He was quiet for such a long time that I thought he was going to hit me. Instead he said, "We'll talk again, Le Ly." He nodded and the guard took me back to my cage.

75 I stayed in the cage two more days. Every morning, a prison worker would splash water on the fetid floor and every evening we were given one bowl of rice with a few greens or pork fat mixed in to sustain us. We were allowed to drink three dippers of water each day and had a few minutes every afternoon to walk around in the compound. Prisoners were forbidden to speak, even in the cages, because the soldiers feared we would coordinate our stories or make plans for breaking out. Given our pathetic condition and the many soldiers and guns that surrounded us, I had trouble imagining how anyone could fear us. Of course, that was exactly why the soldiers worried. The Viet Cong were famous for turning innocent situations into danger for their enemies. Because of our reputation and the countermeasures it demanded, neither jailers nor inmates could relax.

76 Each night I was taken back for interrogation with Sergeant Hoa and each time he asked fewer questions and beat me longer and with more fury. Each morning I was taken to the cell where the second soldier—always kindly and fatherly and good-natured—would show horror at my wounds and ask me different questions about the Viet Cong and life

around Ky La. Compared with Sergeant Hoa and the endless hours in the stinking bamboo cage, these sessions were almost pleasant and I found it harder and harder to play dumb and avoid telling him about my family, whom I now missed very much.

On the third day, after a particularly bad beating the night 77
before, I was summoned for what I thought would be my morning interrogation, but instead was led down the hall toward the shaft of daylight where I found my mother and my sister Ba's husband, Chin, who worked for the government police force in Danang. Despite the toughness I tried to cultivate in prison, I ran weeping to my mother while Chin talked to a soldier about my release. My poor mother, who looked ten years older for my absence, inspected my oozing wounds distastefully—like a shopper sizing up a bad melon. Although I could see she was in almost as much pain as I was, she said nothing, but kept a grim straight face for the soldiers. If I had fooled my jailers into thinking that I was just a naughty, runaway child, my mother's hard look must have convinced them that the beatings I suffered in jail would be nothing compared with the punishment I would get from this heartless woman at home.

Outside, Chin gave me a nasty look and departed on his 78
bicycle. When we got on the bus that would take us near our village and had ridden about a mile, my mother could contain herself no longer and wept as I had done that first night in my cell. She told me Chin was angry at having been disturbed to help his country in-laws, especially since his own house might now be watched and his loyalties questioned because of his shadowy relatives. Although I felt sorry for him, I was so happy to be free that his future troubles—or even my own—just didn't seem to matter.

For Study and Discussion

QUESTIONS FOR RESPONSE

1. What have you been taught about the motives and actions of the combatants in the Vietnam War—the Viet Cong, the Republican Vietnamese, and the Americans?
2. How do you react to Hayslip's portrayal of the Viet Cong as friends, the Republican Vietnamese as pirates, and the Americans as bullies?

QUESTIONS ABOUT PURPOSE

1. Why does Hayslip devote so much attention to her "indoctrination" by the Viet Cong? What is she taught to believe about the "liberation" army?
2. What is her purpose in explaining her parents' attitude toward the war? Why does her father consider her "the first casualty of our new war"?

QUESTIONS ABOUT AUDIENCE

1. What assumptions does Hayslip make about the American readers of her memoir? How much do they know about the average Vietnamese village?
2. How does Hayslip's portrayal of herself as a child caught up in an exciting game affect her readers' view of her behavior?

QUESTIONS ABOUT STRATEGIES

1. How does Hayslip use the scene with the helicopter and the "splendid" American in sunglasses to establish the villagers' view of Americans as a race that "wanted to enslave us"?
2. How does her description of her beating and interrogation demonstrate her ability to follow her mother's advice?

QUESTIONS FOR DISCUSSION

1. What does Hayslip's narrative reveal about loyalty? When does loyalty to family, village, and cause justify criminal behavior? Explain your answer.

2. In what ways does Hayslip's description of the traditional values of the Vietnamese village explain why America did not win the war?

GEORGE ORWELL

George Orwell, the pen name for Eric Blair (1903–1950), was born in Motihari, Bengal, where his father was employed with the Bengal civil service. He was brought to England at an early age for schooling (Eton), but rather than completing his education at the university he served with the Indian imperial police in Burma (1922–1927). He wrote about these experiences in his first novel, *Burmese Days*. Later he returned to Europe and worked at various jobs (described in *Down and Out in Paris and London,* 1933) before fighting on the Republican side in the Spanish civil war (see *Homage to Catalonia,* 1938). Orwell's attitudes toward war and government are reflected in his most famous books: *Animal Farm* (1945), *1984* (1949), and *Shooting an Elephant and Other Essays* (1950). In the title essay from the last volume, Orwell reports a "tiny incident" that gave him deeper insight into his own fears and "the real motives for which despotic governments act."

Shooting an Elephant

In Moulmein, in lower Burma, I was hated by large numbers of people—the only time in my life that I have been important enough for this to happen to me. I was sub-divisional police officer of the town, and in an aimless, petty kind of way anti-European feeling was very bitter. No one had the guts to raise a riot, but if a European woman went through the bazaars alone somebody would probably spit betel juice over her dress. As a police officer I was an obvious target and was baited whenever it seemed safe to do so. When a nimble Burman tripped me up on the football field and the 1 referee (another Burman) looked the other way, the crowd yelled with hideous laughter. This happened more than once. In the end the sneering yellow faces of young men that met me everywhere, the insults hooted after me when I was at a safe distance, got badly on my nerves. The young Buddhist priests were the worst of all. There were several thousands of them in the town and none of them seemed to have anything to do except stand on street corners and jeer at Europeans.

All this was perplexing and upsetting. For at that time I 2
had already made up my mind that imperialism was an evil thing and the sooner I chucked up my job and got out of it the better. Theoretically—and secretly, of course—I was all for the Burmese and all against their oppressors, the British. As for the job I was doing, I hated it more bitterly than I can perhaps make clear. In a job like that you see the dirty work of Empire at close quarters. The wretched prisoners huddling in the stinking cages of the lock-ups, the gray, cowed faces of the long-term convicts, the scarred buttocks of the men who had been flogged with bamboos—all these oppressed me with an intolerable sense of guilt. But I could get nothing into perspective. I was young and ill educated and I had had to think out my problems in the utter silence that is imposed on every Englishman in the East. I did not even know that the British Empire is dying, still less did I know that it is a great deal better than the younger empires that are going to supplant it. All I knew was that I was stuck between my hatred of the empire I served and my rage against the evil-spirited little beasts who tried to make my job impossible. With one part of my mind I thought of the British Raj as an unbreakable tyranny, as something clamped down, in *saecula saeculorum,* upon the will of prostrate peoples; with another part I thought that the greatest joy in the world would be to drive a bayonet into a Buddhist priest's guts. Feelings like these are the normal by-products of imperialism; ask any Anglo-Indian official, if you can catch him off duty.

One day something happened which in a roundabout way 3

was enlightening. It was a tiny incident in itself; but it gave me a better glimpse than I had had before of the real nature of imperialism—the real motives for which despotic governments act. Early one morning the sub-inspector at a police station the other end of town rang me up on the 'phone and said that an elephant was ravaging the bazaar. Would I please come and do something about it? I did not know what I could do, but I wanted to see what was happening and I got on to a pony and started out. I took my rifle, an old .44 Winchester and much too small to kill an elephant, but I thought the noise might be useful *in terrorem.* Various Burmans stopped me on the way and told me about the elephant's doings. It was not, of course, a wild elephant, but a tame one which had gone "must." It had been chained up, as tame elephants always are when their attack of "must" is due, but on the previous night it had broken its chain and escaped. Its mahout, the only person who could manage it when it was in that state, had set out in pursuit, but had taken the wrong direction and was now twelve hours' journey away, and in the morning the elephant had suddenly reappeared in the town. The Burmese population had no weapons and were quite helpless against it. It had already destroyed somebody's bamboo hut, killed a cow and raided some fruit-stalls and devoured the stock; also it had met the municipal rubbish van and, when the driver jumped out and took to his heels, had turned the van over and inflicted violences upon it.

The Burmese sub-inspector and some Indian constables 4
were waiting for me in the quarter where the elephant had been seen. It was a very poor quarter, a labyrinth of squalid bamboo huts, thatched with palm-leaf, winding all over a steep hillside. I remember that it was a cloudy, stuffy morning at the beginning of the rains. We began questioning the people as to where the elephant had gone and, as usual, failed to get any definite information. That is invariably the case in the East; a story always sounds clear enough at a distance, but the nearer you get to the scene of events the vaguer it becomes. Some of the people said that the elephant

had gone in one direction, some said that he had gone in another, some professed not even to have heard of any elephant. I had almost made up my mind that the whole story was a pack of lies, when we heard yells a little distance away. There was a loud, scandalized cry of "Go away, child! Go away this instant!" and an old woman with a switch in her hand came round the corner of a hut, violently shooing away a crowd of naked children. Some more women followed, clicking their tongues and exclaiming; evidently there was something that the children ought not to have seen. I rounded the hut and saw a man's dead body sprawling in the mud. He was an Indian, a black Dravidian coolie, almost naked, and he could not have been dead many minutes. The people said that the elephant had come suddenly upon him round the corner of the hut, caught him with its trunk, put its foot on his back and ground him into the earth. This was the rainy season and the ground was soft, and his face had scored a trench a foot deep and a couple of yards long. He was lying on his belly with arms crucified and head sharply twisted to one side. His face was coated with mud, the eyes wide open, the teeth bared and grinning with an expression of unendurable agony. (Never tell me, by the way, that the dead look peaceful. Most of the corpses I have seen looked devilish.) The friction of the great beast's foot had stripped the skin from his back as neatly as one skins a rabbit. As soon as I saw the dead man I sent an orderly to a friend's house nearby to borrow an elephant rifle. I had already sent back the pony, not wanting it to go mad with fright and throw me if it smelt the elephant.

The orderly came back in a few minutes with a rifle and 5
five cartridges, and meanwhile some Burmans had arrived and told us that the elephant was in the paddy fields below, only a few hundred yards away. As I started forward practically the whole population of the quarter flocked out of the houses and followed me. They had seen the rifle and were all shouting excitedly that I was going to shoot the elephant. They had not shown much interest in the elephant when he was merely ravaging their homes, but it was different now

that he was going to be shot. It was a bit of fun to them, and it would be to an English crowd; besides they wanted the meat. It made me vaguely uneasy. I had no intention of shooting the elephant—I had merely sent for the rifle to defend myself if necessary—and it is always unnerving to have a crowd following you. I marched down the hill, looking and feeling a fool, with the rifle over my shoulder and an ever-growing army of people jostling at my heels. At the bottom, when you got away from the huts, there was a metalled road and beyond that a miry waste of paddy fields a thousand yards across, not yet ploughed but soggy from the first rains and dotted with coarse grass. The elephant was standing eight yards from the road, his left side toward us. He took not the slightest notice of the crowd's approach. He was tearing up bunches of grass, beating them against his knees to clean them, and stuffing them into his mouth.

I had halted on the road. As soon as I saw the elephant I 6
knew with perfect certainty that I ought not to shoot him. It is a serious matter to shoot a working elephant—it is comparable to destroying a huge and costly piece of machinery—and obviously one ought not to do it if it can possibly be avoided. And at that distance, peacefully eating, the elephant looked no more dangerous than a cow. I thought then and I think now that his attack of "must" was already passing off; in which case he would merely wander harmlessly about until the mahout came back and caught him. Moreover, I did not in the least want to shoot him. I decided that I would watch him for a little while to make sure that he did not turn savage again, and then go home.

But at that moment I glanced round at the crowd that 7
had followed me. It was an immense crowd, two thousand at the least and growing every minute. It blocked the road for a long distance on either side. I looked at the sea of yellow faces above the garish clothes—faces all happy and excited over this bit of fun, all certain that the elephant was going to be shot. They were watching me as they would watch a conjurer about to perform a trick. They did not like me, but with the magical rifle in my hands I was momentarily

worth watching. And suddenly I realized that I should have to shoot the elephant after all. The people expected it of me and I had got to do it; I could feel their two thousand wills pressing me forward, irresistibly. And it was at this moment, as I stood there with the rifle in my hands, that I first grasped the hollowness, the futility of the white man's dominion in the East. Here was I, the white man with his gun, standing in front of the unarmed native crowd—seemingly the leading actor of the piece; but in reality I was only an absurd puppet pushed to and fro by the will of those yellow faces behind. I perceived in this moment that when the white man turns tyrant it is his own freedom that he destroys. He becomes a sort of hollow, posing dummy, the conventionalized figure of a sahib. For it is the condition of his rule that he shall spend his life in trying to impress the "natives," and so in every crisis he has got to do what the "natives" expect of him. He wears a mask, and his face grows to fit it. I had got to shoot the elephant. I had committed myself to doing it when I sent for the rifle. A sahib has got to act like a sahib; he has got to appear resolute, to know his own mind and do definite things. To come all that way, rifle in hand, with two thousand people marching at my heels, and then to trail feebly away, having done nothing—no, that was impossible. The crowd would laugh at me. And my whole life, every white man's life in the East, was one long struggle not to be laughed at.

8 But I did not want to shoot the elephant. I watched him beating his bunch of grass against his knees with that preoccupied grandmotherly air that elephants have. It seemed to me that it would be murder to shoot him. At that age I was not squeamish about killing animals, but I had never shot an elephant and never wanted to. (Somehow it always seems worse to kill a *large* animal.) Besides, there was the beast's owner to be considered. Alive, the elephant was worth at least a hundred pounds; dead, he would only be worth the value of his tusks, five pounds, possibly. But I had got to act quickly. I turned to some experienced-looking Burmans who had been there when we arrived, and asked them how the

elephant had been behaving. They all said the same thing: he took no notice of you if you left him alone, but he might charge if you went too close to him.

It was perfectly clear to me what I ought to do. I ought to walk up to within, say, twenty-five yards of the elephant and test his behavior. If he charged, I could shoot; if he took no notice of me, it would be safe to leave him until the mahout came back. But also I knew that I was going to do no such thing. I was a poor shot with a rifle and the ground was soft mud into which one would sink at every step. If the elephant charged and I missed him, I should have about as much chance as a toad under a steam-roller. But even then I was not thinking particularly of my own skin, only of the watchful yellow faces behind. For at that moment, with the crowd watching me, I was not afraid in the ordinary sense, as I would have been if I had been alone. A white man mustn't be frightened in front of "natives"; and so, in general, he isn't frightened. The sole thought in my mind was that if anything went wrong those two thousand Burmans would see me pursued, caught, trampled on, and reduced to a grinning corpse like that Indian up the hill. And if that happened it was quite probable that some of them would laugh. That would never do. There was only one alternative. I shoved the cartridges into the magazine and lay down on the road to get a better aim. 9

The crowd grew very still, and a deep, low, happy sigh, as of people who see the theater curtain go up at last, breathed from innumerable throats. They were going to have their bit of fun after all. The rifle was a beautiful German thing with cross-hair sights. I did not then know that in shooting an elephant one would shoot to cut an imaginary bar running from ear-hole to ear-hole. I ought, therefore, as the elephant was sideways on, to have aimed straight at his ear-hole; actually I aimed several inches in front of this, thinking the brain would be further forward. 10

When I pulled the trigger I did not hear the bang or feel the kick—one never does when a shot goes home—but I heard the devilish roar of glee that went up from the crowd. 11

In that instant, in too short a time, one would have thought, even for the bullet to get there, a mysterious, terrible change had come over the elephant. He neither stirred, nor fell, but every line of his body had altered. He looked suddenly stricken, shrunken, immensely old, as though the frightful impact of the bullet had paralyzed him without knocking him down. At last, after what seemed a long time—it might have been five seconds, I dare say—he sagged flabbily to his knees. His mouth slobbered. An enormous senility seemed to have settled upon him. One could have imagined him thousands of years old. I fired again into the same spot. At the second shot he did not collapse but climbed with desperate slowness to his feet and stood weakly upright, with legs sagging and head drooping. I fired a third time. That was the shot that did for him. You could see the agony of it jolt his whole body and knock the last remnant of strength from his legs. But in falling he seemed for a moment to rise, for as his hind legs collapsed beneath him he seemed to tower upward like a huge rock toppling, his trunk reaching skyward like a tree. He trumpeted, for the first and only time. And then down he came, his belly toward me, with a crash that seemed to shake the ground even where I lay.

I got up. The Burmans were already racing past me across 12
the mud. It was obvious that the elephant would never rise again, but he was not dead. He was breathing very rhythmically with long rattling gasps, his great mound of a side painfully rising and falling. His mouth was wide open—I could see far down into caverns of pale pink throat. I waited a long time for him to die, but his breathing did not weaken. Finally I fired my two remaining shots into the spot where I thought his heart must be. The thick blood welled out of him like red velvet, but still he did not die. His body did not even jerk when the shots hit him, the tortured breathing continued without a pause. He was dying, very slowly and in great agony, but in some world remote from me where not even a bullet could damage him further. I felt that I had got to put an end to that dreadful noise. It seemed dreadful to see the great beast lying there, powerless to move and yet

powerless to die, and not even to be able to finish him. I sent back for my small rifle and poured shot after shot into his heart and down his throat. They seemed to make no impression. The tortured gasps continued as steadily as the ticking of a clock.

In the end I could not stand it any longer and went away. 13 I heard later that it took him half an hour to die. Burmans were bringing dahs and baskets even before I left, and I was told they had stripped his body almost to the bones by the afternoon.

Afterward, of course, there were endless discussions about 14 the shooting of the elephant. The owner was furious, but he was only an Indian and could do nothing. Besides, legally I had done the right thing, for a mad elephant has to be killed, like a mad dog, if its owner fails to control it. Among the Europeans opinion was divided. The older men said I was right, the younger men said it was a damn shame to shoot an elephant for killing a coolie, because an elephant was worth more than any damn Coringhee coolie. And afterward I was very glad that the coolie had been killed; it put me legally in the right and it gave me a sufficient pretext for shooting the elephant. I often wondered whether any of the others grasped that I had done it solely to avoid looking a fool.

For Study and Discussion

QUESTIONS FOR RESPONSE

1. How do you feel when you are laughed at? What do you do in order to avoid looking like a fool?
2. How did you react to Orwell's long introduction (paragraphs 1 and 2) to the incident? Were you attentive, bored, or confused? Now that you have finished the essay, reread these two paragraphs. How does your second reading compare with your first?

QUESTIONS ABOUT PURPOSE

1. What thesis about "the real nature of imperialism" does Orwell prove by narrating this "tiny incident"?
2. List the reasons Orwell considers when he tries to decide what to do. According to his conclusion, what was his main purpose in shooting the elephant?

QUESTIONS ABOUT AUDIENCE

1. How does Orwell wish to present himself to his readers in paragraphs 6 through 9? Do you follow the logic of his argument?
2. Which of the three positions stated in the final paragraph does Orwell expect his readers to agree with? Why is he "glad that the coolie had been killed"?

QUESTIONS ABOUT STRATEGIES

1. Although Orwell begins narrating the incident in paragraph 3, we do not see the elephant until the end of paragraph 5. What details do we see? How do they intensify the dramatic conflict?
2. How does Orwell pace the shooting of the elephant in paragraphs 11 and 12? How does the elephant's slow death affect Orwell's point of view toward what he has done?

QUESTIONS FOR DISCUSSION

1. Orwell was young, frightened, and tormented by strangers in a strange land. What parallels do you see between Orwell's plight and the plight of young American soldiers in Vietnam?
2. Much of Orwell's essay assumes a knowledge of the words *imperialism* and *despotism*. What do these words mean? How do they apply to the essay? What current events can you identify in which these words might also apply?

W. D. WETHERELL

Walter David Wetherell was born in 1948 in Mineola, New York, and was educated at Hofstra University. After working at a variety of odd jobs—movie extra, tour guide, and free-lance journalist—he taught in the creative writing program at the University of Vermont. During this period, Wetherell published short stories in magazines such as *Virginia Quarterly Review, Adventure,* and *New England Quarterly.* His other works include two novels, *Souvenirs* (1981) and *Chekhov's Sister* (1990), and a collection of essays, *Vermont River* (1984). Wetherell's story "The Man Who Loved Levittown" won the O'Henry Prize for best story of the year in 1983, and his collection of stories by the same title won the Heinz Literature Prize in 1985. "The Bass, the River, and Sheila Mant," reprinted from *The Man Who Loved Levittown* (1985), recalls the comic twists in a romantic summer fantasy.

The Bass, the River, and Sheila Mant

There was a summer in my life when the only creature that seemed lovelier to me than a largemouth bass was Sheila Mant. I was fourteen. The Mants had rented the cottage next to ours on the river; with their parties, their frantic games of softball, their constant comings and goings, they appeared to me denizens of a brilliant existence. "Too noisy by half," my mother quickly decided, but I would have given anything to be invited to one of their parties, and when my parents went to bed I would sneak through the woods to their hedge and stare enchanted at the candlelit swirl of white dresses and bright, paisley skirts. 1

Sheila was the middle daughter—at seventeen, all but out 2

of reach. She would spend her days sunbathing on a float my Uncle Sierbert had moored in their cove, and before July was over I had learned all her moods. If she lay flat on the diving board with her hand trailing idly in the water, she was pensive, not to be disturbed. On her side, her head propped up by her arm, she was observant, considering those around her with a look that seemed queenly and severe. Sitting up, arms tucked around her long, suntanned legs, she was approachable, but barely, and it was only in those glorious moments when she stretched herself prior to entering the water that her various suitors found the courage to come near.

These were many. The Dartmouth heavyweight crew would scull by her house on their way upriver, and I think all eight of them must have been in love with her at various times during the summer; the coxswain would curse them through his megaphone, but without effect—there was always a pause in their pace when they passed Sheila's float. I suppose to these jaded twenty-year-olds she seemed the incarnation of innocence and youth, while to me she appeared unutterably suave, the epitome of sophistication. I was on the swim team at school, and to win her attention would do endless laps between my house and the Vermont shore, hoping she would notice the beauty of my flutter kick, the power of my crawl. Finishing, I would boost myself up onto our dock and glance casually over toward her, but she was never watching, and the miraculous day she was, I immediately climbed the diving board and did my best tuck and a half for her, and continued diving until she had left and the sun went down and my longing was like a madness and I couldn't stop. 3

It was late August by the time I got up the nerve to ask her out. The tortured will-I's, won't-I's, the agonized indecision over what to say, the false starts toward her house and embarrassed retreats—the details of these have been seared from my memory, and the only part I remember clearly is emerging from the woods toward dusk while they were playing softball on their lawn, as bashful and frightened as a unicorn. 4

5 Sheila was stationed halfway between first and second, well outside the infield. She didn't seem surprised to see me—as a matter of fact, she didn't seem to see me at all.

6 "If you're playing second base, you should move closer," I said.

7 She turned—I took the full brunt of her long red hair and well-spaced freckles.

8 "I'm playing outfield," she said. "I don't like the responsibility of having a base."

9 "Yeah, I can understand that," I said, though I couldn't. "There's a band in Dixford tomorrow night at nine. Want to go?"

10 One of her brothers sent the ball sailing over the leftfielder's head; she stood and watched it disappear toward the river.

11 "You have a car?" she said, without looking up.

12 I played my master stroke. "We'll go by canoe."

13 I spent all of the following day polishing it. I turned it upside down on our lawn and rubbed every inch with Brillo, hosing off the dirt, wiping it with chamois until it gleamed as bright as aluminum ever gleamed. About five, I slid it into the water, arranging cushions near the bow so Sheila could lean on them if she was in one of her pensive moods, propping up my father's transistor radio by the middle thwart so we could have music when we came back. Automatically, without thinking about it, I mounted my Mitchell reel on my Pfleuger spinning rod and stuck it in the stern.

14 I say automatically, because I never went anywhere that summer without a fishing rod. When I wasn't swimming laps to impress Sheila, I was back in our driveway practicing casts, and when I wasn't practicing casts, I was tying the line to Tosca, our springer spaniel, to test the reel's drag, and when I wasn't doing any of those things, I was fishing the river for bass.

15 Too nervous to sit at home, I got in the canoe early and started paddling in a huge circle that would get me to Sheila's dock around eight. As automatically as I brought along my rod, I tied on a big Rapala plug, let it down into the water, let out some line and immediately forgot all about it.

It was already dark by the time I glided up to the Mants' dock. Even by day the river was quiet, most of the summer people preferring Sunapee or one of the other nearby lakes, and at night it was a solitude difficult to believe, a corridor of hidden life that ran between banks like a tunnel. Even the stars were part of it. They weren't as sharp anywhere else; they seemed to have chosen the river as a guide on their slow wheel toward morning, and in the course of the summer's fishing, I had learned all their names. 16

I was there ten minutes before Sheila appeared. I heard the slam of their screen door first, then saw her in the spotlight as she came slowly down the path. As beautiful as she was on the float, she was even lovelier now—her white dress went perfectly with her hair, and complemented her figure even more than her swimsuit. 17

It was her face that bothered me. It had on its delightful fullness a very dubious expression. 18

"Look," she said. "I can get Dad's car." 19

"It's faster this way," I lied. "Parking's tense up there. Hey, it's safe. I won't tip it or anything." 20

She let herself down reluctantly into the bow. I was glad she wasn't facing me. When her eyes were on me, I felt like diving in the river again from agony and joy. 21

I pried the canoe away from the dock and started paddling upstream. There was an extra paddle in the bow, but Sheila made no move to pick it up. She took her shoes off, and dangled her feet over the side. 22

Ten minutes went by. 23

"What kind of band?" she said. 24

"It's sort of like folk music. You'll like it." 25

"Eric Caswell's going to be there. He strokes number four." 26

"No kidding?" I said. I had no idea who she meant. 27

"What's that sound?" she said, pointing toward shore. 28

"Bass. That splashing sound?" 29

"Over there." 30

"Yeah, bass. They come into the shallows at night to chase frogs and moths and things. Big largemouths. *Micropetrus salmonides,*" I added, showing off. 31

"I think fishing's dumb," she said, making a face. "I mean, it's boring and all. Definitely dumb." 32

Now I have spent a great deal of time in the years since wondering why Sheila Mant should come down so hard on fishing. Was her father a fisherman? Her antipathy toward fishing nothing more than normal filial rebellion? Had she tried it once? A messy encounter with worms? It doesn't matter. What does, is that at that fragile moment in time I would have given anything not to appear dumb in Sheila's severe and unforgiving eyes. 33

She hadn't seen my equipment yet. What I *should* have done, of course, was push the canoe in closer to shore and carefully slide the rod into some branches where I could pick it up again in the morning. Failing that I could have surreptitiously dumped the whole outfit overboard, written off the forty or so dollars as love's tribute. What I actually *did* do was gently lean forward, and slowly, ever so slowly, push the rod back through my legs toward the stern where it would be less conspicuous. 34

It must have been just exactly what the bass was waiting for. Fish will trail a lure sometimes, trying to make up their mind whether or not to attack, and the slight pause in the plug's speed caused by my adjustment was tantalizing enough to overcome the bass's inhibitions. My rod, safely out of sight at last, bent double. The line, tightly coiled, peeled off the spool with the shrill, tearing zip of a high-speed drill. 35

Four things occurred to me at once. One, that it was a bass. Two, that it was a big bass. Three, that it was the biggest bass I had ever hooked. Four, that Sheila Mant must not know. 36

"What was that?" she said, turning half around. 37

"Uh, what was what?" 38

"That buzzing noise." 39

"Bats." 40

She shuddered, quickly drew her feet back into the canoe. Every instinct I had told me to pick up the rod and strike back at the bass, but there was no need to—it was already solidly hooked. Downstream, an awesome distance downstream, it jumped clear of the water, landing with a con- 41 cussion heavy enough to ripple the entire river. For a moment, I thought it was gone, but then the rod was bending again, the tip dancing into the water. Slowly, not making any motion that might alert Sheila, I reached down to tighten the drag.

While all this was going on, Sheila had begun talking and 42
it was a few minutes before I was able to catch up with her train of thought.

"I went to a party there. These fraternity men. Katherine 43
says I could get in there if I wanted. I'm thinking more of UVM or Bennington. Somewhere I can ski."

The bass was slanting toward the rocks on the New 44
Hampshire side by the ruins of Donaldson's boathouse. It had to be an old bass—a young one probably wouldn't have known the rocks were there. I brought the canoe back into the middle of the river, hoping to head it off.

"That's neat," I mumbled. "Skiing. Yeah, I can see that." 45

"Eric said I have the figure to model, but I thought I 46
should get an education first. I mean, it might be a while before I get started and all. I was thinking of getting my hair styled, more swept back? I mean, Ann-Margret? Like hers, only shorter?"

She hesitated. "Are we going backward?" 47

We were. I had managed to keep the bass in the middle 48
of the river away from the rocks, but it had plenty of room there, and for the first time a chance to exert its full strength. I quickly computed the weight necessary to draw a fully loaded canoe backwards—the thought of it made me feel faint.

"It's just the current," I said hoarsely. "No sweat or any- 49
thing."

I dug in deeper with my paddle. Reassured, Sheila began 50
talking about something else, but all my attention was taken up now with the fish. I could feel its desperation as the water grew shallower. I could sense the extra strain on the line, the frantic way it cut back and forth in the water. I could visualize what it looked like—the gape of its mouth, the flared gills and thick, vertical tail. The bass couldn't have encountered

many forces in its long life that it wasn't capable of handling, and the unrelenting tug at its mouth must have been a source of great puzzlement and mounting panic.

Me, I had problems of my own. To get to Dixford, I had 51
to paddle up a sluggish stream that came into the river beneath a covered bridge. There was a shallow sandbar at the mouth of this stream—weeds on one side, rocks on the other. Without doubt, this is where I would lose the fish.

"I have to be careful with my complexion. I tan, but in 52
segments. I can't figure out if it's even worth it. I shouldn't even do it probably. I saw Jackie Kennedy in Boston and she wasn't tan at all."

Taking a deep breath, I paddled as hard as I could for the 53
middle, deepest part of the bar. I could have threaded the eye of a needle with the canoe, but the pull on the stern threw me off and I overcompensated—the canoe veered left and scraped bottom. I pushed the paddle down and shoved. A moment of hesitation . . . a moment more. . . . The canoe shot clear into the deeper water of the stream. I immediately looked down at the rod. It was bent in the same, tight arc—miraculously, the bass was still on.

The moon was out now. It was low and full enough that 54
its beam shone directly on Sheila there ahead of me in the canoe, washing her in a creamy, luminous glow. I could see the lithe, easy shape of her figure. I could see the way her hair curled down off her shoulders, the proud, alert tilt of her head, and all these things were as a tug on my heart. Not just Sheila, but the aura she carried about her of parties and casual touchings and grace. Behind me, I could feel the strain of the bass, steadier now, growing weaker, and this was another tug on my heart, not just the bass but the beat of the river and the slant of the stars and the small of the night, until finally it seemed I would be torn apart between longings, split in half. Twenty yards ahead of us was the road, and once I pulled the canoe up on shore, the bass would be gone, irretrievably gone. If instead I stood up, grabbed the rod and started pumping, I would have it—as tired as the bass was, there was no chance it could get away.

I reached down for the rod, hesitated, looked up to where Sheila was stretching herself lazily toward the sky, her small breasts rising beneath the soft fabric of her dress, and the tug was too much for me, and quicker than it takes to write down, I pulled a penknife from my pocket and cut the line in half.

With a sick, nauseous feeling in my stomach, I saw the 55
rod unbend.

"My legs are sore," Sheila whined. "Are we there yet?" 56

Through a superhuman effort of self-control, I was able 57
to beach the canoe and help Sheila off. The rest of the night is much foggier. We walked to the fair—there was the smell of popcorn, the sound of guitars. I may have danced once or twice with her, but all I really remember is her coming over to me once the music was done to explain that she would be going home in Eric Caswell's Corvette.

"Okay," I mumbled. 58

For the first time that night she looked at me, really looked 59
at me.

"You're a funny kid, you know that?" 60

Funny. Different. Dreamy. Odd. How many times was I 61
to hear that in the years to come, all spoken with the same quizzical, half-accusatory tone Sheila used then. Poor Sheila! Before the month was over, the spell she cast over me was gone, but the memory of that lost bass haunted me all summer and haunts me still. There would be other Sheila Mants in my life, other fish, and though I came close once or twice, it was these secret, hidden tuggings in the night that claimed me, and I never made the same mistake again.

COMMENT ON "THE BASS, THE RIVER, AND SHEILA MANT"

"The Bass, the River, and Sheila Mant" is an excellent illustration of how narration and description are used in short fiction. Although the plot seems arranged in a simple chronology, the narrator indicates that the events took place when he was younger (age fourteen) and that they continue to haunt him. The story is paced at two speeds: the opening is slow and languid as the young boy describes the enchanting moods of Sheila Mant; the action speeds up considerably once they are in the canoe and he accidentally hooks the biggest bass he had ever seen. The complicated situation creates a clear choice—Sheila or the fish. Beguiled by her sensual beauty—even though he suspects it is superficial—the narrator chooses Sheila. Older, wiser, he concludes that he will never make that mistake again.

Narration and Description as a Writing Strategy

1. Recount the details of an accident or disaster in which you were a witness or a victim. You may wish to retell the events as a reporter would for a front-page story in the local newspaper, or you may recount the events from a more personal point of view, as Angelou does in her description of the "disaster" in Mrs. Cullinan's kitchen. If you were a witness, consider the points of view of the other people involved so that you can give your readers an objective perspective on the event. If you were a victim, slow the pace of the major conflict, which probably occurred quickly, so you can show your readers its emotional impact.
2. Report an experience in which you had to commit an extremely difficult or distasteful deed. You may wish to begin, as Orwell does, by telling your readers about the conditions you encountered before you confronted the problem of whether or not to commit the questionable act. Be sure to list all the options you considered before you acted, and conclude by reflecting on your attitude toward your choice. And, of course, make sure to plot your essay so that the *act* is given the central and most dramatic position.
3. In "I Just Wanna Be Average," Mike Rose recounts his experience in the worlds of vocational education and college prep programs. In both worlds, he must come to terms with dismal teachers, defensive peers, and defective learning skills. Study the last few paragraphs, where Rose reminds his readers what it *feels* like to struggle and fail. Then narrate a similar kind of experience, evoking the dramatic details of your attempt to solve a difficult problem.
4. Chronicle a significant event in the life of your family that occurred during a major crisis in the life of the nation—the civil rights movement, the Persian Gulf war, some environmental disaster. Like Hayslip, consider how the personal experience of your family was *similar to* or *different from* the official experience reported by the media

or history books.

5. Narrate an account of your encounter with a culture different from your own. Like N. Scott Momaday, you may want to study the roots of your own culture that seem, from the perspective of your generation, completely different from those of another culture. You may want to focus on the drama of certain ceremonies—weddings, funerals—from another culture or another time to dramatize this difference.
6. Demonstrate the effects of perception on values (how "seeing is believing"). All the writers in this section deal with this subject. Angelou demonstrates how white people's inability to "see" black people distorts their belief about them. Rose demonstrates that the stigma "remedial" encourages students (and their teachers) to believe that they are failures. Momaday recounts how seeing his grandmother's landscape helps him understand why his people believed in the sun god. Hayslip reveals how seeing the splendid man in the sunglasses made her believe in the blindness of Americans. Orwell shows how seeing the crowd's mocking faces convinces him to shoot the elephant. And W. D. Wetherell's young narrator tells how Sheila Mant's beauty made him believe her favorable opinion was worth more than a fish.

PROCESS ANALYSIS

A **process** is an operation that moves through a series of steps to bring about a desired result. You can call almost any procedure a process, whether it is getting out of bed in the morning or completing a transaction on the stock exchange. A useful way to identify a particular kind of process is by its principal function. A process can be *natural* (the birth of a baby), *mechanical* (starting a car engine), *physical* (dancing), or *mental* (reading).

Analysis is an operation for dividing something into its parts in order to understand the whole more clearly. For example, poetry readers analyze the lines of a poem to find meaning. Doctors analyze a patient's symptoms to prescribe treatment. Politicians analyze the opinions of individual voters and groups of voters to plan campaigns.

If you want to write a process-analysis essay, you need to go through three steps: (1) divide the process you are going to explain into its individual steps; (2) show the movement of the process, step by step, from beginning to end; and (3) explain how each step works, how it ties into other steps in the sequence, and how it brings about the desired result.

PURPOSE

Usually you will write a process analysis to accomplish two purposes: *to give directions* and *to provide information.* Sometimes you might find it difficult to separate the two purposes—after all, when you give directions about how to do something (hit a baseball), you also have to provide information on how the whole process works (rules of the game—strike zone, walks, hits, base running, outs, scoring). But usually you can separate the two because you're trying to accomplish different goals. When you give directions, you want to help your readers do something (change a tire). When you give information, you want to satisfy your readers' curiosity about some process they'd like to know about but are unlikely to perform (pilot a space shuttle).

You might also write a process analysis to demonstrate that (1) a task that looks difficult is really easy or (2) a task that looks easy is really quite complex. For instance, you might want to show that selecting a specific tool can simplify a complex process (using a microwave oven to cook a six-course dinner). You might also want to show why it's important to have a prearranged plan to make a process seem simple (explaining the preparations for an informal television interview).

AUDIENCE

When you write a process-analysis essay, you must think carefully about who your audience will be. First, you need to decide whether you're writing *to* an audience (giving directions) or writing *for* an audience (providing information). If you are writing *to* an audience, you can address directly readers who are already interested in your subject: "If you want to plant a successful garden, you must follow these seven steps." If you are writing *for* an audience, you can write from a more detached point of view, but you have to find a way to catch the interest of more casual readers: "Although many Americans say they are concerned about nuclear power, few understand how a nuclear power plant works."

Second, you have to determine how wide the knowledge gap is between you and your readers. Writing about a process suggests you are something of an expert in that area. If you can be sure your readers are also experts, you can write your analysis with certain assumptions. For instance, if you're outlining courtroom procedure to a group of fellow law students, you know you don't have to define the special meaning of the word *brief*.

On the other hand, if you feel sure your intended audience knows almost nothing about a process (or has only general knowledge), you can take nothing for granted. If you are explaining how to operate a VCR to readers who have never used one, you will have to define special terms and explain all procedures. If you presume your readers are experts when they are not, you will confuse or annoy them. If you presume they need to be told everything when they don't, you will bore or antagonize them. And, finally, remember that to analyze a process effectively, you must either research it carefully or have firsthand knowledge of its operation. It's risky to try to explain something you don't really understand.

STRATEGIES

The best way to write a process analysis is to organize your essay according to five steps:

overview
special terms

sequence of steps
examples
results

The first two parts help your readers understand the process, the next two show the process in action, and the last one evaluates the worth of the completed process.

Begin your analysis with an *overview* of the whole process. To make such an overview, you

1. define the objective of the process,
2. identify (and number) the steps in the sequence,
3. group some small steps into larger units, and
4. call attention to the most important steps or units.

For example, William Stafford begins his analysis of writing by pointing out that "a writer is not so much someone who has something to say as he is someone who has found a process that will bring about new things he would not have thought of if he had not started to say them." In Gretel Ehrlich's overview of the rodeo, she lists the traditional order of the events, then goes on to analyze the sequence of steps within each event.

Each process has its own *special terms* to describe tools, tasks, and methods, and you will have to define those terms for your readers. You can define them at the beginning so your readers will understand the terms when you use them, but often you do better to define them as you use them. Your readers may have trouble remembering specialized language out of context, so it's often practical to define your terms throughout the course of the essay, pausing to explain their special meaning or use the first time you introduce them. Tom and Ray Magliozzi follow this strategy in "Inside the Engine" by describing the oil pump, crankcase, journals, and bearings inside the engine and then describing the warning lights on the dashboard.

When you write a process-analysis essay, you must present the *sequence of steps* clearly and carefully. As you do so, give the reason for each step and, where appropriate, provide these reminders:

1. *Do not omit any steps.* A sequence is a sequence because all steps depend on one another. William Stafford explains the importance of the first step, long intervals of uninterrupted time, to the creation of "receptivity," a condition necessary for writing to begin.
2. *Do not reverse steps.* A sequence is a sequence because each step must be performed according to a necessary and logical pattern. Lars Eighner reminds readers that if they start eating something before they have inspected it, they are likely to discover molded bread or sour milk after they have put it into their mouth.
3. *Suspend certain steps.* Occasionally, a whole series of steps must be suspended and another process completed before the sequence can resume. Tom and Ray Magliozzi warn readers that before they can shut off an overheated car, they must "use all necessary caution and get the thing over to the breakdown lane."
4. *Do not overlook steps within steps.* Each sequence is likely to have a series of smaller steps buried within each step. Gretel Ehrlich describes how the "six or seven separate movements [a calf roper] makes are so fluid they look like one continual unfolding."
5. *Avoid certain steps.* It is often tempting to insert steps that are not recommended but that appear "logical." Richard Selzer suggests that following such an impulse in an operating room can produce tragic results.

You may want to use several kinds of *examples* to explain the steps in a sequence:

1. *Pictures.* You can use graphs, charts, and diagrams to illustrate the operation of the process. Although none of the writers in this section uses pictures, the Magliozzis do discuss the warning lights that signal the overheated, glowing-red engine.
2. *Anecdotes.* Since you're claiming some level of expertise

by writing a process analysis, you can clarify your explanation by using examples from your own experience. Eighner uses this method when he describes his experience selecting discarded pizzas and waiting for the "junk" that will be pitched at the end of a semester.

3. *Variants.* You can mention alternative steps to show that the process may not be as rigid or simplistic as it often appears. Stafford's primary purpose is to demonstrate how the writing process always invites new ways to make meaning.
4. *Comparisons.* You can use comparisons to help your readers see that a complex process is similar to a process they already know. Selzer uses this strategy when he suggests that the work of a surgeon is similar to the work of a priest, a poet, or a traveler in a dangerous country.

Although you focus on the movement of the process when you write a process-analysis essay, finally you should also try to evaluate the *results* of that process. You can move to this last step by asking two questions: How do you know it's done? and How do you know it's good? Sometimes the answer is simple—the car starts, the rider stays on the horse. At other times, the answer is not so clear—the patient may need further treatment, the essay may need revision.

Using Process Analysis in a Paragraph

SCOTT RUSSELL SANDERS
from "Digging Limestone"

Dealing with the stone itself involves a whole new set of machines. Great mobile engines called channelers, powered by electricity, chug on rails from one side of the bed to the other, chiseling ten-foot-deep slots. Hammering and puffing along, they look and sound and smell like small locomotives. By shifting rails, the quarriers eventually slice the bed into a grid of blocks. The

Names special tools

first of these to be removed is called the keyblock, and it always provokes a higher than usual proportion of curses. There is no way to get to the base of this first block to cut it loose, so it must be wedged, hacked, splintered and worried at, until something like a clean hole has been excavated. Men can then climb down and, by drilling holes and driving wedges, split the neighboring block free at its base, undoing in an hour a three-hundred-million-year-old cement job.

Identifies first step

Describes subsequent steps

Makes comparison (earth's crust to cement job)

Comment This paragraph, excerpted from "Digging Limestone," analyzes the complicated process of removing large slabs of limestone from the earth. The opening sentences name the special machines required to begin the work. Sanders makes sure his readers understand the importance of removing the keyblock. Only after this slice of stone is removed can the workers proceed with the rest of the process, "undoing in an hour a three-hundred-million-year-old cement job."

TOM AND RAY MAGLIOZZI

Tom (b. 1939) and Ray (b. 1949) Magliozzi—better known as Click and Clack, the Tappet Brothers—were born in East Cambridge, Massachusetts; both were educated at Massachusetts Institute of Technology. Tom earned additional degrees from Northeastern University and Boston University before working in marketing. Ray was a VISTA volunteer, taught junior high school, and worked in the Massachusetts State Consumer Affairs Department. In 1973, the brothers opened a "do-it-yourself" garage in Cambridge called Good News Garage. In 1976, they started a local radio show in which they answered questions about auto repair. This hilarious and informative show, "Car Talk," was syndicated on National Public Radio in 1987. A sampling of their most amusing conversations appears in their book *Car Talk* (1991). In "Inside the Engine," Tom and Ray explain how an engine works and what the warning lights mean.

Inside the Engine

A customer of ours had an old Thunderbird that he used to drive back and forth to New York to see a girlfriend every other weekend. And every time he made the trip he'd be in the shop the following Monday needing to get something fixed because the car was such a hopeless piece of trash. One Monday he failed to show up and Tom said, "Gee, that's kind of unusual." I said jokingly, "Maybe he blew the car up." 1

Well, what happened was that he was on the Merritt Parkway in Connecticut when he noticed that he had to keep the gas pedal all the way to the floor just to go 30 m.p.h., 2 with this big V-8 engine, and he figured something was awry.

So he pulled into one of those filling stations where they sell gasoline and chocolate-chip cookies and milk. And he asked the attendant to look at the engine and, of course, the guy said, "I can't help you. All I know is cookies and milk." But the guy agreed to look anyway since our friend was really desperate. His girlfriend was waiting for him and he needed to know if he was going to make it. Anyway, the guy threw open the hood and jumped back in terror. The engine was glowing red. Somewhere along the line, probably around Hartford, he must have lost all of his motor oil. The engine kept getting hotter and hotter, but like a lot of other things in the car that didn't work, neither did his oil pressure warning light. As a result, the engine got so heated up that it fused itself together. All the pistons melted, and the cylinder heads deformed, and the pistons fused to the cylinder walls, and the bearings welded themselves to the crankshaft—oh, it was a terrible sight! When he tried to restart the engine, he just heard a *click, click, click* since the whole thing was seized up tighter than a drum. 3

That's what can happen in a case of extreme engine neglect. Most of us wouldn't do that, or at least wouldn't do it knowingly. Our friend didn't do it knowingly either, but he learned a valuable lesson. He learned that his girlfriend wouldn't come and get him if his car broke down. Even if he offered her cookies and milk. 4

The oil is critical to keeping things running since it not only acts as a lubricant, but it also helps to keep the engine cool. What happens is that the oil pump sucks the oil out of what's called the sump (or the crankcase or the oil pan), and it pushes that oil, under pressure, up to all of the parts that need lubrication. 5

The way the oil works is that it acts as a cushion. The molecules of oil actually separate the moving metal parts from one another so that they don't directly touch; the crankshaft *journals,* or the hard parts of the crankshaft, never 6 touch the soft connecting-rod *bearings* because there's a film of oil between them, forced in there under pressure. From the pump.

It's pretty high pressure too. When the engine is running at highway speed, the oil, at 50 or 60 pounds or more per square inch (or about 4 bars, if you're of the metric persuasion—but let's leave religion out of this), is coursing through the veins of the engine and keeping all these parts at safe, albeit microscopic, distances from each other. 7

But if there's a lot of dirt in the oil, the dirt particles get embedded in these metal surfaces and gradually the dirt acts as an abrasive and wears away these metal surfaces. And pretty soon the engine is junk. 8

It's also important that the motor oil be present in sufficient quantity. In nontechnical terms, that means there's got to be enough of it in there. If you have too little oil in your engine, there's not going to be enough of it to go around, and it will get very hot, because four quarts will be doing the work of five, and so forth. When that happens, the oil gets overheated and begins to burn up at a greater than normal rate. Pretty soon, instead of having four quarts, you have three and a half quarts, then three quarts doing the work of five. And then, next thing you know, you're down to two quarts and your engine is glowing red, just like that guy driving to New York, and it's chocolate-chip cookie time. 9

In order to avoid this, some cars have gauges and some have warning lights; some people call them "idiot lights." Actually, we prefer to reverse it and call them "idiot gauges." I think gauges are bad. When you drive a car—maybe I'm weird about this—I think it's a good idea to look at the road most of the time. And you can't look at the road if you're busy looking at a bunch of gauges. It's the same objection we have to these stupid radios today that have so damn many buttons and slides and digital scanners and so forth that you need a copilot to change stations. Remember when you just turned a knob? 10

Not that gauges are bad in and of themselves. I think if you have your choice, what you want is idiot lights—or what 11 we call "genius lights"—and gauges too. It's nice to have a gauge that you can kind of keep an eye on for an overview of what's going on. For example, if you know that your engine typically runs at 215 degrees and on this particular day, which is not abnormally hot, it's running at 220 or 225, you might suspect that something is wrong and get it looked at before your radiator boils over.

On the other hand, if that gauge was the only thing you had to rely on and you didn't have a light to alert you when something was going wrong, then you'd look at the thing all the time, especially if your engine had melted on you once. In that case, why don't you take the bus? Because you're not going to be a very good driver, spending most of your time looking at the gauges. 12

Incidentally, if that oil warning light ever comes on, shut the engine off! We don't mean that you should shut it off in rush-hour traffic when you're in the passing lane. Use all necessary caution and get the thing over to the breakdown lane. But don't think you can limp to the next exit, because you can't. Spend the money to get towed and you may save the engine. 13

It's a little-known fact that the oil light does *not* signify whether or not you have oil in the engine. The oil warning light is really monitoring the oil *pressure*. Of course, if you have no oil, you'll have no oil pressure, so the light will be on. But it's also possible to have plenty of oil and an oil pump that's not working for one reason or another. In this event, a new pump would fix the problem, but if you were to drive the car (saying, "It must be a bad light, I just checked the oil!") you'd melt the motor. 14

So if the oil warning light comes on, even if you just had an oil change and the oil is right up to the full mark on the dipstick and is nice and clean—don't drive the car! 15

Here's another piece of useful info. When you turn the key to the "on" position, all the little warning lights *should* 16 *light up:* the temperature light, the oil light, whatever other lights you may have. Because that is the *test mode* for these lights. If those lights *don't* light up when you turn the key to the "on" position (just before you turn it all the way to start the car), does that mean you're out of oil? No. It means that something is wrong with the warning light itself. If the light doesn't work then, it's not going to work at all. Like when you need it, for example.

One more thing about oil: overfilling is just as bad as underfilling. Can you really have too much of a good thing? you ask. Yes. If you're half a quart or even a quart overfilled, it's not a big deal, and I wouldn't be afraid to drive the car under those circumstances. But if you're a quart and a half or two quarts or more overfilled, you could have so much oil in the crankcase that the spinning crankshaft is going to hit the oil and turn it into suds. It's impossible for the pump to pump suds, so you'll ruin the motor. It's kind of like a front-loading washing machine that goes berserk and spills suds all over the floor when you put too much detergent in. That's what happens to your motor oil when you overfill it. 17

With all this talk about things that can go wrong, let's not forget that modern engines are pretty incredible. People always say, "You know, the cars of yesteryear were wonderful. They built cars rough and tough and durable in those days." 18

Horsefeathers. 19

The cars of yesteryear were nicer to look at because they were very individualistic. They were all different, and some were even beautiful. In fact, when I was a kid, you could tell the year, make, and model of a car from a hundred paces just by looking at the taillights or the grille. 20

Nowadays, they all look the same. They're like jellybeans on wheels. You can't tell one from the other. But the truth is, they've never made engines as good as they make them today. Think of the abuse they take! None of the cars of 21 yesteryear was capable of going 60 or 70 miles per hour all day long and taking it for 100,000 miles.

Engines of today—and by today I mean from the late '60s on up—are far superior. What makes them superior is not only the design and the metallurgy, but the lubricants. The oil they had thirty years ago was lousy compared to what we have today. There are magic additives and detergents and long-chain polymers and what-have-you that make them able to hold dirt in suspension and to neutralize acids and to lubricate better than oils of the old days. 22

There aren't too many things that will go wrong, because the engines are made so well and the tolerances are closer. And aside from doing stupid things like running out of oil or failing to heed the warning lights or overfilling the thing, you shouldn't worry. 23

But here's one word of caution about cars that have timing belts: Lots of cars these days are made with overhead camshafts. The camshaft, which opens the valves, is turned by a gear and gets its power from the crankshaft. Many cars today use a notched rubber *timing belt* to connect the two shafts instead of a chain because it's cheaper and easy to change. And here's the caveat: *if you don't change it and the belt breaks, it can mean swift ruin to the engine*. The pistons can hit the valves and you'll have bent valves and possibly broken pistons. 24

So you can do many hundreds of dollars' worth of damage by failing to heed the manufacturer's warning about changing the timing belt in a timely manner. No pun intended. For most cars, the timing belt replacement is somewhere between $100 and $200. It's not a big deal. 25

I might add that there are many cars that have rubber timing belts that will *not* cause damage to the engine when they break. But even if you have one of those cars, make sure that you get the belt changed, at the very least, when the manufacturer suggests it. If there's no specific recommendation and you have a car with a rubber belt, we would recommend that you change it at 60,000 miles. Because even 26 if you don't do damage to the motor when the belt breaks, you're still going to be stuck somewhere, maybe somewhere unpleasant. Maybe even Cleveland! So you want to make sure that you don't fall into that situation.

Many engines that have rubber timing belts also use the belt to drive the water pump. On these, don't forget to change the water pump when you change the timing belt, because the leading cause of premature belt failure is that the water pump seizes. So if you have a timing belt that drives the water pump, get the water pump out of there at the same time. You don't want to put a belt in and then have the water pump go a month later, because it'll break the new belt and wreck the engine. 27

The best way to protect all the other pieces that you can't get to without spending a lot of money is through frequent oil changes. The manufacturers recommend oil changes somewhere between seven and ten thousand miles, depending upon the car. We've always recommended that you change your oil at 3,000 miles. We realize for some people that's a bit of an inconvenience, but look at it as cheap insurance. And change the filter every time too. 28

And last but not least, I want to repeat this because it's important: Make sure your warning lights work. The oil pressure and engine temperature warning lights are your engine's lifeline. Check them every day. You should make it as routine as checking to see if your zipper's up. You guys should do it at the same time. 29

What you do is, you get into the car, check to see that your zipper's up, and then turn the key on and check to see if your oil pressure and temperature warning lights come on. 30

I don't know what women do. 31

For Study and Discussion

QUESTIONS FOR RESPONSE

1. What is your attitude toward cars? For example, do you see them as beautiful objects, mechanical conveniences, financial obligations, or technological puzzles?
2. What is your attitude toward car mechanics? How do you respond to their analysis of your car and its special parts?

QUESTIONS ABOUT PURPOSE

1. What parts of this essay *provide information* about the purpose of engines, oil, and gauges?
2. What parts of this essay *give directions* about how to avoid engine breakdown?

QUESTIONS ABOUT AUDIENCE

1. What assumptions do Tom and Ray make about the technical knowledge of their readers?
2. How do their direct commands—"don't drive the car"—reveal their knowledge of their readers' behavior?

QUESTIONS ABOUT STRATEGIES

1. How do Tom and Ray use the opening example of the Thunderbird to demonstrate the consequences of extreme neglect?
2. How do they use analogies (cushion, veins, suds) to clarify their analysis of how oil helps an eingine work?

QUESTIONS FOR DISCUSSION

1. Why is Tom and Ray's use of humor so effective in helping readers understand and follow instructions? For example, what is the zipper test? Can you think of a test women could use?

QUESTIONS FOR DISCUSSION

2. What is Tom and Ray's attitude toward modern technology? To what extent would the average car owner or car mechanic agree with their opinion?

LARS EIGHNER

Lars Eighner was born in 1948 in Corpus Christi, Texas, and attended the University of Texas, Austin. He held a series of jobs, including work as an attendant at the state mental hospital in Austin, before he became homeless. For five years he drifted between Austin and Hollywood, living on the streets and in abandoned buildings. Then he began to contribute essays to the *Threepenny Review*; these writings will be collected in his yet-to-be-published memoirs *Travels with Lizabeth*. In one of these essays, "My Daily Dives in the Dumpster," Eighner analyzes the "predictable series of stages that a person goes through in learning to scavenge."

My Daily Dives in the Dumpster

I began Dumpster diving about a year before I became homeless. 1

I prefer the term "scavenging" and use the word "scrounging" when I mean to be obscure. I have heard people, evidently meaning to be polite, use the word "foraging," but I prefer to reserve that word for gathering nuts and berries and such which I do also, according to the season and opportunity. 2

I like the frankness of the word "scavenging." I live from the refuse of others. I am a scavenger. I think it a sound and honorable niche, although if I could I would naturally prefer to live the comfortable consumer life, perhaps—and only perhaps—as a slightly less wasteful consumer owing to what I have learned as a scavenger. 3

Except for jeans, all my clothes come from Dumpsters. Boom boxes, candles, bedding, toilet paper, medicine, books, a typewriter, a virgin male love doll, change sometimes 4 amounting to many dollars: All came from Dumpsters. And, yes, I eat from Dumpsters too.

There are a predictable series of stages that a person goes through in learning to scavenge. At first the new scavenger is filled with disgust and self-loathing. He is ashamed of being seen and may lurk around trying to duck behind things, or he may try to dive at night. (In fact, this is unnecessary, since most people instinctively look away from scavengers.) 5

Every grain of rice seems to be a maggot. Everything seems to stink. The scavenger can wipe the egg yolk off the found can, but he cannot erase the stigma of eating garbage from his mind. 6

This stage passes with experience. The scavenger finds a pair of running shoes that fit and look and smell brand-new. He finds a pocket calculator in perfect working order. He finds pristine ice cream, still frozen, more than he can eat or keep. He begins to understand: People do throw away perfectly good stuff, a lot of perfectly good stuff. 7

At this stage he may become lost and never recover. All the Dumpster divers I have known come to the point of trying to acquire everything they touch. Why not take it, they reason, it is all free. This is, of course, hopeless, and most divers come to realize that they must restrict themselves to items of relatively immediate utility. 8

The finding of objects is becoming something of an urban art. Even respectable, employed people will sometimes find something tempting sticking out of a Dumpster or standing beside one. Quite a number of people, not all of them of the bohemian type, are willing to brag that they found this or that piece in the trash. 9

But eating from Dumpsters is the thing that separates the dilettanti from the professionals. Eating safely involves three principles: using the senses and common sense to evaluate the condition of the found materials; knowing the Dumpsters of a given area and checking them regularly; and 10 seeking always to answer the question, Why was this discarded?

Perhaps everyone who has a kitchen and a regular supply of groceries has, at one time or another, eaten half a sandwich before discovering mold on the bread, or has gotten a mouthful of milk before realizing the milk had turned. Nothing of the sort is likely to happen to a Dumpster diver because he is constantly reminded that most food is discarded for a reason. 11

Yet perfectly good food can be found in Dumpsters. Canned goods, for example, turn up fairly often in the Dumpsters I frequent. All except the most phobic people would be willing to eat from a can even if it came from a Dumpster. I have few qualms about dry foods such as crackers, cookies, cereal, chips, and pasta if they are free of visible contaminants and still dry and crisp. Raw fruits and vegetables with intact skins seem perfectly safe to me, excluding, of course, the obviously rotten. Many are discarded for minor imperfections that can be pared away. Chocolate is often discarded only because it has become discolored as the cocoa butter de-emulsified. 12

I began scavenging by pulling pizzas out of the Dumpster behind a pizza delivery shop. In general, prepared food requires caution, but in this case I knew what time the shop closed and went to the Dumpster as soon as the last of the help left. 13

Because the workers at these places are usually inexperienced, pizzas are often made with the wrong topping, baked incorrectly, or refused on delivery for being cold. The products to be discarded are boxed up because inventory is kept by counting boxes: A boxed pizza can be written off; an unboxed pizza does not exist. So I had a steady supply of fresh, sometimes warm pizza. 14

The area I frequent is inhabited by many affluent college students. I am not here by chance; the Dumpsters are very rich. Students throw out many good things, including food, particularly at the end of the semester and before and after 15 breaks. I find it advantageous to keep an eye on the academic calendar.

A typical discard is a half jar of peanut butter—though non-organic peanut butter does not require refrigeration and is unlikely to spoil in any reasonable time. Occasionally I find a cheese with a spot of mold, which, of course, I just pare off, and because it is obvious why the cheese was discarded, I treat it with less suspicion than an apparently perfect cheese found in similar circumstances. One of my favorite finds is yogurt—often discarded, still sealed, when the expiration date has passed—because it will keep for several days, even in warm weather. 16

I avoid ethnic foods I am unfamiliar with. If I do not know what it is supposed to look or smell like when it is good, I cannot be certain I will be able to tell if it is bad. 17

No matter how careful I am I still get dysentery at least once a month, oftener in warm weather. I do not want to paint too romantic a picture. Dumpster diving has serious drawbacks as a way of life. 18

Though I have a proprietary feeling about my Dumpsters, I don't mind my direct competitors, other scavengers, as much as I hate the soda-can scroungers. 19

I have tried scrounging aluminum cans with an able-bodied companion, and afoot we could make no more than a few dollars a day. I can extract the necessities of life from the Dumpsters directly with far less effort than would be required to accumulate the equivalent value in aluminum. Can scroungers, then, are people who *must* have small amounts of cash—mostly drug addicts and winos. 20

I do not begrudge them the cans, but can scroungers tend to tear up the Dumpsters, littering the area and mixing the contents. There are precious few courtesies among scavengers, but it is a common practice to set aside surplus items: pairs of shoes, clothing, canned goods, and such. A true scavenger hates to see good stuff go to waste, and what he cannot use he leaves in good condition in plain sight. Can scroungers lay waste to everything in their path and will stir one of a pair of good shoes to the bottom of a Dumpster to 21 be lost or ruined in the muck. They become so specialized that they can see only cans and earn my contempt by passing up change, canned goods, and readily hockable items.

Can scroungers will even go through individual garbage cans, something I have never seen a scavenger do. Going through individual garbage cans without spreading litter is almost impossible, and litter is likely to reduce the public's tolerance of scavenging. But my strongest reservation about going through individual garbage cans is that this seems to me a very personal kind of invasion, one to which I would object if I were a homeowner. 22

Though Dumpsters seem somehow less personal than garbage cans, they still contain bank statements, bills, correspondence, pill bottles, and other sensitive information. I avoid trying to draw conclusions about the people who dump in the Dumpsters I frequent. I think it would be unethical to do so, although I know many people will find the idea of scavenger ethics too funny for words. 23

Occasionally a find tells a story. I once found a small paper bag containing some unused condoms, several partial tubes of flavored sexual lubricant, a partially used compact of birth control pills, and the torn pieces of a picture of a young man. Clearly, the woman was through with him and planning to give up sex altogether. 24

Dumpster things are often sad—abandoned teddy bears, shredded wedding albums, despaired-of sales kits. I find diaries and journals. College students also discard their papers; I am horrified to discover the kind of paper that now merits an A in an undergraduate course. 25

Dumpster diving is outdoor work, often surprisingly pleasant. It is not entirely predictable; things of interest turn up every day, and some days there are finds of great value. I am always very pleased when I can turn up exactly the thing I most wanted to find. Yet in spite of the element of chance, scavenging, more than most other pursuits, tends to yield returns in some proportion to the effort and intelligence brought to bear. 26

I think of scavenging as a modern form of self-reliance. After ten years of government service, where everything is geared to the lowest common denominator, I find work that rewards initiative and effort refreshing. Certainly I would be happy to have a sinecure again, but I am not heartbroken to be without one. 27

I find from the experience of scavenging two rather deep lessons. The first is to take what I can use and let the rest go. I have come to think that there is no value in the abstract. A thing I cannot use or make useful, perhaps by trading, has no value, however fine or rare it may be. (I mean useful in the broad sense—some art, for example, I would think valuable.) 28

The second lesson is the transience of material being. I do not suppose that ideas are immortal, but certainly they are longer-lived than material objects. 29

The things I find in Dumpsters, the love letters and rag dolls of so many lives, remind me of this lesson. Many times in my travels I have lost everything but the clothes on my back. Now I hardly pick up a thing without envisioning the time I will cast it away. This, I think, is a healthy state of mind. Almost everything I have now has already been cast out at least once, proving that what I own is valueless to someone. 30

I find that my desire to grab for the gaudy bauble has been largely sated. I think this is an attitude I share with the very wealthy—we both know there is plenty more where whatever we have came from. Between us are the rat-race millions who have confounded their selves with the objects they grasp and who nightly scavenge the cable channels looking for they know not what. 31

I am sorry for them. 32

For Study and Discussion

QUESTIONS FOR RESPONSE

1. What assumptions do you make about someone sorting through a Dumpster?
2. What kinds of things do you throw away in the weekly garbage that others might find valuable?

QUESTIONS ABOUT PURPOSE

1. Why does Eighner prefer the term *scavenging* to *scrounging* or *foraging* to characterize the process he analyzes?
2. In what ways does Eighner's analysis demonstrate that Dumpster diving is "a sound and honorable niche"?

QUESTIONS ABOUT AUDIENCE

1. How does Eighner anticipate his audience's reaction to his subject by presenting the "predictable series of stages that a person goes through in learning to scavenge"?
2. How do Eighner's "scavenger ethics" enhance his standing with his readers?

QUESTIONS ABOUT STRATEGIES

1. How does Eighner use the example of pizza to illustrate the three principles of eating from a Dumpster?
2. How does Eighner's analysis of the process of "soda-can scrounging" help distinguish that process from "scavenging"?

QUESTIONS FOR DISCUSSION

1. How do the two lessons Eighner has learned demonstrate that his "work" rewards initiative and effort?

QUESTIONS FOR DISCUSSION

2. What attitudes toward consumption and waste does Eighner claim he shares with the very wealthy? Why does he feel sorry for "the rat-race millions"?

GRETEL EHRLICH

Gretel Ehrlich was born and raised in California and was educated at Bennington College, UCLA Film School, and the New School for Social Research. She now lives on a ranch in Wyoming, where she first went as a documentary filmmaker. She has also been a ranch worker—lambing, branding, herding sheep, and calving. A full-time writer since 1979, she has published prose pieces in the *New York Times*, the *Atlantic, Harper's,* and *New Age Journal. The Solace of Open Spaces,* a collection of her prose, was published in 1985. She has also published two books of poetry and a story collection (with Edward Hoagland) titled *City Tales/Wyoming Stories* (1986). Her most recent book is *Heart Mountain* (1988). In this essay, reprinted from *The Solace of Open Spaces,* Ehrlich describes the traditional events in a rodeo and then analyzes their relationship to life in the West.

Rules of the Game: Rodeo

Instead of honeymooning in Paris, Patagonia, or the Sahara 1
as we had planned, my new husband and I drove through a series of blizzards to Oklahoma City. Each December the National Finals Rodeo is held in a modern, multistoried colosseum next to buildings that house banks and petroleum companies in a state whose flatness resembles a swimming pool filled not with water but with oil.

The National Finals is the "World Series of Professional 2
Rodeo," where not only the best cowboys but also the most athletic horses and bucking stock compete. All year, rodeo cowboys have been vying for the honor to ride here. They've been to Houston, Las Vegas, Pendleton, Tucson, Cheyenne,

San Francisco, Calgary; to as many as eighty rodeos in one season, sometimes making two or three on a day like the Fourth of July, and when the results are tallied up (in money won, not points) the top fifteen riders in each event are invited to Oklahoma City.

We climbed to our peanut gallery seats just as Miss Rodeo America, a lanky brunette swaddled in a lavender pantsuit, gloves, and cowboy hat, loped across the arena. There was a hush in the audience; all the hats swimming down in front of us, like buoys, steadied and turned toward the chutes. "Out of chute number three, Pat Linger, a young cowboy from Miles City, Montana, making his first appearance here on a little horse named Dillinger." And as fast as these words sailed across the colosseum, the first bareback horse bumped into the lights. 3

There's a traditional order to the four timed and three rough stock events that make up a rodeo program. Bareback riders are first, then steer wrestlers, team ropers, saddle bronc riders, barrel racers, and finally, the bull riders. 4

After Pat Linger came Steve Dunham, J. C. Trujillo, Mickey Young, and the defending champ, Bruce Ford, on a horse named Denver. Bareback riders do just that: they ride a horse with no saddle, no halter, no rein, clutching only a handhold riveted into a girth that goes around the horse's belly. A bareback rider's loose style suggests a drunken, comic bout of lovemaking: he lies back on the horse and, with each jump and jolt, flops delightfully, like a libidinous Raggedy Andy, toes turned out, knees flexed, legs spread and pumping, back arched, the back of his hat bumping the horse's rump as if nodding, "Yes, let's do 'er again." My husband, who rode saddle broncs in amateur rodeos, explains it differently: "It's like riding a runaway bicycle down a steep hill and lying on your back; you can't see where you're going or what's going to happen next." 5

Now the steer wrestlers shoot out of the box on their own well-trained horses: there is a hazer on the right to keep the steer running straight, the wrestler on the left, and the steer between them. When the wrestler is neck and neck with the 6 animal, he slides sideways out of his saddle as if he'd been stabbed in the ribs and reaches for the horns. He's airborne for a second; then his heels swing into the dirt, and with his arms around the horns, he skids to a stop twisting the steer's head to one side so the animal loses his balance and falls to the ground. It's a fast-paced game of catch with a thousand-pound ball of horned flesh.

The team ropers are next. Most of them hail from the hilly, oak-strewn valleys of California where dally roping originated.[1] Ropers are the graceful technicians, performing their pas de deux (plus steer) with a precision that begins to resemble a larger clarity—an erudition. Header and heeler come out of the box at the same time, steer between them, but the header acts first: he ropes the horns of the steer, dallies up, turns off, and tries to position the steer for the heeler who's been tagging behind this duo, loop clasped in his armpit as if it were a hen. Then the heeler sets his generous, unsweeping loop free and double-hocks the steer. It's a complicated act which takes about six seconds. Concomitant with this speed and skill is a feminine grace: they don't clutch their stiff loop or throw it at the steer like a bag of dirty laundry the way I do, but hold it gently, delicately, as if it were a hoop of silk. One or two cranks and both arm and loop vault forward, one becoming an appendage of the other, as if the tendons and pulse that travel through the wrist had lengthened and spun forward like fishing line until the loop sails down on the twin horns, then up under the hocks like a repeated embrace that tightens at the end before it releases. 7

The classic event at rodeo is saddle bronc riding. The young men look as serious as academicians: they perch spryly on their high-kicking mounts, their legs flicking forward and back, "charging the point," "going back to the cantle" in a rapid, staccato rhythm. When the horse is at the high point of his buck and the cowboy is stretched out, legs spurring 8

[1]The word dally is a corruption of the Spanish *da la vuelta,* meaning to take a turn, as with a rope around the saddle horn.

above the horse's shoulder, rein-holding arm straight as a board in front, and free hand lifted behind, horse and man look like a propeller. Even their dismounts can look aeronautical: springing off the back of the horse, they land on their feet with a flourish—hat still on—as if they had been ejected mechanically from a burning plane long before the crash.

Barrel racing is the one women's event. Where the men are tender in their movements, as elegant as if Balanchine had been their coach, the women are prodigies of Wayne Gretsky, all speed, bully, and grit. When they charge into the arena, their hats fly off; they ride brazenly, elbows, knees, feet fluttering, and by the time they've careened around the second of three barrels, the whip they've had clenched between their teeth is passed to a hand, and on the home stretch they urge the horse to the finish line. 9

Calf ropers are the whiz kids of rodeo: they're expert on the horse and on the ground, and their horses are as quick-witted. The cowboy emerges from the box with a loop in his hand, a piggin' string in his mouth, coils and reins in the other, and a network of slack line strewn so thickly over horse and rider, they look as if they'd run through a tangle of kudzu before arriving in the arena. After roping the calf and jerking the slack in the rope, he jumps off the horse, sprints down the length of nylon, which the horse keeps taut, throws the calf down, and ties three legs together with the piggin' string. It's said of Roy Cooper, the defending calf-roping champion, that "even with pins and metal plates in his arm, he's known for the fastest groundwork in the business; when he springs down his rope to flank the calf, the resulting action is pure rodeo poetry." The six or seven separate movements he makes are so fluid they look like one continual unfolding. 10

Bull riding is last, and of all the events it's the only one truly dangerous. Bulls are difficult to ride: they're broad-backed, loose-skinned, and powerful. They don't jump balletically the way a horse does; they jerk and spin, and if you fall off, they'll try to gore you with a horn, kick, or trample 11 you. Bull riders are built like the animals they ride: low to the ground and hefty. They're the tough men on the rodeo circuit, and the flirts. Two of the current champs are city men: Charlie Samson is a small, shy black from Watts, and Bobby Del Vecchio, a brash Italian from the Bronx who always throws the audience a kiss after a ride with a Catskill-like showmanship not usually seen here. What a bull rider lacks in technical virtuosity—you won't see the fast spurring action of a saddle bronc rider in this event—he makes up for in personal flamboyance, and because it's a deadlier game they're playing, you can see the belligerence rise up their necks and settle into their faces as the bull starts his first spin. Besides the bull and the cowboy, there are three other men in the ring—the rodeo clowns—who aren't there to make children laugh but to divert the bull from some of his deadlier tricks, and, when the rider bucks off, jump between the two—like secret service men—to save the cowboy's life.

Rodeo, like baseball, is an American sport and has been 12
around almost as long. While Henry Chadwick was writing his first book of rules for the fledgling ball clubs in 1858, ranch hands were paying $25 a dare to a kid who would ride five outlaw horses from the rough string in a makeshift arena of wagons and cars. The first commercial rodeo in Wyoming was held in Lander in 1895, just nineteen years after the National League was formed. Baseball was just as popular as bucking and roping contests in the West, but no one in Cooperstown, New York, was riding broncs. And that's been part of the problem. After 124 years, rodeo is still misunderstood. Unlike baseball, it's a regional sport (although they do have rodeos in New Jersey, Florida, and other eastern states); it's derived from and stands for the western way of life and the western spirit. It doesn't have the universal appeal of a sport contrived solely for the competition and winning; there is no ball bandied about between opposing players.

Rodeo is the wild child of ranch work and embodies some 13
of what ranching is all about. Horsemanship—not gunsling-

ing—was the pride of western men, and the chivalrous ethics they formulated, known as the western code, became the ground rules for every human game. Two great partnerships are celebrated in this Oklahoma arena: the indispensable one between man and animal that any rancher or cowboy takes on, enduring the joys and punishments of the alliance; and the one between man and man, cowboy and cowboy.

Though rodeo is an individualist's sport, it has everything to do with teamwork. The cowboy who "covers" his bronc (stays on the full eight seconds) has become a team with that animal. The cowboys' competitive feelings amongst each other are so mixed with western tact as to appear ambivalent. When Bruce Ford, the bareback rider, won a go-round he said, "The hardest part of winning this year was taking it away from one of my best friends, Mickey Young, after he'd worked so hard all year." Stan Williamson, who'd just won the steer wrestling, said, "I just drew a better steer. I didn't want Butch to get a bad one. I just got lucky, I guess." 14

Ranchers, when working together, can be just as diplomatic. They'll apologize if they cut in front of someone while cutting out a calf, and their thanks to each other at the end of the day has a formal sound. Like those westerners who still help each other out during branding and roundup, rodeo cowboys help each other in the chutes. A bull rider will steady the saddle bronc rider's horse, help measure out the rein or set the saddle, and a bareback rider might help the bull rider set his rigging and pull his rope. Ropers lend each other horses, as do barrel racers and steer wrestlers. This isn't a show they put on; they offer their help with the utmost goodwill and good-naturedness. Once, when a bucking horse fell over backward in the chute with my husband, his friend H.A., who rode bulls, jumped into the chute and pulled him out safely. 15

Another part of the "westernness" rodeo represents is the drifting cowboys do. They're on the road much of their lives the way turn-of-the-century cowboys were on the trail, but these cowboys travel in style if they can—driving pink Lincolns and new pickups with a dozen fresh shirts hanging behind the driver, and the radio on. 16

Some ranchers look down on the sport of rodeo; they don't want these "drugstore cowboys" getting all the attention and glory. Besides, rodeo seems to have less and less to do with real ranch work. Who ever heard of gathering cows on a bareback horse with no bridle, or climbing on a herd bull? Ranchers are generalists—they have to know how to do many things—from juggling the futures market to overhauling a tractor or curing viral scours (diarrhea) in calves—while rodeo athletes are specialists. Deep down, they probably feel envious of each other: the rancher for the praise and big money; the rodeo cowboy for the stay-at-home life among animals to which their sport only alludes. 17

People with no ranching background have even more difficulty with the sport. Every ride goes so fast, it's hard to see just what happened, and perhaps because of the Hollywood mythologizing of the West which distorted rather than distilled western rituals, rodeo is often considered corny, anachronistic, and cruel to animals. Quite the opposite is true. Rodeo cowboys are as sophisticated athletically as Bjorn Borg or Fernando Valenzuela. That's why they don't need to be from a ranch anymore, or to have grown up riding horses. And to undo another myth, rodeo is not cruel to animals. Compared to the arduous life of any "using horse" on a cattle or dude ranch, a bucking horse leads the life of Riley. His actual work load for an entire year, i.e., the amount of time he spends in the arena, totals approximately 4.6 minutes, and nothing done to him in the arena or out could in any way be called cruel. These animals aren't bludgeoned into bucking; they love to buck. They're bred to behave this way, they're athletes whose ability has been nurtured and encouraged. Like the cowboys who compete at the National Finals, the best bulls and horses from all the bucking strings in the country are nominated to appear in Oklahoma, winning money along with their riders to pay their own way. 18

The National Finals run ten nights. Every contestant rides every night, so it is easy to follow their progress and setbacks. One evening we abandoned our rooftop seats and sat behind the chutes to watch the saddle broncs ride. Behind the 19 chutes two cowboys are rubbing rosin—part of their staying power—behind the saddle swells and on their Easter-egg-colored chaps which are pink, blue, and light green with white fringe. Up above, standing on the chute rungs, the stock contractors direct horse traffic: "Velvet Drums" in chute #3, "Angel Sings" in #5, "Rusty" in #1. Rick Smith, Monty Henson, Bobby Berger, Brad Gjermudson, Mel Coleman, and friends climb the chutes. From where I'm sitting, it looks like a field hospital with five separate operating theaters, the cowboys, like surgeons, bent over their patients with sweaty brows and looks of concern. Horses are being haltered; cowboys are measuring out the long, braided reins, saddles are set: one cowboy pulls up on the swells again and again, repositioning his hornless saddle until it sits just right. When the chute boss nods to him and says, "Pull 'em up, boys," the ground crew tightens front and back cinches on the first horse to go, but very slowly so he won't panic in the chute as the cowboy eases himself down over the saddle, not sitting on it, just hovering there. "Okay, you're on." The chute boss nods to him again. Now he sits on the saddle, taking the rein in one hand, holding the top of the chute with the other. He flips the loose bottoms of his chaps over his shins, puts a foot in each stirrup, takes a breath, and nods. The chute gate swings open releasing a flood—not of water, but of flesh, groans, legs kicking. The horse lunges up and out in the first big jump like a wave breaking whose crest the cowboy rides, "marking out the horse," spurs well above the bronc's shoulders. In that first second under the lights, he finds what will be the rhythm of the ride. Once again he "charges the point," his legs pumping forward, then so far back his heels touch behind the cantle. For a moment he looks as though he were kneeling on air, then he's stretched out again, his whole body taut but released, free hand waving in back of his head like a palm frond, rein-holding hand thrust forward: *"En garde!"* he seems to be saying, but he's airborne; he looks like a wing that has sprouted suddenly from the horse's broad back. Eight seconds. The whistle blows. He's covered the horse. Now two gentlemen dressed in white chaps and satin shirts gallop beside the bucking horse. The cowboy hands the rein to one and grabs the waist of the other—the flank strap on the bronc has been undone, so all three horses move at a run—and the pickup man from whom the cowboy is now dangling slows almost to a stop, letting him slide to his feet on the ground.

Rick Smith from Wyoming rides, looking pale and nerv- 20
ous in his white shirt. He's bucked off and so are the brash Monty "Hawkeye" Henson, and Butch Knowles, and Bud Pauley, but with such grace and aplomb, there is no shame. Bobby Berger, an Oklahoma cowboy, wins the go-round with a score of 83.

By the end of the evening we're tired, but in no way as 21
exhausted as these young men who have ridden night after night. "I've never been so sore and had so much fun in my life," one first-time bull rider exclaims breathlessly. When the performance is over we walk across the street to the chic lobby of a hotel chock full of cowboys. Wives hurry through the crowd with freshly ironed shirts for tomorrow's ride, ropers carry their rope bags with them into the coffee shop, which is now filled with contestants, eating mild midnight suppers of scrambled eggs, their numbers hanging crookedly on their backs, their faces powdered with dust, and looking at this late hour prematurely old.

We drive back to the motel, where, the first night, they'd 22
"never heard of us" even though we'd had reservations for a month. "Hey, it's our honeymoon," I told the night clerk and showed him the white ribbons my mother had tied around our duffel bag. He looked embarrassed, then surrendered another latecomer's room.

The rodeo finals in Oklahoma may be a better place to 23
honeymoon than Paris. All week, we've observed some important rules of the game. A good rodeo, like a good marriage, or a musical instrument when played to the pitch of perfection, becomes more than what it started out to be. It is effort transformed into effortlessness; a balance becomes grace, the way love goes deep into friendship.

In the rough stock events such as the one we watched tonight, there is no victory over the horse or bull. The point of the match is not conquest but communion: the rhythm of two beings becoming one. Rodeo is not a sport of opposition; there is no scrimmage line here. No one bears malice—neither the animals, the stock contractors, nor the contestants; no one wants to get hurt. In this match of equal talents, it is only acceptance, surrender, respect, and spiritedness that make for the midair union of cowboy and horse. Not a bad thought when starting out fresh in a marriage. 24

For Study and Discussion

QUESTIONS FOR RESPONSE

1. How do you respond to events where you do not know the "rules of the game"?
2. What surprised you about Ehrlich's revelation that she spent her honeymoon attending a rodeo in Oklahoma City?

QUESTIONS ABOUT PURPOSE

1. What is Ehrlich's purpose in the first part of this essay? Look particularly at paragraphs 4–11.
2. What is her purpose in the second part of the essay? For example, how does this sentence establish her purpose for this section: "After 124 years, rodeo is still misunderstood"?

QUESTIONS ABOUT AUDIENCE

1. What assumptions does Ehrlich make about her readers' knowledge of rodeos? How does her husband help establish her expertise?
2. What does she anticipate are her readers' most common misconceptions about rodeos? What is the source of those misconceptions?

QUESTIONS ABOUT STRATEGIES

1. Ehrlich begins her formal analysis by outlining the traditional order of the rodeo program. Which of the seven events does she omit from her list?
2. How does Ehrlich analyze the multiple stages contained in a short process such as saddle bronc riding? See paragraphs 8 and 19.

QUESTIONS FOR DISCUSSION

1. According to Ehrlich, how does the rodeo exhibit competition and cooperation?
2. How would you reconcile Ehrlich's statement that the rodeo embodies ranch life with her assertion that it has less and less to do with real ranch work?

WILLIAM STAFFORD

William Stafford was born in Hutchinson, Kansas, in 1914 and was educated at the University of Kansas and the State University of Iowa. During World War II he completed his service as a conscientious objector by working for the Brethren Service and the Church World Service. After the war Stafford held faculty positions at several universities before moving to Lewis and Clark College in Portland, Oregon, where he has taught since 1957. Although he published an account of his experiences as a conscientious objector, *Down in My Heart* (1947), when he was thirty-three, Stafford did not publish his first volume of poetry, *West of Your City* (1960), until he was forty-six. He is now considered one of America's most gifted poets. Among his other books are *Traveling Through the Dark* (1962), *The Rescued Year* (1966), *Someday Maybe* (1973), and *Oregon Message* (1987). In "Writing" (first published in *Field* magazine in 1970), Stafford defines the receptivity, risks, and revelations that are part of the writing process.

Writing

A writer is not so much someone who has something to say as he is someone who has found a process that will bring about new things he would not have thought of if he had not started to say them. That is, he does not draw on a reservoir; instead, he engages in an activity that brings to him a whole succession of unforeseen stories, poems, essays, plays, laws, philosophies, religions, or—but wait! 1

Back in school, from the first when I began to try to write things, I felt this richness. One thing would lead to another; the world would give and give. Now, after twenty years or 2 so of trying, I live by that certain richness, an idea hard to pin, difficult to say, and perhaps offensive to some. For there are strange implications in it.

One implication is the importance of just plain receptivity. When I write, I like to have an interval before me when I am not likely to be interrupted. For me, this means usually the early morning, before others are awake. I get pen and paper, take a glance out the window (often it is dark out there), and wait. It is like fishing. But I do not wait very long, for there is always a nibble—and this is where receptivity comes in. To get started I will accept anything that occurs to me. Something always occurs, of course, to any of us. We can't keep from thinking. Maybe I have to settle for an immediate impression: it's cold, or hot, or dark, or bright, or in between! Or—well, the possibilities are endless. If I put down something, that thing will help the next thing come, and I'm off. If I let the process go on, things will occur to me that were not at all in my mind when I started. These things, odd or trivial as they may be, are somehow connected. And if I let them string out, surprising things will happen. 3

If I let them string out. . . . Along with initial receptivity, then, there is another readiness: I must be willing to fail. If I am to keep on writing, I cannot bother to insist on high standards. I must get into action and not let anything stop me, or even slow me much. By "standards" I do not mean "correctness"—spelling, punctuation, and so on. These details become mechanical for anyone who writes for a while. I am thinking about what many people would consider "important" standards, such matters as social significance, positive values, consistency, etc. I resolutely disregard these. Something better, greater, is happening! I am following a process that leads so wildly and originally into new territory that no judgment can at the moment be made about values, significance, and so on. I am making something new, something that has not been judged before. Later others—and maybe I myself—will make judgments. Now, I am headlong to discover. Any distraction may harm the creating. 4

So, receptive, careless of failure, I spin out things on the page. And a wonderful freedom comes. If something occurs to me, it is all right to accept it. It has one justification: it occurs to me. No one else can guide me. I must follow my own weak, wandering, diffident impulses. 5

A strange bonus happens. At times, without my insisting on it, my writings become coherent; the successive elements that occur to me are clearly related. They lead by themselves to new connections. Sometimes the language, even the syllables that happen along, may start a trend. Sometimes the materials alert me to something waiting in my mind, ready for sustained attention. At such times, I allow myself to be eloquent, or intentional, or for great swoops (treacherous! not to be trusted!) reasonable. But I do not insist on any of that; for I know that back of my activity there will be the coherence of my self, and that indulgence of my impulses will bring recurrent patterns and meanings again. 6

This attitude toward the process of writing creatively suggests a problem for me, in terms of what others say. They talk about "skills" in writing. Without denying that I do have experience, wide reading, automatic orthodoxies and maneuvers of various kinds, I still must insist that I am often baffled about what "skill" has to do with the precious little area of confusion when I do not know what I am going to say and then I find out what I am going to say. That precious interval I am unable to bridge by skill. What can I witness about it? It remains mysterious, just as all of us must feel puzzled about how we are so inventive as to be able to talk along through complexities with our friends, not needing to plan what we are going to say, but never stalled for long in our confident forward progress. Skill? If so, it is the skill we all have, something we must have learned before the age of three or four. 7

A writer is one who has become accustomed to trusting that grace, or luck, or—skill. 8

Yet another attitude I find necessary: most of what I write, like most of what I say in casual conversation, will not amount to much. Even I will realize, and even at the time, 9 that it is not negotiable. It will be like practice. In conversation I allow myself random remarks—in fact, as I recall, that is the way I learned to talk—so in writing I launch many expendable efforts. A result of this free way of writing is that I am not writing for others, mostly; they will not see the product at all unless the activity eventuates in something that later appears to be worthy. My guide is the self, and its adventuring in the language brings about communication.

This process-rather-than-substance view of writing invites 10
a final, dual reflection:

1. Writers may not be special—sensitive or talented in 11
any usual sense. They are simply engaged in sustained use of a language skill we all have. Their "creations" come about through confident reliance on stray impulses that will, with trust, find occasional patterns that are satisfying.

2. But writing itself is one of the great, free human activ- 12
ities. There is scope for individuality, and elation, and discovery, in writing. For the person who follows with trust and forgiveness what occurs to him, the world remains always ready and deep, an inexhaustible environment, with the combined vividness of an actuality and flexibility of a dream. Working back and forth between experience and thought, writers have more than space and time can offer. They have the whole unexplored realm of human vision.

For Study and Discussion

QUESTIONS FOR RESPONSE

1. What is your own writing process like? Do you work best at home or in the library, at night or earlier in the day, with a pencil and pad or a word processor? How do ideas come to you? What metaphors might describe the process—perhaps "pulling teeth," "slogging it out," "making a blueprint"?
2. What ideas or beliefs do you have about the way writers work? To what extent does your idea of how a writer works match Stafford's description of his writing?

QUESTIONS ABOUT PURPOSE

1. When Stafford says he must be willing to fail (paragraph 4), what attitude about writing do you think he is encouraging his readers to adopt?
2. How would you summarize what seems to you to be Stafford's most important advice to writers?

QUESTIONS ABOUT AUDIENCE

1. What preconceptions about writing and writers do you think Stafford anticipates most of his readers will have?
2. What questions about his writing and his work do you think Stafford anticipates his readers will want him to answer? How does he try to answer those questions?

QUESTIONS ABOUT STRATEGIES

1. How does Stafford use fishing to illustrate the first few stages in the writing process?
2. How does Stafford use the metaphor of conversation to demonstrate how he assesses the results of his writing?

QUESTIONS FOR DISCUSSION

1. What kind of writing do you think Stafford is discussing in his essay? In what kinds of writing situations do you think a writer might need to use an approach somewhat different from the one Stafford describes? Explain your answer.
2. What are some of the reasons so many people resist writing? How might Stafford's essay be helpful to them?

RICHARD SELZER

Richard Selzer was born in Troy, New York, in 1928 and was educated at Union College and Albany Medical College. In 1960, after his internship and postdoctoral study, Selzer established a private practice in general surgery and became an associate professor of surgery at the Yale University medical school. His articles on various aspects of medicine have appeared in magazines such as *Harper's, Esquire, Redbook,* and *Mademoiselle,* and his books include a volume of short stories, *Rituals of Surgery* (1974), and several collections of essays, including *Mortal Lessons: Notes on the Art of Surgery* (1977), *Letters to a Young Doctor* (1983), *Taking the World in for Repairs* (1986), and a memoir, *Down from Troy: A Doctor Comes of Age* (1992). In "The Knife," reprinted from *Mortal Lessons,* Selzer uses a language of poetic intensity to describe the steps of the surgical process.

The Knife

One holds the knife as one holds the bow of a cello or a tulip—by the stem. Not palmed nor gripped nor grasped, but lightly, with the tips of the fingers. The knife is not for pressing. It is for drawing across the field of skin. Like a slender fish, it waits, at the ready, then, go! It darts, followed by a fine wake of red. The flesh parts, falling away to yellow globules of fat. Even now, after so many times, I still marvel at its power—cold, gleaming, silent. More, I am still struck with a kind of dread that it is I in whose hand the blade travels, that my hand is its vehicle, that yet again this terrible steel-bellied thing and I have conspired for a most unnatural purpose, the laying open of the body of a human being. 1

A stillness settles in my heart and is carried to my hand. It is the quietude of resolve layered over fear. And it is this 2 resolve that lowers us, my knife and me, deeper and deeper into the person beneath. It is an entry into the body that is nothing like a caress; still, it is among the gentlest of acts. Then stroke and stroke again, and we are joined by other instruments, hemostats and forceps, until the wound blooms with strange flowers whose looped handles fall to the sides in steely array.

There is sound, the tight click of clamps fixing teeth into severed blood vessels, the snuffle and gargle of the suction machine clearing the field of blood for the next stroke, the litany of monosyllables with which one prays his way down and in: *clamp, sponge, suture, tie, cut.* And there is color. The green of the cloth, the white of the sponges, the red and yellow of the body. Beneath the fat lies the fascia, the tough fibrous sheet encasing the muscles. It must be sliced and the red beef of the muscles separated. Now there are retractors to hold apart the wound. Hands move together, part, weave. We are fully engaged, like children absorbed in a game or the craftsmen of some place like Damascus. 3

Deeper still. The peritoneum, pink and gleaming and membranous, bulges into the wound. It is grasped with forceps, and opened. For the first time we can see into the cavity of the abdomen. Such a primitive place. One expects to find drawings of buffalo on the walls. The sense of trespassing is keener now, heightened by the world's light illuminating the organs, their secret colors revealed—maroon and salmon and yellow. The vista is sweetly vulnerable at this moment, a kind of welcoming. An arc of the liver shines high and on the right, like a dark sun. It laps over the pink sweep of the stomach, from whose lower border the gauzy omentum is draped, and through which veil one sees, sinuous, slow as just-fed snakes, the indolent coils of the intestine. 4

You turn aside to wash your gloves. It is a ritual cleansing. One enters this temple doubly washed. Here is man as microcosm, representing in all his parts the earth, perhaps the universe. 5

I must confess that the priestliness of my profession has ever been impressed on me. In the beginning there are vows, 6 taken with all solemnity. Then there is the endless harsh novitiate of training, much fatigue, much sacrifice. At last one emerges as celebrant, standing close to the truth lying curtained in the Ark of the body. Not surplice and cassock but mask and gown are your regalia. You hold no chalice, but a knife. There is no wine, no wafer. There are only the facts of blood and flesh.

And if the surgeon is like a poet, then the scars you have made on countless bodies are like verses into the fashioning of which you have poured your soul. I think that if years later I were to see the trace from an old incision of mine, I should know it at once, as one recognizes his pet expressions. 7

But mostly you are a traveler in a dangerous country, advancing into the moist and jungly cleft your hands have made. Eyes and ears are shuttered from the land you left behind; mind empties itself of all other thought. You are the root of groping fingers. It is a fine hour for the fingers, their sense of touch so enhanced. The blind must know this feeling. Oh, there is risk everywhere. One goes lightly. The spleen. No! No! Do not touch the spleen that lurks below the left leaf of the diaphragm, a manta ray in a coral cave, its bloody tongue protruding. One poke and it might rupture, exploding with sudden hemorrhage. The filmy omentum must not be torn, the intestine scraped or denuded. The hand finds the liver, palms it, fingers running along its sharp lower edge, admiring. Here are the twin mounds of the kidneys, the apron of the omentum hanging in front of the intestinal coils. One lifts it aside and the fingers dip among the loops, searching, mapping territory, establishing boundaries. Deeper still, and the womb is touched, then held like a small muscular bottle—the womb and its earlike appendages, the ovaries. How they do nestle in the cup of a man's hand, their power all dormant. They are frailty itself. 8

There is a hush in the room. Speech stops. The hands of the others, assistants and nurses, are still. Only the voice of the patient's respiration remains. It is the rhythm of a quiet sea, the sound of waiting. Then you speak, slowly, the terse entries of a Himalayan climber reporting back. 9

"The stomach is okay. Greater curvature clean. No sign 10

of ulcer. Pylorus, duodenum fine. Now comes the gallbladder. No stones. Right kidney, left, all right. Liver . . . uh-oh."

Your speech lowers to a whisper, falters, stops for a long, long moment, then picks up again at the end of a sigh that comes through your mask like a last exhalation. 11

"Three big hard ones in the left lobe, one on the right. Metastatic deposits. Bad, bad. Where's the primary? Got to be coming from somewhere." 12

The arm shifts direction and the fingers drop lower and lower into the pelvis—the body impaled now upon the arm of the surgeon to the hilt of the elbow. 13

"Here it is." 14

The voice goes flat, all business now. 15

"Tumor in the sigmoid colon, wrapped all around it, pretty tight. We'll take out a sleeve of the bowel. No colostomy. Not that, anyway. But, God, there's a lot of it down there. Here, you take a feel." 16

You step back from the table, and lean into a sterile basin of water, resting on stiff arms, while the others locate the cancer. . . . 17

What is it, then, this thing, the knife, whose shape is virtually the same as it was three thousand years ago, but now with its head grown detachable? Before steel, it was bronze. Before bronze, stone—then back into unremembered time. Did man invent it or did the knife precede him here, hidden under ages of vegetation and hoofprints, lying in wait to be discovered, picked up, used? 18

The scalpel is in two parts, the handle and the blade. Joined, it is six inches from tip to tip. At one end of the handle is a narrow notched prong upon which the blade is slid, then snapped into place. Without the blade, the handle has a blind, decapitated look. It is helpless as a trussed maniac. But slide on the blade, click it home, and the knife springs instantly to life. It is headed now, edgy, leaping to mount the fingers for the gallop to its feast. 19

Now is the moment from which you have turned aside, 20

from which you have averted your gaze, yet toward which you have been hastened. Now the scalpel sings along the flesh again, its brute run unimpeded by germs or other frictions. It is a slick slide home, a barracuda spurt, a rip of embedded talon. One listens, and almost hears the whine—nasal, high, delivered through that gleaming metallic snout. The flesh splits with its own kind of moan. It is like the penetration of rape.

The breasts of women are cut off, arms and legs sliced to 21
the bone to make ready for the saw, eyes freed from sockets, intestines lopped. The hand of the surgeon rebels. Tension boils through his pores, like sweat. The flesh of the patient retaliates with hemorrhage, and the blood chases the knife wherever it is withdrawn.

Within the belly a tumor squats, toadish, fungoid. A gray 22
mother and her brood. The only thing it does not do is croak. It too is hacked from its bed as the carnivore knife lips the blood, turning in it in a kind of ecstasy of plenty, a gluttony after the long fast. It is just for this that the knife was created, tempered, heated, its violence beaten into paper-thin force.

At last a little thread is passed into the wound and tied. 23
The monstrous booming fury is stilled by a tiny thread. The tempest is silenced. The operation is over. On the table, the knife lies spent, on its side, the bloody meal smear-dried upon its flanks. The knife rests.

And waits. 24

For Study and Discussion

QUESTIONS FOR RESPONSE

1. What experiences have you had with doctors and hospitals? How might those experiences precondition your attitude toward an essay on surgery?
2. How does Selzer the writer reveal himself as Selzer the surgeon?

Would you feel comfortable as one of his patients? Explain your answer.

QUESTIONS ABOUT PURPOSE

1. How do you know that Selzer does not intend to give directions on how to perform surgery?
2. Selzer calls surgery "unnatural," but he also calls it "among the gentlest of acts." How do both assertions clarify his purpose in writing the essay?

QUESTIONS ABOUT AUDIENCE

1. The surgeon may be *the* expert in our culture. What effect does Selzer anticipate when he admits to his readers that his "quietude of resolve [is] layered over fear"?
2. Although Selzer does not expect his readers to retrace his steps, he does seem to address them directly on several occasions. To whom is he speaking when he says, "No! No! Do not touch the spleen . . ."?

QUESTIONS ABOUT STRATEGIES

1. Which of the principal steps in the surgical procedure does Selzer describe? How does he use color to make the transition from step to step?
2. On numerous occasions, Selzer uses comparisons to illustrate the process he is analyzing. What characteristics do these comparisons have in common?

QUESTIONS FOR DISCUSSION

1. What kind of dreadful mysteries are usually associated with surgery? In what ways does Selzer's analysis make the process seem less or more terrifying?
2. Analyze Selzer's many references to hands throughout this essay. Besides the work of surgeons, what other jobs require highly skilled hands? What evidence can you present to demonstrate that such skill is the result of natural ability or rigorous training?

CHARLES JOHNSON

Charles Johnson was born in 1948 in Evanston, Illinois, and was educated at Southern Illinois University and the State University of New York at Stony Brook. He worked as a cartoonist and reporter for the *Chicago Tribune* and as a member of the art staff at *St. Louis Proud* before accepting a position as professor of English at the University of Washington, Seattle. Under the tutelage of the late author John Gardner, Johnson published his first novel, *Faith and the Good Thing* (1974), a humorous folk tale of a southern black girl's trip to Chicago. Johnson's second novel, *Oxherding Tale* (1982), a modern, comic, philosophical slave narrative, tells of a young herdsman's search for his rebellious ox. Johnson's third novel, *Middle Passage* (1990), a spellbinding account of the voyage of a slave ship, won the National Book Award for fiction. Johnson has also published a book of essays, *Being and Race: Black Writing Since 1970* (1988), and a collection of short stories, *The Sorcerer's Apprentice: Tales and Conjurations* (1986). The title story from this volume describes a young boy's attempt to understand the various stages of his apprenticeship.

The Sorcerer's Apprentice

There was a time, long ago, when many sorcerers lived in 1
South Carolina, men not long from slavery who remembered the white magic of the Ekpe Cults and the Cameroons, and by far the greatest of these wizards was a blacksmith named Rubin Bailey. Believing he was old, and would soon die, the Sorcerer decided to pass his learning along to an apprentice. From a family near Abbeville he selected a boy, Allan, whose

father, Richard Jackson, Rubin once healed after an accident, and for this Allan loved the Sorcerer, especially the effects of his craft, which comforted the sick, held back evil, and blighted the enemies of newly freed slaves with locusts and bad health. "My house," Richard told the wizard, "has been honored." His son swore to serve his teacher faithfully, then those who looked to the Sorcerer, in all ways. With his father's blessing, the boy moved his belongings into the Sorcerer's home, a houseboat covered with strips of scrap-metal, on the river.

But Rubin Bailey's first teachings seemed to Allan to be no teachings at all. "Bring in fresh water," Rubin told his apprentice. "Scrape barnacles off the boat." He never spoke of sorcery. Around the boy he tied his blacksmith's apron, and guided his hands in hammering out the horseshoes Rubin sold in town, but not once in the first month did Rubin pass along the recipes for magic. Patiently, Allan performed these duties in perfect submission to the Sorcerer, for it seemed rude to express displeasure to a man he wished to emulate, but his heart knocked for the higher knowledge, the techniques that would, he hoped, work miracles. 2

At last, as they finished a meal of boiled pork and collards one evening, he complained bitterly: "You haven't told me anything yet!" Allan regretted this outburst immediately, and lowered his head. "Have I done wrong?" 3

For a moment the Sorcerer was silent. He spiced his coffee with rum, dipped in his bread, chewed slowly, then looked up, steadily, at the boy. "You are the best of students. And you wish to do good, but you can't be too faithful, or too eager, or the good becomes evil." 4

"Now I don't understand," Allan said. "By themselves the tricks aren't good *or* evil, and if you plan to do good, then the results must be good." 5

Rubin exhaled, finished his coffee, then shoved his plate toward the boy. "Clean the dishes," he said. Then, more gently: "What I know has worked I will teach. There is no certainty these things can work for you, or even for me, a second time. White magic comes and goes. I'm teaching you 6 a trade, Allan. You will never starve. This is because after fifty years, I still can't foresee if an incantation will be magic or foolishness."

These were not, of course, the answers Allan longed to hear. He said, "Yes, sir," and quietly cleared away their dishes. If he had replied aloud to Rubin, as he did silently while toweling dry their silverware later that night, he would have told the Sorcerer, "You are the greatest magician in the world because you have studied magic and the long-dead masters of magic, and I believe, even if you do not, that the secret of doing good is a good heart and having a hundred spells at your disposal, so I will study everything—the words and timbre and tone of your voice as you conjure, and listen to those you have heard. Then I, too, will have magic and can do good." He washed his underwear in the moonlight, as is fitting for a fledgling magician, tossed his dishpan water into the river, and, after hanging his washpail on a hook behind Rubin's front door, undressed, and fell asleep with these thoughts: To do good is a very great thing, the *only* thing, but a magician must be able to conjure at a moment's notice. Surely it is all a question of know-how. 7

So it was that after a few months the Sorcerer's apprentice learned well and quickly when Rubin Bailey finally began to teach. In Allan's growth was the greatest joy. Each spell he showed proudly to his father and Richard's friends when he traveled home once a year. Unbeknownst to the Sorcerer, he held simple exhibits for their entertainment—harmless prestidigitation like throwing his voice or levitating logs stacked by the toolshed. However pleased Richard might have been, he gave no sign. Allan's father never joked or laughed too loudly. He was the sort of man who held his feelings in, and people took this for strength. Allan's mother, Beatrice, a tall, thick-waisted woman, had told him (for Richard would not) how when she was carrying Allan, they rode a haywagon to a scrub-ball in Abbeville on Freedom Day. Richard fell beneath the wagon. A wheel smashed his thumb open to the bone. "Somebody better go for Rubin Bailey," was all Richard said, and he stared like it might be 8 a stranger's hand. And Allan remembered Richard toiling so long in the sun he couldn't eat some evenings unless he first emptied his stomach by forcing himself to vomit. His father squirreled away money in their mattresses, saving for seven years to buy the land they worked. When he had $600—half what they needed—he grew afraid of theft, so Beatrice took their money to one of the banks in town. She stood in line behind a northern-looking Negro who said his name was Grady Armstrong. "I work for the bank across the street," he told Beatrice. "You wouldn't be interested in part-time work, would you? We need a woman to clean, someone reliable, but she has to keep her savings with us." Didn't they need the money? Beatrice would ask Allan, later, when Richard left them alone at night. Wouldn't the extra work help her husband? She followed Grady Armstrong, whose easy, loose-hinged walk led them to the second bank across the street. "Have you ever deposited money before?" asked Grady. "No," she said. Taking her envelope, he said, "Then I'll do it for you." On the boardwalk, Beatrice waited. And waited. After five minutes, she opened the door, found no Grady Armstrong, and flew screaming the fifteen miles back to the fields and Richard, who listened and chewed his lip, but said nothing. He leaned, Allan remembered, in the farmhouse door, smoking his cigars and watching only Lord knew what in the darkness—exactly as he stood the following year, when Beatrice, after swallowing rat poison, passed on.

Allan supposed it was risky to feel if you had grown up, 9
like Richard, in a world of nightriders. There was too much to lose. Any attachment ended in separation, grief. If once you let yourself care, the crying might never stop. So he assumed his father was pleased with his apprenticeship to Rubin, though hearing him say this would have meant the world to Allan. He did not mind that somehow the Sorcerer's personality seemed to permeate each spell like sweat staining fresh wood, because this, too, seemed to be the way of things. The magic was Rubin Bailey's, but when pressed, the Sorcerer confessed that the spells had been in circulation for centuries. They were a web of history and culture, like the

king-sized quilts you saw as curiosities at country fairs, sewn by every woman in Abbeville, each having finished only a section, a single flower perhaps, so no man, strictly speaking, could own a mystic spell. "But when you kill a bird by pointing," crabbed Rubin from his rocking chair, "you don't *haveta* wave your left hand in the air and pinch your forefinger and thumb together like I do."

"Did I do that?" asked Allan. 10

Rubin hawked and spit over the side of the houseboat. 11
"Every time."

"I just wanted to get it right." Looking at his hand, he 12
felt ashamed—he was, after all, right-handed—then shoved it deep into his breeches. "The way you do it is so beautiful."

"I know." Rubin laughed. He reached into his coat, 13
brought out his pipe, and looked for matches. Allan stepped inside, and the Sorcerer shouted behind him, "You shouldn't do it because my own teacher, who wore out fifteen flying carpets in his lifetime, told me it was wrong."

"Wrong?" The boy returned. He held a match close to 14
the bowl of Rubin's pipe, cupping the flame. "Then why do you do it?"

"It works best for me that way, Allan. I have arthritis." 15
He slanted his eyes left at his pupil. "Do you?"

The years passed, and Allan improved, even showing a 16
certain flair, a style all his own that pleased Rubin, who praised the boy for his native talent, which did not come from knowledge and, it struck Allan, was wholly unreliable. When Esther Peters, a seamstress, broke her hip, it was not Rubin who the old woman called, but young Allan, who sat stiffly on a fiddle-back chair by her pallet, the fingers of his left hand spread over the bony ledge of her brow and rheumy eyes, whispering the rune that lifted her pain after Esther stopped asking, "Does he know what he doing, Rubin? This ain't how you did when I caught my hand in that cotton gin." Afterwards, as they walked the dark footpath leading back to the river, Rubin in front, the Sorcerer shared a fifth with the boy and paid him a terrifying compliment: "That was the best I've seen anybody do the spell for exorcism."

He stroked his pupil's head. "God took *holt* of you back there—I don't see how you can do it that good again." The smile at the corners of Allan's mouth weighed a ton. He handed back Rubin's bottle, and said, "Me neither." The Sorcerer's flattery, if this was flattery, suspiciously resembled Halloween candy with hemlock inside. Allan could not speak to Rubin the rest of that night.

In the old days of sorcery, it often happened that pupils came to mistrust most their finest creations, those frighteningly effortless works that flew mysteriously from their lips when they weren't looking, and left the apprentice feeling, despite his pride, as baffled as his audience and afraid for his future—this was most true when the compliments compared a fledgling wizard to other magicians, as if the apprentice had achieved nothing new, or on his own. This is how Allan felt. The charm that cured Esther had whipped through him like wind through a reedpipe, or—more exactly, like music struggling to break free, liberate its volume and immensity from the confines of wood and brass. It made him feel unessential, anonymous, like a tool in which the spell sang itself, briefly borrowing his throat, then tossed him, Allan, aside when the miracle ended. To be so used was thrilling, but it gave the boy many bad nights. He lay half on his bed, half off. While Rubin slept, he yanked on his breeches and slipped outside. The river trembled with moonlight. Not far away, in a rowboat, a young man unbuttoned his lover. Allan heard their laughter and fought down the loneliness of a life devoted to discipline and sorcery. So many sacrifices. So many hours spent hunched over yellow, worm-holed scrolls. He pitched small pebbles into the water, and thought, If a conjurer cannot conjure at will, he is worthless. He must have knowledge, an armory of techniques, a thousand strategies, if he is to unfailingly do good. Toward this end the apprentice applied himself, often despising the spontaneity of his first achievement. He watched Rubin Bailey closely until on his fifth year on the river he had stayed by the Sorcerer too long and there was no more to learn. 17

"That can't be," said Allan. He was twenty-five, a full 18

sorcerer himself by most standards, very handsome, more like his father now, at the height of his technical powers, with many honors and much brilliant thaumaturgy behind him, though none half as satisfying as his first exorcism rune for Esther Peters. He had, generally, the respect of everyone in Abbeville. And, it must be said, they waited eagerly for word of his first solo demonstration. This tortured Allan. He paced around the table, where Rubin sat repairing a fishing line. His belongings, rolled in a blanket, lay by the door. He pleaded, "There must be *one* more strategy."

"One more maybe," agreed the Sorcerer. "But what you 19
need to know, you'll learn."

"Without you?" Allan shuddered. He saw himself, in a 20
flash of probable futures, failing Rubin. Dishonoring Richard. Ridiculed by everyone. "How *can* I learn without you?"

"You just do like you did that evening when you helped 21
Esther Peters. . . ."

That wasn't me, thought Allan. I was younger. I don't 22
know how, but everything worked then. You were behind me. I've tried. I've tried the rainmaking charm over and over. *It doesn't rain!* They're only words!

The old Sorcerer stood up and embraced Allan quickly, 23
for he did not like sloppy good-byes or lingering glances or the silly things people said when they had to get across a room and out the door. "You go home and wait for your first caller. You'll do fine."

Allan followed his bare feet away from the houseboat, his 24
head lowered and a light pain in his chest, a sort of flutter like a pigeon beating its wings over his heart—an old pain that first began when he suspected that pansophical knowledge counted for nothing. The apprentice said the spell for fair weather. Fifteen minutes later a light rain fell. He traipsed through mud into Abbeville, shoved his bag under an empty table in a tavern, and sat dripping in the shadows until he dried. A fat man pounded an off-key piano. Boot heels stamped the floor beneath Allan, who ordered tequila. He sucked lemon slices and drained off shot glasses. Gradually, liquor backwashed in his throat and the ache disappeared

and his body felt transparent. Yet still he wondered: Was sorcery a gift given to a few, like poetry? Did the Lord come, lift you up, then drop you forever? If so, then he was finished, bottomed out, bellied up before he even began. He had not been born among the Allmuseri Tribe in Africa, like Rubin, if this was necessary for magic. He had not come to New Orleans in a slave clipper, or been sold at the Cabildo, if this was necessary. He had only, it seemed, a vast and painfully acquired yet hollow repertoire of tricks, and this meant he could be a parlor magician, which paid well enough, but he would never do good. If he could not help, what then? He knew no other trade. He had no other dignity. He had no other means to transform the world and no other influence upon men. His seventh tequila untasted, Allan squeezed the bridge of his nose with two fingers, rummaging through his mind for Rubin's phrase for the transmogrification of liquids into vapor. The demons of drunkenness (Saphathoral) and slow-thinking (Ruax) tangled his thoughts, but finally the words floated topside. Softly, he spoke the phrase, stunned at its beauty—at the Sorcerer's beauty, really—mumbling it under his breath so no one might hear, then opened his eyes on the soaking, square face of a man who wore a blue homespun shirt and butternut trousers, but had not been there an instant before: his father. Maybe he'd said the phrase for telekinesis. "Allan, I've been looking all over. How are you?"

"Like you see." His gaze dropped from his father to the full shot glass and he despaired. 25

"Are you sure you're all right? Your eyelids are puffy." 26

"I'm okay." He lifted the shot glass and made its contents vanish naturally. "I've had my last lesson." 27

"I know—I went looking for you on the river, and Rubin said you'd come home. Since I knew better, I came to Abbeville. There's a girl at the house wants to see you—Lizzie Harris. She was there when you sawed Deacon Wills in half." Richard picked up his son's bag. "She wants you to help her to—" 28

Allan shook his head violently. "Lizzie should see Rubin." 29

"She has." He reached for Allan's hat and placed it on his 30
son's head. "He sent her to you. She's been waiting for hours."

Much rain fell upon Allan and his father, who walked as 31
if his feet hurt, as they left town, but mainly it fell on Allan. His father's confidence in him was painful, his chatter about his son's promising future like the chronicle of someone else's life. This was the night that was bound to come. And now, he thought as they neared the tiny, hip-roofed farmhouse, swimming in fog, I shall fall from humiliation to impotency, from impotency to failure, from failure to death. He leaned weakly against the porch rail. His father scrambled ahead of him, though he was a big man built for endurance and not for speed, and stepped back to open the door for Allan. The Sorcerer's apprentice, stepping inside, decided quietly, definitely, without hope that if this solo flight failed, he would work upon himself the one spell Rubin had described but dared not demonstrate. If he could not help this girl Lizzie—and he feared he could not—he would go back to the river and bring forth demons—horrors that broke a man in half, ate his soul, then dragged him below the ground, where, Allan decided, those who could not do well the work of a magician belonged.

"Allan's here," his father said to someone in the sitting 32
room. "My son is a Conjure Doctor, you know."

"I seen him," said a girl's voice. "Looks like he knows 33
everything there is to know about magic."

The house, full of heirlooms, had changed little since 34
Allan's last year with Rubin. The furniture was darkened by use. All the mirrors in his mother's bedroom were still covered by cloth. His father left week-old dishes on the hob, footswept his cigars under the bare, loose floorboards, and paint on the front porch had begun to peel in large strips. There in the sitting room, Lizzie Harris sat on Beatrice's old flat-bottomed roundabout. She was twice as big as Allan remembered her. Her loose dress and breast exposed as she fed her baby made, he supposed, the difference. Allan looked away while Lizzie drew her dress up, then reached into her

bead purse for a shinplaster—Civil War currency—which she handed to him. "This is all you have?" He returned her money, pulled a milk stool beside her, and said, "Please, sit down." His hands were trembling. He needed to hold something to hide the shaking. Allan squeezed both his knees. "Now," he said, "what's wrong with the child?"

"Pearl don't eat," said Lizzie. "She hasn't touched food in two days, and the medicine Dr. Britton gave her makes her spit. It's a simple thing," the girl assured him. "Make her eat." 35

He lifted the baby off Lizzie's lap, pulling the covering from her face. That she was beautiful made his hands shake even more. She kept her fists balled at her cheeks. Her eyes were light, bread-colored, but latticed by blood vessels. Allan said to his father, without facing him, "I think I need boiled Hound's Tongue and Sage. They're in my bag. Bring me the water from the herbs in a bowl." He hoisted the baby higher on his right arm and, holding the spoon of cold cereal in his left hand, praying silently, began a litany of every spell he knew to disperse suffering and the afflictions of the spirit. From his memory, where techniques lay stacked like crates in a storage bin, Allan unleashed a salvo of incantations. His father, standing nearby with a discolored spoon and the bowl, held his breath so long Allan could hear flies gently beating against the lamp glass of the lantern. Allan, using the spoon like a horseshoe, slipped the potion between her lips. "Eat, Pearl," the apprentice whispered. "Eat and live." Pearl spit up on his shirt. Allan closed his eyes and repeated slowly every syllable of every word of every spell in his possession. And ever he pushed the spoon of cereal against the child's teeth, ever she pushed it away, gagging, swinging her head, and wailing so Allan had to shout each word above her voice. He oozed sweat now. Wind changing direction outside shifted the pressure inside the room so suddenly that Allan's stomach turned violently—it was as if the farmhouse, snatched up a thousand feet, now hung in space. Pearl spit first clear fluids. Then blood. The apprentice attacked this mystery with a dazzling array of devices, analyzed it, looked 36

at her with the critical, wrinkled brow of a philosopher, and
mimed the Sorcerer so perfectly it seemed that Rubin, not
Allan, worked magic in the room. But he was not Rubin
Bailey. And the child suddenly stopped its struggle and relaxed in the apprentice's arms.

Lizzie yelped. "Why ain't Pearl crying?" He began re- 37
peating, futilely, his spells for the fifth time. Lizzie snatched
his arm with such strength her fingers left blue spots on his
skin. "That's enough!" she said. "You give her to me!"

"There's another way," Allan said, "another charm I've 38
seen." But Lizzie Harris had reached the door. She threw a
brusque "Good-bye" behind her to Richard and nothing to
Allan. He knew they were back on the ground when Lizzie
disappeared outside. Within the hour she would be at Rubin's houseboat. In two hours she would be at Esther Peters's
home, broadcasting his failure.

"Allan," said Richard, stunned. "It didn't work." 39

"It's never worked." Allan put away the bowl, looked 40
around the farmhouse for his bag, then a pail, and kissed his
father's rough cheek. Startled, Richard pulled back sharply,
as if he had stumbled sideways against the kiln. "I'm sorry,"
said Allan. It was not an easy thing to touch a man who so
guarded, and for good reason, his emotions. "I'm not much
of a Sorcerer, or blacksmith, or anything else."

"You're not going out this late, are you?" His father strug- 41
gled, and Allan felt guilty for further confusing him with
feeling. "Allan. . . ."

His voice trailed off. 42

"There's one last spell I have to do." Allan touched his 43
arm lightly, once, then drew back his hand. "Don't follow
me, okay?"

On his way to the river Allan gathered the roots and stalks 44
and stones he required to dredge up the demon kings. The
sky was clear, the air dense, and the Devil was in it if he
fouled even this conjuration. For now he was sure that white
magic did not reside in ratiocination, education, or will. Skill
was of no service. His talent was for pa(o)stiche. He could
imitate but never truly heal; impress but never conjure

beauty; ape the good but never again give rise to a genuine spell. For that God or Creation, or the universe—it had several names—had to seize you, *use* you, as the Sorcerer said, because it needed a womb, shake you down, speak through you until the pain pearled into a beautiful spell that snapped the world back together. It had abandoned Allan, this possession. It had taken him, in a way, like a lover, planted one pitiful seed, and said, "'Bye now." This absence, this emptiness, this sterility he felt deep at his center. Beyond all doubt, he owed the universe far more than it owed him. To give was right; to ask wrong. From birth he was indebted to so many, like his father, and for so much. But you could not repay the universe, or anyone, or build a career as a Conjure Doctor on a single, brilliant spell. Talent, Allan saw, was a curse. To have served once—was this enough? Better perhaps never to have served at all than to go on, foolishly, in the wreckage of former grace, glossing over his frigidity with cheap fireworks, window dressing, a trashy display of pyrotechnics, gimmicks designed to distract others from seeing that the magician onstage was dead.

Now the Sorcerer's apprentice placed his stones and herbs 45 into the pail, which he filled with river water; then he built a fire behind a rock. Rags of fog floated over the waste-clogged riverbank as Allan drew a horseshoe in chalk. He sat cross-legged in wet grass that smelled faintly of oil and fish, faced east, and cursed at the top of his voice. "I conjure and I invoke thee, O Magoa, strong king of the East. I order thee to obey me, to send thy servants Onoskelis and Tepheus."

Two froglike shapes stitched from the fumes of Allan's 46 potion began to take form above the pail.

Next he invoked the demon king of the North, who 47 brought Ornia, a beautiful, blue-skinned lamia from the river bottom. Her touch, Allan knew, was death. She wore a black gown, a necklace of dead spiders, and entered through the opening of the enchanted horseshoe. The South sent Rabdos, a griffinlike hound, all teeth and hair, that hurtled toward the apprentice from the woods; and from the West issued Bazazath, and most terrible of all—a collage of horns, cloven feet, and goatish eyes so wild Allan wrenched away his head. Upriver, he saw kerosene lamplight moving from the direction of town. A faraway voice called, "Allan? Allan? Allan, is that you? Allan, are you out there?" His father. The one he had truly harmed. Allan frowned and faced those he had summoned.

"Apprentice," rumbled Bazazath, "*student,* you risk your 48
life by opening hell."

"I am only that, a student," said Allan, "the one who 49
studies beauty, who wishes to give it back, but who cannot serve what he loves."

"You are wretched, indeed," said Bazazath, and he glanced 50
back at the others. "Isn't he wretched?"

They said, as one, "Worse." 51

Allan did not understand. He felt Richard's presence hard 52
by, heard him call from the mystic circle's edge, which no man or devil could break. "How am I worse?"

"Because," said the demon of the West, "to love the good, 53
the beautiful is right, but to labor on and will the work when you are obviously *beneath* this service is to parody them, twist them beyond recognition, to lay hold of what was once beautiful and make it a monstrosity. It becomes *black* magic. Sorcery is relative, student—dialectical, if you like expensive speech. And this, exactly, is what you have done with the teachings of Rubin Bailey."

"No," blurted Allan. 54

The demon of the West smiled. "Yes." 55

"Then," Allan asked, "you must destroy me?" It was less 56
a question than a request.

"That is why we are here." Bazazath opened his arms. 57
"You must step closer."

He had not known before the real criminality of his deeds. 58
How dreadful that love could disfigure the thing loved. Allan's eyes bent up toward Richard. It was too late for apologies. Too late for promises to improve. He had failed everyone, particularly his father, whose face now collapsed into tears, then hoarse weeping like some great animal with

a broken spine. In a moment he would drop to both knees. Don't want me, thought Allan. Don't love me as I am. Could he do nothing right? His work caused irreparable harm—and his death, trivial as it was in his own eyes, that, too, would cause suffering. Why must his choices be so hard? If he returned home, his days would be a dreary marking time for magic, which might never come again, living to one side of what he had loved, and loved still, for fear of creating evil—this was surely the worst curse of all, waiting for grace, but in suicide he would drag his father's last treasure, dirtied as it was, into hell behind him.

"It grows late," said Bazazath. "Have you decided?" 59

The apprentice nodded, yes. 60

He scrubbed away part of the chalk circle with the ball of 61
his foot, then stepped toward his father. The demons waited—two might still be had this night for the price of one. But Allan felt within his chest the first spring of resignation, a giving way of both the hunger to heal and the anxiety to avoid evil. Was this surrender the one thing the Sorcerer could not teach? His pupil did not know. Nor did he truly know, now that he was no longer a Sorcerer's apprentice with a bright future, how to comfort his father. Awkwardly, Allan lifted Richard's wrist with his right hand, for he was right-handed, then squeezed, tightly, the old man's thick, ruined fingers. For a second his father twitched back in an old slave reflex, the safety catch still on, then fell heavily toward his son. The demons looked on indifferently, then glanced at each other. After a moment, they left, seeking better game.

COMMENT ON "THE SORCERER'S APPRENTICE"

"The Sorcerer's Apprentice" questions the reliability of learning a process. Rubin Bailey, a great sorcerer, tries to pass on his knowledge to a young apprentice, Allan Jackson. The process is confusing and disappointing. First, Rubin asks Allan to do chores. Then, once Allan asks for information,

Rubin teaches his young student what has worked for him. But Rubin cautions Allan that he cannot guarantee that any of the spells and incantations will work again. The hard lesson Allan must learn is that he is not important to the process; he is simply a vessel through which the energy is channeled. Even after his dramatic cure of Esther, Allan is discouraged. He is so dependent on Rubin's magic that he does not know what he has done. His insecurities increase when he is unable to cure Lizzie's child. He sees himself falling from "humiliation to impotency, from impotency to failure, from failure to death." He tries one last spell to cure himself, but instead of following the demon Bazazath, he reaches for his father, whose example leads him to independence and knowledge.

Process Analysis as a Writing Strategy

1. Write an essay for the readers of a magazine such as *Popular Mechanics* in which you give directions on how to solve a simple mechanical problem. Like Tom and Ray Magliozzi, you may want to analyze how the process is supposed to work before you give directions on how to correct the process once it goes wrong. You may also want to present the worst-case results if your readers don't take care of this simple problem.
2. Provide information for the members of your writing class on the steps you followed to complete and evaluate an intellectual project such as writing a research paper. Like William Stafford, you may want to explain the wandering impulses and recurrent patterns that you discovered. Unlike Stafford's attempts, your project may well be examined and evaluated by others. Explain how this expectation complicates the steps you followed in your project.
3. Lars Eighner's "My Daily Dives in the Dumpster" raises significant questions about how our culture views the processes of consuming, disposing, and conserving. Construct a portrait of a conscientious consumer and then analyze the processes he or she would use to maintain an ethically responsible relationship to the environment.
4. Analyze the various stages in a political process (casting a ballot) or economic process (balancing your checkbook). Assume that, like the Magliozzi brothers, you are hosting an advice radio program. Use anecdotes, like the one of the man with the Thunderbird, to explain the hilarious consequences that will result if your listener does not follow precisely your step-by-step advice.
5. Analyze a cultural process (such as professional wrestling) for the readers of the section of your local newspaper that deals with topics of general interest. Illustrate how the process serves as a metaphor for a particular set of values. Like Gretel Ehrlich, you may have to correct common misconceptions about the process or answer critics who see the process as degrading or irrelevant. Also, like Ehrlich, you may want to cite the observations of participants

to reveal the hidden details that embody the values you wish to analyze.

6. Analyze a process that confuses, intimidates, or terrifies most people. Richard Selzer's essay on the surgical process is obviously a good resource for this assignment. Your purpose is to clarify (or demystify) the process. Personalize the analysis for your readers by citing your own experience: "I did this and survived to tell the tale. So can you."

COMPARISON AND CONTRAST

Technically speaking, when you **compare** two or more things, you're looking for similarities; when you **contrast** them, you're looking for differences. In practice, of course, the operations are just opposite sides of the same coin, and one implies the other. When you look for what's similar, you will also notice what is different. You can compare things at all levels, from the trivial (plaid shoelaces with plain ones) to the really serious (the differences between a career in medicine and one in advertising). Often when you compare things at a serious level, you do so to make a choice. That's why it's helpful to know how to organize your thinking so that you can analyze similarities and differences in a systematic, useful way that brings out significant differences. It's particularly helpful to have such a system when you are going to write a comparison-and-contrast essay.

PURPOSE

You can take two approaches to writing comparison-and-contrast essays; each has a different purpose. You can make a *strict* comparison, exploring the relationship between things in the same class, or you can do a *fanciful* comparison, looking at the relationship among things from different classes.

When you write a *strict* comparison, you compare only things that are truly alike—actors with actors, musicians with musicians, but *not* actors with musicians. You're trying to find similar information about both your subjects. For instance, what are the characteristics of actors, whether they are movie or stage actors? How are jazz musicians and classical musicians alike, even if their music is quite different? In a strict comparison, you probably also want to show how two things in the same class are different in important ways. Often when you focus your comparison on differences, you do so in order to make a judgment and, finally, a choice. That's one of the main reasons people make comparisons, whether they're shopping or writing.

When you write a *fanciful* comparison, you try to set up an imaginative, illuminating comparison between two things that don't seem at all alike, and you do it for a definite reason: to help explain and clarify a complex idea. For instance, the human heart is often compared to a pump—a fanciful and useful comparison that enables one to envision the heart at work. You can use similar fanciful comparisons to help your readers see new dimensions to events; for instance, you can compare the astronauts landing on the moon to Columbus discovering the new world, or you can compare the increased drug use among young people to an epidemic spreading through part of our culture.

You may find it difficult to construct an entire essay

around a fanciful comparison—such attempts tax the most creative energy and can quickly break down. Probably you can use this method of comparison most effectively as a device for enlivening your writing and highlighting dramatic similarities. When you're drawing fanciful comparisons, you're not very likely to be comparing to make judgments or recommend choices. Instead, your purpose in writing a fanciful comparison is to catch your readers' attention and show new connections between unlike things.

AUDIENCE

As you plan a comparison-and-contrast essay, think ahead about what your readers already know and what they're going to expect. First, ask yourself what they know about the items or ideas you're going to compare. Do they know a good deal about both—for instance, two popular television programs? Do they know very little about either item—for instance, Buddhism and Shintoism? Or do they know quite a bit about one but little about the other—for instance, football and rugby?

If you're confident that your readers know a lot about both items (the television programs), you can spend a little time pointing out similarities and concentrate on your reasons for making the comparison. When readers know little about either (Eastern religions), you'll have to define each, using concepts they are familiar with before you can point out important contrasts. If readers know only one item in a pair (football and rugby), then use the known to explain the unknown. Emphasize what is familiar to them about football and explain how rugby is like it, but also how it is different.

As you think about what your readers need, remember they want your essay to be fairly balanced, not 90 percent about Buddhism and 10 percent about Shintoism, or two paragraphs about tennis and nine or ten about racketball. When your focus seems so unevenly divided, you appear to be using one element in the comparison only as a springboard to talk about the other. Such an imbalance can disappoint your readers, who expect to learn about both.

STRATEGIES

You can use two basic strategies for organizing a comparison-and-contrast essay. The first is the *divided* or *subject-by-subject* pattern. The second is the *alternating* or *point-by-point* pattern. When you use the divided pattern, you present all your information on one topic before you bring in information on the other topic. Mark Twain uses this method in "Two Views of the River." First he gives an apprentice's poetic view, emphasizing the beauty of the river; then he gives the pilot's practical view, emphasizing the technical problems the river poses.

When you use the alternating pattern, however, you work your way through the comparison point by point, giving information first on one aspect of the topic, then on the other. If Mark Twain had written his essay in an alternating pattern, he would have given the apprentice's poetic view of a particular feature of the river, then the pilot's pragmatic view of that same feature. He would have followed that pattern throughout, commenting on each feature—the wind, the surface of the river, the sunset, the color of the water—by alternating between the apprentice's and the pilot's point of view.

Although both methods are useful, you'll find that each has strengths and weaknesses. The divided pattern is strong because you can present each part of your essay as a satisfying whole. It works especially well in short essays, such as Twain's, where you're presenting only two facets of a topic and your reader can easily keep track of the points you want to make. Its weakness, however, is that sometimes you slip into writing what seems like two separate essays. Thus, when you're writing a long comparison essay about a complex topic, you may have trouble organizing your material clearly enough to keep your readers on track.

The alternating pattern works well when you want to

show the two subjects you're comparing side by side, emphasizing the points you're comparing. You'll find it particularly good for longer essays, such as Edward T. Hall's "The Arab World," when you want to show many complex points of comparison and need to help your readers see how those points match up. The weakness of the alternating pattern is that you may reduce your analysis to an exercise. If you use it for making only a few points of comparison in a short essay on a simple topic, your essay sounds choppy and disconnected, like a simple list.

Often you can make the best of both worlds by *combining strategies*. For example, you could start out using a divided pattern to give an overall, unified view of the topics you're going to compare, then shift to an alternating pattern to show how many points of comparison you have found between your subjects. Deborah Tannen uses a version of this strategy in "Rapport-talk and Report-talk." She begins by establishing the difference between private conversations and public speaking; then she uses an alternating pattern within each category to demonstrate the contrasts between the speaking styles of men and women.

When you want to write a good comparison-and-contrast analysis, keep three guidelines in mind: (1) *balance parts,* (2) *include reminders,* and (3) *supply reasons*.

Look, for example, at how Gerald Weissmann designs his comparison of medical charts to the nineteenth- and twentieth-century novel so that each part is illustrated by three extended quotations, approximately equal in length and arranged chronologically. He also uses transitional phrases to show his readers that information he uses in one part of his analysis connects with information appearing elsewhere. Finally, several times in the essay he gives readers his rationale for comparing medical charts and novels.

Rose del Castillo Guilbault uses similar strategies when she contrasts types of male movie stars, reminds readers that cultural distortion is a consistent pattern, and reasons that such distortion "hints at a deeper cultural misunderstanding that extends beyond mere word definitions."

Using Comparison and Contrast in a Paragraph

BRUCE CATTON

From "Grant and Lee: A Study in Contrasts"

So Grant and Lee were in complete contrast, representing two diametrically opposed elements in American life. Grant was the modern man emerging; beyond him, ready to come on the stage, was the great age of steel and machinery, of crowded cities and a restless, burgeoning vitality. Lee might have ridden down from the old age of chivalry, lance in hand, silken banner fluttering over his head. Each man was the perfect champion of his cause, drawing both his strengths and his weaknesses from the people he led.

Establishes differences

Uses alternating pattern
1. Grant (modern man)

2. Lee (chivalric man)

Evokes similarity

Comment This paragraph demonstrates how comparisons can work on several levels at the same time. Catton not only contrasts Grant and Lee, but he also uses these famous generals to contrast two "diametrically opposed elements in American life"—the modern man and the chivalric man. Catton concludes his contrast by evoking a major similarity between the two men: each embodied the strengths and weaknesses of "the people he led."

MARK TWAIN

Mark Twain (the pen name of Samuel Clemens, 1835–1910) was born in Florida, Missouri, and grew up in the river town of Hannibal, Missouri, where he watched the comings and goings of the steamboats he would eventually pilot. Twain spent his young adult life working as a printer, a pilot on the Mississippi, and a frontier journalist. After the Civil War, he began a career as a humorist and storyteller, writing such classics as *The Adventures of Tom Sawyer* (1876), *Life on the Mississippi* (1883), *The Adventures of Huckleberry Finn* (1885), and *A Connecticut Yankee in King Arthur's Court* (1889). His place in American writing was best characterized by editor William Dean Howells, who called Twain the "Lincoln of our literature." In "Two Views of the River," taken from *Life on the Mississippi,* Twain compares the way he saw the river as an innocent apprentice to the way he saw it as an experienced pilot.

Two Views of the River

Now when I had mastered the language of this water, and had come to know every trifling feature that bordered the great river as familiarly as I knew the letters of the alphabet, I had made a valuable acquisition. But I had lost something, too. I had lost something which could never be restored to me while I lived. All the grace, the beauty, the poetry, had gone out of the majestic river! I still keep in mind a certain wonderful sunset which I witnessed when steamboating was new to me. A broad expanse of the river was turned to blood; in the middle distance the red hue brightened into gold, through which a solitary log came floating black and 1 conspicuous; in one place a long, slanting mark lay sparkling upon the water; in another the surface was broken by boiling, tumbling rings that were as many-tinted as an opal; where the ruddy flush was faintest, was a smooth spot that was covered with graceful circles and radiating lines, ever so delicately traced; the shore on our left was densely wooded, and the somber shadow that fell from this forest was broken in one place by a long, ruffled trail that shone like silver; and high above the forest wall a clean-stemmed dead tree waved a single leafy bough that glowed like a flame in the unobstructed splendor that was flowing from the sun. There were graceful curves, reflected images, woody heights, soft distances; and over the whole scene, far and near, the dissolving lights drifted steadily, enriching it every passing moment with new marvels of coloring.

I stood like one bewitched. I drank it in, in a speechless 2
rapture. The world was new to me, and I had never seen anything like this at home. But as I have said, a day came when I began to cease from noting the glories and the charms which the moon and the sun and the twilight wrought upon the river's face; another day came when I ceased altogether to note them. Then, if that sunset scene had been repeated, I should have looked upon it without rapture, and should have commented upon it, inwardly, after this fashion: "This sun means that we are going to have wind to-morrow; that floating log means that the river is rising, small thanks to it; that slanting mark on the water refers to a bluff reef which is going to kill somebody's steamboat one of these nights, if it keeps on stretching out like that; those tumbling 'boils' show a dissolving bar and a changing channel there; the lines and circles in the slick water over yonder are a warning that that troublesome place is shoaling up dangerously; that silver streak in the shadow of the forest is the 'break' from a new snag, and he has located himself in the very best place he could have found to fish for steamboats; that tall dead tree, with a single living branch, is not going to last long, and then how is a body ever going to get through this blind place at night without the friendly old landmark?"

No, the romance and beauty were all gone from the river. All the value any feature of it had for me now was the amount of usefulness it could furnish toward compassing the safe piloting of a steamboat. Since those days, I have pitied doctors from my heart. What does the lovely flush in a beauty's cheek mean to a doctor but a "break" that ripples above some deadly disease? Are not all her visible charms sown thick with what are to him the signs and symbols of hidden decay? Does he ever see her beauty at all, or doesn't he simply view her professionally, and comment upon her unwholesome condition all to himself? And doesn't he sometimes wonder whether he has gained most or lost most by learning his trade? 3

For Study and Discussion

QUESTIONS FOR RESPONSE

1. Mark Twain is one of America's most famous historical personalities. Which of his books or stories have you read? What ideas and images from this selection do you associate with his other works?
2. Do you agree with Twain when he argues that an appreciation of beauty depends on ignorance of danger? Explain your answer.

QUESTIONS ABOUT PURPOSE

1. What does Twain think he has gained and lost by learning the river?
2. What does Twain accomplish by *dividing* the two views of the river rather than *alternating* them beneath several headings?

QUESTIONS ABOUT AUDIENCE

1. Which attitude—poetic or pragmatic—does Twain anticipate his readers have toward the river? Explain your answer.
2. How does he expect his readers to answer the questions he raises in paragraph 3?

QUESTIONS ABOUT STRATEGIES

1. What sequence does Twain use to arrange the points of his comparison?
2. Where does Twain use transitional phrases and sentences to match up the parts of his comparison?

QUESTIONS FOR DISCUSSION

1. Besides the pilot and the doctor, can you identify other professionals who lose as much as they gain by learning their trade?
2. How would people whose job is to create beauty—writers, painters, musicians, architects, gardeners—respond to Twain's assertion that knowledge of their craft destroys their ability to appreciate beauty?

ROSE DEL CASTILLO GUILBAULT

Rose del Castillo Guilbault was born in 1952 in Sonora, Mexico, and was educated at San Jose State University. For the past fourteen years she has worked as director of editorial and public affairs for KGO-TV, the ABC affiliate in San Francisco. For two years, she wrote a column called "Hispanic USA," which appeared in *This World,* a weekly magazine of the *San Francisco Chronicle.* In one of these columns, "Americanization Is Tough on 'Macho,'" Guilbault contrasts American and Hispanic attitudes toward the connotations of the word *macho*.

Americanization Is Tough on "Macho"

1 What is *macho?* That depends which side of the border you come from.

2 Although it's not unusual for words and expressions to lose their subtlety in translation, the negative connotations of *macho* in this country are troublesome to Hispanics.

3 Take the newspaper descriptions of alleged mass murderer Ramon Salcido. That an insensitive, insanely jealous, hard-drinking, violent Latin male is referred to as *macho* makes Hispanics cringe.

4 "*Es muy macho,*" the women in my family nod approvingly, describing a man they respect. But in the United States, when women say, "He's so macho," it's with disdain.

5 The Hispanic *macho* is manly, responsible, hardworking, a man in charge, a patriarch. A man who expresses strength through silence. What the Yiddish language would call a *mensch*.

6 The American *macho* is a chauvinist, a brute, uncouth,

selfish, loud, abrasive, capable of inflicting pain, and sexually promiscuous.

Quintessential *macho* models in this country are Sylvester Stallone, Arnold Schwarzenegger and Charles Bronson. In their movies, they exude toughness, independence, masculinity. But a closer look reveals their machismo is really violence masquerading as courage, sullenness disguised as silence and irresponsibility camouflaged as independence. 7

If the Hispanic ideal of *macho* were translated to American screen roles, they might be Jimmy Stewart, Sean Connery and Laurence Olivier. 8

In Spanish, *macho* ennobles Latin males. In English, it devalues them. This pattern seems consistent with the conflicts ethnic minority males experience in this country. Typically the cultural traits other societies value don't translate as desirable characteristics in America. 9

I watched my own father struggle with these cultural ambiguities. He worked on a farm for twenty years. He laid down miles of irrigation pipe, carefully plowed long, neat rows in fields, hacked away at recalcitrant weeds and drove tractors through whirlpools of dust. He stoically worked twenty-hour days during harvest season, accepting the long hours as part of agricultural work. When the boss complained or upbraided him for minor mistakes, he kept quiet, even when it was obvious the boss had erred. 10

He handled the most menial tasks with pride. At home he was a good provider, helped out my mother's family in Mexico without complaint, and was indulgent with me. Arguments between my mother and him generally had to do with money, or with his stubborn reluctance to share his troubles. He tried to work them out in his own silence. He didn't want to trouble my mother—a course that backfired, because the imagined is always worse than the reality. 11

Americans regarded my father as decidedly un-*macho*. His character was interpreted as nonassertive, his loyalty nonambition, and his quietness ignorance. I once overheard the boss's son blame him for plowing crooked rows in a field. My father merely smiled at the lie, knowing the boy had 12 done it, but didn't refute it, confident his good work was well known. But the boss instead ridiculed him for being "stupid" and letting a kid get away with a lie. Seeing my embarrassment, my father dismissed the incident, saying, "They're the dumb ones. Imagine, me fighting with a kid."

I tried not to look at him with American eyes because sometimes the reflection hurt. 13

Listening to my aunts' clucks of approval, my vision focused on the qualities America overlooked. "He's such a hard worker. So serious, so responsible." My aunts would secretly compliment my mother. The unspoken comparison was that he was not like some of their husbands, who drank and womanized. My uncles represented the darker side of *macho*. 14

In a patriarchal society, few challenge their roles. If men drink, it's because it's the manly thing to do. If they gamble, it's because it's how men relax. And if they fool around, well, it's because a man simply can't hold back so much man! My aunts didn't exactly meekly sit back, but they put up with these transgressions because Mexican society dictated this was their lot in life. 15

In the United States, I believe it was the feminist movement of the early '70s that changed *macho*'s meaning. Perhaps my generation of Latin women was in part responsible. I recall Chicanos complaining about the chauvinistic nature of Latin men and the notion they wanted their women barefoot, pregnant and in the kitchen. The generalization that Latin men embodied chauvinistic traits led to this interesting twist of semantics. Suddenly a word that represented something positive in one culture became a negative prototype in another. 16

The problem with the use of *macho* today is that it's become an accepted stereotype of the Latin male. And like all stereotypes, it distorts truth. 17

The impact of language in our society is undeniable. And the misuse of *macho* hints at a deeper cultural misunderstanding that extends beyond mere word definitions. 18

For Study and Discussion

QUESTIONS FOR RESPONSE

1. How have you heard the word *macho* used in conversation? From your point of view, does the word have primarily positive or negative connotations? Explain your answer.
2. If you have Hispanic friends or your family is Hispanic, would they agree with Guilbault's assertion that *macho* ennobles rather than devalues? How would they define *noble*?

QUESTIONS ABOUT PURPOSE

1. According to Guilbault, why is the Hispanic culture troubled by the negative connotations of the word *macho*?
2. What deeper misunderstanding does Guilbault want to demonstrate about the translation of cultural traits?

QUESTIONS ABOUT AUDIENCE

1. Guilbault wrote this essay for her column "Hispanic USA," which appeared in the Sunday magazine of the *San Francisco Chronicle*. Who does she assume are her primary readers—Hispanics or Americans? How do you know?
2. What assumptions does Guilbault make about the way her readers respond to cultural stereotypes?

QUESTIONS ABOUT STRATEGIES

1. How does Guilbault use movie stars to establish the contrast between American and Hispanic definitions of *macho*?
2. How does Guilbault use her father's behavior to dramatize how Americans distort the meaning of *macho*?

QUESTIONS FOR DISCUSSION

1. Identify other cultural traits that have been distorted by American society. For example, what cultural traits are valued by Africans, Asians, and Arabs but devalued by white Americans?
2. In what ways is the "machismo" problem complicated by issues of gender and class? For example, how do men and women use the word *macho* differently? How might Chicanos use the word differently from the way other Hispanics do?

DEBORAH TANNEN

Deborah Tannen was born in 1945 in Brooklyn, New York, and was educated at the State University of New York, Binghamton; Wayne State University; and the University of California, Berkeley. She has taught English at the Hellenic American Union in Athens, Greece; Herbert H. Lehman College of the City University of New York; and Georgetown University. She has contributed articles on language to numerous scholarly books, including *Language and Social Identity* (1982), and *Languages and Linguistics in Context* (1986). Tannen's *That's Not What I Meant! How Conversational Style Makes or Breaks Your Relations with Others* (1986) achieved national attention because of its engaging study of the breakdown of communication between the sexes. In "Rapport-talk and Report-talk," excerpted from her latest book *You Just Don't Understand* (1989), Tannen compares the public and private conversational styles of men and women.

Rapport-Talk and Report-Talk

Who talks more, then, women or men? The seemingly contradictory evidence is reconciled by the difference between what I call *public* and *private speaking*. More men feel comfortable doing "public speaking," while more women feel comfortable doing "private" speaking. Another way of capturing these differences is by using the terms *report-talk* and *rapport-talk*. 1

For most women, the language of conversation is primarily a language of rapport: a way of establishing connections and negotiating relationships. Emphasis is placed on displaying similarities and matching experiences. From childhood, 2 girls criticize peers who try to stand out or appear better than others. People feel their closest connections at home, or in settings where they *feel* at home—with one or a few people they feel close to and comfortable with—in other words, during private speaking. But even the most public situations can be approached like private speaking.

For most men, talk is primarily a means to preserve independence and negotiate and maintain status in a hierarchical social order. This is done by exhibiting knowledge and skill, and by holding center stage through verbal performance such as story-telling, joking, or imparting information. From childhood, men learn to use talking as a way to get and keep attention. So they are more comfortable speaking in larger groups made up of people they know less well—in the broadest sense, "public speaking." But even the most private situations can be approached like public speaking, more like giving a report than establishing rapport. 3

PRIVATE SPEAKING: THE WORDY WOMAN AND THE MUTE MAN

What is the source of the stereotype that women talk a lot? Dale Spender suggests that most people feel instinctively (if not consciously) that women, like children, should be seen and not heard, so any amount of talk from them seems like too much. Studies have shown that if women and men talk equally in a group, people think the women talked more. So there is truth to Spender's view. But another explanation is that men think women talk a lot because they hear women talking in situations where men would not: on the telephone; or in social situations with friends, when they are not discussing topics that men find inherently interesting; or, like the couple at the women's group, at home alone—in other words, in private speaking. 4

Home is the setting for an American icon that features the silent man and the talkative woman. And this icon, which grows out of the different goals and habits I have been describing, explains why the complaint most often voiced by 5 women about the men with whom they are intimate is "He doesn't talk to me"—and the second most frequent is "He doesn't listen to me."

A woman who wrote to Ann Landers is typical: 6

> *My husband never speaks to me when he comes home from work. When I ask, "How did everything go today?" he says, "Rough . . ." or "It's a jungle out there." (We live in Jersey and he works in New York City.)*
>
> *It's a different story when we have guests or go visiting. Paul is the gabbiest guy in the crowd—a real spellbinder. He comes up with the most interesting stories. People hang on every word. I think to myself, "Why doesn't he ever tell* me *these things?"*
>
> *This has been going on for 38 years. Paul started to go quiet on me after 10 years of marriage. I could never figure out why. Can you solve the mystery?*
>
> —THE INVISIBLE WOMAN

Ann Landers suggests that the husband may not want to talk because he is tired when he comes home from work. Yet women who work come home tired too, and they are nonetheless eager to tell their partners or friends everything that happened to them during the day and what these fleeting, daily dramas made them think and feel.

7 Sources as lofty as studies conducted by psychologists, as down to earth as letters written to advice columnists, and as sophisticated as movies and plays come up with the same insight: Men's silence at home is a disappointment to women. Again and again, women complain, "He seems to have everything to say to everyone else, and nothing to say to me."

8 The film *Divorce American Style* opens with a conversation in which Debbie Reynolds is claiming that she and Dick Van Dyke don't communicate, and he is protesting that he tells her everything that's on his mind. The doorbell interrupts their quarrel, and husband and wife compose themselves before opening the door to greet their guests with cheerful smiles.

Behind closed doors, many couples are having conversations like this. Like the character played by Debbie Reynolds, women feel men don't communicate. Like the husband played by Dick Van Dyke, men feel wrongly accused. How can she be convinced that he doesn't tell her anything, while he is equally convinced he tells her everything that's on his mind? How can women and men have such different ideas about the same conversations? 9

When something goes wrong, people look around for a source to blame: either the person they are trying to communicate with ("You're demanding, stubborn, self-centered") or the group that the other person belongs to ("All women are demanding"; "All men are self-centered"). Some generous-minded people blame the relationship ("We just can't communicate"). But underneath, or overlaid on these types of blame cast outward, most people believe that something is wrong with them. 10

If individual people or particular relationships were to blame, there wouldn't be so many different people having the same problems. The real problem is conversational style. Women and men have different ways of talking. Even with the best intentions, trying to settle the problem through talk can only make things worse if it is ways of talking that are causing trouble in the first place. 11

BEST FRIENDS

Once again, the seeds of women's and men's styles are sown in the ways they learn to use language while growing up. In our culture, most people, but especially women, look to their closest relationships as havens in a hostile world. The center of a little girl's social life is her best friend. Girls' friendships are made and maintained by telling secrets. For grown women too, the essence of friendship is talk, telling each other what they're thinking and feeling, and what happened that day: who was at the bus stop, who called, what they said, how that made them feel. When asked who their best 12 friends are, most women name other women they talk to regularly. When asked the same question, most men will say it's their wives. After that, many men name other men with whom they do things such as play tennis or baseball (but never just sit and talk) or a chum from high school whom they haven't spoken to in a year.

When Debbie Reynolds complained that Dick Van Dyke didn't tell her anything, and he protested that he did, both were right. She felt he didn't tell her anything because he didn't tell her the fleeting thoughts and feelings he experienced throughout the day—the kind of talk she would have with her best friend. He didn't tell her these things because to him they didn't seem like anything to tell. He told her anything that seemed important—anything he would tell his friends. 13

Men and women often have very different ideas of what's important—and at what point "important" topics should be raised. A woman told me, with lingering incredulity, of a conversation with her boyfriend. Knowing he had seen his friend Oliver, she asked, "What's new with Oliver?" He replied, "Nothing." But later in the conversation it came out that Oliver and his girlfriend had decided to get married. "That's nothing?" the woman gasped in frustration and disbelief. 14

For men, "Nothing" may be a ritual response at the start of a conversation. A college woman missed her brother but rarely called him because she found it difficult to get talk going. A typical conversation began with her asking, "What's up with you?" and his replying, "Nothing." Hearing his "Nothing" as meaning "There is nothing personal I want to talk about," she supplied talk by filling him in on her news and eventually hung up in frustration. But when she thought back, she remembered that later in the conversation he had mumbled, "Christie and I got into another fight." This came so late and so low that she didn't pick up on it. And he was probably equally frustrated that she didn't. 15

Many men honestly do not know what women want, and 16

women honestly do not know why men find what they want so hard to comprehend and deliver.

"TALK TO ME!"

Women's dissatisfaction with men's silence at home is captured in the stock cartoon setting of a breakfast table at which a husband and wife are sitting: He's reading a newspaper; she's glaring at the back of the newspaper. In a Dagwood strip, Blondie complains, "Every morning all he sees is the newspaper! I'll bet you don't even know I'm here!" Dagwood reassures her, "Of course I know you're here. You're my wonderful wife and I love you very much." With this, he unseeingly pats the paw of the family dog, which the wife has put in her place before leaving the room. The cartoon strip shows that Blondie is justified in feeling like the woman who wrote to Ann Landers: invisible. 17

Another cartoon shows a husband opening a newspaper and asking his wife, "Is there anything you would like to say to me before I begin reading the newspaper?" The reader knows that there isn't—but that as soon as he begins reading the paper, she will think of something. The cartoon highlights the difference in what women and men think talk is for: To him, talk is for information. So when his wife interrupts his reading, it must be to inform him of something that he needs to know. This being the case, she might as well tell him what she thinks he needs to know before he starts reading. But to her, talk is for interaction. Telling things is a way to show involvement, and listening is a way to show interest and caring. It is not an odd coincidence that she always thinks of things to tell him when he is reading. She feels the need for verbal interaction most keenly when he is (unaccountably, from her point of view) buried in the newspaper instead of talking to her. 18

Yet another cartoon shows a wedding cake that has, on top, in place of the plastic statues of bride and groom in 19 tuxedo and gown, a breakfast scene in which an unshaven husband reads a newspaper across the table from his disgruntled wife. The cartoon reflects the enormous gulf between the romantic expectations of marriage represented by the plastic couple in traditional wedding costume, and the often disappointing reality represented by the two sides of the newspaper at the breakfast table—the front, which he is reading, and the back, at which she is glaring.

These cartoons, and many others on the same theme, are 20
funny because people recognize their own experience in them. What's not funny is that many women are deeply hurt when men don't talk to them at home, and many men are deeply frustrated by feeling they have disappointed their partners, without understanding how they failed or how else they could have behaved.

Some men are further frustrated because, as one put it, 21
"When in the world am I supposed to read the morning paper?" If many women are incredulous that many men do not exchange personal information with their friends, this man is incredulous that many women do not bother to read the morning paper. To him, reading the paper is an essential part of his morning ritual, and his whole day is awry if he doesn't get to read it. In his words, reading the newspaper in the morning is as important to him as putting on makeup in the morning is to many women he knows. Yet many women, he observed, either don't subscribe to a paper or don't read it until they get home in the evening. "I find this very puzzling," he said. "I can't tell you how often I have picked up a woman's morning newspaper from her front door in the evening and handed it to her when she opened the door for me."

To this man (and I am sure many others), a woman who 22
objects to his reading the morning paper is trying to keep him from doing something essential and harmless. It's a violation of his independence—his freedom of action. But when a woman who expects her partner to talk to her is disappointed that he doesn't, she perceives his behavior as a

failure of intimacy: He's keeping things from her; he's lost interest in her; he's pulling away. A woman I will call Rebecca, who is generally quite happily married, told me that this is the one source of serious dissatisfaction with her husband, Stuart. Her term for his taciturnity is *stinginess of spirit*. She tells him what she is thinking, and he listens silently. She asks him what he is thinking, and he takes a long time to answer, "I don't know." In frustration she challenges, "Is there nothing on your mind?"

For Rebecca, who is accustomed to expressing her fleeting 23
thoughts and opinions as they come to her, *saying* nothing means *thinking* nothing. But Stuart does not assume that his passing thoughts are worthy of utterance. He is not in the habit of uttering his fleeting ruminations, so just as Rebecca "naturally" speaks her thoughts, he "naturally" dismisses his as soon as they occur to him. Speaking them would give them more weight and significance than he feels they merit. All her life she has had practice in verbalizing her thoughts and feelings in private conversations with people she is close to; all his life he has had practice in dismissing his and keeping them to himself. . . .

PUBLIC SPEAKING: THE TALKATIVE MAN AND THE SILENT WOMAN

So far I have been discussing the private scenes in which 24
many men are silent and many women are talkative. But there are other scenes in which the roles are reversed. Returning to Rebecca and Stuart, we saw that when they are home alone, Rebecca's thoughts find their way into words effortlessly, whereas Stuart finds he can't come up with anything to say. The reverse happens when they are in other situations. For example, at a meeting of the neighborhood council or the parents' association at their children's school, it is Stuart who stands up and speaks. In that situation, it is Rebecca who is silent, her tongue tied by an acute awareness of all the negative reactions people could have to what she might say, all the mistakes she might make in trying to

express her ideas. If she musters her courage and prepares to say something, she needs time to formulate it and then waits to be recognized by the chair. She cannot just jump up and start talking the way Stuart and some other men can.

Eleanor Smeal, president of the Fund for the Feminist Majority, was a guest on a call-in radio talk show, discussing abortion. No subject could be of more direct concern to women, yet during the hour-long show, all the callers except two were men. Diane Rehm, host of a radio talk show, expresses puzzlement that although the audience for her show is evenly split between women and men, 90 percent of the callers to the show are men. I am convinced that the reason is not that women are uninterested in the subjects discussed on the show. I would wager that women listeners are bringing up the subjects they heard on *The Diane Rehm Show* to their friends and family over lunch, tea, and dinner. But fewer of them call in because to do so would be putting themselves on display, claiming public attention for what they have to say, catapulting themselves onto center stage. 25

I myself have been the guest on innumerable radio and television talk shows. Perhaps I am unusual in being completely at ease in this mode of display. But perhaps I am not unusual at all, because, although I am comfortable in the role of invited expert, I have never called in to a talk show I was listening to, although I have often had ideas to contribute. When I am the guest, my position of authority is granted before I begin to speak. Were I to call in, I would be claiming that right on my own. I would have to establish my credibility by explaining who I am, which might seem self-aggrandizing, or not explain who I am and risk having my comments ignored or not valued. For similar reasons, though I am comfortable lecturing to groups numbering in the thousands, I rarely ask questions following another lecturer's talk, unless I know both the subject and the group very well. 26

My own experience and that of talk show hosts seems to hold a clue to the difference in women's and men's attitudes toward talk: Many men are more comfortable than most women in using talk to claim attention. And this difference 27 lies at the heart of the distinction between report-talk and rapport-talk.

REPORT-TALK IN PRIVATE

Report-talk, or what I am calling public speaking, does not arise only in the literally public situation of formal speeches delivered to a listening audience. The more people there are in a conversation, the less well you know them, and the more status differences among them, the more a conversation is *like* public speaking or report-talk. The fewer the people, the more intimately you know them, and the more equal their status, the more it is like private speaking or rapport-talk. Furthermore, women feel a situation is more "public"—in the sense that they have to be on good behavior—if there are men present, except perhaps for family members. Yet even in families, the mother and children may feel their home to be "backstage" when Father is not home, "on-stage" when he is: Many children are instructed to be on good behavior when Daddy is home. This may be because he is not home often, or because Mother—or Father—doesn't want the children to disturb him when he is. 28

The difference between public and private speaking also explains the stereotype that women don't tell jokes. Although some women are great raconteurs who can keep a group spellbound by recounting jokes and funny stories, there are fewer such personalities among women than among men. Many women who do tell jokes to large groups of people come from ethnic backgrounds in which verbal performance is highly valued. For example, many of the great women stand-up comics, such as Fanny Brice and Joan Rivers, came from Jewish backgrounds. 29

Although it's not true that women don't tell jokes, it is true that many women are less likely than men to tell jokes in large groups, especially groups including men. So it's not surprising that men get the impression that women never tell jokes at all. Folklorist Carol Mitchell studied joke telling on a college campus. She found that men told most of their 30 jokes to other men, but they also told many jokes to mixed groups and to women. Women, however, told most of their jokes to other women, fewer to men, and very few to groups that included men as well as women. Men preferred and were more likely to tell jokes when they had an audience: at least two, often four or more. Women preferred a small audience of one or two, rarely more than three. Unlike men, they were reluctant to tell jokes in front of people they didn't know well. Many women flatly refused to tell jokes they knew if there were four or more in the group, promising to tell them later in private. Men never refused the invitation to tell jokes.

All of Mitchell's results fit in with the picture I have been drawing of public and private speaking. In a situation in which there are more people in the audience, more men, or more strangers, joke telling, like any other form of verbal performance, requires speakers to claim center stage and prove their abilities. These are the situations in which many women are reluctant to talk. In a situation that is more private, because the audience is small, familiar, and perceived to be members of a community (for example, other women), they are more likely to talk. 31

The idea that telling jokes is a kind of self-display does not imply that it is selfish or self-centered. The situation of joke telling illustrates that status and connection entail each other. Entertaining others is a way of establishing connections with them, and telling jokes can be a kind of gift giving, where the joke is a gift that brings pleasure to receivers. The key issue is asymmetry: One person is the teller and the others are the audience. If these roles are later exchanged—for example, if the joke telling becomes a round in which one person after another takes the role of teller—then there is symmetry on the broad scale, if not in the individual act. However, if women habitually take the role of appreciative audience and never take the role of joke teller, the asymmetry of the individual joke telling is diffused through the larger interaction as well. This is a hazard for women. A hazard for men is that continually telling jokes can be distancing. This 32 is the effect felt by a man who complained that when he talks to his father on the phone, all his father does is tell him jokes. An extreme instance of a similar phenomenon is the class clown, who, according to teachers, is nearly always a boy.

RAPPORT-TALK IN PUBLIC

Just as conversations that take place at home among friends can be like public speaking, even a public address can be like private speaking: for example, by giving a lecture full of personal examples and stories. 33

At the executive committee of a fledgling professional organization, the outgoing president, Fran, suggested that the organization adopt the policy of having presidents deliver a presidential address. To explain and support her proposal, she told a personal anecdote: Her cousin was the president of a more established professional organization at the time that Fran held the same position in this one. Fran's mother had been talking to her cousin's mother on the telephone. Her cousin's mother told Fran's mother that her daughter was preparing her presidential address, and she asked when Fran's presidential address was scheduled to be. Fran was embarrassed to admit to her mother that she was not giving one. This made her wonder whether the organization's professional identity might not be enhanced if it emulated the more established organizations. 34

Several men on the committee were embarrassed by Fran's reference to her personal situation and were not convinced by her argument. It seemed to them not only irrelevant but unseemly to talk about her mother's telephone conversations at an executive committee meeting. Fran had approached the meeting—a relatively public context—as an extension of the private kind. Many women's tendency to use personal experience and examples, rather than abstract argumentation, can be understood from the perspective of their orientation to language as it is used in private speaking. 35

A study by Celia Roberts and Tom Jupp of a faculty meeting at a secondary school in England found that the 36 women's arguments did not carry weight with their male colleagues because they tended to use their own experience as evidence, or argue about the effect of policy on individual students. The men at the meeting argued from a completely different perspective, making categorical statements about right and wrong.

The same discussion is found in discussions at home. A man told me that he felt critical of what he perceived as his wife's lack of logic. For example, he recalled a conversation in which he had mentioned an article he had read in *The New York Times* claiming that today's college students are not as idealistic as students were in the 1960s. He was inclined to accept this claim. His wife questioned it, supporting her arugment with the observation that her niece and her niece's friends were very idealistic indeed. He was incredulous and scornful of her faulty reasoning; it was obvious to him that a single personal example is neither evidence nor argumentation—it's just anecdote. It did not occur to him that he was dealing with a different logical system, rather than a lack of logic. 37

The logic this woman was employing was making sense of the world as a more private endeavor—observing and integrating her personal experience and drawing connections to the experiences of others. The logic the husband took for granted was a more public endeavor—more like gathering information, conducting a survey, or devising arguments by rules of formal logic as one might in doing research. 38

Another man complained about what he and his friends call women's "shifting sands" approach to discussion. These men feel that whereas they try to pursue an argument logically, step by step, until it is settled, women continually change course in mid-stream. He pointed to the short excerpt from *Divorce American Style* quoted above as a case in point. It seemed to him that when Debbie Reynolds said, "I can't argue now. I have to take the French bread out of the oven," she was evading the argument because she had made an accusation—"All you do is criticize"—that she could not support. 39

This man also offered an example from his own experi- 40

ence. His girlfriend had told him of a problem she had because her boss wanted her to do one thing and she wanted to do another. Taking the boss's view for the sake of argumentation, he pointed out a negative consequence that would result if she did what she wanted. She countered that the same negative consequence would result if she did what the boss wanted. He complained that she was shifting over to the other field of battle—what would happen if she followed her boss's will—before they had made headway with the first—what would happen if she followed her own.

For Study and Discussion

QUESTIONS FOR RESPONSE

1. How would you characterize your own conversational style?
2. How does context affect the way you talk? What situations make you shift styles?

QUESTIONS ABOUT PURPOSE

1. What does Tannen want to demonstrate about the relationship between communication failure and conversational style?
2. How do size (the number of people) and status (those people claiming authority) contribute to Tannen's comparison of rapport-talk and report-talk?

QUESTIONS ABOUT AUDIENCE

1. What assumptions does Tannen make about the probable gender of most of her readers?
2. How does Tannen's use of subheadings help clarify her comparison for her readers?

QUESTIONS ABOUT STRATEGIES

1. How does Tannen use advice columns, movies, and cartoons to illustrate the problems of domestic communication?

2. How does Tannen use her own experience as a lecturer to compare the way men and women talk in public?

QUESTIONS FOR DISCUSSION

1. Do the men and women you know construct arguments according to Tannen's format? How many men use personal experience as evidence? How many women make categorical assertions?
2. To what extent do conversational styles depend on innate skill (personality type) or learned behavior (social stereotypes)? To what extent is it possible (or desirable) to change styles?

EDWARD T. HALL

Edward T(witchell) Hall was born in 1914 in Webster Groves, Missouri, and was educated at Pomona College, the University of Denver, the University of Arizona, and Columbia University. An anthropologist, he has taught at the University of Denver, Bennington College, Illinois Institute of Technology, and since 1967 has been professor of anthropology at Northwestern University. His books include *Beyond Culture* (1976), a study of the effects of physical settings on human behavior; *The Hidden Dimension* (1977); *The Dance of Life: The Other Dimension of Time* (1983), an exploration of the concept of time from many vantage points; and *Understanding Cultural Differences* (1990), a cross-cultural study of industrial management. In "The Arab World," reprinted from *The Hidden Dimension,* Hall analyzes the hidden assumptions and attitudes that divide the Arab and Western worlds.

The Arab World

In spite of over two thousand years of contact, Westerners and Arabs still do not understand each other. Proxemic research reveals some insights into this difficulty. Americans in the Middle East are immediately struck by two conflicting sensations. In public they are compressed and overwhelmed by smells, crowding, and high noise levels; in Arab homes Americans are apt to rattle around, feeling exposed and often somewhat inadequate because of too much space! (The Arab houses and apartments of the middle and upper classes which Americans stationed abroad commonly occupy are much larger than the dwellings such Americans usually inhabit.) Both the high sensory stimulation which is experienced in 1 public places and the basic insecurity which comes from being in a dwelling that is too large provide Americans with an introduction to the sensory world of the Arab.

BEHAVIOR IN PUBLIC

Pushing and shoving in public places is characteristic of Middle Eastern culture. Yet it is not entirely what Americans think it is (being pushy and rude) but stems from a different set of assumptions concerning not only the relations between people but how one experiences the body as well. Paradoxically, Arabs consider northern Europeans and Americans pushy, too. This was very puzzling to me when I started investigating these two views. How could Americans who stand aside and avoid touching be considered pushy? I used to ask Arabs to explain this paradox. None of my subjects was able to tell me specifically what particulars of American behavior were responsible, yet they all agreed that the impression was widespread among Arabs. After repeated unsuccessful attempts to gain insight into the cognitive world of the Arab on this particular point, I filed it away as a question that only time would answer. When the answer came, it was because of a seemingly inconsequential annoyance. 2

While waiting for a friend in a Washington, D.C., hotel lobby and wanting to be both visible and alone, I had seated myself in a solitary chair outside the normal stream of traffic. In such a setting most Americans follow a rule, which is all the more binding because we seldom think about it, that can be stated as follows: as soon as a person stops or is seated in a public place, there balloons around him a small sphere of privacy which is considered inviolate. The size of the sphere varies with the degree of crowding, the age, sex, and the importance of the person, as well as the general surroundings. Anyone who enters this zone and stays there is intruding. In fact, a stranger who intrudes, even for a specific purpose, acknowledges the fact that he has intruded by 3 beginning his request with "Pardon me, but can you tell me . . . ?"

4 To continue, as I waited in the deserted lobby, a stranger walked up to where I was sitting and stood close enough so that not only could I easily touch him but I could even hear him breathing. In addition, the dark mass of his body filled the peripheral field of vision on my left side. If the lobby had been crowded with people, I would have understood his behavior, but in an empty lobby his presence made me exceedingly uncomfortable. Feeling annoyed by this intrusion, I moved my body in such a way as to communicate annoyance. Strangely enough, instead of moving away, my actions seemed only to encourage him, because he moved even closer. In spite of the temptation to escape the annoyance, I put aside thoughts of abandoning my post, thinking, "To hell with it. Why should I move? I was here first and I'm not going to let this fellow drive me out even if he is a boor." Fortunately, a group of people soon arrived whom my tormentor immediately joined. Their mannerisms explained his behavior, for I knew from both speech and gestures that they were Arabs. I had not been able to make this crucial identification by looking at my subject when he was alone because he wasn't talking and he was wearing American clothes.

5 In describing the scene later to an Arab colleague, two contrasting patterns emerged. My concept and my feelings about my own circle of privacy in a "public" place immediately struck my Arab friend as strange and puzzling. He said, "After all, it's a public place, isn't it?" Pursuing his line of inquiry, I found that in Arab thought I had no rights whatsoever by virtue of occupying a given spot; neither my place nor my body was inviolate! For the Arab, there is no such thing as an intrusion in public. Public means public. With this insight, a great range of Arab behavior that had been puzzling, annoying, and sometimes even frightening began to make sense. I learned, for example, that if *A* is standing on a street corner and *B* wants his spot, *B* is within his rights if he does what he can to make *A* uncomfortable enough to

move. In Beirut only the hardy sit in the last row in a movie theater, because there are usually standees who want seats and who push and shove and make such a nuisance that most people give up and leave. Seen in this light, the Arab who "intruded" on my space in the hotel lobby had apparently selected it for the very reason I had: it was a good place to watch two doors and the elevator. My show of annoyance, instead of driving him away, had only encouraged him. He thought he was about to get me to move.

Another silent source of friction between Americans and Arabs is in an area that Americans treat very informally—the manners and rights of the road. In general, in the United States we tend to defer to the vehicle that is bigger, more powerful, faster, and heavily laden. While a pedestrian walking along a road may feel annoyed he will not think it unusual to step aside for a fast-moving automobile. He knows that because he is moving he does not have the right to the space around him that he has when he is standing still (as I was in the hotel lobby). It appears that the reverse is true with the Arabs, who apparently *take on rights to space as they move.* For someone else to move into a space an Arab is also moving into is a violation of his rights. It is infuriating to an Arab to have someone else cut in front of him on the highway. It is the American's cavalier treatment of moving space that makes the Arab call him aggressive and pushy. 6

CONCEPTS OF PRIVACY

The experience described above and many others suggested to me that Arabs might actually have a wholly contrasting set of assumptions concerning the body and the rights associated with it. Certainly the Arab tendency to shove and push each other in public and to feel and pinch women in public conveyances would not be tolerated by Westerners. It appeared to me that they must not have any concept of a private zone outside the body. This proved to be precisely the case. 7

In the Western world, the person is synonymous with an 8

individual inside a skin. And in northern Europe generally, the skin and even the clothes may be inviolate. You need permission to touch either if you are a stranger. This rule applies in some parts of France, where the mere touching of another person during an argument used to be legally defined as assault. For the Arab the location of the person in relation to the body is quite different. The person exists somewhere down inside the body. The ego is not completely hidden, however, because it can be reached very easily with an insult. It is protected from touch but not from words. The dissociation of the body and the ego may explain why the public amputation of a thief's hand is tolerated as standard punishment in Saudi Arabia. It also sheds light on why an Arab employer living in a modern apartment can provide his servant with a room that is a boxlike cubicle approximately 5 by 10 by 4 feet in size that is not only hung from the ceiling to conserve floor space but has an opening so that the servant can be spied on.

As one might suspect, deep orientations toward the self 9
such as the one just described are also reflected in the language. This was brought to my attention one afternoon when an Arab colleague who is the author of an Arab-English dictionary arrived in my office and threw himself into a chair in a state of obvious exhaustion. When I asked him what had been going on, he said: "I have spent the entire afternoon trying to find the Arab equivalent of the English word 'rape.' There is no such word in Arabic. All my sources, both written and spoken, can come up with no more than an approximation, such as 'He took her against her will.' There is nothing in Arabic approaching your meaning as it is expressed in that one word."

Differing concepts of the placement of the ego in relation 10
to the body are not easily grasped. Once an idea like this is accepted, however, it is possible to understand many other facets of Arab life that would otherwise be difficult to explain. One of these is the high population density of Arab cities like Cairo, Beirut, and Damascus. According to the animal

studies described in the earlier chapters,[1] the Arabs should be living in a perpetual behavioral sink. While it is probable that Arabs are suffering from population pressures, it is also just as possible that continued pressure from the desert has resulted in a cultural adaptation to high density which takes the form described above. Tucking the ego down inside the body shell not only would permit higher population densities but would explain why it is that Arab communications are stepped up as much as they are when compared to northern European communication patterns. Not only is the sheer noise level much higher, but the piercing look of the eyes, the touch of the hands, and the mutual bathing in the warm moist breath during conversation represent stepped-up sensory inputs to a level which many Europeans find unbearably intense.

The Arab dream is for lots of space in the home, which 11
unfortunately many Arabs cannot afford. Yet when he has space, it is very different from what one finds in most American homes. Arab spaces inside their upper middle-class homes are tremendous by our standards. They avoid partitions because Arabs *do not like to be alone*. The form of the home is such as to hold the family together inside a single protective shell, because Arabs are deeply involved with each other. Their personalities are intermingled and take nourishment from each other like the roots and soil. If one is not with people and actively involved in some way, one is deprived of life. An old Arab saying reflects this value: "Paradise without people should not be entered because it is Hell." Therefore, Arabs in the United States often feel socially and sensorially deprived and long to be back where there is human warmth and contact.

Since there is no physical privacy as we know it in the 12
Arab family, not even a word for privacy, one could expect that the Arabs might use some other means to be alone.

[1]I.e., earlier chapters of *The Hidden Dimension*.

Their way to be alone is to stop talking. Like the English, an Arab who shuts himself off in this way is not indicating that anything is wrong or that he is withdrawing, only that he wants to be alone with his own thoughts or does not want to be intruded upon. One subject said that her father would come and go for days at a time without saying a word, and no one in the family thought anything of it. Yet for this very reason, an Arab exchange student visiting a Kansas farm failed to pick up the cue that his American hosts were mad at him when they gave him the "silent treatment." He only discovered something was wrong when they took him to town and tried forcibly to put him on a bus to Washington, D.C., the headquarters of the exchange program responsible for his presence in the U.S.

ARAB PERSONAL DISTANCES

Like everyone else in the world, Arabs are unable to formulate specific rules for their informal behavior patterns. In fact, they often deny that there are any rules, and they are made anxious by suggestions that such is the case. Therefore, in order to determine how the Arab sets distances, I investigated the use of each sense separately. Gradually, definite and distinctive behavioral patterns began to emerge. 13

Olfaction occupies a prominent place in the Arab life. Not only is it one of the distance-setting mechanisms, but it is a vital part of a complex system of behavior. Arabs consistently breathe on people when they talk. However, this habit is more than a matter of different manners. To the Arab, good smells are pleasing and a way of being involved with each other. To smell one's friend is not only nice but desirable, for to deny him your breath is to act ashamed. Americans, on the other hand, trained as they are not to breathe in people's faces, automatically communicate shame in trying to be polite. Who would expect that when our highest diplomats are putting on their best manners they are also communicating shame? Yet this is what occurs constantly, be- 14 cause diplomacy is not only "eyeball to eyeball" but breath to breath.

By stressing olfaction, Arabs do not try to eliminate all the body's odors, only to enhance them and use them in building human relationships. Nor are they self-conscious about telling others when they don't like the way they smell. A man leaving his house in the morning may be told by his uncle, "Habib, your stomach is sour and your breath doesn't smell too good. Better not talk too close to people today." Smell is even considered in the choice of a mate. When couples are being matched for marriage, the man's go-between will sometimes ask to smell the girl, who may be turned down if she doesn't "smell nice." Arabs recognize that smell and disposition may be linked. 15

In a word, the olfactory boundary performs two roles in Arab life. It enfolds those who want to relate and separates those who don't. The Arab finds it essential to stay inside the olfactory zone as a means of keeping tab on changes in emotion. What is more, he may feel crowded as soon as he smells something unpleasant. While not much is known about "olfactory crowding," this may prove to be as significant as any other variable in the crowding complex because it is tied directly to the body chemistry and hence to the state of health and emotions. . . . It is not surprising, therefore, that the olfactory boundary constitutes for the Arabs an informal distance-setting mechanism in contrast to the visual mechanisms of the Westerner. 16

FACING AND NOT FACING

One of my earliest discoveries in the field of intercultural communication was that the position of the bodies of people in conversation varies with the culture. Even so, it used to puzzle me that a special Arab friend seemed unable to walk and talk at the same time. After years in the United States, he could not bring himself to stroll along, facing forward while talking. Our progress would be arrested while he edged 17 ahead, cutting slightly in front of me and turning sideways so we could see each other. Once in this position, he would stop. His behavior was explained when I learned that for the Arabs to view the other person peripherally is regarded as impolite, and to sit or stand back-to-back is considered very rude. You must be involved when interacting with Arabs who are friends.

One mistaken American notion is that Arabs conduct all conversations at close distances. This is not the case at all. On social occasions, they may sit on opposite sides of the room and talk across the room to each other. They are, however, apt to take offense when Americans use what are to them ambiguous distances, such as the four- to seven-foot social-consultative distance. They frequently complain that Americans are cold or aloof or "don't care." This was what an elderly Arab diplomat in an American hospital thought when the American nurses used "professional" distance. He had the feeling that he was being ignored, that they might not take good care of him. Another Arab subject remarked, referring to American behavior, "What's the matter? Do I smell bad? Or are they afraid of me?" 18

Arabs who interact with Americans report experiencing a certain flatness traceable in part to a very different use of the eyes in private and in public as well as between friends and strangers. Even though it is rude for a guest to walk around the Arab home eying things, Arabs look at each other in ways which seem hostile or challenging to the American. One Arab informant said that he was in constant hot water with Americans because of the way he looked at them without the slightest intention of offending. In fact, he had on several occasions barely avoided fights with American men who apparently thought their masculinity was being challenged because of the way he was looking at them. As noted earlier, Arabs look each other in the eye when talking with an intensity that makes most Americans highly uncomfortable. 19

INVOLVEMENT

As the reader must gather by now, Arabs are involved with 20
each other on many different levels simultaneously. Privacy in a public place is foreign to them. Business transactions in the bazaar, for example, are not just between buyer and seller, but are participated in by everyone. Anyone who is standing around may join in. If a grownup sees a boy breaking a window, he must stop him even if he doesn't know him. Involvement and participation are expressed in other ways as well. If two men are fighting, the crowd must intervene. On the political level, *to fail to intervene* when trouble is brewing is to take sides, which is what our State Department always seems to be doing. Given the fact that few people in the world today are even remotely aware of the cultural mold that forms their thoughts, it is normal for Arabs to view *our* behavior as though it stemmed from *their* own hidden set of assumptions.

FEELINGS ABOUT ENCLOSED SPACES

In the course of my interviews with Arabs the term "tomb" 21
kept cropping up in conjunction with enclosed space. In a word, Arabs don't mind being crowded by people but hate to be hemmed in by walls. They show a much greater overt sensitivity to architectural crowding than we do. Enclosed space must meet at least three requirements that I know of if it is to satisfy the Arabs: there must be plenty of unobstructed space in which to move around (possibly as much as a thousand square feet); very high ceilings—so high in fact that they do not normally impinge on the visual field; and, in addition, there must be an unobstructed view. It was spaces such as these in which the Americans referred to earlier felt so uncomfortable. One sees the Arab's need for a view expressed in many ways, even negatively, for to cut off a neighbor's view is one of the most effective ways of spiting him. In Beirut one can see what is known locally as the "spite house." It is nothing more than a thick, four-story wall, built

at the end of a long fight between neighbors, on a narrow strip of land for the express purpose of denying a view of the Mediterranean to any house built on the land behind. According to one of my informants, there is also a house on a small plot of land between Beirut and Damascus which is completely surrounded by a neighbor's wall built high enough to cut off the view from all windows!

BOUNDARIES

Proxemic patterns tell us other things about Arab culture. 22
For example, the whole concept of the boundary as an abstraction is almost impossible to pin down. In one sense, there are no boundaries. "Edges" of towns, yes, but permanent boundaries out in the country (hidden lines), no. In the course of my work with Arab subjects I had a difficult time translating our concept of a boundary into terms which could be equated with theirs. In order to clarify the distinctions between the two very different definitions, I thought it might be helpful to pinpoint acts which constituted trespass. To date, I have been unable to discover anything even remotely resembling our own legal concept of trespass.

Arab behavior in regard to their own real estate is appar- 23
ently an extension of, and therefore consistent with, their approach to the body. My subjects simply failed to respond whenever trespass was mentioned. They didn't seem to understand what I meant by this term. This may be explained by the fact that they organize relationships with each other according to closed social systems rather than spatially. For thousands of years Moslems, Marinites, Druses, and Jews have lived in their own villages, each with strong kin affiliations. Their hierarchy of loyalties is: first to one's self, then to kinsman, townsman, or tribesman, co-religionist and/or countryman. Anyone not in these categories is a stranger. Strangers and enemies are very closely linked, if not synonymous, in Arab thought. Trespass in this context is a matter of who you are, rather than a piece of land or a space with

a boundary that can be denied to anyone and everyone, friend and foe alike.

In summary, proxemic patterns differ. By examining them it is possible to reveal hidden cultural frames that determine the structure of a given people's perceptual world. Perceiving the world differently leads to differential definitions of what constitutes crowded living, different interpersonal relations, and a different approach to both local and international politics. . . . 24

For Study and Discussion

QUESTIONS FOR RESPONSE

1. What characteristics of the Arab world appeal to you? What characteristics would make it impossible for you to feel at home in such a world?
2. What questions would you like to ask Hall about his research methodology? For example, how did a Western anthropologist uncover the "hidden dimension" of the Arab culture?

QUESTIONS ABOUT PURPOSE

1. What is Hall's primary purpose—to describe the unique features of the Arab world, to compare the behavior of Arabs and Westerners, or to demonstrate how hidden cultural frames determine perception? Explain your answer.
2. What connection does Hall establish between the way in which Westerners and Arabs define the ego and the way in which they behave toward one another in public?

QUESTIONS ABOUT AUDIENCE

1. How much does Hall assume his readers know about Arab culture? How much space does he devote to his discussion of Arab culture and how much to his discussion of American (or Western) culture?
2. What assumptions does Hall make about his readers' ability to "formulate specific rules for their informal behavior patterns"?

How is this essay designed to improve his readers' competence in this area?

QUESTIONS ABOUT STRATEGIES

1. Hall does not rigidly adhere to either the subject-by-subject or the point-by-point strategy. In what parts of his essay does he use each method? How do his subject and purpose determine which strategy he uses?
2. How does Hall use the senses of smell and sight to explain the difference between Arab and American social etiquette?

QUESTIONS FOR DISCUSSION

1. Why do Americans place such high value on privacy? Why do Arabs hate to be alone? How do you respond to the old Arab saying "Paradise without people should not be entered because it is Hell"?
2. Hall says that Arabs avoid partitions in their homes, build walls for spite, and fail to understand the concept of boundary. How might these cultural attitudes explain the political difficulties in the Arab world?

GERALD WEISSMANN

Gerald Weissmann was born in Vienna, Austria, in 1930 and subsequently became a U.S. citizen. He received his bachelor's degree from Columbia University and his doctorate in medicine from New York University. He is currently professor of medicine at New York University Medical Center. Although his medical specialty is the diagnosis and treatment of arthritis, his avocation is writing about the growing division between the humanities and the sciences. His graceful essays, most of which were first published in *Hospital Practice,* treat such subjects as crime, bag ladies, plague, and nuclear weapons. They have been collected in *The Woods Hole Cantata: Essays on Science and Society* (1985) and *They All Laughed at Christopher Columbus: Tales of Medicine and the Art of Discovery* (1987). "The Chart of the Novel," reprinted from the first volume, is a fanciful and provocative comparison of medical charts and novels.

The Chart of the Novel

Like other professionals—football scouts, diplomats, and underwriters come to mind—doctors write many words, under pressure of time and for a limited audience. I refer, of course, to the medical charts of our patients. Most of these manuscripts (for even now this material is written almost entirely by hand) are rarely consulted by anyone other than doctors, nurses, or (Heaven forbid!) lawyers. I have always found the libraries of this literature, the record rooms of hospitals, to contain a repository of human, as well as clinical, observations. On their tacky shelves, bound in buff cardboard and sometimes only partially decipherable, are stories of pluck 1 and disaster, muddle and death. If well compressed and described, these *Brief Lives* are more chiseled than Aubrey's. Best of all, I love the conventional paragraph by which the story is introduced. Our tales invariably begin with the chief complaint that brought the patient to the hospital. Consider this sampling from three local hospitals:

> *This is the third MSH admission of a chronically* 2
> *wasted 64-year-old, 98-pound male Hungarian refugee composer, admitted from an unheated residential hotel with the chief complaint of progressive weakness (1945).*

> *This is the second SVH admission of a 39-year-old,* 3
> *obese Welsh male poet, admitted in acute coma after vomiting blood (1953).*

> *This is the first BH admission of a 22-year-old* 4
> *black, female activist transferred from the Women's House of Detention with chief complaints of sharp abdominal pains and an acutely inflamed knee (1968).*

How evocative of time, place, and person—and how dif- 5
ferent in tone and feeling from other sorts of opening lines! They certainly owe little to the news story: "Secretary of State Shultz appeared today before the Foreign Relations Committee of the Senate to urge ratification of . . ." Nor does the description of a chief complaint owe its punch to any derivation from formal scientific prose: "Although the metabolism of arachidonic acid has been less studied in neutrophils than . . ."

The opening sequence of a medical record is unique, and 6
when well written, there's nothing quite like it. These lines localize a human being of defined sex, age, race, occupation, and physical appearance to a moment of extreme crisis: He or she has been "admitted." Attention must therefore be paid, and everything recorded on that chart after the admitting note is a narrative account of that attention, of medical "care."

But this enthusiasm for the products of clinical prose may 7 be unwarranted. There may be other prose forms which, by their nature, tug at the reader with such firm hands: I have not found them. Now, my search has not been exhaustive—indeed, my inquiries are based on a sort of hunt-and-peck excursion amongst the yellowing survivors of my dated library. I must report, however, that no similar jabs of evocative prose hit me from the opening lines of biographer, of critic, of historian—not at all the kind of impact I was looking for. No, the real revelation came from the nineteenth-century novelist. I should not have been surprised:

> *Emma Woodhouse, handsome, clever and rich, with a comfortable home and happy disposition, seemed to unite some of the best blessings of existence, and had lived nearly twenty-one years in the world with very little to distress or vex her.* 8
>
> EMMA *Jane Austen*

> *Madame Vauquer (nee Deconflans) is an elderly person who for the past forty years has kept a lodging house in the Rue Neuve-Sainte-Genevieve, in the district that lies between the Latin Quarter and the Faubourg Saint-Marcel. Her house receives men and women and no word has ever been breathed against her respectable establishment.* 9
>
> LE PÈRE GORIOT *Honoré de Balzac*

> *Fyodor Pavlovitch Karamazov, a landowner well known in our district in his own day, and still remembered among us owing to his mysterious and tragic death, was a strange type, despicable and vicious, and at the same time absurd.* 10
>
> THE BROTHERS KARAMAZOV *Fyodor Dostoyevsky*

Now, that sort of beginning is a little more like the opening paragraphs of our charts. Does this mean that we've been writing nineteenth-century novels all our professional lives, but without knowing it? Do the white, pink, and blue sheets which describe the events between admission and discharge 11

—between beginning and end—constitute a multi-authored *roman à clef*? If we go on to the rest of the record, it is more likely than not that other sources can be identified. The "History of Present Illness," with its chronological listings of coughs, grippes, and disability, owes much to the novelist, but more to the diarist. But the "Past Medical History," drawn to the broader scale of social interactions, returns us again to the world of the novel, and the more detailed "Family and Social History," which describes the ailments of aunts and of nephews, which lists not only military service but the patient's choice of addiction, puts us into the very middle of the realistic novel of 1860.

Now comes the "Physical Examination." Here the world of the clinic or the laboratory intrudes: numbers, descriptions, and measurements. Indeed, from this point on, the record is written in recognition of the debt medicine owes to formal scientific exposition. In this portion of the chart, after all the histories are taken, after the chest has been thumped and the spleen has been fingered, after the white cells have been counted and the potassium surveyed, the doctor can be seen to abandon the position of recorder and to assume that of the natural scientist. He arrives at a "Tentative Diagnosis," a hypothesis, so to speak, to be tested, as time, laboratory procedures, or responses to treatment confirm or deny the initial impression. The revisions of this hypothesis, together with accounts of how doctors and patients learn more about what is *really* wrong, constitute the bulk of our manuscript. 12

So we can argue that our records are an amalgam between the observational norms of the nineteenth-century novelist and the causal descriptions of the physiologist. There is, perhaps, a connection between the two. If we agree that a novelist not only tells a story but weaves a plot, we imply by this the concept of causality. E. M. Forster, in *Aspects of the Novel,* draws the distinction nicely. He suggests that when a writer tells us, "The King dies, and then the Queen died," we are being told a story. When, however, the sentence is altered to read, "The King dies, and therefore the Queen 13 died of grief," we are offered a plot—the notion of causality has been introduced. In much of our medical record keeping we are busy spinning a series of clinical plots: the temperature went down *because* antibiotics were given, etc.

Pick up a chart at random, and you will see what I mean. 14
The sixty-year-old taxi driver has been treated for eight days with antibiotics for his pneumonia. "Intern's Note: Fever down, sputum clearing, will obtain follow-up X-ray." A few days later: "X-ray shows round nodule near segment with resolving infiltrate. Have obtained permission for bronchoscopy and biopsy." Then, "JAR Note: Results of biopsy discussed with patient and family." Months intervene, and at the end of the readmission chart we find the dreary "Intern's Note: 4:00 A.M. Called to see patient . . ." Infection and tumor, hypothesis and test, beginning and end. And so we read these mixtures of story and plot, learning as much along the way about the sensibilities of the doctor as we do of the patient and his disease. The physician-narrator becomes as important to the tale as the unseen Balzac lurking in the boarding house of Madame Vauquer.

An optimistic attempt to reconcile both sources of our 15
clinical narratives, the novel and the scientist's notebook, was made by that great naturalist—and optimist—Émile Zola. After an exhilarating dip into the work of Claude Bernard, Zola decided that the new modes of scientific description and their causal analyses might yield a *method* which would apply to the novel as well. Basing his argument on Bernard's *An Introduction to the Study of Experimental Medicine* (1865), Zola wrote an essay entitled "The Experimental Novel." Zola explained that the novelist customarily begins with an experimental fact: He has observed—so to speak—the behavior of a fictional protagonist. Then, using the inference of character as a sort of hypothesis, the novelist invents a series of lifelike situations which test, as it were, whether the observations of behavior are concordant with the inference. The unfolding of the narrative, interpreted causally as plot, will then naturally, and inevitably, verify the hypothesis. How neat—and how reductionist!

But however simplified this scheme of Zola may appear to us today, it has the merit of suggesting how strong, indeed, is the base of scientific optimism upon which traditional clinical description rests. Our descriptions imply our confidence that detailed observations of individual responses to common disease have a permanent value, which can be used predictively. They reveal an upbeat conviction that causal relations, when appreciated, lead to therapeutic (or narrative) success. Recent views of medicine and the novel seem to challenge these assumptions. 16

If we look at the ways in which we have changed our records in the last decade to the "Problem-Oriented Patient Record," to the "Defined Data Base," we appear to have shifted from a view of patient and disease based on the human, novelistic approach of the last century to one based on the flow sheet of the electronic engineer or the punch card of the computer. No longer do our early narratives end in a tentative diagnosis, a testable hypothesis: we are left with a series of unconnected "problems." The stories dissolve into a sort of diagnostic litany—e.g., anemia, weight loss, fever, skin spots—without the unifying plot that ties these up with the causal thread of leukemia. Worse yet, these records are now frequently transformed into a series of checks scrawled over preprinted sheets which carry in tedious detail a computer-generated laundry list of signs and symptoms. The anomie of impersonal, corporate personnel forms has crept into these records. Added to these forces, which have turned the doctor's prose into institutional slang, is the movement to eliminate reflections on sex preference, race, and social background. In the name of convenience and egalitarianism, we seem to have exchanged the story of the single sick human at a moment of crisis for an impersonal checklist which describes a "case" with "problems." When we fail at words, we fail to understand, we fail to feel. 17

But, I'm afraid that the new novelists have anticipated us here, too. As the naturalistic novel has yielded to the stream of consciousness, to existential angst, and to flat introspection, the anomie of the clinic has been foreshadowed by that 18 of the artist. The opening lines of our major modern novels sound the tones of disengagement as clearly as our clinical records.

> *Today, mother is dead. Or perhaps yesterday. I don't know. I received a telegram from the Home. "Mother dead. Funeral tomorrow. Best Wishes." It means nothing. Perhaps it was yesterday.* 19
>
> THE STRANGER *Albert Camus (1942)*

> *If only I could explain to you how changed I am since those days! Changed yet still the same, but now I can view my old preoccupation with a calm eye.* 20
>
> THE BENEFACTOR *Susan Sontag (1963)*

> *What makes Iago evil? Some people ask. I never ask.* 21
>
> PLAY IT AS IT LAYS *Joan Didion (1970)*

Perhaps as doctors we are now committed to acting as a 22 group of "benefactors" ministering to the sick "strangers"—we cannot, or will not, be involved in the lives of those who have come to us for care; we will now simply describe and solve the problems of the case. We will play it as it lays.

For Study and Discussion

QUESTIONS FOR RESPONSE

1. How did you respond to the illustrations Weissmann cites from patient charts and novels? Did you skip, skim, or study them? Did they enrich or detract from your reading? Explain your answer.
2. As a patient, would you prefer to have your charts written by a doctor-novelist or a doctor-engineer? Speculate on the advantages and disadvantages of each type of writer.

QUESTIONS ABOUT PURPOSE

1. Weissmann's purpose is to discover hidden and striking resemblances between medical charts and other forms of writing. What fundamental similarity does he discover between medical charts and nineteenth-century novels?
2. What changes does Weissmann notice in the composition of contemporary medical charts? How has that change been anticipated by contemporary novelists?

QUESTIONS ABOUT AUDIENCE

1. If, as Weissmann says, doctors write charts for a limited audience, who does he assume are the readers of his essay? To what extent do phrases such as "our patients," "our descriptions," and "we have changed" suggest that he is addressing a limited audience of other doctors?
2. In paragraphs 11 and 12, Weissmann describes the basic divisions of the chart. In what ways does this description suggest that he is writing for a more general audience?

QUESTIONS ABOUT STRATEGIES

1. How does Weissmann use extended quotations from medical charts and nineteenth-century novels to illustrate the basis for his comparison? How do the specific quotations he cites from twentieth-century novels contribute to his conclusion?
2. How does he use other forms of writing—diary, family history, laboratory report—to describe the purpose of the various sections of the chart? What section "constitutes the bulk of our manuscript"?

QUESTIONS FOR DISCUSSION

1. What "upbeat conviction" is at the base of the "Problem-Oriented Patient Record"? What is missing in the "Defined Data Base"? What does this change suggest about the history of medical science?
2. Based on Weissmann's brief citations, which of the six novels quoted in this essay would you enjoy reading? What factors influence your choice?

PAULE MARSHALL

Paule Marshall was born in 1929 in Brooklyn, New York, the daughter of immigrants from Barbados. With degrees from Brooklyn College and Hunter College, Marshall became a writer for the magazine *Our World* while she wrote her first novel, *Brown Girl, Brownstones* (1959). She has taught creative writing and African-American literature at Oxford University, Yale University, Cornell University, and Virginia Commonwealth University. Marshall's fiction—*Soul Clap Hands and Sing* (1961), *The Chosen Place, the Timeless People* (1969), *Praisesong for the Widow* (1983), and *Reena and Other Stores* (1983)—is distinguished by its inclusion of the variety of voices from her cross-cultural heritage. "To Da-duh, In Memoriam," reprinted from *Reena and Other Stories,* contrasts the experience and values of Da-duh, an old woman who has lived her life in the natural beauty of Barbados, with those of her granddaughter, who has grow up amidst the urban splendor of New York City.

To Da-duh, In Memoriam

". . . Oh Nana! all of you is not involved in this evil business 1
Death,
Nor all of us in life."
—From "At My Grandmother's Grave," by Lebert Bethune

I did not see her at first I remember. For not only was it 2
dark inside the crowded disembarkation shed in spite of the daylight flooding in from outside, but standing there waiting for her with my mother and sister I was still somewhat blinded from the sheen of tropical sunlight on the water of

the bay which we had just crossed in the landing boat, leaving behind us the ship that had brought us from New York lying in the offing. Besides, being only nine years of age at the time and knowing nothing of islands I was busy attending to the alien sights and sounds of Barbados, the unfamiliar smells.

I did not see her, but I was alerted to her approach by my mother's hand which suddenly tightened around mine, and looking up I traced her gaze through the gloom in the shed until I finally made out the small, purposeful, painfully erect figure of the old woman headed our way. 3

Her face was drowned in the shadow of an ugly rolled-brim brown felt hat, but the details of her slight body and of the struggle taking place within it were clear enough—an intense, unrelenting struggle between her back which was beginning to bend ever so slightly under the weight of her eighty-odd years and the rest of her which sought to deny those years and hold that back straight, keep it in line. Moving swiftly toward us (so swiftly it seemed she did not intend stopping when she reached us but would sweep past us out the doorway which opened onto the sea and like Christ walk upon the water!), she was caught between the sunlight at her end of the building and the darkness inside—and for a moment she appeared to contain them both: the light in the long severe old-fashioned white dress she wore which brought the sense of a past that was still alive into our bustling present and in the snatch of white at her eye; the darkness in her black high-top shoes and in her face which was visible now that she was closer. 4

It was as stark and fleshless as a death mask, that face. The maggots might have already done their work, leaving only the framework of bone beneath the ruined skin and deep wells at the temple and jaw. But her eyes were alive, unnervingly so for one so old, with a sharp light that flicked out of the dim clouded depths like a lizard's tongue to snap up all in her view. Those eyes betrayed a child's curiosity about the world, and I wondered vaguely seeing them, and seeing the way the bodice of her ancient dress had collapsed in on her flat chest (what had happened to her breasts?), whether she 5 might not be some kind of child at the same time that she was a woman, with fourteen children, my mother included, to prove it. Perhaps she was both, both child and woman, darkness and light, past and present, life and death—all the opposites contained and reconciled in her.

"My Da-duh," my mother said formally and stepped forward. The name sounded like thunder fading softly in the distance. 6

"Child," Da-duh said, and her tone, her quick scrutiny of my mother, the brief embrace in which they appeared to shy from each other rather than touch, wiped out the fifteen years my mother had been away and restored the old relationship. My mother, who was such a formidable figure in my eyes, had suddenly with a word been reduced to my status. 7

"Yes, God is good," Da-duh said with a nod that was like a tic. "He has spared me to see my child again." 8

We were led forward then, apologetically because not only did Da-duh prefer boys but she also liked her grandchildren to be "white," that is, fair-skinned; and we had, I was to discover, a number of cousins, the outside children of white estate managers and the like, who qualified. We, though, were as black as she. 9

My sister being the oldest was presented first. "This one takes after the father," my mother said and waited to be reproved. 10

Frowning, Da-duh tilted my sister's face toward the light. But her frown soon gave way to a grudging smile, for my sister with her large mild eyes and little broad winged nose, with our father's high-cheeked Barbadian cast to her face, was pretty. 11

"She's goin' be lucky," Da-duh said and patted her once on the cheek. "Any girl child that takes after the father does be lucky." 12

She turned then to me. But oddly enough she did not touch me. Instead leaning close, she peered hard at me, and then quickly drew back. I thought I saw her hand start up as though to shield her eyes. It was almost as if she saw not only me, a thin truculent child who it was said took after no 13 one but myself, but something in me which for some reason she found disturbing, even threatening. We looked silently at each other for a long time there in the noisy shed, our gaze locked. She was the first to look away.

"But Adry," she said to my mother and her laugh was cracked, thin, apprehensive. "Where did you get this one here with this fierce look?" 14

"We don't know where she came out of, my Da-duh," my mother said, laughing also. Even I smiled to myself. After all I had won the encounter. Da-duh had recognized my small strength—and this was all I ever asked of the adults in my life then. 15

"Come, soul," Da-duh said and took my hand. "You must be one of those New York terrors you hear so much about." 16

She led us, me at her side and my sister and mother behind, out of the shed into the sunlight that was like a bright driving summer rain and over to a group of people clustered beside a decrepit lorry. They were our relatives, most of them from St. Andrews although Da-duh herself lived in St. Thomas, the women wearing bright print dresses, the colors vivid against their darkness, the men rusty black suits that encased them like straitjackets. Da-duh, holding fast to my hand, became my anchor as they circled round us like a nervous sea, exclaiming, touching us with their calloused hands, embracing us shyly. They laughed in awed bursts: "But look Adry got big-big children!"/ "And see the nice things they wearing, wrist watch and all!"/ "I tell you, Adry has done all right for sheself in New York. . . ." 17

Da-duh, ashamed at their wonder, embarrassed for them, admonished them the while. "But oh Christ," she said, "why you all got to get on like you never saw people from 'Away' before? You would think New York is the only place in the world to hear wunna. That's why I don't like to go anyplace with you St. Andrews people, you know. You all ain't been colonized." 18

We were in the back of the lorry finally, packed in among the barrels of ham, flour, cornmeal and rice and the trunks of clothes that my mother had brought as gifts. We made our way slowly through Bridgetown's clogged streets, part 19 of a funereal procession of cars and open-sided buses, bicycles and donkey carts. The dim little limestone shops and offices along the way marched with us, at the same mournful pace, toward the same grave ceremony—as did the people, the women balancing huge baskets on top their heads as if they were no more than hats they wore to shade them from the sun. Looking over the edge of the lorry I watched as their feet slurred the dust. I listened, and their voices, raw and loud and dissonant in the heat, seemed to be grappling with each other high overhead.

Da-duh sat on a trunk in our midst, a monarch amid her court. She still held my hand, but it was different now. I had suddenly become her anchor, for I felt her fear of the lorry with its asthmatic motor (a fear and distrust, I later learned, she held of all machines) beating like a pulse in her rough palm. 20

As soon as we left Bridgetown behind though, she relaxed, and while the others around us talked she gazed at the canes standing tall on either side of the winding marl road. "C'dear," she said softly to herself after a time. "The canes this side are pretty enough." 21

They were too much for me. I thought of them as giant weeds that had overrun the island, leaving scarcely any room for the small tottering houses of sunbleached pine we passed or the people, dark streaks as our lorry hurtled by. I suddenly feared that we were journeying, unaware that we were, toward some dangerous place where the canes, grown as high and thick as a forest, would close in on us and run us through with their stiletto blades. I longed then for the familiar: for the street in Brooklyn where I lived, for my father who had refused to accompany us ("Blowing out good money on foolishness," he had said of the trip), for a game of tag with my friends under the chestnut tree outside our aging brownstone house. 22

"Yes, but wait till you see St. Thomas canes," Da-duh was saying to me. "They's canes father, bo," she gave a proud arrogant nod. "Tomorrow, God willing, I goin' take you out in the ground and show them to you." 23

True to her word Da-duh took me with her the following 24

day out into the ground. It was a fairly large plot adjoining
her weathered board and shingle house and consisting of a
small orchard, a good-sized canepiece and behind the canes,
where the land sloped abruptly down, a gully. She had purchased it with Panama money sent her by her eldest son, my
uncle Joseph, who had died working on the canal. We entered the ground along a trail no wider than her body and
as devious and complex as her reasons for showing me her
land. Da-duh strode briskly ahead, her slight form filled out
this morning by the layers of sacking petticoats she wore
under her working dress to protect her against the damp. A
fresh white cloth, elaborately arranged around her head,
added to her height, and lent her a vain, almost roguish air.

Her pace slowed once we reached the orchard, and glanc- 25
ing back at me occasionally over her shoulder, she pointed
out the various trees.

"This is a breadfruit," she said. "That one yonder is a 26
papaw. Here's a guava. This is a mango. I know you don't
have anything like these in New York. Here's a sugar apple."
(The fruit looked more like artichokes than apples to me.)
"This one bears limes. . . ." She went on for some time,
intoning the names of the trees as though they were those
of her gods. Finally, turning to me, she said, "I know you
don't have anything this nice where you come from." Then,
as I hesitated: "I said I know you don't have anything this
nice where you come from. . . ."

"No," I said and my world did seem suddenly lacking. 27

Da-duh nodded and passed on. The orchard ended and 28
we were on the narrow cart road that led through the canepiece, the canes clashing like swords above my cowering
head. Again she turned and her thin muscular arms spread
wide, her dim gaze embracing the small field of canes, she
said—and her voice almost broke under the weight of her
pride, "Tell me, have you got anything like these in that place
where you were born?"

"No." 29

"I din' think so. I bet you don't even know that these 30
canes here and the sugar you eat is one and the same thing.

That they does throw the canes into some damn machine at the factory and squeeze out all the little life in them to make sugar for you all so in New York to eat. I bet you don't know that."

"I've got two cavities and I'm not allowed to eat a lot of 31
sugar."

But Da-duh didn't hear me. She had turned with an 32
inexplicably angry motion and was making her way rapidly out of the canes and down the slope at the edge of the field which led to the gully below. Following her apprehensively down the incline amid a stand of banana plants whose leaves flapped like elephants' ears in the wind, I found myself in the middle of a small tropical wood—a place dense and damp and gloomy and tremulous with the fitful play of light and shadow as the leaves high above moved against the sun that was almost hidden from view. It was a violent place, the tangled foliage fighting each other for a chance at the sunlight, the branches of the trees locked in what seemed an immemorial struggle, one both necessary and inevitable. But despite the violence, it was pleasant, almost peaceful in the gully, and beneath the thick undergrowth the earth smelled like spring.

This time Da-duh didn't even bother to ask her usual 33
question, but simply turned and waited for me to speak.

"No," I said, my head bowed. "We don't have anything 34
like this in New York."

"Ah," she cried, her triumph complete. "I din' think so. 35
Why, I've heard that's a place where you can walk till you near drop and never see a tree."

"We've got a chestnut tree in front of our house," I said. 36

"Does it bear?" She waited. "I ask you, does it bear?" 37

"Not anymore," I muttered. "It used to, but not any- 38
more."

She gave the nod that was like a nervous twitch. "You 39
see," she said. "Nothing can bear there." Then, secure behind her scorn, she added, "But tell me, what's this snow like that you hear so much about?"

Looking up, I studied her closely, sensing my chance, and 40 then I told her, describing at length and with as much drama as I could summon not only what snow in the city was like, but what it would be like here, in her perennial summer kingdom.

". . . And you see all these trees you got here," I said. "Well, they'd be bare. No leaves, no fruit, nothing. They'd be covered in snow. You see your canes. They'd be buried under tons of snow. The snow would be higher than your head, higher than your house, and you wouldn't be able to come down into this here gully because it would be snowed under. . . ." 41

She searched my face for the lie, still scornful but intrigued. "What a thing, huh?" she said finally, whispering it softly to herself. 42

"And when it snows you couldn't dress like you are now," I said. "Oh no, you'd freeze to death. You'd have to wear a hat and gloves and galoshes and ear muffs so your ears wouldn't freeze and drop off, and a heavy coat. I've got a Shirley Temple coat with fur on the collar. I can dance. You wanna see?" 43

Before she could answer I began, with a dance called the Truck which was popular back then in the 1930s. My right forefinger waving, I trucked around the nearby trees and around Da-duh's awed and rigid form. After the Truck I did the Suzy-Q, my lean hips swishing, my sneakers sidling zigzag over the ground. "I can sing," I said and did so, starting with "I'm Gonna Sit Right Down and Write Myself a Letter," then without pausing, "Tea for Two," and ending with "I Found a Million Dollar Baby in a Five and Ten Cent Store." 44

For long moments afterwards Da-duh stared at me as if I were a creature from Mars, an emissary from some world she did not know but which intrigued her and whose power she both felt and feared. Yet something about my performance must have pleased her, because bending down she slowly lifted her long skirt and then, one by one, the layers of petticoats until she came to a drawstring purse dangling at the end of a long strip of cloth tied round her waist. 45

Opening the purse she handed me a penny. "Here," she said half-smiling against her will. "Take this to buy yourself a sweet at the shop up the road. There's nothing to be done with you, soul."

From then on, whenever I wasn't taken to visit relatives, I accompanied Da-duh out into the ground, and alone with her amid the canes or down in the gully I told her about New York. It always began with some slighting remark on her part: "I know they don't have anything this nice where you come from," or "Tell me, I hear those foolish people in New York does do such and such. . . ." But as I answered, re-creating my towering world of steel and concrete and machines for her, building the city out of words, I would feel her give way. I came to know the signs of her surrender: the total stillness that would come over her little hard dry form, the probing gaze that like a surgeon's knife sought to cut through my skull to get at the images there, to see if I were lying; above all, her fear, a fear nameless and profound, the same one I had felt beating in the palm of her hand that day in the lorry. 46

Over the weeks I told her about refrigerators, radios, gas stoves, elevators, trolley cars, wringer washing machines, movies, airplanes, the cyclone at Coney Island, subways, toasters, electric lights: "At night, see, all you have to do is flip this little switch on the wall and all the lights in the house go on. Just like that. Like magic. It's like turning on the sun at night." 47

"But tell me," she said to me once with a faint mocking smile, "do the white people have all these things too or it's only the people looking like us?" 48

I laughed. "What d'ya mean," I said. "The white people have even better." Then: "I beat up a white girl in my class last term." 49

"Beating up white people!" Her tone was incredulous. 50

"How you mean!" I said, using an expression of hers. "She called me a name." 51

For some reason Da-duh could not quite get over this and repeated in the same hushed, shocked voice, "Beating up 52 white people now! Oh, the lord, the world's changing up so I can scarce recognize it anymore."

One morning toward the end of our stay, Da-duh led me into a part of the gully that we had never visited before, an area darker and more thickly overgrown than the rest, almost impenetrable. There in a small clearing amid the dense bush, she stopped before an incredibly tall royal palm which rose cleanly out of the ground, and drawing the eye up with it, soared high above the trees around it into the sky. It appeared to be touching the blue dome of sky, to be flaunting its dark crown of fronds right in the blinding white face of the late morning sun. 53

Da-duh watched me a long time before she spoke, and then she said very quietly, "All right, now, tell me if you've got anything this tall in that place you're from." 54

I almost wished, seeing her face, that I could have said no. "Yes," I said. "We've got buildings hundreds of times this tall in New York. There's one called the Empire State Building that's the tallest in the world. My class visited it last year and I went all the way to the top. It's got over a hundred floors. I can't describe how tall it is. Wait a minute. What's the name of that hill I went to visit the other day, where they have the police station?" 55

"You mean Bissex?" 56

"Yes, Bissex. Well, the Empire State Building is way taller than that." 57

"You're lying now!" she shouted, trembling with rage. Her hand lifted to strike me. 58

"No, I'm not," I said. "It really is, if you don't believe me I'll send you a picture postcard of it soon as I get back home so you can see for yourself. But it's way taller than Bissex." 59

All the fight went out of her at that. The hand poised to strike me fell limp to her side, and as she stared at me, seeing not me but the building that was taller than the highest hill she knew, the small stubborn light in her eyes (it was the same amber as the flame in the kerosene lamp she lit at dusk) began to fail. Finally, with a vague gesture that even in the midst of her defeat still tried to dismiss me and my world, 60 she turned and started back through the gully, walking slowly, her steps groping and uncertain, as if she were suddenly no longer sure of the way, while I followed triumphant yet strangely saddened behind.

The next morning I found her dressed for our morning walk but stretched out on the Berbice chair in the tiny drawing room where she sometimes napped during the afternoon heat, her face turned to the window beside her. She appeared thinner and suddenly indescribably old. 61

"My Da-duh," I said. 62

"Yes, nuh," she said. Her voice was listless and the face she slowly turned my way was, now that I think back on it, like a Benin mask, the features drawn and almost distorted by an ancient abstract sorrow. 63

"Don't you feel well?" I asked. 64

"Girl, I don't know." 65

"My Da-duh, I goin' boil you some bush tea," my aunt, Da-duh's youngest child, who lived with her, called from the shed roof kitchen. 66

"Who tell you I need bush tea?" she cried, her voice assuming for a moment its old authority. "You can't even rest nowadays without some malicious person looking for you to be dead. Come girl," she motioned me to a place beside her on the old-fashioned lounge chair, "give us a tune." 67

I sang for her until breakfast at eleven, all my brash irreverent Tin Pan Alley songs, and then just before noon we went out into the ground. But it was a short, dispirited walk. Da-duh didn't even notice that the mangoes were beginning to ripen and would have to be picked before the village boys got to them. And when she paused occasionally and looked out across the canes or up at her trees it wasn't as if she were seeing them but something else. Some huge, monolithic shape had imposed itself, it seemed, between her and the land, obstructing her vision. Returning to the house she slept the entire afternoon on the Berbice chair. 68

She remained like this until we left, languishing away the mornings on the chair at the window gazing out at the land 69 as if it were already doomed; then, at noon, taking the brief stroll with me through the ground during which she seldom spoke, and afterwards returning home to sleep till almost dusk sometimes.

On the day of our departure she put on the austere, ankle- 70
length white dress, the black shoes and brown felt hat (her town clothes she called them), but she did not go with us to town. She saw us off on the road outside her house and in the midst of my mother's tearful protracted farewell, she leaned down and whispered in my ear, "Girl, you're not to forget now to send me the picture of that building, you hear."

By the time I mailed her the large colored picture postcard 71
of the Empire State Building she was dead. She died during the famous '37 strike which began shortly after we left. On the day of her death England sent planes flying low over the island in a show of force—so low, according to my aunt's letter, that the downdraft from them shook the ripened mangoes from the trees in Da-duh's orchard. Frightened, everyone in the village fled into the canes. Except Da-duh. She remained in the house at the window so my aunt said, watching as the planes came swooping and screaming like monstrous birds down over the village, over her house, rattling her trees and flattening the young canes in her field. It must have seemed to her lying there that they did not intend pulling out of their dive, but like the hard-back beetles which hurled themselves with suicidal force against the walls of the house at night, those menacing silver shapes would hurl themselves in an ecstasy of self-immolation onto the land, destroying it utterly.

When the planes finally left and the villagers returned they 72
found her dead on the Berbice chair at the window.

She died and I lived, but always, to this day even, within 73
the shadow of her death. For a brief period after I was grown I went to live alone, like one doing penance, in a loft above a noisy factory in downtown New York and there painted seas of sugar-cane and huge swirling Van Gogh suns and palm trees striding like brightly-plumed Tutsi warriors across

a tropical landscape, while the thunderous tread of the machines downstairs jarred the floor beneath my easel, mocking my efforts.

COMMENT ON "TO DA-DUH, IN MEMORIAM"

Paule Marshall's "To Da-duh, In Memoriam" sets up a comparison between the natural world of Da-duh and the urban world of the young narrator. For Da-duh, Barbados is a magnificent, magical place that she is eager to show her visiting granddaughter. As they walk between the canes or among the banana plants, she wants to know whether her companion has "anything this nice where you come from." The narrator says no to most of these questions but eventually begins "describing at length and with as much drama as I could summon" all the marvels of New York—from snow to electrical appliances to the Empire State Building. The once proud Da-duh learns a lesson, slowly surrendering to the new world where trees do not bear fruit, black people beat up white people, and a building is "taller than the highest hill she knew." The story concludes as she dies trying to face down the English airplanes that invade her world. But the last lesson is reserved for the narrator, who, when she is grown, moves into a noisy loft in downtown New York to paint Da-duh's world: "seas of sugar-cane and high swirling Van Gogh suns and palm trees striding like brightly-plumed Tutsi warriors across a tropical landscape."

Comparison and Contrast as a Writing Strategy

1. Select a place in your childhood neighborhood—perhaps a garden, a playground, or a movie theater. Then, in an essay addressed to your writing class, write a short comparison of the same place: the way it used to be and the way it is now. Consider the example of Mark Twain's "Two Views of the River" as you compare your childhood and adult visions. Consider also what you have learned about the place or yourself by making the comparison. That lesson should help control your decisions about purpose and audience.
2. Select a person who embodies many admirable characteristics—a grandparent, teacher, movie star, or historical figure. Consider such points as behavior, education, work, dress, and style. Then, like Rose del Castillo Guilbault, compare and contrast how this character would be perceived by two *different* communities or cultures. Try to account for the differences and distortions you discover in your point-by-point comparison.
3. Conduct some research on the conversational patterns in your home (or dormitory) and in your classroom. Keep track of who talks, what they talk about, and how they use conversation—for example, to make friends, to report information, to win approval. Keep track of who doesn't talk and in what situations they are likely to stay silent. Then write an essay in which you compare the patterns of home and school conversation.
4. Gerald Weissmann's "The Chart of the Novel" depends on the careful selection of quotations from medical charts and novels. He also relies on E. M. Forster's distinction between *story* and *plot* to emphasize the importance of causal analysis (see pp. 202–203). Use this distinction to demonstrate how the quotations from the nineteenth- and twentieth-century novels support Weissmann's thesis that medical charts have changed.
5. Write an essay comparing the way two magazines or newspapers cover the same news story. You could select

magazines that have opposing political philosophies or newspapers that are published in different parts of the country. Or, like Edward T. Hall, you may wish to analyze how two cultures see the same problem. For example, compare American and Libyan statements on terrorism, American and Russian views on economic aid, or American and Mexican policies on immigration.

6. Compare and contrast arguments on both sides of a controversial issue such as welfare or health care. Such issues produce controversy because there are legitimate arguments on each side. They also produce controversy because people can simplify them in slogans (reading is good, television is bad). Select two slogans that present the opposing sides of the controversy you are writing about. Compare and contrast the assumptions, evidence, and logic of both slogans. Like Tannen, avoid choosing sides. Maintain a neutral tone as you assess the motives, methods, and reasons for each argument.

DIVISION AND CLASSIFICATION

Division and **classification** are mental processes that often work together. When you *divide,* you separate something (a college, a city) into sections (departments, neighborhoods). When you *classify,* you place examples of something (restaurants, jobs) into categories or classes (restaurants: moderately expensive, very expensive; jobs: unskilled, semiskilled, and skilled).

When you *divide,* you move downward from a concept to the subunits of that concept. When you *classify,* you move upward from specific examples to classes or categories that share a common characteristic. For example, you could divide a television news program into subunits such as news, features, editorials, sports, and weather. You would, however, classify some element of that program—for example, the editorial commentator on the six o'clock news—according to his or her style, knowledge, and trustworthiness. Although you can use either division or classification singly, depending on your purpose, most of the time you will probably use them together when you are writing a classification essay. For example, first you might discover the subunits in a college sports program—football, basketball, hockey, volleyball, tennis, for example—then you could classify them according to their budgets—most money budgeted for football, the least budgeted for volleyball.

PURPOSE

When you write a classification essay, your chief purpose is to ***explain***. You might want to explain an established method for organizing information, such as the Library of Congress system, or a new plan for arranging data such as the Internal Revenue Service's latest schedule for itemizing tax deductions. On one level, your purpose in such an essay is simply to show how the system works. At a deeper level, however, your purpose is to define, analyze, and justify the organizing principle that underlies the system.

You can also write a classification essay to ***entertain*** or to ***persuade***. If you classify to entertain, you have an opportunity to be clever and witty; if you classify to persuade, you have a chance to be cogent and forceful. If you want to entertain, for example, you might concoct an elaborate scheme for classifying fools, pointing out the distinguishing features of each category and giving particularly striking examples of each type. If you want to persuade, however, you could explain how some new or controversial plan, such as the metric system or congressional redistricting, is organized, pointing out how the schemes use new principles to identify and organize information. Again, although you may give your readers a great deal of information in such an essay, your main purpose is to persuade your readers that the new plan is better than the old one.

AUDIENCE

As with any writing assignment, when you write a classification essay you need to think carefully about what your readers already know and what they need to get from your writing. If you're writing on a new topic (social patterns in a primitive society) or if you're explaining a specialized system of classification (the botanist's procedure for identifying plants), your readers need precise definitions and plenty of illustrations for each subcategory. If your readers already know about your subject and the system it uses for classification (the movies' G, PG, R, and X rating code), then you don't need to give them an extensive demonstration. In that kind of writing situation, you might want to sketch the system briefly to refresh your readers' memory but then move on, using examples of specific movies to analyze whether the system really works.

You also need to think about how your readers might use the classification system you explain in your essay. If you're classifying rock musicians, your readers are probably going to regard the system you create as something self-enclosed—interesting and amusing, perhaps something to quibble about, but not something they're likely to use in their everyday lives. On the other hand, if you write an essay classifying stereo equipment, your readers may want to use your system when they shop. For the first audience, you can use an informal approach to classification, dividing your subject into interesting subcategories and illustrating them with vivid examples. For the other audience, you need to be careful and strict in your approach, making sure you divide your topic into all its possible classes and illustrating each class with concrete examples.

STRATEGIES

When you write a classification essay, your basic strategy for organization should be to *divide your subject* into major categories that exhibit a common trait, then subdivide those categories into smaller units. Next, *arrange your categories* into a sequence that shows a logical or a dramatic progression. Finally, *define each of your categories*. First, show how a category is different from the others, and second, discuss its most vivid examples. In order to make this strategy succeed, however, you must be sure that your classification system is *consistent, complete, emphatic,* and *significant*. Here is a method for achieving this goal.

First, when you divide your subject into categories, *apply the same principle of selection to each class*. You may find this hard to do if you're trying to explain a system that someone else has already established but that is actually inconsistent. You have only to visit a few record stores to realize that they often classify music according to many overlapping and inconsistent systems (for example, Linda Ronstadt albums may be classified as country, rock, pop, standard, or female vocal). You can avoid such tangles, however, if you create and control your own classification system.

For instance, in this section Russell Baker classifies objects by their ability to "resist man and ultimately to defeat him." The other writers follow a similar strategy. Lewis Thomas classifies medical technologies by their cost-effectiveness; John Holt classifies discipline by the degree of human intervention; Gail Sheehy classifies human development by predictable stages of growth. Even Joseph Epstein, who argues that class labels have lost their descriptive power, uses the traditional markers of social class to make his argument.

After you have divided your subject into separate and consistent categories, *make sure that your division is complete*. The simplest kind of division separates a subject into two categories: A and Not-A (for example, conformists and nonconformists). This kind of division, however, is rarely encouraged because although it allows you to tell your readers about category A (conformists), you won't tell them much about Not-A (noncomformists). For this reason, you should try to "exhaust" your subject by finding at least three separate categories and by acknowledging those examples that won't fit into the system. When an author writes a formal classification essay, such as Sheehy does when she analyzes stages of growth, he or she tries to be definitive—that is, to include everything significant. Even when authors are writing less formal classification essays, such as Baker does in "The Plot Against People" and Epstein does in "They Told Me You Was High Class," they try to set up a reasonably complete system.

Once you have completed your process of division, *arrange your categories and examples in an emphatic order*. Sheehy arranges her categories of human development chronologically, from the rebellion of eighteen-year-olds to the mellowing of fifty-year-olds. Thomas arranges his categories of medical technology dramatically, from least effective to most effective. John Holt arranges his three kinds of discipline logically, from most simple to complex. The author of each of these essays reveals the principal purpose underlying any classification process: to show variety in similarity, to distinguish good from bad, and to point out how a form changes.

Finally, *you need to show the significance of your system of classification*. The strength of the classifying process is that you can use it to analyze a subject by any number of systems. Its weakness is that it also allows you to classify a subject by all kinds of trivial or pointless categories. You can classify people by their educational backgrounds, their work experience, or their significant achievements; you can also classify them by their shoe size, the kind of socks they wear, or their tastes in ice cream. Notice that when a writer such as Lewis Thomas classifies a subject according to a particular system, he asserts that the system is significant, that it tells us something important about the money we spend on medical technologies. Even when a writer chooses a subject that doesn't seem particularly significant—as Russell Baker does when he classifies objects—that writer still must convince readers that his or her *system* counts in some way, if only because it lays out and demonstrates, consistently and completely, the significant subdivisions of the subject.

Using Division and Classification in a Paragraph

HERBERT J. GANS
From *Deciding What's News*

Identifies principles of division (suitability)

The New York Times announces every day that it contains "All the News That's Fit to Print." The wording is arrogant, but the phrase makes the point that the news consists of suitable stories. To determine story suitability, journalists employ a large number of suitability considerations, all of which are interrelated. These can be divided into three categories: substantive considerations judge story content and the newsworthiness of what sources supply; product considerations evaluate the "goodness" of stories; and competitive considerations test stories for their ability to serve in the continuing rivalry among news organizations to provide the most suitable news.

Establishes three categories:
1. substantive
2. product
3. competitive

Comment In this excerpt from his study of the media, Herbert J. Gans divides the suitability of news stories into three categories. Although he admits that the categories are "interrelated," Gans suggests that journalists classify a story by three considerations: (1) substantive—whether the story is newsworthy; (2) product—whether the story is "good"; and (3) competitive—whether the story improves the paper's standing against other newspapers.

RUSSELL BAKER

Russell Baker was born in 1925 in rural Loudoun County, Virginia; graduated from Johns Hopkins University; and served in the navy during World War II. He began his newspaper career in 1947, covering the State Department, White House, and Congress for *The New York Times* until, as he recounts, "I just got bored. I had done enough reporting." The *Times* offered him a thrice-weekly column, which came to be called "Observer" and which Baker continues to write today. His text is a happy combination of humor and substantive comment on such diverse topics as politicians and government bureaucrats, unreadable menus, and vacationing with children. Many of his columns have been collected in book form: *No Cause for Panic* (1969), *Poor Russell's Almanac* (1972), *So This Is Depravity* (1980), *The Rescue of Miss Yaskell and Other Pipe Dreams* (1983), and *There's a Country in My Cellar* (1990). His autobiography, *Growing Up* (1982), was awarded the Pulitzer Prize. *The Good Times* (1989) continues his reminiscences. In "The Plot Against People," Baker employs his wry humor to classify inanimate objects into three categories.

The Plot Against People

Inanimate objects are classified into three major categories—those that don't work, those that break down and those that get lost. 1

The goal of all inanimate objects is to resist man and ultimately to defeat him, and the three major classifications are based on the method each object uses to achieve its purpose. As a general rule, any object capable of breaking 2 down at the moment when it is most needed will do so. The automobile is typical of the category.

With the cunning typical of its breed, the automobile never breaks down while entering a filling station with a large staff of idle mechanics. It waits until it reaches a downtown intersection in the middle of the rush hour, or until it is fully loaded with family and luggage on the Ohio Turnpike. 3

Thus it creates maximum misery, inconvenience, frustration and irritability among its human cargo, thereby reducing its owner's life span. 4

Washing machines, garbage disposals, lawn mowers, light bulbs, automatic laundry dryers, water pipes, furnaces, electrical fuses, television tubes, hose nozzles, tape recorders, slide projectors—all are in league with the automobile to take their turn at breaking down whenever life threatens to flow smoothly for their human enemies. 5

Many inanimate objects, of course, find it extremely difficult to break down. Pliers, for example, and gloves and keys are almost totally incapable of breaking down. Therefore, they have had to evolve a different technique for resisting man. 6

They get lost. Science has still not solved the mystery of how they do it, and no man has ever caught one of them in the act of getting lost. The most plausible theory is that they have developed a secret method of locomotion which they are able to conceal the instant a human eye falls upon them. 7

It is not uncommon for a pair of pliers to climb all the way from the cellar to the attic in its single-minded determination to raise its owner's blood pressure. Keys have been known to burrow three feet under mattresses. Women's purses, despite their great weight, frequently travel through six or seven rooms to find hiding space under a couch. 8

Scientists have been struck by the fact that things that break down virtually never get lost, while things that get lost hardly ever break down. 9

A furnace, for example, will invariably break down at the 10 depth of the first winter cold wave, but it will never get lost. A woman's purse, which after all does have some inherent capacity for breaking down, hardly ever does; it almost invariably chooses to get lost.

Some persons believe this constitutes evidence that inanimate objects are not entirely hostile to man, and that a negotiated peace is possible. After all, they point out, a furnace could infuriate a man even more thoroughly by getting lost than by breaking down, just as a glove could upset him far more by breaking down than by getting lost. 11

Not everyone agrees, however, that this indicates a conciliatory attitude among inanimate objects. Many say it merely proves that furnaces, gloves and pliers are incredibly stupid. 12

The third class of objects—those that don't work—is the most curious of all. These include such objects as barometers, car clocks, cigarette lighters, flashlights and toy-train locomotives. It is inaccurate, of course, to say that they never work. They work once, usually for the first few hours after being brought home, and then quit. Thereafter, they never work again. 13

In fact, it is widely assumed that they are built for the purpose of not working. Some people have reached advanced ages without ever seeing some of these objects—barometers, for example—in working order. 14

Science is utterly baffled by the entire category. There are many theories about it. The most interesting holds that the things that don't work have attained the highest state possible for an inanimate object, the estate to which things that break down and things that get lost can still only aspire. 15

They have truly defeated man by conditioning him never to expect anything of them, and in return they have given man the only peace he receives from inanimate society. He does not expect his barometer to work, his electric locomotive to run, his cigarette lighter to light or his flashlight to illuminate, and when they don't, it does not raise his blood pressure. 16

He cannot attain that peace with furnaces and keys and cars and women's purses as long as he demands that they work for their keep. 17

For Study and Discussion

QUESTIONS FOR RESPONSE

1. What experiences have you had with objects that don't work, break down, or get lost?
2. How does Baker's title, "The Plot Against People," prepare you for the subject of this classification of things?

QUESTIONS ABOUT PURPOSE

1. How does Baker's introduction of his first category (paragraph 2) and his illustrative example (paragraph 3) demonstrate that his primary purpose is to entertain?
2. In what ways do Baker's repeated references to science reinforce or alter his purpose?

QUESTIONS ABOUT AUDIENCE

1. How does Baker's use of examples reveal his assumptions about the common experience of his audience?
2. How does Baker expect his readers to use his classification system? Look particularly at paragraphs 11, 12, and 16.

QUESTIONS ABOUT STRATEGIES

1. What is the principle by which Baker divides objects into three categories?
2. What does Baker accomplish by scrambling the sequence of categories he presents in his opening sentence?

QUESTIONS FOR DISCUSSION

1. What evidence can you supply to confirm Baker's thesis that "the highest state possible for an inanimate object" occurs when it can condition people not to expect anything from it?
2. What evidence can you suggest to defeat Baker's thesis? That is, how would you support the argument that objects do not defeat people but provide them with ways to extend their creative powers?

LEWIS THOMAS

Lewis Thomas was born in 1913 in Flushing, New York, and was educated at Princeton University and Harvard University Medical School. He held appointments at numerous research hospitals and medical schools before assuming his present position as president of the Sloan-Kettering Cancer Center in New York City. Thomas's early writing, on the subject of pathology, appeared in scientific journals. In 1971 he began contributing a popular column, "Notes of a Biology Watcher," to the *New England Journal of Medicine*. In 1974 his collection of these essays, *The Lives of a Cell: Notes of a Biology Watcher,* won the National Book Award for Arts and Letters. His other books include *The Medusa and the Snail: More Notes of a Biology Watcher* (1979), *The Youngest Science* (1983), *Late Night Thoughts on Listening to Mahler's Ninth Symphony* (1983), and *The Fragile Species* (1992). In "The Technology of Medicine," from *The Lives of a Cell,* Thomas classifies "three quite different levels of technology in medicine."

The Technology of Medicine

Technology assessment has become a routine exercise for the scientific enterprises on which the country is obliged to spend vast sums for its needs. Brainy committees are continually evaluating the effectiveness and cost of doing various things in space, defense, energy, transportation, and the like, to give advice about prudent investments for the future. 1

Somehow medicine, for all the $80-odd billion that it is said to cost the nation, has not yet come in for much of this analytical treatment. It seems taken for granted that the technology of medicine simply exists, take it or leave it, and the 2 only major technologic problem which policy-makers are interested in is how to deliver today's kind of health care, with equity, to all the people.

When, as is bound to happen sooner or later, the analysts get around to the technology of medicine itself, they will have to face the problem of measuring the relative cost and effectiveness of all the things that are done in the management of disease. They make their living at this kind of thing, and I wish them well, but I imagine they will have a bewildering time. For one thing, our methods of managing disease are constantly changing—partly under the influence of new bits of information brought in from all corners of biologic science. At the same time, a great many things are done that are not so closely related to science, some not related at all. 3

In fact, there are three quite different levels of technology in medicine, so unlike each other as to seem altogether different undertakings. Practitioners of medicine and the analysts will be in trouble if they are not kept separate. 4

1. First of all, there is a large body of what might be termed "nontechnology," impossible to measure in terms of its capacity to alter either the natural course of disease or its eventual outcome. A great deal of money is spent on this. It is valued highly by the professionals as well as the patients. It consists of what is sometimes called "supportive therapy." It tides patients over through diseases that are not, by and large, understood. It is what is meant by the phrases "caring for" and "standing by." It is indispensable. It is not, however, a technology in any real sense, since it does not involve measures directed at the underlying mechanism of disease. 5

It includes the large part of any good doctor's time that is taken up with simply providing reassurance, explaining to patients who fear that they have contracted one or another lethal disease that they are, in fact, quite healthy. 6

It is what physicians used to be engaged in at the bedside of patients with diphtheria, meningitis, poliomyelitis, lobar pneumonia, and all the rest of the infectious diseases that have since come under control. 7

It is what physicians must now do for patients with 8

intractable cancer, severe rheumatoid arthritis, multiple sclerosis, stroke, and advanced cirrhosis. One can think of at least twenty major diseases that require this kind of supportive medical care because of the absence of an effective technology. I would include a large amount of what is called mental disease, and most varieties of cancer, in this category.

The cost of this nontechnology is very high, and getting 9
higher all the time. It requires not only a great deal of time but also very hard effort and skill on the part of physicians; only the very best of doctors are good at coping with this kind of defeat. It also involves long periods of hospitalization, lots of nursing, lots of involvement of nonmedical professionals in and out of the hospital. It represents, in short, a substantial segment of today's expenditures for health.

2. At the next level up is a kind of technology best termed 10
"halfway technology." This represents the kinds of things that must be done after the fact, in efforts to compensate for the incapacitating effects of certain diseases whose course one is unable to do very much about. It is a technology designed to make up for disease, or to postpone death.

The outstanding examples in recent years are the trans- 11
plantations of hearts, kidneys, livers, and other organs, and the equally spectacular inventions of artificial organs. In the public mind, this kind of technology has come to seem like the equivalent of the high technologies of the physical sciences. The media tend to present each new procedure as though it represented a breakthrough and therapeutic triumph, instead of the makeshift that it really is.

In fact, this level of technology is, by its nature, at the 12
same time highly sophisticated and profoundly primitive. It is the kind of thing that one must continue to do until there is a genuine understanding of the mechanisms involved in disease. In chronic glomerulonephritis, for example, a much clearer insight will be needed into the events leading to the destruction of glomeruli by the immunologic reactants that now appear to govern this disease, before one will know how to intervene intelligently to prevent the process, or turn

it around. But when this level of understanding has been reached, the technology of kidney replacement will not be much needed and should no longer pose the huge problem of logistics, cost, and ethics that it poses today.

An extremely complex and costly technology for the management of coronary heart disease has evolved—involving specialized ambulances and hospital units, all kinds of electronic gadgetry, and whole platoons of new professional personnel—to deal with the end results of coronary thrombosis. Almost everything offered today for the treatment of heart disease is at this level of technology, with the transplanted and artificial hearts as ultimate examples. When enough has been learned to know what really goes wrong in heart disease, one ought to be in a position to figure out ways to prevent or reverse the process, and when this happens the current elaborate technology will probably be set to one side. 13

Much of what is done in the treatment of cancer, by surgery, irradiation, and chemotherapy, represents halfway technology, in the sense that these measures are directed at the existence of already established cancer cells, but not at the mechanisms by which cells become neoplastic. 14

It is a characteristic of this kind of technology that it costs an enormous amount of money and requires a continuing expansion of hospital facilities. There is no end to the need for new, highly trained people to run the enterprise. And there is really no way out of this, at the present state of knowledge. If the installation of specialized coronary-care units can result in the extension of life for only a few patients with coronary disease (and there is no question that this technology is effective in a few cases), it seems to me an inevitable fact of life that as many of these as can be will be put together, and as much money as can be found will be spent. I do not see that anyone has much choice in this. The only thing that can move medicine away from this level of technology is new information, and the only imaginable source of this information is research. 15

3. The third type of technology is the kind that is so 16

effective that it seems to attract the least public notice; it has come to be taken for granted. This is the genuinely decisive technology of modern medicine, exemplified best by modern methods for immunization against diphtheria, pertussis, and the childhood virus diseases, and the contemporary use of antibiotics and chemotherapy for bacterial infections. The capacity to deal effectively with syphilis and tuberculosis represents a milestone in human endeavor, even though full use of this potential has not yet been made. And there are, of course, other examples: the treatment of endocrinologic disorders with appropriate hormones, the prevention of hemolytic disease of the newborn, the treatment and prevention of various nutritional disorders, and perhaps just around the corner the management of Parkinsonism and sickle-cell anemia. There are other examples, and everyone will have his favorite candidates for the list, but the truth is that there are nothing like as many as the public has been led to believe.

The point to be made about this kind of technology—the real high technology of medicine—is that it comes as the result of a genuine understanding of disease mechanisms, and when it becomes available, it is relatively inexpensive, and relatively easy to deliver. 17

Offhand, I cannot think of any important human disease for which medicine possesses the outright capacity to prevent or cure where the cost of the technology is itself a major problem. The price is never as high as the cost of managing the same diseases during the earlier stages of no-technology or halfway technology. If a case of typhoid fever had to be managed today by the best methods of 1935, it would run to a staggering expense. At, say, around fifty days of hospitalization, requiring the most demanding kind of nursing care, with the obsessive concern for details of diet that characterized the therapy of that time, with daily laboratory monitoring, and, on occasion, surgical intervention for abdominal catastrophe, I should think $10,000 would be a conservative estimate for the illness, as contrasted with today's cost of a bottle of chloramphenicol and a day or two of fever. The halfway technology that was evolving for poliomyelitis in the early 1950s, just before the emergence of 18 the basic research that made the vaccine possible, provides another illustration of the point. Do you remember Sister Kenny, and the cost of those institutes for rehabilitation, with all those ceremonially applied hot fomentations, and the debates about whether the affected limbs should be totally immobilized or kept in passive motion as frequently as possible, and the masses of statistically tormented data mobilized to support one view or the other? It is the cost of that kind of technology, and its relative effectiveness, that must be compared with the cost and effectiveness of the vaccine.

Pulmonary tuberculosis had similar episodes in its history. 19
There was a sudden enthusiasm for the surgical removal of infected lung tissue in the early 1950s, and elaborate plans were being made for new and expensive installations for major pulmonary surgery in tuberculosis hospitals, and the INH and streptomycin came along and the hospitals themselves were closed up.

It is when physicians are bogged down by their incomplete 20
technologies, by the innumerable things they are obliged to do in medicine when they lack a clear understanding of disease mechanisms, that the deficiencies of the health-care system are most conspicuous. If I were a policy-maker, interested in saving money for health care over the long haul, I would regard it as an act of high prudence to give high priority to a lot more basic research in biologic science. This is the only way to get the full mileage that biology owes to the science of medicine, even though it seems, as used to be said in the days when the phrase still had some meaning, like asking for the moon.

For Study and Discussion

QUESTIONS FOR RESPONSE

1. What kind of medical tests have you experienced or seen conducted on friends or family? What kind of emotional reaction do you feel toward the imposing machines used for such tests?

2. What does the word *technology* mean? What do you expect when you hear phrases such as "the latest in medical technology"?

QUESTIONS ABOUT PURPOSE

1. Is Thomas's primary purpose to explain the various kinds of medical technology or to argue that certain technologies are more useful than others? Explain your answer.
2. What does Thomas demonstrate about the relationship between cost-effective technology and a genuine understanding of the disease mechanism?

QUESTIONS ABOUT AUDIENCE

1. How does Thomas's assertion that policy makers are interested in "how to deliver today's kind of health care, with equity, to all the people" suggest that he is aware of his readers' interest in the issue he will discuss?
2. To what extent does Thomas assume that his readers are familiar with the diseases he uses to illustrate each category? How does he provide assistance to his readers when the disease may be unfamiliar? See, for example, his discussion of typhoid fever in paragraph 18.

QUESTIONS ABOUT STRATEGIES

1. How does Thomas's definition of his three categories—nontechnology, halfway technology, and effective technology—clarify the single principle he has used to establish his classification system?
2. How does Thomas's discussion of specific diseases demonstrate that his divisions are complete? What aspect of his system enables him to discuss cancer as an illustration in two categories?

QUESTIONS FOR DISCUSSION

1. Why does Thomas believe so strongly in "basic research in biologic science"? Why would an investment in such research save money for "health care over the long haul"?
2. What is Thomas's attitude toward his second category, halfway technology? Why does he call it "at the same time highly sophisticated and profoundly primitive"?

JOHN HOLT

John Holt (1923–1985) was born in New York City, attended Yale University, and served on the submarine USS *Barbero* during World War II. After the war, he worked for World Federalists, U.S.A., a group that advocated world government. His interests soon turned to education; he taught in a private elementary school in Colorado and later in an elementary school and a high school in Boston. The diaries and letters he wrote during his teaching career formed the basis for his two best-selling books on American education, *How Children Fail* (1964) and *How Children Learn* (1967). His other books include *Freedom and Beyond* (1972), *Escape from Childhood* (1974), *Instead of Education* (1976), and *Teach Your Own* (1981). As the last title suggests, Holt was interested in helping parents assume responsibility for the education of their children. In "Types of Discipline," excerpted from *Freedom and Beyond,* Holt distinguishes among three uses of the word *discipline*.

Types of Discipline

A child, in growing up, may meet and learn from three different kinds of disciplines. The first and most important is what we might call the Discipline of Nature or of Reality. When he is trying to do something real, if he does the wrong thing or doesn't do the right one, he doesn't get the result he wants. If he doesn't pile one block right on top of another, or tries to build on a slanting surface, his tower falls down. If he hits the wrong key, he hears the wrong note. If he doesn't hit the nail squarely on the head, it bends, and he has to pull it out and start with another. If he doesn't measure 1 properly what he is trying to build, it won't open, close, fit, stand up, fly, float, whistle, or do whatever he wants it to do. If he closes his eyes when he swings, he doesn't hit the ball. A child meets this kind of discipline every time he tries to *do* something, which is why it is so important in school to give children more chances to do things, instead of just reading or listening to someone talk (or pretending to). This discipline is a great teacher. The learner never has to wait long for his answer; it usually comes quickly, often instantly. Also it is clear, and very often points toward the needed correction; from what happened he can not only see that what he did was wrong, but also why, and what he needs to do instead. Finally, and most important, the giver of the answer, call it Nature, is impersonal, impartial, and indifferent. She does not give opinions, or make judgments; she cannot be wheedled, bullied, or fooled; she does not get angry or disappointed; she does not praise or blame; she does not remember past failures or hold grudges; with her one always gets a fresh start, this time is the one that counts.

The next discipline we might call the Discipline of Cul- 2
ture, of Society, of What People Really Do. Man is a social, a cultural animal. Children sense around them this culture, this network of agreements, customs, habits, and rules binding the adults together. They want to understand it and be a part of it. They watch very carefully what people around them are doing and want to do the same. They want to do right, unless they become convinced they can't do right. Thus children rarely misbehave seriously in church, but sit as quietly as they can. The example of all those grownups is contagious. Some mysterious ritual is going on, and children, who like rituals, want to be part of it. In the same way, the little children that I see at concerts or operas, though they may fidget a little, or perhaps take a nap now and then, rarely make any disturbance. With all those grownups sitting there, neither moving nor talking, it is the most natural thing in the world to imitate them. Children who live among adults who are habitually courteous to each other, and to them, will soon learn to be courteous. Children who live sur-

rounded by people who speak a certain way will speak that way, however much we may try to tell them that speaking that way is bad or wrong.

The third discipline is the one most people mean when 3
they speak of discipline—the Discipline of Superior Force, of sergeant to private, of "you do what I tell you or I'll make you wish you had." There is bound to be some of this in a child's life. Living as we do surrounded by things that can hurt children, or that children can hurt, we cannot avoid it. We can't afford to let a small child find out from experience the danger of playing in a busy street, or of fooling with the pots on the top of a stove, or of eating up the pills in the medicine cabinet. So, along with other precautions, we say to him, "Don't play in the street, or touch things on the stove, or go into the medicine cabinet, or I'll punish you." Between him and the danger too great for him to imagine we put a lesser danger, but one he can imagine and maybe therefore want to avoid. He can have no idea of what it would be like to be hit by a car, but he can imagine being shouted at, or spanked, or sent to his room. He avoids these substitutes for the greater danger until he can understand it and avoid it for its own sake. But we ought to use this discipline only when it is necessary to protect the life, health, safety, or well-being of people or other living creatures, or to prevent destruction of things that people care about. We ought not to assume too long, as we usually do, that a child cannot understand the real nature of the danger from which we want to protect him. The sooner he avoids the danger, not to escape our punishment, but as a matter of good sense, the better. He can learn that faster than we think. In Mexico, for example, where people drive their cars with a good deal of spirit, I saw many children no older than five or four walking unattended on the streets. They understood about cars, they knew what to do. A child whose life is full of the threat and fear of punishment is locked into babyhood. There is no way for him to grow up, to learn to take responsibility for his life and acts. Most important of all, we should not assume that having to yield to the threat of our superior

force is good for the child's character. It is never good for *anyone's* character. To bow to superior force makes us feel impotent and cowardly for not having had the strength or courage to resist. Worse, it makes us resentful and vengeful. We can hardly wait to make someone pay for our humiliation, yield to us as we were once made to yield. No, if we cannot always avoid using the Discipline of Superior Force, we should at least use it as seldom as we can.

There are places where all three disciplines overlap. Any 4
very demanding human activity combines in it the disciplines of Superior Force, of Culture, and of Nature. The novice will be told, "Do it this way, never mind asking why, just do it that way, that is the way we always do it." But it probably *is* just the way they always do it, and usually for the very good reason that it is a way that has been found to work. Think, for example, of ballet training. The student in a class is told to do this exercise, or that; to stand so; to do this or that with his head, arms, shoulders, abdomen, hips, legs, feet. He is constantly corrected. There is no argument. But behind these seemingly autocratic demands by the teacher lie many decades of custom and tradition, and behind that, the necessities of dancing itself. You cannot make the moves of classical ballet unless over many years you have acquired, and renewed every day, the needed strength and suppleness in scores of muscles and joints. Nor can you do the difficult motions, making them look easy, unless you have learned hundreds of easier ones first. Dance teachers may not always agree on all the details of teaching these strengths and skills. But no novice could learn them all by himself. You could not go for a night or two to watch the ballet and then, without any other knowledge at all, teach yourself how to do it. In the same way, you would be unlikely to learn any complicated and difficult human activity without drawing heavily on the experience of those who know it better. But the point is that the authority of these experts or teachers stems from, grows out of their greater competence and experience, the fact that what they do *works,* not the fact that they happen to be the teacher and as such have the

power to kick a student out of the class. And the further point is that children are always and everywhere attracted to that competence, and ready and eager to submit themselves to a discipline that grows out of it. We hear constantly that children will never do anything unless compelled to by bribes or threats. But in their private lives, or in extracurricular activities in school, in sports, music, drama, art, running a newspaper, and so on, they often submit themselves willingly and wholeheartedly to very intense disciplines, simply because they want to learn to do a given thing well. Our Little-Napoleon football coaches, of whom we have too many and hear far too much, blind us to the fact that millions of children work hard every year getting better at sports and games without coaches barking and yelling at them.

For Study and Discussion

QUESTIONS FOR RESPONSE

1. How have you felt when you have been disciplined or had to discipline someone else?
2. On those occasions when you had to discipline yourself—to learn something, to change your behavior—how did you motivate yourself?

QUESTIONS ABOUT PURPOSE

1. What theory of education does Holt demonstrate by classifying these three types of discipline?
2. What is the main reason to avoid using the "Discipline of Superior Force"?

QUESTIONS ABOUT AUDIENCE

1. What does Holt assume about the knowledge and interest of his readers when he offers numerous examples from educational settings?

2. How does Holt's use of *we* in his discussion of the third type of discipline intensify his relationship with his readers?

QUESTIONS ABOUT STRATEGIES

1. How does Holt's use of examples of the "Discipline of Nature" differ from his use of examples of the "Discipline of Culture"?
2. How does Holt use the example of ballet training to illustrate how the three types of discipline overlap?

QUESTIONS FOR DISCUSSION

1. To what extent do you agree with Holt's assessment that children are eager to join the "network of agreements, customs, habits, and rules binding the adults together"? What factors discourage children from imitating such behavior?
2. What does Holt's analysis suggest about the relationship between knowledge and power?

GAIL SHEEHY

Gail Sheehy was born in 1937, attended the University of Vermont and Columbia University Journalism School, and worked as contributing editor for *New York* magazine for ten years. Her writing has appeared in *Esquire, McCall's, Ms.,* and *Rolling Stone.* Although Sheehy's first book was a novel, *Lovesounds* (1970), she soon turned to nonfiction, writing *Panthermania: The Clash of Black Against Black in One American City* (1971), *Hustling: Prostitution in Our Wide Open Society* (1973), and her best-selling *Passages: Predictable Crises of Adult Life* (1976). Her more recent books include a history of Cambodia, *The Spirit of Survival* (1986); an analysis of the presidential candidates, *Character: America's Search for Leadership* (1988); and a study of Mikhail Gorbachev, *The Man Who Changed the World* (1990). In "Predictable Crises of Adulthood," excerpted from the second chapter of *Passages,* Sheehy identifies six stages most adults experience between the ages of eighteen and fifty.

Predictable Crises of Adulthood

We are not unlike a particularly hardy crustacean. The lobster grows by developing and shedding a series of hard, protective shells. Each time it expands from within, the confining shell must be sloughed off. It is left exposed and vulnerable until, in time, a new covering grows to replace the old. 1

With each passage from one stage of human growth to the next we, too, must shed a protective structure. We are left exposed and vulnerable—but also yeasty and embryonic again, capable of stretching in ways we hadn't known before. These sheddings may take several years or more. Coming 2 out of each passage, though, we enter a longer and more stable period in which we can expect relative tranquillity and a sense of equilibrium regained. . . .

As we shall see, each person engages the steps of development in his or her own characteristic *step-style*. Some people never complete the whole sequence. And none of us "solves" with one step—by jumping out of the parental home into a job or marriage, for example—the problems in separating from the caregivers of childhood. Nor do we "achieve" autonomy once and for all by converting our dreams into concrete goals, even when we attain those goals. The central issues or tasks of one period are never fully completed, tied up, and cast aside. But when they lose their primacy and the current life structure has served its purpose, we are ready to move on to the next period. 3

Can one catch up? What might look to others like listlessness, contrariness, a maddening refusal to face up to an obvious task may be a person's own unique detour that will bring him out later on the other side. Developmental gains won can later be lost—and rewon. It's plausible, though it can't be proven, that the mastery of one set of tasks fortifies us for the next period and the next set of challenges. But it's important not to think too mechanistically. Machines work by units. The bureaucracy (supposedly) works step by step. Human beings, thank God, have an individual inner dynamic that can never be precisely coded. 4

Although I have indicated the ages when Americans are likely to go through each stage, and the differences between men and women where they are striking, do not take the ages too seriously. The stages are the thing, and most particularly the sequence. 5

Here is the briefest outline of the developmental ladder. 6

PULLING UP ROOTS

Before 18, the motto is loud and clear: "I have to get away from my parents." But the words are seldom connected to action. Generally still safely part of our families, even if away 7 at school, we feel our autonomy to be subject to erosion from moment to moment.

After 18, we begin Pulling Up Roots in earnest. College, military service, and short-term travels are all customary vehicles our society provides for the first round trips between family and a base of one's own. In the attempt to separate our view of the world from our family's view, despite vigorous protestations to the contrary—"I know exactly what I want!"—we cast about for any beliefs we can call our own. And in the process of testing those beliefs we are often drawn to fads, preferably those most mysterious and inaccessible to our parents. 8

Whatever tentative memberships we try out in the world, the fear haunts us that we are really kids who cannot take care of ourselves. We cover that fear with acts of defiance and mimicked confidence. For allies to replace our parents, we turn to our contemporaries. They become conspirators. So long as their perspective meshes with our own, they are able to substitute for the sanctuary of the family. But that doesn't last very long. And the instant they diverge from the shaky ideals of "our group," they are seen as betrayers. Rebounds to the family are common between the ages of 18 and 22. 9

The tasks of this passage are to locate ourselves in a peer group role, a sex role, an anticipated occupation, an ideology or world view. As a result, we gather the impetus to leave home physically and the identity to *begin* leaving home emotionally. 10

Even as one part of us seeks to be an individual, another part longs to restore the safety and comfort of merging with another. Thus one of the most popular myths of this passage is: We can piggyback our development by attaching to a Stronger One. But people who marry during this time often prolong financial and emotional ties to the family and relatives that impede them from becoming self-sufficient. 11

A stormy passage through the Pulling Up Roots years will probably facilitate the normal progression of the adult life cycle. If one doesn't have an identity crisis at this point, 12 it will erupt during a later transition, when the penalties may be harder to bear.

THE TRYING TWENTIES

The Trying Twenties confront us with the question of how to take hold in the adult world. Our focus shifts from the interior turmoils of late adolescence—"Who am I?" "What is truth?"—and we become almost totally preoccupied with working out the externals. "How do I put my aspirations into effect?" "What is the best way to start?" "Where do I go?" "Who can help me?" "How did *you* do it?" 13

In this period, which is longer and more stable compared with the passage that leads to it, the tasks are as enormous as they are exhilarating: To shape a Dream, that vision of ourselves which will generate energy, aliveness, and hope. To prepare for a lifework. To find a mentor if possible. And to form the capacity for intimacy, without losing in the process whatever consistency of self we have thus far mustered. The first test structure must be erected around the life we choose to try. 14

Doing what we "should" is the most pervasive theme of the twenties. The "shoulds" are largely defined by family models, the press of the culture, or the prejudices of our peers. If the prevailing cultural instructions are that one should get married and settle down behind one's own door, a nuclear family is born. If instead the peers insist that one should do one's own thing, the 25-year-old is likely to harness himself onto a Harley-Davidson and burn up Route 66 in the commitment to have no commitments. 15

One of the terrifying aspects of the twenties is the inner conviction that the choices we make are irrevocable. It is largely a false fear. Change is quite possible, and some alteration of our original choices is probably inevitable. 16

Two impulses, as always, are at work. One is to build a firm, safe structure for the future by making strong commitments, to "be set." Yet people who slip into a ready-made 17 form without much self-examination are likely to find themselves *locked in*.

The other urge is to explore and experiment, keeping any structure tentative and therefore easily reversible. Taken to the extreme, these are people who skip from one trial job and one limited personal encounter to another, spending their twenties in the *transient* state. 18

Although the choices of our twenties are not irrevocable, they do set in motion a Life Pattern. Some of us follow the locked-in pattern, others the transient pattern, the wunderkind pattern, the caregiver pattern, and there are a number of others. Such patterns strongly influence the particular questions raised for each person during each passage. . . . 19

Buoyed by powerful illusions and belief in the power of the will, we commonly insist in our twenties that what we have chosen to do is the one true course in life. Our backs go up at the merest hint that we are like our parents, that two decades of parental training might be reflected in our current actions and attitudes. 20

"Not me," is the motto, "I'm different." 21

CATCH-30

Impatient with devoting ourselves to the "shoulds," a new vitality springs from within as we approach 30. Men and women alike speak of feeling too narrow and restricted. They blame all sorts of things, but what the restrictions boil down to are the outgrowth of career and personal choices of the twenties. They may have been choices perfectly suited to that stage. But now the fit feels different. Some inner aspect that was left out is striving to be taken into account. Important new choices must be made, and commitments altered or deepened. The work involves great change, turmoil, and often crisis—a simultaneous feeling of rock bottom and the urge to bust out. 22

One common response is the tearing up of the life we spent most of our twenties putting together. It may mean striking out on a secondary road toward a new vision or 23 converting a dream of "running for president" into a more realistic goal. The single person feels a push to find a partner. The woman who was previously content at home with children chafes to venture into the world. The childless couple reconsiders children. And almost everyone who is married, especially those married for seven years, feels a discontent.

If the discontent doesn't lead to a divorce, it will, or should, call for a serious review of the marriage and of each partner's aspirations in the Catch-30 condition. The gist of that condition was expressed by a 29-year-old associate with a Wall Street law firm: 24

"I'm considering leaving the firm. I've been there four years now; I'm getting good feedback, but I have no clients of my own. I feel weak. If I wait much longer, it will be too late, too close to that fateful time of decision on whether or not to become a partner. I'm success-oriented. But the concept of being 55 years old and stuck in a monotonous job drives me wild. It drives me crazy now, just a little bit. I'd say that 85 percent of the time I thoroughly enjoy my work. But when I get a screwball case, I come away from court saying, 'What am I doing here?' It's a *visceral* reaction that I'm wasting my time. I'm trying to find some way to make a social contribution or a slot in city government. I keep saying, 'There's something more.'" 25

Besides the push to broaden himself professionally, there is a wish to expand his personal life. He wants two or three more children. "The concept of a home has become very meaningful to me, a place to get away from troubles and relax. I love my son in a way I could not have anticipated. I never could live alone." 26

Consumed with the work of making his own critical life-steering decisions, he demonstrates the essential shift at this age: an absolute requirement to be more self-concerned. The self has new value now that his competency has been proved. 27

His wife is struggling with her own age-30 priorities. She wants to go to law school, but he wants more children. If she is going to stay home, she wants him to make more time for the family instead of taking on even wider professional 28 commitments. His view of the bind, of what he would most like from his wife, is this:

"I'd like not to be bothered. It sounds cruel, but I'd like not to have to worry about what she's going to do next week. Which is why I've told her several times that I think she should do something. Go back to school and get a degree in social work or geography or whatever. Hopefully that would fulfill her, and then I wouldn't have to worry about her line of problems. I want her to be decisive about herself." 29

The trouble with his advice to his wife is that it comes out of concern with *his* convenience, rather than with *her* development. She quickly picks up on this lack of goodwill: He is trying to dispose of her. At the same time, he refuses her the same latitude to be "selfish" in making an independent decision to broaden her own horizons. Both perceive a lack of mutuality. And that is what Catch-30 is all about for the couple. 30

ROOTING AND EXTENDING

Life becomes less provisional, more rational and orderly in the early thirties. We begin to settle down in the full sense. Most of us begin putting down roots and sending out new shoots. People buy houses and become very earnest about climbing career ladders. Men in particular concern themselves with "making it." Satisfaction with marriage generally goes downhill in the thirties (for those who have remained together) compared with the highly valued, vision-supporting marriage of the twenties. This coincides with the couple's reduced social life outside the family and the in-turned focus on raising their children. 31

THE DEADLINE DECADE

In the middle of the thirties we come upon a crossroads. We have reached the halfway mark. Yet even as we are reaching our prime, we begin to see there is a place where it finishes. Time starts to squeeze. 32

The loss of youth, the faltering of physical powers we have always taken for granted, the fading purpose of stereotyped roles by which we have thus far identified ourselves, the spiritual dilemma of having no absolute answers—any or all of these shocks can give this passage the character of crisis. Such thoughts usher in a decade between 35 and 45 that can be called the Deadline Decade. It is a time of both danger and opportunity. All of us have the chance to rework the narrow identity by which we defined ourselves in the first half of life. And those of us who make the most of the opportunity will have a full-out authenticity crisis. 33

To come through this authenticity crisis, we must reexamine our purposes and reevaluate how to spend our resources from now on. "Why am I doing all this? What do I really believe in?" No matter what we have been doing, there will be parts of ourselves that have been suppressed and now need to find expression. "Bad" feelings will demand acknowledgment along with the good. 34

It is frightening to step off onto the treacherous footbridge leading to the second half of life. We can't take everything with us on this journey through uncertainty. Along the way, we discover that we are alone. We no longer have to ask permission because we are the providers of our own safety. We must learn to give ourselves permission. We stumble upon feminine or masculine aspects of our natures that up to this time have usually been masked. There is grieving to be done because an old self is dying. By taking in our suppressed and even our unwanted parts, we prepare at the gut level for the reintegration of an identity that is ours and ours alone—not some artificial form put together to please the culture or our mates. It is a dark passage at the beginning. But by disassembling ourselves, we can glimpse the light and gather our parts into a renewal. 35

Women sense this inner crossroads earlier than men do. The time pinch often prompts a woman to stop and take an all-points survey at age 35. Whatever options she has already played out, she feels a "my last chance" urgency to review those options she has set aside and those that aging and 36 biology will close off in the *now foreseeable* future. For all her qualms and confusion about where to start looking for a new future, she usually enjoys an exhilaration of release. Assertiveness begins rising. There are so many firsts ahead.

Men, too, feel the time push in the mid-thirties. Most 37
men respond by pressing down harder on the career accelerator. It's "my last chance" to pull away from the pack. It is no longer enough to be the loyal junior executive, the promising young novelist, the lawyer who does a little *pro bono* work on the side. He wants now to become part of top management, to be recognized as an established writer, or an active politician with his own legislative program. With some chagrin, he discovers that he has been too anxious to please and too vulnerable to criticism. He wants to put together his own ship.

During this period of intense concentration on external 38
advancement, it is common for men to be unaware of the more difficult, gut issues that are propelling them forward. The survey that was neglected at 35 becomes a crucible at 40. Whatever rung of achievement he has reached, the man of 40 usually feels stale, restless, burdened, and unappreciated. He worries about his health. He wonders, "Is this all there is?" He may make a series of departures from well-established lifelong base lines, including marriage. More and more men are seeking second careers in midlife. Some become self-destructive. And many men in their forties experience a major shift of emphasis away from pouring all their energies into their own advancement. A more tender, feeling side comes into play. They become interested in developing an ethical self.

RENEWAL OR RESIGNATION

Somewhere in the mid-forties, equilibrium is regained. A 39
new stability is achieved, which may be more or less satisfying.

If one has refused to budge through the midlife transition, 40
the sense of staleness will calcify into resignation. One by

one, the safety and supports will be withdrawn from the person who is standing still. Parents will become children; children will become strangers; a mate will grow away or go away; the career will become just a job—and each of these events will be felt as an abandonment. The crisis will probably emerge again around 50. And although its wallop will be greater, the jolt may be just what is needed to prod the resigned middle-ager toward seeking revitalization.

On the other hand . . . 41

If we have confronted ourselves in the middle passage and found a renewal of purpose around which we are eager to build a more authentic life structure, these may well be the best years. Personal happiness takes a sharp turn upward for partners who can now accept the fact: "I cannot expect *anyone* to fully understand me." Parents can be forgiven for the burdens of our childhood. Children can be let go without leaving us in collapsed silence. At 50, there is a new warmth and mellowing. Friends become more important than ever, but so does privacy. Since it is so often proclaimed by people past midlife, the motto of this stage might be "No more bullshit." 42

For Study and Discussion

QUESTIONS FOR RESPONSE

1. Does it reassure or infuriate you when what you assume is your own idiosyncratic behavior is classified as "normal" for your age? Explain your answer.
2. How much confidence do you have in Sheehy's system? What kinds of evidence do you think she used to organize it?

QUESTIONS ABOUT PURPOSE

1. What is Sheehy's purpose—to define the various stages of human development or to analyze the process of moving (or the consequences of not moving) from one stage to another?

2. What do the words *predictable* and *crisis* contribute to Sheehy's purpose?

QUESTIONS ABOUT AUDIENCE

1. Who does Sheehy imagine as the readers of her essay: general readers, psychologists, people who are stuck in one stage, or people who have successfully navigated the passage from stage to stage?
2. How does Sheehy use the pronoun *we* to establish a relationship with her readers?

QUESTIONS ABOUT STRATEGIES

1. How does Sheehy use the opening metaphor of the lobster shedding its shell to clarify the system of development she intends to classify?
2. How effective are the headings Sheehy uses to identify the six stages of development?

QUESTIONS FOR DISCUSSION

1. What assumptions about growth does Sheehy make by stopping her system at age fifty? Suggest some crises (and stages) for the years after fifty.
2. What problems do psychologists encounter when they try to make generalizations about human behavior? For example, how does Sheehy's classification system compare with those designed for early childhood and adolescence?

JOSEPH EPSTEIN

Joseph Epstein was born in 1937 in Chicago and was educated at the University of Chicago. He edits *American Scholar,* the quarterly journal of the national honor society Phi Beta Kappa, and is a visiting lecturer in English at Northwestern University. His learned essays on American life and letters, sometimes written under the pseudonym Aristides, have appeared in magazines such as *American Scholar, Harper's,* the *New Yorker,* and the *New York Times Magazine.* His books include *Divorced in America: Marriage in an Age of Possibility* (1974), *Ambition: The Secret Passion* (1981), *The Middle of My Tether: Familiar Essays* (1983), *Plausible Prejudices: Essays on American Writing* (1985), and *Partial Payments* (1989). In "They Told Me You Was High Class," reprinted from *American Scholar,* Epstein explains why the divisions in America's social class system have "lost much of their descriptive power."

They Told Me You Was High Class

Karl, Friedrich, forgive me, fellas, for never having taken much interest in your class struggle, but the truth is that for the better part of my life I have been a bit unclear about what class I myself belong to. If the phrase didn't imply that I was of a higher social class than I am—and make me sound like an Englishman into the bargain—I should call the whole thing a frightful muddle. More than a mite confusing it is, though. How nice to be able to say with confidence, as George Orwell once did, that one is "lower-upper-middle class." Yet, unless I am quite wrong, such terms have now lost much of their descriptive power. The social pace has quickened; nowadays people move in and out of social classes 1 with greater rapidity than ever before. Sometimes I wonder if today social class, at least as we used to think of it in this country, has about as much relevance as an electric salad fork and as bright a future as a cha-cha instructor in Montana.

Social mobility—the jumping or, more commonly, sliding from one class to another—is scarcely a new phenomenon. Chekhov, to cite an interesting instance, had a grandfather who bought himself out of serfdom and a nephew who became a Hollywood producer. I myself have a cousin, ten years older than I, named Moe and a niece, thirty years younger than I, named Nicole; and to go from Moe to Nicole in only forty years is in some respects to travel farther than the Chekhovs did from Voronezh Province to Beverly Hills. Other evidence of our whirring social flux can readily be adduced. The janitor of the apartment building I live in has published a book; it is not, granted, a slender little volume on the poetry of the Comte Robert de Montesquiou but instead a book about the martial arts; yet the same man is a janitor and a published author. The other day, in Manhattan, I had the bite put on me by a panhandler wearing a rumpled but still a real Ralph Lauren shirt; and it occurred to me shortly afterward that, should I ever hit the skids, I may not have the wardrobe to go on the bum. Just when you begin to think you understand a thing or two about the drama of life, they change the scenery and send in a whole new cast of characters. 2

Cracks, major fault lines, in the class system, may be a world-wide phenomenon. Peregrine Worsthorne, the British political writer, recently noted in *The Spectator* that "the class system has changed out of all recognition in my lifetime." Certainly, social distinctions in America have become vastly less clear in my own. When does a child first notice such distinctions? My own first realization that the world was a place filled with social differences might have been the gross recognition that some people lived rather better than we and others rather worse. It might have been the woman, whose name was Emma, who came in to clean for us on Tuesdays, for I seem to recall thinking it peculiar that someone would 3 clean a place not her own. It might have had to do with automobiles, for we lived on a street that was a thoroughfare, and the first organized knowledge I acquired as a child had to do with telling the difference between cars; and it could not have been long before I also learned that some cars (Cadillacs, Packards, Lincolns) were held in higher regard than others (Fords, Studebakers, Plymouths). These were the years of World War II, during which my father drove a green 1942 Dodge sedan.

If our family had a crest, that green 1942 Dodge sedan ought to be at its center. That car placed us—socially, financially, and stylistically—and where it placed us was slam-bang in the middle. Our family was not so much socially uninteresting as socially uninterested. If life is in some sense a status race, my parents never noticed the flag drop. While we owned possessions roughly comparable to those owned by our neighbors, we showed no passion for the subtleties of social life. Even when the money was there to do so, it would never have occurred to my parents to join a city club or country club or to move to a fashionable address—a residence with social resonance. Their notion of the good life was to live comfortably, always well within their means, and insofar as possible never to pay for pretension. Then as now that seems to me quite sensible—though I must add, I myself have not had the character to live up to it. 4

I have omitted a social fact of no small significance and even greater complication. The fact is that I am Jewish. I was born thus, and thus I shall remain; and it is exceedingly difficult to be Jewish and not have a somewhat heightened sense of social and class distinctions. Not for nothing was the keenest modern observer of such distinctions, Marcel Proust, half Jewish and fully homosexual; after all, a man who is in danger of being despised from two different directions learns to devise sensitive antennae. Another sharp observer of social gradations, Anton Chekhov, was neither Jewish nor homosexual; but he was lowborn, the son of a bankrupt grocer, the grandson of a serf, and that put the antennae permanently on his roof. In a famous letter to his friend and publisher, Alexey Suvorin, Chekhov explained his 5 own social unease when he wrote that "what aristocratic writers take from nature gratis, the less privileged must pay for with their youth," adding that he had had to squeeze "the slave out of himself drop by drop" before he "finds that the blood coursing through his veins is no longer the blood of a slave, but that of a real human being."

Let me hasten to insert that I never for a moment felt the 6
least like a slave. Doubtless this was in large part owing to having a father who was successful yet in no way tyrannical or crushing, on the model, say, of Papa Kafka. My father, along with giving me the reassuring sense that I was working with a net under me, encouraged me to believe that I came of a family capable of serious achievement. But my father also alerted me early to the alarming fact that people might detest me for reasons having nothing to do with my character or conduct and everything to do with my religion. I must have been four or five years old when the potential social consequences of being Jewish were thus impinged upon me. In the 1940s and early 1950s the word—the euphemism, really—for de facto anti-Semitic arrangements was "restricted"; and in those years many neighborhoods and suburbs, clubs and resorts, fraternities and sororities were restricted.

I would be a liar if I said that knowledge of such things 7
didn't bother me. But I would be an even greater liar if I said that it bothered me very much. When I was growing up, we lived in neighborhoods that tended to be at least 50 percent Jewish, and the same was true of the public schools I attended. If anything, this encouraged me in the belief that Jews were rather superior—a belief based, unknowingly, on social class. What I didn't know was that the non-Jews who remained in the neighborhoods we lived in were mainly people who for one reason or another were probably unable to depart them. In other words, most of the non-Jews I went to grade school and high school with were the sons and daughters of the working class or the lower white-collar classes, while the Jews tended to be among the newly surging middle classes, still very much on the make.

Although so far as I know I have never been the victim 8

of any serious anti-Semitic acts, the first time I recall feeling rather out of the social mainstream because I was Jewish was during a year I spent as a freshman student at the University of Illinois in the middle 1950s. Illinois was very much a school of fraternities and sororities—a "Greek campus," as it was called—and I, who had not yet developed socially to the point of knowing there was something in the world called nonconformity, accepted an invitation to join what was thought to be the best of the Jewish fraternities. (All non-Jewish fraternities and sororities at Illinois were then "restricted.") The reigning spirit at the university in those days, far from being the Jewish and metropolitan one I was used to, was Protestant and small town—a midwestern, somewhat more yokelish version of the muscular Christianity that George Santayana found several decades earlier prevailing at Yale. The student who seemed to me best to represent this spirit was a young man from Peoria named Hiles Stout. Stout was a Sigma Chi and played three major sports for the university and resembled e. e. cummings's conscientious objector Olaf only in being "more brave than me:more blond than you"—though perhaps it would be more accurate to say that he was "more Hiles than me:more Stout than you."

I did not so much feel outclassed or declassed at the University of Illinois as I felt myself on the outside of a house I had no particular desire to enter. For while attending the University of Illinois, I had informally enrolled at good old Mencken-Lewis-Dreiser University, where I learned a haughty if not especially original disdain for the middle class, that inartistic and uninspired group also known as the booboisie—that is to say, a disdain for the social class and culture from which, apart from being Jewish, I myself had derived. From MLDU, beloved alma mater, I learned not to join the class struggle but instead to disassociate myself, insofar as possible, from my own class. 9

As a step in that direction, I transferred to the University of Chicago, which was perhaps as close as I have ever come to living in a classless society—I refer to the student segment of university society—and rather closer than I ever again care 10 to come. A few fraternities remained at the University of Chicago at that time, but far from being thought in any way admirable, the chief attitude toward them was a mixture of mild contempt and apathy. Wealth and genteel birth counted for naught at the University of Chicago; apart from books and classical records, material possessions were thought the sign of a cramped spirit. Physical beauty and social graces were held to be beside the point, and the standard joke of the day had it that a panty raid on one of the women's dormitories netted a fatigue jacket and a single combat boot. A passionate bohemianism was what the University of Chicago student body aspired to; a grim scruffiness was what it often achieved.

Intellectually, the University of Chicago strove much higher, holding four tasks in life to be worthwhile: to be an artist, to be a scientist, to be a statesman, or to be a teacher of artists, scientists, or statesmen. In this regard the University of Chicago was not anti-middle class in the abrasive manner of Sinclair Lewis and H. L. Mencken; it was para-middle class by its tacit implication that there were higher things in life than getting a good job, earning a living, raising a family, and getting on. Chamfort once said that society was divided between those who had more dinners than appetite and those who had more appetite than dinners, but at the University of Chicago the division was between those who loved art and learning and those who did not, and those who loved it were thought better. 11

If the University of Chicago was relatively free of conventional social-class considerations, the United States Army, the institution in which I was to spend the next two years of my life, was, at least formally, as class-bound as any society I have ever lived in. The first—and chief—class distinction was the patent one between officers and enlisted men. Officers ate, slept, dressed, and were paid better. Obeisance needed to be paid them in the form of salutes and in addressing them as "sir." Theirs was a strikingly better deal; one didn't have to be Alexis de Tocqueville to notice that. As an enlisted man who as a boy was never required to learn 12 the habits of obeisance, I could not help marveling at the vast social discrepancies between officers and enlisted men. I did not so much resent them as wonder how career noncommissioned officers managed to tolerate them, especially in a peacetime army, when an officer's responsibilities were less and the call on his bravery nonexistent. Confronted for the first time with a codified class system, I found myself more of a democrat than I had imagined.

At the same time that the U.S. Army was rigidly hierar- 13
chical and held together by the idea of rank, no American institution was, at its core, more democratic. Well in advance of the larger society of which it was a part, the U.S. Army had integrated its facilities and was color-blind in its promotions and other procedures. As an enlisted man, one was really thrown into the stew of American life. In my own basic-training platoon I lived with Missouri farmers, Appalachian miners, an American Indian auto mechanic, a black car salesman from Detroit, a Jewish lawyer from Chicago, a fundamentalist high school teacher from Kansas, and others no less varied but now lost to memory. It felt, at moments, like living in a badly directed screen version of *Leaves of Grass*. Although I groaned and cursed, questioning the heavens for putting me through the torture in tedium that I then took my time in the Army to be, I have since come to view that time as one of the most interesting interludes in my life—among other reasons because it jerked me free, if only for a few years, from the social classes in which I have otherwise spent nearly all my days. It jerked everyone free from his social class, however high or low that class may have been, and yet somehow, despite the jolt, it seemed to work.

Or at least it seemed to work most of the time. A case 14
where it didn't was that of Samuel Schuyler III, whom I worked with as a fellow enlisted man in the Public Information Office at Fort Hood, Texas. The Third, as I always thought of him, had gone to the Wharton School of Business, hungered for the country-club ease he was missing while in the Army, and drove a black Cadillac convertible, the current year's model. Despite the numeral affixed to his name, the Third was without social pretensions; he was a

simple hedonist and a straight money man. How he had come to own that Cadillac convertible at the age of twenty-three I never discovered—my own social-class manners, I now suppose, prevented me from asking—but he played the stock market fairly often, calling his broker in Pittsburgh to place his orders.

What was not difficult to discover was the Third's con- 15
tempt for everyone around him, officers and enlisted men both. (Only a few acquaintances, of whom for some reason I was one, were spared.) Forms through which to express this contempt were not wanting to him. The Third had developed a salute that, while formally correct, made every officer to whom he tendered it think at least twice about it; there was about this salute the faint yet almost unmistakable suggestion that its recipient go forth to exercise an anatomical impossibility upon himself. Driving on the post in his black Cadillac, the Third was everywhere taken for the post commander—who himself drove a more modest car, a Buick—and everyone, even up to the rank of bird colonel, dropped everything to salute him, only to receive in turn the Third's own extraordinary salute. The Third even dressed with contempt. If there is a word that is the antonym of "panache," I should avail myself of it to describe the deliberately slovenly way that he wore his uniform. In mufti, meanwhile, no muted Ivy League dresser, the Third preferred draped trousers, alligator shoes, and in shirts showed an unfortunate penchant for the color known as dubonnet. Toward the close of his enlistment, the Third was promoted from Pfc. to Sp4c. but refused the promotion on the grounds that the additional money wasn't worth the trouble of sewing new patches on his uniforms. No gesture better summed up his refusal to partake of military class arrangements; he scoffed at them every chance he got, making clear that, short of doing anything that could land him in the stockade, he chose not to play the game. His lofty contempt earned him a great deal of not-so-lofty hatred. The Third knew he was hated and felt about this much as he did about his promotion—he could not, that is, have cared less.

I cared rather more, in the Army and elsewhere, because 16

social class has always seemed to me intrinsically fascinating. I have inevitably been interested in attempting to take the measure of any class system in which I found myself, though when young I must often have been, as Henry James might have put it, destitute of the materials requisite for measurement. A fantasy about social class said to be common among children, especially children fed ample rations of fairy tales, is that one's parents are not one's real parents but instead that one is much higher born—and is probably, as will surely one day be revealed, a prince or princess. My fantasy, taken up in early adolescence and not quite dropped to this day, is that I can roam freely from social class to social class, comfortable everywhere and everywhere welcome. Sometimes I think it would be more realistic to believe that one is the last of the Romanovs.

Not that I am a proletarian fancier, the American equiv- 17
alent of a Narodnik or a Slavophile. There is something inherently condescending in assigning special qualities to the lower class. Dorothy Parker, after being told that Clare Boothe Luce was always kind to her inferiors, is supposed to have asked, "And where does she find them?" But I like to view myself as being able to slip from class to class because I detest the notion of one's destiny being absolutely determined by birth and social upbringing; I readily grant the importance of both but not their decisiveness. I myself dislike being labeled too easily, being understood too quickly. Neither a strict Marxist nor a straight Freudian be—such is the advice of this old Polonius. Accept the possibility of all influences; reject the fiats of all absolute determinants.

The old, received wisdom about social class is that one is 18
supposed to dislike the class just below one's own and gaze yearningly upon those above one's own. But I find that the only class whose members can sometimes get me worked up are the upper classes, or what is left of them after taxes and the Zeitgeist have done their work. A plummy upper-class English accent with nothing behind it but enormous self-satisfaction can, in the proper mood, still bring out the residual Red in me. My Anglophilia, which may have had

behind it a certain social-class longing, seems to have slipped badly in recent years; today, apart from being somewhat regretful about not having gone to an Oxbridge college when a boy, I have only one regret about not being English, which is that, because I am not, I cannot be permitted to use the word "whilst" without seeming affected. The upper class of my own country now seems to me, when it is not sad, mostly comic. The traditional WASP-ocracy seems to have left the field without firing a shot; they resemble nothing so much as white Russians, with the serious proviso that they appear to have been forced into exile without actually leaving their own country. One reads about them nowadays at play in Newport or in Charleston, or in repose at the Somerset Club in Boston, or sees them decked out for a photographer from *Town & Country,* but they seem rather desiccated and plain tuckered out.

It is a bit difficult to have a serious class system when, as in this country at present, you don't have a convincing upper class. So long as there is a convincing upper class, other classes in the society at least know what to imitate, however absurd the imitation. I can attest to this when I recall that, in 1950, as a boy of thirteen growing up in a middle-class, mostly Jewish neighborhood, I and several of my pals attended a class in ballroom dancing called Fortnightly. It was held at the field house of a public park, was taught by a couple of very correct posture and general deportment whom I now think would be best described as "shabby genteel," and, despite the name Fortnightly, met every Saturday afternoon. What we did in this class was, in effect, prepare for a cotillion none of us would ever attend. Young ladies sat on one side of the room, young gentlemen on the other; young gentlemen crossed the room to ask young ladies to dance, and to dance waltzes, fox trots, and other, rather intricate dances and steps that this young gentleman, aging fast, has still never had to press into service. 19

The decisive moment in the defeat of upper-class, capital-*S* Society may have come when, in newspapers all over the nation, what used to be called the Society page was replaced by 20 the Style section. The old Society page, with its accounts of engagements and weddings, charity balls and coming-out parties, tended to be boring and silly; while the new Style section, with its accounts of designer clothing, gourmandizing, and the trend of the moment, tends to be lively and silly. The Society page, like Society itself, began to go under sometime in the middle 1960s, which was not exactly a felicitous time for establishments of many kinds. Not that the sixties did away with class consciousness; it attempted instead to reorient such consciousness in favor of other classes. The animus of the sixties generation, expressed in its popular culture, was against both upper- and middle-class life. In their place it wished to substitute ethnic pride and, as expressed by such groups as the Beatles and the Rolling Stones, something of a working-class ethos, with sexual freedom and drug use added. Even in England, that most traditional of class-bound countries, according to the English journalist Jilly Cooper, "working-class became beautiful and everyone from Princess Anne downwards spat the plums out of their mouths, embraced the flat 'a' and talked with a working-class accent."

Not many people outside of it are likely to have been sorry 21 to see the old upper class in this country pushed rudely to the sidelines. The upper class had a lot to apologize for, and in many ways it is still apologizing. In wealthy Fairfield County, Connecticut, in the town of Darien (the setting for Laura Hobson's novel about genteel anti-Semitism, *Gentleman's Agreement*), a local newspaper, according to *The New York Times,* ran an article by a high school girl attacking the town for its lack of social diversity. "I am," this girl wrote, "a white Protestant living in a basically white Protestant community. I lack the richness and cultural background gained from a diversified environment. What are you, the townspeople, going to do about it?" Few things so lower the morale, and raise the gorge, as being lectured to by one's own children. One of these things may be being lectured to on the same grounds by the clergymen of one's church, and no church in America has gone at this task more relentlessly than the Episcopalian church, once *the* church of the old upper classes if there is truth in the one-sentence sociology of religion that holds: A Methodist is a Baptist with shoes, a Presbyterian is a Methodist who has gone to college, and an Episcopalian is a Presbyterian living off his investments.

Although much that was once thought to represent upper- 22
class life appears to have been routed, much more lives on, often in attenuated and snobbish form. Contemned the old upper class may be, yet the line of people hopefully awaiting their children's enrollment in such formerly exclusively upper-class prep schools as Choate, Groton, Exeter, and Saint Paul's has not, my guess is, in any serious way diminished. Most middle-class students who have a wide choice will tend to choose universities favored by the old upper classes; and most university professors, given a similar choice in institutions, will do the same—a tenured professor who has left Princeton for Purdue, or Harvard for Hofstra, or Yale for Ypsilanti Community College is a fit candidate for the television show called "That's Incredible."

Freud said that it was better to be an ancestor, which he 23
turns out to have been, than to have ancestors, which he lacked. But surely better still is both to be an ancestor and to have ancestors. In literary life I can think of at least three living writers whose careers owe more than a little to upper-class cachet: Gore Vidal, who at every opportunity brings his family connections into his writing; William F. Buckley, who attempts to live like an aristocrat, though without much in the way of aristocratic leisure; and George Plimpton, whose many autobiographical books on the subject of sports have about them something of the aura of slumming. (I do not count Louis Auchincloss, a novelist whose subject is often the eclipse of the upper class in which he grew up.) All three men are, in accent, neither chummy nor unplummy.

If he were still alive, I should most certainly count in 24
Robert Lowell, whose ancestors were reputed to speak only to God and who, before his death, was generally conceded to be this country's first poet. Without for a moment claiming that Lowell set out to exploit his upper-class genealogy,

neither can one for another moment disclaim the importance of that genealogy to Lowell's poetry. Elizabeth Bishop once told Lowell: "All you have to do is put down the names! And the fact that it seems significant, illustrative, American, etc., gives you, I think, the confidence you display about tackling any idea or theme, *seriously,* in both writing and conversation. In some ways you are the luckiest poet I know." Was Elizabeth Bishop correct? Let us change some of those names she claimed Lowell had only to mention. What if Lowell's poem "My Last Afternoon with Uncle Devereux Winslow" were instead entitled "My Last Afternoon with Uncle Morris Shapiro," or his "Terminal Days at Beverly Farms" were instead entitled "Terminal Days at Grossinger's"? (Actually, given that resort's famously rich provender, any day at Grossinger's could be terminal.) Not quite the same, perhaps you will agree.

But then neither is anti-Semitism in the United States 25
quite the same as it once was, or else I could not make the kind of easy joke that I just did about the titles of Robert Lowell's poems, at least not in print. Whether anti-Semitism is today less, whether racism has greatly diminished, cannot be known with certainty; my sense is that they both are much reduced. But what can be known is that neither is any longer officially recognized in restricted or segregated arrangements, and this, along with marking impressive progress, has made for significant changes in the American class system. Whereas the retreat of the old upper class has blown the roof off the system, the demise of official and quasi-official discrimination has uprooted the basement. The metaphor I seem to be building toward here is a class system that resembles an open-air ranch house. Strange edifice, this, but then socially many strange things appear to have taken place in recent years. In many industries union wages have placed many union workers, financially at least, into the upper reaches of the middle class, while attending college, once the ultimate rite of passage into solid middle-class respectability, no longer inevitably accomplishes this task—owing doubtless to the spread and watering down of higher

education. There is a great deal of senseless and haphazard luxury in the land. Athletes and rock stars, many of them made millionaires before they are thirty, are removed from the financial wars for all their days. Meanwhile a servant class has all but disappeared. A daughter from the working class uses part of her wages from working at the supermarket to buy designer jeans, while a son of Scarsdale comes into Manhattan to acquire his duds at a Salvation Army thrift shop. The other day, in a parking lot near where I live, I noted a rather dingy Saab automobile, with an antenna for a telephone on its roof, an Oberlin College decal on its back window, and bumper stickers reading "National Computer Camp" and "I Support Greenpeace." Now there is a vehicle with a lot of class—and, symbolic of our time, a lot of class confusions.

If that car isn't owned by someone from what today passes 26 for the upper-middle class, I'll buy you a salmon mousse and a manual on how your children can raise their SAT scores fully thirty points. "The upper-middle classes," writes Jilly Cooper, "are the most intelligent and highly educated of all the classes, and therefore the silliest and most sensitive to every new trend: radical chic, health food, ethnic clothes, bra-lessness, gifted children, French cooking." The members of the upper-middle class that Miss Cooper has in mind are mostly newly risen and, not always sure where they are, insecure about where they are headed. This upper-middle class is not to be confused with the nouveau riche. The former tends to be rather better educated, immensely concerned with what it understands to be good taste, and serious if also a little worried about culture—very little that one could think of, in fact, would be more wounding to members of this upper-middle class than to be taken for nouveau riche. I think I know what I am talking about here; this upper-middle class is my milieu—or, as the writer Josephine Herbst used to call it, my "maloo."

When I say that the upper-middle class is my maloo, I do 27 not mean that I am quite of that class. Strictly speaking, I am fairly sure that I do not qualify financially. I do not drive a BMW, a Mercedes, or a Jaguar; I do not dream of driving such cars, and if I leave the earth without owning one or the other of them, I shall not, for that reason, die with a frown on my face (I cannot otherwise promise to depart smiling). I own no works of art, nor do I aspire to own anything above the level of an unnumbered print. No espresso machine sits on the counter of my kitchen, no mousse molds sit upon the shelves of my cabinets. From the tax standpoint, I do not earn enough money now, nor do I soon expect to earn enough, to cry out, in the words of the rock 'n' roll song, "Gimme shelter." Do not get me wrong. I should not in the least mind driving off in a Mercedes 380 SL, a Turner watercolor locked in its trunk, on my way to have a cappuccino with my tax lawyer. But my mind, the great wanderer, does not linger long on such things. Expensive good taste, that sine qua non of the new upper-middle class, is not my sine qua non. I do not despise it; I am not in the least uncomfortable around it; but I do not live for it.

What, then, do I live for? Apart from love for my family 28
and friends, I live for words. I live for the delights of talking and reading and writing. I am content when talking with people I adore or admire or at least feel I can learn a little something from; I am happy when I am reading something fine or subtle or powerful; and I am delirious when I am writing something of which I am not altogether ashamed. If one's social class is defined, at least in part, by one's wishes, then I ought perhaps to be defined as a member of what I think of as the verbal class—someone, that is, who both earns his livelihood and derives his greatest pleasure from words. Membership in the verbal class has its advantages and its disadvantages: the hours are a bit crazy, but, like the village idiot posted at the town gates to await the arrival of the messiah, at least you are never out of work.

The term "verbal class" is meant to be almost purely de- 29
scriptive; nothing, certainly, honorific is intended by it. Orwell, who did not use the term "verbal class," did once refer to "the new aristocracy" of professors, publicists, and journalists who in large part comprise the verbal class; he did so

in the portion of *1984* that purports to be from Emmanuel Goldstein's manuscript, where this new aristocracy is described as "less tempted by luxury, hungrier for pure power" than their opposite numbers in past ages. In Chekhov's time the verbal class of our day and the new aristocracy of *1984* would have been described as the intelligentsia. This is the same intelligentsia of whom Chekhov, in a letter to a friend, writes: "I have no faith in our intelligentsia; it is hypocritical, dishonest, hysterical, ill-bred, and lazy." Which made them, in Chekhov's view, quite as wretched as any other social class, though perhaps a bit worse because the pretensions of the intelligentsia were more extravagant and its complaints better formulated and more insistently expressed. Read Chekhov and, in questions of social class, one soon becomes a Chekhovian. "I have faith in individuals," he wrote. "I see salvation in individuals scattered here and there . . . be they intellectuals or peasants, for they're the ones who really matter, though they are few."

Yet my sense is that the verbal class has risen slightly in 30
recent years. It has not done so, near as I can make out, because of any improvement in its members' general mental acuity or civic valor. The verbal class appears instead to be rising by default. Members of the verbal class, odd fish that they are, seem able to swim easily through a fluid social scene—and the American social scene at present seems extremely fluid. John Adams spoke of his studying "politics and war that my sons may have the liberty to study mathematics and philosophy," but what would he have thought of men who studied real estate and the stock market that their daughters may have the liberty to study Marxist historiography and their sons become, through downward mobility, carpenters in Vancouver? He would probably think his wife, Abigail, very clever for describing the American people as "the mobility."

"Classless Soviet Is Far Off, Siberian Scholar Says." So 31
read a recent headline in *The New York Times*. It is difficult to doubt such authority, for surely one of the quickest ways of telling that a classless society is far off is merely to live in

Siberia. My guess is that a classless society is roughly as near completion in the Soviet Union as it is in the United States—which isn't very near at all. Not that this even remotely suggests the need for intensifying the class struggle. Take it from a member of the verbal class: in a real class struggle one is lucky to end up with a draw, except that it inevitably turns out to have been a very bloody draw.

I see the serious class struggle as that of men and women singly fighting off being entirely shaped by the social class into which they were born. Insularity, unimaginativeness, self-satisfaction—each social class has its own special drawbacks, blindnesses, vices. "Vices" reminds me of a story a friend of mine, a man born into the English working class, used to tell about a shop class he was required to take at a grammar school in London. It was taught by a flinty little Scotsman who, when he wanted the class's attention in order to make an announcement, used to cry out, "Stand by your vices, boys!" When we think too exclusively as members of our social class, we all, essentially, stand by our vices. I should have thought the trick of becoming a human being is to stand away from them. 32

For Study and Discussion

QUESTIONS FOR RESPONSE

1. How would you characterize your social class? What clues (income, education, possessions) do you use to identify your class?
2. How would you characterize the people in the class above you and the class below you? What is your attitude toward these people?

QUESTIONS ABOUT PURPOSE

1. What does Epstein want to demonstrate about the "descriptive power" of class labels?
2. How does his assertion that most people attempt to fight off

"being entirely shaped by the social class into which they were born" modify his purpose?

QUESTIONS ABOUT AUDIENCE

1. This essay was written for *American Scholar,* the official journal of the Phi Beta Kappa Society. What is the "class" standing of the readers of this publication?
2. How do Epstein's allusions and examples—for example, "Karl, Friedrich, forgive me,"—identify his assumptions about the "verbal class" of his readers?

QUESTIONS ABOUT STRATEGIES

1. How does Epstein use his experience at the University of Illinois and the University of Chicago to illustrate two different class systems?
2. How does his discussion of the army and Samuel Schuyler III demonstrate his thesis that the class system has lost much of its power?

QUESTIONS FOR DISCUSSION

1. What does the change from Society page to Style section in the newspaper indicate about how class is currently defined in our culture?
2. To what extent is class determined by birth and upbringing? What factors enable or prevent people from roaming "freely from social class to social class"?

FLANNERY O'CONNOR

Flannery O'Connor (1925–1964) was born in Savannah, Georgia, and was educated at the Women's College of Georgia and the University of Iowa. She returned to her mother's farm near Milledgeville, Georgia, when she discovered that she had contracted lupus erythematosus, the systemic disease that had killed her father and of which she herself was to die. For the last fourteen years of her life, she lived a quiet, productive life on the farm—raising peacocks, painting, and writing the extraordinary stories and novels that won her worldwide acclaim. Her novels, *Wise Blood* (1952), which was adapted to film in 1979, and *The Violent Bear It Away* (1960), deal with fanatical preachers. Her thirty-one carefully crafted stories, combining grotesque comedy and violent tragedy, appear in *A Good Man Is Hard to Find* (1955), *Everything That Rises Must Converge* (1965), and *The Complete Stories* (1971), which won the National Book Award. "Revelation" dramatizes the ironic discoveries a woman makes about how different classes of people fit into the order of things.

Revelation

1 The doctor's waiting room, which was very small, was almost full when the Turpins entered and Mrs. Turpin, who was very large, made it look even smaller by her presence. She stood looming at the head of the magazine table set in the center of it, a living demonstration that the room was inadequate and ridiculous. Her little bright black eyes took in all the patients as she sized up the seating situation. There was one vacant chair and a place on the sofa occupied by a

blond child in a dirty blue romper who should have been told to move over and make room for the lady. He was five or six, but Mrs. Turpin saw at once that no one was going to tell him to move over. He was slumped down in the seat, his arms idle at his sides and his eyes idle in his head; his nose ran unchecked.

Mrs. Turpin put a firm hand on Claud's shoulder and said 2
in a voice that included anyone who wanted to listen, "Claud, you sit in that chair there," and gave him a push down into the vacant one. Claud was florid and bald and sturdy, somewhat shorter than Mrs. Turpin, but he sat down as if he were accustomed to doing what she told him to.

Mrs. Turpin remained standing. The only man in the 3
room besides Claud was a lean stringy old fellow with a rusty hand spread out on each knee, whose eyes were closed as if he were asleep or dead or pretending to be so as not to get up and offer her his seat. Her gaze settled agreeably on a well-dressed gray-haired lady whose eyes met hers and whose expression said: if that child belonged to me, he would have some manners and move over—there's plenty of room there for you and him too.

Claud looked up with a sigh and made as if to rise. 4

"Sit down," Mrs. Turpin said. "You know you're not 5
supposed to stand on that leg. He has an ulcer on his leg," she explained.

Claud lifted his foot onto the magazine table and rolled 6
his trouser leg up to reveal a purple swelling on a plump marble-white calf.

"My!" the pleasant lady said. "How did you do that?" 7

"A cow kicked him," Mrs. Turpin said. 8

"Goodness!" said the lady. 9

Claud rolled his trouser leg down. 10

"Maybe the little boy would move over," the lady sug- 11
gested, but the child did not stir.

"Somebody will be leaving in a minute," Mrs. Turpin said. 12
She could not understand why a doctor—with as much money as they made charging five dollars a day to just stick their head in the hospital door and look at you—couldn't

afford a decent-sized waiting room. This one was hardly bigger than a garage. The table was cluttered with limp-looking magazines and at one end of it there was a big green glass ash tray full of cigarette butts and cotton wads with little blood spots on them. If she had had anything to do with the running of the place, that would have been emptied every so often. There were no chairs against the wall at the head of the room. It had a rectangular-shaped panel in it that permitted a view of the office where the nurse came and went and the secretary listened to the radio. A plastic fern in a gold pot sat in the opening and trailed its fronds down almost to the floor. The radio was softly playing gospel music.

Just then the inner door opened and a nurse with the highest stack of yellow hair Mrs. Turpin had ever seen put her face in the crack and called for the next patient. The woman sitting beside Claud grasped the two arms of her chair and hoisted herself up; she pulled her dress free from her legs and lumbered through the door where the nurse had disappeared. 13

Mrs. Turpin eased into the vacant chair, which held her tight as a corset. "I wish I could reduce," she said, and rolled her eyes and gave a comic sigh. 14

"Oh, *you* aren't fat," the stylish lady said. 15

"Ooooo I am too," Mrs. Turpin said. "Claud he eats all he wants to and never weighs over one hundred and seventy-five pounds, but me I just look at something good to eat and I gain some weight," and her stomach and shoulders shook with laughter. "You can eat all you want to, can't you, Claud?" she asked, turning to him. 16

Claud only grinned. 17

"Well, as long as you have such a good disposition," the stylish lady said, "I don't think it makes a bit of difference what size you are. You just can't beat a good disposition." 18

Next to her was a fat girl of eighteen or nineteen, scowling into a thick blue book which Mrs. Turpin saw was entitled *Human Development*. The girl raised her head and directed her scowl at Mrs. Turpin as if she did not like her looks. She 19

appeared annoyed that anyone should speak while she tried
to read. The poor girl's face was blue with acne and Mrs.
Turpin thought how pitiful it was to have a face like that at
that age. She gave the girl a friendly smile but the girl only
scowled the harder. Mrs. Turpin herself was fat but she had
always had good skin, and, though she was forty-seven years
old, there was not a wrinkle in her face except around her
eyes from laughing too much.

Next to the ugly girl was the child, still in exactly the same 20
position, and next to him was a thin leathery old woman in
a cotton print dress. She and Claud had three sacks of chicken
feed in their pump house that was in the same print. She
had seen from the first that the child belonged with the old
woman. She could tell by the way they sat—kind of vacant
and white-trashy, as if they would sit there until Doomsday
if nobody called and told them to get up. And at right angles
but next to the well-dressed pleasant lady was a lank-faced
woman who was certainly the child's mother. She had on a
yellow sweat shirt and wine-colored slacks, both gritty-look-
ing, and the rims of her lips were stained with snuff. Her
dirty yellow hair was tied behind with a little piece of red
paper ribbon. Worse than niggers any day, Mrs. Turpin
thought.

The gospel hymn playing was, "When I looked up and 21
He looked down," and Mrs. Turpin, who knew it, supplied
the last line mentally, "And wona these days I know I'll weear
a crown."

Without appearing to, Mrs. Turpin always noticed peo- 22
ple's feet. The well-dressed lady had on red and gray suede
shoes to match her dress. Mrs. Turpin had on her good black
patent leather pumps. The ugly girl had on Girl Scout shoes
and heavy socks. The old woman had on tennis shoes and
the white-trashy mother had on what appeared to be bedroom slippers, black straw with gold braid threaded through
them—exactly what you would have expected her to have
on.

Sometimes at night when she couldn't go to sleep, Mrs. 23
Turpin would occupy herself with the question of who she

would have chosen to be if she couldn't have been herself. If Jesus had said to her before he made her, "There's only two places available for you. You can either be a nigger or white-trash," what would she have said? "Please, Jesus, please," she would have said, "just let me wait until there's another place available," and he would have said, "No, you have to go right now and I have only those two places so make up your mind." She would have wiggled and squirmed and begged and pleaded but it would have been no use and finally she would have said, "All right, make me a nigger then—but that don't mean a trashy one." And he would have made her a neat clean respectable Negro woman, herself but black.

Next to the child's mother was a red-headed youngish woman, reading one of the magazines and working a piece of chewing gum, hell for leather, as Claud would say. Mrs. Turpin could not see the woman's feet. She was not white-trash, just common. Sometimes Mrs. Turpin occupied herself at night naming the classes of people. On the bottom of the heap were most colored people, not the kind she would have been if she had been one, but most of them; then next to them—not above, just away from—were the white-trash; then above them were the home-owners, and above them the home-and-land-owners, to which she and Claud belonged. Above she and Claud were people with a lot of money and much bigger houses and much more land. But here the complexity of it would begin to bear in on her, for some of the people with a lot of money were common and ought to be below she and Claud and some of the people who had good blood had lost their money and had to rent and then there were colored people who owned their homes and land as well. There was a colored dentist in town who had two red Lincolns and a swimming pool and a farm with registered white-face cattle on it. Usually by the time she had fallen asleep all the classes of people were moiling and roiling around in her head, and she would dream they were all crammed in together in a box car, being ridden off to be put in a gas oven. 24

"That's a beautiful clock," she said and nodded to her 25
right. It was a big wall clock, the face encased in a brass sunburst.

"Yes, it's very pretty," the stylish lady said agreeably. "And 26
right on the dot too," she added, glancing at her watch.

The ugly girl beside her cast an eye upward at the clock, 27
smirked, then looked directly at Mrs. Turpin and smirked again. Then she returned her eyes to her book. She was obviously the lady's daughter because, although they didn't look anything alike as to disposition, they both had the same shape of face and the same blue eyes. On the lady they sparkled pleasantly but in the girl's seared face they appeared alternately to smolder and to blaze.

What if Jesus had said, "All right, you can be white-trash 28
or a nigger or ugly"!

Mrs. Turpin felt an awful pity for the girl, though she 29
thought it was one thing to be ugly and another to act ugly.

The woman with the snuff-stained lips turned around in 30
her chair and looked up at the clock. Then she turned back and appeared to look a little to the side of Mrs. Turpin. There was a cast in one of her eyes. "You want to know wher you can get you one of themther clocks?" she asked in a loud voice.

"No, I already have a nice clock," Mrs. Turpin said. Once 31
somebody like her got a leg in the conversation, she would be all over it.

"You can get you one with green stamps," the woman 32
said. "That's most likely wher he got hisn. Save you up enough, you can get you most anythang. I got me some joo'ry."

Ought to have got you a wash rag and some soap, Mrs. 33
Turpin thought.

"I get contour sheets with mine," the pleasant lady said. 34

The daughter slammed her book shut. She looked straight 35
in front of her, directly through Mrs. Turpin and on through the yellow curtain and the plate glass window which made the wall behind her. The girl's eyes seemed lit all of a sudden with a peculiar light, an unnatural light like night road signs

give. Mrs. Turpin turned her head to see if there was anything going on outside that she should see, but she could not see anything. Figures passing cast only a pale shadow through the curtain. There was no reason the girl should single her out for her ugly looks.

"Miss Finley," the nurse said, cracking the door. The gum- 36
chewing woman got up and passed in front of her and Claud and went into the office. She had on red high-heeled shoes.

Directly across the table, the ugly girl's eyes were fixed on 37
Mrs. Turpin as if she had some very special reason for disliking her.

"This is wonderful weather, isn't it?" the girl's mother 38
said.

"It's good weather for cotton if you can get the niggers 39
to pick it," Mrs. Turpin said, "but niggers don't want to pick cotton any more. You can't get the white folks to pick it and now you can't get the niggers—because they got to be right up there with the white folks."

"They gonna *try* anyways," the white-trash woman said, 40
leaning forward.

"Do you have one of the cotton-picking machines?" the 41
pleasant lady asked.

"No," Mrs. Turpin said, "they leave half the cotton in the 42
field. We don't have much cotton anyway. If you want to make it farming now, you have to have a little of everything. We got a couple of acres of cotton and a few hogs and chickens and just enough white-face that Claud can look after them himself."

"One thang I don't want," the white-trash woman said, 43
wiping her mouth with the back of her hand. "Hogs. Nasty stinking things, a-gruntin and a-rootin all over the place."

Mrs. Turpin gave her the merest edge of her attention. 44
"Our hogs are not dirty and they don't stink," she said. "They're cleaner than some children I've seen. Their feet never touch the ground. We have a pig-parlor—that's where you raise them on concrete," she explained to the pleasant lady, "and Claud scoots them down with the hose every afternoon and washes off the floor." Cleaner by far than that

child right there, she thought. Poor nasty little thing. He had not moved except to put the thumb of his dirty hand into his mouth.

The woman turned her face away from Mrs. Turpin. "I 45
know I wouldn't scoot down no hog with no hose," she said to the wall.

You wouldn't have no hog to scoot down, Mrs. Turpin 46
said to herself.

"A-gruntin and a-rootin and a-groanin," the woman mut- 47
tered.

"We got a little of everything," Mrs. Turpin said to the 48
pleasant lady. "It's no use in having more than you can handle yourself with help like it is. We found enough niggers to pick our cotton this year but Claud he has to go after them and take them home again in the evening. They can't walk that half a mile. No they can't. I tell you," she said and laughed merrily, "I sure am tired of buttering up niggers, but you got to love em if you want em to work for you. When they come in the morning, I run out and I say, 'Hi yawl this morning?' and when Claud drives them off to the field I just wave to beat the band and they just wave back." And she waved her hand rapidly to illustrate.

"Like you read out of the same book," the lady said, 49
showing she understood perfectly.

"Child, yes," Mrs. Turpin said. "And when they come in 50
from the field, I run out with a bucket of icewater. That's the way it's going to be from now on," she said. "You may as well face it."

"One thang I know," the white-trash woman said. "Two 51
thangs I ain't going to do: love no niggers or scoot down no hog with no hose." And she let out a bark of contempt.

The look that Mrs. Turpin and the pleasant lady ex- 52
changed indicated they both understood that you had to *have* certain things before you could *know* certain things. But every time Mrs. Turpin exchanged a look with the lady, she was aware that the ugly girl's peculiar eyes were still on her, and she had trouble bringing her attention back to the conversation.

"When you got something," she said, "you got to look after it." And when you ain't got a thing but breath and britches, she added to herself, you can afford to come to town every morning and just sit on the Court House coping and spit. 53

A grotesque revolving shadow passed across the curtain behind her and was thrown palely on the opposite wall. Then a bicycle clattered down against the outside of the building. The door opened and a colored boy glided in with a tray from the drugstore. It had two large red and white paper cups on it with tops on them. He was a tall, very black boy in discolored white pants and a green nylon shirt. He was chewing gum slowly, as if to music. He set the tray down in the office opening next to the fern and stuck his head through to look for the secretary. She was not in there. He rested his arms on the ledge and waited, his narrow bottom stuck out, swaying to the left and right. He raised a hand over his head and scratched the base of his skull. 54

"You see that button there, boy?" Mrs. Turpin said. "You can punch that and she'll come. She's probably in the back somewhere." 55

"Is thas right?" the boy said agreeably, as if he had never seen the button before. He leaned to the right and put his finger on it. "She sometime out," he said and twisted around to face his audience, his elbows behind him on the counter. The nurse appeared and he twisted back again. She handed him a dollar and he rooted in his pocket and made the change and counted it out to her. She gave him fifteen cents for a tip and he went out with the empty tray. The heavy door swung to slowly and closed at length with the sound of suction. For a moment no one spoke. 56

"They ought to send all them niggers back to Africa," the white-trash woman said. "That's wher they come from in the first place." 57

"Oh, I couldn't do without my good colored friends," the pleasant lady said. 58

"There's a heap of things worse than a nigger," Mrs. Turpin agreed. "It's all kinds of them just like it's all kinds of us." 59

"Yes, and it takes all kinds to make the world go round," the lady said in her musical voice. 60

As she said it, the raw-complexioned girl snapped her teeth together. Her lower lip turned downwards and inside out, revealing the pale pink inside of her mouth. After a second it rolled back up. It was the ugliest face Mrs. Turpin had ever seen anyone make and for a moment she was certain that the girl had made it at her. She was looking at her as if she had known and disliked her all her life—all of Mrs. Turpin's life, it seemed too, not just all the girl's life. Why, girl, I don't even know you, Mrs. Turpin said silently. 61

She forced her attention back to the discussion. "It wouldn't be practical to send them back to Africa," she said. "They wouldn't want to go. They got it too good here." 62

"Wouldn't be what they wanted—if I had anythang to do with it," the woman said. 63

"It wouldn't be a way in the world you could get all the niggers back over there," Mrs. Turpin said. "They'd be hiding out and lying down and turning sick on you and wailing and hollering and raring and pitching. It wouldn't be a way in the world to get them over there." 64

"They got over here," the trashy woman said. "Get back like they got over." 65

"It wasn't so many of them then," Mrs. Turpin explained. 66

The woman looked at Mrs. Turpin as if here was an idiot indeed but Mrs. Turpin was not bothered by the look, considering where it came from. 67

"Nooo," she said, "they're going to stay here where they can go to New York and marry white folks and improve their color. That's what they all want to do, every one of them, improve their color." 68

"You know what comes of that, don't you?" Claud asked. 69

"No, Claud, what?" Mrs. Turpin said. 70

Claud's eyes twinkled. "White-faced niggers," he said with never a smile. 71

Everybody in the office laughed except the white-trash and the ugly girl. The girl gripped the book in her lap with white fingers. The trashy woman looked around her from face to face as if she thought they were all idiots. The old 72 woman in the feed sack dress continued to gaze expressionless across the floor at the high-top shoes of the man opposite her, the one who had been pretending to be asleep when the Turpins came in. He was laughing heartily, his hands still spread out on his knees. The child had fallen to the side and was lying now almost face down in the old woman's lap.

73 While they recovered from their laughter, the nasal chorus on the radio kept the room from silence.

"You go to blank blank
And I'll go to mine
But we'll all blank along
To-geth-ther,
And all along the blank
We'll hep eachother out
Smile-ling in any kind of
Weath-ther!"

74 Mrs. Turpin didn't catch every word but she caught enough to agree with the spirit of the song and it turned her thoughts sober. To help anybody out that needed it was her philosophy of life. She never spared herself when she found somebody in need, whether they were white or black, trash or decent. And of all she had to be thankful for, she was most thankful that this was so. If Jesus had said, "You can be high society and have all the money you want and be thin and svelte-like, but you can't be a good woman with it," she would have had to say, "Well don't make me that then. Make me a good woman and it don't matter what else, how fat or how ugly or how poor!" Her heart rose. He had not made her a nigger or white-trash or ugly! He had made her herself and given her a little of everything. Jesus, thank you! she said. Thank you thank you thank you! Whenever she counted her blessings she felt as buoyant as if she weighed one hundred and twenty-five pounds instead of one hundred and eighty.

75 "What's wrong with your little boy?" the pleasant lady asked the white-trashy woman.

76 "He has a ulcer," the woman said proudly. "He ain't give me a minute's peace since he was born. Him and her are just

alike," she said, nodding at the old woman, who was running her leathery fingers through the child's pale hair. "Look like I can't get nothing down them two but Co' Cola and candy."

That's all you try to get down em, Mrs. Turpin said to herself. Too lazy to light the fire. There was nothing you could tell her about people like them that she didn't know already. And it was not just that they didn't have anything. Because if you gave them everything, in two weeks it would all be broken or filthy or they would have chopped it up for lightwood. She knew all this from her own experience. Help them you must, but help them you couldn't. 77

All at once the ugly girl turned her lips inside out again. Her eyes fixed like two drills on Mrs. Turpin. This time there was no mistaking that there was something urgent behind them. 78

Girl, Mrs. Turpin exclaimed silently, I haven't done a thing to you! The girl might be confusing her with somebody else. There was no need to sit by and let herself be intimidated. "You must be in college," she said boldly, looking directly at the girl. "I see you reading a book there." 79

The girl continued to stare and pointedly did not answer. 80

Her mother blushed at this rudeness. "The lady asked you a question, Mary Grace," she said under her breath. 81

"I have ears," Mary Grace said. 82

The poor mother blushed again. "Mary Grace goes to Wellesley College," she explained. She twisted one of the buttons on her dress. "In Massachusetts," she added with a grimace. "And in the summer she just keeps right on studying. Just reads all the time, a real book worm. She's done real well at Wellesley; she's taking English and Math and History and Psychology and Social Studies," she rattled on, "and I think it's too much. I think she ought to get out and have fun." 83

The girl looked as if she would like to hurl them all through the plate glass window. 84

"Way up north," Mrs. Turpin murmured and thought, well, it hasn't done much for her manners. 85

"I'd almost rather to have him sick," the white-trash 86

woman said, wrenching the attention back to herself. "He's so mean when he ain't. Look like some children just take natural to meanness. It's some gets bad when they get sick but he was the opposite. Took sick and turned good. He don't give me no trouble now. It's me waitin to see the doctor," she said.

If I was going to send anybody back to Africa, Mrs. Turpin thought, it would be your kind, woman. "Yes, indeed," she said aloud, but looking up at the ceiling, "it's a heap of things worse than a nigger." And dirtier than a hog, she added to herself. 87

"I think people with bad dispositions are more to be pitied than anyone on earth," the pleasant lady said in a voice that was decidedly thin. 88

"I thank the Lord he has blessed me with a good one," Mrs. Turpin said. "The day has never dawned that I couldn't find something to laugh at." 89

"Not since she married me anyways," Claud said with a comical straight face. 90

Everybody laughed except the girl and the white-trash. 91

Mrs. Turpin's stomach shook. "He's such a caution," she said, "that I can't help but laugh at him." 92

The girl made a loud ugly noise through her teeth. 93

Her mother's mouth grew thin and tight. "I think the worst thing in the world," she said, "is an ungrateful person. To have everything and not appreciate it. I know a girl," she said, "who has parents who would give her anything, a little brother who loves her dearly, who is getting a good education, who wears the best clothes, but who can never say a kind word to anyone, who never smiles, who just criticizes and complains all day long." 94

"Is she too old to paddle?" Claud asked. 95

The girl's face was almost purple. 96

"Yes," the lady said, "I'm afraid there's nothing to do but leave her to her folly. Some day she'll wake up and it'll be too late." 97

"It never hurt anyone to smile," Mrs. Turpin said. "It just makes you feel better all over." 98

"Of course," the lady said sadly, "but there are just some people you can't tell anything to. They can't take criticism." 99

"If it's one thing I am," Mrs. Turpin said with feeling, "it's grateful. When I think who all I could have been besides myself and what all I got, a little of everything, and a good disposition besides, I just feel like shouting, 'Thank you, Jesus, for making everything the way it is!' It could have been different!" For one thing, somebody else could have got Claud. At the thought of this, she was flooded with gratitude and a terrible pang of joy ran through her. "Oh thank you, Jesus, Jesus, thank you!" she cried aloud. 100

The book struck her directly over her left eye. It struck almost at the same instant that she realized the girl was about to hurl it. Before she could utter a sound, the raw face came crashing across the table toward her, howling. The girl's fingers sank like clamps into the soft flesh of her neck. She heard the mother cry out and Claud shout, "Whoa!" There was an instant when she was certain that she was about to be in an earthquake. 101

All at once her vision narrowed and she saw everything as if it were happening in a small room far away, or as if she were looking at it through the wrong end of a telescope. Claud's face crumpled and fell out of sight. The nurse ran in, then out, then in again. Then the gangling figure of the doctor rushed out of the inner door. Magazines flew this way and that as the table turned over. The girl fell with a thud and Mrs. Turpin's vision suddenly reversed itself and she saw everything large instead of small. The eyes of the white-trashy woman were staring hugely at the floor. There the girl, held down on one side by the nurse and on the other by her mother, was wrenching and turning in their grasp. The doctor was kneeling astride her, trying to hold her arm down. He managed after a second to sink a long needle into it. 102

Mrs. Turpin felt entirely hollow except for her heart which swung from side to side as if it were agitated in a great empty drum of flesh. 103

"Somebody that's not busy call for the ambulance," the doctor said in the off-hand voice young doctors adopt for terrible occasions. 104

Mrs. Turpin could not have moved a finger. The old man who had been sitting next to her skipped nimbly into the office and made the call, for the secretary still seemed to be gone. 105

"Claud!" Mrs. Turpin called. 106

He was not in his chair. She knew she must jump up and find him but she felt like some one trying to catch a train in a dream, when everything moves in slow motion and the faster you try to run the slower you go. 107

"Here I am," a suffocated voice, very unlike Claud's, said. 108

He was doubled up in the corner on the floor, pale as paper, holding his leg. She wanted to get up and go to him but she could not move. Instead, her gaze was drawn slowly downward to the churning face on the floor, which she could see over the doctor's shoulder. 109

The girl's eyes stopped rolling and focused on her. They seemed a much lighter blue than before, as if a door that had been tightly closed behind them was now open to admit light and air. 110

Mrs. Turpin's head cleared and her power of motion returned. She leaned forward until she was looking directly into the fierce brilliant eyes. There was no doubt in her mind that the girl did know her, knew her in some intense and personal way, beyond time and place and condition. "What you got to say to me?" she asked hoarsely and held her breath, waiting, as for a revelation. 111

The girl raised her head. Her gaze locked with Mrs. Turpin's. "Go back to hell where you came from, you old wart hog," she whispered. Her voice was low but clear. Her eyes burned for a moment as if she saw with pleasure that her message had struck its target. 112

Mrs. Turpin sank back in her chair. 113

After a moment the girl's eyes closed and she turned her head wearily to the side. 114

The doctor rose and handed the nurse the empty syringe. 115

He leaned over and put both hands for a moment on the mother's shoulders, which were shaking. She was sitting on the floor, her lips pressed together, holding Mary Grace's hand in her lap. The girl's fingers were gripped like a baby's around her thumb. "Go on to the hospital," he said. "I'll call and make the arrangements."

"Now let's see that neck," he said in a jovial voice to Mrs. Turpin. He began to inspect her neck with his first two fingers. Two little moon-shaped lines like pink fish bones were indented over her windpipe. There was the beginning of an angry red swelling above her eye. His fingers passed over this also. 116

"Lea' me be," she said thickly and shook him off. "See about Claud. She kicked him." 117

"I'll see about him in a minute," he said and felt her pulse. He was a thin gray-haired man, given to pleasantries. "Go home and have yourself a vacation the rest of the day," he said and patted her on the shoulder. 118

Quit your pattin me, Mrs. Turpin growled to herself. 119

"And put an ice pack over that eye," he said. Then he went and squatted down beside Claud and looked at his leg. After a moment he pulled him up and Claud limped after him into the office. 120

Until the ambulance came, the only sounds in the room were the tremulous moans of the girl's mother, who continued to sit on the floor. The white-trash woman did not take her eyes off the girl. Mrs. Turpin looked straight ahead at nothing. Presently the ambulance drew up, a long dark shadow, behind the curtain. The attendants came in and set the stretcher down beside the girl and lifted her expertly onto it and carried her out. The nurse helped the mother gather up her things. The shadow of the ambulance moved silently away and the nurse came back in the office. 121

"That ther girl is going to be a lunatic, ain't she?" the white-trash woman asked the nurse, but the nurse kept on to the back and never answered her. 122

"Yes, she's going to be a lunatic," the white-trash woman said to the rest of them. 123

"Po' critter," the old woman murmured. The child's face was still in her lap. His eyes looked idly out over her knees. He had not moved during the disturbance except to draw one leg up under him. 124

"I thank Gawd," the white-trash woman said fervently, "I ain't a lunatic." 125

Claud came limping out and the Turpins went home. 126

As their pick-up truck turned into their own dirt road and made the crest of the hill, Mrs. Turpin gripped the window ledge and looked out suspiciously. The land sloped gracefully down through a field dotted with lavender weeds and at the start of the rise their small yellow frame house, with its little flower beds spread out around it like a fancy apron, sat primly in its accustomed place between two giant hickory trees. She would not have been startled to see a burnt wound between two blackened chimneys. 127

Neither of them felt like eating so they put on their house clothes and lowered the shade in the bedroom and lay down, Claud with his leg on a pillow and herself with a damp washcloth over her eye. The instant she was flat on her back, the image of a razor-backed hog with warts on its face and horns coming out behind its ears snorted into her head. She moaned, a low quiet moan. 128

"I am not," she said tearfully, "a wart hog. From hell." But the denial had no force. The girl's eyes and her words, even the tone of her voice, low but clear, directed only to her, brooked no repudiation. She had been singled out for the message, though there was trash in the room to whom it might justly have been applied. The full force of this fact struck her only now. There was a woman there who was neglecting her own child but she had been overlooked. The message had been given to Ruby Turpin, a respectable, hard-working, church-going woman. The tears dried. Her eyes began to burn instead with wrath. 129

She rose on her elbow and the washcloth fell into her hand. Claud was lying on his back, snoring. She wanted to tell him what the girl had said. At the same time, she did not wish to put the image of herself as a wart hog from hell into his mind. 130

"Hey, Claud," she muttered and pushed his shoulder. 131

Claud opened one pale baby blue eye. 132

She looked into it warily. He did not think about any- 133
thing. He just went his way.

"Wha, whasit?" he said and closed the eye again. 134

"Nothing," she said. "Does your leg pain you?" 135

"Hurts like hell," Claud said. 136

"It'll quit terreckly," she said and lay back down. In a 137
moment Claud was snoring again. For the rest of the afternoon they lay there. Claud slept. She scowled at the ceiling.
Occasionally she raised her fist and made a small stabbing
motion over her chest as if she was defending her innocence
to invisible guests who were like the comforters of Job,
reasonable-seeming but wrong.

About five-thirty Claud stirred. "Got to go after those 138
niggers," he sighed, not moving.

She was looking straight up as if there were unintelligible 139
handwriting on the ceiling. The protuberance over her eye
had turned a greenish-blue. "Listen here," she said.

"What?" 140

"Kiss me." 141

Claud leaned over and kissed her loudly on the mouth. 142
He pinched her side and their hands interlocked. Her expression of ferocious concentration did not change. Claud
got up, groaning and growling, and limped off. She continued to study the ceiling.

She did not get up until she heard the pick-up truck 143
coming back with the Negroes. Then she rose and thrust her
feet in her brown oxfords, which she did not bother to lace,
and stumped out onto the back porch and got her red plastic
bucket. She emptied a tray of ice cubes into it and filled it
half full of water and went out into the back yard. Every
afternoon after Claud brought the hands in, one of the boys
helped him put out hay and the rest waited in the back of
the truck until he was ready to take them home. The truck
was parked in the shade under one of the hickory trees.

"Hi yawl this evening?" Mrs. Turpin asked grimly, ap- 144
pearing with the bucket and the dipper. There were three
women and a boy in the truck.

"Us doin nicely," the oldest woman said. "Hi you doin?" and her gaze stuck immediately on the dark lump on Mrs. Turpin's forehead. "You done fell down, ain't you?" she asked in a solicitous voice. The old woman was dark and almost toothless. She had on an old felt hat of Claud's set back on her head. The other two women were younger and lighter and they both had new bright green sunhats. One of them had hers on her head; the other had taken hers off and the boy was grinning beneath it. 145

Mrs. Turpin set the bucket down on the floor of the truck. "Yawl hep yourselves," she said. She looked around to make sure Claud had gone. "No, I didn't fall down," she said, folding her arms. "It was something worse than that." 146

"Ain't nothing bad happen to you!" the old woman said. She said it as if they all knew that Mrs. Turpin was protected in some special way by Divine Providence. "You just had you a little fall." 147

"We were in town at the doctor's office for where the cow kicked Mr. Turpin," Mrs. Turpin said in a flat tone that indicated they could leave off their foolishness. "And there was this girl there. A big fat girl with her face all broke out. I could look at that girl and tell she was peculiar but I couldn't tell how. And me and her mama was just talking and going along and all of a sudden WHAM! She throws this big book she was reading at me and . . ." 148

"Naw!" the old woman cried out. 149

"And then she jumps over the table and commences to choke me." 150

"Naw!" they all exclaimed, "naw!" 151

"Hi come she do that?" the old woman asked. "What ail her?" 152

Mrs. Turpin only glared in front of her. 153

"Somethin ail her," the old woman said. 154

"They carried her off in an ambulance," Mrs. Turpin continued, "but before she went she was rolling on the floor and they were trying to hold her down to give her a shot and she said something to me." She paused. "You know what she said to me?" 155

"What she say?" they asked. 156

"She said," Mrs. Turpin began, and stopped, her face very 157
dark and heavy. The sun was getting whiter and whiter, blanching the sky overhead so that the leaves of the hickory tree were black in the face of it. She could not bring forth the words. "Something real ugly," she muttered.

"She sho shouldn't said nothin ugly to you," the old 158
woman said. "You so sweet. You the sweetest lady I know."

"She pretty too," the one with the hat on said. 159

"And stout," the other one said. "I never knowed no 160
sweeter white lady."

"That's the truth befo' Jesus," the old woman said. "Amen! 161
You des as sweet and pretty as you can be."

Mrs. Turpin knew exactly how much Negro flattery was 162
worth and it added to her rage. "She said," she began again and finished this time with a fierce rush of breath, "that I was an old wart hog from hell."

There was an astounded silence. 163

"Where she at?" the youngest woman cried in a piercing 164
voice.

"Lemme see her. I'll kill her!" 165

"I'll kill her with you!" the other one cried. 166

"She b'long in the sylum," the old woman said emphati- 167
cally. "You the sweetest white lady I know."

"She pretty too," the other two said. "Stout as she can be 168
and sweet. Jesus satisfied with her!"

"Deed he is," the old woman declared. 169

Idiots! Mrs. Turpin growled to herself. You could never 170
say anything intelligent to a nigger. You could talk at them but not with them. "Yawl ain't drunk your water," she said shortly. "Leave the bucket in the truck when you're finished with it. I got more to do than just stand around and pass the time of day," and she moved off and into the house.

She stood for a moment in the middle of the kitchen. The 171
dark protuberance over her eye looked like a miniature tornado cloud which might any moment sweep across the horizon of her brow. Her lower lip protruded dangerously. She squared her massive shoulders. Then she marched into the

front of the house and out the side door and started down the road to the pig parlor. She had the look of a woman going single-handed, weaponless, into battle.

The sun was a deep yellow now like a harvest moon and 172
was riding westward very fast over the far tree line as if it meant to reach the hogs before she did. The road was rutted and she kicked several good-sized stones out of her path as she strode along. The pig parlor was on a little knoll at the end of a lane that ran off from the side of the barn. It was a square of concrete as large as a small room, with a board fence about four feet high around it. The concrete floor sloped slightly so that the hog wash could drain off into a trench where it was carried to the field for fertilizer. Claud was standing on the outside, on the edge of the concrete, hanging onto the top board, hosing down the floor inside. The hose was connected to the faucet of a water trough nearby.

Mrs. Turpin climbed up beside him and glowered down 173
at the hogs inside. There were seven long-snouted bristly shoats in it—tan with liver-colored spots—and an old sow a few weeks off from farrowing. She was lying on her side grunting. The shoats were running about shaking themselves like idiot children, their little slit pig eyes searching the floor for anything left. She had read that pigs were the most intelligent animal. She doubted it. They were supposed to be smarter than dogs. There had even been a pig astronaut. He had performed his assignment perfectly but died of a heart attack afterwards because they left him in his electric suit, sitting upright throughout his examination when naturally a hog should be on all fours.

A-gruntin and a-rootin and a-groanin. 174

"Gimme that hose," she said, yanking it away from Claud. 175
"Go on and carry them niggers home and then get off that leg."

"You look like you might have swallowed a mad dog," 176
Claud observed, but he got down and limped off. He paid no attention to her humors.

Until he was out of earshot, Mrs. Turpin stood on the 177

side of the pen, holding the hose and pointing the stream of water at the hind quarters of any shoat that looked as if it might try to lie down. When he had had time to get over the hill, she turned her head slightly and her wrathful eyes scanned the path. He was nowhere in sight. She turned back again and seemed to gather herself up. Her shoulders rose and she drew in her breath.

"What do you send me a message like that for?" she said 178
in a low fierce voice, barely above a whisper but with the force of a shout in its concentrated fury. "How am I a hog and me both? How am I saved and from hell too?" Her free fist was knotted and with the other she gripped the hose, blindly pointing the stream of water in and out of the eye of the old sow whose outraged squeal she did not hear.

The pig parlor commanded a view of the back pasture 179
where their twenty beef cows were gathered around the hay-bales Claud and the boy had put out. The freshly cut pasture sloped down to the highway. Across it was their cotton field and beyond that a dark green dusty wood which they owned as well. The sun was behind the wood, very red, looking over the paling of trees like a farmer inspecting his own hogs.

"Why me?" she rumbled. "It's no trash around here, black 180
or white, that I haven't given to. And break my back to the bone every day working. And do for the church."

She appeared to be the right size woman to command the 181
arena before her. "How am I a hog?" she demanded. "Exactly how am I like them?" and she jabbed the stream of water at the shoats. "There was plenty of trash there. It didn't have to be me.

"If you like trash better, go get yourself some trash then," 182
she railed. "You could have made me trash. Or a nigger. If trash is what you wanted why didn't you make me trash?" She shook her fist with the hose in it and a watery snake appeared momentarily in the air. "I could quit working and take it easy and be filthy," she growled. "Lounge about the sidewalks all day drinking root beer. Dip snuff and spit in every puddle and have it all over my face. I could be nasty.

"Or you could have made me a nigger. It's too late for 183
me to be a nigger," she said with deep sarcasm, "but I could act like one. Lay down in the middle of the road and stop traffic. Roll on the ground."

In the deepening light everything was taking on a mys- 184
terious hue. The pasture was growing a peculiar glassy green and the streak of highway had turned lavender. She braced herself for a final assault and this time her voice rolled out over the pasture. "Go on," she yelled, "call me a hog! Call me a hog again. From hell. Call me a wart hog from hell. Put that bottom rail on top. There'll still be a top and bottom!"

A garbled echo returned to her. 185

A final surge of fury shook her and she roared, "Who do 186
you think you are?"

The color of everything, field and crimson sky, burned for 187
a moment with a transparent intensity. The question carried over the pasture and across the highway and the cotton field and returned to her clearly like an answer from beyond the wood.

She opened her mouth but no sound came out of it. 188

A tiny truck, Claud's, appeared on the highway, heading 189
rapidly out of sight. Its gears scraped thinly. It looked like a child's toy. At any moment a bigger truck might smash into it and scatter Claud's and the niggers' brains all over the road.

Mrs. Turpin stood there, her gaze fixed on the highway, 190
all her muscles rigid, until in five or six minutes the truck reappeared, returning. She waited until it had had time to turn into their own road. Then like a monumental statue coming to life, she bent her head slowly and gazed, as if through the very heart of mystery, down into the pig parlor at the hogs. They had settled all in one corner around the old sow who was grunting softly. A red glow suffused them. They appeared to pant with a secret life.

Until the sun slipped finally behind the tree line, Mrs. 191
Turpin remained there with her gaze bent to them as if she were absorbing some abysmal life-giving knowledge. At last

she lifted her head. There was only a purple streak in the sky, cutting through a field of crimson and leading, like an extension of the highway, into the descending dusk. She raised her hands from the side of the pen in a gesture hieratic and profound. A visionary light settled in her eyes. She saw the streak as a vast swinging bridge extending upward from the earth through a field of living fire. Upon it a vast horde of souls were rumbling toward heaven. There were whole companies of white-trash, clean for the first time in their lives, and bands of black niggers in white robes, and battalions of freaks and lunatics shouting and clapping and leaping like frogs. And bringing up the end of the procession was a tribe of people whom she recognized at once as those who, like herself and Claud, had always had a little of everything and the God-given wit to use it right. She leaned forward to observe them closer. They were marching behind the others with great dignity, accountable as they had always been for good order and common sense and respectable behavior. They alone were on key. Yet she could see by their shocked and altered faces that even their virtues were being burned away. She lowered her hands and gripped the rail of the hog pen, her eyes small but fixed unblinkingly on what lay ahead. In a moment the vision faded but she remained where she was, immobile.

At length she got down and turned off the faucet and 192
made her slow way on the darkening path to the house. In the woods around her the invisible cricket choruses had struck up, but what she heard were the voices of the souls climbing upward into the starry field and shouting hallelujah.

COMMENT ON "REVELATION"

Ruby Turpin, the central character in Flannery O'Connor's "Revelation," is obsessed with the classification process. At night she occupies herself "naming the classes of people": most "colored people" are on the bottom; "next to them—not above, just away from—are the white trash"; and so on. Mrs. Turpin puzzles about the exceptions to her system—

the black dentist who owns property and the decent white folks who have lost their money—but for the most part she is certain about her system and her place in it. In the doctor's waiting room, she sizes up the other patients, placing them in their appropriate class. But her internal and external dialogue reveals the ironies and inconsistencies in her rigid system. Self-satisfied, pleased that Jesus is on her side, she is not prepared for the book on *Human Development* that is thrown at her or the events that follow—the transparent flattery of the black workers, her cleaning of the pig parlor, and finally her vision of the highway to heaven that reveals her real place in God's hierarchy.

Division and Classification as a Writing Strategy

1. Write a column for your local newspaper in which you develop a system for classifying a concept such as trash. You may decide to interpret this word literally, developing a scheme to categorize the type of objects people throw away. Or you may decide to interpret the word figuratively, focusing on activities people consider worthless—gossip columns, romance magazines, game shows. As Russell Baker did, develop a clever thesis about the subject you are classifying, such as, although people throw trash away, it won't go away; people's distaste for trash is the cause of its creation; people are so saturated by trash that they accept it as part of their culture with its own subtle subcategories.
2. In an essay that might be submitted to a psychology class, classify various kinds of dependency. Follow the pattern John Holt uses in his essay on discipline by arranging the kinds of dependency in an ascending order of complexity. You may want to illustrate your categories with personal experience or cite various historical figures who were extraordinarily dependent personalities. You may want to justify your categories by analyzing the power of the people, customs, or ideas that created the dependent relationship.
3. Joseph Epstein argues that "one's social class is defined, at least in part, by one's wishes." Divide a social group—small (your writing class) or large (American society)—according to their wishes. Then establish categories (labels) for each kind of wish. As you analyze the wish of each group, determine whether the wish is an *end* (physical comfort) or a *means* (wealth) toward some other *end* (social status). You may want to ask Aristotle's old question about wishes: Is there an end which is an end unto itself? His answer was happiness. How would each of the groups in your categories define *happiness*?
4. Analyze Gail Sheehy's essay from the perspective of gender. That is, does her use of the pronoun *we*, her descrip-

tion of examples, and her concepts of growth and adulthood suggest that she is outlining "predictable crises" for both men and women? Reconsider her six stages by pointing out how each one may need substantial revision when seen from a woman's point of view.

5. Select one of Lewis Thomas's categories in "The Technology of Medicine" and classify it into smaller subcategories. For example, you may wish to draft an editorial in which you explain that the various kinds of "supportive therapy," while costly, time-consuming, and ineffective by one set of standards, are nevertheless the most valuable medical technology. As you consider each subcategory, demonstrate how it contributes to the well-being, though not necessarily the health, of the patient.
6. Using Gail Sheehy's crisis/growth model, write an essay in which you classify the predictable crises of a college education. Although you may divide the period into the traditional four years (age eighteen to twenty-one), remember that the average student takes six years to complete a college education and that the nontraditional student population is the fastest-growing group within the university. Use this information to expand and enrich your classification system. But use your system, as Sheehy does, to illustrate some theory of intellectual development. What are the factors that permit or prevent students from moving from stage to stage?

DEFINITION

As a writer, both in and out of college, you're likely to spend a good deal of time writing definitions. In an astronomy class, you may be asked to explain what the Doppler effect is or what a white dwarf star is; in a literature class, you may be asked to define a sonnet and identify its different forms. If you become an engineer, you may write to define problems your company proposes to solve or to define a new product your company has developed; if you become a junior business executive, you may have to write a brochure to describe a new service your company offers or draft a letter that defines the company's policy on credit applications.

So definitions are everywhere. Writers use them to establish boundaries, to show the essential nature of something, and to explain the special qualities that identify a purpose, place, object, or concept and distinguish it from others similar to it. Writers often write extended definitions, definitions that go beyond the one-sentence or one-paragraph explanations that you find in a dictionary or encyclopedia to expand on and examine the essential qualities of a policy, an event, a group, or a trend. Sometimes an extended definition becomes an entire book. Some books are written to define the good life; others are written to define the ideal university or the best kind of government. In fact, many of the books on any current nonfiction best-seller list are primarily definitions. The essays in this section of the book are all extended definitions.

PURPOSE

When you write, you can use definitions in several ways. For instance, you can define to *point out the special nature* of something. You may want to show the special flavor of San Francisco that makes it different from other major cities in the world, or you may want to describe the unique features that make the Macintosh computer different from other personal computers.

You can also define to *explain.* In an essay about cross-country skiing, you might want to show your readers what the sport is like and point out why it's less hazardous and less expensive than downhill skiing, but better exercise. You might also define to *entertain*—to describe the essence of what it means to be a "good old boy," for instance. Often you define to *inform;* that is what you are doing in college papers when you write about West Virginia folk art or post-modern architecture. Often you write to *establish a standard,* perhaps for a good exercise program, a workable environmental policy, or even the ideal pair of running shoes. Notice that when you define to set a standard, you may also be defining to *persuade,* to convince your reader to accept the ideal you describe. Many definitions are essentially arguments.

Sometimes you may even write to define yourself. That is what you are doing when you write an autobiographical statement for a college admissions officer or a scholarship committee, or when you write a job application letter. You hope to give your readers the special information that will distinguish you from all other candidates. When that is your task, you'll profit by knowing the common strategies for defining and by recognizing how other writers have used them.

AUDIENCE

When you're going to use definition in your writing, you can benefit by thinking ahead of time about what your readers expect from you. Why are they reading and what questions will they want you to answer? You can't anticipate all their questions, but you should plan on responding to at least two kinds of queries.

First, your readers are likely to ask, "What distinguishes what you're writing about? What's typical or different about it? How do I know when I see one?" For example, if you were writing about the Olympic games, your readers would probably want to know the difference between today's Olympic games and the original games in ancient Greece. With a little research, you could tell them about several major differences.

Second, for more complex topics you should expect that your readers will also ask, "What is the basic character or the essential nature of what you're writing about? What do you mean when you say 'alternative medicine,' 'Marxist theory,' or 'white-collar crime?'" Answering questions such as these is more difficult, but if you're going to use terms like these in an essay, you have an obligation to define them, using as many strategies as you need to clarify your terms. To define white-collar crime, for instance, you could specify that it is nonviolent, likely to happen within businesses, and involves illegal manipulation of funds or privileged information. You should also strengthen your definition by giving examples that your readers might be familiar with.

STRATEGIES

You can choose from a variety of strategies for defining and use them singly or in combination. Probably a favorite strategy for all of us is *giving examples,* a strategy as natural as pointing to a picture of a horse or an elephant in a children's book. Writers use the same technique when they describe a scene or an event to help readers get a visual image. Every writer in this section defines by giving examples, but Loren Eiseley probably uses them most in "Man the Firemaker" as he helps his readers visualize how the human being has evolved from a primitive maker of campfires to an intellectual genius who now knows how to burn up the planet. Raymond Carver's short story "What We Talk About When We Talk About Love" also focuses on defining through examples.

You can define by *analyzing qualities* to show what features distinguish your topic. When you do that, you pick out particular qualities that you want your readers to associate with the person, concept, or object you're defining. Verlyn Klinkenborg does this in "The Western Saddle," and David Gates does it in his essay "Who Was Columbus?" by showing that Columbus was a man of his time: deeply religious but at the same time exploitative, a modern adventurer but also pious enough to accept the Bible as a reliable source of geographical knowledge. A writer uses a similar strategy when he or she begins *attributing characteristics.* Alison Lurie does this in "Folktale Liberation" when she describes the elements of fairy tales that support the ideas of women's liberation. Francine du Plessix Gray also uses this strategy in "On Friendship" when she identifies the special characteristics that we need in our friends: trust and selflessness.

Du Plessix Gray's essay also demonstrates *defining negatively,* using the important strategy of saying what something is not. She points out that friendship, unlike romantic love, is not possessive or jealous. Raymond Carver also defines negatively when his main character insists that love is *not* dragging someone around by her hair. You can also define by *using analogies,* a favorite strategy with many writers. In "Man the Firemaker," Loren Eiseley uses rich analogies comparing human evolution to an ascent up the heat ladder and human life on our planet to a flame.

Finally, you can define by *giving functions.* Sometimes the most significant fact about a person, object, or institution is what he, she, or it does. In "The Western Saddle," Verlyn Klinkenborg shows how the changing functions of western saddles have controlled the way they have developed. In "Folktale Liberation," Alison Lurie claims that one of the main functions of fairy tales in their original forms was to help children cope with the problems in their lives.

COMBINING STRATEGIES

Even when you're writing an article or essay that is primarily a definition, you're not limited to the strategies we've just mentioned. You may want to combine them with other patterns, as professional writers do. For instance, in "Rules of the Game: Rodeo" (in Process Analysis), Gretel Ehrlich is defining as well as analyzing a process—the two go together well. In "Secession of the Successful" (in Persuasion and Argument), Robert Reich starts by defining the nation's economic elite and then goes on to argue that they are seceding from the rest of the country. Writers can also use narration and description as ways of defining—Maya Angelou defines a certain kind of racist attitude in her narrative "My Name Is Margaret," and N. Scott Momaday uses description to define a way of life in "The Way to Rainy Mountain."

As you read the essays in this section, and especially as you reread them, keep part of your mind alert to spot the strategies the writer is using. You may want to incorporate some of them into your own writing; for instance, you could use the patterns Klinkenborg uses in "The Western Saddle" to show how the changing needs of riders have brought about the development of today's mountain bikes. When you start drafting an essay that will be mainly definition, it may help for you to read this introduction again to refresh your memory about what strategies are available to you.

Using Definition in a Paragraph

SUSAN SONTAG
From *AIDS and Its Metaphors*

Negative definition: AIDS not illness, but a condition

Contrasts with cancer and syphilis

Requires presence of other illnesses

We think of AIDS as having a single cause

Strictly speaking, AIDS—acquired immune deficiency syndrome—is not the name of an illness at all. It is the name of a medical condition, whose consequences are a spectrum of illnesses. In contrast to syphilis and cancer, which provide prototypes for most of the images and metaphors attached to AIDS, the very definition of AIDS requires the presence of other illnesses, so-called opportunistic infections and malignancies. But though not in that sense a single disease, AIDS lends itself to being regarded as one—in part because, unlike cancer and like syphilis, it is thought to have a single cause.

Comment In this early paragraph from her book *AIDS and Its Metaphors* (1989), Susan Sontag lays a foundation for her exploration of the topic by making a negative definition. Calmly, without using metaphors or emotional language, she specifies that AIDS is *not* a disease or an illness; rather it is a condition that allows the body to be invaded by infections and malignancies. She extends her negative definition by showing that AIDS is *not* like cancer and syphilis, because it necessarily involves other illnesses. Nevertheless, we tend to bracket AIDS with those dreaded diseases and consider it a single disease, partially because we mistakenly believe that it has a single cause.

VERLYN KLINKENBORG

Verlyn Klinkenborg was born in 1952 in Meeker, Colorado, raised in Iowa and California, and attended Pomona College and Princeton University. He has worked as the assistant curator at the Pierpont Morgan Library and as a teacher of creative writing at Fordham University and Harvard University. He is a recent winner of the Lila Wallace *Reader's Digest* Writer's Award. Klinkenborg's essays have appeared in magazines such as the *New Yorker, Harper's, Esquire,* and *Smithsonian.* His books include *Making Hay* (1986) and *Last Fine Time* (1990). In "The Western Saddle," reprinted from *Esquire,* Klinkenborg defines the parts of this functional and mythical western gear.

The Western Saddle

1 Like any piece of completely functional and completely mythic gear, the western saddle has become invisible. When most of us get a glimpse of that familiar shape—the saddle horn, the heavy stirrups, perhaps a rope tied on the fork—what we really see is a Hollywood vision, a cigarette scene of the cowboy West. We had might as well be looking at a six-gun or a shot glass or Miss Kitty's garter belt.

2 But nothing speaks more truly of the working West than a western stockman's saddle. It solves the cowboy's basic problem: How do you tie a cow to a horse? The answer is not so obvious. The llaneros—barefoot Venezuelan cowboys who rode in stirrups with room for only the big toe—used to catch cattle with a rawhide rope braided into the horse's tail. For a time, the vaqueros of colonial New Spain did not bother connecting cow and horse at all—they hamstrung cattle with long spears or rode up behind the beast, grabbed

the tail, slung it under a stirrup, and galloped off in another direction.

Like the cow pony itself, the western saddle descended directly from Spanish colonists in the New World. It may have evolved from some combination of the conquistador's saddle, the *estradiota,* a massive, thigh-binding combat rig, and the *jineta,* a light leather pad that was brought to Spain by the Moors. In its early forms, the vaquero's saddle was a homemade rig: just a tree—a skeleton of wood and rawhide—and a separate leather covering. Because vaqueros rode in cactus country, they also used tapaderos, stirrup covers now seen mainly on fancy parade saddles, and the heavy leather armor that evolved into cowboy's chaps. 3

Because its deep seat and prominent horn—sometimes large enough to be called a dinner plate—were so well suited to the cattleman's work, the Spanish saddle spread rapidly through Texas, New Mexico, and California, and on into the heart of the West. Everywhere it went it met with regional adaptations, some inspired by terrain, some by the way local cowboys handled their ropes. If you tie one end of your rope to the horn, a Texas specialty called roping hard and fast, you don't need as tall a horn as you do if you dally, which means taking several wraps around the horn without a knot. Another regional difference concerns the location of the cinch, the strap that passes under a horse's ribs and keeps the whole contraption—cowboy and all—from flying into the cactus. Hard-and-fast roping puts a lot of strain on the saddle, so in Texas they like a full, double rig—one cinch under the horn and a looser one under the cantle (the leather crescent that keeps the rider from slipping onto the horse's rump). Many cowboys, especially those in California and Montana, use a single cinch set a little farther back behind the horn—a three-quarter rig. "In cow country," says Chas Weldon, a highly regarded custom saddler, "and in places where they still buckaroo, people stay traditional. Even now you can pretty much tell where a cowboy's from by the look of his saddle." 4

Weldon turns out some forty saddles a year, all hand-built, 5 from his shop in Billings, Montana. They are beautiful, but not cheap. The average price is about $2,500, and it rises quickly as you add special touches. Factory-made saddles are like factory-built autos: They offer a small range of highly standardized options, and most people buy what's on the showroom floor. But when you order a custom saddle from Chas Weldon, or from his peers in the business, you face a two-year wait for delivery. You also face a bewildering array of choices, most of them directly related to the way you ride and the job you have to do on a horse.

The first thing you specify is the type of tree you want the saddle built on. There are dozens of varieties—Low Association, Old Association, Wade, 3B, Weatherly, Butch Cassidy, Rocky Mountain Roper, Brannaman, et cetera—but they differ mainly in the shape of the fork, that little bridge of leather and wood under the saddle horn. You may want a swell fork like the kind rodeo bronc riders use—the shoulders of the fork bulge sharply outward to give your thighs something to clamp onto when things, as they say, get western—or you may want a slick fork, with no swell at all. 6

And that is just the first decision. You've chosen the tree, but what about the horn? Do you dally or not? (Has the question ever occurred to you?) Do you want it wrapped in mulehide or latigo leather, or will you do what many ranchers do—wind the horn with a strip of inner tube? Do you want the cantle to go straight up or do you want a Cheyenne roll, the cantle breaking downward at the top like a wave? What kind of stirrups—bells, ropers, Visalias, oxbows—and how wide, and in brass or Monel or leather-covered? What kind of saddle leather: rough-out, plain, or tooled? Do you want a pocket for fencing pliers on the back billet? A pocket for fencing staples on the back of the cantle? How about a quilted seat? Do you prefer buckles or laces on the stirrup leathers? The questions go on and on, and every decision answers the larger question of who you are and how you ride and whether you plan to catch a cow with a rope. 7

But then that's the point of a western saddle. Every part of it has a name, and behind every name there is an origin, 8 a story, a historical model. In every bend of leather, every embellishment of form, you can find a purpose that takes you right back to a time when the Old West of popular imagination had not yet been born, when the true character of the western saddle did not yet lie hidden in myth.

For Study and Discussion

QUESTIONS FOR RESPONSE

1. What images and associations do you connect with the western saddle? Where do you think you got those images and associations? What specific sources do you remember?
2. What objects or tools that you use regularly in your everyday life have developed and changed since you first began to use them? (Think about phones, televisions, or bicycles, for instance.) What circumstances or developments do you think brought about those changes?

QUESTIONS ABOUT PURPOSE

1. What major realization about the western saddle do you think Klinkenborg wants to leave with his readers when they finish this essay?
2. How do you think the new information Klinkenborg has given you will affect the way you look at a western saddle the next time you see one firsthand, at a rodeo, or in a western movie?

QUESTIONS ABOUT AUDIENCE

1. This essay originally appeared in *Esquire* magazine. Who do you assume to be the principal audience for *Esquire*? What background information about western saddles does Klinkenborg assume these readers have? Where would they have gotten that information?
2. Frequently professional writers like Klinkenborg decide they want to write an article on a particular topic and then send a query letter to a magazine editor asking if he or she would be interested in publishing such an article. If you were the *Esquire*

editor who received a query letter from Klinkenborg about the idea for this article, what reasons might you have for thinking the article might be a good one for your magazine?

QUESTIONS ABOUT STRATEGIES

1. How does Klinkenborg catch his readers' attention in the first two paragraphs? What does he implicitly promise to tell the reader in the rest of the article? Do you think he fulfills that promise?
2. What kinds of details in the essay catch your attention and stay in your memory after you've finished reading it? What does Klinkenborg achieve by using those details? What impression about Klinkenborg himself do those details give you?

QUESTIONS FOR DISCUSSION

1. Probably few Americans have actually ridden on a western saddle or even seen one close up, yet Klinkenborg assumes that Americans—and probably millions of people in other countries as well—share a store of common knowledge about western saddles. To what extent do you think he is justified in this assumption? Why?
2. Klinkenborg refers to the "myth" of the western saddle in both the first and last sentences of the essay. What is that myth, and how does Klinkenborg seek to get behind it and show the saddle for what it really is? Why do you think he wants to do that?

DAVID GATES

David Gates was born in 1947 in Middletown, Connecticut, and was educated at the University of Connecticut. He taught English at the University of Virginia and Harvard University and then began a career as a journalist, eventually joining the staff of *Newsweek,* where he serves as a general editor of book reviews and music stories. He has published a novel, *Jennigan,* and his stories and articles have appeared in magazines such as *Esquire, Ploughshares, Smithsonian, Rolling Stone,* and *Virginia Quarterly Review.* In "Who Was Columbus?" reprinted from *Newsweek,* Gates sorts through the many myths and legends about Columbus to identify the "first American."

Who Was Columbus?

Forget the lettering at the top of Sebastiano del Piombo's famous painting, identifying that pursed-lipped, peevish-looking character as Columbus. It was probably added, years after the fact, to a portrait of some long-forgotten Italian nobleman. And forget the yarns in which he has to persuade stubborn monarchs that the earth is round, and face down a mutinous crew terrified they're going to sail off the edge. In 1492 educated people already knew, in theory, that you could reach the East by sailing west; sailors had long ceased to smite their brows when ships and land masses popped into sight from below the horizon. And he probably never heard the name Columbus, a Latinizing of his likely birth name, Cristoforo Colombo; Richard Hakluyt's "Principall navigations" (1598) popularized this fancy-dan form among English speakers. He was generally called Cristóbal Colón, as he still is among Spanish speakers. He signed himself simply Xρ̃o FERENS, a Greek-Latin hybrid clearly meant to 1 suggest his self-assigned mission of bringing Christ to the naked people across the ocean. His son, who was also his biographer, called him Colonus.

Like heroes from Julius Caesar to John Kennedy, Christopher Columbus has mostly been who people wanted him to be. To Renaissance humanists, he was the open-minded explorer, the arch-empiricist; to North American revolutionaries, he was the Founding Fathers' father, standing toe to toe with Old World monarchs and making them see things his way. Even 20th-century historiography hasn't quite humanized him—even when it's demythologized him. Samuel Eliot Morison's worshipful "Admiral of the Ocean Sea" (1942) acknowledges Columbus's slave trading and his disastrous stint as a colonial governor; still, his Columbus is not only a master seaman—Morison traced the voyages himself in a variety of boats—but a visionary "who carried Christian civilization across the Ocean Sea." In Kirkpatrick Sale's hostile "The Conquest of Paradise" (1990), Columbus becomes the embodiment of every political, spiritual and ecological sin imaginable to a founder of the New York Green Party: Eurocentrism, speciesism, capitalism, estrangement from both nature and self. "Perhaps most revealing of all," Sale writes, "this is a man without a settled *name,* and it is hard not to believe that a confusion, or at least inconstancy, of that kind reflects . . . psychological instability." Oh, right: he's an incompetent sailor, too. 2

The real Columbus, according to people who had seen him in the flesh, was a tall, red-faced man; he might've looked something like a 1512 portrait by Lorenzo Lotto, painted six years after Columbus's death. (We're not dead certain *this* portrait was meant to be Columbus, either.) He was probably born in Genoa, in 1451. His father was a wool weaver and tavernkeeper. In his early 20s, Columbus went to Portugal, then the most adventurous seafaring nation; at least once he sailed down the coast of West Africa. He married, had a son and was widowed; later he had a second son (Fernando, the biographer) by a woman he didn't marry. (That and the miracles he didn't perform killed his proposed 3 canonization in the 19th century.) At some point, for some reason, he made it his life's goal to reach Asia by sailing west across the Atlantic. After years of lobbying in the royal courts of both Portugal and Spain, he managed to get funding from the Spanish monarchs Ferdinand and Isabella. On four separate expeditions, he explored various Caribbean islands from which he sent back plants, minerals and slaves. Once he claimed to have found the Terrestrial Paradise: it was actually the mainland of South America. Under his stewardship, the first permanent Spanish settlement in the New World became so cruel and chaotic that he was returned to Europe in chains. He made one final, anticlimactic voyage and died, embittered, with plenty of money.

What was he like? Ambitious, obviously. Despite relatively humble beginnings—Genoese wool weavers didn't have the prestige or political clout of their Florentine or Venetian counterparts—he managed to marry a Portuguese woman whose family had influence at court. (Only after King João II turned him down did Columbus approach Spain's Ferdinand and Isabella.) He seems to have craved not just wealth but, as his first-name-only signature suggests, instant nobility. He campaigned, successfully, to be styled "Don," and Spain still honors his request to pass the title "Admiral of the Ocean Sea" on to his descendants. His ambition may or may not explain why he married Felipa Perestrello e Moniz, but it could well explain why he *didn't* marry Beatriz Enríquez de Arana, the mother of his son Fernando. "Marriage to a low-born orphan," write University of Minnesota historians William and Carla Phillips in the forthcoming "The Worlds of Christopher Columbus," "would do nothing to enhance his prestige and would surely impede his search for noble status." 4

If that seems distasteful—even after we've corrected for the 15th century's less enlightened views on both women and social class—consider that Columbus supported her in part with money he'd chiseled from the sailor who'd raised the cry of *"Tierra!"* on his 1492 voyage. Columbus had 5 promised a 10,000-maravedi annuity (perhaps $1,400 today) to whoever first sighted land; at first he credited one Juan Rodríguez Bermejo, but he later argued that he himself should get the annuity, since he'd spotted, or thought he spotted, a distant light some hours earlier. Perhaps the real issue wasn't the money but the credit for being first: for Columbus, as for most people, money seems to have been mixed up with self-esteem. (Wealthy but neglected in his last days, he claimed to be "without a single blanca.") The Phillipses speculate that Columbus may have turned the annuity over to de Arana because he felt guilty about his treatment of Bermejo. It's possible—though it's equally possible he cheated the man to channel some money to his mistress. We'll never know.

One thing does seem certain: that Columbus sometimes exaggerated, misrepresented and just plain lied, particularly in overselling the islands he discovered. One often-cited instance of his deviousness may be a bum rap: the confession in his journal of the first voyage that he underreported the distance the ship made each day so as not to alarm the sailors. The Phillipses argue that this part of the journal may be garbled. (It doesn't exist in manuscript, but in a 16th-century paraphrase of an unreliable copy.) But there are enough other instances—like his forcing sailors on the second voyage to swear that Cuba was not an island—to justify Sale's claim that Columbus's indifference to the distinction between truth and falsehood sometimes verged on madness. 6

Yet where Columbus seems looniest to us, he's actually at his most orthodox. World maps in his day *did* place the Garden of Eden near Asia—where he always insisted his islands were—and he was sufficiently a man of the Middle Ages to deem the Bible a reliable (if sibylline) source of geographical knowledge. As the Phillipses show, Columbus's picture of the world was a collage of Scripture, Ptolemy, contemporary maps, his own observations and wishful thinking. Similarly, we should take seriously the stated purpose of his explorations: to bring the unconverted to Christ and 7 to raise funds in order to capture Jerusalem, thereby ushering in the Second Coming. It's hard for moderns to ignore the dissonance between these pious aims and the reality: the Admiral of the Ocean Sea brutalizing and enslaving the "Indians" and enriching himself. It's safe to say he never saw it that way. Despite his posthumous status as empiricist exemplar, he put a lot of energy into *not* seeing things as they were.

It's become commonplace to regard Columbus as a representative man of his time, with one foot in the Middle Ages and one in the Renaissance. It's safer than making inferences about his personality, beyond such hard-to-miss traits as the grandiosity and self-pity he showed late in life. Consequently, today's Columbus is more "complex" than the imaginary hero who stood the egg on end, but also more remote. Only imagination can bring us close to him again: not by resurrecting discredited yarns, but by using the verifiable facts to reconstruct what his experience must have been like. 8

So put yourself in Columbus's shoes. You're 41—in those days, an old man—and at last your dream comes true. They've given you your ships, the winds are favorable, you reach the land you always knew was there. But it's not the way you thought it would be, and not what you promised when they put up the money. There's island after island after island, but you can't find Cipango (Japan), where the cities and the gold mines are, and you can't get a straight answer out of the locals. So you deliver what you can: a little gold, some plants you thought (mistakenly) you recognized and a few natives. You're vindicated; they give you more ships, more men. But something's not right, and your sponsors soon get suspicious. You should be dealing with Eastern potentates, not these naked people who've started to hate you. You try to keep order in your pitiful settlement, but things get out of hand. You wind up in chains, accused of brutality and, worse, incompetence. And you started out with the best intentions. You were going to get rich *and* save 9 the world. You didn't see any contradiction there. You were the first American.

For Study and Discussion

QUESTIONS FOR RESPONSE

1. What opinions and ideas about Columbus did you have before your read this essay? What do you think is the source of those opinions?
2. In what ways did Gates's essay modify your views about Columbus? What would you say is your impression about him now? What new information did you acquire that contributed to that change?

QUESTIONS ABOUT PURPOSE

1. At the time Gates wrote this essay for a special commemorative issue of *Newsweek,* some groups were protesting the celebration of the five hundredth anniversary of Columbus's arrival in America. They claimed that Americans, particularly Native Americans, should not celebrate his achievements because he exploited the Indians and harmed the environment. In what ways does this essay seem to be a response to such charges?
2. What do you think Gates wants his readers to conclude about Columbus's character and his place in history?

QUESTIONS ABOUT AUDIENCE

1. In writing for *Newsweek* readers, what assumptions about his audience do you think Gates can reasonably make? How much historical information do you think such readers are likely to have? Why would Gates assume they have an interest in his topic?
2. At the end, Gates asks the reader to imagine that he or she is Columbus and see his world and his ambitions from that point of view. What obstacles do you think a twentieth-century reader faces in doing this? Are they so serious that Gates is really asking for an impossible exercise? Why?

QUESTIONS ABOUT STRATEGIES

1. How does Gates use the first two paragraphs of his essay to set the stage for the picture of Columbus he presents in the rest of the essay?
2. What details does Gates use to persuade his readers that he is a careful historian who wants to present a balanced picture of Columbus? How does his tone contribute to that same goal?

QUESTIONS FOR DISCUSSION

1. To what extent does Gates succeed in winning your sympathies for Columbus? How does he accomplish that?
2. At the end Gates suggests that Columbus was a typical American—ambitious, adventuresome, a risk taker, and greedy for fame and fortune. How do you react to that intepretation of Columbus and of Americans?

ALISON LURIE

Alison Lurie was born in Chicago in 1926 and was educated in New York, Connecticut, and at Radcliffe College. She began to write at an early age and continued to do so during the early years of her marriage and child-rearing. Her first novel, *Love and Friendship,* was published in 1962. The title of the book was borrowed from an early Jane Austen novel, and over the years reviewers have pointed to similarities between the two writers—their detached observations, ironic wit, and precision of statement. Lurie's tendency to write about the closed community she knows best—the wealthy and educated segment of American society—is also reminiscent of Austen. Her fifth novel, *The War Between the Tates* (1974), was the first to find a sizable audience. Her seventh novel, *Foreign Affairs* (1984), was awarded a Pulitzer Prize. Alison Lurie has also published three collections of stories for children; a witty social history of apparel, *The Language of Clothes* (1981); and a study of children's literature, *Don't Tell the Grown-ups* (1990). In "Folktale Liberation," excerpted from this last work, Lurie defines the "most subversive texts in children's literature"—fairy tales.

Folktale Liberation

Folktales are the oldest and most widely known form of literature for children. "Beauty and the Beast" was told in classical Greece and ancient India; "Hansel and Gretel" has been collected in the West Indies, in African villages, and among the American Indians. 1

These tales also have another distinction: they are among the most subversive texts in children's literature. Often, 2 though usually in disguised form, they support the rights of disadvantaged members of the population—children, women, and the poor—against the establishment. Law and order are not always respected: the master thief fools the count and the parson, and Jack kills the giant and steals his treasure. Rich people are often unlucky, afflicted, or helpless: kings and queens cannot have children or suffer from strange illnesses, while the poor are healthy and enterprising and fortunate.

As long as these stories remained part of an oral culture, related to small audiences of unimportant people, they were largely overlooked by the literary and educational establishment. But as soon as they began to surface in printed texts there were outcries of horror and disapproval; cries that have continued to this day. 3

The late-eighteenth-century author and educational authority Sarah Trimmer cautioned parents against allowing their children to hear or read fairy tales, which she considered immoral because they taught ambition, violence, a love of wealth, and the desire to marry above one's station. Cinderella, she wrote, "paints some of the worst passions that can enter into the human breast, and of which little children should, if possible, be totally ignorant; such as envy, jealousy, a dislike of step-mothers and half-sisters, vanity, a love of dress, etc." Other critics complained that these tales were unscientific and confused truth with fiction, and that they wasted time that would be better spent learning facts, skills, and good manners. 4

More than 150 years later it was still believed in high-minded progressive circles that fairy tales were unsuitable for children. "Does not 'Cinderella' interject a social and economic situation which is both confusing and vicious? . . . Does not 'Jack and the Beanstalk' delay a child's rationalizing of the world and leave him longer than is desirable without the beginnings of scientific standards?" As one child education expert, Lucy Sprague Mitchell, put it in the introduction to her *Here and Now Story Book,* which I received for my fifth birthday. It would be much better, she and her colleagues 5 thought, for children to read simple, pleasant, realistic tales that would help to prepare us for the adult world.

Mrs. Mitchell's own contribution to literature was a squat volume, sunny orange in color, with an idealized city scene on the cover. Inside I could read about the Grocery Man ("This is John's Mother. Good morning, Mr. Grocery Man") and How Spot Found a Home. The children and parents in these stories were exactly like the ones I knew, only more boring. They never did anything really wrong, and nothing dangerous or surprising ever happened to them—no more than it did to Dick and Jane, whom I and my friends were soon to meet in first grade. 6

After we grew up, of course, we found out how unrealistic these stories had been. The simple, pleasant adult society they had prepared us for did not exist. As we had suspected, the fairy tales had been right all along—the world was full of hostile, stupid giants and perilous castles and people who abandoned their children in the nearest forest. To succeed in this world you needed some special skill or patronage, plus remarkable luck; and it didn't hurt to be very good-looking. The other qualities that counted were wit, boldness, stubborn persistence, and an eye for the main chance. Kindness to those in trouble was also advisable—you never knew who might be useful to you later on. 7

The fairy tales were also way ahead of Mrs. Mitchell with respect to women's liberation. In her stories men drove wagons and engines and boats, built skyscrapers, worked in stores, and ran factories; women did nothing except keep house, look after children, and go shopping. Fairy tales, on the other hand, portrayed a society in which women were as competent and active as men, at every age and in every class. Gretel, not Hansel, defeated the witch; and for every clever youngest son there was a youngest daughter equally resourceful. The contrast continued in maturity, when women were often more powerful than men. Real help for the hero or heroine came most often from a fairy godmother or wise woman, and real trouble from a witch or wicked stepmother. With a frequency that recalls current feminist polemics, the 8 significant older male figures were either dumb macho giants or malevolent little dwarfs.

Yet in spite of this, some contemporary feminists have joined the chorus of critics and attacked fairy tales as a male chauvinist form of literature: they believe that giving children stories like "Cinderella" and "Snow White" is a sort of brainwashing, intended to convince them that all little girls must be gentle, obedient, passive, and domestic while they wait patiently for their princes to come. 9

In a way these objections are understandable, since some of the tales we know best—those that have been popularized by Walt Disney, for instance—do have this kind of heroine. But from the point of view of European (and world) folklore, such stories are highly unrepresentative. The traditional tale, in fact, is exactly the sort of subversive literature of which a feminist should approve. 10

For one thing, these stories are in a literal sense women's literature. Charles Perrault, who was one of the first to write them down, called them "old wives' tales, governesses' and grannies' tales." Later, throughout Europe (except in Ireland), the storytellers from whom the Grimm brothers and their followers collected their material were most often women; in some areas, they were all women. For hundreds of years, while written literature was almost exclusively in the hands of men, these tales were being invented and passed on orally by women. 11

In content too fairy tales are women's literature. Writers like Robert Graves have seen them as survivals of an older, matriarchal culture and faith; but whether they are right or not, it is women who most often are the central characters in many of these stories, and women who have the supernatural power. In the Grimms' original *Children's and Household Tales* (1812), there are sixty-one women and girl characters who have magic powers as against only twenty-one men and boys: and these men are usually dwarfs and not humans. 12

Another thing that separates the folktale from the printed literature of its time is that it is a middle- and working-class genre. The world it portrays and the problems it deals with 13 are those of farmers, artisans, shopkeepers, and the working poor: survival, employment, family unity. The heroes and heroines of these tales are often very badly off, while the supernatural villains—the giants and ogres and witches—are rich. "Kings" and "queens," who lack supernatural powers and have human problems—infertility, exterior enemies, serious illness—seem from internal evidence to be merely well-to-do farmers. Literary retellings of the tales, however, from Perrault to the present, usually give their royalty a convincingly aristocratic setting.

The handful of folktales that most readers today know are not typical of the genre. They are the result of a more insidious sort of critical attack than that mounted by Sarah Trimmer and her heirs: the skewed selection and silent revision of subversive texts. At first this selection and revision were open and acknowledged. Perrault rewrote the stories he had heard from his "old wives" in elegant seventeenth-century French, adding witty morals in verse and turning the wise women of folk tradition into pretty fairies in court dress with sparkling wands and butterfly wings. In midnineteenth-century England, George Cruikshank made his four favorite tales into temperance tracts—at Cinderella's wedding, he reported, a great bonfire was made of all the bottles of wine and spirits in the castle. Even the Grimm brothers openly bowdlerized their stories to make them "suitable for childhood," and, as time went on, altered them in other ways. In each subsequent edition of the tales, for instance, women were given less to say and do. 14

Most compilers of books of fairy tales, unfortunately, have been less direct. For nearly two hundred years tales have been omitted and unacknowledged changes made in the original texts. The stories we know best today reflect the taste of the literary men who edited the first popular collections of fairy stories for children during the nineteenth century. They read the hundreds of folktales that had been gathered by scholars, chose the ones that most appealed to them as conventional upper-middle-class Victorians, and then rewrote these tales to make them suitable for Victorian children. 15

By the late nineteenth century a canon had been estab- 16

lished, and the dozen or so tales these editors had liked best were reprinted again and again. "Sleeping Beauty" was retold over and over, always without its original ending, in which the heroine gives birth to two children as the result of the prince's passionate awakening of her. Meanwhile, "The Sleeping Prince," a parallel story about a passive hero rescued from enchantment by an active heroine, was forgotten.

Folktales recorded in the field are full of everything the Victorian editors left out: sex, death, low humor, and especially female initiative. In some more recent and comprehensive books of tales—as well as in Andrew Lang's famous fairy books named after colors, the later volumes of which were largely compiled and revised by his wife—there are more active heroines. They travel to the world's end, cross oceans on a wild goose's back, climb mountains of glass, enter giants' castles and steal magic objects, outwit false suitors, and defeat all kinds of supernatural enemies. They work for years to release their lovers or relatives from enchantments and help them to escape from witches and ogres. They are in effect liberated women who have courage, intelligence, resourcefulness, endurance, and kind hearts. 17

For Study and Discussion

QUESTIONS FOR RESPONSE

1. What folktales do you know? "Hansel and Gretel"? "Little Red Riding Hood"? "Beauty and the Beast"? In what ways do you think these or other folktales or fairy tales "support the rights of disadvantaged members of the population—children, women, and the poor—against the establishment," as Lurie suggests?
2. Today's young people may encounter folktales in the form of movies or television cartoons. If that is the form in which most folktales and fairy tales are familiar to you, to what extent do you think these popular versions have altered the liberating messages that Lurie sees in the originals?

QUESTIONS ABOUT PURPOSE

1. What function does Lurie think stories about enchantment and magical powers can serve in the lives of the children who read them?
2. How does Lurie think it would help today's children if they were able to read folktales and fairy stories such as "Sleeping Beauty" in their original forms rather than the bland and sanitized versions found in many modern storybooks and in Disney films?

QUESTIONS ABOUT AUDIENCE

1. This essay comes from Lurie's book *Don't Tell the Grown-ups,* a book about children's literature that she might use as a text in the children's literature course she teaches at Cornell University. What experiences with children's books does Lurie seem to assume her readers have had?
2. Folktales originated in preprint, oral cultures in which people were taught and entertained through stories and myths. To what degree is there still an oral culture in our modern world? Under those circumstances, how can folktales and fairy tales still be a force in the lives of today's children?

QUESTIONS ABOUT STRATEGIES

1. What early appeal does Lurie make to the rebellious adolescent streak that she suspects most of her readers share with her?
2. What evidence does Lurie present to support her claim that folktales and fairy tales are essentially a literature of women's liberation?

QUESTIONS FOR DISCUSSION

1. What connections can young readers make between the original folk stories Lurie mentions and elements in their own lives? How could that be helpful?
2. Who does Lurie portray as the "villains" when she bemoans the changes in fairy stories from their original forms to censored Victorian versions to Disney World versions of today? What does she see as the major motives for changing the stories?

FRANCINE du PLESSIX GRAY

Francine du Plessix Gray was born in 1930 in Warsaw, Poland, and came to the United States in 1941. She was educated at Bryn Mawr, Black Mountain College, and Barnard College. She worked as a reporter for UPI, an editorial assistant for *Realities,* a book editor for *Art in America,* and a staff writer for the *New Yorker.* She has also taught writing at Yale University and Columbia University. Her articles, stories, and reviews have appeared in magazines such as *Vogue,* the *New Yorker,* and the *New York Times Book Review.* Her nonfiction includes *Divine Disobedience: Profiles in Catholic Radicalism* (1970), *Hawaii: The Sugar-Coated Fortress* (1972), *Adam and Eve and the City* (1987), and *Soviet Women: Walking the Tightrope* (1990). She has also written three novels: *Lovers and Tyrants* (1976), *World Without End* (1981), and *October Blood* (1985). "On Friendship," reprinted from *Adam and Eve and the City,* defines the central role of friendship in achieving human happiness.

On Friendship

I saw Madame Bovary at Bloomingdale's the other morning, or rather, I saw many incarnations of her. She was hovering over the cosmetic counters, clutching the current issue of *Cosmopolitan,* whose cover line read "New Styles of Coupling, Including Marriage." Her face already ablaze with numerous products advertised to make her irresistible to the opposite sex, she looked anguished, grasping, overwrought, and terribly lonely. And I thought to myself: Poor girl! With all the reams of literature that have analyzed her plight (victimized by double standards, by a materialistic middle-class glutting on the excesses of romantic fiction), notwithstand- 1 ing all these diagnoses, one fact central to her tragic fate has never been stressed enough: Emma Bovary had a faithful and boring husband and a couple of boring lovers—not so intolerable a condition—but she did not have a friend in the world. And when I think of the great solitude which the original Emma and her contemporaries exude, one phrase jumps to my mind. It comes from an essay by Francis Bacon, and it is one of the finest statements ever penned about the human need for friendship: "Those who have no friends to open themselves unto are cannibals of their own hearts."

In the past years the theme of friendship has been increas- 2
ingly prominent in our conversations, in our books and films, even in our college courses. It is evident that many of us are yearning with new fervor for this form of bonding. And our yearning may well be triggered by the same disillusionment with the reign of Eros that destroyed Emma Bovary. Emma was eating her heart out over a fantasy totally singular to the Western world, and only a century old at that: the notion that sexual union between men and women who believe that they are passionately in love, a union achieved by free choice and legalized by marriage, tends to offer a life of perpetual bliss and is the most desirable human bond available on earth. It is a notion bred in the same frenzied climate of the romantic epoch that caused countless young Europeans to act like the characters of their contemporary literature. Goethe's *Werther* is said to have triggered hundreds of suicides. Numerous wives glutted on the fantasies of George Sand's heroines demanded separations because their husbands were unpoetic. And Emma Bovary, palpitating from that romantic fiction which precurses our current sex manuals in its outlandish hopes for the satiation of desire, muses in the third week of her marriage: Where is "the felicity, the passion, the intoxication" that had so enchanted her in the novels of Sir Walter Scott?

This frenzied myth of love which has also led to the 3
downfall of Cleopatra, Juliet, Romeo, and King Kong continues to breed, in our time, more garbled thinking, wretched verse, and nonsensical jingles than any emotion under the sun: "All You Need Is Love," or as we heard it in our high-

school days, "Tell me you'll love me forever, if only tonight." As Flaubert put it, we are all victims of romanticism. And if we still take for granted its cult of heterosexual passion, it is in part because we have been victimized, as Emma was, by the propaganda machine of the Western novel. It was the power and the genius of the novel form to fuse medieval notions of courtly love with the idealization of marriage that marked the rise of the eighteenth-century middle class. (By "romantic love," I mean an infatuation that involves two major ingredients: a sense of being "enchanted" by another person through a complex process of illusion, and a willingness to totally surrender to that person.)

One hardly needs a course in anthropology to realize that 4
this alliance of marriage and romantic love is restricted to a small segment of the Western world, and would seem sheer folly in most areas of this planet. The great majority of humans—be it in China, Japan, Africa, India, the Moslem nations—still engage in marriages prearranged by their elders or dictated by pragmatic reasons of money, land, tribal politics, or (as in the Socialist countries) housing shortages. Romantically motivated marriage as the central ingredient of the good life is almost as novel in our own West. In popular practice, it remained restricted to a narrow segment of the middle class until the twentieth century. And on the level of philosophical reflection, it was always friendship between members of the same sex, never any bonding of sexual affection, which from Greek times to the Enlightenment was held to be the cornerstone of human happiness. Yet this central role allotted to friendship for two thousand years has been progressively eroded by such factors as the nineteenth-century exaltation of instinct; science's monopoly on our theories of human sentiment; the massive eroticizing of society; and that twentieth-century celebration of the body that reaches its peak in the hedonistic solitude of the multiple orgasm.

To Aristotle, friendship can be formed only by persons of 5
virtue: A man's capacity for friendship is the most accurate

measure of his virtue; it is the foundation of the state, for great legislators care even more for friendship than they care for justice. To Plato, as we know, passionate affection untainted by physical relations is the highest form of human bonding. To Cicero, *Amicitia* is more important than either money, power, honors, or health because each of these gifts can bring us only one form of pleasure, whereas the pleasures of friendship are marvelously manifold; and friendship being based on equity, the tyrant is the man least capable of forming that bond because of his need to wield power over others. Montaigne's essay, along with Bacon's, is the most famous of many that glorify our theme in the Renaissance. And like the ancients, he stresses the advantages of friendship over any kind of romantic and physical attachment. Love for members of the opposite sex, in Montaigne's words, is "an impetuous and fickle flame, undulating and variable, a fever flame subject to fits and lulls." Whereas the fire of friendship produces "a general and universal warmth, moderate and even," and will always forge bonds superior to those of marriage because marriage's continuance is "constrained and forced, depending on factors other than our free will."

A century later, even La Rochefoucauld, that great cynic 6
who described the imperialism of the ego better than any other precursor of Freud, finds that friendship is the only human bond in which the tyrannical cycle of our self-love seems broken, in which "we can love each other even more than love ourselves." One of the last classic essays on friendship I can think of before it loses major importance as a philosophical theme is by Ralph Waldo Emerson. And it's interesting to note that by mid-nineteenth century, the euphoric absolutes which had previously described this form of bonding are sobered by many cautious qualifications. A tinge of modern pragmatism sets in. Emerson tends to distrust any personal friendship unless it functions for the purpose of some greater universal fraternity.

Yet however differently these thinkers focused on our 7
theme, they all seemed to reach a consensus on the qualities of free will, equity, trust, and selflessness unique to the

affection of friendship. They cannot resist comparing it to physical passion, which yearns for power over the other, seeks possession and the state of being possessed, seeks to devour, breeds on excess, can easily become demonic, is closely allied to the death wish, and is often a form of agitated narcissism quite unknown to the tranquil, balanced rule of friendship. And rereading the sagas of Tristan and Iseult, Madame Bovary, and many other romantic lovers, it is evident that their passions tend to breed as much on a masturbatory excitement as on a longing for the beloved. They are in love with love, their delirium is involved with a desire for self-magnification through suffering, as evidenced in Tristan's words, "Eyes with joy are blinded. I myself am the world." There is confrontation, turmoil, aggression, in the often militaristic language of romantic love: Archers shoot fatal arrows or unerring shafts; the male enemy presses, pursues, and conquers; women surrender after being besieged by amorous assaults. Friendship on the other hand is the most pacifist species in the fauna of human emotions, the most steadfast and sharing. No wonder then that the finest pacifist ideology in the West was devised by a religious group—the Quakers—which takes as its official name the Religious Society of Friends; the same temperate principle of fraternal bonding informs that vow demanded by the Benedictine Order—the Oath of Stability—which remains central to the monastic tradition to this day. No wonder, also, that the kind of passionate friendship shared by David and Jonathan has inspired very few masterpieces of literature, which seem to thrive on tension and illicitness. For until they were relegated to the dissecting rooms of the social sciences, our literary views of friendship tended to be expressed in the essay form, a cool, reflective mode that never provided friendship with the motive, democratic, propagandistic force found by Eros in novel, verse, and stage. To this day, friendship totally resists commercial exploitation, unlike the vast businesses fueled by romantic love that support the couture, perfume, cosmetic, lingerie, and pulp-fiction trades.

One should note, however, that most views of friendship 8

expressed in the past twenty centuries of Western thought have dealt primarily with the male's capacity for affection. And they tend to be extremely dubious about the possibility of women ever being able to enjoy genuine friendships with members of their own sex, not to speak of making friends with male peers. Montaigne expressed a prejudice that lasts well into our day when he wrote, "The ordinary capacity of women is inadequate for that communion and fellowship which is the nurse of that sacred bond, nor does their soul feel firm enough to endure the strain of so tight and durable a knot." It is shocking, though not surprising, to hear prominent social scientists paraphrase that opinion in our own decades. Konrad Lorenz and Lionel Tiger, for instance, seem to agree that women are made eminently unsociable by their genetic programming; their bondings, in Lorenz's words, "must be considered weak imitations of the exclusively male associations." Given the current vogue for sociobiology, such assertions are often supported by carefully researched papers on the courtship patterns of Siberian wolves, the prevalence of eye contact among male baboons, and the vogue for gangbanging among chimpanzees.

Our everyday language reflects the same bias: "Fraternity" 9
is a word that goes far beyond its collegiate context and embraces notions of honor, dignity, loyalty. "Sorority" is something we might have belonged to as members of the University of Oklahoma's bowling team in the early 1950s. So I think it is high time that the same feminist perspective that has begun to correct the biases of art history and psychoanalysis should be brought to bear on this area of anthropology. We have indeed been deprived of those official, dramatically visible rites offered to men in pub, poolroom, Elks, hunting ground, or football league. And having been brought up in a very male world, I'm ashamed to say it took me a decade of feminist consciousness to realize that the few bonding associations left to twentieth-century women—garden clubs, church suppers, sewing circles (often derided by men because they do not deal with power)—have been activities considerably more creative and life-enhancing than

the competition of the poolroom, the machismo of beer drinking, or the bloodshed of hunting.

Among both sexes, the rites and gestures of friendship seemed to have been decimated in the Victorian era, which brought a fear of homosexuality unprecedented in the West. (They also tended to decrease as rites of heterosexual coupling became increasingly permissive.) Were Dr. Johnson and James Boswell gay, those two men who constantly exhibited their affection for each other with kisses, tears, and passionate embraces? I suspect they were as rabidly straight as those tough old soldiers described by Tacitus begging for last kisses when their legion broke up. Since Freud, science has tended to dichotomize human affection along lines of deviance and normalcy, genitality and platonic love, instead of leaving it as a graduated spectrum of emotion in which love, friendship, sensuality, sexuality, can freely flow into each other as they did in the past. This may be another facet of modern culture that has cast coolness and self-consciousness on our gestures of friendship. The 1960s brought us some hope for change, both in its general emotional climate and in our scientists' tendency to relax their definitions of normalcy and deviance. For one of the most beautiful signs of that decade's renewed yearning for friendship and community, particularly evident among the groups who marched in civil-rights or antiwar demonstrations, was the sight of men clutching, kissing, embracing each other unabashedly as Dr. Johnson and James Boswell. 10

Which leads me to reflect on the reasons why I increasingly turn to friendship in my own life: In a world more and more polluted by the lying of politicians and the illusions of the media, I occasionally crave to hear and to tell the truth. To borrow a beautiful phrase from Friedrich Nietzsche, I look upon my friend as "the beautiful enemy" who alone is able to offer me total candor. I look for the kind of honest friend Emma Bovary needed: one who could have told her that her lover was a jerk. 11

Friendship is by its very nature freer of deceit than any other relationship we can know because it is the bond least 12 affected by striving for power, physical pleasure, or material profit, most liberated from any oath of duty or of constancy. With Eros the *body* stands naked, in friendship our *spirit* is denuded. Friendship, in this sense, is a human condition resembling what may be humanity's most beautiful and necessary lie—the promise of an afterlife. It is an almost celestial sphere in which we most resemble that society of angels offered us by Christian theology, in which we can sing the truth of our inner thoughts in relative freedom and abundance. No wonder then that the last contemporary writers whose essays on friendship may remain classics are those religiously inclined, scholars relatively unaffected by positivism or behaviorism, or by the general scientificization of human sentiment. That marvelous Christian maverick, C. S. Lewis, tells us: "Friendship is unnecessary, like philosophy, like art, like the universe itself (since God did not *need* to create). It has no survival value; rather it is one of those things that give value to survival." And the Jewish thinker Simone Weil focuses on the classic theme of free consent when she writes: "Friendship is a miracle by which a person consents to view from a certain distance, and without coming any nearer, the very being who is necessary to him as food."

The quality of free consent and self-determination inher- 13
ent in friendship may be crucial to the lives of twentieth-century women beginning their vocations. But in order to return friendship to an absolutely central place in our lives, we might have to wean ourselves in part from the often submissive premises of romantic passion. I suspect that we shall always need some measure of swooning and palpitating, of ecstasy and trembling, of possessing and being possessed. But, I also suspect that we've been bullied and propagandized into many of these manifestations by the powerful modern organism that I call the sexual-industrial complex and that had an antecedent in the novels that fueled Emma Bovary's deceitful fantasies. For one of the most treacherous aspects of the cult of romantic love has been its complex idealization and exploitation of female sexuality. There is now a new school of social scientists who are militantly questioning the

notion that Western romantic love is the best foundation for human bonding, and their criticism seems much inspired by feminist perspectives. The Australian anthropologist Robert Brain, for instance, calls romantic love "a lunatic relic of medieval passions . . . the handmaiden of a moribund capitalistic culture and of an equally dead Puritan ethic."

What exactly would happen if we women remodeled our concepts of ideal human bonding on the ties of friendship and abandoned the premises of enchantment and possession? Such a restructuring of our ideals of happiness could be extremely subversive. It might imply a considerable de-eroticizing of society. It could bring about a minor revolution against the sexual-industrial complex that brings billions of dollars to thousands of men by brainwashing us into the roles of temptress and seductress, and estranges us from the plain and beautiful Quaker ideal of being a sister to the world. How topsy-turvy the world would be! Dalliance, promiscuity, all those more sensationalized aspects of the Women's Movement that were once seen as revolutionary might suddenly seem most bourgeois and old-fashioned activities. If chosen in conditions of rigorous self-determination, the following values, considered up to now as reactionary, could suddenly become the most radical ones at hand: Virginity. Celibacy. Monastic communities. And that most endangered species of all, fidelity in marriage, which has lately become so exotically rare that it might soon become very fashionable, and provide the cover story for yet another publication designed to alleviate the seldom-admitted solitude of swinging singles: "Mick Jagger Is into Fidelity." 14

For Study and Discussion

QUESTIONS FOR RESPONSE

1. As a late twentieth-century man or woman, how do you respond to Montaigne's sixteenth-century point of view that women

don't have the capacity for real friendship or to Konrad Lorenz's assertion that women's friendships are weak imitations of men's? How does your own experience support or refute such statements?

2. Du Plessix Gray makes some strong claims for friendship, saying that the qualities of free will, equity, trust, and selflessness are unique to it. Drawing on your own experiences with your friends, explain why you, on the whole, agree or disagree with her.

QUESTIONS ABOUT PURPOSE

1. How does du Plessix Gray want to change her readers' view of romantic love? What difficulties does she have to overcome in order to do so?
2. This essay argues that in our culture we should focus more on friendship and less on erotic love. Which of those purposes do you think the author feels more strongly about? What about the essay makes you think that?

QUESTIONS ABOUT AUDIENCE

1. What influences and forces in our society make nearly every American reader familiar with what du Plessix Gray calls "the sexual-industrial complex"?
2. What preconceptions and biases about romantic love do you think an audience of college readers is likely to have? How do you think their responses to du Plessix Gray's arguments are going to be affected by those biases?

QUESTIONS ABOUT STRATEGIES

1. Why do you think du Plessix Gray starts her essay with "I saw Madame Bovary at Bloomingdale's the other morning"? What is the immediate picture you get? How does the author expand her comments in the first two paragraphs to reach readers who may not have read *Madame Bovary*?
2. What effect does du Plessix Gray get by pointing out the militaristic language of romantic love in paragraph 7? How does this effect serve her purpose?

QUESTIONS FOR DISCUSSION

1. Describe the various elements of du Plessix Gray's "sexual-industrial complex." How powerful do you think it is? Who would you say is most affected by it?
2. What changes in our society would you expect if it were to be "de-eroticized," as du Plessix Gray puts it? How do you think you would react to those changes?

LOREN EISELEY

Loren Eiseley (1907–1977) was born in Lincoln, Nebraska, and was educated at the University of Pennsylvania. He held faculty positions at the University of Kansas, Oberlin College, and the University of Pennsylvania, where he was Franklin Professor of Anthropology and History of Science. He contributed articles to scientific journals, such as *American Anthropologist* and *Scientific Monthly,* and popular magazines, such as *Holiday* and the *Ladies' Home Journal.* His books include *The Immense Journey* (1957), *Darwin's Century* (1958), *The Mind as Nature* (1962), *Francis Bacon and the Modern Dilemma* (1963), and *The Unexpected Universe* (1969). In these books, and in all his writing, Eiseley conveys the scrupulousness of scientific inquiry in beautifully crafted language; his vision is simultaneously that of scientist and poet. In "Man the Firemaker," reprinted from *The Star Thrower* (1978), Eiseley defines the uniqueness of the human species by its manipulation and consumption of fire.

Man the Firemaker

Man, it is well to remember, is the discoverer but not the inventor of fire. Long before this meddling little Prometheus took to experimenting with flints, then matches, and finally (we hope not too finally) hydrogen bombs, fires had burned on this planet. Volcanoes had belched molten lava, lightning had struck in dry grass, winds had rubbed dead branches against each other until they burst into flame. There are evidences of fire in ancient fossil beds that lie deep below the time of man. 1

Man did not invent fire but he did make it one of the 2

giant powers on the earth. He began this experiment long ago in the red morning of the human mind. Today he continues it in the midst of coruscating heat that is capable of rending the very fabric of his universe. Man's long adventure with knowledge has, to a very marked degree, been a climb up the heat ladder, for heat alone enables man to mold metals and glassware, to create his great chemical industries, to drive his swift machines. It is my intention here to trace man's manipulation of this force far back into its ice-age beginnings and to observe the part that fire has played in the human journey across the planet. The torch has been carried smoking through the ages of glacial advance. As we follow man on this journey, we shall learn another aspect of his nature: that he is himself a consuming fire.

At just what level in his intellectual development man 3
mastered the art of making fire is still unknown. Neanderthal man of 50,000 years ago certainly knew the art. Traces of the use of fire have turned up in a cave of Peking man, the primitive human being of at least 250,000 years ago who had a brain only about two-thirds the size of modern man's. And in 1947 Raymond Dart of Witwatersrand University announced the discovery in South Africa of *Australopithecus prometheus,* a man-ape cranium recovered from deposits which he believed showed traces of burned bone.

This startling announcement of the possible use of fire by 4
a subhuman creature raised a considerable storm in anthropological circles. The chemical identifications purporting to indicate evidence of fire are now considered highly questionable. It has also been intimated that the evidence may represent only traces of a natural brush fire. Certainly, so long as the South African man-apes have not been clearly shown to be tool users, wide doubts about their use of fire will remain. There are later sites of tool-using human beings which do not show traces of fire.

Until there is proof to the contrary, it would seem wise 5
to date the earliest use of fire to Peking man—*Sinanthropus.* Other human sites of the same antiquity have not yielded evidence of ash, but this is not surprising, for as a new

discovery the use of fire would have taken time to diffuse from one group to another. Whether it was discovered once or several times we have no way of knowing. The fact that fire was in worldwide use at the beginning of man's civilized history enables us to infer that it is an old human culture trait—doubtless one of the earliest. Furthermore, it is likely that man used fire long before he became sophisticated enough to produce it himself.

In 1865 Sir John Lubbock, a British banker who made a 6
hobby of popular writing on science, observed: "There can be no doubt that man originally crept over the earth's surface, little by little, year by year, just, for instance, as the weeds of Europe are now gradually but surely creeping over the surface of Australia." This remark was, in its time, a very shrewd and sensible observation. We know today, however, that there have been times when man suddenly made great strides across the face of the earth. I want to review one of those startling expansions—a lost episode in which fire played a tremendous part. To make its outlines clear we shall have to review the human drama in three acts.

The earliest humanlike animals we can discern are the 7
man-apes of South Africa. Perhaps walking upright on two feet, this creature seems to have been roaming the East African grasslands about one million years ago. Our ancestor, proto-man, probably emerged from the tropics and diffused over the region of warm climate in Eurasia and North Africa. He must have been dependent upon small game, insects, wild seeds, and fruits. His life was hard, his search for food incessant, his numbers were small.

The second stage in human history is represented by the 8
first true men. Paleoanthropic man is clearly a tool user, a worker in stone and bone, but there is still something of the isolated tinkerer and fumbler about him. His numbers are still sparse, judging from the paucity of skeletal remains. Short, stocky, and powerful, he spread over the most temperate portions of the Afro-Eurasiatic land mass but never attempted the passage through the high Arctic to America. Through scores of millennia he drifted with the seasons,

seemingly content with his troglodyte existence, making little serious change in his array of flint tools. It is quite clear that some of these men knew the use of fire, but many may not have.

The third act begins some 15,000 or 20,000 years ago. 9
The last great ice sheet still lies across northern Europe and North America. Roving on the open tundra and grasslands below those ice sheets is the best-fed and most varied assemblage of grass-eating animals the world has ever seen. Giant long-horned bison, the huge wild cattle of the Pleistocene, graze on both continents. Mammoth and mastodon wander about in such numbers that their bones are later to astonish the first American colonists. Suddenly, into this late paradise of game, there erupts our own species of man—*Homo sapiens.* Just where he came from we do not know. Tall, lithe, long-limbed, he is destined to overrun the continents in the blink of a geological eye. He has an excellent projectile weapon in the shape of the spear thrower. His flint work is meticulous and sharp. And the most aggressive carnivore the world has ever seen comes at a time made for his success: the grasslands are alive with seemingly inexhaustible herds of game.

Yet fire as much as flesh was the magic that opened the 10
way for the supremacy of *Homo sapiens.* We know that he was already the master of fire, for the track of it runs from camp to buried camp: the blackened bones of the animals he killed, mute testimony to the relentless step of man across the continents, lie in hundreds of sites in the Old and the New Worlds. Meat, more precious than the gold for which men later struggled, supplied the energy that carried man across the world. Had it not been for fire, however, all that enormous source of life would have been denied to him: he would have gone on drinking the blood from small kills, chewing wearily at uncooked bone ends or masticating the crackling bodies of grasshoppers.

Fire shortens the digestive process. It breaks down tough 11
masses of flesh into food that the human stomach can easily assimilate. Fire made the difference that enabled man to expand his numbers rapidly and to press on from hunting

to more advanced cultures. Yet we take fire so much for granted that this first great upswing in human numbers, this first real gain in the seizure of vast quantities of free energy, has to a remarkable degree eluded our attention.

With fire primitive man did more than cook his meat. He 12
extended the pasture for grazing herds. A considerable school of thought, represented by such men as the geographer Carl Sauer and the anthropologist Omer Stewart, believes that the early use of fire by the aborigines of the New World greatly expanded the grassland areas. Stewart says: "The number of tribes reported using fire leads one to the conclusion that burning of vegetation was a universal culture pattern among the Indians of the U.S. Furthermore, the amount of burning leads to the deduction that nearly all vegetation in America at the time of discovery and exploration was what ecologists would call fire vegetation. That is to say, fire was a major factor, along with soil, moisture, temperature, wind, animals, and so forth, in determining the types of plants occurring in any region. It follows, then, that the vegetation of the Great Plains was a fire vegetation." In short, the so-called primeval wilderness which awed our forefathers had already felt the fire of the Indian hunter. Here, as in many other regions, man's fire altered the ecology of the earth.

It had its effect not only on the flora but also on the fauna. 13
Of the great herds of grazing animals that flourished in America in the last Ice Age, not a single trace remains—the American elephants, camels, long-horned bison are all gone. Not all of them were struck down by the hunters' weapons. Sauer argues that a major explanation of the extinction of the great American mammals may be fire. He says that the aborigines used fire drives to stampede game, and he contends that this weapon would have worked with peculiar effectiveness to exterminate such lumbering creatures as the mammoth. I have stood in a gully in western Kansas and seen outlined in the earth the fragmented black bones of scores of bison who had perished in what was probably a man-made conflagration. If, at the end of Pleistocene times, vast ecological changes occurred, if climates shifted, if lakes

dried and in other places forests sprang up, and if, in this uncertain and unsteady time, man came with flint and fire upon the animal world about him, he may well have triggered a catastrophic decline and extinction. Five thousand years of man and his smoking weapon rolling down the wind may have finished the story for many a slow-witted animal species. In the great scale of geological time this act of destruction amounts to but one brief hunt.

Man, as I have said, is himself a flame. He has burned 14
through the animal world and appropriated its vast stores of protein for his own. When the great herds failed over many areas, he had to devise new ways to feed his increase or drop back himself into a precarious balance with nature. Here and there on the world's margins there have survived into modern times men who were forced into just such local adjustments. Simple hunters and collectors of small game in impoverished areas, they maintain themselves with difficulty. Their numbers remain the same through generations. Their economy permits no bursts of energy beyond what is necessary for the simple age-old struggle with nature. Perhaps, as we view the looming shadow of atomic disaster, this way of life takes on a certain dignity today.

Nevertheless there is no road back; the primitive way is 15
no longer our way. We are the inheritors of an aggressive culture which, when the great herds disappeared, turned to agriculture. Here again the magic of fire fed the great human wave and built up man's numbers and civilization.

Man's first chemical experiment involving the use of heat 16
was to make foods digestible. He had cooked his meat; now he used fire to crack his grain. In the process of adopting the agricultural way of life he made his second chemical experiment with heat: baking pottery. Ceramics may have sprung in part from the need for storage vessels to protect harvested grain from the incursions of rats and mice and moisture. At any rate, the potter's art spread with the revolutionary shift in food production in early Neolithic times.

People who have only played with mud pies or made little 17
sun-dried vessels of clay are apt to think of ceramics as a

simple art. Actually it is not. The sun-dried vessels of our childhood experiments would melt in the first rain that struck them. To produce true pottery one must destroy the elasticity of clay through a chemical process which can be induced only by subjecting the clay to an intense baking at a temperature of at least 400 or 500 degrees centigrade. The baking drives out the so-called water of constitution from the aluminum silicate in the clay. Thereafter the clay will no longer dissolve in water; a truly fired vessel will survive in the ground for centuries. This is why pottery is so important to the archaeologist. It is impervious to the decay that overtakes many other substances, and, since it was manufactured in quantity, it may tell tales of the past when other clues fail us.

Pottery can be hardened in an open campfire, but the 18
results can never be so excellent as those achieved in a kiln. At some point the early potter must have learned that he could concentrate and conserve heat by covering his fire—perhaps making it in a hole or trench. From this it was a step to the true closed kiln, in which there was a lower chamber for the fire and an upper one for the pottery. Most of the earthenware of simple cultures was fired at temperatures around 500 degrees centigrade, but really thorough firing demands temperatures in the neighborhood of 900 degrees.

After man had learned to change the chemical nature of 19
clay, he began to use fire to transform other raw materials—ores into metals, for instance. One measure of civilization is the number of materials manipulated. The savage contents himself with a few raw materials which can be shaped without the application of high temperatures. Civilized man uses fire to extract, alter, or synthesize a multitude of substances.

By the time metals came into extended use, the precious 20
flame no longer burned in the open campfire, radiating its heat away into the dark or flickering on the bronzed faces of the hunters. Instead it roared in confined furnaces and was fed oxygen through crude bellows. One of the by-products of more intensified experiments with heat was glass—the

strange, impassive substance which, in the form of the chemist's flask, the astronomer's telescope, the biologist's microscope, and the mirror, has contributed so vastly to our knowledge of ourselves and the universe.

We hear a good deal about the Iron Age, or age of metals, 21
as a great jump forward in man's history; actually the metals themselves played a comparatively small part in the rise of the first great civilizations. While men learned to use bronze, which demands little more heat than is necessary to produce good ceramics, and later iron, for tools and ornaments, the use of metal did not make a really massive change in civilization for well over 1,500 years. It was what Leslie White of the University of Michigan calls the "Fuel Revolution" that brought the metals into their own. Coal, oil, and gas, new sources of energy, combined with the invention of the steam and combustion engines, ushered in the new age. It was not metals as tools, but metals combined with heat in new furnaces and power machinery that took human society off its thousand-year plateau and made possible another enormous upswing in human numbers, with all the social repercussions.

Today the flames grow hotter in the furnaces. Man has 22
come far up the heat ladder. The creature that crept furred through the glitter of blue glacial nights lives surrounded by the hiss of steam, the roar of engines, and the bubbling of vats. Like a long-armed crab, he manipulates the tongs in dangerous atomic furnaces. In asbestos suits he plunges into the flaming debris of hideous accidents. With intricate heat-measuring instruments he investigates the secrets of the stars, and he has already found heat-resistant alloys that have enabled him to hurl himself into space.

How far will he go? Three hundred years of the scientific 23
method have built the great sky-touching buildings and nourished the incalculable fertility of the human species. But man is also *Homo duplex,* as they knew in the darker ages. He partakes of evil and of good, of god and of man. Both struggle in him perpetually. And he is himself a flame—a great, roaring, wasteful furnace devouring irreplaceable sub-

stances of the earth. Before this century is out, either *Homo duplex* must learn that knowledge without greatness of spirit is not enough for man, or there will remain only his calcined cities and the little charcoal of his bones.

For Study and Discussion

QUESTIONS FOR RESPONSE

1. As you go about your daily activities, in what ways are you a firemaker? How would your life be changed if you were not a firemaker in any way?
2. How do you react to Eiseley's suggestions that we must curb our firemaking if we are to survive? What specific measures would you suggest?

QUESTIONS ABOUT PURPOSE

1. What does Eiseley point out as some of the current costs of our "climb up the heat ladder"?
2. What impact on his readers do you think Eiseley wants to achieve by characterizing the human being as "a flame—a great, roaring, wasteful furnace"?

QUESTIONS ABOUT AUDIENCE

1. What relevant knowledge and awareness about our society's development and modern living habits does Eiseley depend on his readers having? Why is such information necessary for the essay to work?
2. How do you think anti-nuclear-power groups would respond to this essay? How might utility company executives respond? Nuclear physicists? Why?

QUESTIONS ABOUT STRATEGIES

1. Eiseley's writing is rich in metaphor. Select several from the first two paragraphs and analyze how they contribute to the impact of the opening section.

2. What is the "plot line" in the drama Eiseley creates about human evolution and firemaking? What are the elements of conflict in it?

QUESTIONS FOR DISCUSSION

1. What contemporary manmade fires (in the broadest sense) do you know about that are affecting our environment and probably our future? What is their purpose?
2. Eiseley finishes the essay by asking "How far will he [man the firemaker] go?" What is your answer and what do you see as the consequences?

RAYMOND CARVER

Raymond Carver (1938–1988) was born in Clatskanie, Oregon, and was educated at Humboldt State College (now California State University, Arcata). After further study at the University of Iowa, Carver worked briefly as an editor for Science Research Associates before accepting several positions as lecturer in creative writing at the University of California, Berkeley, the Writing Workshop at the University of Iowa, and the University of Texas at El Paso. In 1980 he became a professor of English at Syracuse University. He died in the summer of 1988, at the age of fifty, at his home in Port Angeles, Washington. He contributed poems and stories to many literary periodicals and such national magazines as *Esquire* and *Harper's*. His poems are collected in *Near Klamath* (1968), *Winter Insomnia* (1970), and *At Night the Salmon Move* (1976). Carver's stories, which received many awards, are collected in *Will You Please Be Quiet, Please?* (1976), *Furious Seasons* (1977), *What We Talk About When We Talk About Love* (1981), *Cathedral* (1983), *The Stories of Raymond Carver* (1985), and *Where I'm Calling From,* completed shortly before his death. In "What We Talk About When We Talk About Love," Carver records a "kitchen-table symposium" on the subject of love.

What We Talk About When We Talk About Love

My friend Mel McGinnis was talking. Mel McGinnis is a cardiologist, and sometimes that gives him the right. 1

The four of us were sitting around his kitchen table drinking gin. Sunlight filled the kitchen from the big window behind the sink. There were Mel and me and his second wife, Teresa—Terri, we called her—and my wife, Laura. We lived in Albuquerque then. But we were all from somewhere else. 2

There was an ice bucket on the table. The gin and the tonic water kept going around, and we somehow got on the subject of love. Mel thought real love was nothing less than spiritual love. He said he'd spent five years in a seminary before quitting to go to medical school. He said he still looked back on those years in the seminary as the most important years in his life. 3

Terri said the man she lived with before she lived with Mel loved her so much he tried to kill her. Then Terri said, "He beat me up one night. He dragged me around the living room by my ankles. He kept saying, 'I love you, I love you, you bitch.' He went on dragging me around the living room. My head kept knocking on things." Terri looked around the table. "What do you do with love like that?" 4

She was a bone-thin woman with a pretty face, dark eyes, and brown hair that hung down her back. She liked necklaces made of turquoise, and long pendant earrings. 5

"My God, don't be silly. That's not love, and you know it," Mel said. "I don't know what you'd call it, but I sure know you wouldn't call it love." 6

"Say what you want to, but I know it was," Terri said. "It may sound crazy to you, but it's true just the same. People are different, Mel. Sure, sometimes he may have acted crazy. Okay. But he loved me. In his own way maybe, but he loved me. There was love there, Mel. Don't say there wasn't." 7

Mel let out his breath. He held his glass and turned to Laura and me. "The man threatened to kill me," Mel said. He finished his drink and reached for the gin bottle. "Terri's a romantic. Terri's of the kick-me-so-I'll-know-you-love-me school. Terri, hon, don't look that way." Mel reached across the table and touched Terri's cheek with his fingers. He grinned at her. 8

"Now he wants to make up," Terri said. 9

"Make up what?" Mel said. "What is there to make up? I 10
know what I know. That's all."

"How'd we get started on this subject, anyway?" Terri 11
said. She raised her glass and drank from it. "Mel always has
love on his mind," she said. "Don't you, honey?" She smiled.
And I thought that was the last of it.

"I just wouldn't call Ed's behavior love. That's all I'm 12
saying, honey," Mel said. "What about you guys?" Mel said
to Laura and me. "Does that sound like love to you?"

"I'm the wrong person to ask," I said. "I didn't even know 13
the man. I've only heard his name mentioned in passing. I
wouldn't know. You'd have to know the particulars. But I
think what you're saying is that love is an absolute."

Mel said, "The kind of love I'm talking about is. The kind 14
of love I'm talking about, you don't try to kill people."

Laura said, "I don't know anything about Ed, or anything 15
about the situation. But who can judge anyone else's situation?"

I touched the back of Laura's hand. She gave me a quick 16
smile. I picked up Laura's hand. It was warm, the nails
polished, perfectly manicured. I encircled the broad wrist
with my fingers, and I held her.

"When I left, he drank rat poison," Terri said. She clasped 17
her arms with her hands. "They took him to the hospital in
Santa Fe. That's where we lived then, about ten miles out.
They saved his life. But his gums went crazy from it. I mean
they pulled away from his teeth. After that, his teeth stood
out like fangs. My God," Terri said. She waited a minute,
then let go of her arms and picked up her glass.

"What people won't do!" Laura said. 18

"He's out of the action now," Mel said. "He's dead." 19

Mel handed me the saucer of limes. I took a section, 20
squeezed it over my drink, and stirred the ice cubes with my
finger.

"It gets worse," Terri said. "He shot himself in the mouth. 21
But he bungled that too. Poor Ed," she said. Terri shook
her head.

"Poor Ed nothing," Mel said. "He was dangerous." 22

Mel was forty-five years old. He was tall and rangy with curly soft hair. His face and arms were brown from the tennis he played. When he was sober, his gestures, all his movements, were precise, very careful. 23

"He did love me though, Mel. Grant me that," Terri said. "That's all I'm asking. He didn't love me the way you love me. I'm not saying that. But he loved me. You can grant me that, can't you?" 24

"What do you mean, he bungled it?" I said. 25

Laura leaned forward with her glass. She put her elbows on the table and held her glass in both hands. She glanced from Mel to Terri and waited with a look of bewilderment on her open face, as if amazed that such things happened to people you were friendly with. 26

"How'd he bungle it when he killed himself?" I said. 27

"I'll tell you what happened," Mel said. "He took this twenty-two pistol he'd bought to threaten Terri and me with. Oh, I'm serious, the man was always threatening. You should have seen the way we lived in those days. Like fugitives. I even bought a gun myself. Can you believe it? A guy like me? But I did. I bought one for self-defense and carried it in the glove compartment. Sometimes I'd have to leave the apartment in the middle of the night. To go to the hospital, you know? Terri and I weren't married then, and my first wife had the house and kids, the dog, everything, and Terri and I were living in this apartment here. Sometimes, as I say, I'd get a call in the middle of the night and have to go in to the hospital at two or three in the morning. It'd be dark out there in the parking lot, and I'd break into a sweat before I could even get to my car. I never knew if he was going to come up out of the shrubbery or from behind a car and start shooting. I mean, the man was crazy. He was capable of wiring a bomb, anything. He used to call my service at all hours and say he needed to talk to the doctor, and when I'd return the call, he'd say, 'Son of a bitch, your days are numbered.' Little things like that. It was scary, I'm telling you." 28

"I still feel sorry for him," Terri said. 29

"It sounds like a nightmare," Laura said. "But what exactly 30
happened after he shot himself?"

Laura is a legal secretary. We'd met in a professional 31
capacity. Before we knew it, it was a courtship. She's thirty-five, three years younger than I am. In addition to being in love, we like each other and enjoy one another's company. She's easy to be with.

"What happened?" Laura said.

Mel said, "He shot himself in the mouth in his room. 33
Someone heard the shot and told the manager. They came in with a passkey, saw what had happened, and called an ambulance. I happened to be there when they brought him in, alive but past recall. The man lived for three days. His head swelled up to twice the size of a normal head. I'd never seen anything like it, and I hope I never do again. Terri wanted to go in and sit with him when she found out about it. We had a fight over it. I didn't think she should see him like that. I didn't think she should see him, and I still don't."

"Who won the fight?" Laura said. 34

"I was in the room with him when he died," Terri said. 35
"He never came up out of it. But I sat with him. He didn't have anyone else."

"He was dangerous," Mel said. "If you call that love, you 36
can have it."

"It was love," Terri said. "Sure, it's abnormal in most 37
people's eyes. But he was willing to die for it. He did die for it."

"I sure as hell wouldn't call it love," Mel said. "I mean, 38
no one knows what he did it for. I've seen a lot of suicides, and I couldn't say anyone ever knew what they did it for."

Mel put his hands behind his neck and tilted his chair 39
back. "I'm not interested in that kind of love," he said. "If that's love, you can have it."

Terri said, "We were afraid. Mel even made a will out and 40
wrote to his brother in California who used to be a Green

Beret. Mel told him who to look for if something happened to him."

Terri drank from her glass. She said, "But Mel's right— 41
we lived like fugitives. We were afraid. Mel was, weren't you, honey? I even called the police at one point, but they were no help. They said they couldn't do anything until Ed actually did something. Isn't that a laugh?" Terri said.

She poured the last of the gin into her glass and waggled 42
the bottle. Mel got up from the table and went to the cupboard. He took down another bottle.

"Well, Nick and I know what love is," Laura said. "For 43
us, I mean," Laura said. She bumped my knee with her knee. "You're supposed to say something now," Laura said, and turned her smile on me.

For an answer, I took Laura's hand and raised it to my 44
lips. I made a big production out of kissing her hand. Everyone was amused.

"We're lucky," I said. 45

"You guys," Terri said. "Stop that now. You're making 46
me sick. You're still on the honeymoon, for God's sake. You're still gaga, for crying out loud. Just wait. How long have you been together now? How long has it been? A year? Longer than a year?"

"Going on a year and a half," Laura said, flushed and 47
smiling.

"Oh, now," Terri said. "Wait awhile." 48

She held her drink and gazed at Laura. 49

"I'm only kidding," Terri said. 50

Mel opened the gin and went around the table with the 51
bottle.

"Here, you guys," he said. "Let's have a toast. I want to 52
propose a toast. A toast to love. To true love," Mel said.

We touched glasses. 53

"To love," we said. 54

Outside in the backyard, one of the dogs began to bark. 55
The leaves of the aspen that leaned past the window ticked

against the glass. The afternoon sun was like a presence in this room, the spacious light of ease and generosity. We could have been anywhere, somewhere enchanted. We raised our glasses again and grinned at each other like children who had agreed on something forbidden.

"I'll tell you what real love is," Mel said. "I mean, I'll give 56
you a good example. And then you can draw your own conclusions." He poured more gin into his glass. He added an ice cube and a sliver of lime. We waited and sipped our drinks. Laura and I touched knees again. I put a hand on her warm thigh and left it there.

"What do any of us really know about love?" Mel said. 57
"It seems to me we're just beginners at love. We say we love each other and we do, I don't doubt it. I love Terri and Terri loves me, and you guys love each other too. You know the kind of love I'm talking about now. Physical love, that impulse that drives you to someone special, as well as love of the other person's being, his or her essence, as it were. Carnal love and, well, call it sentimental love, the day-to-day caring about the other person. But sometimes I have a hard time accounting for the fact that I must have loved my first wife too. But I did, I know I did. So I suppose I am like Terri in that regard. Terri and Ed." He thought about it and then he went on. "There was a time when I thought I loved my first wife more than life itself. But now I hate her guts. I do. How do you explain that? What happened to that love? What happened to it, is what I'd like to know. I wish someone could tell me. Then there's Ed. Okay, we're back to Ed. He loves Terri so much he tries to kill her and he winds up killing himself." Mel stopped talking and swallowed from his glass. "You guys have been together eighteen months and you love each other. It shows all over you. You glow with it. But you both loved other people before you met each other. You've both been married before, just like us. And you probably loved other people before that too, even. Terri and I have been together five years, been married for four. And the terrible thing, the terrible thing is, but the good thing too, the saving grace, you might say, is that if some-

thing happened to one of us—excuse me for saying this—but if something happened to one of us tomorrow, I think the other one, the other person, would grieve for a while, you know, but then the surviving party would go out and love again, have someone else soon enough. All this, all of this love we're talking about, it would just be a memory. Maybe not even a memory. Am I wrong? Am I way off base? Because I want you to set me straight if you think I'm wrong. I want to know. I mean, I don't know anything, and I'm the first one to admit it."

"Mel, for God's sake," Terri said. She reached out and took hold of his wrist. "Are you getting drunk? Honey? Are you drunk?" 58

"Honey, I'm just talking," Mel said. "All right? I don't have to be drunk to say what I think. I mean, we're all just talking, right?" Mel said. He fixed his eyes on her. 59

"Sweetie, I'm not criticizing," Terri said. 60

She picked up her glass. 61

"I'm not on call today," Mel said. "Let me remind you of that. I am not on call," he said. 62

"Mel, we love you," Laura said. 63

Mel looked at Laura. He looked at her as if he could not place her, as if she was not the woman she was. 64

"Love you too, Laura," Mel said. "And you, Nick, love you too. You know something?" Mel said. "You guys are our pals," Mel said. 65

He picked up his glass. 66

Mel said, "I was going to tell you about something. I mean, I was going to prove a point. You see, this happened a few months ago, but it's still going on right now, and it ought to make us feel ashamed when we talk like we know what we're talking about when we talk about love." 67

"Come on now," Terri said. "Don't talk like you're drunk if you're not drunk." 68

"Just shut up for once in your life," Mel said very quietly. "Will you do me a favor and do that for a minute? So as I was saying, there's this old couple who had this car wreck 69 out on the interstate. A kid hit them and they were all torn to shit and nobody was giving them much chance to pull through."

Terri looked at us and then back at Mel. She seemed 70
anxious, or maybe that's too strong a word.

Mel was handing the bottle around the table. 71

"I was on call that night," Mel said. "It was May or maybe 72
it was June. Terri and I had just sat down to dinner when the hospital called. There'd been this thing out on the interstate. Drunk kid, teenager, plowed his dad's pickup into this camper with this old couple in it. They were up in their mid-seventies, that couple. The kid—eighteen, nineteen, something—he was DOA. Taken the steering wheel through his sternum. The old couple, they were alive, you understand. I mean, just barely. But they had everything. Multiple fractures, internal injuries, hemorrhaging, contusions, lacerations, the works, and they each of them had themselves concussions. They were in a bad way, believe me. And, of course, their age was two strikes against them. I'd say she was worse off than he was. Ruptured spleen along with everything else. Both kneecaps broken. But they'd been wearing their seatbelts and, God knows, that's what saved them for the time being."

"Folks, this is an advertisement for the National Safety 73
Council," Terri said. "This is your spokesman, Dr. Melvin R. McGinnis, talking." Terri laughed. "Mel," she said, "sometimes you're just too much. But I love you, hon," she said.

"Honey, I love you," Mel said. 74

He leaned across the table. Terri met him halfway. They 75
kissed.

"Terri's right," Mel said as he settled himself again. "Get 76
those seatbelts on. But seriously, they were in some shape, those oldsters. By the time I got down there, the kid was dead, as I said. He was off in a corner, laid out on a gurney. I took one look at the old couple and told the ER nurse to get me a neurologist and an orthopedic man and a couple of surgeons down there right away."

He drank from his glass. "I'll try to keep this short," he 77 said. "So we took the two of them up to the OR and worked like fuck on them most of the night. They had these incredible reserves, those two. You see that once in a while. So we did everything that could be done, and toward morning we're giving them a fifty-fifty chance, maybe less than that for her. So here they are, still alive the next morning. So, okay, we move them into the ICU, which is where they both kept plugging away at it for two weeks, hitting it better and better on all the scopes. So we transfer them out to their own room."

Mel stopped talking. "Here," he said, "let's drink this cheapo gin the hell up. Then we're going to dinner, right? Terri and I know a new place. That's where we'll go, to this new place we know about. But we're not going until we finish up this cut-rate, lousy gin." 78

Terri said, "We haven't actually eaten there yet. But it looks good. From the outside, you know." 79

"I like food," Mel said. "If I had it to do all over again, I'd be a chef, you know? Right, Terri?" Mel said. 80

He laughed. He fingered the ice in his glass. 81

"Terri knows," he said. "Terri can tell you. But let me say this. If I could come back again in a different life, a different time and all, you know what? I'd like to come back as a knight. You were pretty safe wearing all that armor. It was all right being a knight until gunpowder and muskets and pistols came along." 82

"Mel would like to ride a horse and carry a lance," Terri said. 83

"Carry a woman's scarf with you everywhere," Laura said. 84

"Or just a woman," Mel said. 85

"Shame on you," Laura said. 86

Terri said, "Suppose you came back as a serf. The serfs didn't have it so good in those days," Terri said. 87

"The serfs never had it good," Mel said. "But I guess even the knights were vessels to someone. Isn't that the way it worked? But then everyone is always a vessel to someone. Isn't that right? Terri? But what I liked about knights, besides 88 their ladies, was that they had that suit of armor, you know, and they couldn't get hurt very easy. No cars in those days, you know? No drunk teenagers to tear into your ass."

"Vassals," Terri said. 89

"What?" Mel said. 90

"Vassals," Terri said. "They were called vassals, not ves- 91
sels."

"Vassals, vessels," Mel said, "what the fuck's the differ- 92
ence? You knew what I meant anyway. All right," Mel said. "So I'm not educated. I learned my stuff. I'm a heart surgeon, sure, but I'm just a mechanic. I go in and I fuck around and I fix things. Shit," Mel said.

"Modesty doesn't become you," Terri said. 93

"He's just a humble sawbones," I said. "But sometimes 94
they suffocated in all that armor, Mel. They'd even have heart attacks if it got too hot and they were too tired and worn out. I read somewhere that they'd fall off their horses and not be able to get up because they were too tired to stand with all that armor on them. They got trampled by their own horses sometimes."

"That's terrible," Mel said. "That's a terrible thing, Nicky. 95
I guess they'd just lay there and wait until somebody came along and made a shish kebab out of them."

"Some other vessel," Terri said. 96

"That's right," Mel said. "Some vassal would come along 97
and spear the bastard in the name of love. Or whatever the fuck it was they fought over in those days."

"Same things we fight over these days," Terri said. 98

Laura said, "Nothing's changed." 99

The color was still high in Laura's cheeks. Her eyes were 100
bright. She brought her glass to her lips.

Mel poured himself another drink. He looked at the label 101
closely as if studying a long row of numbers. Then he slowly put the bottle down on the table and slowly reached for the tonic water.

"What about the old couple?" Laura said. "You didn't 102
finish that story you started."

Laura was having a hard time lighting her cigarette. Her 103
matches kept going out.

The sunshine inside the room was different now, chang- 104
ing, getting thinner. But the leaves outside the window were still shimmering, and I stared at the pattern they made on the panes and on the Formica counter. They weren't the same patterns, of course.

"What about the old couple?" I said. 105

"Older but wiser," Terri said. 106

Mel stared at her. 107

Terri said, "Go on with your story, hon. I was only kid- 108
ding. Then what happened?"

"Terri, sometimes," Mel said. 109

"Please Mel," Terri said. "Don't always be so serious, 110
sweetie. Can't you take a joke?"

"Where's the joke?" Mel said. 111

He held his glass and gazed steadily at his wife. 112

"What happened?" Laura said. 113

Mel fastened his eyes on Laura. He said, "Laura, if I didn't 114
have Terri and if I didn't love her so much, and if Nick wasn't my best friend, I'd fall in love with you. I'd carry you off, honey," he said.

"Tell your story," Terri said. "Then we'll go to that new 115
place, okay?"

"Okay," Mel said. "Where was I?" he said. He stared at 116
the table and then he began again.

"I dropped in to see each of them every day, sometimes 117
twice a day if I was up doing other calls anyway. Casts and bandages, head to foot, the both of them. You know, you've seen it in the movies. That's just the way they looked, just like in the movies. Little eye-holes and nose-holes and mouth-holes. And she had to have her legs slung up on top of it. Well, the husband was very depressed for the longest while. Even after he found out that his wife was going to pull through, he was still very depressed. Not about the accident, though. I mean, the accident was one thing, but it wasn't everything. I'd get up to his mouth-hole, you know, and he'd say no, it wasn't the accident exactly but it was

because he couldn't see her through his eye-holes. He said that was what was making him feel so bad. Can you imagine? I'm telling you, the man's heart was breaking because he couldn't turn his goddamn head and *see* his goddamn wife."

Mel looked around the table and shook his head at what 118
he was going to say.

"I mean, it was killing the old fart just because he couldn't 119
look at the fucking woman."

We all looked at Mel. 120

"Do you see what I'm saying?" he said. 121

Maybe we were a little drunk by then. I know it was hard 122
keeping things in focus. The light was draining out of the room, going back through the window where it had come from. Yet nobody made a move to get up from the table to turn on the overhead light.

"Listen," Mel said. "Let's finish this fucking gin. There's 123
about enough left here for one shooter all around. Then let's go eat. Let's go to the new place."

"He's depressed," Terri said. "Mel, why don't you take a 124
pill?"

Mel shook his head. "I've taken everything there is." 125

"We all need a pill now and then," I said. 126

"Some people are born needing them," Terri said. 127

She was using her finger to rub at something on the table. 128
Then she stopped rubbing.

"I think I want to call my kids," Mel said. "Is that all right 129
with everybody? I'll call my kids," he said.

Terri said, "What if Marjorie answers the phone? You 130
guys, you've heard us on the subject of Marjorie? Honey, you know you don't want to talk to Marjorie. It'll make you feel even worse."

"I don't want to talk to Marjorie," Mel said. "But I want 131
to talk to my kids."

"There isn't a day goes by that Mel doesn't say he wishes 132
she'd get married again. Or else die," Terri said. "For one thing," Terri said, "she's bankrupting us. Mel says it's just to

spite him that she won't get married again. She has a boyfriend who lives with her and the kids, so Mel is supporting the boyfriend too."

"She's allergic to bees," Mel said. "If I'm not praying she'll 133
get married again, I'm praying she'll get herself stung to death by a swarm of fucking bees."

"Shame on you," Laura said. 134

"Bzzzzzzz," Mel said, turning his fingers into bees and 135
buzzing them at Terri's throat. Then he let his hands drop all the way to his sides.

"She's vicious," Mel said. "Sometimes I think I'll go up 136
there dressed like a beekeeper. You know, that hat that's like a helmet with the plate that comes down over your face, the big gloves, and the padded coat? I'll knock on the door and let loose a hive of bees in the house. But first I'd make sure the kids were out, of course."

He crossed one leg over the other. It seemed to take him 137
a lot of time to do it. Then he put both feet on the floor and leaned forward, elbows on the table, his chin cupped in his hands.

"Maybe I won't call the kids, after all. Maybe it isn't such 138
a hot idea. Maybe we'll just go eat. How does that sound?"

"Sounds fine to me," I said. "Eat or not eat. Or keep 139
drinking. I could head right on out into the sunset."

"What does that mean, honey?" Laura said. 140

"It just means what I said," I said. "It means I could just 141
keep going. That's all it means."

"I could eat something myself," Laura said. "I don't think 142
I've ever been so hungry in my life. Is there something to nibble on?"

"I'll put out some cheese and crackers," Terri said. 143

But Terri just sat there. She did not get up to get anything. 144

Mel turned his glass over. He spilled it out on the table. 145

"Gin's gone," Mel said. 146

Terri said, "Now what?" 147

I could hear my heart beating. I could hear everyone's 148
heart. I could hear the human noise we sat there making, not one of us moving, not even when the room went dark.

COMMENT ON "WHAT WE TALK ABOUT WHEN WE TALK ABOUT LOVE"

In "What We Talk About When We Talk About Love," Carver creates a kitchen-table symposium on love. The participants are familiar ones in our society—two couples who have been divorced and remarried, but who still seem to believe in romantic love as much as did the knights of chivalry Mel admires. All of them, but particularly Mel, keep trying to figure out what it is we mean when we talk about love, and, not surprisingly, they use the most common of definition strategies: they give examples, positive and negative. Love is physical attraction like Nick and Laura's; love is a romantic ideal like the knight fighting for his lady; it's the pity Terri felt for her dying husband. Most of all, for Mel, it's the devotion of the elderly couple together in the hospital room. Love is *not,* he insists, physical violence and abuse of someone you claim to love. Toward the end of the story, Carver hints that Mel's compulsion to define love may be a symptom of his desperate search for real love. Whatever it is, he doesn't seem to have found it. He's drinking heavily, and he's depressed even though, as he says, "I've taken everything there is."

Definition as a Writing Strategy

1. Research the development of something you use often and know quite well—perhaps ski boots, roller blades, the mountain bicycle, a truck or recreational vehicle, a stereo system, or something similar—and write an essay showing how its design has developed and changed because of the changing needs and expectations of the people who use it. You might write such an essay for a specialized magazine that is targeted toward the users of the object you choose.
2. For a challenging assignment that you might find especially interesting, pick a celebrity you admire—perhaps an athlete, a scientist, a writer, a television personality, or a musician or singer—and read several magazine or newspaper articles on that person. Be sure to include some in-depth articles; don't depend on the snippets that come from the sports or entertainment pages. Then write an essay of about the length of Gates's essay on Columbus in which you describe that person in a way that defines him or her and gives his or her standing in that person's profession. Remember that anecdotes can be useful in this kind of essay. A hypothetical audience for this kind of essay might be readers of the entertainment or sports section of your college or local newspaper.
3. If as a child you enjoyed folktales, fairy tales, or imaginative chronicles like C. S. Lewis's *Narnia Chronicles* or Tolkien's *Lord of the Ring* series, reread a few of those stories and take notes. If you didn't read such literature as a child, you might find current examples of stories you like that are also a kind of folk literature: popular soap operas such as "Days of Our Lives" or popular television comedies such as "Cheers" or "The Simpsons." Watch a few episodes of these and take notes. Then write an essay similar to Alison Lurie's in which you analyze how the stories you have chosen present women and men, children and adults, the powerful and the weak, the rulers and the ruled. As Lurie does, theorize about the comment these stories make about the culture or society they portray.
4. In an essay for the members of your writing class, define

what some abstract concept such as friendship, sportsmanship, chutzpah, or class means to you. What are its necessary components? What is its opposite? You may find the analysis of different ways to define (pp. 306–307) helpful in getting started on this assignment. Remember that you'll enliven your writing by using people and anecdotes to illustrate your points.

5. As an anthropologist, Loren Eiseley has frequently used the metaphor of a journey to describe people's progress through time. In "Man the Firemaker" he evokes that metaphor again, starting in the second paragraph. Trace and analyze the human journey Eiseley describes by identifying the most important events in it that show humankind changing the world through the mastery of fire. How does he enrich this account with specific metaphors?
6. Writers and speakers often argue from definition, trying to convince their audiences to agree with or approve of something by defining it positively (for example, a good education) or to disagree or reject something by defining it negatively (for example, a bad grading policy). Drawing on material and information you are getting in another course, write a paper suitable for that course defining a concept, policy, theory, or event either negatively or positively. For example, for a physical education course, you could define a good exercise program; for an experimental psychology course, you could define a well-designed experiment. For a government course, you could define an ineffective political campaign; for a speech course, you could define a poor speaking style.

CAUSE AND EFFECT

If you are like most people, you are born curious and stay that way all your life, always wondering why things happen, wanting to know reasons. You want to know why the wind blows or what makes some young people dye their hair green, but you also want to know how to control your life and your environment. You can't have that control unless you understand **causes**. That is why so much writing is cause-and-effect writing. You need it to help you understand more about your world so you can improve it. Writing about causes plays an important role in almost all the professions, and it certainly figures prominently in writing in college.

You also want to know about **effects**. Will A lead to B?

And also to C, D, and E? Such questions also arise partly from pure curiosity—a youngster will pull any string or push any button just to find out what will happen—but they stem too from a need to regulate your life, to understand how your acts affect the lives of others. You want to predict consequences so you can manage your existence in ways that other creatures cannot. You see an effect and look for explanations, usually in writing; and when you try to explain an effect to someone else, you often do it in writing.

PURPOSE

When you write cause-and-effect essays, you're likely to have one of three purposes. Frequently, you will write *to explain*. You want your readers to know how and why things happen, to satisfy their curiosity or to educate them on some issue. You could write a paper in science or economics to lay out logical explanations and show connections for your readers. At other times, you might use a cause-and-effect pattern simply *to speculate* about an interesting topic—for example, to theorize about why a new style has become popular or what the effects will be of a new "no pass/no play" law for high school athletes.

You can also use cause-and-effect writing *to argue*. In fact, that may be the way you will use it most often, particularly when you are making an argument to pragmatic people who will pay attention to practical, common-sense reasons. When you cannot get someone to listen to arguments that something is right or wrong, you may be able to persuade by arguing not that a policy is wrong but that it is foolish or impractical—it will have bad effects.

AUDIENCE

You can assume that cause-and-effect arguments appeal to most audiences because the pattern is such a natural one that readers are used to seeing it. Whether they are teachers, lawyers, parents, doctors, or politicians, your readers will expect you to explain and argue from cause and effect.

When you are thinking about your readers for such arguments, you will find that it helps greatly to think about them as *jurors* for whom you are going to present a case. You can make up a list of questions about your readers just as a lawyer would to help him or her formulate an argument.

Here are some suggested questions: How ready are your readers to hear your arguments? Do you need to give them background information to prepare them? How skeptical are they likely to be? How much evidence will they require? What kind of evidence? Factual? Statistical? Are they bright and well informed, likely to see the connections you want them to make, or will you have to spell them out? Like a lawyer, you're trying to establish *probable* cause-and-effect sequences; you have the best chance of doing that if you think ahead of time about the expectations, questions, and doubts your readers will have.

STRATEGIES

You can use at least two approaches to get started on your cause-and-effect paper. With one approach, you may start by identifying some event or idea you're interested in and begin to speculate about its causes and its impact. Working from only a hazy idea of where your speculations might lead, you can brainstorm and free-write until you find a thesis you want to develop, then take it from there. You may come up with some fascinating hypothesis that, with research and patience, you can turn into an original and interesting paper. You can choose your audience and focus your purpose as you work.

With the other approach, you may have a clear idea from the start about the claims you want to make about cause and effect and know precisely who your audience will be. Your writing task then is to lay out your argument, show the connections between your claim and your data, and find supporting evidence or examples to strengthen your argument. Either approach can work well.

When you make a cause-and-effect argument, you want your readers to accept your analysis—to agree that when A occurs, then B will probably follow. Sam Keen makes such an analysis in "The High Price of Success" when he argues that "if life is a battle, if winning is the only thing, sooner or later you are going to come down with battle fatigue." Later he asks, "At what cost to the life of our body and spirit do we purchase corporate and professional success?"; he spends the rest of the essay supporting his theory with examples and drawing analogies to convince his readers that although work is important and can be rewarding, it now threatens to usurp our souls. You could use the same kind of argument if you wanted to persuade readers that overemphasis on sports in middle and high school warps the values of boys and even girls—sometimes those of a whole community. You could model your essay after Keen's, outlining the unwritten rules of competitive sports in high school and citing a book such as H. G. Bissinger's *Friday Night Lights*.

When you are arguing about effects, you want your readers to accept your analysis of a situation and agree that activity X has been a major contributor to problem Y. Notice that Gloria Steinem is using this kind of pattern in her essay "Why Young Women Are More Conservative." She was surprised to find that young college women were conservative and went looking for reasons to explain the finding. Another argument in the same pattern could point out that more and more young athletes are using anabolic steroids and theorize that this has happened because of widespread publicity about steroid use by professional athletes and because of the growing perception that sports is about making money, not about playing games. You would have to do considerable research to support your claims here and rely on newspaper stories and the accounts of professional athletes themselves to make a strong case.

Some of the strategies you can use for cause-and-effect papers resemble those used by lawyers in making an argument. For instance, it's a good idea to *state your claim early,* then *show the connection* you're setting up. Then *present supporting evidence*—past experience, research findings, documentation, personal observation, expert testimony, and so on. Pay special attention to establishing links between the claim and the evidence. It's crucial to establish that connection. Stephen Jay Gould uses this approach in "Carrie Buck's Daughter."

You don't have to write every cause-and-effect paper to prove something or as if you were conducting a case in court. You can also write interesting speculative papers in which you theorize or fantasize possible effects of certain trends—for example, the way punk-rock hair styles have spread to some groups of college students—or in which you speculate satirically about some of the annoyances in our culture—for instance, the reasons for impenetrable plastic packages or why hotels insist on locking coat hangers to the rack in a $150-a-day room.

POTENTIAL PITFALLS IN CAUSE-AND-EFFECT PAPERS

Although cause and effect is a powerful writing strategy, it can also be a hazardous one. When it comes to dealing with the difficult, ongoing problems of people and societies, you can almost never prove simple cause-and-effect relationships. Many serious human problems really have no good, single solutions because our lives and cultures are so complex. Thus, to avoid looking naive or poorly informed, avoid hasty statements such as "I know what causes X and we can fix it if we just do Y." To avoid such pitfalls, you should observe the following cautions in writing about cause and effect.

First, as in all expository writing, be careful about how

much you claim. Instead of insisting that if A happens, B is inevitable, write, "I believe if A occurs, B is very likely to happen" or "B will probably follow if A happens." For instance, you might be absolutely sure that if the university opened a child-care center for students' children, attendance at classes would be higher, but you can't absolutely prove it. You would gain more credibility with university administrators if you were careful not to overstate your case.

Second, be careful not to oversimplify cause-and-effect connections. Experienced observers and writers know that most significant acts and events have not one cause but several. Gloria Steinem makes this clear in "Why Young Women Are More Conservative" as she examines the several forces in American culture that contribute to making young college women less angry and rebellious than one might expect. A less complicated, because more easily analyzed, effect that one might explore is the significant decline in deaths from heart disease in the United States in the last thirty years. There are many reasons for this decline, not just one or two. Increasingly, people smoke less, eat healthier foods, exercise more, and try to control their blood pressure. New treatments for heart problems also make a difference. Similarly, when major events occur, such as the disintegration of Eastern European socialism or the Los Angeles riots of May 1992, knowledgeable observers know that they have multiple and complex causes. Thus, wise writers qualify their claims about causes and effects by using phrases such as "a major cause," "an important result," or "an immediate effect."

You should also take care to distinguish between immediate, obvious causes for something and more remote, less apparent causes. You may feel that the immediate cause of the distressing rise in teen-age pregnancies in the United States is movies and television programs that are much more sexually explicit than those of fifteen years ago, but it's important to recognize that there are more far-reaching, long-term reasons, such as poor sex education programs, many taboos on dispensing birth control information, and the increased focus on sexuality in ads.

Third, avoid confusing coincidence or simple sequence for cause and effect. Just because X follows Y doesn't mean Y causes X—that assumption is the basis of superstitions. If an increase in the automobile accident rate follows a drop in gasoline prices, you can't conclude there is a necessary connection between the two events. There might be, but a prudent investigator would want much more data before drawing such a conclusion. If you jump to quick conclusions about causes and effects, you risk falling into the "false cause" or "after this, therefore because of this" fallacy.

So working with cause and effect in a paper can be tricky and complex. That doesn't mean, however, that you should refrain from using cause-and-effect explanations or arguments until you are absolutely sure of your ground. You can't always wait for certainty to make an analysis or a forecast. The best you can do is observe carefully, speculate intelligently, and add qualifications.

For an annotated example of using cause and effect in a paragraph, turn to the next page.

Using Cause and Effect in Paragraphs

HEDRICK SMITH
From *The New Russians*

Thesis: reform in USSR came from internal forces

Effect

Cause

Specific examples

Hidden discontent at every level. E.g., housewives, miners, farmers, etc., angry about shortages and corruption

The evidence is overwhelming that Gorbachev's reforms [in the Soviet Union] blossomed forth from forces germinating within Russia itself. . . . In fact, by the time Gorbachev became the top man in the Kremlin, reform had hidden constituencies at every level of Soviet society: mine workers and housewives incensed about and weary of chronic consumer shortages and the dismal quality of Soviet goods; farmers and teachers demoralized by rural decay; little people outraged by the arrogant, pervasive, Mafia-like corruption of ministers and party officials; others embittered by the rampant black market, and by underground millionaires profiting from the gaping inefficiency of Stalinist economics.

Scientists, engineers, intellectuals angry about poor technology and being fourth-rate power

More examples

Cynicism

Scientists and engineers were worried about the Soviet Union's industrial stagnation and its growing technological inferiority to the West. Intellectuals and young military veterans were sickened by the futile war in Afghanistan. Army generals, intelligence chiefs, and civilian technocrats were alarmed by the Soviet inability to compete in the world market and by the prospect of becoming a fourth-rate power in the twenty-first century, outstripped not only by the United States, Western Europe, and Japan, but even by China. Cab drivers and poets alike were sick of the blatant hypocrisy of Soviet propaganda. There was a pervasive cynicism about the widening chasm between the pompous pretensions of Brezhnev and the bleak reality of a Russian's everyday life.

Comment In these paragraphs from *The New Russians* (1990), former *New York Times* Moscow correspondent Hedrick Smith begins by identifying a major effect, Gor-

bachev's reforms in the Soviet Union, and asserts that the cause of those reforms was dissatisfaction at every level of Soviet society. He backs up his claim with rich supporting detail, bringing in mine workers and housewives, farmers and teachers, scientists and engineers, intellectuals and military veterans, cab drivers and poets. He strengthens his analysis with a series of strong verbs—*incensed, demoralized, outraged, embittered, sickened, alarmed*—and he lists the Russians' specific complaints, such as chronic shortages, dismal quality of Soviet goods, corruption, gaping inefficiency, industrial stagnation, and blatant hypocrisy. In fewer than two hundred words, he builds a convincing case of cause and effect, just as a lawyer would in court.

BRENT STAPLES

Brent Staples was born in Chester, Pennsylvania, in 1951 and was educated at Widener College and the University of Chicago. He worked for several years as a reporter for the *Chicago Sun-Times* before moving on to an editorial position with the *New York Times Book Review.* He currently serves as assistant editor of the Metropolitan section of the *Times.* He has contributed articles to journals such as the *New York Times Magazine* and *Harper's* and is currently at work on *Parallel Time,* an autobiography of his family and hometown. In "Black Men and Public Space," reprinted from *Ms.* magazine, Staples analyzes the effects of being perceived as dangerous.

Black Men and Public Space

My first victim was a woman—white, well dressed, probably in her early twenties. I came upon her late one evening on a deserted street in Hyde Park, a relatively affluent neighborhood in an otherwise mean, impoverished section of Chicago. As I swung onto the avenue behind her, there seemed to be a discreet, uninflammatory distance between us. Not so. She cast back a worried glance. To her, the youngish black man—a broad six feet two inches with a beard and billowing hair, both hands shoved into the pockets of a bulky military jacket—seemed menacingly close. After a few more quick glimpses, she picked up her pace and was soon running in earnest. Within seconds she disappeared into a cross street. 1

That was more than a decade ago. I was twenty-two years old, a graduate student newly arrived at the University of Chicago. It was in the echo of that terrified woman's footfalls that I first began to know the unwieldy inheritance I'd come into—the ability to alter public space in ugly ways. It was 2 clear that she thought herself the quarry of a mugger, a rapist, or worse. Suffering a bout of insomnia, however, I was stalking sleep, not defenseless wayfarers. As a softy who is scarcely able to take a knife to a raw chicken—let alone hold one to a person's throat—I was surprised, embarrassed, and dismayed all at once. Her flight made me feel like an accomplice in tyranny. It also made it clear that I was indistinguishable from the muggers who occasionally seeped into the area from the surrounding ghetto. That first encounter, and those that followed, signified that a vast, unnerving gulf lay between nighttime pedestrians—particularly women—and me. And I soon gathered that being perceived as dangerous is a hazard in itself. I only needed to turn a corner into a dicey situation, or crowd some frightened, armed person in a foyer somewhere, or make an errant move after being pulled over by a policeman. Where fear and weapons meet—and they often do in urban America—there is always the possibility of death.

In that first year, my first away from my hometown, I was 3
to become thoroughly familiar with the language of fear. At dark, shadowy intersections, I could cross in front of a car stopped at a traffic light and elicit the *thunk, thunk, thunk, thunk* of the driver—black, white, male, or female—hammering down the door locks. On less traveled streets after dark, I grew accustomed to but never comfortable with people crossing to the other side of the street rather than pass me. Then there were the standard unpleasantries with policemen, doormen, bouncers, cab drivers, and others whose business it is to screen out troublesome individuals *before* there is any nastiness.

I moved to New York nearly two years ago and I have 4
remained an avid night walker. In central Manhattan, the near-constant crowd cover minimizes tense one-on-one street encounters. Elsewhere—in SoHo, for example, where sidewalks are narrow and tightly spaced buildings shut out the sky—things can get very taut indeed.

After dark, on the warrenlike streets of Brooklyn where I 5
live, I often see women who fear the worst from me. They

seem to have set their faces on neutral, and with their purse straps strung across their chests bandolier-style, they forge ahead as though bracing themselves against being tackled. I understand, of course, that the danger they perceive is not a hallucination. Women are particularly vulnerable to street violence, and young black males are drastically overrepresented among the perpetrators of that violence. Yet these truths are no solace against the kind of alienation that comes of being ever the suspect, a fearsome entity with whom pedestrians avoid making eye contact.

It is not altogether clear to me how I reached the ripe old age of twenty-two without being conscious of the lethality nighttime pedestrians attributed to me. Perhaps it was because in Chester, Pennsylvania, the small, angry industrial town where I came of age in the 1960s, I was scarcely noticeable against a backdrop of gang warfare, street knifings, and murders. I grew up one of the good boys, had perhaps a half-dozen fistfights. In retrospect, my shyness of combat has clear sources. 6

As a boy, I saw countless tough guys locked away; I have since buried several, too. They were babies, really—a teenage cousin, a brother of twenty-two, a childhood friend in his mid-twenties—all gone down in episodes of bravado played out in the streets. I came to doubt the virtues of intimidation early on. I chose, perhaps unconsciously, to remain a shadow—timid, but a survivor. 7

The fearsomeness mistakenly attributed to me in public places often has a perilous flavor. The most frightening of these confusions occurred in the late 1970s and early 1980s, when I worked as a journalist in Chicago. One day, rushing into the office of a magazine I was writing for with a deadline story in hand, I was mistaken for a burglar. The office manager called security and, with an ad hoc posse, pursued me through the labyrinthine halls, nearly to my editor's door. I had no way of proving who I was. I could only move briskly toward the company of someone who knew me. 8

Another time I was on assignment for a local paper and 9

killing time before an interview. I entered a jewelry store on the city's affluent Near North Side. The proprietor excused herself and returned with an enormous red Doberman pinscher straining at the end of a leash. She stood, the dog extended toward me, silent to my questions, her eyes bulging nearly out of her head. I took a cursory look around, nodded, and bade her good night.

Relatively speaking, however, I never fared as badly as 10
another black male journalist. He went to nearby Waukegan, Illinois, a couple of summers ago to work on a story about a murderer who was born there. Mistaking the reporter for the killer, police officers hauled him from his car at gunpoint and but for his press credentials would probably have tried to book him. Such episodes are not uncommon. Black men trade tales like this all the time.

Over the years, I learned to smother the rage I felt at so 11
often being taken for a criminal. Not to do so would surely have led to madness. I now take precautions to make myself less threatening. I move about with care, particularly late in the evening. I give a wide berth to nervous people on subway platforms during the wee hours, particularly when I have exchanged business clothes for jeans. If I happen to be entering a building behind some people who appear skittish, I may walk by, letting them clear the lobby before I return, so as not to seem to be following them. I have been calm and extremely congenial on those rare occasions when I've been pulled over by the police.

And on late-evening constitutionals I employ what has 12
proved to be an excellent tension-reducing measure: I whistle melodies from Beethoven and Vivaldi and the more popular classical composers. Even steely New Yorkers hunching toward nighttime destinations seem to relax, and occasionally they even join in the tune. Virtually everybody seems to sense that a mugger wouldn't be warbling bright, sunny selections from Vivaldi's *Four Seasons.* It is my equivalent of the cowbell that hikers wear when they know they are in bear country.

For Study and Discussion

QUESTIONS FOR RESPONSE

1. What experiences of your own were you reminded of by Staples's account? How did you respond in those situations?
2. If you could talk to Staples about his article, what would you say to him? What questions would you ask him? Would you feel that you owe him an apology or an explanation? Why?

QUESTIONS ABOUT PURPOSE

1. What racial and sexual assumptions does Staples want to dispel?
2. What do you think Staples hopes his readers will learn from this article? How do you think he wants them to respond?

QUESTIONS ABOUT AUDIENCE

1. In what ways does Staples anticipate that men and women might respond differently to his essay?
2. What groups of readers does Staples want to address most directly in his essay?

QUESTIONS ABOUT STRATEGIES

1. What effect does Staples achieve with his first paragraph? What is your response to it?
2. How does Staples use personal details to intensify the effects of his analysis?

QUESTIONS FOR DISCUSSION

1. What are some of the elements in American culture that cause many people to react to black men in the way Staples describes? How could some of those elements be changed?
2. How do you think it affects people's feelings about themselves to know that other people fear them? How can it affect their behavior?

GLORIA STEINEM

Gloria Steinem was born in Toledo, Ohio, in 1934 and was educated at Smith College. Her byline first appeared in *Esquire* in 1962, and it soon began appearing in *Vogue, Glamour, McCall's, Ladies' Home Journal, Life,* and *Cosmopolitan*. She was hired as a contributing editor for *New York* magazine in 1968 and shortly began writing a column called "The City Politic." During this period Steinem became involved in the women's movement: She helped found the National Women's Political Caucus and the Women's Action Alliance, and in 1972 she launched *Ms.* magazine. She wrote *Marilyn,* a book about Marilyn Monroe, in 1987. In *Outrageous Acts and Everyday Rebellions* (1983), a collection of articles, Steinem charts her development as a journalist and a feminist; in *Revolution from Within* (1991), she assesses the cost of her public life on her private life. In "Why Young Women Are More Conservative," reprinted from *Outrageous Acts and Everyday Rebellions,* Steinem speculates on the causes that delay women's declarations of independence until middle age.

Why Young Women Are More Conservative

If you had asked me a decade or more ago, I certainly would have said the campus was the first place to look for the feminist or any other revolution. I also would have assumed that student-age women, like student-age men, were much more likely to be activist and open to change than their parents. After all, campus revolts have a long and well- 1 publicized tradition, from the students of medieval France, whose "heresy" was suggesting that the university be separate from the church, through the anticolonial student riots of British India; from students who led the cultural revolution of the People's Republic of China, to campus demonstrations against the Shah of Iran. Even in this country, with far less tradition of student activism, the populist movement to end the war in Vietnam was symbolized by campus protests and mistrust of anyone over thirty.

It has taken me many years of traveling as a feminist speaker and organizer to understand that I was wrong about women; at least, about women acting on their own behalf. In activism, as in so many other things, I had been educated to assume that men's cultural pattern was the natural or the only one. If student years were the peak time of rebellion and openness to change for men, then the same must be true for women. In fact, a decade of listening to every kind of women's group—from brown-bag lunchtime lectures organized by office workers to all-night rap sessions at campus women's centers; from housewives' self-help groups to campus rallies—has convinced me that the reverse is more often true. Women may be the one group that grows more radical with age. Though some students are big exceptions to this rule, women in general don't begin to challenge the politics of our own lives until later. 2

Looking back, I realize that this pattern has been true for my life, too. My college years were full of uncertainties and the personal conservatism that comes from trying to win approval and fit into the proper grown-up and womanly role, whether that means finding a well-to-do man to be supported by or a male radical to support. Nonetheless, I went right on assuming that brave exploring youth and cowardly conservative old age were the norms for everybody, and that I must be just an isolated and guilty accident. Though every generalization based on female culture has many exceptions, and should never be used as a crutch or excuse, I think we might be less hard on ourselves and each other as students, feel better about our potential for change 3 as we grow older—and educate reporters who announce feminism's demise because its red-hot center is not on campus—if we figured out that for most of us as women, the traditional college period is an unrealistic and cautious time. Consider a few of the reasons.

As students, women are probably treated with more equality than we ever will be again. For one thing, we're consumers. The school is only too glad to get the tuitions we pay, or that our families or government grants pay on our behalf. With population rates declining because of women's increased power over childbearing, that money is even more vital to a school's existence. Yet more than most consumers, we're too transient to have much power as a group. If our families are paying our tuition, we may have even less power. 4

As young women, whether students or not, we're still in the stage most valued by male-dominant cultures: we have our full potential as workers, wives, sex partners, and childbearers. 5

That means we haven't yet experienced the life events that are most radicalizing for women: entering the paid-labor force and discovering how women are treated there; marrying and finding out that it is not yet an equal partnership; having children and discovering who is responsible for them and who is not; and aging, still a greater penalty for women than for men. 6

Furthermore, new ambitions nourished by the rebirth of feminism may make young women feel and behave a little like a classical immigrant group. We are determined to prove ourselves, to achieve academic excellence, and to prepare for interesting and successful careers. More noses are kept to more grindstones in an effort to demonstrate newfound abilities, and perhaps to allay suspicions that women still have to have more and better credentials than men. This doesn't leave much time for activism. Indeed, we may not yet know that it is necessary. 7

In addition, the very progress into previously all-male careers that may be revolutionary for women is seen as conservative and conformist by outside critics. Assuming male 8 radicalism to be the measure of change, they interpret any concern with careers as evidence of "campus conservatism." In fact, "dropping out" may be a departure for men, but "dropping in" is a new thing for women. Progress lies in the direction we have not been.

Like most groups of the newly arrived or awakened, our faith in education and paper degrees also has yet to be shaken. For instance, the percentage of women enrolled in colleges and universities has been increasing at the same time that the percentage of men has been decreasing. Among students entering college in 1978, women *outnumbered* men for the first time. This hope of excelling at the existing game is probably reinforced by the greater cultural pressure on females to be "good girls" and observe somebody else's rules. 9

Though we may know intellectually that we need to have new games with new rules, we probably haven't quite absorbed such facts as the high unemployment rate among female Ph.D.s; the lower average salary among women college graduates of all races than among counterpart males who graduated from high school or less; the middle-management ceiling against which even those eagerly hired new business-school graduates seem to bump their heads after five or ten years; and the barrier-breaking women in nontraditional fields who become the first fired when recession hits. Sadly enough, we may have to personally experience some of these reality checks before we accept the idea that lawsuits, activism, and group pressure will have to accompany our individual excellence and crisp new degrees. 10

Then there is the female guilt trip, student edition. If we're not sailing along as planned, it must be *our* fault. If our mothers didn't "do anything" with their educations, it must have been *their* fault. If we can't study as hard as we think we must (because women still have to be better prepared than men), and have a substantial personal and sexual life at the same time (because women are supposed to care more about relationships than men do), then we feel inadequate, as if each of us were individually at fault for a problem that is actually culture-wide. 11

I've yet to be on a campus where most women weren't worrying about some aspect of combining marriage, children, and a career. I've yet to find one where many men were worrying about the same thing. Yet women will go right on suffering from the double-role problem and terminal guilt until men are encouraged, pressured, or otherwise forced, individually and collectively, to integrate themselves into the "women's work" of raising children and homemaking. Until then, and until there are changed job patterns to allow equal parenthood, children will go right on growing up with the belief that only women can be loving and nurturing, and only men can be intellectual or active outside the home. Each half of the world will go on limiting the full range of its human talent. 12

Finally, there is the intimate political training that hits women in the teens and early twenties: the countless ways we are still brainwashed into assuming that women are dependent on men for our basic identities, both in our work and our personal lives, much more than vice versa. After all, if we're going to enter a marriage system that's still legally designed for a person and a half, submit to an economy in which women still average about fifty-nine cents on the dollar earned by men, and work mainly as support staff and assistants, or *co*-directors and *vice*-presidents at best, then we have to be convinced that we are not whole people on our own. 13

In order to make sure that we will see ourselves as half-people, and thus be addicted to getting our identity from serving others, society tries hard to convert us as young women into "man junkies"; that is, into people who are addicted to regular shots of male approval and presence, both professionally and personally. We need a man standing next to us, actually and figuratively, whether it's at work, on Saturday night, or throughout life. (If only men realized how little it matters *which* man is standing there, they would understand that this addiction depersonalizes them, too.) Given the danger to a male-dominant system if young women stop internalizing this political message of derived identity, it's no wonder that those who try to kick the ad- 14 diction—and, worse yet, to help other women do the same—are likely to be regarded as odd or dangerous by everyone from parents to peers.

With all that pressure combined with little experience, it's no wonder that younger women are often less able to support each other. Even young women who espouse feminist goals as individuals may refrain from identifying themselves as "feminist": It's okay to want equal pay for yourself (just one small reform) but it's not okay to want equal pay for women as a group (an economic revolution). Some retreat into individualized career obsessions as a way of avoiding this dangerous discovery of shared experience with women as a group. Others retreat into the safe middle ground of "I'm not a feminist but . . . " Still others become politically active, but only on issues that are taken seriously by their male counterparts. 15

The same lesson about the personal conservatism of younger women is taught by the history of feminism. If I hadn't been conned into believing the masculine stereotype of youth as the "natural" time for freedom and rebellion, a time of "sowing wild oats" that actually is made possible by the assurance of power and security later on, I could have figured out the female pattern of activism by looking at women's movements of the past. 16

In this country, for instance, the nineteenth-century wave of feminism was started by older women who had been through the radicalizing experience of getting married and becoming the legal chattel of their husbands (or the equally radicalizing experience of *not* getting married and being treated as spinsters). Most of them had also worked in the antislavery movement and learned from the political parallels between race and sex. In other countries, that wave was also led by women who were past the point of maximum pressure toward marriageability and conservatism. 17

Looking at the first decade of this second wave, it's clear that the early feminist activist and consciousness-raising groups of the 1960s were organized by women who had experienced the civil rights movement, or homemakers who 18 had discovered that raising kids and cooking didn't occupy all their talents. While most campuses of the late sixties were still circulating the names of illegal abortionists privately (after all, abortion could damage our marriage value), slightly older women were holding press conferences and speak-outs about the reality of abortions (including their own, even though that often meant confessing to an illegal act) and demanding reform or repeal of antichoice laws. Though rape had been a quiet epidemic on campus for generations, younger women victims were still understandably fearful of speaking up, and campuses encouraged silence in order to retain their reputation for safety with tuition-paying parents. It took many off-campus speak-outs, demonstrations against laws of evidence and police procedures, and testimonies in state legislatures before most student groups began to make demands on campus and local cops for greater rape protection. In fact, "date rape"—the common campus phenomenon of a young woman being raped by someone she knows, perhaps even by several students in a fraternity house—is just now being exposed. Marital rape, a more difficult legal issue, was taken up several years ago. As for battered women and the attendant exposé of husbands and lovers as more statistically dangerous than unknown muggers in the street, that issue still seems to be thought of as a largely noncampus concern, yet at many of the colleges and universities where I've spoken, there has been at least one case within current student memory of a young woman beaten or murdered by a jealous lover.

This cultural pattern of youthful conservatism makes the growing number of older women going back to school very important. They are life examples and pragmatic activists who radicalize women young enough to be their daughters. Now that the median female undergraduate age in this country is twenty-seven because so many older women have returned, the campus is becoming a major place for cross-generational connections. 19

None of this should denigrate the courageous efforts of young women, especially women on campus, and the many 20 changes they've pioneered. On the contrary, they should be seen as even more remarkable for surviving the conservative pressures, recognizing societal problems they haven't yet fully experienced, and organizing successfully in the midst of a transient student population. Every women's history course, rape hot line, or campus newspaper that is finally covering *all* the news; every feminist professor whose job has been created or tenure saved by student pressure, or male administrator whose consciousness has been permanently changed; every counselor who's stopped guiding women one way and men another; every lawsuit that's been fueled by student energies against unequal athletic funds or graduate school requirements: all those accomplishments are even more impressive when seen against the backdrop of the female pattern of activism.

Finally, it would help to remember that a feminist revo- 21
lution rarely resembles a masculine-style one—just as a young woman's most radical act toward her mother (that is, connecting as women in order to help each other get some power) doesn't look much like a young man's most radical act toward his father (that is, breaking the father-son connection in order to separate identities or take over existing power).

It's those father-son conflicts at a generational, national 22
level that have often provided the conventional definition of revolution; yet they've gone on for centuries without basically changing the role of the female half of the world. They have also failed to reduce the level of violence in society, since both fathers and sons have included some degree of aggressiveness and superiority to women in their definition of masculinity, thus preserving the anthropological model of dominance.

Furthermore, what current leaders and theoreticians define 23
as revolution is usually little more than taking over the army and the radio stations. Women have much more in mind than that. We have to uproot the sexual caste system that is the most pervasive power structure in society, and that means transforming the patriarchal values of those who run the

institutions, whether they are politically the "right" or the "left," the fathers or the sons. This cultural part of the change goes very deep, and is often seen as too intimate, and perhaps too threatening, to be considered as either serious or possible. Only conflicts among men are "serious." Only a takeover of existing institutions is "possible."

That's why the definition of "political," on campus as elsewhere, tends to be limited to who's running for president, who's demonstrating against corporate investments in South Africa, or which is the "moral" side of some conventional revolution, preferably one that is thousands of miles away. 24

As important as such activities are, they are also the most comfortable ones when we're young. They provide a sense of virtue without much disruption in the power structure of our daily lives. Even when the most consistent energies on campus are actually concentrated around feminist issues, they may be treated as apolitical and invisible. Asked "What's happening on campus?" a student may reply, "The antinuke movement," even though that resulted in one demonstration of two hours, while student antirape squads have been patrolling the campus every night for two years and women's studies have begun to transform the very textbooks we read. 25

No wonder reporters and sociologists looking for revolution on campus often miss the depth of feminist change and activity that is really there. Women students themselves may dismiss it as not political and not serious. Certainly, it rarely comes in the masculine sixties' style of bombing buildings or burning draft cards. In fact, it goes much deeper than protesting a temporary symptom—say, the draft—and challenges the right of one group to dominate another, which is the disease itself. 26

Young women have a big task of resisting pressures and challenging definitions. Their increasing success is a miracle of foresight and courage that should make us all proud. But they should know that they, too, may grow more radical with age. 27

One day, an army of gray-haired women may quietly take over the earth. 28

For Study and Discussion

QUESTIONS FOR RESPONSE

1. If you're a woman, what comments did you want to make to Steinem after you read this essay? If there are other women students in your class who are significantly older or younger than you, how do their responses compare to yours?
2. Describe a woman you know who made surprising changes in her life when she was in her late thirties or forties. How do you think her life illustrates some of the claims Steinem makes about why women change?

QUESTIONS ABOUT PURPOSE

1. Why do you think it is important to Steinem to explain the roots of the conservatism she has noticed in young college women? What does she hope to achieve by the explanation?
2. Political issues are issues about power. What does Steinem mean when she says that "women in general don't begin to challenge the politics of our own lives until later"?

QUESTIONS ABOUT AUDIENCE

1. How does Steinem anticipate that her readers will respond to her claim that "the traditional college period is an unrealistic and cautious time"? Explain your answer.
2. What groups of college women do you think Steinem most hopes to reach with this essay? Why?

QUESTIONS ABOUT STRATEGIES

1. What specific cause-and-effect arguments does Steinem set up to develop her thesis in this essay?
2. How does Steinem try to avoid antagonizing or seeming to blame her young women readers?

QUESTIONS FOR DISCUSSION

1. How are the life patterns of most women in college today different from those of their mothers and especially their grand-

mothers? To what extent do you think some women would like their lives to be more like those of women in earlier generations?

2. Considering your own experiences and knowledge of other college students, how do you respond to Steinem's claim that young men are likely to be more rebellious than young women? What supporting or contradicting examples can you give?

SAM KEEN

Sam Keen was born in 1931 and was educated at Harvard Divinity School and Princeton University. In the late 1960s, Keen left a successful teaching career to become a contributing editor to *Psychology Today* and conduct seminars on personal mythology. His books include *Apology for Wonder* (1969), *To a Dancing God* (1970), *The Passionate Life* (1983), *Faces of the Enemy* (1986), and *Fire in the Belly: On Being a Man* (1992). *Faces of the Enemy* was the basis of a PBS documentary that was nominated for an Emmy, and *Fire in the Belly: On Being a Man* propelled Keen on to the talk-show circuit to discuss male consciousness. In "The High Price of Success," excerpted from *Fire in the Belly,* Keen analyzes the "cost to the life of our body and spirit . . . [of purchasing] corporate and professional success."

The High Price of Success

At the moment the world seems to be divided between those countries that are suffering from failed economies and those that are suffering from successful economies. After a half century of communism the USSR, Eastern Europe, and China are all looking to be saved from the results of stagnation by a change to market economies. Meanwhile, in the U.S., Germany, and Japan we are beginning to realize that our success has created an underclass of homeless and unemployed, and massive pollution of the environment. As the Dow rises to new heights everyone seems to have forgotten the one prophetic insight of Karl Marx: where the economy creates a class of winners it will also create a class of losers, where wealth gravitates easily into the hands of the haves, the fortunes of the have-nots become more desperate. 1

On the psychological level, the shadow of our success, the flip side of our affluence, is the increasing problem of stress and burnout. Lately, dealing with stress and burnout has become a growth industry. Corporations are losing many of their best men to the "disease" of stress. Every profession seems to have its crisis: physician burnout, teacher burnout, lawyer burnout. Experts in relaxation, nutrition, exercise, and meditation are doing a brisk business. 2

But finally, stress cannot be dealt with by psychological tricks, because for the most part it is a philosophical rather than a physiological problem, a matter of the wrong worldview. Perhaps the most common variety of stress can best be described as "rustout" rather than burnout. It is a product, not of an excess of fire, but of a deficiency of passion. We, human beings, can survive so long as we "make a living," but we do not thrive without a sense of significance that we gain only by creating something we feel is of lasting value—a child, a better mousetrap, a computer, a space shuttle, a book, a farm. When we spend the majority of our time doing work that gives us a paycheck but no sense of meaning we inevitably get bored and depressed. When the requirements of our work do not match our creative potential we rust out. The second kind of burnout is really a type of combat fatigue that is the inevitable result of living for an extended period within an environment that is experienced as a battle zone. If the competition is always pressing you to produce more and faster, if life is a battle, if winning is the only thing, sooner or later you are going to come down with battle fatigue. Like combat veterans returning from Vietnam, businessmen who live for years within an atmosphere of low-intensity warfare begin to exhibit the personality traits of the warrior. They become disillusioned and numb to ethical issues; they think only of survival and grow insensitive to pain. You may relax, breathe deeply, take time for R and R, and remain a warrior. But ultimately the only cure for stress is to leave the battlefield. 3

The feminist revolution made us aware of how the economic order has discriminated against women, but not of 4

how it cripples the male psyche. In ancient China
upper-class women were broken, bent backwards, an
to make them more "beautiful." Have the best and b
men of our time had their souls broken and bent to
them "successful"?

Let's think about the relation between the wounds m
suffer, our overidentification with work, and our captivit
within the horizons of the economic myth.

Recently, a lament has gone out through the land that
men are becoming too tame, if not limp. The poet Robert
Bly, who is as near as we have these days to a traveling bard
and shaman for men, says we have raised a whole generation
of soft men—oh-so-sensitive, but lacking in thunder and
lightning. He tells men they must sever the ties with mother,
stop looking at themselves through the eyes of women, and
recover the "wild man" within themselves.

I suspect that if men lack the lusty pride of self-affirmation, 7
if we say "yes" too often but without passion, if we are
burned out without ever having been on fire, it is mostly
because we have allowed ourselves to be engulfed by a
metabody, a masculine womb—The Corporation. Our fragile,
tender, wild, and succulent bodies are being deformed to
suit the needs of the body corporate. Climbing the economic
or corporate ladder has replaced the hero's journey up Mt.
Analogue. Upward mobility has usurped the ascent of the
Seven-Story Mountain, the quest to discover the heights and
depths of the human psyche.

At what cost to the life of our body and spirit do we 8
purchase corporate and professional success? What sacrifices
are we required to make to these upstart economic gods?

Here are some of the secrets they didn't tell you at the 9
Harvard Business School, some of the hidden, largely unconscious, tyrannical, unwritten rules that govern success in
professional and corporate life:

> **Cleanliness is next to prosperity.** *Sweat is lower* 10
> *class, lower status. Those who shower before work and*

use deodorant make more than those who shower after work and smell human throughout the day. As a nation we are proud that only three percent of the population has to work on the land—get soiled, be earthy—to feed the other ninety-seven percent.

Look but don't touch. *The less contact you have with real stuff—raw material, fertilizer, wood, steel, chemicals, making things that have moving parts—the more money you will make. Lately, as we have lost our edge in manufacturing and production, we have comforted ourselves with the promise that we can prosper by specializing in service and information industries. Oh, so clean.* 11

Prefer abstractions. *The further you move up toward the catbird seat, the penthouse, the office with the view of all Manhattan, the more you live among abstractions. In the brave new world of the market you may speculate in hog futures without ever having seen a pig, buy out an airline without knowing how to fly a plane, grow wealthy without having produced anything.* 12

Specialize. *The modern economy rewards experts, men and women who are willing to become focused, concentrated, tightly bound, efficient. Or to put the matter more poignantly, we succeed in our professions to the degree that we sacrifice wide-ranging curiosity and fascination with the world at large, and become departmental in our thinking. The professions, like medieval castles, are small kingdoms sealed off from the outer world by walls of jargon. Once initiated by the ritual of graduate school, MBAs, economists, lawyers, and physicians speak only to themselves and theologians speak only to God.* 13

Sit still and stay indoors. *The world is run largely by urban, sedentary males. The symbol of power is the chair. The chairman of the board sits and manages. As a general rule those who stay indoors and move the least make the most money. Muscle doesn't pay.* 14

Worse yet, anybody who has to work in the sun and rain is likely to make the minimum wage. With the exception of quarterbacks, boxers, and race car drivers, whose bodies are broken for our entertainment, men don't get ahead by moving their bodies.

Live by the clock. *Ignore your intimate body time,* 15
body rhythms, and conform to the demands of corporate time, work time, professional time. When "time is money," we bend our bodies and minds to the demands of EST (economic standard time). We interrupt our dreams when the alarm rings, report to work at nine, eat when the clock strikes twelve, return to our private lives at five, and retire at sixty-five—ready or not. As a reward we are allowed weekends and holidays for recreation. Conformity to the sacred routine, showing up on time, is more important than creativity. Instead of "taking our time" we respond to deadlines. Most successful men, and lately women, become Type A personalities, speed freaks, addicted to the rush of adrenaline, filled with a sense of urgency, hard driven, goal oriented, and stressed out. The most brutal example of this rule is the hundred-hour week required of physicians in their year of residency. This hazing ritual, like circumcision, drives home the deep mythic message that your body is no longer your own.

Wear the uniform. *It wouldn't be so bad if those* 16
who earned success and power were proud enough in their manhood to peacock their colors. But no. Success makes drab. The higher you rise in the establishment the more colorless you become, the more you dress like an undertaker or a priest. Bankers, politicians, CEOs wear black, gray, or dark blue, with maybe a bold pinstripe or a daring "power tie." And the necktie? That ultimate symbol of the respectable man has obviously been demonically designed to exile the head from the body and restrain all deep and passionate breath. The more a corporation, institution, or profession requires the sacrifice of the individuality of its members, the more it requires uniform wear. The corp isn't really looking for a few good men. It's looking for

a few dedicated Marines, and it knows exactly how to transform boys into uniform men. As monks and military men have known for centuries, once you get into the habit you follow the orders of the superior.

Keep your distance, stay in your place. *The hierarchy of power and prestige that governs every profession and corporation establishes the proper distance between people. There are people above you, people below you, and people on your level, and you don't get too close to any of them. Nobody hugs the boss. What is lacking is friendship. I know of no more radical critique of economic life than the observation by Earl Shorris that nowhere in the vast literature of management is there a single chapter on friendship.* 17

Desensitize yourself. *Touch, taste, smell—the realm of the senses—receive little homage. What pays off is reason, willpower, planning, discipline, control. There has, of course, recently been a move afoot to bring in potted plants and tasteful art to make corporate environments more humane. But the point of these exercises is aesthetics, like the development of communication skills by practitioners of organizational development, is to increase production. The bottom line is still profit, not pleasure or persons.* 18

Don't trouble yourself with large moral issues. *The more the world is governed by experts, specialists, and professionals, the less anybody takes responsibility for the most troubling consequences of our success-failure. Television producers crank out endless cop and killing tales, but refuse to consider their contribution to the climate of violence. Lawyers concern themselves with what is legal, not what is just. Physicians devote themselves to kidneys or hearts of individual patients while the health delivery system leaves masses without medicine. Physicists invent new generations of genocidal weapons which they place in the eager arms of the military. The military hands the responsibility for their use over to politicians. Politicians plead that they have no choice—the enemy makes them do it. Profes-* 19 *sors publish esoterica while students perish from poor teaching. Foresters, in cahoots with timber companies, clear-cut or manage the forest for sustained yield, but nobody is in charge of oxygen regeneration. Psychologists heal psyches while communities fall apart. Codes of professional ethics are for the most part, like corporate advertisements, high sounding but self-serving.*

When we live within the horizons of the economic myth, we begin to consider it honorable for a man to do whatever he must to make a living. Gradually we adopt what Erich Fromm called "a marketing orientation" toward our selves. We put aside our dreams, forget the green promise of our young selves, and begin to tailor our personalities to what the market requires. When we mold ourselves into commodities, practice smiling and charm so we will have "winning personalities," learn to sell ourselves, and practice the silly art of power dressing, we are certain to be haunted by a sense of emptiness. 20

Men, in our culture, have carried a special burden of unconsciousness, of ignorance of the self. The unexamined life has been worth quite a lot in economic terms. It has enabled us to increase the gross national product yearly. It may not be necessary to be a compulsive extrovert to be financially successful, but it helps. Especially for men, ours is an outer-directed culture that rewards us for remaining strangers to ourselves, unacquainted with feeling, intuition, or the subtleties of sensation and dreams. 21

Many of the personality characteristics that have traditionally been considered "masculine"—aggression, rationality—are not innate or biological components of maleness but are products of a historical era in which men have been socially assigned the chief roles in warfare and the economic order. As women increasingly enter the quasimilitary world of the economic system they are likely to find themselves governed by the logic of the system. Some feminists, who harbor a secret belief in the innate moral superiority of women, believe that women will change the rules of business and bring the balm of communication and human kindness into the board- 22 room. To date this has been a vain hope. Women executives have proven themselves the equal of men in every way—including callousness. The difference between the sexes is being eroded as both sexes become defined by work. It is often said that the public world of work is a man's place and that as women enter it they will become increasingly "masculine" and lose their "femininity." To think this way is to miss the most important factor of the economic world. Economic man, the creature who defines itself within the horizons of work and consumption, is not man in any full sense of the word, but a being who has been neutralized, degendered, rendered subservient to the laws of the market. The danger of economics is not that it turns women into men but that it destroys the fullness of both manhood and womanhood.

History is a game of leapfrog in which yesterday's gods 23
regularly become today's demons, and the rectitude of the fathers becomes the fault of the sons. The Greeks invented the idea of nemesis to show how any single virtue stubbornly maintained gradually changes into a destructive vice. Our success, our industry, our habit of work have produced our economic nemesis. In our current economic crisis we are driving to the poorhouse in new automobiles, spending our inflated dollars for calorie-free food, lamenting our falling productivity in an environment polluted by our industry. Work made modern men great, but now threatens to usurp our souls, to inundate the earth in things and trash, to destroy our capacity to love and wonder. According to an ancient myth, Hephaestus (Vulcan) the blacksmith, the only flawed immortal who worked, was born lame.

Somehow men got so lost in the doing that we forgot to 24
pause and ask, "What is worth doing? What of value are we creating—and destroying—within the economic order?" Work has always been our womb—the fertile void out of which we give birth to our visions. Today we need to stop the world for a while and look carefully at where our industry is taking us. We have a hopeful future only if we stop asking what we can produce and begin to ask what we want to

create. Our dignity as men lies not in exhausting ourselves in work but in discovering our vocation.

Remembering Dr. Faust, it might be a good idea to pause and ask ourselves how much of our psyches we will trade for how much profit, power, and prestige. Maybe we should require graduate schools, professional organizations, places of labor, and corporations to put a warning over their doors. Caution: Excessive work may be hazardous to the health of your body and spirit. 25

I fear that something beautiful, terrible, and complex about work has escaped me. Some part of the mixed blessing I cannot capture in words. 26

A friend who is a successful entrepreneur asked me, "Are you antibusiness? Business is where I create. It is where the excitement and juice is for me. I can hardly wait to get to my office." My literary agent, Ned Leavitt, tells me: "My work is my art. When I dress in my suit each morning I feel like a knight going forth to battle, and I love to fight hard and win in a hard bargaining session with a publisher and get the best deal for my clients." 27

I know. I know. I am also one of the work-driven men. And I am lucky to have work that fits skintight over my spirit. I hardly know how to separate work from self. Even when I subtract the long hours, the fatigue, the uncertainties about money, the irritation of having to deal with a million nit-shit details, the long hours in the limbo of jet planes and airports, the compromises I have to make, the sum is overwhelmingly positive. I don't know who I would be without the satisfaction of providing for my family, the occasional intoxication of creativity, the warm companionship of colleagues, the pride in a job well done, and the knowledge that my work has been useful to others. 28

But there is still something unsaid, something that forces me to ask questions about my life that are, perhaps, tragic: In working so much have I done violence to my being? How often, doing work that is good, have I betrayed what is better in myself and abandoned what is best for those I love? 29

How many hours would have been better spent walking in silence in the woods or wrestling with my children? Two decades ago, near the end of what was a good but troubled marriage, my wife asked me: "Would you be willing to be less efficient?" The question haunts me.

For Study and Discussion

QUESTIONS FOR RESPONSE

1. What is your reaction to the ten unwritten rules that Keen claims govern success in professional and corporate life? How well do you think you would fit into an environment that operates by these rules? Why?
2. On November 20, 1991, the *Chronicle of Higher Education* reported on a survey about the values and career hopes of college freshmen. One of the findings was that 75.6 percent of these students listed "being well off financially" as one of their major goals. What initial response do you think these students would be likely to have to Keen's essay? Why?

QUESTIONS ABOUT PURPOSE

1. What does Keen mean when he says in paragraph 24 that people should stop asking what they can produce and ask what they can create? What essential difference do you think he sees in the two activities?
2. In the last section of the essay, paragraphs 26 to 29, Keen introduces a new point of view. What is it? Why do you think he does this?

QUESTIONS ABOUT AUDIENCE

1. Although most college students who read this essay have probably not been directly involved in the corporate or professional world, they are likely to be aware of the pressures and conflicts Keen describes. What would their sources of such knowledge be? How influential are those sources in shaping their attitudes?
2. The book from which this essay is taken, *Fire in the Belly,* is

directed toward men. What relevance do you think the essay can have for women as well, including those who do not plan to go into the corporate or professional world?

QUESTIONS ABOUT STRATEGIES

1. What effect does Keen create by listing nine of his ten unwritten rules as brusque imperatives? What reactions do you think he wants to trigger from his readers?
2. Examine these metaphors in the essay: "our fragile, tender . . . bodies are being deformed to suit the needs of the body corporate" in paragraph 7; "cripples the male psyche" in paragraph 4; and "we mold ourselves into commodities" in paragraph 20. What does Keen hope to achieve with such figurative language?

QUESTIONS FOR DISCUSSION

1. What questions, if any, does reading Keen's essay make you ask about the profession you are planning to go into? What pressures and conflicts do you anticipate facing?
2. Reread Keen's expansion of his tenth unwritten rule: "Don't trouble yourself with large moral issues" (paragraph 19). How valid do you find the claims he makes here? What could any of the individuals in the professions he names do about the charges he makes?

ALICE STEWART TRILLIN

Alice Stewart Trillin was born in 1938 in Rye, New York, and was educated at Wellesley College and Yale University. Trillin worked for several years as a college English teacher in New York City. The experience was the basis for her book about teaching underprepared students, *Teaching Basic Skills* (1980). She then began producing educational programming for public television. Her first series, "Writers Writing" (1985), is a dramatic portrayal of the writing process; her second, "Behind the Scenes" (1992), is a ten-part series presenting the arts to children. She first delivered "Of Dragons and Garden Peas" as a talk to medical students at both Cornell and Albert Einstein medical schools; she then published it in the *New England Journal of Medicine*. Using her own experience as a cancer patient, Trillin analyzes how her illness affected her attitude toward doctors, patients, friends, and family.

Of Dragons and Garden Peas

When I first realized that I might have cancer, I felt immediately that I had entered a special place, a place I came to call "The Land of the Sick People." The most disconcerting thing, however, was not that I found that place terrifying and unfamiliar, but that I found it so ordinary, so banal. I didn't feel different, didn't feel that my life had radically changed at the moment the word *cancer* became attached to it. The same rules still held. What had changed, however, was other people's perceptions of me. Unconsciously, even with a certain amount of kindness, everyone—with the single rather extraordinary exception of my husband—regarded me as someone who had been altered irrevocably. I don't want 1 to exaggerate my feeling of alienation or to give the impression that it was in any way dramatic. I have no horror stories of the kind I read a few years ago in the *New York Times;* people didn't move their desks away from me at the office or refuse to let their children play with my children at school because they thought that cancer was catching. My friends are all too sophisticated and too sensitive for that kind of behavior. Their distance from me was marked most of all by their inability to understand the ordinariness, the banality of what was happening to me. They marveled at how well I was "coping with cancer." I had become special, no longer like them. Their genuine concern for what had happened to me, and their complete separateness from it, expressed exactly what I had felt all my life about anyone I had ever known who had experienced tragedy.

When asked to speak to a group of doctors and medical 2
students about what it was like to be a cancer patient, I worried for a long time about what I should say. It was a perfect opportunity—every patient's fantasy—to complain about doctors' insensitivity, nurses who couldn't draw blood properly, and perhaps even the awful food in hospitals. Or, instead, I could present myself as the good patient, full of uplifting thoughts about how much I had learned from having cancer. But, unlike many people, I had had very good experiences with doctors and hospitals. And the role of the brave patient troubled me, because I was afraid that all the brave things I said might no longer hold if I got sick again. I had to think about this a great deal during the first two years after my operation as I watched my best friend live out my own worst nightmares. She discovered that she had cancer several months after I did. Several months after that, she discovered that it had metastasized; she underwent eight operations during the next year and a half before she died. All my brave talk was tested by her illness as it has not yet been tested by mine.

And so I decided not to talk about the things that separate 3
those of us who have cancer from those who do not. I decided that the only relevant thing for me to talk about was

the one thing that we all have most in common. We are all afraid of dying.

Our fear of death makes it essential to maintain a distance between ourselves and anyone who is threatened by death. Denying our connection to the precariousness of others' lives is a way of pretending that we are immortal. We need this deception—it is one of the ways we stay sane—but we also need to be prepared for the times when it doesn't work. For doctors, who confront death when they go to work in the morning as routinely as other people deal with balance sheets and computer printouts, and for me, to whom a chest x-ray or a blood test will never again be a simple, routine procedure, it is particularly important to face the fact of death squarely, to talk about it with one another. 4

Cancer connects us to one another because having cancer is an embodiment of the existential paradox that we all experience: we feel that we are immortal, yet we know that we will die. To Tolstoy's Ivan Ilyich, the syllogism he had learned as a child, "'Caius is a man, men are mortal, therefore Caius is mortal,' had always seemed . . . correct as applied to Caius but certainly not as applied to himself." Like Ivan Ilyich, we all construct an elaborate set of defense mechanisms to separate ourselves from Caius. To anyone who has had cancer, these defense mechanisms become talismans that we invest with a kind of magic. These talismans are essential to our sanity, and yet they need to be examined. 5

First of all, we believe in the magic of doctors and medicine. The purpose of a talisman is to give us control over the things we are afraid of. Doctors and patients are accomplices in staging a kind of drama in which we pretend that doctors have the power to keep us well. The very best doctors—and I have had the very best—share their power with their patients and try to give us the information that we need to control our own treatment. Whenever I am threatened by panic, my doctor sits me down and tells me something concrete. He draws a picture of my lung, or my lymph nodes; he explains as well as he can how cancer cells work and what might be happening in my body. Together, 6 we approach my disease intelligently and rationally, as a problem to be solved, an exercise in logic to be worked out. Of course, through knowledge, through medicine, through intelligence, we do have some control. But at best this control is limited, and there is always the danger that the disease I have won't behave rationally and respond to the intelligent argument we have constructed. Cancer cells, more than anything else in nature, are likely to behave irrationally. If we think that doctors and medicine can always protect us, we are in danger of losing faith in doctors and medicine when their magic doesn't work. The physician who fails to keep us well is like an unsuccessful witch doctor; we have to drive him out of the tribe and look for a more powerful kind of magic.

The reverse of this, of course, is that the patient becomes 7
a kind of talisman for the doctor. Doctors defy death by keeping people alive. To a patient, it becomes immediately clear that the best way to please a doctor is to be healthy. If you can't manage that, the next best thing is to be well-behaved. (Sometimes the difference between being healthy and being well-behaved becomes blurred in a hospital, so that it almost seems as if being sick were being badly behaved.) If we get well, we help our doctors succeed; if we are sick, we have failed. Patients often say that their doctors seem angry with them when they don't respond to treatment. I think that this phenomenon is more than patients' paranoia or the result of overdeveloped medical egos. It is the fear of death again. It is necessary for doctors to become a bit angry with patients who are dying, if only as a way of separating themselves from someone in whom they have invested a good bit of time and probably a good bit of caring. We all do this to people who are sick. I can remember being terribly angry with my mother, who was prematurely senile, for a long time. Somehow I needed to think that it was her fault that she was sick, because her illness frightened me so much. I was also angry with my friend who died of cancer. I felt that she had let me down, that perhaps she hadn't fought hard enough. It was important for me to find reasons for

her death, to find things that she might have done to cause it, as a way of separating myself from her and as a way of thinking that I would somehow have behaved differently, that I would somehow have been able to stay alive.

So, once we have recognized the limitations of the magic of doctors and medicine, where are we? We have to turn to our own magic, to our ability to "control" our bodies. For people who don't have cancer, this often takes the form of jogging and exotic diets and transcendental meditation. For people who have cancer, it takes the form of conscious development of the will to live. For a long time after I found out that I had cancer, I loved hearing stories about people who had simply decided that they would not be sick. I remember one story about a man who had a lung tumor and a wife with breast cancer and several children to support; he said, "I simply can't afford to be sick." Somehow the tumor went away. I think I suspected that there was a missing part to this story when I heard it, but there was also something that sounded right to me. I knew what he meant. I also found the fact that I had cancer unacceptable; the thought that my children might grow up without me was as ridiculous as the thought that I might forget to make appointments for their dental checkups and polio shots. I simpy had to be there. Of course, doctors give a lot of credence to the power of the will over illness, but I have always suspected that the stories in medical books about this power might also have missing parts. My friend who died wanted to live more than anyone I have ever known. The talisman of will didn't work for her. 8

The need to exert some kind of control over the irrational forces that we imagine are loose in our bodies also results in what I have come to recognize as the "brave act" put on by people who have cancer. We all do it. The blood-count line at Memorial Hospital can be one of the cheeriest places in New York on certain mornings. It was on this line, during my first visit to Memorial, that a young leukemia patient in remission told me, "They treat lung cancer like the common cold around here." (Believe me, that was the cheeriest thing 9 anyone had said to me in months.) While waiting for blood counts, I have heard stories from people with lymphoma who were given up for dead in other hospitals and who are feeling terrific. The atmosphere in that line suggests a gathering of knights who have just slain a bunch of dragons. But there are always people in the line who don't say anything at all, and I always wonder if they have at other times felt the exhilaration felt by those of us who are well. We all know, at least, that the dragons are never quite dead and might at any time be aroused, ready for another fight. But our brave act is important. It is one of the ways we stay alive, and it is the way that we convince those who live in "The Land of the Well People" that we aren't all that different from them.

As much as I rely on the talisman of the will, I know that believing in it too much can lead to another kind of deception. There has been a great deal written (mostly by psychiatrists) about why people get cancer and which personality types are most likely to get it. Susan Sontag has pointed out that this explanation of cancer parallels the explanations for tuberculosis that were popular before the discovery of the tubercle bacillus. But it is reassuring to think that people get cancer because of their personalities, because that implies that we have some control over whether we get it. (On the other hand, if people won't give up smoking to avoid cancer, I don't see how they can be expected to change their personalities on the basis of far less compelling evidence.) The trouble with this explanation of cancer is the trouble with any talisman: it is only useful when its charms are working. If I get sick, does that mean that my will to live isn't strong enough? Is being sick a moral and psychological failure? If I feel successful, as if I had slain a dragon, because I am well, should I feel guilty, as if I have failed, if I get sick? 10

One of the ways that all of us avoid thinking about death is by concentrating on the details of our daily lives. The work that we do every day and the people we love—the fabric of our lives—convince us that we are alive and that we will stay alive. William Saroyan said in a recent book, "Why am I writing this book? To save my life, to keep from dying, of 11 course. That is why we get up in the morning." Getting up in the morning seems particularly miraculous after having seriously considered the possibility that these mornings might be limited. A year after I had my lung removed, my doctors asked me what I cared about most. I was about to go to Nova Scotia, where we have a summer home, and where I had not been able to go the previous summer because I was having radiation treatments, and I told him that what was most important to me was garden peas. Not the peas themselves, of course, though they were particularly good that year. What was extraordinary to me after that year was that I could again think that peas were important, that I could concentrate on the details of when to plant them and how much mulch they would need instead of thinking about platelets and white cells. I cherished the privilege of thinking about trivia. Thinking about death can make the details of our lives seem unimportant, and so, paradoxically, they become a burden—too much trouble to think about. This is the real meaning of depression: feeling weighed down by the concrete, unable to make the effort to move objects around, overcome by ennui. It is the fear of death that causes that ennui, because the fear of death ties us too much to the physical. We think too much about our bodies, and our bodies become too concrete—machines not functioning properly.

The other difficulty with the talisman of the moment is 12
that it is often the very preciousness of these moments that makes the thought of death so painful. As my friend got closer to death she became rather removed from those she loved the most. She seemed to have gone to some place where we couldn't reach her—to have died what doctors sometimes call a "premature death." I much preferred to think of her enjoying precious moments. I remembered the almost ritualistic way she had her hair cut and tied in satin ribbons before brain surgery, the funny, somehow joyful afternoon that we spent trying wigs on her newly shaved head. Those moments made it seem as if it wasn't so bad to have cancer. But of course it was bad. It was unspeakably

bad, and toward the end she couldn't bear to speak about it or to be too close to the people she didn't want to leave. The strength of my love for my children, my husband, my life, even my garden peas has probably been more important than anything else in keeping me alive. The intensity of this love is also what makes me so terrified of dying.

For many, of course, a response to the existential paradox 13
is religion—Kierkegaard's irrational leap toward faith. It is no coincidence that such a high number of conversions take place in cancer hospitals; there is even a group of Catholic nurses in New York who are referred to by other members of their hospital staff as "the death squad." I don't mean to belittle such conversions or any help that religion can give to anyone. I am at this point in my life simply unqualified to talk about the power of this particular talisman.

In considering some of the talismans we all use to deny 14
death, I don't mean to suggest that these talismans should be abandoned. However, their limits must be acknowledged. Ernest Becker, in *The Denial of Death,* says that "skepticism is a more radical experience, a more manly confrontation of potential meaninglessness than mysticism." The most important thing I know now that I didn't know four years ago is that this "potential meaninglessness" can in fact be confronted. As much as I rely on my talismans—my doctors, my will, my husband, my children, and my garden peas—I know that from time to time I will have to confront what Conrad described as "the horror." I know that we can—all of us—confront that horror and not be destroyed by it, even, to some extent, be enhanced by it. To quote Becker again: "I think that taking life seriously means something such as this: that whatever man does on this planet has to be done in the lived truth of the terror of creation, of the grotesque, of the rumble of panic underneath everything. Otherwise it is false."

It astonishes me that having faced the terror, we continue 15
to live, even to live with a great deal of joy. It is commonplace for people who have cancer—particularly those who feel as well as I do—to talk about how much richer their lives are

because they have confronted death. Yes, my life is very rich. I have even begun to understand that wonderful line in *King Lear,* "Ripeness is all." I suppose that becoming ripe means finding out that none of the really important questions have answers. I wish that life had devised a less terrifying, less risky way of making me ripe. But I wasn't given any choice about this.

William Saroyan said recently, "I'm growing old! I'm falling apart! And it's VERY INTERESTING!" I'd be willing to bet that Mr. Saroyan, like me, would much rather be young and all in one piece. But somehow his longing for youth and wholeness doesn't destroy him or stop him from getting up in the morning and writing, as he says, to save his life. We will never kill the dragon. But each morning we confront him. Then we give our children breakfast, perhaps put a bit more mulch on the peas, and hope that we can convince the dragon to stay away for a while longer. 16

For Study and Discussion

QUESTIONS FOR RESPONSE

1. If you know someone who has had cancer or another life-threatening illness such as lupus, kidney disease, or AIDS, to what extent does Trillin's essay help you understand their problems better? How?
2. What do you learn about Trillin's personality and values from this essay? How does that knowledge affect the way you react to her essay?

QUESTIONS ABOUT PURPOSE

1. Trillin first wrote this essay as a talk to be given to an audience of medical students, then published it in the *New England Journal of Medicine,* a major medical publication. What special insights do you think she hopes physicians will gain from this very personal essay?

2. What comfort do you think someone with cancer might find in reading this essay? Why?

QUESTIONS ABOUT AUDIENCE

1. What attitude about cancer does Trillin assume her nonmedical audience may have? What do you think are the sources of those attitudes?
2. Even though most of the nonmedical readers of this essay are probably healthy people, what experiences does Trillin assume they share with her that will make them an interested and sympathetic audience?

QUESTIONS ABOUT STRATEGIES

1. Trillin has considerable experience in making films. How does she use the cinematic techniques of narration, scene setting, and dramatization to tell her story?
2. How does Trillin's repeated comparisons of her own experience with cancer to that of her friend who died make her account more poignant?

QUESTIONS FOR DISCUSSION

1. Often it is difficult to convey one's experience of illness to another person. How well do you think Trillin succeeds? What contributes to that success?
2. Why do you think people so often want to detach themselves from friends or family who are seriously ill? To what extent does Trillin help you understand that reaction?

STEPHEN JAY GOULD

Stephen Jay Gould was born in New York City in 1941 and attended Antioch College and Columbia University. Trained as a paleontologist, Gould has been a professor of geology at Harvard University since 1967. Throughout his teaching and writing career he has been known for his ability to translate challenging scientific theories into understandable terms. His books include *The Panda's Thumb: More Reflections in Natural History* (1980); *Hen's Teeth and Horse's Toes: Further Reflections in Natural History* (1983); *The Flamingo's Smile: Reflections in Natural History* (1985); *An Urchin in the Storm: Essays About Books and Ideas* (1987), and *Bully for Brontosaurus* (1991). Several of these books are collections of his monthly column for *Natural History* magazine, "This View of Life." In "Carrie Buck's Daughter," reprinted from *The Flamingo's Smile,* Gould traces the tragic consequences of a simplistic assessment of the chain of cause and effect.

Carrie Buck's Daughter

The Lord really put it on the line in his preface to that prototype of all prescription, the Ten Commandments: 1

> *. . . for I, the Lord thy God, am a jealous God, visiting the iniquity of the fathers upon the children unto the third and fourth generation of them that hate me (Exod. 20:5).*

The terror of this statement lies in its patent unfairness—its promise to punish guiltless offspring for the misdeeds of their distant forebears. 2

A different form of guilt by genealogical association 3

attempts to remove this stigma of injustice by denying a cherished premise of Western thought—human free will. If off-spring are tainted not simply by the deeds of their parents but by a material form of evil transferred directly by biological inheritance, then "the iniquity of the fathers" becomes a signal or warning for probable misbehavior of their sons. Thus Plato, while denying that children should suffer directly for the crimes of their parents, nonetheless defended the banishment of a personally guiltless man whose father, grandfather, and great-grandfather had all been condemned to death.

It is, perhaps, merely coincidental that both Jehovah and Plato chose three generations as their criterion for establishing different forms of guilt by association. Yet we maintain a strong folk, or vernacular, tradition for viewing triple occurrences as minimal evidence of regularity. Bad things, we are told, come in threes. Two may represent an accidental association; three is a pattern. Perhaps, then, we should not wonder that our own century's most famous pronouncement of blood guilt employed the same criterion—Oliver Wendell Holmes's defense of compulsory sterilization in Virginia (Supreme Court decision of 1927 in *Buck v. Bell*): "three generations of imbeciles are enough." 4

Restrictions upon immigration, with national quotas set to discriminate against those deemed mentally unfit by early versions of IQ testing, marked the greatest triumph of the American eugenics movement—the flawed hereditarian doctrine, so popular earlier in our century and by no means extinct today, that attempted to "improve" our human stock by preventing the propagation of those deemed biologically unfit and encouraging procreation among the supposedly worthy. But the movement to enact and enforce laws for compulsory "eugenic" sterilization had an impact and success scarcely less pronounced. If we could debar the shiftless and the stupid from our shores, we might also prevent the propagation of those similarly afflicted but already here. 5

The movement for compulsory sterilization began in earnest during the 1890s, abetted by two major factors—the 6 rise of eugenics as an influential political movement and the perfection of safe and simple operations (vasectomy for men and salpingectomy, the cutting and tying of Fallopian tubes, for women) to replace castration and other socially unacceptable forms of mutilation. Indiana passed the first sterilization act based on eugenic principles in 1907 (a few states had previously mandated castration as a punitive measure for certain sexual crimes, although such laws were rarely enforced and usually overturned by judicial review). Like so many others to follow, it provided for sterilization of afflicted people residing in the state's "care," either as inmates of mental hospitals and homes for the feeble-minded or as inhabitants of prisons. Sterilization could be imposed upon those judged insane, idiotic, imbecilic, or moronic, and upon convicted rapists or criminals when recommended by a board of experts.

By the 1930s, more than thirty states had passed similar 7
laws, often with an expanded list of so-called hereditary defects, including alcoholism and drug addiction in some states, and even blindness and deafness in others. These laws were continually challenged and rarely enforced in most states; only California and Virginia applied them zealously. By January 1935, some 20,000 forced "eugenic" sterilizations had been performed in the United States, nearly half in California.

No organization crusaded more vociferously and success- 8
fully for these laws than the Eugenics Record Office, the semiofficial arm and repository of data for the eugenics movement in America. Harry Laughlin, superintendent of the Eugenics Record Office, dedicated most of his career to a tireless campaign of writing and lobbying for eugenic sterilization. He hoped, thereby, to eliminate in two generations the genes of what he called the "submerged tenth"—"the most worthless one-tenth of our present population." He proposed a "model sterilization law" in 1922, designed

> *to prevent the procreation of persons socially inadequate from defective inheritance, by authorizing and*

> *providing for eugenical sterilization of certain potential parents carrying degenerate hereditary qualities.*

This model bill became the prototype for most laws passed 9
in America, although few states cast their net as widely as Laughlin advised. (Laughlin's categories encompassed "blind, including those with seriously impaired vision; deaf, including those with seriously impaired hearing; and dependent, including orphans, ne'er-do-wells, the homeless, tramps, and paupers.") Laughlin's suggestions were better heeded in Nazi Germany, where his model act inspired the infamous and stringently enforced *Erbgesundheitsrecht,* leading by the eve of World War II to the sterilization of some 375,000 people, most for "congenital feeble-mindedness," but including nearly 4,000 for blindness and deafness.

The campaign for forced eugenic sterilization in America 10
reached its climax and height of respectability in 1927, when the Supreme Court, by an 8–1 vote, upheld the Virginia sterilization bill in *Buck v. Bell.* Oliver Wendell Holmes, then in his mid-eighties and the most celebrated jurist in America, wrote the majority opinion with his customary verve and power of style. It included the notorious paragraph, with its chilling tag line, cited ever since as the quintessential statement of eugenic principles. Remembering with pride his own distant experiences as an infantryman in the Civil War, Holmes wrote:

> *We have seen more than once that the public welfare may call upon the best citizens for their lives. It would be strange if it could not call upon those who already sap the strength of the state for these lesser sacrifices. . . . It is better for all the world, if instead of waiting to execute degenerate offspring for crime, or to let them starve for their imbecility, society can prevent those who are manifestly unfit from continuing their kind. The principle that sustains compulsory vaccination is broad enough to cover cutting the Fallopian tubes. Three generations of imbeciles are enough.*

Who, then, were the famous "three generations of imbe- 11
ciles," and why should they still compel our interest?

When the state of Virginia passed its compulsory sterilization law in 1924, Carrie Buck, an eighteen-year-old white woman, lived as an involuntary resident at the State Colony for Epileptics and Feeble-Minded. As the first person selected for sterilization under the new act, Carrie Buck became the focus for a constitutional challenge launched, in part, by conservative Virginia Christians who held, according to eugenical "modernists," antiquated views about individual preferences and "benevolent" state power. (Simplistic political labels do not apply in this case, and rarely in general for that matter. We usually regard eugenics as a conservative movement and its most vocal critics as members of the left. This alignment has generally held in our own decade. But eugenics, touted in its day as the latest in scientific modernism, attracted many liberals and numbered among its most vociferous critics groups often labeled as reactionary and antiscientific. If any political lesson emerges from these shifting allegiances, we might consider the true inalienability of certain human rights.) 12

But why was Carrie Buck in the State Colony and why was she selected? Oliver Wendell Holmes upheld her choice as judicious in the opening lines of his 1927 opinion: 13

> *Carrie Buck is a feeble-minded white woman who was committed to the State Colony. . . . She is the daughter of a feeble-minded mother in the same institution, and the mother of an illegitimate feeble-minded child.*

In short, inheritance stood as the crucial issue (indeed as the driving force behind all eugenics). For if measured mental deficiency arose from malnourishment, either of body or mind, and not from tainted genes, then how could sterilization be justified? If decent food, upbringing, medical care, and education might make a worthy citizen of Carrie Buck's daughter, how could the State of Virginia justify the severing of Carrie's Fallopian tubes against her will? (Some forms of mental deficiency are passed in inheritance in family lines, but most are not—a scarcely surprising conclusion when we consider the thousand shocks that beset us all during our lives, from abnormalities in embryonic growth to traumas of 14 birth, malnourishment, rejection, and poverty. In any case, no fair-minded person today would credit Laughlin's social criteria for the identification of hereditary deficiency—ne'er-do-wells, the homeless, tramps, and paupers—although we shall soon see that Carrie Buck was committed on these grounds.)

When Carrie Buck's case emerged as the crucial test of 15
Virginia's law, the chief honchos of eugenics understood that the time had come to put up or shut up on the crucial issue of inheritance. Thus, the Eugenics Record Office sent Arthur H. Estabrook, their crack fieldworker, to Virginia for a "scientific" study of the case. Harry Laughlin himself provided a deposition, and his brief for inheritance was presented at the local trial that affirmed Virginia's law and later worked its way to the Supreme Court as *Buck v. Bell.*

Laughlin made two major points to the court. First, that 16
Carrie Buck and her mother, Emma Buck, were feeble-minded by the Stanford-Binet test of IQ then in its own infancy. Carrie scored a mental age of nine years, Emma of seven years and eleven months. (These figures ranked them technically as "imbeciles" by definitions of the day, hence Holmes's later choice of words—though his infamous line is often misquoted as "three generations of idiots." Imbeciles displayed a mental age of six to nine years; idiots performed worse, morons better, to round out the old nomenclature of mental deficiency.) Second, that most feeble-mindedness resides ineluctably in the genes, and that Carrie Buck surely belonged with this majority. Laughlin reported:

> *Generally, feeble-mindedness is caused by the inheritance of degenerate qualities; but sometimes it might be caused by environmental factors which are not hereditary. In the case given, the evidence points strongly toward the feeble-mindedness and moral delinquency of Carrie Buck being due, primarily, to inheritance and not to environment.*

Carrie Buck's daughter was then, and has always been, the 17
pivotal figure of this painful case. I noted in beginning this

essay that we tend (often at our peril) to regard two as potential accident and three as an established pattern. The supposed imbecility of Emma and Carrie might have been an unfortunate coincidence, but the diagnosis of similar deficiency for Vivian Buck (made by a social worker, as we shall see, when Vivian was but six months old) tipped the balance in Laughlin's favor and led Holmes to declare the Buck lineage inherently corrupt by deficient heredity. Vivian sealed the pattern—*three* generations of imbeciles are enough. Besides, had Carrie not given illegitimate birth to Vivian, the issue (in both senses) would never have emerged.

Oliver Wendell Holmes viewed his work with pride. The man so renowned for his principle of judicial restraint, who had proclaimed that freedom must not be curtailed without "clear and present danger"—without the equivalent of falsely yelling "fire" in a crowded theater—wrote of his judgment in *Buck v. Bell:* "I felt that I was getting near the first principle of real reform." 18

And so *Buck v. Bell* remained for fifty years, a footnote to a moment of American history perhaps best forgotten. Then, in 1980, it reemerged to prick our collective conscience, when Dr. K. Ray Nelson, then director of the Lynchburg Hospital where Carrie Buck had been sterilized, researched the records of his institution and discovered that more than 4,000 sterilizations had been performed, the last as late as 1972. He also found Carrie Buck, alive and well near Charlottesville, and her sister Doris, covertly sterilized under the same law (she was told that her operation was for appendicitis), and now, with fierce dignity, dejected and bitter because she had wanted a child more than anything else in her life and had finally, in her old age, learned why she had never conceived. 19

As scholars and reporters visited Carrie Buck and her sister, what a few experts had known all along became abundantly clear to everyone. Carrie Buck was a woman of obviously normal intelligence. For example, Paul A. Lombardo of the School of Law at the University of Virginia, and a leading scholar of *Buck v. Bell,* wrote in a letter to me: 20

> *As for Carrie, when I met her she was reading newspapers daily and joining a more literate friend to assist at regular bouts with the crossword puzzles. She was not a sophisticated woman, and lacked social graces, but mental health professionals who examined her in later life confirmed my impressions that she was neither mentally ill nor retarded.*

On what evidence, then, was Carrie Buck consigned to the State Colony for Epileptics and Feeble-Minded on January 23, 1924? I have seen the text of her commitment hearing; it is, to say the least, cursory and contradictory. Beyond the bald and undocumented say-so of her foster parents, and her own brief appearance before a commission of two doctors and a justice of the peace, no evidence was presented. Even the crude and early Stanford-Binet test, so fatally flawed as a measure of innate worth (see my book *The Mismeasure of Man,* although the evidence of Carrie's own case suffices) but at least clothed with the aura of quantitative respectability, had not yet been applied. 21

When we understand why Carrie Buck was committed in January 1924, we can finally comprehend the hidden meaning of her case and its message for us today. The silent key, again as from the first, is her daughter Vivian, born on March 28, 1924, and then but an evident bump on her belly. Carrie Buck was one of several illegitimate children borne by her mother, Emma. She grew up with foster parents, J. T. and Alice Dobbs, and continued to live with them as an adult, helping out with chores around the house. She was raped by a relative of her foster parents, then blamed for the resulting pregnancy. Almost surely, she was (as they used to say) committed to hide her shame (and her rapist's identity), not because enlightened science had just discovered her true mental status. In short, she was sent away to have her baby. Her case never was about mental deficiency; Carrie Buck was persecuted for supposed sexual immorality and social deviance. The annals of her trial and hearing reek with the contempt of the well-off and well-bred for poor people of "loose 22 morals." Who really cared whether Vivian was a baby of normal intelligence; she was the illegitimate child of an illegitimate woman. Two generations of bastards are enough. Harry Laughlin began his "family history" of the Bucks by writing: "These people belong to the shiftless, ignorant and worthless class of anti-social whites of the South."

We know little of Emma Buck and her life, but we have no more reason to suspect her than her daughter Carrie of true mental deficiency. Their supposed deviance was social and sexual; the charge of imbecility was a cover-up, Mr. Justice Holmes notwithstanding. 23

We come then to the crux of the case, Carrie's daughter, Vivian. What evidence was ever adduced for her mental deficiency? This and only this: At the original trial in late 1924, when Vivian Buck was seven months old, a Miss Wilhelm, social worker for the Red Cross, appeared before the court. She began by stating honestly the true reason for Carrie Buck's commitment: 24

> *Mr. Dobbs, who had charge of the girl, had taken her when a small child, had reported to Miss Duke [the temporary secretary of Public Welfare for Albemarle County] that the girl was pregnant and that he wanted to have her committed somewhere—to have her sent to some institution.*

Miss Wilhelm then rendered her judgment of Vivian Buck by comparing her with the normal granddaughter of Mrs. Dobbs, born just three days earlier: 25

> *It is difficult to judge probabilities of a child as young as that, but it seems to me not quite a normal baby. In its appearance—I should say that perhaps my knowledge of the mother may prejudice me in that regard, but I saw the child at the same time as Mrs. Dobbs' daughter's baby, which is only three days older than this one, and there is a very decided difference in the development of the babies. That was about two weeks ago. There is a look about it that is not quite normal, but just what it is, I can't tell.*

This short testimony, and nothing else, formed all the evidence for the crucial third generation of imbeciles. Cross-examination revealed that neither Vivian nor the Dobbs grandchild could walk or talk, and that "Mrs. Dobbs' daughter's baby is a very responsive baby. When you play with it or try to attract its attention—it is a baby that you can play with. The other baby is not. It seems very apathetic and not responsive." Miss Wilhelm then urged Carrie Buck's sterilization: "I think," she said, "it would at least prevent the propagation of her kind." Several years later, Miss Wilhelm denied that she had ever examined Vivian or deemed the child feeble-minded. 26

Unfortunately, Vivian died at age eight of "enteric colitis" (as recorded on her death certificate), an ambiguous diagnosis that could mean many things but may well indicate that she fell victim to one of the preventable childhood diseases of poverty (a grim reminder of the real subject in *Buck v. Bell*). She is therefore mute as a witness in our reassessment of her famous case. 27

When *Buck v. Bell* resurfaced in 1980, it immediately struck me that Vivian's case was crucial and that evidence for the mental status of a child who died at age eight might best be found in report cards. I have therefore been trying to track down Vivian Buck's school records for the past four years and have finally succeeded. (They were supplied to me by Dr. Paul A. Lombardo, who also sent other documents, including Miss Wilhelm's testimony, and spent several hours answering my questions by mail and Lord knows how much time playing successful detective in re Vivian's school records. I have never met Dr. Lombardo; he did all this work for kindness, collegiality, and love of the game of knowledge, not for expected reward or even requested acknowledgment. In a profession—academics—so often marred by pettiness and silly squabbling over meaningless priorities, this generosity must be recorded and celebrated as a sign of how things can and should be.) 28

Vivian Buck was adopted by the Dobbs family, who had raised (but later sent away) her mother, Carrie. As Vivian 29

Alice Elaine Dobbs, she attended the Venable Public Elementary School of Charlottesville for four terms, from September 1930 until May 1932, a month before her death. She was a perfectly normal, quite average student, neither particularly outstanding nor much troubled. In those days before grade inflation, when C meant "good, 81–87" (as defined on her report card) rather than barely scraping by, Vivian Dobbs received A's and B's for deportment and C's for all academic subjects but mathematics (which was always difficult for her, and where she scored D) during her first term in Grade 1A, from September 1930 to January 1931. She improved during her second term in 1B, meriting an A in deportment, C in mathematics, and B in all other academic subjects; she was placed on the honor roll in April 1931. Promoted to 2A, she had trouble during the fall term of 1931, failing mathematics and spelling but receiving A in deportment, B in reading, and C in writing and English. She was "retained to 2A" for the next term—or "left back" as we used to say, and scarcely a sign of imbecility as I remember all my buddies who suffered a similar fate. In any case, she again did well in her final term, with B in deportment, reading, and spelling, and C in writing, English, and mathematics during her last month in school. This daughter of "lewd and immoral" women excelled in deportment and performed adequately, although not brilliantly, in her academic subjects.

In short, we can only agree with the conclusion that Dr. 30
Lombardo has reached in his research on *Buck v. Bell*—there were no imbeciles, not a one, among the three generations of Bucks. I don't know that such correction of cruel but forgotten errors of history counts for much, but I find it both symbolic and satisfying to learn that forced eugenic sterilization, a procedure of such dubious morality, earned its official justification (and won its most quoted line of rhetoric) on a patent falsehood.

Carrie Buck died last year. By a quirk of fate, and not by 31
memory or design, she was buried just a few steps from her only daughter's grave. In the umpteenth and ultimate verse

of a favorite old ballad, a rose and a brier—the sweet and the bitter—emerge from the tombs of Barbara Allen and her lover, twining about each other in the union of death. May Carrie and Vivian, victims in different ways and in the flower of youth, rest together in peace.

For Study and Discussion

QUESTIONS FOR RESPONSE

1. What do you know about the Nazis' attempt to create a "master race" in Germany in the 1930s? If you have information on that program, how does it affect the way you respond to this essay?
2. Gould is writing almost seventy years after the case of *Bell v. Buck*. How do you think the public, including your social group, would respond to having the same issues raised today? How much have times changed since the time of the case?

QUESTIONS ABOUT PURPOSE

1. What connections does Gould draw between the eugenics movement in the United States and the goals of the Nazi regime in Germany in the 1930s?
2. What attitudes of the society in which Carrie Buck was reared does Gould want to analyze? Why? To what extent are those attitudes outmoded today?

QUESTIONS ABOUT AUDIENCE

1. What knowledge about the racial policies of the Nazi regime in Germany in the 1930s does Gould depend on his readers having? How well can one appreciate the essay without that knowledge?
2. How does Gould connect his analysis of Carrie Buck to his readers' knowledge of contemporary social problems?

QUESTIONS ABOUT STRATEGIES

1. What evidence does Gould bring in to support his belief that Carrie Buck's treatment was motivated by prejudice and shame, not concern over her mental abilities?
2. In what particular sections do you notice Gould's own feelings about the Buck case surfacing throughout the essay? How does his showing those feelings influence your opinion of him as a scientist?

QUESTIONS FOR DISCUSSION

1. Now, almost seventy years after the event, in what ways can or should the case of *Bell v. Buck,* involving "three generations of imbeciles," as Chief Justice Holmes put it, still compel our interest and be worth discussing? What issues about it are timeless?
2. Poll your class to find out whether the men and women in it have different responses to this essay. In what ways and to what extent are they different, and what do you think might cause such differences?

GAIL GODWIN

Gail Godwin was born in Birmingham, Alabama, in 1937 and was educated at the University of North Carolina and the University of Iowa. She has taught English at several universities and has also worked as a travel consultant with the U.S. embassy in London and as a reporter for the *Miami Herald.* A versatile writer, Godwin has published essays and short stories in such magazines as *Harper's, Esquire, Cosmopolitan,* and *Ms.,* and she has written librettos for four musical compositions by Robert Starer. She has published eight novels, the most recent of which are *Violet Clay* (1978), *A Mother and Two Daughters* (1981), *The Finishing School* (1985), *A Southern Family* (1987), and *Father Melancholy's Daughter* (1991). In all of her novels, Godwin captures the consciousness of contemporary women. In "Dream Children," the title story from her 1976 collection of short stories, Godwin recounts a young woman's attempts to find happiness after she has been victimized by a terrible freakish accident.

Dream Children

1 *The worst thing. Such a terrible thing to happen to a young woman. It's a wonder she didn't go mad.*

2 As she went about her errands, a cheerful, neat young woman, a wife, wearing pants with permanent creases and safari jackets and high-necked sweaters that folded chastely just below the line of the small gold hoops she wore in her ears, she imagined people saying this, or thinking it to themselves. But nobody knew. Nobody knew anything, other than that she and her husband had moved here a year ago, as so

many couples were moving farther away from the city, the husband commuting, or staying in town during the week—as hers did. There was nobody here, in this quaint, unspoiled village, nestled in the foothills of the mountains, who could have looked at her and guessed that anything out of the ordinary, predictable, auspicious spectrum of things that happen to bright, attractive young women had happened to her. She always returned her books to the local library on time; she bought liquor at the local liquor store only on Friday, before she went to meet her husband's bus from the city. He was something in television, a producer? So many ambitious young couples moving to this Dutch farming village, founded in 1690, to restore ruined fieldstone houses and plant herb gardens and keep their own horses and discover the relief of finding oneself insignificant in Nature for the first time!

A terrible thing. So freakish. If you read it in a story or saw it on TV, you'd say no, this sort of thing could never happen in an American hospital. 3

DePuy, who owned the old Patroon farm adjacent to her land, frequently glimpsed her racing her horse in the early morning, when the mists still lay on the fields, sometimes just before the sun came up and there was a frost on everything. "One woodchuck hole and she and that stallion will both have to be put out of their misery," he told his wife. "She's too reckless. I'll bet you her old man doesn't know she goes streaking to hell across the fields like that." Mrs. DePuy nodded, silent, and went about her business. She, too, watched that other woman ride, a woman not much younger than herself, but with an aura of romance—of tragedy, perhaps. The way she looked: like those heroines in English novels who ride off their bad tempers and unrequited love affairs, clenching their thighs against the flanks of spirited horses with murderous red eyes. Mrs. DePuy, who had ridden since the age of three, recognized something beyond recklessness in that elegant young woman, in her crisp checked shirts and her dove-gray jodhpurs. *She has nothing* 4 *to fear anymore,* thought the farmer's wife, with sure feminine instinct; she both envied and pitied her. "What she needs is children," remarked DePuy.

"A Dry Sack, a Remy Martin, and . . . let's see, a half- 5
gallon of the Chablis, and I think I'd better take a Scotch . . . and the Mouton-Cadet . . . and maybe a dry vermouth." Mrs. Frye, another farmer's wife, who runs the liquor store, asks if her husband is bringing company for the weekend. "He sure is; we couldn't drink all that by ourselves," and the young woman laughs, her lovely teeth exposed, her small gold earrings quivering in the light. "You know, I saw his name—on the television the other night," says Mrs. Frye. "It was at the beginning of that new comedy show, the one with the woman who used to be on another show with her husband and little girl, only they divorced, you know the one?" "Of course I do. It's one of my husband's shows. I'll tell him you watched it." Mrs. Frye puts the bottles in an empty box, carefully inserting wedges of cardboard between them. Through the window of her store she sees her customer's pert bottle-green car, some sort of little foreign car with the engine running, filled with groceries and weekend parcels, and that big silver-blue dog sitting up in the front seat just like a human being. "I think that kind of thing is so sad," says Mrs. Frye; "families breaking up, poor little children having to divide their loyalties." "I couldn't agree more," replies the young woman, nodding gravely. Such a personable, polite girl! "Are you sure you can carry that, dear? I can get Earl from the back. . . ." But the girl has it hoisted on her shoulder in a flash, is airily maneuvering between unopened cartons stacked in the aisle, in her pretty boots. Her perfume lingers in Mrs. Frye's store for a half-hour after she has driven away.

After dinner, her husband and his friends drank brandy. 6
She lay in front of the fire, stroking the dog, and listening to Victoria Darrow, the news commentator, in person. A few minutes ago, they had all watched Victoria on TV.

"That's right; thirty-nine!" Victoria now whispered to her. "What? That's kind of you. I'm photogenic, thank God, or I'd have been put out to pasture long before. . . . I look five, maybe seven years younger on the screen . . . but the point I'm getting at is, I went to this doctor and he said, 'If you want to do this thing, you'd better go home today and get started.' He told me—did you know this? Did you know that a woman is born with all the eggs she'll ever have, and when she gets to my age, the ones that are left have been rattling around so long they're a little shopworn; then every time you fly you get an extra dose of radioactivity, so those poor eggs. He told me when a woman over forty comes into his office pregnant, his heart sinks; that's why he quit practicing obstetrics, he said; he could still remember the screams of a woman whose baby he delivered . . . she was having natural childbirth and she kept saying, 'Why won't you let me see it, I insist on seeing it,' and so he had to, and he says he can still hear her screaming."

"Oh, what was—what was wrong with it?" 7

But she never got the answer. Her husband, white around the lips, was standing over Victoria ominously, offering the Remy Martin bottle. "Vicky, let me pour you some more," he said. And to his wife, "I think Blue Boy needs to go out." 8

"Yes, yes, of course. Please excuse me, Victoria. I'll just be . . ." 9

Her husband followed her to the kitchen, his hand on the back of her neck. "Are you okay? That stupid yammering bitch. She and her twenty-six-year-old lover! I wish I'd never brought them, but she's been hinting around the studio for weeks." 10

"But I like them, I like having them. I'm fine. Please go back. I'll take the dog out and come back. Please . . ." 11

"All right. If you're sure you're okay." He backed away, hands dangling at his sides. A handsome man, wearing a pink shirt with Guatemalan embroidery. Thick black hair and a face rather boyish, but cunning. Last weekend she had sat beside him, alone in this house, just the two of them, and watched him on television: a documentary, in several parts, 12 in which TV "examines itself." There was his double, sitting in an armchair in his executive office, coolly replying to the questions of Victoria Darrow. *"Do you personally watch all the programs you produce, Mr. McNair?"* She watched the man on the screen, how he moved his lips when he spoke, but kept the rest of his face, his body perfectly still. Funny, she had never noticed this before. He managed to say that he did and did not watch all the programs he produced.

Now, in the kitchen, she looked at him backing away, a little like a renegade in one of his own shows—a desperate man, perhaps, who had just killed somebody and is backing away, hands dangling loosely at his sides, Mr. McNair, her husband. That man on the screen. Once a lover above her in bed. That friend who held her hand in the hospital. One hand in hers, the other holding the stopwatch. For a brief instant, all the images coalesce and she feels something again. But once outside, under the galaxies of autumn-sharp stars, the intelligent dog at her heels like some smart gray ghost, she is glad to be free of all that. She walks quickly over the damp grass to the barn, to look in on her horse. She understands something: her husband, Victoria Darrow lead double lives that seem perfectly normal to them. But if she told her husband that she, too, is in two lives, he would become alarmed; he would sell this house and make her move back to the city where he could keep an eye on her welfare. 13

She is discovering people like herself, down through the centuries, all over the world. She scours books with titles like *The Timeless Moment, The Sleeping Prophet, Between Two Worlds, Silent Union: A Record of Unwilled Communication;* collecting evidence, weaving a sort of underworld net of colleagues around her. 14

A rainy fall day. Too wet to ride. The silver dog asleep beside her in her special alcove, a padded window seat filled with pillows and books. She is looking down on the fields of dried lithrium, and the fir trees beyond, and the mountains gauzy with fog and rain, thinking, in a kind of terror and 15 ecstasy, about all these connections. A book lies face down on her lap. She has just read the following:

> *Theodore Dreiser and his friend John Cowper Powys had been dining at Dreiser's place on West Fifty Seventh Street. As Powys made ready to leave and catch his train to the little town up the Hudson, where he was then living, he told Dreiser, "I'll appear before you here, later in the evening."*
>
> *Dreiser laughed. "Are you going to turn yourself into a ghost, or have you a spare key?" he asked. Powys said he would return "in some form," he didn't know exactly what kind.*
>
> *After his friend left, Dreiser sat up and read for two hours. Then he looked up and saw Powys standing in the doorway to the living room. It was Powys' features, his tall stature, even the loose tweed garments which he wore. Dreiser rose at once and strode toward the figure, saying, "Well, John, you kept your word. Come on in and tell me how you did it." But the figure vanished when Dreiser came within three feet of it.*
>
> *Dreiser then went to the telephone and called Powys' house in the country. Powys answered. Dreiser told him what had happened and Powys said, "I told you I'd be there and you oughtn't to be surprised." But he refused to discuss how he had done it, if, indeed, he knew how.*

"But don't you get frightened, up here all by yourself, alone with all these creaky sounds?" asked Victoria, the next morning. 16

"No, I guess I'm used to them," she replied, breaking eggs into a bowl. "I know what each one means. The wood expanding and contracting . . . the wind getting caught between the shutter and the latch . . . Sometimes small animals get lost in the stone walls and scratch around till they find their way . . . or die." 17

"Ugh. But don't you imagine things? I would, in a house like this. How old? That's almost three hundred years of lived lives, people suffering and shouting and making love 18 and giving birth, under this roof. . . . You'd think there'd be a few ghosts around."

"I don't know," said her hostess blandly. "I haven't heard 19
any. But of course, I have Blue Boy, so I don't get scared." She whisked the eggs, unable to face Victoria. She and her husband had lain awake last night, embarrassed at the sounds coming from the next room. No ghostly moans, those. "Why can't that bitch control herself, or at least lower her voice," he said angrily. He stroked his wife's arm, both of them pretending not to remember. She had bled for an entire year afterward, until the doctor said they would have to remove everything. "I'm empty," she had said when her husband had tried again, after she was healed. "I'm sorry, I just don't feel anything." Now they lay tenderly together on these weekends, like childhood friends, like effigies on a lovers' tomb, their mutual sorrow like a sword between them. She assumed he had another life, or lives, in town. As she had here. Nobody is just one person, she had learned.

"I'm sure I would imagine things," said Victoria. "I would 20
see things and hear things inside my head much worse than an ordinary murderer or rapist."

The wind caught in the shutter latch . . . a small animal 21
dislodging pieces of fieldstone in its terror, sending them tumbling down the inner walls, from attic to cellar . . . a sound like a child rattling a jar full of marbles, or small stones . . .

"I have so little imagination," she said humbly, warming 22
the butter in the omelet pan. She could feel Victoria Darrow's professional curiosity waning from her dull country life, focusing elsewhere.

Cunning! 23

As a child of nine, she had gone through a phase of 24
walking in her sleep. One summer night, they found her bed empty, and after an hour's hysterical search they had found her in her nightgown, curled up on the flagstones beside the fishpond. She woke, baffled, in her father's tense clutch, the stars all over the sky, her mother repeating over and over again to the night at large, "Oh, my God, she could have

drowned!" They took her to a child psychiatrist, a pretty Austrian woman who spoke to her with the same vocabulary she used on grownups, putting the child instantly at ease. "It is not at all uncommon what you did. I have known so many children who take little night journeys from their beds, and then they awaken and don't know what all the fuss is about! Usually these journeys are quite harmless, because children are surrounded by a magical reality that keeps them safe. Yes, the race of children possesses magically sagacious powers! But the grownups, they tend to forget how it once was for them. They worry, they are afraid of so many things. You do not want your mother and father, who love you so anxiously, to live in fear of you going to live with the fishes." She had giggled at the thought. The woman's steady gray-green eyes were trained on her carefully, suspending her in a kind of bubble. Then she had rejoined her parents, a dutiful "child" again, holding a hand up to each of them. The night journeys had stopped.

A thunderstorm one night last spring. Blue Boy whining in his insulated house below the garage. She had lain there, strangely elated by the nearness of the thunderclaps that tore at the sky, followed by instantaneous flashes of jagged light. Wondering shouldn't she go down and let the dog in; he hated storms. Then dozing off again . . . 25

She woke. The storm had stopped. The dark air was quiet. Something had changed, some small thing—what? She had to think hard before she found it: the hall light, which she kept burning during the week-nights when she was there alone, had gone out. She reached over and switched the button on her bedside lamp. Nothing. A tree must have fallen and hit a wire, causing the power to go off. This often happened here. No problem. The dog had stopped crying. She felt herself sinking into a delicious, deep reverie, the kind that sometimes came just before morning, as if her being broke slowly into tiny pieces and spread itself over the world. It was a feeling she had not known until she had lived by herself in this house: this weightless though conscious state 26 in which she lay, as if in a warm bath, and yet was able to send her thoughts anywhere, as if her mind contained the entire world.

And as she floated in this silent world, transparent and buoyed upon the dream layers of the mind, she heard a small rattling sound, like pebbles being shaken in a jar. The sound came distinctly from the guest room, a room so chosen by her husband and herself because it was the farthest room from their bedroom on this floor. It lay above what had been the old side of the house, built seventy-five years before the new side, which was completed in 1753. There was a bed in it, and a chair, and some plants in the window. Sometimes on weekends when she could not sleep, she went and read there, or meditated, to keep from waking her husband. It was the room where Victoria Darrow and her young lover would not sleep the following fall, because she would say quietly to her husband, "No . . . not that room. I—I've made up the bed in the other room." "What?" he would want to know. "The one next to ours? Right under our noses?" 27

She did not lie long listening to this sound before she understood it was one she had never heard in the house before. It had a peculiar regularity to its rhythm; there was nothing accidental about it, nothing influenced by the wind, or the nerves of some lost animal. *K-chunk, k-chunk, k-chunk,* it went. At intervals of exactly a half-minute apart. She still remembered how to time such things, such intervals. She was as good as any stopwatch when it came to timing certain intervals. 28

K-chunk, k-chunk, k-chunk. That determined regularity. Something willed, something poignantly repeated, as though the repetition was a means of consoling someone in the dark. Her skin began to prickle. Often, lying in such states of weightless reverie, she had practiced the trick of sending herself abroad, into rooms of the house, out into the night to check on Blue Boy, over to the barn to look in on her horse, who slept standing up. Once she had heard a rather frightening noise, as if someone in the basement had turned on a faucet, and so she forced herself to "go down," floating 29 down two sets of stairs into the darkness, only to discover what she had known all the time: the hookup system between the hot-water tank and the pump, which sounded like someone turning on the water.

Now she went through the palpable, prickly darkness, without lights, down the chilly hall in her sleeveless gown, into the guest room. Although there was no light, not even a moon shining through the window, she could make out the shape of the bed and then the chair, the spider plants on the window, and a small dark shape in one corner, on the floor, which she and her husband had painted a light yellow. 30

K-chunk, k-chunk, k-chunk. The shapes moved with the noise. 31

Now she knew what they meant, that "someone's hair stood on end." It was true. As she forced herself across the borders of a place she had never been, she felt, distinctly, every single hair on her head raise itself a millimeter or so from her scalp. 32

She knelt down and discovered him. He was kneeling, a little cold and scared, shaking a small jar filled with some kind of pebbles. (She later found out, in a subsequent visit, that they were small colored shells, of a triangular shape, called coquinas: she found them in a picture in a child's nature book at the library.) He was wearing pajamas a little too big for him, obviously hand-me-downs, and he was exactly two years older than the only time she had ever held him in her arms. 33

The two of them knelt in the corner of the room, taking each other in. His large eyes were the same as before: dark and unblinking. He held the small jar close to him, watching her. He was not afraid, but she knew better than to move too close. 34

She knelt, the tears streaming down her cheeks, but she made no sound, her eyes fastened on that small form. And then the hall light came on silently, as well as the lamp beside her bed, and with wet cheeks and pounding heart she could not be sure whether or not she had actually been out of the room. 35

But what did it matter, on the level where they had met? He traveled so much farther than she to reach that room. *("Yes, the race of children possesses magically sagacious powers!")* 36

She and her husband sat together on the flowered chintz sofa, watching the last of the series in which TV purportedly examined itself. She said, "Did you ever think that the whole thing is really a miracle? I mean, here we sit, eighty miles away from your studios, and we turn on a little machine and there is Victoria, speaking to us as clearly as she did last weekend when she was in this very room. Why, it's magic, it's time travel and space travel right in front of our eyes, but because it's been 'discovered,' because the world understands that it's only little dots that transmit Victoria electrically to us, it's *all right*. We can bear it. Don't you sometimes wonder about all the miracles that haven't been officially approved yet? I mean, who knows, maybe in a hundred years everybody will take it for granted that they can send an image of themselves around in space by some perfectly natural means available to us now. I mean, when you think about it, what *is* space? What *is* time? Where do the so-called boundaries of each of us begin and end? Can anyone explain it?" 37

He was drinking Scotch and thinking how they had decided not to renew Victoria Darrow's contract. Somewhere on the edges of his mind hovered an anxious, growing certainty about his wife. At the local grocery store this morning, when he went to pick up a carton of milk and the paper, he had stopped to chat with DePuy. "I don't mean to interfere, but she doesn't know those fields," said the farmer. "Last year we had to shoot a mare, stumbled into one of those holes. . . . It's madness, the way she rides." 38

And look at her now, her face so pale and shining, speaking of miracles and space travel, almost on the verge of tears. . . . 39

And last night, his first night up from the city, he had wandered through the house, trying to drink himself into this slower weekend pace, and he had come across a pile of 40 her books, stacked in the alcove where, it was obvious, she lay for hours, escaping into science fiction, and the occult.

Now his own face appeared on the screen. "I want to be fair," he was telling Victoria Darrow. "I want to be objective. . . . Violence has always been part of the human makeup. I don't like it any more than you do, but there it is. I think it's more a question of whether we want to face things as they are or escape into fantasies of how we would like them to be." 41

Beside him, his wife uttered a sudden bell-like laugh. 42

("*. . . It's madness, the way she rides.*") 43

He did want to be fair, objective. She had told him again and again that she liked her life here. And he—well, he had to admit he liked his own present setup. 44

"I am a pragmatist," he was telling Victoria Darrow on the screen. He decided to speak to his wife about her riding and leave her alone about the books. She had the right to some escape, if anyone did. But the titles: *Marvelous Manifestations, The Mind Travellers, A Doctor Looks at Spiritualism, The Other Side* . . . Something revolted in him, he couldn't help it; he felt an actual physical revulsion at this kind of thinking. Still it was better than some other escapes. His friend Barnett, the actor, who said at night he went from room to room, after his wife was asleep, collecting empty glasses. ("Once I found one by the Water Pik, a second on the ledge beside the tub, a third on the back of the john, and a fourth on the floor beside the john. . . .") 45

He looked sideways at his wife, who was absorbed, it seemed, in watching him on the screen. Her face was tense, alert, animated. She did not look mad. She wore slim gray pants and a loose-knit pullover made of some silvery material, like a knight's chain mail. The lines of her profile were clear and silvery themselves, somehow sexless and pure, like a child's profile. He no longer felt lust when he looked at her, only a sad determination to protect her. He had a mistress in town, whom he loved, but he had explained, right from the beginning, that he considered himself married for the rest of his life. He told this woman the whole story. "And I 46 am implicated in it. I could never leave her." An intelligent, sensitive woman, she had actually wept and said, "Of course not."

He always wore the same pajamas, a shade too big, but always clean. Obviously washed again and again in a machine that went through its cycles frequently. She imagined his "other mother," a harassed woman with several children, short on money, on time, on dreams—all the things she herself had too much of. The family lived, she believed, somewhere in Florida, probably on the west coast. She had worked that out from the little coquina shells: their bright colors, even in moonlight shining through a small window with spider plants in it. His face and arms had been suntanned early in the spring and late into the autumn. They never spoke or touched. She was not sure how much of this he understood. She tried and failed to remember where she herself had gone, in those little night journeys to the fishpond. Perhaps he never remembered afterward, when he woke up, clutching his jar, in a roomful of brothers and sisters. Or with a worried mother or father come to collect him, asleep by the sea. Once she had a very clear dream of the whole family, living in a trailer, with palm trees. But that was a dream; she recognized its difference in quality from those truly magic times when, through his own childish powers, he somehow found a will strong enough, or innocent enough, to project himself upon her still-floating consciousness, as clearly and as believably as her own husband's image on the screen. 47

There had been six of those times in six months. She dared to look forward to more. So unafraid he was. The last time was the day after Victoria Darrow and her young lover and her own good husband had returned to the city. She had gone farther with the child than ever before. On a starry-clear, cold September Monday, she had coaxed him down the stairs and out of the house with her. He held to the banisters, a child unused to stairs, and yet she knew there was no danger; he floated in his own dream with her. She 48 took him to see Blue Boy. Who disappointed her by whining and backing away in fear. And then to the barn to see the horse. Who perked up his ears and looked interested. There was no touching, of course, no touching or speaking. Later she wondered if horses, then, were more magical than dogs. If dogs were more "realistic." She was glad the family was poor, the mother harassed. They could not afford any expensive child psychiatrist who would hypnotize him out of his night journeys.

He loved her. She knew that. Even if he never remembered her in his other life. 49

"At last I was beginning to understand what Teilhard de Chardin meant when he said that man's true home is the mind. I understood that when the mystics tell us that the mind is a place, they *don't mean it as a metaphor.* I found these new powers developed with practice. I had to detach myself from my ordinary physical personality. The intelligent part of me had to remain wide awake, and move down into this world of thoughts, dreams and memories. After several such journeyings I understood something else: dream and reality aren't competitors, but reciprocal sources of consciousness." This she read in a "respectable book," by a "respectable man," a scientist, alive and living in England, only a few years older than herself. She looked down at the dog, sleeping on the rug. His lean silvery body actually ran as he slept! Suddenly his muzzle lifted, the savage teeth snapped. Where was he "really" now? Did the dream rabbit in his jaws know it was a dream? There was much to think about, between her trips to the nursery. 50

Would the boy grow, would she see his body slowly emerging from its child's shape, the arms and legs lengthening, the face thinning out into a man's—like a certain advertisement for bread she had seen on TV where a child grows up, in less than a half-minute of sponsor time, right before the viewer's eyes? Would he grow into a man, grow a beard . . . outgrow the nursery region of his mind where they had been able to meet? 51

And yet, some daylight part of his mind must have re- 52

tained an image of her from that single daylight time they had looked into each other's eyes.

The worst thing, such an awful thing to happen to a young woman . . . She was having this natural childbirth, you see, her husband in the delivery room with her, and the pains were coming a half-minute apart, and the doctor had just said, "This is going to be a breeze, Mrs. McNair," and they never knew exactly what went wrong, but all of a sudden the pains stopped and they had to go in after the baby without even time to give her a saddle block or any sort of anesthetic. . . . They must have practically had to tear it out of her . . . the husband fainted. The baby was born dead, and they gave her a heavy sedative to put her out all night. 53

When she woke the next morning, before she had time to remember what had happened, a nurse suddenly entered the room and laid a baby in her arms. "Here's your little boy," she said cheerfully, and the woman thought, with a profound, religious relief, *So that other nightmare was a dream,* and she had the child at her breast feeding him before the nurse realized her mistake and rushed back into the room, but they had to knock the poor woman out with more sedatives before she would let the child go. She was screaming and so was the little baby and they clung to each other till she passed out. 54

They would have let the nurse go, only it wasn't entirely her fault. The hospital was having a strike at the time; some of the nurses were outside picketing and this nurse had been working straight through for forty-eight hours, and when she was questioned afterward she said she had just mixed up the rooms, and yet, she said, when she had seen the woman and the baby clinging to each other like that, she had undergone a sort of revelation in her almost hallucinatory exhaustion: the nurse said she saw that all children and mothers were interchangeable, that nobody could own anybody or anything, any more than you could own an idea that happened to be passing through the air and caught on your mind, or any more than you owned the rosebush that grew 55 in your back yard. There were only mothers and children, she realized; though, afterward, the realization faded.

It was the kind of freakish thing that happens once in a million times, and it's a wonder the poor woman kept her sanity. 56

In the intervals, longer than those measured by any stop-watch, she waited for him. In what the world accepted as "time," she shopped for groceries, for clothes; she read; she waved from her bottle-green car to Mrs. Frye, trimming the hedge in front of the liquor store, to Mrs. DePuy, hanging out her children's pajamas in the back yard of the old Patroon farm. She rode her horse through the fields of the waning season, letting him have his head; she rode like the wind, a happy, happy woman. She rode faster than fear because she was a woman in a dream, a woman anxiously awaiting her child's sleep. The stallion's hoofs pounded the earth. Oiling his tractor, DePuy resented the foolish woman and almost wished for a woodchuck hole to break that arrogant ride. Wished deep in a violent level of himself he never knew he had. For he was a kind, distracted father and husband, a practical, hard-working man who would never descend deeply into himself. Her body, skimming through time, felt weightless to the horse. 57

Was she a woman riding a horse and dreaming she was a mother who anxiously awaited her child's sleep; or was she a mother dreaming of herself as a free spirit who could ride her horse like the wind because she had nothing to fear? 58

I am a happy woman, that's all I know. Who can explain such things? 59

COMMENT ON "DREAM CHILDREN"

In "Dream Children," Gail Godwin shows her readers a young woman who leads two lives: one in an affluent suburb, the other in a fantasy world where she meets the spirit of a young child she once thought was hers. Gradually, Godwin reveals to us the tragedy that has driven the young wife to this fantasy life and to the edge of a nervous breakdown. Through the narrative Godwin skillfully merges causes and effects. The woman had been a sleepwalker as a child, one who thought she had magical powers; now, under stress, she has reverted to her childhood again. She has lost her sexuality and lives with her husband as a friend, not a lover. She has secrets as she did as a child. The greatest of those secrets is that she has a secret, imaginary companion, the lost child who comes to her occasionally. Like a child, she feels that she and he are magical creatures, beyond ordinary boundaries of reality. By the end of the story, we understand the cruel shock that has pushed this young woman to these extremes and realize that the effects of that shock, though apparently bizarre, represent her way of adapting to a tragedy that would otherwise have killed her.

Cause and Effect as a Writing Strategy

1. In his essay "Black Men and Public Space," Brent Staples shows how serious misunderstandings can come about because we so often stereotype people by categorizing them in a certain group, then treating them as if they have the characteristics we ascribe to that group. In a paper written for possible publication in the Opinion column of your daily newspaper or in the newsletter of an organization you belong to, write about your own experiences in being stereotyped as a member of a group and treated unpleasantly—or at least inappropriately—as a result. To be worth writing about, your experiences need not be as unsettling or as dangerous as Staples's were. Some possibilities could include being categorized because of your age, your accent or dialect, your style of dress, your sex, or your hometown.
2. In her essay "Why Young Women Are More Conservative," Gloria Steinem claims that most young women on college campuses today are worried about how they are going to combine a career, marriage, and children. If you are a woman who has juggled or is currently trying to juggle these elements in your life, write an essay that describes your problems and, perhaps, some of the strategies you have worked out for coping with them. Discuss, too, how you feel these experiences have changed you. If you are a man whose life has been affected by the same problems, write a similar essay. Think of your audience as the readers of a popular family magazine you see at the checkout counter of grocery stores.
3. You may strongly disagree with one of the cause-and-effect essays in this section and want to refute what the author is saying or at least argue against a part of his or her thesis. If so, develop a paper by supposing that the writer has appeared as a speaker in your college's Ideas and Issues lecture series and given his or her essay as a talk. Write your counterargument as a guest editorial for your campus newspaper, assuming that your readers will be other students and the college faculty.

Here are some of the strategies you might use for your argument:

a. Challenge the cause-and-effect relationships that the author claims.
b. Citing information you have from different sources or from your experience, argue that the writer's conclusions are faulty.
c. Challenge the accuracy of some of the author's evidence or show weak links in his or her reasoning.
d. Show that the writer has failed to take certain things into account about his or her readers or their situation and has thus weakened the thesis of the essay.
e. Demonstrate that the writer has let his or her biases distort the argument.
f. Show that the writer claims too much, more than the evidence warrants.

Keep in mind how skillfully the writers use facts and examples to support their essays and be sure you do the same.

4. Write an essay for your classmates giving your reasons for choosing the profession you expect to go into. In what ways do you think you will find it rewarding? What kind of training and education will be necessary, and what sacrifices, both financial and psychological, will be involved? What conflicts, if any, do you anticipate between your personal and professional lives? How do you hope to resolve them?
5. If, like Alice Trillin, you have had personal experience with a serious or painful illness or have been close to someone who has suffered through such an illness, analyze and describe what that experience was like and how you or that person dealt with it. Some possible illnesses are diabetes, rheumatic fever, cancer, lupus—of course, there are many others. Try to give your readers a sense of how the experience feels by showing its effects or by telling stories and try to help them understand more about the illness. A newsletter distributed by a support group for families of people with the disease would be a good target publication.

6. In "Carrie Buck's Daughter," Stephen Jay Gould argues that Carrie Buck was sterilized not because she, her mother, and her daughter were feeble-minded but because of a combination of injustices inflicted on her both by individuals and by the community. In an essay written to be shared with your classmates and instructor, write a paper analyzing what you perceive those injustices to be and theorizing about what real issues were hidden behind the public excuses. If you know of similar kinds of injustices that have occurred within your own social group or subculture, you might bring them in as modern-day examples of such practices.

PERSUASION AND ARGUMENT

Intuitively, you already know a good deal about **argument.** For one thing, you use it all the time yourself as you go through the day talking or writing and making claims and giving reasons. But you also live surrounded by arguments. They come not only from people you talk to and deal with in everyday personal or business situations, but also from television, radio, newspapers, subway posters, billboards, and signs and brochures of all kinds. Any time someone is trying to persuade you to buy something, contribute money, take action, make a judgment, or change your mind about anything, that person is arguing with you.

People write entire books showing how to argue effectively, how to analyze arguments, and how to refute them.

Colleges offer complete courses in the subject. Obviously, then, the subject is too complex and extensive to do more than skim the surface in this brief discussion. This introduction offers a quick overview of some important argument theory, tips about the kinds of arguments you can make, some concerns and strategies to keep in mind as you write arguments, and a reminder about pitfalls to avoid. If you want to learn more about making better arguments and criticizing them effectively, you can find useful books in your college bookstore or library or take an argumentation course in your speech department.

Some Kinds of Arguments. In college writing, at least, you're not likely to spend time writing arguments about matters of taste—that is, debates in which you're saying little more than "I like it" or "I don't like it." You may enjoy talking with friends about whether you'd rather watch soccer or rugby, but mere preferences don't make workable topics for writing arguments in college. Nor do matters of fact, such as whether Mount Hood or Mount Whitney is the highest peak in the United States. Such disputes can be quickly settled by research and aren't worth the time it takes to write about them.

But in college you will probably write a wide variety of other kinds of arguments, ranging from strong personal-opinion essays to closely reasoned position statements. At one extreme, in the personal-opinion essays, you may make emotional claims and support them with moving and colorful language. At the other extreme, in the position statements, you try to make strictly logical claims and support them with factual, research-based data. Traditionally, your emotional argument would be classified as *persuasive,* and your logical argument would be classified as *rational.* In practice, however, most arguments mix emotion and reason in various degrees. In this section, the argumentative essays are arranged along a continuum; the more emotional, opinion-focused essays appear at the beginning, and the more objective, fact-focused essays are at the end of the section.

It's also important to remember that writing which is primarily rational isn't necessarily better than writing which is mainly emotional. Some occasions call for appeals to pride, loyalty, or compassion; for using vivid metaphors that reach the senses; and for strong language that touches the passions. When someone is speaking at a political rally or graduation ceremony or giving a eulogy, the audience wants not statistics and intellectual reasoning but emotional satisfaction and inspiration. The kind of writing done for such occasions is called *ceremonial discourse,* and often it is successful precisely because it is emotional.

When you write arguments for college instructors or your fellow students, however, you should assume that you face a skeptical audience, one that wants explanations and good reasons. Thus you need to write primarily rational arguments built mostly on evidence and logical appeal, although at times you might bring in emotional elements. You can take your cue from lawyers pleading a courtroom case; you should argue as persuasively as you can, but you also want to make reasonable claims and support them with strong evidence.

PURPOSE

When you hear the term *argument,* you may automatically connect it with controversy and conflict. That's not necessarily the case, however, particularly in academic writing. There—and at other times too—you may have many purposes other than winning a dispute.

Sometimes you may argue *to support a cause.* For instance, you might write an editorial in favor of subsidized child care on your campus. You may also argue *to urge people to action* or *to promote change*—for instance, when you write a campaign brochure or a petition to reduce student fees. Sometimes you may argue *to refute a theory*—perhaps a history paper claiming that antislavery sentiment was not the chief cause of the Civil War. You can also write arguments *to arouse sympathy*—for better laws against child abuse, for example; *to stimulate interest*—for more participation in student government; *to win agreement*—to get condominium residents to agree to abolish regulations against pets; and *to provoke anger*—to arouse outrage against a proposed tax. And, of course, you might incorporate several of these purposes into one piece of writing.

AUDIENCE

When you write arguments, you must think about your readers—who are they, what do they know, what do they believe, what do they expect? Unless you can answer these questions at least partially, you cannot expect to write an effective argument. There simply is no such thing as a good argument in the abstract, separated from its purpose and its audience. Any argument you write is a good one only if it does what you want it to do with the particular readers who are going to read it. So by no later than the second draft of any argument you write, you need to know why you are writing and for whom you are writing.

Often it's not easy to analyze your readers. You have to work partly by instinct. Sometimes you adjust the tone of your writing almost automatically to suit a particular group of readers, and often you know intuitively that certain strategies won't work with certain readers. But you don't have to depend only on hunches. Working through a set of questions as part of your preparation to write will yield important information about your readers and will help you gradually form a sense of audience to guide you as you write and revise.

If you are trying to choose an audience for your paper, ask yourself the following questions:

> Who is likely to be interested in what I am writing about?
>
> What groups could make the changes I'm arguing for?

When you know the answers to these questions, you can direct your writing to readers to whom you have something to say—otherwise, there's little point in writing.

Once you have settled on your audience, ask yourself these questions:

- What do my readers already know about my topic?
  - What experience and knowledge do they have that I can use?
  - Can I use specialized language? Should I?
  - How can I teach them something they want to know?
- How do my readers feel about my topic?
  - What shared values can I appeal to?
  - What prejudices or preconceptions must I pay attention to?
  - What kind of approach will work best with them—casual or formal, objective or personal, factual or anecdotal?
- What questions will my readers want me to answer?

You may find it especially useful to write out the answers to this last question.

When you have worked your way through all of these questions, either as a brainstorming exercise or in a prewriting group discussion, you'll have a stronger sense of who your readers are and how you can appeal to them.

STRATEGIES

When you are writing arguments, you can use a wide range of strategies, but most of them will fall into one of these three categories: *emotional appeal, logical appeal,* or *ethical appeal*.

Emotional appeal You argue by emotional or nonlogical appeal when you appeal to the emotions, the senses, and to personal biases or prejudices. You incorporate such appeals into your writing when you use *connotative language* that elicits feelings or reactions—words like "melancholy," "crimson," "slovenly," or "villainous." Usually you're also using nonlogical appeal when you use *figurative language*—metaphors, allusions, or colorful phrases that make the reader draw comparisons or make associations. Phrases like "environmental cancer" or "industrial Goliath" evoke images and comparisons and play on the emotions.

Creating a tone is also a nonlogical strategy and an important one. The tone you choose can exert a powerful force on your readers, catching their attention, ingratiating you into their favor, conveying an air of authority and confidence. You can establish a friendly, close-to-your-reader tone by using contractions and the pronouns "I," "we," and "you." You can create a relaxed tone by bringing in humor or personal anecdote, or you can give your writing an air of authority and detachment by avoiding personal pronouns and writing as objectively as possible.

All the writers in this section use emotional appeals, but those who rely on them most heavily are Martin Luther King, Jr. and Brigid Brophy. In "I Have a Dream," King appeals to the passions and hopes of his listeners through extensive use of metaphor and fervent language. In "The Rights of Animals," Brophy appeals to her readers' compassion and sense of fairness through her vivid descriptions of animal suffering and her frequent use of words like "sacrifice," "torture," and "exploit." Lynne Sharon Schwartz's "Beggaring Our Better Selves" has a more restrained emotional appeal because her language is not highly connotative and her stories about beggars are not overdramatized, but her argument is still an emotional one, focusing on how we are affected by the constant impact of the outstretched hand.

Logical appeal You argue with logical or rational strategies when you appeal mainly to your readers' intelligence, reason, and common sense. Here you depend heavily on *making claims* and *using supporting evidence*. Like a lawyer arguing a case, you may *bring in testimony* (including statistics and reports), *cite authorities,* and *argue from precedent.* You *make comparisons* and *use analogies* to strengthen your presentation, and you *theorize about cause and effect.* You also *de-emphasize personal feelings,* although you may not eliminate them completely, and *focus on facts and research.*

Robert Reich's "Secession of the Successful" and Marjorie Kelly's "Revolution in the Market Place" are the most logical essays in this section. Reich makes strong claims about the growing split between the affluent top 20 percent of our society and the other four-fifths, supporting his case with an array of statistics and documented evidence, and he also relies heavily on cause-and-effect arguments, many of which can be reinforced by his readers' own experiences. But he also advances his argument by appealing to his readers' guilt and to their moral sense. Marjorie Kelly uses a variety of logical appeals in "Revolution in the Market Place," using facts and citing a wide range of instances in which industry and business are working to improve education, the environment, and literacy. But she also makes a subtle emotional appeal to her readers by using phrases like "business might be the last best hope of humanity" and describing many business projects in favorable terms.

In "White Guilt," Shelby Steele argues logically for a new way of looking at special preferments based on race, depending heavily on cause-and-effect analysis and analogies to support his case, but he adds a strong emotional element to his essay by citing personal experience and appeals to fairness. In "Murder, Inc." Robert Sherrill makes a logical argument in his indictment of business, using a barrage of facts and documented cases in which he cites authorities, testimony, and legal evidence, but his tone is so angry and his descriptions so damning that the impact of the essay is highly emotional.

Ethical appeal This kind of appeal is probably the most subtle and also the most powerful. As a writer, your ethical appeal comes from your ability to convince your readers that you are reliable, well informed, sincere, and qualified to write on your topic. You persuade your readers because you make them believe in you and respect what you have to say. As you might suspect, building this kind of appeal into your arguments isn't easy. You have to demonstrate that you put time and thought into preparing your argument and that you know your readers, respect them, and care about communicating with them. Simply put, you have to show you've done your homework.

Most of the writers in this section demonstrate strong ethical appeal, partly because all of them have excellent credentials in their fields, but also because they show that they care about their readers and that they know their subjects. Reich's obvious expertise in political economics and his knowledge of social and economic conditions greatly strengthen his warnings about trends in the United States. Both Robert Sherrill and Marjorie Kelly show they've thought seriously about their topic and deserve their readers' attention. Kelly enhances her ethical appeal by freely acknowledging evidence on the other side. Martin Luther King's record as a pioneer fighter for civil rights and his own history of persecution add a strong ethical element to his appeal for racial justice. In the companion essay on the struggles of African-Americans, "White Guilt," Shelby Steele's own experience with racism and his considerable achievements as an educator and writer give him credibility and stature. But none of these writers depends primarily on their reputations to carry their arguments; they're all careful to cite evidence, argue from precedent and analogy, and make thoughtful arguments that show their respect for their readers' intelligence.

Ultimately, ethical appeal is the strongest of all argument strategies because it comes from the character and background of the author. If you can demonstrate to your readers that you are honest, knowledgeable, and genuinely committed to your position, you are likely to convince them with your arguments.

POTENTIAL PITFALLS IN ARGUMENT

This brief introduction to argument cannot point out all the things that can go wrong in arguments, the so-called logical fallacies, but adhering to the following guidelines should keep you from getting into too much trouble.

1. *Don't claim too much.* Avoid suggesting that the proposal you're arguing for will solve all the problems involved—for instance, implying that legalizing drugs would get rid of drug-related crimes or that paying football players openly would eliminate recruitment scandals. Settle for suggesting that your ideas may be worth considering or that you have thought of a new approach.

2. *Don't oversimplify complex issues.* Usually when an issue is serious enough and interesting enough for you to spend your time writing about it, it's a complicated matter with a tangled history and involves difficult issues. If you try to reduce it to simplistic terms and come up with an easy solution, you'll lose credibility quickly. Instead, acknowledge that the matter defies easy analysis but suggest that some things could be done.

3. *Support your arguments with concrete evidence and specific proposals, not with generalizations and conventional sentiments.* Always assume you are arguing for skeptical readers who expect you to demonstrate your case and won't be impressed by opinion alone. You can hold their interest and gain their respect only if you teach them something as you argue and present an old problem in a new light.

As you read the essays in this section, try to identify how these writers are arguing and what strategies they are using to convince you. As you get in the habit of reading arguments analytically and appreciatively, you will move toward writing arguments more easily and effectively. None of these strategies is new, after all, and seeing what other writers have done can give you an idea of what is possible.

Using Persuasion and Argument in a Paragraph

LEWIS LAPHAM
From "A Political Opiate"

To politicians in search of sound opinions and sustained applause, the war on drugs presents itself as a gift from heaven. Because the human craving for intoxicants cannot be suppressed—not by priests or jailers or acts of Congress—the politicians can bravely confront an allegorical enemy rather than an enemy that takes the corporeal form of the tobacco industry, say, or the oil and banking lobbies. The war against drugs provides them with something to say that offends nobody, requires them to do nothing difficult, and allows them to postpone, perhaps indefinitely, the more urgent and specific questions about the state of the nation's schools, housing, employment opportunities for young black men—i.e., the conditions to which drug addiction speaks as a tragic symptom, not a cause. They remain safe in the knowledge that they might as well be denouncing Satan or rain, and so they can direct the voices of prerecorded blame at metaphors and apparitions who, unlike Jessie Helms and his friends at the North Carolina tobacco auctions, can be transformed into demonic spirits riding north across the Caribbean on an evil wind. The war on drugs thus becomes the perfect war for people who would rather not fight a war, a war in which the politicians who stand so fearlessly on the side of the good, the true, and the beautiful need do nothing else but strike noble poses as protectors of the people and defenders of the public trust.

Politicians love the war on drugs because they don't have to take on real enemies

Popular & harmless

Can use war on drugs to avoid facing real problems: housing, education, unemployment

Largely for show

Lets them do nothing and look good

Comment In this opening paragraph of his essay, Lapham severely criticizes United States politicians. He argues that they have mounted a phony war on drugs in order to keep

from having to deal with the real problems of our country: poor schools, inadequate housing, unemployment among young black men. All of these are more serious and more threatening to our society than drug addiction, but pontificating about drugs and evil drug dealers appeals to the politicians because it's safe. No one can be *for* drugs, after all. Thus everyone can look good and sound virtuous without having to worry about fighting really powerful interests such as the tobacco industry, whose products kill more Americans than drugs do, or the powerful oil and banking lobbies, which contribute so much money to political campaigns.

Lapham's argument is based on logic: humans have always craved intoxicants and found them in spite of prohibition or other attempts to stop them. The only long-term solutions for drug addiction are education and alleviating social conditions that encourage it. His argument is also strongly emotional, however, full of irony and scathing indictments of those who haven't the courage to address the hard problems. He uses phrases such as "the politicians can bravely confront an allegorical enemy," "safe in the knowledge that they might as well be denouncing Satan," and "politicians who stand so fearlessly on the side of the good, the true, and the beautiful need do nothing else but strike noble poses." One of Lapham's goals is to show how foolish the United States is to keep posturing about the war on drugs when it should be working on its real social problems; his other goal is to denounce politicians as cowardly, more interested in their public image than they are in the truth.

MARTIN LUTHER KING, JR.

Martin Luther King, Jr. (1929–1968) was born in Atlanta, Georgia, and was educated at Morehouse College, Crozer Theological Seminary, and Boston University. Ordained a Baptist minister in his father's church in 1947, King soon became involved in civil rights activities in the South. In 1957 he founded the Southern Christian Leadership Conference and established himself as America's most prominent spokesman for nonviolent racial integration. In 1963 he was named *Time* magazine's Man of the Year; in 1964 he was given the Nobel Peace Prize. In 1968 he was assassinated in Memphis, Tennessee. His writing includes *Letter from Birmingham City Jail* (1963), *Why We Can't Wait* (1964), and *Where Do We Go from Here: Chaos or Community?* (1967). "I Have a Dream" is the famous speech King delivered at the Lincoln Memorial at the end of the "March on Washington" in 1963 to commemorate the one hundredth anniversary of the Emancipation Proclamation. King argues that realization of the dream of freedom for all American citizens is long overdue.

I Have a Dream

Five score years ago, a great American, in whose symbolic 1 shadow we stand, signed the Emancipation Proclamation. This momentous decree came as a great beacon light of hope to millions of Negro slaves who had been seared in the flames of withering injustice. It came as a joyous daybreak to end the long night of captivity.

But one hundred years later, we must face the tragic fact 2 that the Negro is still not free. One hundred years later, the

life of the Negro is still sadly crippled by the manacles of segregation and the chains of discrimination. One hundred years later, the Negro lives on a lonely island of poverty in the midst of a vast ocean of material prosperity. One hundred years later, the Negro is still languishing in the corners of American society and finds himself an exile in his own land. So we have come here today to dramatize an appalling condition.

In a sense we have come to our nation's Capitol to cash a check. When the architects of our republic wrote the magnificent words of the Constitution and the Declaration of Independence, they were signing a promissory note to which every American was to fall heir. This note was a promise that all men would be guaranteed the unalienable rights of life, liberty, and the pursuit of happiness. 3

It is obvious today that America has defaulted on this promissory note insofar as her citizens of color are concerned. Instead of honoring this sacred obligation, America has given the Negro people a bad check; a check which has come back marked "insufficient funds." But we refuse to believe that the bank of justice is bankrupt. We refuse to believe that there are insufficient funds in the great vaults of opportunity of this nation. So we have come to cash this check—a check that will give us upon demand the riches of freedom and the security of justice. We have also come to this hallowed spot to remind America of the fierce urgency of *now*. This is no time to engage in the luxury of cooling off or to take the tranquilizing drug of gradualism. *Now* is the time to make real the promises of Democracy. *Now* is the time to rise from the dark and desolate valley of segregation to the sunlit path of racial justice. *Now* is the time to open the doors of opportunity to all of God's children. *Now* is the time to lift our nation from the quicksands of racial injustice to the solid rock of brotherhood. 4

It would be fatal for the nation to overlook the urgency of the moment and to underestimate the determination of the Negro. This sweltering summer of the Negro's legitimate discontent will not pass until there is an invigorating autumn 5 of freedom and equality. 1963 is not an end, but a beginning. Those who hope that the Negro needed to blow off steam and will now be content will have a rude awakening if the nation returns to business as usual. There will be neither rest nor tranquility in America until the Negro is granted his citizenship rights. The whirlwinds of revolt will continue to shake the foundations of our nation until the bright day of justice emerges.

But there is something I must say to my people who stand 6
on the warm threshold which leads into the palace of justice. In the process of gaining our rightful place we must not be guilty of wrongful deeds. Let us not seek to satisfy our thirst for freedom by drinking from the cup of bitterness and hatred. We must forever conduct our struggle on the high plane of dignity and discipline. We must not allow our creative protest to degenerate into physical violence. Again and again we must rise to the majestic heights of meeting physical force with soul force. The marvelous new militancy which has engulfed the Negro community must not lead us to a distrust of all white people, for many of our white brothers, as evidenced by their presence here today, have come to realize that their destiny is tied up with our destiny and their freedom is inextricably bound to our freedom. We cannot walk alone.

And as we walk, we must make the pledge that we shall 7
march ahead. We cannot turn back. There are those who are asking the devotees of civil rights, "When will you be satisfied?" We can never be satisfied as long as the Negro is the victim of the unspeakable horrors of police brutality. We can never be satisfied as long as our bodies, heavy with the fatigue of travel, cannot gain lodging in the motels of the highways and the hotels of the cities. We cannot be satisfied as long as the Negro's basic mobility is from a smaller ghetto to a larger one. We can never be satisfied as long as a Negro in Mississippi cannot vote and a Negro in New York believes he has nothing for which to vote. No, no, we are not satisfied, and we will not be satisfied until justice rolls down like waters and righteousness like a mighty stream.

I am not unmindful that some of you have come here out 8
of great trials and tribulations. Some of you have come fresh from narrow jail cells. Some of you have come from areas where your quest for freedom left you battered by the storms of persecution and staggered by the winds of police brutality. You have been the veterans of creative suffering. Continue to work with the faith that unearned suffering is redemptive.

Go back to Mississippi, go back to Alabama, go back to 9
South Carolina, go back to Georgia, go back to Louisiana, go back to the slums and ghettoes of our northern cities, knowing that somehow this situation can and will be changed. Let us not wallow in the valley of despair.

I say to you today, my friends, that in spite of the diffi- 10
culties and frustrations of the moment I still have a dream. It is a dream deeply rooted in the American dream.

I have a dream that one day this nation will rise up and 11
live out the true meaning of its creed: "We hold these truths to be self-evident; that all men are created equal."

I have a dream that one day on the red hills of Georgia 12
the sons of former slaves and the sons of former slaveowners will be able to sit down together at the table of brotherhood.

I have a dream that the state of Mississippi, a desert state 13
sweltering with the heat of injustice and oppression, will be transformed into an oasis of freedom and justice.

I have a dream that my four little children will one day 14
live in a nation where they will not be judged by the color of their skin but by the content of their character.

I have a dream today. 15

I have a dream that the state of Alabama, whose governor's 16
lips are presently dripping with the words of interposition and nullification, will be transformed into a situation where little black boys and black girls will be able to join hands with little white boys and white girls and walk together as sisters and brothers.

I have a dream today. 17

I have a dream that one day every valley shall be exalted, 18
every hill and mountain shall be made low, the rough places will be made plain, and the crooked places will be made

straight, and the glory of the Lord shall be revealed, and all flesh shall see it together.

This is our hope. This is the faith with which I return to 19
the South. With this faith we will be able to hew out of the mountain of despair a stone of hope. With this faith we will be able to transform the jangling discords of our nation into a beautiful symphony of brotherhood. With this faith we will be able to work together, to pray together, to struggle together, to go to jail together, to stand up for freedom together, knowing that we will be free one day.

This will be the day when all of God's children will be 20
able to sing with new meaning.

My country, 'tis of thee
Sweet land of liberty,
Of thee I sing:
Land where my fathers died,
Land of the pilgrims' pride,
From every mountainside
Let freedom ring.

And if America is to be a great nation this must become 21
true. So let freedom ring from the prodigious hilltops of New Hampshire. Let freedom ring from the mighty mountains of New York. Let freedom ring from the heightening Alleghenies of Pennsylvania!

Let freedom ring from the snowcapped Rockies of Col- 22
orado!

Let freedom ring from the curvaceous peaks of California! 23

But not only that; let freedom ring from Stone Mountain 24
of Georgia!

Let freedom ring from Lookout Mountain of Tennessee! 25

Let freedom ring from every hill and molehill of Missis- 26
sippi. From every mountainside, let freedom ring.

When we let freedom ring, when we let it ring from every 27
village and every hamlet, from every state and every city, we will be able to speed up that day when all of God's children, black men and white men, Jews and Gentiles, Protestants and Catholics, will be able to join hands and sing in the

words of the old Negro spiritual, "Free at last! free at last! thank God almighty, we are free at last!"

For Study and Discussion

QUESTIONS FOR RESPONSE

1. What experiences of discrimination or injustice have you had (or perhaps witnessed or read about) that help you to identify with King's dreams and feel the force of his speech?
2. What do you know about the life of Martin Luther King, Jr., and of his place in modern U.S. history that helped you to anticipate what you would encounter in reading the "I Have a Dream" speech? How well did the speech live up to your expectations?

QUESTIONS ABOUT PURPOSE

1. King has at least two strong messages: one message is local and immediate, and one is national and long-range. How would you summarize those messages?
2. How does King use his speech to reinforce his belief in nonviolence as the appropriate tool in the civil rights movement?

QUESTIONS ABOUT AUDIENCE

1. When King gave this speech he spoke to a huge live, predominantly black audience that had come to Washington, D.C., on a march for freedom and civil rights. What much larger audience is he addressing, and why is that audience also important?
2. What do you think King's immediate audience expected of and hoped for from him on that occasion? To what extent does the speech seem to you to meet those expectations?

QUESTIONS ABOUT STRATEGIES

1. How does King draw on the power of metaphor to engage his listeners' feelings of injustice and give them hope for a new day?

2. How and why does King use the language of religious sermons and patriotic speeches in this speech?

QUESTIONS FOR DISCUSSION

1. If King were alive today, some thirty years after his famous speech, how much of his dream do you think he would feel has come true? Look particularly at the visions he speaks of in paragraph 7 and paragraphs 11 through 16.
2. What elements in the speech reveal those qualities that contributed to King's power as a major civil rights leader, effective with whites as well as blacks?

SHELBY STEELE

Shelby Steele was born in 1946 in Chicago, attended the University of Utah, and currently serves as a professor of English at San Jose State University. His writing, which often contests or revises the traditional view of racial issues in the United States, has appeared in magazines such as *American Scholar, Black World, Harper's,* and *Commentary.* He has also served as the host for a PBS special, "Seven Days in Bensonhurst." His first book, *The Content of Our Character: A New Vision of Race in America* (1990), won the National Book Critics Circle Award but created considerable controversy for its criticism of social entitlements and affirmative action. In "White Guilt," excerpted from *The Content of Our Character,* Steele argues that the combination of black power and white guilt has created racial policies that encourage dependency rather than development.

White Guilt

I don't remember hearing the phrase "white guilt" very much before the mid-sixties. Growing up black in the fifties, I never had the impression that whites were much disturbed by guilt when it came to blacks. When I would stray into the wrong restaurant in pursuit of a hamburger, it didn't occur to me that the waitress was unduly troubled by guilt when she asked me to leave. I can see now that possibly she was, but then all I saw was her irritability at having to carry out so unpleasant a task. If there was guilt, it was mine for having made an imposition of myself. Frankly, I can remember feeling a certain sympathy for such people, as if *I* was victimizing *them* by drawing them out of an innocent anonymity into the unasked-for role of racial policemen. Occasionally, they 1 came right out and asked me to feel sorry for them. A caddy master at a country club told my brother and me that he was doing us a favor by not letting us caddy at this white club, and that we should try to understand his position, "put yourselves in my shoes." Our color had brought this man anguish and, if a part of that anguish was guilt, it was not as immediate to me as my own guilt. I smiled at the man to let him know he shouldn't feel bad and then began the long walk home. Certainly, I also judged him a coward, but in that era his cowardice was something I had to absorb.

In the sixties, particularly the black-is-beautiful late sixties, 2
this sort of absorption was no longer necessary. The lines of moral power, like plates in the earth, had shifted. White guilt became so palpable you could see it on people. At the time, what it looked like to my eyes was a remarkable loss of authority. And what whites lost in authority, blacks gained. You cannot feel guilty toward anyone without giving away power to them. So, suddenly, this huge vulnerability opened up in whites and, as a black, you had the power to step right into it. In fact, black power all but demanded that you do so. What shocked me in the late sixties, after the helplessness I had felt in the fifties, was that guilt had changed the nature of the white man's burden from the administration of inferiors to the uplift of equals, from the obligations of dominance to the urgencies of repentance.

I think what made the difference between the fifties and 3
sixties, as far as white guilt was concerned, was that whites in the sixties underwent an archetypal Fall. Because of the immense turmoil of the civil rights movement, and later the black power movement, whites were confronted for more than a decade with their willingness to participate in or comply with the oppression of blacks, their indifference to human suffering and denigration, their capacity to abide evil for their own benefit, and in defiance of their own sacred principles. The 1964 Civil Rights Act that bestowed equality under the law on blacks was also, in a certain sense, an admission of white guilt. Had white society not been wrong, there would have been no need for such an act. In this act,

the nation acknowledged its fallen state, its lack of racial innocence, and confronted the incriminating self-knowledge that it had rationalized flagrant injustice. Denial is a common way of handling guilt, but in the sixties there was little will left for denial except in the most recalcitrant whites. And with this defense lost, there was really only one road back to innocence—through actions and policies that would bring redemption.

I believe that in the sixties the need for white redemption from racial guilt became the most poweful, yet unspoken, element in America's social-policy-making process, first giving rise to the Great Society and then to a series of programs, policies, and laws that sought to make black equality and restitution a national mission. Once America could no longer deny guilt, it went after redemption, or at least the look of redemption, with a vengeance. Yet today, some twenty years later, study after study tells us that, by many measures, the gap between blacks and whites is widening rather than narrowing. A University of Chicago study indicates that segregation is more entrenched in American cities today than ever imagined. A National Research Council study says the "status of blacks relative to whites (in housing and education) has stagnated or regressed since the early seventies." A follow-up to the famous Kerner Commission Report says we are as much at risk today of becoming a "nation within a nation" as we were twenty years ago when the original report was made. 4

I think the white need for redemption has contributed to this tragic situation by shaping our policies regarding blacks in ways that might deliver the look of innocence to society and its institutions, but that do very little to actually uplift blacks. Specifically, the effect of this hidden need has been to bend social policy more toward reparation for black oppression than toward the much harder and more mundane work of black uplift and development. Rather than facilitate the development of blacks to parity with whites, these programs and policies—affirmative action is a good example—have tended to give blacks special entitlements that in many 5 cases are of no use because we lack the development that would put us in a position to take advantage of them. I think the reason there has been more entitlement than development is (along with black power) the unacknowledged white need for redemption—not true redemption, which would have focused policy on black development, but the appearance of redemption, which requires only that society, in the name of development, seem to be paying back its former victims with preferences. One of the effects of entitlements, I believe, has been to encourage in blacks a dependency both on the entitlements and on the white guilt that generates them. Even when it serves ideal justice, bounty from another man's guilt weakens. This is not the only factor in black "stagnation" and "regression," but I do believe it is one factor.

It is easy enough the say that white guilt too often has the effect of bending social policies in the wrong direction. But what exactly is this guilt, and how does it work in American life? 6

I think that white guilt, in its broad sense, springs from a *knowledge* of ill-gotten advantage. More precisely, it comes from the juxtaposition of this knowledge with the inevitable gratitude one feels for being white rather than black in America. Given the moral instincts of human beings, it is all but impossible to enjoy an ill-gotten advantage, much less to feel at least secretly grateful for it, without consciously or unconsciously experiencing guilt. If, as Kierkegaard says, "innocence is ignorance," then guilt must always involve knowledge. White Americans *know* that their historical advantage comes from the subjugation of an entire people. So, even for whites today for whom racism is anathema, there is no escape from the knowledge that makes for guilt. Racial guilt simply accompanies the condition of being white in America. 7

I do not believe that this guilt is a crushing anguish for most whites, but I do believe it constitutes an ongoing racial vulnerability, an openness to racial culpability, that is a thread in white life, sometimes felt, sometimes not, but ever present 8 as a potential feeling. In the late sixties almost any black could charge this thread with enough current for a white to feel it. I had a friend who developed this activity into a sort of specialty. I don't think he meant to be mean, though certainly he was mean. I think he was, in that hyperbolic era, exhilarated by the discovery that his race, which had long been a liability, now gave him a certain edge—that white guilt was black power. To feel this power he would sometimes set up what he called "race experiments." Once I watched him stop a white businessman in a large hotel men's room and convince him to increase his tip to the black attendant from one to twenty dollars.

My friend's tact in this was very simple, even corny. Out of the attendant's earshot he asked the man to simply look at the attendant, a frail, elderly, and very dark man in a starched white smock that made the skin on his neck and face look as leathery as a turtle's. He sat listlessly, pathetically, on a straight-backed chair next to a small table on which sat a stack of hand towels and a silver plate for tips. Since he offered no service beyond the handing out of towels, one could only conclude the hotel management offered his lowly presence as flattery to their patrons, as an opportunity for that easy noblesse oblige that could reassure even the harried, wrung-out traveling salesman of his superior station. My friend was quick to make this point to the businessman and to say that no white man would do in this job. But when the businessman put the single back in his wallet and took out a five, my friend only sneered. Did he understand the tragedy of a life spent this way, of what it must be like to earn one's paltry living as a symbol of inferiority? And did he realize that his privilege as an affluent white businessman (ironically, he had just spent the day trying to sell a printing press to the Black Muslims for their newspaper *Muhammad Speaks*) was connected to the deprivation of this man and others like him? 9

But then my friend made a mistake that ended the game. In the heat of argument, which until then had only been playfully challenging, he inadvertently mentioned his father. 10

This stopped him cold and his eyes turned inward. "What about your father?" the businessman asked. "He had a hard life, that's all." "How did he have a hard life?" Now my friend was on the defensive. I knew he did not get along with his father, a bitter man who worked nights in a factory and demanded that the house be dark and silent all day. My friend blamed his father's bitterness on racism, but I knew he had not meant to exploit his own pain in this silly "experiment." Things had gotten too close to home, but he didn't know how to get out of the situation without losing face. Now, caught in his own trap, he did what he least wanted to do. He gave forth the rage he truly felt to a white stranger in a public men's room. "My father never had a chance," he said with the kind of anger that could easily turn to tears. "He never had a fuckin' chance. Your father had all the goddamn chances, and you know he did. You sell printing presses to black people and make thousands and your father probably lives down in Fat City, Florida, somewhere, all because you're white." On and on he went in this vein, using—against all that was honorable in him—his own profound racial pain to extract a flash of guilt from a white man he didn't even know.

He got more than a flash. The businessman was touched. 11
His eyes became mournful and finally he simply said, "You're right. Your people got a raw deal." He took a twenty-dollar bill from his wallet, then walked over and dropped it in the old man's tip plate. When he was gone my friend and I could not look at the old man, nor could we look at each other.

It is obvious that this was a rather shameful encounter for 12
all concerned—my friend and I as his silent accomplice—trading on our racial pain, tampering with a stranger for no reason, and the stranger then buying his way out of the situation for twenty dollars, a sum that was generous by one count and cheap by another. It was not an encounter of people but of historical grudges and guilts. Yet, when I think about it now, twenty years later, I see that it had all the elements of a paradigm that I believe has been very much at the heart of racial policymaking in America since the sixties.

13 My friend did two things that made this businessman vulnerable to his guilt, that brought his guilt into the situation as a force. First, he put this man in touch with his own *knowledge* of his ill-gotten advantage as a white. The effect of this was to disallow the man any pretense of racial innocence, to let him know that even if he was not the sort of white who used the word *nigger* around the dinner table, he still had reason to feel racial guilt. But as disarming as this might have been, it was too abstract to do much more than crack open his vulnerability, to expose him to the logic of white guilt. This was the five-dollar intellectual sort of guilt. The twenty dollars required something more visceral. In achieving this, the second thing my friend did was something that he had not intended to do, something that ultimately brought him as much shame as he was passing out. He made a display of his own racial pain and anger. (What brought him shame was not the pain and anger but his trading on them for what turned out to be a mere twenty bucks.) The effect of this display was to reinforce the man's knowledge of ill-gotten advantage, to give credibility and solidity to it by putting a face on it. Here was human testimony, a young black beside himself at the thought of his father's racially constricted life. The pain of one man evidenced the knowledge of the other. When the businessman listened to my friend's pain, his racial guilt—normally one guilt lying dormant among others—was called out like a neglected debt he would finally have to settle. An ill-gotten advantage is not hard to bear—it can be marked up to fate—until it touches the human pain it brought into the world. This is the pain that hardens guilty knowledge.

14 Such knowledge is a powerful pressure when it becomes conscious. And what makes it so powerful is the element of fear that guilt always carries, fear of what the guilty knowledge says about us. Guilt makes us afraid for ourselves and so generates as much self-preoccupation as concern for others. The nature of this preoccupation is always the redemption of innocence, the reestablishment of good feeling about oneself.

In this sense, the fear for the self that is buried in all guilt is a pressure toward selfishness. It can lead us to put our own need for innocence above our concern for the problem that made us feel guilt in the first place. But this fear for the self not only inspires selfishness; it also becomes a pressure to *escape* the guilt-inducing situation. When selfishness and escapism are at work, we are no longer interested in the source of our guilt and, therefore, no longer concerned with an authentic redemption from it. Now we only want the *look* of redemption, the gesture of concern that will give us the appearance of innocence and escape from the situation. Obviously, the businessman did not put twenty dollars in the tip plate because he thought it would go to the uplift of black Americans. He did it selfishly for the appearance of concern and for the escape it afforded him. 15

This is not to say that guilt is never the right motive for doing good works or showing concern, only that it is a very dangerous one because of its tendency to draw us into self-preoccupation and escapism. Guilt is a civilizing emotion when the fear for the self it carries is contained—a containment that allows guilt to be more selfless and that makes genuine concern possible. I think this was the kind of guilt that, along with other forces, made the 1964 Civil Rights Act possible. But, since then, I believe too many of our social policies related to race have been shaped by the fearful underside of guilt. 16

Black power evoked white guilt and made it a force in American institutions, just as my friend brought it to life in the businessman. Not many volunteer for guilt. Usually, it is others that make us feel it. It was the expression of black anger and pain that hardened the guilty knowledge of white ill-gotten advantage. And black power—whether from militant fringe groups, the civil rights establishment, or big city political campaigns—knew exactly the kind of white guilt it was after. It wanted to trigger the kind of white guilt in which whites fear for their own decency and innocence; it wanted the guilt of white self-preoccupation and escapism. Always at the heart of black power, in whatever form, there has been a profound anger at what was done to blacks and 17 an equally profound feeling that there should be reparations. But a sober white guilt in which fear for the self is contained is only good for strict fairness—the 1964 Civil Rights Act that guaranteed equality under the law. It is of little value when one is after more than fairness. So black power made it its mission to have whites fear for their innocence, to feel a visceral guilt from which they would have to seek a more profound redemption. In such redemption was the possibility of black reparation. Black power upped the ante on white guilt.

With black power, all the elements of the hidden paradigm 18
that shapes America's race-related social policy were in place. Knowledge of ill-gotten advantage could now be evidenced and deepened by black power into the sort of guilt from which institutions could redeem themselves only by offering more than fairness—by offering forms of reparation and compensation for past injustice. I believe this was the paradigm that bent our policies toward racial entitlements at the expense of racial development. In 1964, one of the assurances that Senator Hubert Humphrey and other politicians had to give Congress in order to get the landmark Civil Rights Bill passed was that the bill would not in any way require employers to use racial preferences to rectify racial imbalances. But this was before the explosion of black power in the late sixties, before the hidden paradigm was set in motion. After black power, racial preferences became the order of the day.

If this paradigm brought blacks entitlements, it also 19
brought us the continuation of our most profound problem in American society: our invisibility as a people. The white guilt that this paradigm elicits is the kind of guilt that preoccupies whites with their own innocence and pressures them toward escapism—twenty dollars in the plate and out the door. With this guilt, as opposed to the contained guilt of genuine concern, whites tend to see only their own need for quick redemption. Blacks, then, become a means to this redemption and, as such, they must be seen as generally "less than" others. Their needs are "special," "unique," "different." They are seen exclusively along the dimension of their victimization, so they become "different" people with whom

whites can negotiate entitlements, but never fully see as people like themselves. Guilt that preoccupies people with their own innocence blinds them to those who make them feel guilty. This, of course, is not racism, and yet it has the same effect as racism since it makes blacks something of a separate species for whom normal standards and values do not automatically apply.

Nowhere is this more evident today than in American universities. At some of America's most elite universities, administrators have granted concessions in response to black student demands (black power) that all but sanction racial separatism on campus—black "theme" dorms, black student unions, black yearbooks, homecoming dances, and so on. I don't believe administrators sincerely believe in these separatist concessions. Most of them are liberals who see racial separatism as wrong. But black student demands pull them into the paradigm of self-preoccupied white guilt whereby they seek a quick redemption by offering special entitlements that go beyond fairness. In this black students become invisible to them. Though blacks have the lowest grade point average of any group in American universities, administrators never sit down with them and "demand" in kind that they bring their grades up to par. The paradigm of white guilt makes the real problems of black students secondary to the need for white redemption. It also cuts these administrators off from their own values, which would most certainly discourage racial separatism and encourage higher black performance. Lastly, it makes for escapist policies; there is little difference between giving black students a separate graduation ceremony or student lounge and leaving twenty dollars in the tip plate on the way out the door. 20

What demonstrates more than anything the degree to which university administrators (and faculties) have been subdued by this paradigm is their refusal to lead black students, to tell them what they honestly think, to insist that they perform at a higher level, and to ask them to integrate themselves fully into campus life. This marks the difference between self-preoccupied guilt and the guilt of genuine con- 21 cern, where fear for one's innocence is contained. The former grants entitlements as a means to easy innocence and escape from judgment; the latter refuses the entanglements and blindness of self-concerned guilt and, out of honest concern, demands black development.

Escapist racial policies—policies whereby institutions favor black entitlement over development out of a preoccupation with their own innocence—have, I believe, a dispiriting impact on blacks. Such policies have the effect of transforming whites from victimizers into patrons and keeping blacks where they have always been—dependent on the largesse of whites. This was made evident in a famous statement by President Lyndon Johnson at Howard University in 1965: "You do not take a person who, for years, had been hobbled by chains and liberate him, bring him up to the starting line of a race and then say, 'You're free to compete with others,' and justly believe that you have been fair." 22

On its surface this seems to be the most reasonable of statements, but on closer examination we can see how it deflects the emphasis away from black responsibility and toward white responsibility. The actors in this statement—"You [whites] do not *take* a person [blacks] . . ."—are whites; blacks are the passive recipients of white action. The former victimizers are challenged now to be patrons, but where is the black challenge? This is really a statement to and about white people, their guilt, their responsibility, and their road to redemption. Not only does it not enunciate a black mission, but it sees blacks only in the dimension of their victimization—"hobbled by chains"—and casts them once again in the role of receivers of white beneficence. Nowhere in this utterance does President Johnson show respect for black resilience, or faith in the capacity of blacks to run fast once they get to the "starting line." This statement, which launched Johnson's Great Society, had the two ever-present signposts of white guilt—white self-preoccupation and black invisibility. 23

White guilt has pressured many of America's racial policies toward a paternalism that makes it difficult for blacks to find their true mettle or develop a faith in their own capacity to 24 run as fast as others. The most vivid examples of this are the many forms of preferential treatment that come under the heading of affirmative action—an escapist racial policy, I believe, that offers entitlements, rather than development, to blacks. A preference is not a training program; it teaches no skills, instills no values. It only makes a color a passport. But the worst aspect of racial preferences is that they encourage dependency on entitlements rather than on our own initiative, a situation that has already led many blacks to believe that we cannot have fairness without entitlements. And here we fall into an Orwellian double-speak where preference means equality. At the heart of this confusion, I believe, is an unspoken black doubt about our ability to compete that is covered over by a preoccupation with racial discrimination. Since there are laws to protect us against discrimination, preferences only impute a certain helplessness to blacks that diminishes our self-esteem. The self-preoccupied form of white guilt that is behind racial preferences always makes us lower so that we can be lifted up.

Recently, Penn State launched a program that actually 25
pays black students for improving their grades—a C to C+ average brings \$550, and anything more brings \$1,100. Here is the sort of guilty kindness that kills. What kind of self-respect is a black student going to have as he or she reaches out to take \$550 for C work when many white students would be embarrassed by so average a performance? What better way to drive home the nail of inferiority? And what more Pavlovian system of conditioning blacks to dependency than shelling out cash for grades? Here, black students learn to hustle their victimization rather than overcome it while their patrons escape with the cheapest sort of innocence. Not all preferential treatment is this insidious, but the same dynamic is always at work when color brings entitlement.

I think effective racial policies can only come from the sort 26
of white guilt where fear for the self is contained so that genuine concern can emerge. The test for this healthy guilt is simply a heartfelt feeling of concern without any compro-

mise of one's highest values and principles. But how can whites reach this more selfless form of guilt? I believe the only way is to slacken one's grip on innocence. Guilt has always been the lazy man's way to innocence—I feel guilt *because* I am innocent, guilt confirms my innocence. It is the compulsion to always think of ourselves as innocent that binds us to self-preoccupied guilt. Whites in general, and particularly those public and private institutions (not necessarily white) that make racial policy, must not be so preoccupied with their image of innocence or, put another way, their public relations of good intentions. What is needed now is a new spirit of pragmatism in racial matters where blacks are seen simply as American citizens who deserve complete fairness and in some cases developmental assistance, but in no case special entitlements based on color. We need de-racinated social policies that attack poverty rather than *black* poverty and that instill those values that make for self-reliance. The white message to blacks must be: America hurt you badly and that is wrong, but entitlements only prolong the hurt while development overcomes it.

Selfish white guilt is really self-importance. It has no humility and it asks for an unreasonable, egotistical innocence. Nothing diminishes a black more than this sort of guilt in a white, which to my mind amounts to sort of moral colonialism. We used to say in the sixties that at least in the South you knew where you stood. I always thought this was a little foolish since I didn't like where I stood there. But I think one of the things we meant by this—at the time—was that the South had little investment in its racial innocence and that this was very liberating in an ironical sort of way. It meant there would be no undercurrent of enmeshment with white need. It gave us back ourselves. The selfishly guilty white is drawn to what blacks least like in themselves—their suffering, victimization, and dependency. This is no good for anyone. 27

For Study and Discussion

QUESTIONS FOR RESPONSE

1. If you are white, to what extent are you aware of feeling the white guilt that Steele says accompanies the condition of being white in America? How, if at all, does such guilt affect your behavior? If you are not white, how conscious are you of white guilt? Do you think it is a constructive or destructive emotion? Why?
2. What preferential treatment programs for minorities are you aware of on your campus? How do they affect minority students? What is your feeling about these programs?

QUESTIONS ABOUT PURPOSE

1. Steele claims that programs designed to compensate for past injustices are demeaning to blacks and, in the long run, don't really benefit them. How does he want administrators and legislators to change their policies to provide what he would consider real help?
2. What does Steele see as the drawbacks of the members of any group—women, minorities, gays, disabled—seeing themselves as victims and using that status to receive benefits from another group?

QUESTIONS ABOUT AUDIENCE

1. Many readers prefer to avoid reading any writing that criticizes them, and "White Guilt" criticizes both blacks and whites. Yet *The Content of Our Character,* the book from which this essay was taken, was on the nonfiction best-seller list for months. What concerns and interests do you think general readers have that would draw them to read about the issues that Steele raises here?
2. Because many people feel so strongly about preferential programs for any racial group, the issue has provoked heated political arguments in recent years. What biases for or against the programs do you think readers might bring to this essay? How effective do you think Steele's arguments are in combating those biases?

QUESTIONS ABOUT STRATEGIES

1. How does Steele establish an early advantage with his readers by his story about not being allowed to caddie at an all-white country club?
2. Identify two of the logical appeals Steele uses to support his thesis that preferential programs harm blacks in the long run. What details does he use to back up those logical arguments?

QUESTIONS FOR DISCUSSION

1. For a number of reasons, Steele believes that many black college students need help in the form of developmental programs and that colleges should work to provide such help. Do you agree and, if so, what form do you think such programs should take?
2. The United States is now home to millions of immigrants from Asia, Latin America, and the Near East. To what extent do you think whites feel white guilt toward these groups? How do the situations of various groups differ?

BRIGID BROPHY

Brigid Brophy was born in London, England, in 1929 and attended St. Paul's Girls' School and St. Hugh's College, Oxford University. Quick-witted and keenly intelligent, she soon became a writer, following the family tradition established by her father, novelist John Brophy. Her novels include *Hackenfeller's Ape* (1954), *The King of Rainy County* (1957), *Flesh* (1962), and *Palace Without Chairs* (1978). Her nonfiction includes works as diverse as *Mozart the Dramatist: A New View of Mozart's Operas and His Age* (1964), *Black Ship to Hell* (1962), *The Rights of Animals* (1969), and *Baroque 'n' Roll and Other Essays* (1987). A regular contributor to the *New Statesman, London Magazine,* and the *Times Literary Supplement,* Brophy is an astute literary critic and an impassioned defender of her moral and political opinions. In "The Rights of Animals," reprinted from *Don't Never Forget: Collected Views and Reviews* (1966), she argues one of her favorite causes—the responsibility of the superior species (human beings) to behave decently toward the inferior species (animals).

The Rights of Animals

1 Were it announced tomorrow that anyone who fancied it might, without risk of reprisals or recriminations, stand at a fourth-storey window, dangle out of it a length of string with a metal (labelled "Free") on the end, wait till a chance passer-by took a bite and then, having entangled his cheek or gullet on a hook hidden in the food, haul him up to the fourth floor and there batter him to death with a knobkerry, I do not think there would be many takers.

Most sane adults would, I imagine, sicken at the mere thought. Yet sane adults do the equivalent to fish every day: not in panic, sexual jealousy, ideological frenzy or even greed—many of our freshwater fish are virtually inedible, and not one of them constitutes a threat to the life, love or ideology of a human on the bank—but for amusement. Civilisation is not outraged at their behaviour. On the contrary: that a person's hobby is fishing is often read as a guarantee of his sterling and innocent character. 2

The relationship of *homo sapiens* to the other animals is one of unremitting exploitation. We employ their work; we eat and wear them. We exploit them to serve our superstitions: whereas we used to sacrifice them to our gods and tear out their entrails in order to foresee the future, we now sacrifice them to Science and experiment on their entrails in the hope—or on the mere off chance—that we might thereby see a little more clearly into the present. When we can think of no pretext for causing their death and no profit to turn it to, we often cause it nonetheless, wantonly, the only gain being a brief pleasure for ourselves, which is usually only marginally bigger than the pleasure we could have had without killing anything; we could quite well enjoy our marksmanship or crosscountry galloping without requiring a real dead wild animal to shew for it at the end. 3

It is rare for us to leave wild animals alive; when we do, we often do not leave them wild. Some we put on display in a prison just large enough for them to survive, but not in any full sense to live, in. Others we trundle about the country in their prisons, pausing every now and then to put them on public exhibition performing, like clockwork, "tricks" we have "trained" into them. However, animals are not clockwork but instinctual beings. Circus "tricks" are spectacular or risible as the case may be precisely *because* they violate the animals' instinctual nature—which is precisely why they ought to violate both our moral and our aesthetic sense. 4

But where animals are concerned humanity seems to have switched off its morals and aesthetics—indeed, its very imagination. Goodness knows those faculties function erratically 5 enough in our dealings with one another. But at least we recognise their faultiness. We spend an increasing number of our cooler moments trying to forestall the moral and aesthetic breakdowns which are liable, in a crisis, to precipitate us into atrocities against each other. We have bitter demarcation disputes about where the rights of one man end and those of the next man begin, but most men now acknowledge that there are such things as the rights of the next man. Only in relation to the next animal can civilised humans persuade themselves that they have absolute and arbitrary rights—that they may do anything whatever that they can get away with.

The reader will have guessed in some detail by now what 6
sort of person he confronts in me: a sentimentalist; probably a killjoy; a person with no grasp on economic realities; a twee anthropomorphist, who attributes human feelings (and no doubt human names and clothes as well) to animals, and yet actually prefers animals to humans and would sooner succour a stray cat than an orphan child; a latter-day version of those folklore English spinsters who in the nineteenth century excited the ridicule of the natives by walking round Florence requesting them not to ill-treat their donkeys; and *par excellence,* of course, a crank.

Well. To take the last item first: if by "crank" you mean 7
"abnormal," yes. My views are shared by only a smallish (but probably not so small as you think) part of the citizenry—as yet. Still, that proves nothing either way about the validity of our views. It is abnormal to be a lunatic convinced you are Napoleon, but equally (indeed, numerically considered, probably even more) abnormal to be a genius. The test of a view is its rationality, not the number of people who endorse it. It would have been cranky indeed in the ancient world to raise the question of the rights of slaves—so cranky that scarcely a voice went on record as doing so. To us it seems incredible that the Greek philosophers should have scanned so deep into right and wrong and yet never *noticed* the immorality of slavery. Perhaps three thousand years from now it will seem equally incredible that we do not notice the immorality of our oppression of animals.

Slavery was the ancient world's patch of moral and aesthetic insensitivity. Indeed, it was not until the eighteenth and nineteenth centuries of our own era that the human conscience was effectively and universally switched on in that respect. Even then, we went on with economic and social exploitations which stopped short of slavery only in constitutional status, and people were found to justify them. But by then the exploiters had at least been forced onto the defensive and felt obliged to produce the feeble arguments that had never even been called for in the ancient world. Perhaps it is a sign that our conscience is about to be switched on in relation to animals that some animal-exploiters are now seeking to justify themselves. When factory farmers tell us that animals kept in "intensive" (i.e. concentration) camps are being kindly spared the inclemency of a winter outdoors, and that calves do not mind being tethered for life on slats because they have never known anything else, an echo should start in our historical consciousness: do you remember how childlike blackamoors were kindly spared the harsh responsibilities of freedom, how the skivvy didn't feel the hardship of scrubbing all day because she was used to it, how the poor didn't mind their slums because they had never known anything else? 8

The first of the factory farmers' arguments is, of course, an argument for ordinary farms to make better provision for animals in winter, not for ordinary farms to be replaced by torture chambers. As for the one about the animals' never having known anything else, I still shan't believe it valid but I shall accept that the factory farmers genuinely believe it themselves when they follow out its logic by using their profits to finance the repatriation of every circus and zoo animal that was caught in the wild, on the grounds that those *have* known something else. 9

Undismayed by being a crank, I will make you a free gift of another stick to beat me with, by informing you that I am a vegetarian. Now, surely, you have me. Not only am I a more extreme crank, a member of an even smaller minority, than you had realised; surely I *must,* now, be a killjoy. Yet 10 which, in fact, kills more joy: the killjoy who would deprive you of your joy in eating steak, which is just one of the joys open to you, or the kill-animal who puts an end to all the animal's joys along with its life?

Beware, however (if we may now take up the first item in your Identikit portrait of me), how you call me a sentimentalist in this matter. I may be less of one than you are. I won't kill an animal in order to eat it, but I am no respecter of dead bodies as such. If our chemists discovered (as I'm sure they quickly would were there a demand) how to give tenderness and hygiene to the body of an animal which had died of old age, I would willingly eat it; and in principle that goes for human animals, too. In practice I suspect I should choke on a rissole which I knew might contain bits of Great-Aunt Emily (whether through love for or repulsion from her I am not quite sure), and I admit I might have to leave rational cannibalism to future generations brought up without my irrational prejudice (which is equally irrational whether prompted by love or by repulsion for the old lady). But you were accusing me, weren't you, of sentimentality and ignorance of economic realities. Have you thought how much of the world's potential food supply *you* unrealistically let go waste because of your sentimental compunction about eating your fellow citizens after they have lived out their natural lives? 11

If we are going to rear and kill animals for our food, I think we have a moral obligation to spare them pain and terror in both processes, simply because they are sentient. I can't *prove* they are sentient; but then I have no proof *you* are. Even though you are articulate, whereas an animal can only scream or struggle, I have no assurance that your "It hurts" expresses anything like the intolerable sensations I experience in pain. I know, however, that when I visit my dentist and say "It hurts," I am grateful that he gives me the benefit of the doubt. 12

I don't myself believe that, even when we fulfill our minimum obligation not to cause pain, we have the right to kill animals. I know I would have no right to kill you, however 13 painlessly, just because I liked your flavour, and I am not in a position to judge that your life is worth more to you than the animal's to it. If anything, you probably value yours less; unlike the animal, you are capable of acting on an impulse to suicide. Christian tradition would permit me to kill the animal but not you, on the grounds that you have, and it hasn't, an immortal soul. I am not a Christian and do not avail myself of this licence; but if I were, I should in elementary justice see the soul theory as all the more reason to let the animal live out the one mortal life it has.

The only genuine moral problem is where there is a direct clash between an animal's life and a human one. Our diet proposes no such clash, meat not being essential to a human life; I have sustained a very healthy one for ten years without. And in fact such clashes are much rarer in reality than in exam papers, where we are always being asked to rescue either our grandmother or a Rubens from a blazing house. . . . 14

The most genuine and painful clash is, of course, on the subject of vivisection. To hold vivisection never justified is a hard belief. But so is its opposite. I believe it is never justified because I can see nothing (except our being able to get away with it) which lets us pick on animals that would not equally let us pick on idiot humans (who would be more useful) or, for the matter of that, on a few humans of any sort whom we might sacrifice for the good of the many. If we do permit vivisection, here if anywhere we are under the most stringent minimum obligations. The very least we must make sure of is that no experiment is ever duplicated, or careless, or done for mere teaching's sake or as a substitute for thinking. Knowing how often, in every other sphere, pseudowork proliferates in order to fill time and jobs, and how often activity substitutes for thought, and then reading the official statistics about vivisection, do you truly believe we *do* make sure? . . . 15

Our whole relation to animals is tinted by a fantasy—and a fallacy—about our toughness. We feel obliged to demonstrate we can take it; in fact, it is the animals who take it. 16

So shy are we of seeming sentimental that we often disguise our humane impulses under "realistic" arguments: foxhunting is snobbish; factory-farmed food doesn't taste so nice. But foxhunting would still be an atrocity if it were done by authenticated, pedigreed proletarians, and so would factory-farming even if a way were found of making its corpses tasty. So, incidentally, would slavery, even if it were proved a hundred times more economically realistic than freedom.

The saddest and silliest of the superstitions to which we sacrifice animals is our belief that by killing them we ourselves somehow live more fully. We might live more fully by entering imaginatively into their lives. But shedding their blood makes us no more full-blooded. It is a mere myth, often connected with our myth about the *savoir vivre* and sexiness of the sunny south (which is how you manged to transform me into a frustrated British virgin in Florence). There is no law of nature which makes *savoir vivre* incompatible with "live and let live." The bullfighter who torments a bull to death and then castrates it of an ear has neither proved nor increased his own virility; he has merely demonstrated that he is a butcher with balletic tendencies. 17

Superstition and dread of sentimentality weight all our questions against the animals. We *don't* scrutinise vivisection rigorously—we somehow think it would be soft of us to do so, which we apparently think a worse thing to be than cruel. When, in February of this year, the House of Lords voted against a Bill banning animal acts from circuses, it was pointed out that animal-trainers would lose their jobs. (Come to think of it, many human-trainers must have lost theirs when it was decided to ban gladiator acts from circuses.) No one pointed out how many unemployed acrobats and jugglers would *get* jobs to replace the animals. (I'm not, you see by the way, the sort of killjoy who wants to abolish the circus as such.) Similarly with the anthropomorphism argument, which works in both directions but is always wielded in one only. In the same House of Lords debate, Lady Summerskill, who had taken the humane side, was mocked by a noble lord on the grounds that were *she* shut 18 up in a cage she would indeed suffer from mortification and the loss of her freedom, but an animal, not being human, wouldn't. Why did no one point out that a human, in such circumstances, dreadful as they are, would have every consolation of the human intellect and imagination, from reading books to analysing his circumstances and writing to the Home Secretary about them, whereas the animal suffers the raw terror of not comprehending what is being done to it?

In point of fact, I am the very opposite of an anthropo- 19
morphist. I don't hold animals superior or even equal to humans. The whole case for behaving decently to animals rests on the fact that we are the superior species. We are the species uniquely capable of imagination, rationality and moral choice—and that is precisely why we are under the obligation to recognise and respect the rights of animals.

For Study and Discussion

QUESTIONS FOR RESPONSE

1. How do you react to Brophy's assertion that "the relationship of *homo sapiens* to the other animals is one of unremitting exploitation"? In what ways do you think you or your family may share in such exploitation?
2. If you or any of your family hunts or fishes, how do you feel about Brophy's charge that such acts are immoral? What arguments can you make for hunting and fishing?

QUESTIONS ABOUT PURPOSE

1. What policies regarding animals would Brophy like to see outlawed in England and elsewhere? How could such policies be interpreted as exploitative?
2. Since Brophy is unlikely to persuade people to stop eating meat, poultry, or fish, what changes in the ways such products are raised would she consider a good step in the right direction?

QUESTIONS ABOUT AUDIENCE

1. This essay first appeared in the London *Times*. What do you know about the British that might make them sympathetic to Brophy's arguments? Do you think they would be more sympathetic than Americans? Why?
2. What groups of college students who read Brophy's essay are likely to hold the values similar to the ones she expresses here? What shared knowledge about the way animals are sometimes treated do you think she can depend on those students having?

QUESTIONS ABOUT STRATEGIES

1. How does Brophy go about trying to get her readers to put themselves in the situation of animals?
2. Why does Brophy introduce a humorous tone in anticipating possible objections and accusations from her readers (paragraphs 6, 7, 10, and 11)? What does she gain by this tactic?

QUESTIONS FOR DISCUSSION

1. What economic effects would follow if legislation were passed to adopt all or even some of Brophy's proposals about animal rights?
2. How do you react to the persona Brophy projects in this essay? Do you see her as a crackpot or an impractical and sentimental idealist? How persuaded are you by her arguments?

VICKI HEARNE

Vicki Hearne was born in 1946 in Austin, Texas, and was educated at the University of California, Riverside, and Stanford University. She has taught creative writing at the University of California, Davis, and Yale University. Her own writing includes two volumes of poetry, *Nervous Horses* (1980) and *In Absence of Horses* (1984); a novel, *The White German Shepherd* (1988); and two extraordinary books of nonfiction, *Adam's Task: Calling Animals by Name* (1986) and *Bandit: Dossier of a Dangerous Dog* (1991)—all of which focus on the complicated relationship between humans and animals. An expert animal trainer, and lately "the Pit Bull Lady," Hearne has established the National Pit Bull Terrier Defense Association and Literary Society. In "What's Wrong with Animal Rights?", reprinted from *Harper's*, Hearne argues that animal-rights activists have "got it all wrong" because they are preoccupied with the problems of animal suffering rather than the possibility of animal happiness.

What's Wrong with Animal Rights?

Not all happy animals are alike. A Doberman going over a hurdle after a small wooden dumbbell is sleek, all arcs of harmonious power. A basset hound cheerfully performing the same exercise exhibits harmonies of a more lugubrious nature. There are chimpanzees who love precision the way musicians or fanatical housekeepers or accomplished hypochondriacs do; others for whom happiness is a matter of invention and variation—chimp vaudevillians. There is a rhinoceros whose happiness, as near as I can make out, is in needing to be trained every morning, all over again, or else 1 he "forgets" his circus routine, and in this you find a clue to the slow, deep, quiet chuckle of his happiness and to the glory of the beast. Happiness for Secretariat is in his ebullient bound, that joyful length of stride. For the draft horse or the weight-pull dog, happiness is of a different shape, more awesome and less obviously intelligent. When the pulling horse is at its most intense, the animal goes into himself, allocating all of the educated power that organizes his desire to dwell in fierce and delicate intimacy with that power, leans into the harness, and MAKES THAT SUCKER *MOVE*.

If we are speaking of human beings and use the phrase "animal happiness," we tend to mean something like "creature comforts." The emblems of this are the golden retriever rolling in the grass, the horse with his nose deep in the oats, the kitty by the fire. Creature comforts are important to animals—"Grub first, then ethics" is a motto that would describe many a wise Labrador retriever, and I have a pit bull named Annie whose continual quest for the perfect pillow inspires her to awesome feats. But there is something more to animals, a capacity for satisfactions that come from work in the fullest sense—what is known in philosophy and in this country's Declaration of Independence as "happiness." This is a sense of personal achievement, like the satisfaction felt by a good wood-carver or a dancer or a poet or an accomplished dressage horse. It is a happiness that, like the artist's, must come from something within the animal, something trainers call "talent." Hence, it cannot be imposed on the animal. But it is also something that does not come *ex nihilo*. If it had not been a fairly ordinary thing, in one part of the world, to teach young children to play the pianoforte, it is doubtful that Mozart's music would exist. 2

Happiness is often misunderstood as a synonym for pleasure or as an antonym for suffering. But Aristotle associated happiness with ethics—codes of behavior that urge us toward the sensation of getting it right, a kind of work that yields the "click" of satisfaction upon solving a problem or surmounting an obstacle. In his *Ethics,* Aristotle wrote, "If happiness is activity in accordance with excellence, it is reasonable that it should be in accordance with the highest 3 excellence." Thomas Jefferson identified the capacity for happiness as one of the three fundamental rights on which all others are based: "life, liberty, and the pursuit of happiness."

I bring up this idea of happiness as a form of work because I am an animal trainer, and work is the foundation of the happiness a trainer and an animal discover together. I bring up these words also because they cannot be found in the lexicon of the animal-rights movement. This absence accounts for the uneasiness toward the movement of most people, who sense that rights advocates have a point but take it too far when they liberate snails or charge that goldfish at the county fair are suffering. But the problem with the animal-rights advocates is not that they take it too far, it's that they've got it all wrong. 4

Animal rights are built upon a misconceived premise that rights were created to prevent us from unnecessary suffering. You can't find an animal-rights book, video, pamphlet, or rock concert in which someone doesn't mention the Great Sentence, written by Jeremy Bentham in 1789. Arguing in favor of such rights, Bentham wrote: "The question is not, Can they *reason*? nor, can they *talk*? but, can they suffer?" 5

The logic of the animal-rights movement places suffering at the iconographic center of a skewed value system. The thinking of its proponents—given eerie expression in a virtually sado-pornographic sculpture of a tortured monkey that won a prize for its compassionate vision—has collapsed into a perverse conundrum. Today the loudest voices calling for—demanding—the destruction of animals are the humane organizations. This is an inevitable consequence of the apotheosis of the drive to relieve suffering: Death is the ultimate release. To compensate for their contradictions, the humane movement has demonized, in this century and the last, those who made animal happiness their business: veterinarians, trainers, and the like. We think of Louis Pasteur as the man whose work saved you and me and your dog and cat from rabies, but antivivisectionists of the time claimed that rabies increased in areas where there were Pasteur Institutes. 6

An anti-rabies public-relations campaign mounted in Eng- 7

land in the 1880s by the Royal Society for the Prevention of Cruelty to Animals and other organizations led to orders being issued to club any dog found not wearing a muzzle. England still has her cruel and unnecessary law that requires an animal to spend six months in quarantine before being allowed loose in the country. Most of the recent propaganda about pit bulls—the crazy claim that they "take hold with their front teeth while they chew away with their rear teeth" (which would imply, incorrectly, that they have double jaws)—can be traced to literature published by the Humane Society of the United States during the fall of 1987 and earlier. If your neighbors want your dog or horse impounded and destroyed because he is a nuisance—say the dog barks, or the horse attracts flies—it will be the local Humane Society to whom your neighbors turn for action.

In a way, everyone has the opportunity to know that the history of the humane movement is largely a history of miseries, arrests, prosecutions, and death. The Humane Society is the pound, the place with the decompression chamber or the lethal injections. You occasionally find worried letters about this in Ann Landers's column. 8

Animal-rights publications are illustrated largely with photographs of two kinds of animals—"Helpless Fluff" and "Agonized Fluff," the two conditions in which some people seem to prefer their animals, because any other version of an animal is too complicated for propaganda. In the introduction to his book *Animal Liberation,* Peter Singer says somewhat smugly that he and his wife have no animals and, in fact, don't much care for them. This is offered as evidence of his objectivity and ethical probity. But it strikes me as an odd, perhaps obscene, underpinning for an ethical project that encourages university and high school students to cherish their ignorance of, say, great bird dogs as proof of their devotion to animals. 9

I would like to leave these philosophers behind, for they are inept connoisseurs of suffering who might revere my Airedale for his capacity to scream when subjected to a blowtorch but not for his wit and courage, not for his natural 10 good manners that are a gentle rebuke to ours. I want to celebrate the moment not long ago when, at his first dog show, my Airedale, Drummer, learned that there can be a public place where his work is respected. I want to celebrate his meticulousness, his happiness upon realizing at the dog show that no one would swoop down upon him and swamp him with the goo-goo excesses known as the "teddy-bear complex" but that people actually got out of his way, gave him room to work. I want to say, "There can be a six-and-a-half-month-old puppy who can care about accuracy, who can be fastidious, and whose fastidiousness will be a foundation for courage later." I want to say, "Leave my puppy alone!"

I want to leave the philosophers behind, but I cannot, in part because the philosophical problems that plague academicians of the animal-rights movement are illuminating. They wonder, do animals have rights or do they have interests? Or, if these rightists lead particularly unexamined lives, they dismiss that question as obvious (yes, of course, animals have rights, prima facie) and proceed to enumerate them, James Madison style. This leads to the issuance of bills of rights—the right to an environment, the right not to be used in medical experiments—and other forms of trivialization. 11

The calculus of suffering can be turned against the philosophers of festering flesh, even in the case of food animals, or exotic animals who perform in movies and circuses. It is true that it hurts to be slaughtered by man, but it doesn't hurt nearly as much as some of the cunningly cruel arrangements meted out by "Mother Nature." In Africa, 75 percent of the lions cubbed do not survive to the age of two. For those who make it to two, the average age at death is ten years. Asali, the movie and TV lioness, was still working at age twenty-one. There are fates worse than death, but twenty-one years of a close working relationship with Hubert Wells, Asali's trainer, is not one of them. Dorset sheep and polled Herefords would not exist at all were they not in a symbiotic relationship with human beings. 12

A human being living in the "wild"—somewhere, say, 13

without the benefits of medicine and advanced social organizations—would probably have a life expectancy of from thirty to thirty-five years. A human being living in "captivity"—in, say, a middle-class neighborhood of what the Centers for Disease Control call a Metropolitan Statistical Area—has a life expectancy of seventy or more years. For orangutans in the wild in Borneo and Malaysia, the life expectancy is thirty-five years; in captivity, fifty years. The wild is not a suffering-free zone or all that frolicsome a location.

The questions asked by animal-rights activists are flawed, 14 because they are built on the concept that the origin of rights is in the avoidance of suffering rather than in the pursuit of happiness. The question that needs to be asked—and that will put us in closer proximity to the truth—is not, do they have rights? or, what are those rights? but rather, what is a right?

Rights originate in committed relationships and can be 15 found, both intact and violated, wherever one finds such relationships—in social compacts, within families, between animals, and between people and nonhuman animals. This is as true when the nonhuman animals in question are lions or parakeets as when they are dogs. It is my Airedale whose excellencies have my attention at the moment, so it is with reference to him that I will consider the question, what is a right?

When I imagine situations in which it naturally arises that 16 A defends or honors or respects B's rights, I imagine situations in which the relationship between A and B can be indicated with a possessive pronoun. I might say, "Leave her alone, she's my daughter" or, "That's what she wants, and she is my daughter. I think I am bound to honor her wants." Similarly, "Leave her alone, she's my mother." I am more tender of the happiness of my mother, my father, my child, than I am of other people's family members; more tender of my friends' happiness than your friends' happinesses, unless you and I have a mutual friend.

Possession of a being by another has come into more and 17 more disrepute, so that the common understanding of one person possessing another is slavery. But the important detail about the kind of possessive pronoun that I have in mind is reciprocity: If I have a friend, she has a friend. If I have a daughter, she has a mother. The possessive does not bind one of us while freeing the other; it cannot do that. Moreover, should the mother reject the daughter, the word that applies is "disown." The form of disowning that most often appears in the news is domestic violence. Parents abuse children; husbands batter wives.

Some cases of reciprocal possessives have built-in limitations, such as "my patient / my doctor" or "my student / my teacher" or "my agent / my client." Other possessive relations are extremely limited but still remarkably binding: "my neighor" and "my country" and "my president." 18

The responsibilities and the ties signaled by reciprocal possession typically are hard to dissolve. It can be as difficult to give up an enemy as to give up a friend, and often the one becomes the other, as though the logic of the possessive pronoun outlasts the forms it chanced to take at a given moment, as though we were stuck with one another. In these bindings, nearly inextricable, are found the origin of our rights. They imply a possessiveness but also recognize an acknowledgment by each side of the other's existence. 19

The idea of democracy is dependent on the citizens' having knowledge of the government; that is, realizing that the government exists and knowing how to claim rights against it. I know this much because I get mail from the government and see its "representatives" running about in uniforms. Whether I actually have any rights in relationship to the government is less clear, but the idea that I do is symbolized by the right to vote. I obey the government, and, in theory, it obeys me, by counting my ballot, reading the *Miranda* warning to me, agreeing to be bound by the Constitution. My friend obeys me as I obey her; the government "obeys" me to some extent, and, to a different extent, I obey it. 20

What kind of thing can my Airedale, Drummer, have knowledge of? He can know that I exist and through that knowledge can claim his happiness, with varying degrees of 21 success, both with me and against me. Drummer can also know about larger human or dog communities than the one that consists only of him and me. There is my household—the other dogs, the cats, my husband. I have had enough dogs on campuses to know that he can learn that Yale exists as a neighborhood or village. My older dog, Annie, not only knows that Yale exists but can tell Yalies from townies, as I learned while teaching there during labor troubles.

Dogs can have elaborate conceptions of human social structures, and even of something like their rights and responsibilities within them, but these conceptions are never elaborate enough to construct a rights relationship between a dog and the state, or a dog and the Humane Society. Both of these are concepts that depend on writing and memoranda, officers in uniform, plaques and seals of authority. All of these are literary constructs, and all of them are beyond a dog's ken, which is why the mail carrier who doesn't also happen to be a dog's friend is forever an intruder—this is why dogs bark at mailmen. 22

It is clear enough that natural rights relations can arise between people and animals. Drummer, for example, can insist, "Hey, let's go outside and do something!" if I have been at my computer several days on end. He can both refuse to accept various of my suggestions and tell me when he fears for his life—such as the time when the huge, white flapping flag appeared out of nowhere, as it seemed to him, on the town green one evening when we were working. I can (and do) say to him either, "Oh, you don't have to worry about that" or, "Uh oh, you're right, Drum, that guy looks dangerous." Just as the government and I—two different species of organism—have developed improvised ways of communicating, such as the vote, so Drummer and I have worked out a number of ways to make our expressions known. Largely through obedience, I have taught him a fair amount about how to get responses from me. Obedience is reciprocal; you cannot get responses from a dog to whom you do not respond accurately. I have enfranchised him in a 23 relationship to me by educating him, creating the conditions by which he can achieve a certain happiness specific to a dog, maybe even specific to an Airedale, inasmuch as this same relationship has allowed me to plumb the happiness of being a trainer and writing this article.

Instructions in this happiness are given terms that are alien to a culture in which liver treats, fluffy windup toys, and miniature sweaters are confused with respect and work. Jack Knox, a sheepdog trainer originally from Scotland, will shake his crook at a novice handler who makes a promiscuous move to praise a dog, and will call out in his Scottish accent, "Eh! Eh! Get back, get BACK! Ye'll no be abusin' the dogs like that in my clinic." America is a nation of abused animals, Knox says, because we are always swooping at them with praise, "no gi'ing them their freedom." I am reminded of Rainer Maria Rilke's account in which the Prodigal Son leaves—has to leave—because everyone loves him, even the dogs love him, and he has no path to the delicate and fierce truth of himself. Unconditional praise and love, in Rilke's story, disenfranchise us, distract us from what truly excites our interest. 24

In the minds of some trainers and handlers, praise is dishonesty. Paradoxically, it is a kind of contempt for animals that masquerades as a reverence for helplessness and suffering. The idea of freedom means that you do not, at least not while Jack Knox is nearby, helpfully guide your dog through the motions of, say, herding over and over—what one trainer calls "explainy-wainy." This is rote learning. It works tolerably well on some handlers, because people have vast unconscious minds and can store complex pre-programmed behaviors. Dogs, on the other hand, have almost no unconscious minds, so they can learn only by thinking. Many children are like this until educated out of it. 25

If I tell my Airedale to sit and stay on the town green, and someone comes up and burbles, "What a pretty thing you are," he may break his stay to go for a caress. I pull him back and correct him for breaking. Now he holds his stay because I have blocked his way to movement but not because 26

I have punished him. (A correction blocks one path as it opens another for desire to work; punishment blocks desire and opens nothing.) He holds his stay now, and—because the stay opens this possibility of work, new to a heedless young dog—he watches. If the person goes on talking, and isn't going to gush with praise, I may heel Drummer out of his stay and give him an "Okay" to make friends. Sometimes something about the person makes Drummer feel that reserve is in order. He responds to an insincere approach by sitting still, going down into himself, and thinking, "This person has no business pawing me. I'll sit very still, and he will go away." If the person doesn't take the hint from Drummer, I'll give the pup a little backup by saying, "Please don't pet him, he's working," even though he was not under any command.

The pup reads this, and there is a flicker of a working trust now stirring in the dog. Is the pup grateful? When the stranger leaves, does he lick my hand, full of submissive blandishments? This one doesn't. This one says nothing at all, and I say nothing much to him. This is a working trust we are developing, not a mutual-congratulation society. My backup is praise enough for him; the use he makes of my support is praise enough for me. 27

Listening to a dog is often praise enough. Suppose it is just after dark and we are outside. Suddenly there is a shout from the house. The pup and I both look toward the shout and then toward each other: "What do you think?" I don't so much as cock my head, because Drummer is growing up, and I want to know what he thinks. He takes a few steps toward the house, and I follow. He listens again and comprehends that it's just Holly, who at fourteen is much given to alarming cries and shouts. He shrugs at me and goes about his business. I say nothing. To praise him for this performance would make about as much sense as praising a human being for the same thing. Thus: 28

A. What's that?
B. I don't know. [*Listens*] *Oh, it's just Holly.*

C. What a goooooood human being!
B. Huh?

This is one small moment in a series of like moments that will culminate in an Airedale who on a Friday will have the discrimination and confidence required to take down a man who is attacking me with a knife and on Saturday clown and play with the children at the annual Orange Empire Dog Club Christmas party. 29

People who claim to speak for animal rights are increasingly devoted to the idea that the very keeping of a dog or a horse or a gerbil or a lion is in and of itself an offense. The more loudly they speak, the less likely they are to be in a rights relation to any given animal, because they are spending so much time in airplanes or transmitting fax announcements of the latest Sylvester Stallone anti-fur rally. In a 1988 *Harper's* forum, for example, Ingrid Newkirk, the national director of People for the Ethical Treatment of Animals, urged that domestic pets be spayed and neutered and ultimately phased out. She prefers, it appears, wolves—and wolves someplace else—to Airedales and, by a logic whose interior structure is both emotionally and intellectually forever closed to Drummer, claims thereby to be speaking for "animal rights." 30

She is wrong. I am the only one who can own up to my Airedale's inalienable rights. Whether or not I do it perfectly at any given moment is no more refutation of this point than whether I am perfectly my husband's mate at any given moment refutes the fact of marriage. Only people who know Drummer, and whom he can know, are capable of this relationship. PETA and the Humane Society and the ASPCA and the Congress and NOW—as institutions—do have the power to affect my ability to grant rights to Drummer but are otherwise incapable of creating conditions or laws or rights that would increase his happiness. Only Drummer's owner has the power to obey him—to obey who he is and 31 what he is capable of—deeply enough to grant him his rights and open up the possibility of happiness.

For Study and Discussion

QUESTIONS FOR RESPONSE

1. What kind of impression does the author of this essay, Vicki Hearne, make on you? How do you think her being an animal trainer affects her ideas and attitudes toward animal-rights advocates?
2. How do you react to Hearne's belief that animals can have work in which they take satisfaction? If you can, give examples of animals for whom this seems to be true and describe their work.

QUESTIONS ABOUT PURPOSE

1. What kinds of animal-rights activists is Hearne most critical of? What does she object to most?
2. What kind of relationship between animals and their owners would Hearne like to see? How does that ideal relationship fit with her ideas about animal rights?

QUESTIONS ABOUT AUDIENCE

1. What groups of people do you think are likely to respond positively to Hearne's essay? Why?
2. If you are or have been an animal owner, what experiences do you bring to this essay that would reinforce or contradict Hearne's claims about how animals should be treated?

QUESTIONS ABOUT STRATEGIES

1. Hearne's images and language in the first paragraph of this essay are highly anthropomorphic; that is, through her choice of language she attributes human qualities and emotions to the animals she describes. What effect do you think she wants this opening to achieve with her readers?
2. In paragraphs 9 and 30, Hearne uses a sarcastic tone and ex-

treme examples when she criticizes certain animal-rights activists. What effect does this strategy have on you? What do you think she hopes to accomplish with it?

QUESTIONS FOR DISCUSSION

1. What are the major differences between the kind of animal rights Brigid Brophy argues for in "The Rights of Animals" and the kind of animal rights Hearne is talking about in her essay? On what guidelines for dealing with animals do you think the two authors would probably agree?
2. To what extent does Hearne's essay deal effectively with the main point Brophy makes in her essay: that people have no right to exploit animals for pleasure or profit?

Robert Sherrill was born in 1925 in Frogtown, Georgia, and was educated at Pepperdine University and the University of Texas. After teaching English at Texas A & M and the University of Missouri, Sherrill began a career as a journalist with the *Texas Observer,* the *Miami Herald,* and as the Washington editor for the *Nation.* He has written about many controversial political issues in such books as *The Accidental President* (1967), *Military Justice Is to Justice as Military Music Is to Music* (1971), *The Saturday Night Special, and Other Guns with Which America Won the West, Protected Bootleg Franchises, Slew Wildlife, Robbed Countless Banks, Shot Husbands Purposely and by Mistake, and Killed Presidents: Together with the Debate over Continuing Same* (1973), and *The Oil Follies of 1970–1980: How the Petroleum Industry Stole the Show (and Much More Besides)* (1983). In "Murder, Inc.," reprinted from *Grand Street,* Sherrill argues that we need a new category of crime that would allow irresponsible corporate executives to be charged with murder.

Murder, Inc.

There are something over fifteen hundred men and women on the death rows of America. Given the social context in which they operated, one might reasonably assume that they were sentenced to be executed not because they are murderers but because they were inefficient. Using guns and knives and the usual footpad paraphernalia, they dispatched only a few more than their own number. Had they used asbestos, mislabeled pharmaceutical drugs and devices, defective autos, and illegally used and illegally disposed chemicals, they could 1 have killed, crippled, and tortured many thousands of people. And they could have done it without very much fuss.

Corporate criminals, as we all know, live charmed lives. 2
Not until 1978 had a corporation ever been indicted for murder (Ford Motor Company, which was acquitted), and not until 1985 had corporate executives ever been brought to trial for murder because of the lethal mischief done by their company.

The executives who made history last year were the pres- 3
ident, plant manager, and plant foreman of Film Recovery Systems Corporation, a ratty little silver-rendering operation in Elm Grove Village outside Chicago. The silver was recovered by cooking used X-ray films in vats of boiling cyanide. Film Recovery hired mostly illegal immigrants, who were afraid to protest working conditions so foul that they made employees vomit and faint. The illegals were preferred also because they couldn't read much English and would not be spooked by the written warnings on the drums of cyanide. To make doubly sure that fright wouldn't drive workers away, management had the skull-and-crossbones signs scraped off the drums. Although the antidote for cyanide poisoning is cheap and easy to obtain, Film Recovery Systems didn't keep any on hand.

So it came to pass that Stefan Golab, a sixty-one-year-old 4
illegal immigrant from Poland, took too hefty a lungful of cyanide fumes and died. Charged with murder on the grounds that they had created such unsafe working conditions as to bring about "a strong probability of death and great bodily harm," the three officials were convicted and sentenced to twenty-five years in prison.

Will executives at other villainous corporations be simi- 5
larly charged and convicted? Don't bet on it. In this instance the law was applied so properly, so rightly, so commonsensically that one would be foolish to expect such usage to appear again soon. It was a sort of Halley's Comet of Justice.

The idea of treating corporate murderers as just plain 6
murderers strikes many people as excessive. Some lawyers who cautiously approved the conviction in principle said they

were afraid it would confuse people generally because a bald murder charge is usually associated with a bullet in the gut or an ice pick in the neck, and nice people would have a hard time adapting the charge to the way things are sometimes accomplished in the front office. Speaking for this timid viewpoint, Alan Dershowitz, Harvard's celebrated criminal law specialist, said he thought the Film Recovery case showed we need a new category of crime. "We should have one that specifically reflects our condemnation of this sort of behavior," he said, "without necessarily assimilating it into the most heinous forms of murder"—as if the St. Valentine's Day massacre were any more heinous than Bhopal.

During the trial, the Illinois prosecutor accused the defendants of "callousness, disregard of human lives, and exposing people to dangerous products all for the sake of profits." No wonder the verdict has been so modestly praised. If that's enough to rate a murder charge, our whole commercial system is at risk. If it were to become the rule, we could look forward to a lineup of accused corporate executives extending out the courthouse and around the block several times. Since there is no statute of limitations on murder, prosecutors would be obliged to charge those executives at Firestone who, a few years back, allegedly killed and injured no telling how many people by flooding the market with ten million tires they knew to be defective; and the executives at Ford who sent the Pinto into circulation knowing its gas tank was so poorly designed that a rear-end collision could turn the car into a fire trap (several dozen men, women, and children were burned alive). From the pharmaceutical fraternity would come such as Dr. William Shedden, former vice-president and chief medical officer for Eli Lily Research Laboratories, who recently pleaded guilty to fifteen criminal counts relating to the marketing of Oraflex, an arthritis drug that the Food and Drug Administration says has been "possibly" linked to forty-nine deaths in the United States and several hundred abroad, not to mention the hundreds who have suffered nonfatal liver and kidney failure. Seems as how 7 the folks at Lilly, when they sought approval from the FDA, forgot to mention that the drug was already known to have killed at least twenty-eight people in Europe. (Shedden was fined $15,000; Lilly, which earned $3.1 billion in 1984, was fined $25,000.) And let's be sure to save an early murder indictment for those three sly dogs at SmithKline Beckman Corporation who whizzed their product, Selacryn, through the FDA without mentioning that it had caused severe liver damage in some patients in France. False labels were used to peddle it in this country, where it has been linked to thirty-six deaths and five hundred cases of liver and kidney damage.

Now comes a ripple of books that, were there any justice, would put a dozen or so hangdog executives in the dock. Three of the books make particularly persuasive cases. Paul Brodeur's *Outrageous Misconduct: The Asbestos Industry on Trial* (Pantheon) is an account of how the largest manufacturer of asbestos products, Manville Corporation (previously known as Johns-Manville Corporation), and other asbestos companies committed over the years what one plaintiff's attorney called "the greatest mass murder in history," which is possibly true if one means industrial mass murder, not political. People who regularly inhale asbestos fibers are likely to die, or at least be crippled, from the lung disease called asbestosis or the even worse (at least it sounds worse) mesothelioma. It sometimes takes twenty to thirty years for asbestosis to appear, so a measure of the slaughter from it is somewhat vague. But the best experts in the field, which means Dr. Irving J. Selikoff and his staff at the Mount Sinai Hospital in New York City, estimate that aside from the many thousands who have died from asbestos diseases in the past, there will be between eight and ten thousand deaths from asbestos-related cancer each year for the next twenty years. These deaths are not accidental. Manville et al. knew exactly what they were doing. Brodeur's book is mainly an account of how the asbestos companies, though they claimed to be ignorant of the deadly quality of their product until a study by Dr. Selikoff was released in 1964, had for forty years known about, and had suppressed or disregarded, hundreds of studies that clearly showed what asbestos was doing to the people who inhaled it. Did the companies even care what was happening? Typically, at a Manville asbestos mine in Canada, company doctors found that of seven hundred and eight workers, only four—who had worked there less than four years—had normal lungs. Those who were dying of asbestosis were not told of their ailment.

The other two books, Susan Perry and Jim Dawson's *Nightmare: Women and the Dalkon Shield* (Macmillan) and Morton Mintz's *At Any Cost: Corporate Greed, Women, and the Dalkon Shield* (Pantheon), remind me of what Dr. Jules Amthor said to my favorite detective: "I'm in a very sensitive profession, Mr. Marlowe. I'm a quack." The murderous quackery of the Dalkon Shield, an intrauterine device, was committed by A. H. Robins, a company that should have stuck to making Chap Stick and Sergeant's Flea & Tick Collars, and left birth-control gadgets to those who knew how to make them properly. These two books should convince anyone, I think, that compared to the fellows at A. H. Robins, the Film Recovery executives were pikers when it came to showing disregard for human lives for the sake of profits. Profits were plentiful, that's for sure. A. H. Robins sold more than 4.5 million Dalkon Shields worldwide (2.8 million in the United States) for $4.35 each; not bad for a device that cost only twenty-five cents to produce. The death count among women who wore the shield still isn't complete; the last I heard it was twenty. But wearers of the shield also have reported stillbirths, babies with major congenital defects, punctured uteri, forced hysterectomies, sterilization from infection, and various tortures and illnesses by the thousands—some generous portion, we may presume, of the 9,230 lawsuits that A. H. Robins has settled out of court. And as both books make clear, the company launched the Dalkon Shield fully aware of the shield's dangers, sold it with false advertising, kept on selling it for several years after the company knew what its customers were going through, and pulled a complicated cover-up of guilt. 9

10 Dershowitz is right in one respect: corporate murderers are not like your typical killer on death row. Corporate murderers do not set out to kill. There's no profit in that. They are simply willing to accept a certain amount of death and physical torment among their workers and customers as a sometimes necessary byproduct of the free enterprise system. Mintz has uncovered a dandy quote from history to illustrate this attitude. When it was suggested to Alfred P. Sloan, Jr., president of General Motors circa 1930, that he should have safety glass installed in Chevrolets, he refused with the explanation, "Accidents or no accidents, my concern in this matter is a matter of profit and loss."

11 The Sloan spirit is everywhere. Brodeur quotes from a deposition of Charles H. Roemer, once a prominent New Jersey attorney who handled legal matters for the Union Asbestos and Rubber Company. Roemer reveals that around 1942, when Union Asbestos discovered a lot of its workers coming down with asbestos disease, he and some of Union Asbestos's top officials went to Johns-Manville and asked Vandiver Brown, Manville's attorney, and Lewis Brown, president of Manville, if their physical examination program had turned up similar results. According to Roemer, Vandiver Brown said, in effect, Sure, our X-rays show many of our workers have that disease, but we don't tell them they are sick because if we did, they would stop working and sue us. Roemer recalled asking, "Mr. Brown, do you mean to tell me you would let them work until they dropped dead?" and Brown answering, "Yes, we save a lot of money that way."

12 Saving money, along with making money, was obviously the paramount objective of A. H. Robins, too. This was evident from the beginning, when Robins officials learned—*six months before marketing the device nationally*—that the Dalkon Shield's multifilament tail had a wicking tendency and could carry potentially deadly bacteria into the uterus. Did the company hold up marketing the shield until it could be further tested and made safe? No, no. That would have meant a delay, for one thing, in recovering the $750,000 they had

paid the shield's inventors. Though Robins knew it was putting its customers in great jeopardy, it hustled the shield onto the market with promotional claims that it was "safe" and "superior" to all other intrauterine devices; and never, during the four years the shield was on the market, did A. H. Robins conduct wicking studies of the string. The shield's promotional literature, by the way, was a classic example of phony drugstore hype. A. H. Robins claimed the shield kept the pregnancy rate at 1.1 percent; the company was well aware that the shield allowed at least a 5 percent pregnancy rate, one of the most slipshod in the birth-control business. A. H. Robins also advertised that the device could be easily inserted in "even the most sensitive woman," although in fact many doctors, before inserting the shield, had to give patients an anesthetic, and many women were in pain for months.

Not long after the shield went on the market, Wayne 13
Crowder, one of the few heroes in this sorry tale, a quality-control engineer at Chap Stick, which manufactured many of the shields for its parent firm, rejected ten thousand of them because he was convinced the strings could wick bacteria. His boss overruled him with the remark, "Your conscience doesn't pay your salary." Crowder also suggested a method for stopping the wicking, but his technique was rejected because it would have cost an extra five cents per device. Crowder kept on complaining (he would ultimately be fired as an irritant) and he finally stirred Daniel French, president of Chap Stick, to convey Crowder's criticisms to the home office. French was told to mind his own business and not worry about the safety of the shield, which prompted him to go into the corporate softshoe routine he knew would please. He wrote A. H. Robins: "It is not the intention of Chap Stick Company to attempt any unauthorized improvements in the Dalkon Shield. My only interest in the Dalkon Shield is to produce it at the lowest possible price and, therefore, increase Robins' gross profit level."

Of course, when thousands of women begin dying, scream- 14
ing, cursing, and suing, it gets a little difficult to pretend

that all is well with one's product, but for more than a decade A. H. Robins did its best, never recalling the gadget, never sending a warning to doctors about possible deadly side effects, and continuing to the last—continuing right up to the present even after losing hundreds of millions of dollars in lawsuits—to argue that the shield is just hunkydory. The A. H. Robins school spirit was beautifully capsulated by one of its officials who told the *National Observer,* "But after all, we are in business to sell the thing, to make a profit. I don't mean we're trying to go out and sell products that are going to be dangerous, fatal, or what have you. But you don't put all the bad things in big headlines."

15 Where is the corporate executive who will not savor the easy insouciance of "or what have you"?

16 One of the more fascinating characteristics of corporate murderers is the way these fellows cover up their dirty work. They are really quite bold and successful in their deviousness. When one considers how many top officials there are at places like Manville and Robins, and when one assumes (obviously naïvely) among the lot of them surely there must be at least one or two with a functioning conscience, the completeness of their cover-ups is indeed impressive. Which isn't to say that their techniques are very sophisticated. They simply lie, or hide or burn the incriminating material. When the litigation flood began to break over Manville Corporation in the late 1960s, the asbestos gang began thwarting their victims' attorneys by claiming certain Manville executives couldn't give depositions because they were dead (when they were very much alive), by refusing to produce documents ordered by the court, and by denying that certain documents existed when in fact they did. A. H. Robins was just as expert at that sort of thing. According to Mintz, "Thousands of documents sought by lawyers for victims of the Dalkon Shield sank from sight in suspicious circumstances. A few were hidden for a decade in a home basement in Tulsa, Oklahoma. Other records were destroyed, some admittedly in a city dump in Columbus, Indiana, and some

allegedly in an A. H. Robins furnace. And despite court orders, the company did not produce truckloads of documents for judicial rulings on whether the women's lawyers could see the papers."

A. H. Robins's most notorious effort at a cover-up ultimately failed, thanks to one Roger Tuttle, a classic example of what can happen when the worm turns. 17

Tuttle was an attorney for A. H. Robins in the early 1970s. He says that immediately after the company lost its first Dalkon Shield lawsuit, his superiors ordered him (they deny it) to search through the company's files and burn every document that he thought might be used against A. H. Robins in future lawsuits—documents that, in Tuttle's words, indicated "knowledge and complicity, if any, of top officials in what at that stage of the game appeared to be a grim situation." Unfortunately for the company, Tuttle did not fully obey orders. He took possession of some of the juiciest documents and kept them. Just why he rebelled isn't clear. Perhaps it was because Tuttle, a plain little guy who admits he isn't the smartest attorney in the world, was tired of having his employers push him around, which they often did. He says he did it because he was ashamed that "I personally lacked the courage" to challenge the order and "I wanted some sop for my own conscience as an attorney." Whatever his motivation, Tuttle sat on the purloined files for nearly ten years. He moved on to other jobs, finally winding up, a born-again Christian, on the Oral Roberts University law faculty. Watching the Dalkon Shield trials from afar, troubled by the plaintiffs' inability to cope with A. H. Robins's cover-up, Tuttle finally decided to step forward and provide the material their attorneys needed for the big breakthrough. 18

A lucky windfall like that is the only way victims can overcome the tremendous imbalance in legal firepower. In the way they muster defense, corporate murderers bear no resemblance to the broken-down, half-nuts, penniless drifters on death row, dozens of whom have no attorney at all. Corporate killers are like the Mafia in the way they come to 19 court with a phalanx of attorneys. They are fronted by the best, or at least the best known. Griffin Bell, President Carter's Attorney General, has been one of A. H. Robins's attorneys.

There are two other significant differences between cor- 20
porate killers and the habitués of death rows. In the first place, the latter generally did not murder as part of doing business, except for the relatively few who killed coincidental to a holdup. They did not murder to protect their rackets or territory, as the Mafia does, and they did not murder to exploit a patent or to increase production and sales, as corporate murderers do. One judge accused A. H. Robins officials of taking "the bottom line as your guiding beacon and the low road as your route." Killing for the bottom line has probably not sent a single murderer to death row anywhere. In the second place, most of the men and women on death row were lonely murderers. No part of society supported what they did. But just as the Mafia can commit murder with impunity only because it has the cooperation of police and prosecutors, so too corporate murderers benefit from the collusion of respectable professions, particularly doctors (who, for a price, keep quiet), and insurance companies (who, to help Manville, did not reveal what their actuarial tables told about the risks to asbestos workers; and, for Robins, worked actively backstage to conceal the Dalkon Shield's menace to public health), and government agencies who are supposed to protect public health but look the other way.

It was an old, and in its way valid, excuse that Film 21
Recovery's officials gave the court: "We were just operating like other plants, and none of the government health and safety inspectors who dropped around—neither the Elm Grove Village Public Health Department nor the Environmental Protection Agency—told us we shouldn't be letting our workers stick their heads in vats of boiling cyanide." They were probably telling the truth. That's the way health and safety regulators have usually operated.

Brodeur tells us that a veritable parade of government inspectors marched through the Pittsburgh Corning asbestos plant in Tyler, Texas, over a period of six and a half years without warning the workers that the asbestos dust levels were more than twenty times the maximum recommended for health safety. One Department of Labor official later admitted he had not worn a respirator when inspecting the plant because he did not want to excite the workers into asking questions about their health. Though the Public Health Service several times measured the fallout of asbestos dust, never did it warn the workers that the stuff was eating up their lungs. Finally things got so bad at Tyler that federal inspectors, forced to bring charges against the owners for appalling infractions of health standards, recommended that they be fined $210. Today the men and women who worked in that plant (since closed) are dying of lung cancer at a rate five times greater than the national average. 22

The most impressive bureaucratic collusion A. H. Robins received was, not surprisingly, from the Food and Drug Administration. When trial attorneys brought evidence that the Dalkon Shield's rotting tail strings were endangering thousands of women and asked FDA officials to remove the device from the market, the agency did nothing. When the National Women's Health Network petitioned the FDA for a recall—paid for by Robins—that would remove the shield from all women then wearing it, the FDA did nothing. For a full decade it pretended to be helpless. 23

There is one more significant difference between the people on death row and the corporate murderers: the former sometimes say they are sorry; the latter never do. Midway through 1985, Texas executed Charles Milton, thirty-four, because when he stuck up a liquor store the owner and his wife wrestled Milton for the gun, it went off, and the woman died. Shortly before the state killed him with poison, Milton said, "I am sorry Mrs. Denton was killed in the struggle over the gun." There. He said it. It wasn't much, but he said it. And that's more than the folks at Manville have ever said about the thousands of people they killed with asbestos. When it comes to feeling no remorse, A. H. Robins doesn't 24 take a back seat to anybody. In a famous courtroom confrontation between Federal Judge Miles W. Lord and three A. H. Robins officials, including company president E. Claiborne Robins, Jr., Judge Lord asked them to read silently to themselves a long reprimand of their actions. The most scathing passage, quoted both by Mintz and by Perry and Dawson, was this:

> *Today as you sit here attempting once more to extricate yourselves from the legal consequences of your acts, none of you has faced up to the fact that more than nine thousand women [the figure two years ago (in 1984)] have made claims that they gave up part of their womanhood so that your company might prosper. It is alleged that others gave their lives so you might so prosper. And there stand behind them legions more who have been injured but who had not sought relief in the courts of this land. . . .* 25
>
> *If one poor young man were by some act of his—without authority or consent—to inflict such damage upon one woman, he would be jailed for a good portion of the rest of his life. And yet your company, without warning to women, invaded their bodies by the millions and caused them injuries by the thousands. And when the time came for these women to make their claims against your company, you attacked their characters. You inquired into their sexual practices and into the identity of their sex partners. You exposed these women—and ruined families and reputations and careers—in order to intimidate those who would raise their voices against you. You introduced issues that had no relationship whatsoever to the fact that you planted in the bodies of these women instruments of death, of mutilation, of disease.* 26

Judge Lord admitted that he did not have the power to make them recall the shield but he begged them to do it on their own: "You've got lives out there, people, women, wives, moms, and some who will never be moms. . . . You are the corporate conscience. Please, in the name of humanity, lift your eyes above the bottom line." 27

It was a pretty stirring piece of writing (later, when Judge 28

Lord got so pissed off he read it aloud, they say half the courtroom was in tears), and the judge asked them if it had had any impact on them.

Looking sulky, they just stared at him and said nothing. 29

A few weeks later, at A. H. Robins's annual meeting, 30
E. Claiborne Robins, Jr., dismissed Lord's speech as a "poisonous attack." The company did not recall the shield for another eight months.

Giving deposition in 1984, Ernest L. Bender, Jr., senior 31
vice-president for corporate planning and development, was asked if he had ever heard an officer or employee say he or she was "sorry or remorseful about any infection that's been suffered by any Dalkon Shield wearer." He answered, "I've never heard anyone make such remarks because I've never heard anyone that said the Dalkon Shield was the cause."

What punishment is fitting for these fellows? 32

If they are murderers, why not the death sentence? Polls 33
show that 84 percent of Americans favor the death penalty, but half think the penalty is unfairly applied. Let's restore their faith by applying justice equally and poetically. In Georgia recently it took the state two 2,080 volts spaced over nineteen minutes to kill a black man who murdered during a burglary. How fitting it would be to use the same sort of defective electric chair to execute, for example, auto manufacturers and tire manufacturers who knowingly kill people with defective merchandise. In Texas recently it took the state executioners forty minutes to administer the lethal poison to a drifter who had killed a woman. Could anything be more appropriate than to tie down drug and device manufacturers who have killed many women and let slow-witted executioners poke around their bodies for an hour or so, looking for just the right blood vessel to transport the poison? At a recent Mississippi execution, the prisoner's protracted gasping for breath became such an ugly spectacle that prison authorities, in a strange burst of decorum, ordered witnesses out of the death chamber. That sort of execution for Manville executives who specialized in spreading long-

term asphyxiation over thousands of lives would certainly be appropriate.

But these things will never happen. For all our popular declarations of democracy, most Americans are such forelock-tugging toadies that they would be horrified to see, say, Henry Ford II occupying the same electric chair that cooked black, penniless Alpha Otis Stephens. 34

Nor will we incarcerate many corporate murderers. Though some of us with a mean streak may enjoy fantasizing the reception that our fat-assed corporate killers would get from some of their cellmates in America's more interesting prisons—I like to think of the pious chaps from A. H. Robins spending time in Tennessee's notorious Brushy Mountain Prison—that is not going to happen very often either, the precedent of Film Recovery to the contrary notwithstanding. The Film Recovery trio had the misfortune of working for a crappy little corporation that has since gone defunct. Judges will not be so stern with killers from giant corporations. 35

So long as we have an army of crassly aggressive plaintiff attorneys to rely on, however, there is always the hope that we can smite the corporations and the men who run them with a punishment they probably fear worse than death or loss of freedom: to wit, massive loss of profits. Pamela C. Van Duyn, whose use of the Dalkon Shield at the age of twenty-six destroyed one Fallopian tube and critically damaged the other (her childbearing chances are virtually nil), says: "As far as I'm concerned, the last dime that is in Claiborne Robins's pocket ought to be paid over to all the people that have suffered." Author Brodeur dreams of an even broader financial punishment for the industry he hates: 36

> *When I was a young man, out of college in 1953, I went into the Army Counterintelligence Corps and went to Germany, where I saw one of the death camps, Dachau. And I saw what the occupational army had done to Dachau. They had razed it, left the chimneys standing, and the barbed wire as a monument—quite the same way the Romans left Carthage. What I would do with some of these companies that are noth-*

ing more or less than killing grounds would be to sell their assets totally, reimburse the victims, and leave the walls as a reminder—just the way Dachau was—that a law-abiding and decent society will not tolerate this kind of conduct.

He added, "I know perfectly well that this is not going to happen in the private enterprise system." 37

How right he is. The laws, the court system, federal and state legislature, most of the press, the unions—most of the establishment is opposed to applying the final financial solution to killer corporations. 38

As it became evident that juries were inclined to agree with Mrs. Van Duyn's proposal to wring plenty of money from A. H. Robins, the corporation in 1985 sought protection under Chapter 11 of the Federal Bankruptcy Code. It was a sleazy trick they had picked up from Manville Corporation, which had declared bankruptcy in August 1982. Although both corporations had lost hundreds of millions in court fights, neither was actually in financial trouble. Indeed, at the time it copped out under Chapter 11, Manville was the nation's 181st largest corporation and had assets of more than $2 billion. Bankruptcy was a transparent ploy—or, as plaintiff attorneys put it, a fraudulent abuse and perversion of the bankruptcy laws—but with the connivance of the federal courts it is a ploy that has worked. Not a penny has been paid to the victims of either corporation since they declared bankruptcy, and the 16,500 pending lawsuits against Manville and the five thousand lawsuits pending against A. H. Robins (those figures are climbing every day) have been frozen. 39

Meanwhile, companies are not even mildly chastised. Quite the contrary. Most major newspapers have said nothing about Manville's malevolent cover-up but have clucked sympathetically over its courtroom defeats. *The New York Times* editorially seemed to deplore the financial problems of the asbestos industry almost as much as it deplored the industry's massacre of workers: "Asbestos is a tragedy, most of all for the victims and their families but also for the companies, which are being made to pay the price for deci- 40 sions made long ago." Senator Gary Hart, whose home state, Colorado, is corporate headquarters for Manville, pitched in with legislation that would lift financial penalty from the asbestos companies and dump it on the taxpayers. And in Richmond, Virginia, corporate headquarters for the makers of the Dalkon Shield, civic leaders threw a banquet for E. Claiborne Robins, Sr. The president of the University of Virginia assured Robins that "Your example will cast its shadow into eternity, as the sands of time carry the indelible footprint of your good works. We applaud you for always exhibiting a steadfast and devoted concern for your fellow man. Truly, the Lord has chosen you as one of His most essential instruments."

After similar encomiums from other community leaders, 41
the top man behind the marketing of the Dalkon Shield was given the Great American Tradition Award.

For Study and Discussion

QUESTIONS FOR RESPONSE

1. What is your first reaction to Sherrill's essay—outrage, disbelief, a sense of hopelessness, disillusionment, or a cynical "Well, I'm not surprised"? Compare your responses with those of your classmates. How do you account for differences?
2. What is your response to Sherrill as a person? Based on this essay, how would you describe him? Why?

QUESTIONS ABOUT PURPOSE

1. What long-range goals do you think Sherrill had in writing this exposé?
2. What immediate changes do you think he hopes to bring about in his readers?

QUESTIONS ABOUT AUDIENCE

1. Sherrill makes dramatic charges against several American business executives, calling them "corporate murderers," and even

suggests they deserve the death penalty for the harm they have done. What questions and challenges does he seem to anticipate these accusations will bring from his readers? How can you tell? How does he respond to those challenges?

2. Sherrill seems to be writing for an audience who is already antibusiness and would be predisposed to agree with him. If he wanted to adapt the article for a different group of readers, what changes could be made and still keep the facts he uses?

QUESTIONS ABOUT STRATEGIES

1. How would you describe Sherrill's tone in this essay? How do you think it affects the impact of his article? Why?
2. What does Sherrill hope to accomplish with his detailed accounts of executions by electrocution and lethal injection?

QUESTIONS FOR DISCUSSION

1. Which, if any, of Sherrill's claims would you challenge? On what grounds would you make such a challenge?
2. What is the effect of Sherrill's comparison of business executives to the Mafia?

MARJORIE KELLY

Marjorie Kelly was born in 1953 in Columbia, Missouri, and was educated at the University of Missouri. She has worked as a reporter for the *Clarksville Leaf Chronicle;* as an editor for *Bread and Roses: A Woman's Journal on Issues and the Arts* and *The Freedom of Information Digest;* and as associate publisher for Magna Publications. In 1987 she founded *Business Ethics,* "the magazine of socially responsible business," which features writing about model companies and hands-on advice for fostering ethical business practices. In "Revolution in the Market Place," reprinted from the *Utne Reader,* Kelly points to signs that business is changing the way it thinks about its ethical responsibilities to society and the environment.

Revolution in the Market Place

1 The names come like a litany: Bhopal, the Dalkon Shield, Ivan Boesky, Three Mile Island. It is a litany of the tragedy of business in our time, the tragedy of ruined lives and a tainted earth. And not only in our time, but throughout modern history. The trail of industrialization has been a trail of bloody footprints: stripping native Americans of their homeland, raping the earth, polluting the rivers and the skies and the soil. The history of business is a tale of child labor, robber barons, snake oil salesmen, and sweat shops. In the future, our history will tell of plant closings, nuclear accidents, toxic waste, and ozone depletion.

2 Business is destroying the earth: if that seems to you an inescapable conclusion, it is with good reason. But there are some today who suggest a surprising sequel to this tale of destruction. There are some who say business might be the last best hope of humanity.

If business has the power to destroy the earth, might it also have the power to heal it? If business has the ability to ruin human lives, might it also have the ability to save them? 3

The answer may be yes. From many sectors—inside and outside the corporation, among academics, activists, and New Age thinkers—there are signs that a new life-affirming paradigm is emerging for business. Just as physics is shifting paradigms of the physical world from matter to energy, and as medicine is shifting paradigms of health care from treatment to prevention, so too is a shift under way in business. It is a shift from the inhuman to the human or, in consultant Michael Ducey's phrase, "from jungle to community." 4

The new paradigm has to do with respect for the human resources in business, and the acknowledgment that workers aren't obedient automatons but team players. It concerns employees demanding jobs with substance and meaning, and with corporations beginning to offer flextime, day care, and worker ownership. The new paradigm has corporations taking a role in helping the schools, reducing pollution, or fighting illiteracy. And it means tougher community standards, with public outcry against animal testing, nuclear power, and business in South Africa. The new paradigm has to do, in short, with making a better world—and using business as a tool. 5

No, the millennium has not arrived. But there are signs that the way we think about business—and the way business thinks about itself—are beginning to change. 6

A good example is the idea of "stakeholders," an increasingly popular concept in corporate circles. The premise is that it's not only stockholders who count, but all who have a stake in a company: employees, customers, suppliers, government, the community, anyone affected by corporate actions. NCR is one corporation that has been carrying this banner high, taking out a series of full-page ads in the *Wall Street Journal* and *Business Week,* proclaiming its commitment to various stakeholder groups. And in June, 1988, NCR sponsored the First International Symposium on Stakeholders, inviting corporate leaders to examine questions like this 7 one, taken verbatim from the program: "Can Marxist claims about the 'internal contradictions of capitalism' be countered with a stakeholder approach to management?" Also: "Is stakeholder goodwill a fundamental component of success?"

It's respectable these days to be a good corporate citizen. When *Fortune* magazine ranks America's Most Admired Corporations each year, it uses a list of "Eight Key Attributes of Reputation." Right up there alongside "Financial Soundness" is "Community and Environmental Responsibility." 8

Even conservative *Forbes* shows a few signs of change. In its May 1988 cover story on "The 800 Most Powerful People in Corporate America," it used a headline that could have come straight from a New Age workshop: "Not power but empower." *Forbes* told readers, "The most efficient way to wield power is to democratize it." Describing its talks with powerful corporate leaders, the magazine reported: "These executives reached reflexively for words like 'participatory management,' 'collegiality,' and 'consensus-building' to describe what they do." 9

A more humane vocabulary seems to be entering the management lexicon. According to *Business Week*'s April article on "Management for the 1990s," leadership today calls for "a new ingredient, caring." The magazine quoted one corporate chairman as saying, "The more you want people to have creative ideas and solve difficult problems, the less you can afford to manage them with terror." 10

In management practices, a key sign of change is the move toward decentralization, and giving workers a greater voice. In union-management relations, for example, an adversarial stance is giving way to a spirit of cooperation in some sectors. Since 1980, the United Steelworkers and a handful of steelmakers have been experimenting with labor-management participation teams (LMPT), where ten to fifteen workers meet each week to explore how to do their jobs better—and how to improve life in the mills. One LMPT reduced the chances for burns from a caustic solution by devising a better delivery system: driving the truck directly to the bath, eliminating a messy transfer step. "I think both sides feel that 11

LMPTs can improve the industry," said one union official. Recently, eight companies and the United Steelworkers began an unusual joint effort to set up LMPTs throughout the industry.

At Pitney Bowes, communication lines are kept open with the Council of Personnel Relations, which brings together an equal number of managers and employees twice each month to discuss issues ranging from salaries to new products. Kollmorgen Corporation believes so strongly in decentralization that it keeps even key decisions—such as capital expansion, the research and development budget, and the hiring of senior management—at the division level. And divisions are kept deliberately small, so employees can feel part of a group where their contribution matters. 12

From inhuman to human. From jungle to community. A new corporate ethic may be gradually emerging—and it has to do with external as well as internal constituencies. Indeed, the very idea of a corporate "constituency" is being broadened to include the local community, the nation, even the Earth itself. 13

"The terms of the contract between business and society are changing," Henry Ford II observed. "Now we are being asked to serve a wider range of human values and to accept an obligation to members of the public with whom we have no commercial transactions." 14

Du Pont seems to have been acting in that spirit, responding to its global constituency, when it decided in the late 1980s to phase out the production of chlorofluorocarbons (CFCs), which destroy ozone. Similarly responsive moves were made by McDonald's, when it decided to eliminate styrofoam cartons made with CFCs, and by Toys "R" Us, when it decided to stop selling realistic toy guns. If operating from a jungle mentality—as many corporations still do—these companies might have dug in and refused to change, leaving society's problems to society. But operating from a community mindset, they realized that society's problems *are* their problems. 15

Increasingly, the terms of the new contract between business and society are being written into law. Much has been made of former president Ronald Reagan's move to deregulate industry, but in addition new legislation is quietly being enacted that places greater demands on companies, and holds them to higher standards of accountability. In the wake of Bhopal and Chernobyl, the new Community Right to Know Act requires companies to inform the public about hazardous materials in use. When the law took effect in 1988, Pennsylvania residents had the surprising experience of seeing a full-page ad from Rohm & Haas, saying that it releases one million pounds of chemicals into the environment each year. Texas residents heard Texaco tell about its annual release of seventy-six thousand pounds of benzene, which is known to cause leukemia. The ultimate intent of the law is for public pressure to force companies to reduce their use of toxic materials. 16

In other legislation from the late 1980s, one law sharply restricts employers' use of polygraph tests, and another requires advance notice of plant closings. Communities in California and New York have banned certain kinds of plastic packaging, and a dozen states are considering similar restrictions—moving chemical companies to work faster on developing biodegradable plastics. Pending legislation would raise the minimum wage, and require businesses above a certain size to offer health insurance to workers. 17

The public welfare is increasingly becoming a private concern. We're accustomed to thinking that nonprofit institutions do good, while profit-making companies are greedy and uncaring. But as futurist Hazel Henderson says, we're beginning to tear down the wall between the two. Nonprofits are developing profit-making businesses to help themselves survive, while corporations are taking a greater hand in community welfare. 18

One example is the growing role of business in education. General Electric, the nation's largest defense contractor and the target of a national consumers boycott, spends fifty thou- 19 sand dollars a year working with top students at a public school in New York's Spanish Harlem, helping its GE Scholars get into prestigious universities. The well-known Boston Compact—a pledge by Boston businesses to hire one thousand graduates a year from inner-city schools—has added a new Compact Ventures program, providing remedial education and mentors for high school students in an effort to stem dropout rates.

Another area where public and private interests blend is in pollution cleanup. The public problem of hazardous waste has been solved in an ingenious way by the private company Marine Shale Processors, which turns toxic materials like paint solvent and chemicals into street paving. In a different approach, Detox Industries of Sugarland, Texas, has developed a method that breaks down polychlorinated biphenyls, or PCBs, biologically—using microorganisms. Even more elegantly, the Environmental Concern company restores native wetlands on the Atlantic Coast, building new marshes, reconstructing lost habitat, and planting vegetation. 20

Outside of industry, there are further signs of change. Activists have brought nuclear power to a virtual standstill and successfully fought for animal rights. Revlon, Bausch & Lomb, and Clorox are among the companies now supporting research into alternatives to the Draize test, which calls for toxic substances to be tested on the eyes of rabbits. Colgate has reduced animal use 80 percent in six years, while Avon and Procter & Gamble have eliminated animal tests entirely. 21

In the religious community, the Interfaith Center on Corporate Responsibility acts as a central clearinghouse for shareholder activism by churches—and in recent years, that activism has reached all-time highs, with record numbers of resolutions on topics like South African divestment, poison-pill takeover defenses, and the environment. Churches have also been active in the Royal Dutch/Shell boycott, with the United Church of Christ, United Methodist, and the Episcopal Church, among others, endorsing a boycott against Shell's presence in South Africa. 22

In the financial community, the field of socially responsible investing has grown geometrically, from forty billion dollars in investments in 1985 to ten times that amount today. It's been called the fastest growing new niche in the investing world—supporting some two dozen funds, a number of specialty newsletters, and a trade association called the Social Investment Forum. 23

Academia has shown a burgeoning interest in business ethics, with a growing number of universities offering required courses in the topic, several conferences being offered each year, and three dozen campus centers of ethics enjoying rising popularity. 24

In the alternative community, socially responsible companies find a national market for their goods and services through Co-op America, which lets thousands of consumers put their dollars where their hearts are. Co-op America director Paul Freundlich has created a new entity called Fair Trade, to bring wider U.S. distribution to products from the Third World. 25

The growing trend toward employee ownership is nourished by the Industrial Cooperative Association of Massachusetts, which offers both financial and technical assistance to worker-owned firms. When a brass company in Connecticut was threatened with closure, for example, ICA helped structure an Employee Stock Ownership Plan that put control of the company in the hands of its 227 employees. And in the first eight months after the company agreed to sell to the workers, the mill made more money than in the previous three years. 26

In the New Age community, there are groups like the Business Initiative—part of the Open Center in New York—which critically examines topics like "manipulation and trust in the field of sales," or "personal growth within large corporations." In Santa Monica, the company InSynergy runs "summit teams"—ongoing support groups where executives can explore their own spiritual growth, and work on being more effective and sensitive leaders. In 1988 Boulder's 27

Buddhist-inspired Naropa Institute sponsored a conference called Good Work, exploring "the relationship of spiritual journey and business."

All this activity on so many fronts adds up to an emerging new paradigm—a new picture of what's expected of business, and what's possible. It's a picture of workplaces that are healthy for employees, of corporate citizens who are powerful yet responsive, of companies that are tools for social change, and of a corporate community that is a humane presence on the earth. 28

Beyond this new picture, there seems to be a groundswell of change, driven by a variety of powerful forces. In this age of environmental limits, we simply cannot afford widespread corporate carelessness anymore. And with the coming of age of the baby boom generation, sixties values are being transformed into responsible professional values of the eighties. Faced with coming shortages of skilled labor, corporations need all available hands—and they need them functioning at their best. To reverse America's trade imbalance, companies need creativity at every level, including the shop floor. And that makes union-management cooperation a necessity. With the rise of service industries, employees are coming to function more as autonomous professionals, requiring a wholly new style of management: less autocratic, more democratic, more collegial. 29

Society *needs* a more humane business environment—and it's beginning to develop. But that's not to say everything is sliding effortlessly into place; far from it. Even companies that appear to espouse new values may be operating from the same old jungle mentality. 30

Some companies do good with their right hand only to do harm with the left. Tobacco companies, for instance, are dragged into court for product liability lawsuits, while they're lauded as the darling philanthropists of the art world. Other companies specialize in window dressing—as in IBM's "departure" from South Africa, which, through transfer of assets to an independent company, left sales intact. 31

There are grand schemes that sound good but will never go anywhere—like a plan for Universal Stock Ownership, which would solve poverty by handing corporate equity around like food stamps. There are corporations that institute employee stock ownership plans merely as fancy tax dodges. Others set up generous severance benefits for workers—tin parachutes to match executive golden parachutes—which turn out to be nothing but take-over defenses. We may have a new picture of what we want from business, yet we certainly don't have the full reality. Yet if we allow ourselves a flight of optimism, the possibilities are tantalizing. 32

If it's illiteracy we want to tackle, business can help. Dayton Hudson has spent millions on a literacy program, encouraging employees to serve as tutors, and is working to recruit thousands of volunteers at other companies. The New York ad agency of Benton & Bowles put together a public service campaign about literacy—and McGraw-Hill's chairman funded a clearinghouse to handle calls the ads generated. 33

If homelessness is the issue, business can help. Meredith Corporation's *Better Homes & Gardens* has set up a foundation to help homeless families, with a goal of raising ten million dollars from its eight million readers. Meredith also hopes to convince advertisers in areas like home furnishings and building materials to donate both supplies and money. 34

If poverty is the problem, business can help. The South Shore Bank in Chicago is channeling funds into development of its decaying inner-city neighborhood, and has succeeded in sparking a real estate renaissance—with benefits going not to outsiders, but to the largely minority community. IBM has a network of sixty job training centers for disadvantaged youth, and has graduated more than fourteen thousand students—with a job placement record of better than 80 percent. 35

There's no denying that we live in a troubled world, and that the corporate community has had a hand in creating those troubles. With its soiled past and its powerful self-interest, business may never be a wholly reliable force for the public good. But in a search for the most powerful tool for 36 social change in the world, the most effective lever available might just turn out to be business. It may be an unavoidable truth: business is our last best hope.

For Study and Discussion

QUESTIONS FOR RESPONSE

1. What attitudes, positive or negative, do you have toward corporations in America today? What do you think are the sources of those attitudes?
2. If you have ever held a job with a large business corporation—for example, Sears, Burger King, Walmart, or some hotel chain—what evidence have you found that a new business paradigm (model) may exist that encourages respect for the workers and concern for the community? What are some examples?

QUESTIONS ABOUT PURPOSE

1. As the publisher of the magazine *Business Ethics,* Kelly has an interest in making American businesses more ethical and more involved in their communities. What specific activities does she suggest that a business executive could sponsor if he or she wanted to improve the community?
2. What new knowledge about business and industry does Kelly want to communicate to her nonbusiness readers?

QUESTIONS ABOUT AUDIENCE

1. Kelly's original audience was the readers of *Utne,* a relatively small magazine with strong appeal to educated and well-informed readers. What elements in the essay reveal that she is writing for this kind of audience?
2. What different reactions to this essay would you expect from an audience of college freshmen and an audience made up of subscribers to Kelly's magazine, *Business Ethics*?

QUESTIONS ABOUT STRATEGIES

1. Why does Kelly start out with a strong criticism of a group she is going to praise?
2. What kind of evidence does Kelly assemble to support her claim that corporate America is becoming more ethical and more community-minded? How convincing do you find her evidence?

QUESTIONS FOR DISCUSSION

1. What groups do you know of among consumer advocates or community activists who are working to make businesses more active in community affairs and environmental projects? What are those groups' specific goals for your community?
2. What seems to you to be the best way to encourage local or national businesses to take an active role in solving social problems? Where would be a good place to start?

ROBERT REICH

Robert Reich was born in 1946 in Scranton, Pennsylvania, and was educated at Dartmouth College, Oxford University, and Yale University. He has worked as assistant to the solicitor general of the United States during the Ford administration and as director of policy planning for the Federal Trade Commission in the Carter administration. He currently serves as professor of economics at the Kennedy School of Government, Harvard University. His books on various aspects of political economics include *Industrial Policy for America: Is It Needed?* (1983), *Next American Frontier* (1984), *Education and the Next Economy* (1988), and *Work of Nations: Preparing Ourselves for the Twenty-first Century* (1991). In "Secession of the Successful," reprinted from *The New York Times Magazine,* Reich argues that Americans in the top income brackets are "quietly seceding from the rest of the nation."

Secession of the Successful

The idea of "community" has always held a special attraction for Americans. In a 1984 speech, President Ronald Reagan celebrated America's "bedrock"—"its communities where neighbors help one another, where families bring up kids together, where American values are born." Gov. Mario M. Cuomo of New York, with a very different political leaning, has been almost as lyrical. "Community . . . is the reality on which our national life has been founded," he said in 1987. 1

There is only one problem with this picture. Most Americans no longer live in traditional communities. They live in suburban subdivisions bordered by highways and sprinkled with shopping malls, or in tony condominiums and residen- 2 tial clusters, or in ramshackle apartment buildings and housing projects. Most of them commute to work and socialize on some basis other than geographic proximity. And most people pick up and move to a different neighborhood every five years or so.

But Americans generally have one thing in common with their neighbors: they have similar incomes. And that simple fact lies at the heart of the new community. This means that their educational backgrounds are likely to be similar, that they pay roughly the same in taxes, and that they indulge in the same consumer impulses. "Tell me someone's ZIP code," the founder of a direct-mail company once bragged, "and I can predict what they eat, drink, drive—even think." 3

Americans who own their homes usually share one political cause with their neighbors: a near obsessive concern with maintaining or upgrading property values. And this common interest is responsible for much of what has brought neighbors together in recent years. Complete strangers, although they may live on the same street or in the same condominium complex, suddenly feel intense solidarity when it is rumored that low-income housing will be constructed in their midst or that a poorer school district will be consolidated with their own. 4

The renewed emphasis on "community" in American life has justified and legitimized these economic enclaves. If generosity and solidarity end at the border of similarly valued properties, then the most fortunate can be virtuous citizens at little cost. Since most people in one neighborhood or town are equally well off, there is no cause for a guilty conscience. If inhabitants of another area are poorer, let them look to one another. Why should *we* pay for *their* schools? 5

So the argument goes, without acknowledging that the critical assumption has already been made: "we" and "they" belong to fundamentally different communities. Through such reasoning, it has become possible to maintain a self-image of generosity toward, and solidarity with, one's "community" without bearing any responsibility to "them"—the other "community." 6

America's high earners—the fortunate top fifth—thus feel increasingly justified in paying only what is necessary to ensure that everyone in their community is sufficiently well educated and has access to the public services they need to succeed. 7

Last year, the top fifth of working Americans took home more money than the other four-fifths put together—the highest portion in postwar history. These high earners will relinquish somewhat more of their income to the Federal Government this year than in 1990 as a result of last fall's tax changes, although considerably less than in the late 1970's, when the tax code was more progressive. But the continuing debate over whether the wealthy are paying their fair share of taxes obscures a larger issue, with more profound implications for America: the fortunate fifth is quietly seceding from the rest of the nation. 8

This is occurring gradually, without much awareness by members of the top group—or, for that matter, by anyone else. And the Government is speeding this process as Washington shifts responsibility for many public services to state and local governments. 9

The secession is taking several forms. In many cities and towns, the wealthy have in effect withdrawn their dollars from the support of public spaces and institutions shared by all and dedicated the savings to their own private services. As public parks and playgrounds deteriorate, there is a proliferation of private health clubs, golf clubs, tennis clubs, skating clubs and every other type of recreational association in which costs are shared among members. Condominiums and the omnipresent residential communities dun their members to undertake work that financially strapped local governments can no longer afford to do well—maintaining roads, mending sidewalks, pruning trees, repairing street lights, cleaning swimming pools, paying for lifeguards and, notably, hiring security guards to protect life and property. (The number of private security guards in the United States now exceeds the number of public police officers.) 10

Of course, wealthier Americans have been withdrawing into their own neighborhoods and clubs for generations. But the new secession is more dramatic because the highest earners now inhabit a different economy from other Americans. The new elite is linked by jet, modem, fax, satellite and fiber-optic cable to the great commercial and recreational centers of the world, but it is not particularly connected to the rest of the nation. 11

That is because the work this group does is becoming less tied to the activities of other Americans. Most of their jobs consist of analyzing and manipulating symbols—words, numbers or visual images. Among the most prominent of these "symbolic analysts" are management consultants, lawyers, software and design engineers, research scientists, corporate executives, financial advisers, strategic planners, advertising executives, television and movie producers, and other workers whose job titles include terms like "strategy," "planning," "consultant," "policy," "resources" or "engineer." 12

These workers typically spend long hours in meetings or on the telephone and even longer hours in planes or hotels—advising, making presentations, giving briefings and making deals. Periodically, they issue reports, plans, designs, drafts, briefs, blueprints, analyses, memorandums, layouts, renderings, scripts or projections. In contrast with people whose jobs tend to be tedious and repetitive, symbolic analysts find their work varied and intellectually challenging. In fact, the work is often enjoyable. 13

These symbolic analysts are in ever greater demand in a world market that places an increasing value on identifying and solving problems. Requests for their software designs, financial advice or engineering blueprints come from all parts of the globe. This largely explains why most (but by no means all) symbolic analysts have become wealthier, even as the ever-growing worldwide supply of unskilled labor continues to depress the wages of other Americans. 14

Successful Americans have not completely disengaged themselves from the lives of their less fortunate compatriots. 15

Some devote substantial resources and energies to helping the rest of society, not through their tax payments, but through voluntary efforts. "Generosity is a reflection of what one does with his or her resources—and not what he or she advocates the government do with everyone's money," Ronald Reagan said in 1984.

The argument is fair enough. Government is not the only device for redistributing wealth. In his speech accepting the Presidential nomination at the Republican National Convention in 1988, George Bush said that the real magnanimity of America was to be found in a "brilliant diversity" of private charities, "spread like stars, like a thousand points of light in a broad and peaceful sky." 16

No nation congratulates itself more enthusiastically on its charitable acts than America: none engages in a greater number of charity balls, bake sales, benefit auctions and border-to-border hand holdings for good causes. Much of this is sincerely motivated and admirable. 17

But close examination reveals that many of these acts of benevolence do not help the needy. Particularly suspect is the private giving of those in the top income-tax bracket. Studies have revealed that their largess does not flow mainly to social services for the poor—to better schools, health clinics or recreational centers. Instead, most voluntary contributions of wealthy Americans go to the places and institutions that entertain, inspire, cure or educate wealthy Americans—art museums, opera houses, theaters, orchestras, ballet companies, private hospitals and elite universities. 18

And even these charitable contributions are relatively skimpy. Last year, American households with incomes of less than $10,000 gave an average of 3.3 percent of their earnings to charity or to a religious organization; those making more than $100,000 a year gave only 2.9 percent. After the 1986 tax-code overhaul reduced the benefits of charitable giving, the very rich became even stingier. According to Internal Revenue Service data, taxpayers earning $500,000 or more slashed their average donations to $16,062 in 1988 from $47,432 in 1980. 19

Corporate philanthropy is following the same general pattern. In recent years, the largest American corporations have been sounding the alarm about the nation's fast deteriorating primary and secondary schools. Few are more eloquent and impassioned about the need for better schools than American executives. "How well we educate all of our children will determine our competitiveness globally, and our economic health domestically, and our communities' character and vitality," said a report of The Business Roundtable, a New York-based association of top executives. 20

Accordingly, there are numerous "partnerships" between corporations and public schools: scholarships for poor children qualified to attend college, and programs in which businesses adopt individual schools by making conspicuous donations of computers, books, and, on occasion, even money. That such activities are loudly touted by corporate public relations staffs should not detract from the good they do. 21

Despite the hoopla, business donations to education and charitable causes actually tapered off markedly in the 1980's, even as the economy boomed. In the 1970's, corporate giving to education jumped an average of 15 percent a year. In 1990, however, giving was only 5 percent over that in 1989; in 1989 it was 3 percent over 1988. Moreover, most of this money goes to colleges and universities—in particular, to the alma maters of symbolic analysts, who expect their children and grandchildren to follow in their footsteps. Only 1.5 percent of corporate giving in the late 1980's was to public primary and secondary schools. 22

Notably, these contributions have been smaller than the amounts corporations are receiving from states and communities in the form of subsidies or tax breaks. Companies are quietly procuring such deals by threatening to move their operations—and jobs—to places around the world with a more congenial tax climate. The paradoxical result has been even less corporate revenue to spend on schools and other community services than before. The executives of General Motors, for example, who have been among the loudest to proclaim the need for better schools, have also been among 23 the most relentless in pursuing local tax abatements and in challenging their tax assessments. G.M.'s successful efforts to reduce its taxes in North Tarrytown, N.Y., where the company has had a factory since 1914, cut local revenues by $1 million in 1990, part of a larger shortfall that forced the town to lay off scores of teachers.

The secession of the fortunate fifth has been most apparent in how and where they have chosen to work and live. In effect, most of America's large urban centers have splintered into two separate cities. One is composed of those whose symbolic and analytic services are linked to the world economy. The other consists of local service workers—custodians, security guards, taxi drivers, clerical aides, parking attendants, sales people, restaurant employees—whose jobs are dependent on the symbolic analysts. Few blue-collar manufacturing workers remain in American cities. Between 1953 and 1984, for example, New York City lost about 600,000 factory jobs; in the same interval, it added about 700,000 jobs for symbolic analysts and service workers. 24

The separation of symbolic analysts from local service workers within cities has been reinforced in several ways. Most large cities now possess two school systems—a private one for the children of the top-earning group and a public one for the children of service workers, the remaining blue-collar workers and the unemployed. Symbolic analysts spend considerable time and energy insuring that their children gain entrance to good private schools, and then small fortunes keeping them there—dollars that under a more progressive tax code might finance better public education. 25

People with high incomes live, shop and work within areas of cities that, if not beautiful, are at least esthetically tolerable and reasonably safe; precincts not meeting these minimum standards of charm and security have been left to the less fortunate. 26

Here again, symbolic analysts have pooled their resources to the exclusive benefit of themselves. Public funds have been spent in earnest on downtown "revitalization" projects, en- 27 tailing the construction of clusters of post-modern office buildings (complete with fiber-optic cables, private branch exchanges, satellite dishes and other communications equipment linking them to the rest of the world), multilevel parking garages, hotels with glass-enclosed atriums, upscale shopping plazas and galleries, theaters, convention centers and luxury condominiums.

Ideally, these complexes are entirely self-contained, with air-conditioned walkways linking residences, businesses and recreational space. The lucky resident is able to shop, work and attend the theater without risking direct contact with the outside world—that is, the other city. 28

Carrying the principle a step further, several cities have begun authorizing property owners in certain affluent districts to assess a surtax on local residents and businesses for amenities unavailable to other urban residents, services like extra garbage collections, street cleaning and security. One such New York district, between 38th and 48th Streets and Second and Fifth Avenues, raised $4.7 million from its residents in 1989, of which $1 million underwrote a private force of uniformed guards and plainclothes investigators. The new community of people with like incomes and with the power to tax and enforce the law is thus becoming a separate city within the city. 29

When not living in urban enclaves, symbolic analysts are increasingly congregating in suburbs and exurbs where corporate headquarters have been relocated, research parks have been created, and where bucolic universities have spawned entrepreneurial ventures. Among the most desirable of such locations are Princeton, N.J.; northern Westchester and Putnam Counties in New York; Palo Alto, Calif.; Austin, Tex.; Bethesda, Md., and Raleigh-Durham, N.C. 30

Engineers and strategists of American auto companies, for example, do not live in Flint or Saginaw, Mich., where the blue-collar workers reside; they cluster in their own towns of Troy, Warren, and Auburn Hills. Likewise, the vast majority of the financial specialists, lawyers and executives working for the insurance companies of Hartford would never 31 consider living there; after all, Hartford is the nation's fourth-poorest city. Instead, they flock to Windsor, Middlebury, West Hartford and other towns that are among the wealthiest in the country.

This trend, too, has been growing for decades. But technology has accelerated it. Today's symbolic analysts linked directly to the rest of the globe can choose to live and work in the most pastoral of settings. 32

The secession has been encouraged by the Federal Government. For the last decade, Washington has in effect shifted responsibility for many public services to local governments. At their peak, Federal grants made up 25 percent of state and local spending in the late 1970's. Today, the Federal share has dwindled to 17 percent. Direct aid to local governments, in the form of programs introduced in the Johnson and Nixon Administrations, has been the hardest hit by budget cuts. In the 1980's, Federal dollars for clean water, job training and transfers, low-income housing, sewage treatment and garbage disposal shrank by some $50 billion a year, and Washington's share of spending on local transit declined by 50 percent. (The Bush Administration has proposed that states and localities take on even more of the costs of building and maintaining roads, and wants to cut Federal aid for mass transit.) In 1990, New York City received only 9.6 percent of all its revenue from the Federal Government, compared with 16 percent in 1981. 33

States have quickly transferred many of these new expenses to fiscally strapped cities and towns, with a result that by the start of the 1990's, localities were bearing more than half of the costs of water and sewage, roads, parks, welfare and public schools. In New York State, the local communities' share has risen to about 75 percent of these costs. 34

Cities and towns with affluent inhabitants can bear these burdens relatively easily. Poorer ones, faced with the twin problems of lower incomes and greater demand for social services, have had far more difficulty. And as the gap between the richest and poorest communities has widened, the shift in responsibility for public services to cities and towns has 35

functioned as another means of relieving wealthier Americans of the cost of aiding less fortunate citizens.

The result has been a growing inequality in basic social and community services. While the city tax rate in Philadelphia, for example, is about triple that of communities around it, the suburbs enjoy far better schools, hospitals, recreation and police protection. Eighty-five percent of the richest families in the greater Philadelphia area live outside the city limits, and 80 percent of the region's poorest live inside. The quality of a city's infrastructure—roads, bridges, sewage, water treatment—is likewise related to the average income of its inhabitants. 36

The growing inequality in government services has been most apparent in the public schools. The Federal Government's share of the costs of primary and secondary education has dwindled to about 6 percent. The bulk of the cost is divided about equally between the states and local school districts. States with a higher concentration of wealthy residents can afford to spend more on their schools than other states. In 1989, the average public-school teacher in Arkansas, for example, received $21,700; in Connecticut, $37,300. 37

Even among adjoining suburban towns in the same state the differences can be quite large. Consider three Boston-area communities located within minutes of one another. All are predominantly white, and most residents within each town earn about the same as their neighbors. But the disparity of incomes between towns is substantial. 38

Belmont, northwest of Boston, is inhabited mainly by symbolic analysts and their families. In 1988, the average teacher in its public schools earned $36,100. Only 3 percent of Belmont's 18-year-olds dropped out of high school, and more than 80 percent of graduating seniors chose to go on to a four-year college. 39

Just east of Belmont is Somerville, most of whose residents are low-wage service workers. In 1988, the average Somerville teacher earned $29,400. A third of the town's 18-year-olds did not finish high school, and fewer than a third planned to attend college. 40

Chelsea, across the Mystic River from Somerville, is the poorest of the three towns. Most of its inhabitants are unskilled, and many are unemployed or only employed part time. The average teacher in Chelsea, facing tougher educational challenges than his or her counterparts in Belmont, earned $26,200 in 1988, almost a third less than the average teacher in the more affluent town just a few miles away. More than half of Chelsea's 18-year-olds did not graduate from high school, and only 10 percent planned to attend college. 41

Similar disparities can be found all over the nation. Students at Highland Park High School in a wealthy suburb of Dallas, for example, enjoy a campus with a planetarium, indoor swimming pool, closed-circuit television studio and state-of-the-art science laboratory. Highland Park spends about $6,000 a year to educate each student. This is almost twice that spent per pupil by the towns of Wilmer and Hutchins in southern Dallas County. According to Texas education officials, the richest school district in the state spends $19,300 a year per pupil; its poorest, $2,100 a year. 42

The courts have become involved in trying to repair such imbalances, but the issues are not open to easy judicial remedy. 43

The four-fifths of Americans left in the wake of the secession of the fortunate fifth include many poor blacks, but racial exclusion is neither the primary motive for the separation nor a necessary consequence. Lower-income whites are similarly excluded, and high-income black symbolic analysts are often welcomed. The segregation is economic rather than racial, although economically motivated separation often results in *de facto* racial segregation. Where courts have found a pattern of racially motivated segregation, it usually has involved lower-income white communities bordering on lower-income black neighborhoods. 44

In states where courts have ordered equalized state spending in school districts, the vast differences in a town's property values—and thus local tax revenues—continue to result in substantial inequities. Where courts or state governments 45 have tried to impose limits on what affluent communities can pay their teachers, not a few parents in upscale towns have simply removed their children from the public schools and applied the money they might otherwise have willingly paid in higher taxes to private school tuitions instead. And, of course, even if state-wide expenditures were better equalized, poorer states would continue to be at a substantial disadvantage.

In all these ways, the gap between America's symbolic 46
analysts and everyone else is widening into a chasm. Their secession from the rest of the population raises fundamental questions about the future of American society. In the new global economy—in which money, technologies and corporations cross borders effortlessly—a citizen's standard of living depends more and more on skills and insights, and on the infrastructure needed to link these abilities to the rest of the world. But the most skilled and insightful Americans, who are already positioned to thrive in the world market, are now able to slip the bonds of national allegiance, and by so doing disengage themselves from their less favored fellows. The stark political challenge in the decades ahead will be to reaffirm that, even though America is no longer a separate and distinct economy, it is still a society whose members have abiding obligations to one another.

For Study and Discussion

QUESTIONS FOR RESPONSE

1. Approximately where do you think you and your family fit into the income scale Reich uses? (If your family income is more than $65,000 a year, you're in the top 20 percent.) If you're in the top 20 percent, how do you react to Reich's assertions about that group? If you're in the lower 80 percent, how justified do you think Reich's claims are?
2. Which statistics in Reich's economic analysis made the greatest impression on you—that those in the top one-fifth take home

more money than the rest combined, that those with incomes under $10,000 give a higher percentage of their incomes to charity than those with incomes over $100,000, that there are more security guards than public police officers in the United States, or his figures about the disparity of spending on schools and teachers between rich school districts and poor ones? Why do you think you reacted this way?

QUESTIONS ABOUT PURPOSE

1. What specific changes in their behavior do you think Reich wants affluent Americans to agree to? What changes in government policy does he want to see?
2. Reich was an economic adviser in the 1992 presidential campaign. What points in this essay would be important for a political candidate?

QUESTIONS ABOUT AUDIENCE

1. Reich first published this essay in the magazine section of *The New York Times,* one of the nation's most prestigious and influential papers. How would you characterize the readers of this publication? Where do you think they would fall on his economic scale?
2. What group of readers beyond those of *The New York Times* do you think Reich most wants to reach with his message? Why?

QUESTIONS ABOUT STRATEGIES

1. What kind of arguments does Reich use to get his readers to accept this disturbing picture of our society? Identify two or three and give examples.
2. Although Reich is a professor of political economics, a complex and abstract discipline, his prose style is easy to read and understand. How does Reich make his essay readable and interesting to a nonacademic audience?

QUESTIONS FOR DISCUSSION

1. Identify what you feel to be your own community. How much community spirit does it have? What elements unite it? How

much support do you think community members give each other?

2. What examples can you think of that illustrate the "we/them" mentality that Reich claims is common among the economic top 20 percent of U.S. citizens? How could that attitude be changed?

LYNNE SHARON SCHWARTZ

Lynne Sharon Schwartz was born in 1939 in New York City and was educated at Barnard College, Bryn Mawr College, and New York University. She has worked as an editor for *Writer,* as a writer for Operation Open City (a civil rights–fair housing operation), and as a professor of English at Hunter College, Columbia University, and Rice University. Her books include *Rough Strife* (1980), *Balancing Acts* (1981), *Disturbances in the Field* (1983), *We Are Talking About Homes: A Great University Against Its Neighbors* (1985), and *Leaving Brooklyn* (1989). She has contributed stories, articles, translations, and reviews to literary journals and popular magazines such as *Transatlantic Review, Ploughshares, New York Times Book Review,* and *Redbook.* In "Beggaring Our Better Selves," reprinted from *Harper's,* Schwartz argues that because today's beggars "baffle" us, we "harden our hearts" into indifference.

Beggaring Our Better Selves

A family legend: New York, the Bowery, early 1950s, a man comes up to my father and asks for money for something to eat. What most Bowery beggars really want is a drink, my father knows. But food is healthier. "You're hungry? Okay, come on, I'll buy you lunch." And he does. 1

The story was meant to be touching—how generous my father was with time, money, wisdom—and for a long time I found it so. I could hear my father's voice, like the snapping of a finger—"Come on, I'll buy you lunch"—and picture the swift, peremptory jerk of his head in the direction of the nearest restaurant, a simple but decent place. How gallantly he led the beggar to a table, appropriating two illustrated 2 menus coated in plastic and handing him one. "Anything you like," he would say rather grandly. Did the beggar order a substantial meal, steaming pot roast nestled in simmered carrots and onions, or something more austere, like an egg salad sandwich?

Knowing my father, I assumed they did not eat in silence. 3
Did he use the opportunity to expound on his political views, making provocative statements, raising his voice and blood pressure? And was the beggar gregarious, eager to tell his tale of adversity, or taciturn, paying for the meal with his only abundant possession, his endurance?

Did my father finally dab suavely at his mustache, toss 4
down his napkin, and extend his hand for a gentlemanly parting? And how did the beggar respond to that? Alas, the story was never told as I would have liked to hear it, with each nuance of gesture and dialogue, setting and timing, the shifting underpinnings of emotion and small stirrings of heart and mind as revealed in the face and voice, all of which, to me, *were* the story, as opposed to the bare events. Still, it was a good story, despite its ambiguities.

Until many years later, that is, when I told it to my friend 5
A. She was aghast. My father's act showed the worst kind of condescension, she informed me heatedly. Giving was his free choice, but how to spend the gift was the beggar's choice. Otherwise giving is an abuse of power. An ego trip.

A. had a good case, and I was downcast, my moment of 6
nostalgia ruined. Yet wasn't my father's behavior valid in his life and times? His own scramble for success proved that he knew how to go about things; doing good, by his lights, was scattering abroad his earned knowledge. How could I scorn him when I myself would not have given my time to an unappealing stranger? True, A. might have done it. She would have taken him to a bar, I thought bitterly.

Long after my father's episode, I happened to see, from a 7
third-floor window, another lunch given away on the Bowery. A raggedy grizzled man shuffled northward across Delancey Street. A young black woman wearing shorts and a halter and biting into a frankfurter crossed in the opposite

direction. When they met, he held out his hand, palm up. Barely breaking stride—for the light was changing and four lanes of impatient traffic would instantly engulf them—she handed him the half-eaten frankfurter. Between the north and south corners of Delancey Street the frankfurter passed from one pair of lips to another, as the milk from Rose of Sharon's breast passed to the lips of the dying man in *The Grapes of Wrath*.

Now, of course, our streets are so thick with beggars that people of my father's virtuous persuasion could take a beggar to lunch every day, ten times a day, incensing the politically correct. Or, in keeping with "lite" aesthetics, they might follow B.'s strategy: Overcome by the clamor of the hungry, she has begun fixing daily packets of sandwiches—whatever she herself is having for lunch—and hands out the neat tinfoil squares to whoever asks. "What's in it today?" one of her regulars inquired. "Peanut butter and jelly." He scowled, hesitated, but in the end accepted it indulgently, as if *she* were the beggar, asking to be relieved of the burden of good fortune. 8

Indeed, social roles have become so fluid that askers and givers change places with the agility of partners at a square dance. As the numbers of beggars increased, C., like B., came to loathe the impotence of his assigned role. No more awkward doling out of futile coins, he decided. He would give a significant sum every couple of weeks, like paying a bill, a sum that might make a real, if temporary, difference in a beggar's life. No class-bound judgments either: He wouldn't choose the apparently deserving or speculate on how the money might be spent. A gratuitous act, a declaration of freedom from the conventional etiquette of beggardom. The first time he tried it, the beggar looked at the bill handed to him, then up at C. "But this is twenty dollars." "Yes, I know," said C. "Hey, this is terrific! Come on, I'll take you to lunch." 9

Some hold that begging is a job, not one which anyone would aspire to but which a share of the population regularly 10 does, through family tradition, lack of drive or opportunity, possibly even natural talent. George Orwell puts it best in *Down and Out in Paris and London:*

> 11 *There is no* essential *difference between a beggar's livelihood and that of numberless respectable people. Beggars do not work, it is said; but then, what is* work? *A navvy works by swinging a pick. An accountant works by adding up figures. A beggar works by standing out of doors in all weathers and getting varicose veins, chronic bronchitis, etc. It is a trade like any other; quite useless, of course—but, then, many reputable trades are quite useless . . . A beggar . . . has not, more than most modern people, sold his honour; he has merely made the mistake of choosing a trade at which it is impossible to grow rich.*

12 But in the United States begging evokes too much shock and horror ever to be accepted as a career. The pursuit of happiness works as a command as well as a right, and part of the pursuit is ambition, labor, sweat. Then there is the famous liberal guilt at being privileged in a supposedly classless society. Above all, our horror is attached to a certain pride: We are enlightened enough to be horrified at beggary, if not enough to do anything significant about it.

13 Before the First World War, according to my mother's sentimental stories, hoboes turning up on her parents' doorstep were given lunch in exchange for sweeping the yard or hauling the garbage—a fairly clear and guilt-free transaction compared with begging and giving. These days few city people are at home to offer lunch—they're out doing what Orwell so disparagingly calls "work"—while those who are would hardly open their doors to a stranger.

14 Today's beggars baffle us. Unlike the working poor, they haven't always been with us, not lining the streets, at any rate, in such a vast and variegated array: from bedraggled to shabbily decent to casually hip; sick or drugged-out to robust; pathetic to friendly to arrogant.

15 To confuse matters further, not all beggars see their situ-

ation in an Orwellian light, as my friend D.'s experience illustrates. The opposite of shy, D. can say with impunity virtually anything to anybody. She marches up to the regular on her street corner and asks, "Look here, why can't a healthy, strapping young man like you get a job?" He talks about the sad state of the job market, how demoralizing it is to be turned away. "Look here," says D., undaunted, very much like my father in her certainty of what is right, "we've all had some bad luck with jobs. You've got to get back in there and keep trying." So the conversation goes. And, as in my father's time, enduring it is how the beggar earns his keep. When he feels he's put in enough time for the money, he says, "Look here, I'll decide when the vacation is over."

The beggars become an index of our state of affairs: Who 16
we are is revealed in our response. We range from open-handed A., who sets forth staunchly with a pocketful of change and gives democratically to all—"If they're desperate enough to ask . . ."—to otherwise kindly Z., who never gives because she suspects every beggar is making a fool of her. To give, she feels, is to be taken.

In themselves, A. and Z. do not represent extremes of 17
generosity and meanness, wealth and poverty, or political left and right. A. may have more money, but Z. is far from penury. Nor is she stingy and insensitive; a therapist working in a social agency, she gives at the office, as it were. What can be read from their actions is their degree of suspicion of the world and safety in it, their reflexive response to the unexpected and unwelcome. Maybe their whole psychic structure could be discovered, had we enough data.

On my way to the supermarket recently I saw a familiar 18
beggar approach—a tall, slender, woebegone man with watery eyes, graying hair, and neat gray clothes, whose beat was slightly to the south. Immediately came the usual and wearisome chain of thoughts. Do I have any change on me? Do I feel like it today? How am I today anyway, that is, how firm is my place in the world?—a question usually reserved for the murky insomniac hours. The unsettling thing about beggars is that, unless one has a very thick skin or, like A.

and Z., a strict policy, their presence compels such questions many times a day. Like public clocks that drive compulsives to check their watches, beggars make us check our inner dials of plenitude or neediness, well-being or instability. The readings determine whether and what we give.

In the midst of my reckonings, the man passed me by without even an acknowledgment. Imagine! I was just another face in the crowd. He wasn't soliciting because he wasn't yet at work. Why assume begging is a twenty-four-hour-a-day job any more than plumbing or typing? Any more an identity than grocer or engineer? Maybe I assume it because quite a few beggars in mufti—spiffy, sprightly—stroll past with such a gracious good morning that I'm moved to answer in kind. Then, with my attention snagged, comes the touch, a mutual joke at my expense: Ha, ha, and you thought I was only being friendly. 19

Some in rags, and some in tags. And one in a velvet gown. 20

It didn't begin, this age of beggary, on an appointed day, the way Errol Flynn in an old movie announced with a flourish of his sword the opening thrust of the Thirty Years' War, but sneaked up some seven or eight years ago, just as the cult of money was enjoying a passionate revival. At first people were appalled. Not here; this wasn't Calcutta, after all. There was sympathy, naturally. We stared uneasily, clucked somberly, catalogued: young, old, black, white, male, female. Sickly and strong. Addicts? Hard to tell. In rags and tags and velvet gowns. 21

There was curiosity, too. The beggars offered a new genre of performance art amid other lively street phenomena, and we the audience compared offerings, whipped up impromptu reviews around our dinner tables. As with any art form, early samples ranged from the banal—I'm not really a beggar but an unemployed carpenter with five hungry children—to the memorable—pardon my odor but I have no place to take a shower like you folks. Successful beggars, like successful stand-up comics, must display uniqueness of personality in a few swift, arresting strokes. Their stories require a certain narrative flair. Verisimilitude aside, we treasure sheer inventiveness. 22

A justly renowned beggar works the rowdy nocturnal subway cars returning from New York's Shea Stadium during the baseball season. He enters ominously, carrying a tarnished trumpet blotched with holes. He brings it to his lips; the sound that emerges is a Dantean assault. The passengers blink and shudder, like romping children startled by an ogre. At last he mercifully lowers the trumpet and announces genially, "I'm not going to stop till you folks give me some money." A tense moment? Not at all. The crowd laughs, and gives. A good-humored crowd, they've paid for their tickets and beer and hot dogs and subway ride; they'll shell out for peace too, and for a laugh. It's part of the price of the sportive outing, a surtax. By some mad urban alchemy it is acceptable to be assailed by this grotesque noise and have to pay to make it stop. He plays a few more measures, goading the recalcitrant, then moves on to the next car to repeat the performance, becoming part of the legend of the city, O splendiferous city full of assaults and of relief, where you pay for both. 23

Our reactions followed a predictable trajectory. As the initial surprise wore off along with the entertainment value, as we got used to seeing beggars everywhere (but not for long, surely—whatever political glitch brought them out would soon be repaired), our interest became more defined. Refined. We found we have *tastes* in beggars as in everything else. E. will not give to those who look young and healthy, for why are they not out hustling for a living as he is? F. always gives to women because they seem more vulnerable, their lot harder to bear than men's. G. gives only outside his immediate neighborhood so as not to encourage beggars to congregate there, while H., careful of her spiritual integrity, will give only out of genuine sympathy, not to get rid of a nuisance. J. will not give to anyone who comes too close: she has strong feelings about her personal "space" being invaded. K. is too afraid to take out her purse on the street: She views beggars and, in fact, all passersby as potential thieves. 24

L. gives exclusively to those who ask humbly and politely. 25

If he must be solicited and possibly "taken" (shades of Z.), he feels the beggars should at the very least make a pretense of a civil transaction, to save face all around. Anyone claiming his contribution as if by right is out of luck. If L. is not thanked, he will not give again. Sensitive M. prefers not to be thanked. "There but for the grace of God . . . ," she murmurs. She will gladly engage in non-grateful repartee, though, while N., who also shuns gratitude, wants the briefest verbal exchange: He gives willingly but cannot stomach long-winded explanations or autobiography.

Quite unlike O., who must say a few words with his donation and wants a few in return; he needs to act out an ordinary exchange between ordinary people, one of whom happens to be in straitened circumstances. P. went still further: He made friends with a local beggar, learned his story, occasionally met him for coffee, and introduced him around. Now living elsewhere, P. inquires after him and sends news through friends. 26

Q. resists giving when pressured or manipulated—for instance, when beggars act as obsequious doormen at the threshold of banks, an explicit reminder: You have reason to enter a bank while I do not, and what is a bank but the stony emblem of what distinguishes us? R., too, resists urgent pleas but yields to the beggar who with grinning aplomb requests ten dollars for a steak dinner or five hundred for a trip to Hawaii. An epicure, he waits for a beggar worthy of his attentions, a beggar of kindred, subtle sensibility, an accomplice. Then he can forget the mutual mortification. 27

With the passage of time, sympathy and selective appreciation slid into frustration. We had given, we were giving, yet the beggars remained rooted to their posts, holding out the everlasting Styrofoam cups. (S., in an expansive mood, dropped a quarter into a Styrofoam cup and coffee splashed forth.) Our tone, when we spoke of them, was somewhat distraught. 28

So we cast around for reasons to harden our hearts. In all probability, our handouts encouraged the drug trade, crime, and personal degeneration. Shouldn't legitimate beggars avail 29 themselves of social services through official channels? (A. Brechtian notion, given the nature of the services.) One way or another, we tempered generosity with righteousness.

Meanwhile the beggars grew intemperate. No more meek charm and witty eccentricities. Their banter took on a hard edge. A nagging beggar trailed T. until she announced firmly, "Look, I'm having a really bad day. I feel lousy, would you please leave me alone?" "Oh, I'm sorry," he replied. "Anything I can do?" "No thanks, I'll be okay. Just let me alone." "Well, in that case how about a dollar sixty-five for a hamburger?" Caving in, T. fished around and came up with sixty cents. "Here." "But it's not enough," the man said evenly. 30

Irritation took root. We had given and given, surely enough to expiate our blessings. Now could we have our streets back? As if we needed to give only to a certain point, as we need to give taxes or suffer unto the death. In response the beggars became aggressive—after all, they had been asking for as long as we had been giving. They implored, nagged, demanded. They hounded, pursued, and menaced, accepting small change grudgingly, muttering, even shouting their contempt, a form of blackmail, embarrassing us publicly as if we—we!—were the outcasts. Once I had no bills less than five dollars and gave my only coin, a dime, to a sickly young beggar wrapped in a blanket. "You can keep your ten cents, lady," he shouted through the crowd. Maybe he threw it back at me—I didn't turn to look. It would have cost me less to give him a five. 31

As I lugged my crammed shopping cart home, I was stopped by the woebegone man who had earlier failed to recognize me. This time my first thought was atavistic—those stories about hoboes sweeping the porch for a hot lunch. If only he would offer to pull my cart home. Yes, by rights he should earn the money with dignity for a change. But this is not 1910: The social contract has altered, along with the connotations of "rights" and "earn" and "dignity." Whatever tasks I might need done were not his concern. If he noticed at all, chances are he resented my cornucopia on wheels. Or perhaps he prized his freedom from the banality 32 of shopping carts, like the hoboes of legend. I gave him some coins and he drifted past and away—to the bar, to McDonald's, the crack dealer, or his hungry family? We were farther apart than my grandmother and her pre-war vagrants, the distance greater with each step: no common life, no basis for business, between us.

Nowadays we want to pick and choose our stimuli. Sealed cars and windows, shopping malls, suburbs, and retirement communities shut out the natural inevitabilities of weather, noise, dirt, and chaos, while the technology of exclusion is hard at work on pain and death. But the beggars simply will not vanish. And when they are truculent and defy our wishes, we sullenly withhold our aid. In turn, when we deny the full measure of their requests, they withhold their gratitude. 33

In the end the beggars became tiresome, like TV sitcoms. Their plots were always the same, leaning heavily on flashback and ending with the extended cup. We got bored. Soon came boredom's handmaiden: We are indifferent. Yes, a few, like A., still give with a kind of moral fervor. Some try to renovate housing, others work in soup kitchens or hand out used clothing. But no matter what small efforts we make, still the beggars remain. They line the crazed streets, a serpentine fun-house mirror, confounding us, giving us our images *in extremis,* distorting our best instincts, exaggerating our worst. 34

At jarring moments they reflect us all too well. My friend U.'s street is a gathering place for beggars, among them a relentless badgerer. In a vindictive mood, she gave a pittance every few feet but bypassed this least favorite. He chased after her, yelling, "Hey, what about me? I'm a person too!" A cry from the soul. A universal truth that brought U. to a repentant halt. She turned, her hand already burrowing in the grit of her pocket, but the imploring face, the timbre of his plea resounding in her ears, sent a streak of revulsion through her. That endless self-assertion, that merciless need: Why, he was a replica of the inexhaustibly demanding hus- 35 band she was on the point of leaving. She wheeled around and walked on.

I think all the forms of giving, with their elaborate rationales, come down to two modes, the way art can be crudely divided into classic and romantic. We give from a feeling that the beggars are different from us or that they are the same. Social philosopher Philip Slater has written that love of others is what we have left over when self-love has been satisfied. To give from a feeling of plenitude and aloofness adds to our self-satisfaction. To give out of kinship is the more accurate impulse, though, as well as the more raw and painful. 36

I tend to give when feeling least in need, when the world has provided me with my share and maybe more. When I feel neglected, abused, invisible, unloved, and surly—a bit like a beggar myself—I resist. What makes you think I'm any different from you? I want to say. That I have anything to spare, that I don't need help too? Of course my feelings are irrelevant to beggars (though theirs are not irrelevant to me, making for a deeper inequity and unease). They are not asking for my existential well-being but for my spare change, and while my well-being may vary from day to day, I always have spare change. I can afford subtle distinctions. To the beggars, though, money is not metaphor. 37

Just as slavery imprisons masters as well as slaves, beggary beggars us. We are solicited and must solicit in turn, asking that the performances represent the world as we wish it to be, so that our place in it holds steady. We beg the beggars not to jostle too noticeably the abstractions we have constituted in our heads and imprinted on the physical matter around us. 38

Small wonder that beggars are resented. Unlike slaves, they appear to have opted out, gotten away with something, while we earn our bread by the sweat of our brow. And yet they certainly sweat, and also shiver. A paradox. Often we would like not to work either—more than a dash of envy sours our tangled response—but we surely don't want to sweat quite so much. There they outdo us. We imagine what 39 kinds of beggars we would make, as we have idly imagined what kinds of politicians or pitchers or violinists we would make, and shrink from the image. What a relief, then, how glad we are of our lives. The next instant brings a faint needling: But are we living right? Do our lives make sense? Any more than theirs? What do their lives say about our own? The worst suspicion, the one we must not look at too closely, is that our lives and theirs amount to more or less the same thing—sweating, shivering, waiting to die, only some far more comfortably than others. For then we would have to wonder, in more than a glancing way, why as a people we feel no need to remedy this.

Our finely wrought distinctions, from A. to Z., shape a 40
peculiar aesthetics of giving, fittingly traced on the urban fresco of blank or battered faces. The pattern reveals how much we can give without feeling destitute, how far we can unclench our fists without feeling powerless. It becomes a moral fever chart, as morality always underlies aesthetics, showing what we feel ourselves entitled to and how much we feel the entitlement of others falls on us to fulfill. In the end its import is quite simple: Either we are our brothers' keepers or we are not. The government's answer has the virtue of being cruelly clear: It is no one's keeper but its own. Our individual answers are not cruel, only ambiguous. Like aesthetics.

For Study and Discussion

QUESTIONS FOR RESPONSE

1. What is your reaction to street beggars who solicit you for money? Which of the responses Schwartz mentions seems most like yours?
2. To what extent do you agree with Schwartz that how you respond to indigent or homeless people depends on what kind of day you are having?

QUESTIONS ABOUT PURPOSE

1. What new light on our contemporary social problems does Schwartz's essay trigger for you?
2. How, if at all, did Schwartz's analysis of different people's responses to beggars help you to learn something about yourself? In what ways might you behave differently next time you encounter such a person?

QUESTIONS ABOUT AUDIENCE

1. How do you feel about Schwartz's use of "we"? Are you willing to be included when she makes statements like "[we feel] liberal guilt at being privileged," "we cast around for reasons to harden our hearts," and "we [become] indifferent"? Why do you feel this way?
2. Schwartz lives in New York City, a place where most people encounter beggars and homeless people dozens of times a day. If you live in a small town or in a city where the homeless and poor are seldom visible, what impression does this essay make on you? How relevant is it to your life?

QUESTIONS ABOUT STRATEGIES

1. How does Schwartz's opening anecdote about her father and her reflections on it draw the reader into the essay?
2. Schwartz is a novelist as well as an essayist and a teacher. How does her use of narrative and drama contribute to the impact of her essay? Which specific scenes do you find particularly effective?

QUESTIONS FOR DISCUSSION

1. What does Schwartz mean when she says "beggary beggars us"? How do you think you would be affected if you walked among the poor and homeless every day, as she does? What would you do?
2. What specific steps, even if small, do you think should be taken to reduce the number of people begging on city streets? What are the civil and human rights of such people?

ARTHUR C. CLARKE

Arthur C. Clarke was born in 1917 in Somerset, England. Although he was interested in science at an early age, building his first telescope at the age of thirteen, he could not afford a formal university education. He went to work for the British Civil Service as an auditor and became treasurer for the British Interplanetary Society. During World War II, he was a radar specialist with the Royal Air Force. After the war he received educational assistance and entered King's College, University of London, where in two years he graduated with honorary degrees in math and physics. He worked briefly as an editor for *Science Abstracts* but soon devoted his full attention to his lifetime vocation, writing about science. His nonfiction publications, such as *Interplanetary Flight* (1950), *The Exploration of Space* (1951), and *The Making of a Moon* (1957), explain space travel, but his science fiction is concerned with the complex effect of such travel on human emotions and values. His novels include *The Sounds of Mars* (1951) and *Rendezvous with Rama* (1974); and his screenplay for Stanley Kubrick's *2001: A Space Odyssey* is considered a classic. In "The Star," reprinted from *The Nine Billion Names of God* (1955), a Jesuit astronomer tells of a space journey that challenges his faith in God.

The Star

It is three thousand light-years to the Vatican. Once, I believed that space could have no power over faith, just as I believed that the heavens declared the glory of God's 1 handiwork. Now I have seen that handiwork, and my faith is sorely troubled. I stare at the crucifix that hangs on the cabin wall above the Mark VI Computer, and for the first time in my life I wonder if it is no more than an empty symbol.

I have told no one yet, but the truth cannot be concealed. 2
The facts are there for all to read, recorded on the countless miles of magnetic tape and the thousands of photographs we are carrying back to Earth. Other scientists can interpret them as easily as I can, and I am not one who would condone that tampering with the truth which often gave my order a bad name in the olden days.

The crew were already sufficiently depressed: I wonder 3
how they will take this ultimate irony. Few of them have any religious faith, yet they will not relish using this final weapon in their campaign against me—that private, good-natured, but fundamentally serious war which lasted all the way from Earth. It amused them to have a Jesuit as chief astrophysicist: Dr. Chandler, for instance, could never get over it. (Why are medical men such notorious atheists?) Sometimes he would meet me on the observation deck, where the lights are always low so that the stars shine with undiminished glory. He would come up to me in the gloom and stand staring out of the great oval port, while the heavens crawled slowly around us as the ship turned end over end with the residual spin we had never bothered to correct.

"Well, Father," he would say at last, "it goes on forever 4
and forever, and perhaps *Something* made it. But how you can believe that Something has a special interest in us and our miserable little world—that just beats me." Then the argument would start, while the stars and nebulae would swing around us in silent, endless arcs beyond the flawlessly clear plastic of the observation port.

It was, I think, the apparent incongruity of my position 5
that caused most amusement to the crew. In vain I would point to my three papers in the *Astrophysical Journal,* my five in the *Monthly Notices of the Royal Astronomical Society.* I would remind them that my order has long been famous for its

scientific works. We may be few now, but ever since the eighteenth century we have made contributions to astronomy and geophysics out of all proportion to our numbers. Will my report on the Phoenix Nebula end our thousand years of history? It will end, I fear, much more than that.

I do not know who gave the nebula its name, which seems 6
to me a very bad one. If it contains a prophecy, it is one that cannot be verified for several billion years. Even the word "nebula" is misleading: this is a far smaller object than those stupendous clouds of mist—the stuff of unborn stars—that are scattered throughout the length of the Milky Way. On the cosmic scale, indeed, the Phoenix Nebula is a tiny thing—a tenuous shell of gas surrounding a single star.

Or what is left of a star . . . 7

The Rubens engraving of Loyola seems to mock me as it 8
hangs there above the spectrophotometer tracings. What would *you,* Father, have made of this knowledge that has come into my keeping, so far from the little world that was all the Universe you knew? Would your faith have risen to the challenge, as mine has failed to do?

You gaze into the distance, Father, but I have traveled a 9
distance beyond any that you could have imagined when you founded our order a thousand years ago. No other survey ship has been so far from Earth: we are at the very frontiers of the explored Universe. We set out to reach the Phoenix Nebula, we succeeded, and we are homeward bound with our burden of knowledge. I wish I could lift that burden from my shoulders, but I call to you in vain across the centuries and the light-years that lie between us.

On the book you are holding the words are plain to read. 10
AD MAIOREM DEI GLORIAM, the message runs, but it is a message I can no longer believe. Would you still believe it, if you could see what we have found?

We knew, of course, what the Phoenix Nebula was. Every 11
year, in our Galaxy alone, more than a hundred stars explode, blazing for a few hours or days with thousands of times their normal brilliance before they sink back into death and obscurity. Such are the ordinary novae—the commonplace dis-

asters of the Universe. I have recorded the spectrograms and light curves of dozens since I started working at the Lunar Observatory.

But three or four times in every thousand years occurs something beside which even a nova pales into total insignificance. 12

When a star becomes a *supernova,* it may for a little while outshine all the massed suns of the Galaxy. The Chinese astronomers watched this happen in A.D. 1054, not knowing what it was they saw. Five centuries later, in 1572, a supernova blazed in Cassiopeia so brilliantly that it was visible in the daylight sky. There have been three more in the thousand years that have passed since then. 13

Our mission was to visit the remnants of such a catastrophe, to reconstruct the events that led up to it, and, if possible, to learn its cause. We came slowly in through the concentric shells of gas that had been blasted out six thousand years before, yet were expanding still. They were immensely hot, radiating even now with a fierce violet light, but were far too tenuous to do us any damage. When the star had exploded, its outer layers had been driven upward with such speed that they had escaped completely from its gravitational field. Now they formed a hollow shell large enough to engulf a thousand solar systems, and at its center burned the tiny, fantastic object which the star had now become—a White Dwarf, smaller than the Earth, yet weighing a million times as much. 14

The glowing gas shells were all around us, banishing the normal night of interstellar space. We were flying into the center of the cosmic bomb that had detonated millennia ago and whose incandescent fragments were still hurtling apart. The immense scale of the explosion, and the fact that the debris already covered a volume of space many billions of miles across, robbed the scene of any visible movement. It would take decades before the unaided eye could detect any motion in these tortured wisps and eddies of gas, yet the sense of turbulent expansion was overwhelming. 15

We had checked our primary drive hours before, and were 16

drifting slowly toward the fierce little star ahead. Once it had been a sun like our own, but it had squandered in a few hours the energy that should have kept it shining for a million years. Now it was a shrunken miser, hoarding its resources as if trying to make amends for its prodigal youth.

No one seriously expected to find planets. If there had 17
been any before the explosion, they would have been boiled into puffs of vapor, and their substance lost in the greater wreckage of the star itself. But we made the automatic search, as we always do when approaching an unknown sun, and presently we found a single small world circling the star at an immense distance. It must have been the Pluto of this vanished Solar System, orbiting on the frontiers of the night. Too far from the central sun ever to have known life, its remoteness had saved it from the fate of all its lost companions.

The passing fires had seared its rocks and burned away 18
the mantle of frozen gas that must have covered it in the days before the disaster. We landed, and we found the Vault.

Its builders had made sure that we should. The monolithic 19
marker that stood above the entrance was now a fused stump, but even the first long-range photographs told us that here was the work of intelligence. A little later we detected the continent-wide pattern of radioactivity that had been buried in the rock. Even if the pylon above the vault had been destroyed, this would have remained, an immovable and all but eternal beacon calling to the stars. Our ship fell toward this gigantic bull's-eye like an arrow into its target.

The pylon must have been a mile high when it was built, 20
but now it looked like a candle that had melted down into a puddle of wax. It took us a week to drill through the fused rock, since we did not have the proper tools for a task like this. We were astronomers, not archaeologists, but we could improvise. Our original purpose was forgotten: this lonely monument, reared with such labor at the greatest possible distance from the doomed sun, could have only one meaning. A civilization that knew it was about to die had made its last bid for immortality.

It will take us generations to examine all the treasures that were placed in the Vault. They had plenty of time to prepare, for their sun must have given its first warnings many years before the final detonation. Everything that they wished to preserve, all the fruit of their genius, they brought here to this distant world in the days before the end, hoping that some other race would find it and that they would not be utterly forgotten. Would we have done as well, or would we have been too lost in our own misery to give thought to a future we could never see or share? 21

If only they had had a little more time! They could travel freely enough between the planets of their own sun, but they had not yet learned to cross the interstellar gulfs, and the nearest Solar System was a hundred light-years away. Yet even had they possessed the secret of the Transfinite Drive, no more than a few millions could have been saved. Perhaps it was better thus. 22

Even if they had not been so disturbingly human as their sculpture shows, we could not have helped admiring them and grieving for their fate. They left thousands of visual records and the machines for projecting them, together with elaborate pictorial instructions from which it will not be difficult to learn their written language. We have examined many of these records, and brought to life for the first time in six thousand years the warmth and beauty of a civilization that in many ways must have been superior to our own. Perhaps they only showed us the best, and one can hardly blame them. But their worlds were very lovely, and their cities were built with a grace that matches anything of man's. We have watched them at work and play, and listened to their musical speech sounding across the centuries. One scene is still before my eyes—a group of children on a beach of strange blue sand, playing in the waves as children play on Earth. Curious whiplike trees line the shore, and some very large animal is wading in the shallows yet attracting no attention at all. 23

And sinking into the sea, still warm and friendly and life-giving, is the sun that will soon turn traitor and obliterate all this innocent happiness. 24

Perhaps if we had not been so far from home and so 25
vulnerable to loneliness, we should not have been so deeply moved. Many of us had seen the ruins of ancient civilizations on other worlds, but they had never affected us so profoundly. This tragedy was unique. It is one thing for a race to fail and die, as nations and cultures have done on Earth. But to be destroyed so completely in the full flower of its achievement, leaving no survivors—how could that be reconciled with the mercy of God?

My colleagues have asked me that, and I have given what 26
answers I can. Perhaps you could have done better, Father Loyola, but I have found nothing in the *Exercitia Spiritualia* that helps me here. They were not an evil people: I do not know what gods they worshiped, if indeed they worshiped any. But I have looked back at them across the centuries, and have watched while the loveliness they used their last strength to preserve was brought forth again into the light of their shrunken sun. They could have taught us much: why were they destroyed?

I know the answers that my colleagues will give when 27
they get back to Earth. They will say that the Universe has no purpose and no plan, that since a hundred suns explode every year in our Galaxy, at this very moment some race is dying in the depths of space. Whether that race has done good or evil during its lifetime will make no difference in the end: there is no divine justice, for there is no God.

Yet, of course, what we have seen proves nothing of the 28
sort. Anyone who argues thus is being swayed by emotion, not logic. God has no need to justify His actions to man. He who built the Universe can destroy it when He chooses. It is arrogance—it is perilously near blasphemy—for us to say what He may or may not do.

This I could have accepted, hard though it is to look upon 29
whole worlds and peoples thrown into the furnace. But there comes a point when even the deepest faith must falter, and now, as I look at the calculations lying before me, I know I have reached that point at last.

We could not tell, before we reached the nebula, how long 30
ago the explosion took place. Now, from the astronomical

evidence and the record in the rocks of that one surviving planet, I have been able to date it very exactly. I know in what year the light of this colossal conflagration reached our Earth. I know how brilliantly the supernova whose corpse now dwindles behind our speeding ship once shone in terrestrial skies. I know how it must have blazed low in the east before sunrise, like a beacon in that oriental dawn.

There can be no reasonable doubt: the ancient mystery is 31
solved at last. Yet, oh God, there were so many stars you could have used. What was the need to give these people to the fire, that the symbol of their passing might shine above Bethlehem?

COMMENT ON "THE STAR"

The distressed narrator of this story is a Jesuit scientist who, on the basis of evidence that he cannot refute professionally or ethically, finds himself forced to acknowledge a scientific discovery that he fears may destroy his religious faith, the rock of his very existence. Two arguments are going on in the story. The first is a vocal one between the Jesuit and the crew, particularly a medical doctor who represents the traditional scientific view that although there may be order in the universe, there is no God who takes a special interest in the affairs of humans. The Jesuit represents the argument for faith in God and His concern for humankind. The second argument is the silent one that the Jesuit astrophysicist has seen building as his spaceship penetrated the outer reaches of space to investigate the origins of the Phoenix Nebula. He collects evidence from three sources: from the interstellar space debris that testifies to the explosion of a supernova; from irrefutable evidence left purposefully by a superior, cultured civilization that flourished on a lost planet several thousand years before; and, finally, from the evidence that allows him to calculate the date of the explosion that destroyed that planet. When he puts all the pieces together, the Jesuit sees the conclusion of the second argument. Ironically, it destroys the first argument but almost destroys the Jesuit also. God does indeed take special interest in the affairs of humans; the proof is that the date of the supernova that destroyed the beautiful lost civilization coincides precisely with the Star of Bethlehem announcing the birth of Jesus.

Persuasion and Argument as a Writing Strategy

1. Reread several of the essays in this section and decide which one or two appeal to you most. Then analyze your response to those essays—to their topic, their tone, their vocabulary, their use of personal anecdotes or narratives, and to the kind of arguments the author presented. Why do you think you liked these one or two better than the rest or found them most convincing? What was it about them that appealed to you, a college student, even though you were not the original reader for that essay? Finally, draw a general conclusion about what you think the author or authors have done that made their work effective for you and what lesson you could take for your own writing.
2. Reread "I Have a Dream" by Martin Luther King, Jr.; then consider how King's dreams and hopes for black people compare with the dreams and hopes Shelby Steele expresses in "White Guilt." How are they similar? How are they different? Outline and argue for a development program for college students that would respect the dignity and individuality of black students and help them achieve the goals King envisions in his speech.
3. If you are interested in the welfare and rights of animals, visit your local humane society and see what kind of operation it is running. Talk to the administrators and to some of the citizens who hold nonpaying positions on its board of trustees or as volunteers. Find out what these people see as the chief problems for their society and what they hope to achieve. Then write an editorial for your local newspaper in which you explain to the general public how your humane society operates, what its functions and goals are, and what it does for animals. If you are favorably impressed by the society, argue for the city and the citizens to give it more support. If you are not favorably impressed, argue for changes you think need to be made.
4. Write a persuasive article for either your hometown news-

paper or your campus newspaper in which you try to get a local company or industry to contribute its support to a civic project, either one that exists or one you design. Such a project might be restoring dilapidated homes for people who need housing, sponsoring a literacy project, sponsoring a remodeling project for a public playground, or something similar. Be specific about how the company could help and how it would benefit. You might reread the introduction to this section to help you frame your argument and establish your tone.

5. For an audience of your classmates, write an essay in which you examine and discuss how Schwartz uses narration in "Beggaring Our Better Selves." Focusing on a few examples, explain how this strategy enhances both the emotional and the ethical appeal of her essay.
6. Both Reich and Schwartz argue that affluent Americans are detaching themselves from the disadvantaged in our society and forgetting what should be our common goals. Using your own experiences and perhaps new information you are getting in some college course, pick some particular areas in your community—schools, hospitals and clinics, transportation, recreational facilities, and housing are possibilities—and argue for or against Reich's and Schwartz's claims. If you think they're true, cite specific examples and show how those affect the community. If you think such claims are exaggerated or false, pick some specific project that bears out your contention and show how it was carried out and how it benefits the community.

RESOURCES FOR WRITING

As you have worked your way through this book, you have discovered that you already possess many resources for reading and writing. You have read essays on a wide variety of subjects. You have encountered new and complicated information shaped by unusual and unsettling assertions. But you have also discovered experiences and feelings you recognize—the challenge of learning, the ordeal of disappointment, the cost of achievement. As you have examined these essays, you realized that you had something to say about your reading, something to contribute to the writers' interpretation of some fairly substantial subjects. Your reading revealed your resources for writing.

Your work with this book has also enabled you to identify

and practice using patterns that at each stage of the writing process have helped you transform your resources into writing. In the beginning, these patterns serve as questions you might ask about any body of information. Suppose you want to write an essay on women's contributions to science. You might begin by asking why so few women are ranked among the world's great scientists. You might continue asking questions: What historical forces have discouraged women from becoming scientists (cause and effect)? How do women scientists define problems, analyze evidence, formulate conclusions (process analysis), and do they go about these processes in ways different from men scientists (comparison and contrast)? If women scientists look at the world differently from the way men do, does this have an effect on the established notions of inquiry (argument)? These questions work like the different lenses you attach to a camera: each lens gives you a slightly different perspective on your subject.

Your initial questions enable you to envision your subject from different perspectives. Answering one question encourages you to develop your subject according to a purpose associated with one of the common patterns of organization. For instance, if you decide to write about your first scuba dive, your choice of purpose seems obvious: to answer the question, What happened? You would then proceed to write a narrative essay. In drafting this essay, however, you may discover questions you had not anticipated, such as: What factors led to the development of scuba diving? How do you use scuba equipment? How is scuba diving similar to or different from swimming?

Responding to these new questions forces you to decide whether your new information develops or distorts your draft. The history of underwater diving—from diving bells to diving suits to self-contained equipment—may help your readers see a context for your narrative. On the other hand, such information may confuse them, distracting them from your original purpose: to tell what happened.

As you struggle with your new resources, you may decide that your original purpose no longer drives your writing. You may decide to change your purpose and write a cause-

and-effect essay. Instead of telling what happened on your first scuba dive, you might decide to use your personal experience, together with some reading, to write a more scientific essay analyzing the effects of underwater swimming on your senses of sight and hearing.

This book has helped you make such decisions by showing you how the common patterns of organization evoke different purposes, audiences, and strategies. In this final section of the book, you will have the opportunity to make such decisions about a new collection of resources—an anthology of writing on the subject of crime.

Before you begin reading these selections, take an initial inventory. What kind of direct experience have you had with crime? (Have you ever been robbed? Have you ever witnessed a mugging?) What kind of indirect experience have you had with crime? (What sorts of crimes have you seen portrayed in novels, on television, and in the movies?) What do you know about the criminal justice system and where did you learn it? (Who taught you about how police capture criminals? Where did you learn about criminal law, trials, and punishment?) What is your attitude toward some of the more famous crimes in your community or our country? (What is your attitude toward the criminals, victims, accusers, and defenders?)

Thinking about such questions will remind you of the extensive resources you bring to the subject of crime. Unfortunately, it is a subject that touches all of our lives in some way. And it affects our behavior in countless other ways—where we decide to live, what we think of our neighbors, when we decide to travel, how we spend our money, who we elect to political office, and why we believe in certain values.

After you have made a preliminary inventory of your knowledge and attitudes toward crime, read the writing in this section. You will notice that each selection asks you to look at crime from a different perspective:

1. *What happened? (narration and description)* Calvin Trillin recounts a murder in Kentucky and then describes the

reaction of all those involved to the prosecution of the murderer.

2. *How do you do it? (process analysis)* Edward Hoagland analyzes the steps in how a jury is selected and how it performs its responsibilities.
3. *How is it similar to or different from something else? (comparison and contrast)* Stephen Chapman compares the methods of criminal punishment in Islamic cultures with those in Western countries.
4. *What kind of subdivision does it contain? (division and classification)* David Hage and his team of writers classify various corporate monopolies by the way they have exploited American consumers.
5. *How would you characterize it? (definition)* Barbara Ehrenreich defines "marginal men" by characterizing the lives of those who live in the suburbs, are unemployed, and, because they have nothing better to do, commit crimes.
6. *How did it happen? (cause and effect)* Lucy Kavaler explains how temperature, especially excessive heat, can trigger riot, murder, and crimes of passion.
7. *How can you prove it? (persuasion and argument)* Diane Johnson uses evidence from three studies to demonstrate how cultural and personal histories have conditioned attitudes toward rape.

The collection concludes with Frank O'Connor's short story "Guests of the Nation." Although the story focuses on a political conflict, the main character asks many of the same questions about crime that prompted the other essays in this section: What crime did my enemies commit? How am I supposed to guard them? Why do I have to kill them? What have I proved by doing my duty? How will my actions alter my life?

As you examine these selections, keep track of how your reading expands your resources—provoking memories, adding information, and suggesting questions you had not considered when you made your initial inventory about crime. Because this information will give you new ways to think about your original questions, you will want to explore your thinking in writing.

The assignments that follow each selection suggest several ways that you can use these resources for writing:

1. You can *respond* to the essay by shaping a similar experience according to its method of organization.
2. You can *analyze* the essay to discover how the author uses specific strategies to communicate a purpose to an audience.
3. You can use the essay as a springboard for an essay that *argues* a similar thesis in a different context.
4. You can *compare* the essay to other selections in the anthology that raise similar questions about crime. At the end of each assignment, two selections are suggested as **resources for comparison**.
5. You can *explore* some aspect of crime by *combining* several writing strategies.

Drawing on your experience, reading, and familiarity with writing strategies, you are ready to work up a writing assignment on any subject.

CALVIN TRILLIN

Calvin Trillin was born in Kansas City, Missouri, in 1935 and was educated at Yale University. He began his career by working as a reporter for *Time* magazine, then as a columnist for the *New Yorker.* In recent years, he has written a national newspaper column and staged a one-man show off-Broadway. His writing includes two novels, *Runestruck* (1977) and *Floater* (1980); several collections of reporting, *U.S. Journal* (1971), *Killings* (1982), and *American Stories* (1991); and numerous books of humor, *American Fried: Adventures of a Happy Eater* (1974), *Alice, Let's Eat: Further Adventures of a Happy Eater* (1978), *With All Disrespect: More Uncivil Liberties* (1985), *If You Can't Say Something Nice* (1987), *Enough's Enough (and Other Rules of Life)* (1990). In "A Stranger with a Camera," reprinted from *Killings,* Trillin describes the crime that resulted from a film crew's attempt to document poverty.

A Stranger with a Camera
(Narration and Description)

On a bright afternoon in September, in 1967, a five-man film crew working in the mountains of Eastern Kentucky stopped to take pictures of some people near a place called Jeremiah. In a narrow valley, a half-dozen dilapidated shacks—each one a tiny square box with one corner cut away to provide a cluttered front porch—stood alongside the county blacktop. Across the road from the shacks, a mountain rose abruptly. In the field that separated them from the mountain behind them, there were a couple of ramshackle privies and some clotheslines tied to trees and a railroad track and a rusted automobile body and a dirty river called Rockhouse Creek. The leader of the film crew was a Canadian named Hugh 1

O'Connor. Widely acclaimed as the co-producer of the Labyrinth show at Expo 67 in Montreal, O'Connor had been hired by Francis Thompson, an American filmmaker, to work on a film Thompson was producing for the American pavilion at HemisFair in San Antonio. O'Connor went up to three of the shacks and asked the head of each household for permission to take pictures. When each one agreed, O'Connor had him sign the customary release forms and gave him a token payment of ten dollars—a token that, in this case, happened to represent a month's rent. The light was perfect in the valley, and the shooting went well. Theodore Holcomb, the associate producer of the film, was particularly struck by the looks of a miner, still in his work clothes and still covered with coal dust, sitting in a rocking chair on one of the porches. "He was just sitting there scratching his arm in a listless way," Holcomb said later. "He had an expression of total despair. It was an extraordinary shot—so evocative of the despair of that region."

The shot of the coal miner was good enough to be included in the final version of the film, and so was a shot of 2
a half-dozen children who, somehow, lived with their parents in one of the tiny shacks. After about an hour and a half, the crew was ready to leave, but someone had noticed a woman come out of one of the shacks and go to the common well to draw some water, and she was asked to repeat the action for filming. As that last shot was being completed, a woman drove up and told the filmmakers that the man who owned the property was coming to throw them off of it. Then she drove away. A couple of minutes later, another car arrived, and a man—a thin, bald man—leaped out. He was holding a pistol. "Get off my property!" he shouted again and again. Then he shot twice. No one was hit. The filmmakers kept moving their equipment toward their cars across the road while trying to tell the man that they were leaving. One of them said that the man must be shooting blanks. "Get off my property!" he kept screaming. Hugh O'Connor, who was lugging a heavy battery across the highway, turned to say that they were going. The man held the pistol in both

hands and pulled the trigger again. "Mr. O'Connor briefly looked down in amazement, and I saw a hole in his chest," Holcomb later testified in court. "He saw it and he looked up in despair and said, 'Why did you have to do that?' and, with blood coming from his mouth, he fell to the ground."

Whitesburg, a town about twelve miles from Jeremiah, is 3
the county seat of Letcher County—headquarters for the county court, the sheriff, and assorted coal companies and anti-poverty agencies. Word that someone had been killed reached Whitesburg quickly, but for a couple of hours there was some confusion about just who the victim was. According to various stories, the dead man had been a representative of the Army Corps of Engineers, a Vista volunteer, or a C.B.S. cameraman—any of whom might qualify as a candidate for shooting in Letcher County. The Corps of Engineers had proposed building the Kingdom Come Dam across Rockhouse Creek, thereby flooding an area that included Jeremiah, and some opponents of the dam had been saying that the first government man who came near their property had better come armed. Throughout Eastern Kentucky, local political organizations and coal-mining interests had warned that community organizers who called themselves Vistas or Appalachian Volunteers or anything else were nothing but another variety of Communists—three of them had been arrested on charges of attempting to overthrow the government of Pike County—and even some of the impoverished people whom the volunteers were supposedly in Kentucky to help viewed them with fear and suspicion. A number of television crews had been to Letcher County to record the despair that Holcomb saw in the face of the miner sitting on the front porch. Whitesburg happens to be the home of Harry M. Caudill, a lawyer who drew attention to the plight of the mountain people in 1963 with an eloquent book called *Night Comes to the Cumberlands*. Television crews and reporters on a tour of Appalachia are tempted to start with Letcher County in order to get the benefit of Caudill's counsel, which is ordinarily expressed in a tone of sustained rage—

rage at the profit ratio of out-of-state companies that take the region's natural resources while paying virtually no taxes, rage at the strip mines that are gouged across the mountains and at the mud slides and floods and pollution and ugliness they cause, rage at the local merchants and politicians who make a good living from the trade of welfare recipients or the retainers of coal companies and insist that there is nothing wrong with the economy, and, most of all, rage at the country that could permit it all to happen. "Look what man hath wrought on *that* purple mountain's majesty," he will say as he points out the coal waste on the side of a mountain that had once been beautiful. "A country that treats its land and people this way deserves to perish from the earth."

In the view of Caudill and of Tom Gish, the liberal editor 4 of the *Mountain Eagle,* a Letcher County weekly, the reactions of people in Jeremiah to the presence of O'Connor's film crew—cooperation by the poor people being photographed in their squalid shacks, rage by the man who owned the shacks—were characteristic of Letcher County: a lot of people who are still in Eastern Kentucky after years of welfare or subsistence employment have lost the will to treat their situation as an embarrassment, but outside journalists are particularly resented by the people who have managed to make a living—running a country store or a filling station or a small truck mine, working for the county administration, managing some rental property. They resent the impression that everyone in Eastern Kentucky is like the people who are desperately poor—people whose condition they tend to blame on "just sorriness, mostly." In Letcher County, fear of outsiders by people who are guarding reputations or economic interests blends easily into a deep-rooted suspicion of outsiders by all Eastern Kentucky mountain people, who have always had a fierce instinct to protect their property and a distrust of strangers that has often proved to have been justified. All of the people in Letcher County—people who live in the shacks up remote hollows or people who run stores on Main Street in Whitesburg—consider themselves mountain people, and, despite an accurate story in the *Moun-*

tain Eagle, many of them instinctively believed that the mountaineer who killed Hugh O'Connor was protecting his property from smart-aleck outsiders who wouldn't leave when they were told.

5 The mountaineer's name was Hobart Ison. There have always been Isons in Letcher County, and many of them have managed somewhat better than their neighbors. Hobart Ison had inherited a rather large piece of land in Jeremiah—he raised chickens and rented out shacks he himself had built and at one time ran a small sawmill—but he was known mainly as an eccentric, mean-tempered old man. Everyone in Letcher County knew that Hobart Ison had once built and furnished a house for his future bride and—having been rejected or having been afraid to ask or having had no particular future bride in mind—had let the house remain as it was for thirty years, the grass growing up around it and the furniture still in the packing crates. He had occasionally painted large signs attacking the people he thought had wronged him. He was easily enraged by people hunting on his property, and he despised all of the local Democrats, whom he blamed for injustices that included dismissing him from a post-office job. A psychiatrist who examined him after the shooting said, "Any reference to 'game warden' or 'Democrat' will provoke him tremendously." Once, when some local youths were taunting him, he took a shot at them, hitting one in the shoulder. "A lot of people around here would have welcomed them," Caudill said of the filmmakers. "They just happened to pick the wrong place."

6 Streams of people came to visit Ison in the Letcher County jail before he was released on bail. Women from around Jeremiah baked him cakes. When his trial came up, it proved impossible to find a jury. The Letcher County commonwealth's attorney and Caudill, who had been retained by Francis Thompson, Inc., secured a change of venue. They argued that Ison's family relationship in Letcher County was "so extensive as to comprise a large segment of the population," and, through an affidavit signed by three citizens in position to know public opinion, they stated that "the over-

whelming expression of sentiment has been to the effect that the defendant did right in the slaying of Hugh O'Connor and that he ought to be acquitted of the offense of murder."

Harlan County is a mountain or two away from Letcher County. In the town of Harlan, benches advertising Bunny Enriched Bread stand outside the front door of the county courthouse, flanking the First World War monument and the Revolutionary War monument and the plaque recalling how many Kentucky courthouses were burned down by each side during the Civil War. On the ground floor of the courthouse, the men who habitually gather on the plain wooden benches to pass the time use old No. 5 cans for ashtrays or spittoons and a large container that once held Oscar Mayer's Pure Lard as a wastebasket. In the courtroom, a plain room with all of its furnishings painted black, the only decoration other than pictures of the men who have served as circuit judge is a framed poster in praise of the country lawyer—and also in praise, it turns out upon close reading, of the Dun & Bradstreet Corporation. The front door of the courthouse is almost always plastered with election stickers. In the vestibule just inside, an old man sits on the floor behind a display of old pocketknives and watchbands and billfolds and eyeglass cases offered for sale or trade. 7

The commonwealth's attorney of Harlan County is Daniel Boone Smith. Eight or nine years ago, Smith got curious about how many people he had prosecuted or defended for murder, and counted up seven hundred and fifty. He was able to amass that total partly because of longevity (except for a few years in the service during the Second World War, he has been commonwealth's attorney continuously since 1933), partly because he has worked in an area that gives anyone interested in trying murder cases plenty of opportunity (the wars between the unions and the coal operators in Harlan County during the thirties were almost as bloody as the mountain feuds earlier in the century), and partly because he happens to be a quick worker ("Some people will take three days to try a murder case," he has said. "I usually 8 get my case on in a day"). During his first week as commonwealth's attorney of Harlan and an adjoining county, Smith tried five murder cases. These days, Harlan County may have about that many a year, but it remains a violent place. The murders that do occur in mountain counties like Harlan and Letcher often seem to occur while someone is in a drunken rage, and often among members of the same family—a father shooting a son over something trivial, one member of a family mowing down another who is breaking down the door trying to get at a third. "We got people in this county today who would kill you as quick as look at you," Smith has said. "But most of 'em are the type that don't bother you if you leave them alone." Smith is known throughout Eastern Kentucky for his ability to select jurors—to remember which prospective juror's uncle may have had a boundary dispute with which witness's grandfather twenty years ago—and for his ability to sum up the case for them in their own language once the evidence has been heard. He is an informal, colloquial, storytelling man who happens to be a graduate of the Harvard Law School.

A lack of fervor about convicting Hobart Ison was as- 9
sumed in Harlan County when he came up for trial there in May 1968. "Before the case, people were coming up and saying, 'He *should've* killed the son of a bitch,'" Smith said later. "People would say, 'They oughtn't to make fun of mountain people. They've made enough fun of mountain people. Let me on the jury, Boone, and I'll turn him loose.'" Smith saw his task as persuading the citizens and the jurors that the case was not what it appeared to be—that the filmmakers were not "a bunch of privateers and pirates" but respectable people who had been commissioned by the United States government, that the film was not another study of how poor and ignorant people were in Eastern Kentucky but a film about the whole United States in which the shots of Eastern Kentucky would take up only a few seconds, that the filmmakers had behaved properly and politely to those they were photographing. "Why, if they had been smart alecks come to hold us up to ridicule, I'd be the

last man to try him," Smith assured everyone. It took Smith only a day or so to present his case against Hobart Ison, although it took three days to pick the jury. On the witness stand, the surviving filmmakers managed to avoid admitting to Ison's lawyers that it was the appalling poverty of his tenants that had interested them; they talked about being attracted by expressive family groups and by the convenience of not having to move their equipment far from the road. The defense asked if they were planning to take pictures of the Bluegrass as well as Appalachia. Were they going to make a lot of money from the film? How many millions of viewers would see the pictures of poor Eastern Kentucky people? Had they refused to move? Had they taunted Ison by saying he was shooting blanks? Did the people who signed the release forms really know what they were signing? (At least one of the signers was, like one out of four of his neighbors, unable to read.)

Except for the underlying issue of Eastern Kentucky v. 10
Outsiders, the only issue seriously in contention was Ison's sanity. The director of a nearby mental-health clinic, testifying for the defense, said that Ison was a paranoid schizophrenic. He told of Ison showing up for one interview with long socks worn on the outside of his trouser legs and of his altercations with his neighbors and of his lack of remorse. The prosecution's psychiatrist—an impressive woman from the University of Kentucky who had been retained by Francis Thompson, Inc.—said that Ison had grown up at a time when it was common practice to run people off of property with a gun, and, because he had lived with aging parents or alone ever since childhood, he still followed that practice. Some of Ison's ideas did have "paranoid coloring," she said, but that could be traced to his being a mountaineer, since people in isolated mountain pockets normally had a suspicion of strangers and even of each other. "Socio-cultural circumstances," she concluded, "lead to the diagnosis of an individual who is normal for his culture, the shooting and the paranoid color both being present in other individuals in this culture who are considered normal." In the trial and in the insanity

hearing that had earlier found Ison competent to stand trial, Smith insisted that Ison was merely peculiar, not crazy. "I said, 'Now, I happen to like mayonnaise on my beans. Does that make *me* crazy?'" Smith later recalled. "I turned to one of the jurors, a man named Mahan Fields, and I said, 'Mahan, you remember Uncle Bob Woolford, who used to work up at Evarts? Did you ever see Uncle Bob in the winter when he didn't have his socks pulled up over his pants legs to keep out the cold? Now, was Uncle Bob crazy? Why, Mahan, I bet on many a winter morning *you* wore *your* socks over your pants legs.'"

In his summation, Smith saved his harshest words not for the defendant but for the person who was responsible for bringing Hobart Ison, a mountaineer who was not quite typical of mountaineers, and Hugh O'Connor, a stranger with a camera who was not quite typical of strangers with cameras, into violent conflict. Judy Breeding—the operator of a small furniture store near Ison's shacks, and the wife of Ison's cousin—had testified that she was not only the woman who told the film crew that Ison was coming but also the woman who had told Ison that the film crew was on his property. "Hobart," she recalled saying, "there is some men over there taking pictures of your houses, with out-of-state license." Smith looked out toward the courtroom spectators and suddenly pointed his finger at Judy Breeding. He told her that he would like to be prosecuting her, that if it hadn't been for her mouth Hugh O'Connor would not be in his grave and Hobart Ison would be back home where he belonged. Later, Smith caught a glimpse of Mrs. Breeding in the hall, and he thought he saw her shake her fist at him, smiling. "You know," he said, "I believe the idea that she had anything to do with bringing that about had never occurred to her till I mentioned it." 11

The jury was eleven to one for conviction, but the one held out. Some people were surprised that Ison had come that close to being convicted, although it was generally agreed that the prosecution's psychiatrist had out-talked the psychiatrist who testified for the defense. Smith believed that 12 his case had been greatly strengthened by the fact that the filmmakers had been respectful, soft-spoken witnesses—not at all smart-alecky. "If there was anything bigheaded about them," he said, "it didn't show."

The retrial was postponed once, and then was stopped suddenly during jury selection when Smith became ill. On March 24th, Hobart Ison came to trial again. The filmmakers, who had been dreading another trip to Kentucky, were at the county courthouse in Harlan at nine in the morning, ready to repeat their testimony. Although Smith had anticipated even more trouble finding a jury, he was prepared to go to trial. But Ison's lawyers indicated to Smith and Caudill that their client, now seventy, would be willing to plead guilty to voluntary manslaughter, and they finally met Smith's insistence on a ten-year sentence. Ison—wearing a baggy brown suit, his face pinched and red—appeared only briefly before the judge to plead guilty. A couple of hours after everyone arrived, Caudill was on his way back to Whitesburg, where he was working on the case of a Vietnam veteran accused of killing two men during an argument in the street, and the filmmakers were driving to Knoxville to catch the first plane to New York. 13

The following day, the clerk of the court, a strong-looking woman with a strong Kentucky accent, happened to get into a discussion about the filmmakers with another citizen who had come to know them in the year and a half since Hugh O'Connor's death—a woman with a softer accent and a less certain tone to her voice. 14

"You know, I asked those men yesterday morning if they were happy with the outcome," the clerk said. "And they said, 'Yes.' And I said, 'Well, you know, us hillbillies is a queer breed. We are. I'm not offering any apologies when I say that. Us hillbillies *are* a queer breed, and I'm just as proud as punch to be one.'" 15

"Not all of us are like that," the other woman said. "Mean like that." 16

"Well, I wouldn't say that man is mean," the clerk said. 17

"I don't guess he ever harmed anybody in his life. They were very nice people. I think it was strictly a case of misunderstanding. I think that the old man thought they were laughing and making fun of him, and it was more than he could take. I know this: a person isolated in these hills, they often grow old and eccentric, which I think they have a right to do."

"But he didn't have a right to kill," the other woman said. 18

"Well, no," the clerk said. "But us hillbillies, we don't 19
bother nobody. We go out of our way to help people. But we don't want nobody pushin' us around. Now, that's the code of the hills. And he felt like—that old man felt like—he was being pushed around. You know, it's like I told those men: 'I wouldn't have gone on that old man's land to pick me a mess of wild greens without I'd asked him.' They said, 'We didn't know all this.' I said, 'I bet you know it now. I bet you know it now.'"

Topics for Writing

1. *Respond.* React to Trillin's essay by recalling some occasion when you were cast in the role of an outsider. In an essay designed for the travel section of your local newspaper, describe how it felt to be an outsider, what customs you failed to notice or understand, and what sorts of behavior created communication problems. (*Resources for comparison:* George Orwell, "Shooting an Elephant"; Lynne Sharon Schwartz, "Beggaring Our Better Selves.")
2. *Analyze.* Trillin narrates the murder in the first few pages but devotes the rest of the essay to describing the character and culture of the murderer. Analyze the kind of information he gathers from Harry M. Caudill, Daniel Boone Smith, the two psychiatrists, and other citizens of Letcher and Harlan counties. Then, in an essay that might be submitted to a sociology class, assess the evidence Trillin uses to "explain" why the crime occurred. (*Resources for comparison:* Mike Rose, "I Just Wanna Be Average"; David Gates, "Who Was Columbus?")
3. *Argue.* A major theme in Trillin's narrative is that outsiders—business executives, government workers, and media personnel—victimize poor people, even when they are trying to help them. This behavior proceeds from distorted assumptions about what's wrong with poor people and how their situation should be corrected. Construct an argument addressed to a specific government agency outlining the kind of "local" knowledge it requires to design and administer effective programs for the poor. (*Resources for comparison:* Maya Angelou, "My Name Is Margaret"; Rose del Castillo Guilbault, "Americanization Is Tough on 'Macho.'")

EDWARD HOAGLAND

Edward Hoagland was born in New York City in 1932 and was educated at Harvard University. Although he has written several novels and books on travel, Hoagland considers himself a personal essayist, a writer who is concerned with expressing "what I think" and "what I am." He has published essays in *Commentary, Newsweek,* the *Village Voice,* and *The New York Times* on an intriguing range of subjects such as tugboats, turtles, circuses, city life in Cairo, and his own stutter. His essays have been collected in five critically acclaimed volumes: *The Courage of Turtles* (1971), *Walking the Dead Diamond River* (1973), *Red Wolves and Black Bears* (1976), *The Edward Hoagland Reader* (1979), *The Tugman's Passage* (1982), and *Notes from the Century Before: A Journal from British Columbia* (1982). He has also published a collection of stories, *City Tales/Wyoming Stories* (1986), with Gretel Ehrlich. In "In the Toils of the Law," reprinted from *Walking the Dead Diamond River,* Hoagland uses his own experience to explain the process of being selected for and serving on a jury.

In the Toils of the Law

(Process Analysis)

Lately people seem to want to pigeonhole themselves ("I'm 'into' this," "I'm 'into' that"), and the anciently universal experiences like getting married or having a child, like voting or jury duty, acquire a kind of poignancy. We hardly believe that our vote will count, we wonder whether the world will 1 wind up uninhabitable for the child, but still we do vote with a rueful fervor and look at new babies with undimmed tenderness, because who knows what will become of these old humane responsibilities? . . .

Jury duty. Here one sits listening to evidence: thumbs up for a witness or thumbs down. It's unexpectedly moving; everybody tries so hard to be fair. For their two weeks of service people really try to be better than themselves. In Manhattan eighteen hundred are called each week from the voters' rolls, a third of whom show up and qualify. Later this third is divided into three groups of two hundred, one for the State Supreme Court of New York County, one for the Criminal Court, and one for the Civil Court. At Civil Court, 111 Centre Street, right across from the Tombs, there are jury rooms on the third and eleventh floors, and every Monday a new pool goes to one or the other. The building is relatively modern, the chairs upholstered as in an airport lounge, and the two hundred people sit facing forward like a school of fish until the roll is called. It's like waiting six or seven hours a day for an unscheduled flight to leave. They read and watch the clock, go to the drinking fountain, strike up a conversation, dictate business letters into the pay telephones. When I served, one man in a booth was shouting, "I'll knock your teeth down your throat! I don't want to hear, I don't want to know!" 2

. . . There are lots of retired men and institutional employees from banks, the Post Office or the Transit Authority whose bosses won't miss them, as well as people at loose ends who welcome the change. But some look extremely busy, rushing back to the office when given a chance or sitting at the tables at the front of the room, trying to keep up with their work. They'll write payroll checks, glancing to see if you notice how important they are, or pore over statistical charts or contact sheets with a magnifying glass, if they are in public relations or advertising. Once in a while a clerk emerges to rotate a lottery box and draw the names of jurors, who go into one of the challenge rooms—six jurors, six alternates—to be interviewed by the plaintiff's and de- 3 fendant's lawyers. Unless the damages asked are large, in civil cases the jury has six members, only five of whom must agree on a decision, and since no one is going to be sentenced to jail, the evidence for a decision need merely seem preponderant, not "beyond a reasonable doubt."

The legal fiction is maintained that the man or woman you see as defendant is actually going to have to pay, but the defense attorneys are generally insurance lawyers from a regular battery which each big company keeps at the courthouse to handle these matters, or from the legal corps of the City of New York, Con Edison, Hertz Rent A Car, or whoever. If so, they act interchangeably and you may see a different face in court than you saw in the challenge room, and still another during the judge's charge. During my stint most cases I heard about went back four or five years, and the knottiest problem for either side was producing witnesses who were still willing to testify. In negligence cases, so many of which involve automobiles, there are several reasons why the insurers haven't settled earlier. They've waited for the plaintiff to lose hope or greed, and to see what cards each contestant will finally hold in his hands when the five years have passed. More significantly, it's a financial matter. The straight-arrow companies that do right by a sufferer and promptly pay him off lose the use as capital of that three thousand dollars or so meanwhile—multiplied perhaps eighty thousand times, for all the similar cases they have. 4

Selecting a jury is the last little battle of nerves between the two sides. By now the opposing attorneys know who will testify and have obtained pretrial depositions; this completes the hand each of them holds. Generally they think they know what will happen, so to save time and costs they settle the case either before the hearing starts or out of the jury's earshot during the hearing with the judge's help. Seeing a good sober jury waiting to hear them attempt to justify a bad case greases the wheels. 5

In the challenge room, though, the momentum of confrontation goes on. With a crowded court calendar, the judge in these civil cases is not present, as a rule. It's a small room, 6

and there's an opportunity for the lawyers to be folksy or emotional in ways not permitted them later on. For example, in asking the jurors repeatedly if they will "be able to convert pain and suffering into dollars and cents" the plaintiff's attorney is preparing the ground for his more closely supervised presentation in court. By asking them if they own any stock in an insurance company he can get across the intelligence, which is otherwise *verboten,* that not the humble "defendant" but some corporation is going to have to pay the tab. His opponent will object if he tells too many jokes and wins too many friends, but both seek not so much a sympathetic jury as a jury that is free of nuts and grudge-holders, a jury dependably ready to give everybody "his day in court"—a phrase one hears over and over. The questioning we were subjected to was so polite as to be almost apologetic, however, because of the danger of unwittingly offending any of the jurors who remained. Having to size up a series of strangers, on the basis of some monosyllabic answers and each fellow's face, profession and address, was hard work for these lawyers. Everybody was on his best behavior, the jurors too, because the procedure so much resembled a job interview, and no one wanted to be considered less than fair-minded, unfit to participate in the case; there was a vague sense of shame about being excused.

The six alternates sat listening. The lawyers could look at 7
them and draw any conclusions they wished, but they could neither question them until a sitting juror had been challenged, nor know in advance which one of the alternates would be substituted first. Each person was asked about his work, about any honest bias or special knowledge he might have concerning cases of the same kind, or any lawsuits he himself might have been involved in at one time. Some questions were probably partly designed to educate us in the disciplines of objectivity, lest we think it was all too easy, and one or two lawyers actually made an effort to educate us in the majesty of the law, since, as they said, the judges sometimes are "dingbats" and don't. We were told there should be no opprobrium attached to being excused, that

we must not simply assume a perfect impartiality in ourselves but should help them to examine us. Jailhouse advocates, or Spartan types who might secretly believe that the injured party should swallow his misfortune and grin and bear a stroke of bad luck, were to be avoided, of course, along with the mingy, the flippant, the grieved and the wronged, as well as men who might want to redistribute the wealth of the world by finding for the plaintiff, or who might not limit their deliberations to the facts of the case, accepting the judge's interpretation of the law as law. We were told that our common sense and experience of life was what was wanted to sift out the likelihood of the testimony we heard.

Most dismissals were caused just by a lawyer's hunch—or figuring the percentages as baseball managers do. After the first day's waiting in the airport lounge, there wasn't anybody who didn't want to get on a case; even listening as an alternate in the challenge room was a relief. I dressed in a suit and tie and shined my shoes. I'd been afraid that when I said I was a novelist no lawyer would have me, on the theory that novelists favor the underdog. On the contrary, I was accepted every time; apparently a novelist was considered ideal, having no allegiances at all, no expertise, no professional link to the workaday world. I stutter and had supposed that this too might disqualify me [but] these lawyers did not think it so. What they seemed to want was simply a balanced group, because when a jury gets down to arguing there's no telling where its leadership will arise. The rich man from Sutton Place whom the plaintiff's lawyer almost dismissed, fearing he'd favor the powers that be, may turn out to be a fighting liberal whose idea of what constitutes proper damages is much higher than what the machinist who sits next to him has in mind. In one case I heard about, a woman was clonked by a Christmas tree in a department store and the juror whose salary was lowest suggested an award of fifty dollars, and the man who earned the most, fifty thousand dollars (they rounded it off to fifteen hundred dollars). These were the kind of cases Sancho Panza did so well on when he was governor of Isle Barataria, and as I was questioned about my prejudices, and solemnly looking into each lawyer's 8 eyes, shook my head—murmuring, No, I had no prejudices—all the time my true unreliable quirkiness filled my head. All I could do was resolve to try to be fair.

By the third day, we'd struck up shipboard friendships. 9
There was a babbling camaraderie in the jury pool, and for lunch we plunged into that old, eclipsed, ethnic New York near City Hall—Chinese roast ducks hanging in the butcher's windows on Mulberry Street next door to an Italian store selling religious candles. We ate at Cucina Luna and Giambone's. Eating at Ping Ching's, we saw whole pigs, blanched white, delivered at the door. We watched an Oriental funeral with Madame Nhu the director waving the limousines on. The deceased's picture, heaped with flowers, was in the lead car, and all his beautiful daughters wept with faces disordered and long black hair streaming down. One of the Italian bands which plays on feast days was mourning over a single refrain—two trumpets, a clarinet, a mellophone and a drum.

As an alternate I sat in on the arguments for a rent-a-car 10
crash case, with four lawyers, each of whom liked to hear himself talk, representing the different parties. The theme was that we were New Yorkers and therefore streetwise and no fools. The senior fellow seemed to think that all his years of trying these penny-ante negligence affairs had made him very good indeed, whereas my impression was that the reason he was still trying them was because he was rather bad. The same afternoon I got on a jury to hear the case of a cleaning woman, sixty-four, who had slipped on the floor of a Harlem ballroom in 1967 and broken her ankle. She claimed the floor was overwaxed. She'd obviously been passed from hand to hand within the firm that had taken her case and had wound up with an attractive young man who was here cutting his teeth. What I liked about her was her abusive manner, which expected no justice and made no distinction at all between her own lawyer and that of the ballroom owner, though she was confused by the fact that the judge was black. He was from the Supreme Court, assigned to help cut through this backlog, had a clerk with an Afro, and was exceedingly brisk and effective.

The porter who had waxed the floor testified—a man of 11

good will, long since at another job. The ballroom owner had operated the hall for more than thirty years, and his face was fastidious, Jewish, sensitive, sad, like that of a concert-goer who is not unduly pleased with his life. He testified, and it was not *his* fault. Nevertheless the lady had hurt her ankle and been out of pocket and out of work. It was a wedding reception, and she'd just stepped forward, saying, "Here comes the bride!"

The proceedings were interrupted while motions were heard in another case, and we sat alone in a jury room, trading reading material, obeying the injunction not to discuss the case, until after several hours we were called back and thanked by the judge. "They also serve who stand and wait." He said that our presence next door as a deliberative body, passive though we were, had pressured a settlement. It was for seven hundred and fifty dollars, a low figure to me (the court attendant told me that there had been a legal flaw in the plaintiff's case), but some of the other jurors thought she'd deserved no money; they were trying to be fair to the ballroom man. Almost always that's what the disputes boiled down to: one juror trying to be fair to one person, another to another. 12

On Friday of my first week I got on a jury to hear the plight of a woman who had been standing at the front of a bus and had been thrown forward and injured when she stooped to pick up some change that had spilled from her purse. The bus company's lawyer was a ruddy, jovial sort. "Anybody here have a bone to pick with our New York City buses?" We laughed and said, no, we were capable of sending her away without any award if she couldn't prove negligence. Nevertheless, he settled with her attorney immediately after we left the challenge room. (These attorneys did not necessarily run to type. There was a Transit Authority man who shouted like William Kunstler; five times the judge had an officer make him sit down, and once threatened to have the chap bound to his chair.) 13

I was an alternate for another car crash. With cases in progress all over the building, the jury pool had thinned out, 14 so that no sooner were we dropped back into it than our names were called again. Even one noteworthy white-haired fellow who was wearing a red velvet jump suit, a dragon-colored coat and a dangling gold talisman had some experiences to talk about. I was tabbed for a panel that was to hear from a soft-looking, tired, blond widow of fifty-seven who, while walking home at night five years before from the shop where she worked, had tripped into an excavation only six inches deep but ten feet long and three feet wide. She claimed that the twists and bumps of this had kept her in pain and out of work for five months. She seemed natural and truthful on the witness stand, yet her testimony was so brief and flat that one needed to bear in mind how much time had passed. As we'd first filed into the courtroom she had watched us with the ironic gravity that a person inevitably would feel who has waited five years for a hearing and now sees the cast of characters who will decide her case. This was a woeful low point of her life, but the memory of how badly she'd felt was stale.

The four attorneys on the case were straightforward youngsters getting their training here. The woman's was properly aggressive; Con Edison's asked humorously if we had ever quarreled with Con Edison over a bill; the city's, who was an idealist with shoulder-length hair, asked with another laugh if we disliked New York; and the realty company's, whether we fought with our landlords. Of course, fair-minded folk that we were, we told them no. They pointed out that just as the code of the law provides that a lone woman, fifty-seven, earning a hundred dollars a week, must receive the same consideration in court as a great city, so must the city be granted an equal measure of justice as that lone woman was. 15

Our panel included a bank guard, a lady loan officer, a young black Sing Sing guard, a pale, slim middle-aged executive from Coca-Cola, a hale fellow who sold package tours from an airline and looked like the Great Gildersleeve, and me. If her attorney had successfully eliminated Spartans from the jury, we'd surely award her something; the question was 16 how much. I wondered about the five months. No bones broken—let's say, being rather generous, maybe two months of rest. But couldn't the remainder be one of those dead-still intermissions that each of us must stop and take once or twice in a life, not from any single blow but from the accumulating knocks and scabby disappointments that pile up, the harshness of winning a living, and the rest of it—for which the government in its blundering wisdom already makes some provision through unemployment insurance?

But there were no arguments. The judge had allowed the 17
woman to testify about her injuries on the condition that her physician appear. When, the next day, he didn't, a mistrial was declared.

Topics for Writing

1. *Respond.* Respond to Hoagland's analysis of our trial system by examining the process of jury selection dramatized in a particular television show or film. What predictable characteristics do the opposing lawyers want in the jurors they select? What questions do they ask to determine a juror's values? Write your analysis for the readers of the entertainment section of your local newspaper. (*Resources for comparison:* Deborah Tannen, "Rapport-talk and Report-talk"; Gail Sheehy, "Predictable Crises of Adulthood.")
2. *Analyze.* Hoagland's analysis rests on many assumptions about the rights of individuals and corporations within our culture. Uncover these assumptions by examining the evaluation and resolution of the five cases he uses as illustrations. Analyze these cases to explain to business-law students why Hoagland's evidence suggests that the courts protect the individual or the corporation. (*Resources for comparison:* Flannery O'Connor, "Revelation"; Martin Luther King, Jr., "I Have a Dream.")
3. *Argue.* Hoagland is assigned to civil court, where most cases are at least five years old. But you have read about criminal cases where the appeals process has postponed the final judgment even longer. Conduct some research in professional journals or study a local trial. Then draft a speech for the local bar association in which you evaluate the effectiveness of the American legal system. (*Resources for comparison:* Stephen Jay Gould, "Carrie Buck's Daughter"; Arthur C. Clarke "The Star.")

STEPHEN CHAPMAN

Stephen Chapman was born in 1954 in Brady, Texas, and was educated at Harvard University and the University of Chicago School of Business. For several years he worked as an associate editor for the *New Republic.* In 1981, he began writing a column on national and international affairs for the *Chicago Tribune.* His other writing has been published in magazines such as *American Spectator, Atlantic,* and *Harper's.* In "The Prisoner's Dilemma," reprinted from the *New Republic,* Chapman compares Eastern and Western traditions of punishing criminals.

The Prisoner's Dilemma

(Comparison and Contrast)

If the punitive laws of Islam were applied for only one year, all the devastating injustices would be uprooted. Misdeeds must be punished by the law of retribution: cut off the hands of the thief; kill the murderers; flog the adulterous woman or man. Your concerns, your "humanitarian" scruples are more childish than reasonable. Under the terms of Koranic law, any judge fulfilling the seven requirements (that he have reached puberty, be a believer, know the Koranic laws perfectly, be just, and not be affected by amnesia, or be a bastard, or be of the female sex) is qualified to be a judge in any type of case. He can thus judge and dispose of twenty trials in a single day, whereas the Occidental justice might take years to argue them out. 1

—from SAYINGS OF THE AYATOLLAH KHOMEINI
(Bantam Books)

One of the amusements of life in the modern West is the opportunity to observe the barbaric rituals of countries that are attached to the customs of the dark ages. Take Pakistan, for example, our newest ally and client state in Asia. Last October President Zia, in harmony with the Islamic fervor that is sweeping his part of the world, revived the traditional Moslem practice of flogging lawbreakers in public. In Pakistan, this qualified as mass entertainment, and no fewer than 10,000 law-abiding Pakistanis turned out to see justice done to 26 convicts. To Western sensibilities the spectacle seemed barbaric—both in the sense of cruel and in the sense of precivilized. In keeping with Islamic custom each of the unfortunates—who had been caught in prostitution raids the previous night and summarily convicted and sentenced—was stripped down to a pair of white shorts, which were painted with a red stripe across the buttocks (the target). Then he was shackled against an easel, with pads thoughtfully placed over the kidneys to prevent injury. The floggers were muscular, fierce-looking sorts—convicted murderers, as it happens—who paraded around the flogging-platform in colorful loincloths. When the time for the ceremony began, one of the floggers took a running start and brought a five-foot stave down across the first victim's buttocks, eliciting screams from the convict and murmurs from the audience. Each of the 26 received from five to 15 lashes. One had to be carried from the stage unconscious. 2

Flogging is one of the punishments stipulated by Koranic law, which has made it a popular penological device in several Moslem countries, including Pakistan, Saudi Arabia, and, most recently, the ayatollah's Iran. Flogging, or *ta'zir,* is the general punishment prescribed for offenses that don't carry an explicit Koranic penalty. Some crimes carry automatic *hadd* punishments—stoning or scourging (a severe whipping) for illicit sex, scourging for drinking alcoholic beverages, amputation of the hands for theft. Other crimes—as varied as murder and abandoning Islam—carry the death penalty (usually carried out in public). Colorful practices like 3 these have given the Islamic world an image in the West, as described by historian G. H. Jansen, "of blood dripping from the stumps of amputated hands and from the striped backs of malefactors, and piles of stones barely concealing the battered bodies of adulterous couples." Jansen, whose book *Militant Islam* is generally effusive in its praise of Islamic practices, grows squeamish when considering devices like flogging, amputations, and stoning. But they are given enthusiastic endorsements by the Koran itself.

Such traditions, we all must agree, are no sign of an advanced civilization. In the West, we have replaced these various punishments (including the death penalty in most cases) with a single device. Our custom is to confine criminals in prison for varying lengths of time. In Illinois, a reasonably typical state, grand theft carries a punishment of three to five years; armed robbery can get you from six to 30. The lowest form of felony theft is punishable by one to three years in prison. Most states impose longer sentences on habitual offenders. In Kentucky, for example, habitual offenders can be sentenced to life in prison. Other states are less brazen, preferring the more genteel sounding "indeterminate sentence," which allows parole boards to keep inmates locked up for as long as life. It was under an indeterminate sentence of one to 14 years that George Jackson served 12 years in California prisons for committing a $70 armed robbery. Under a Texas law imposing an automatic life sentence for a third felony conviction, a man was sent to jail for life last year because of three thefts adding up to less than $300 in property value. Texas also is famous for occasionally imposing extravagantly long sentences, often running into hundreds or thousands of years. This gives Texas a leg up on Maryland, which used to sentence some criminals to life plus a day—a distinctive if superfluous flourish. 4

The punishment *intended* by Western societies in sending their criminals to prison is the loss of freedom. But, as everyone knows, the actual punishment in most American prisons is of a wholly different order. The February 2 riot at New Mexico's state prison in Santa Fe, one of several bloody 5 prison riots in the nine years since the Attica bloodbath, once again dramatized the conditions of life in an American prison. Four hundred prisoners seized control of the prison before dawn. By sunset the next day 33 inmates had died at the hands of other convicts and another 40 people (including five guards) had been seriously hurt. Macabre stories came out of prisoners being hanged, murdered with blowtorches, decapitated, tortured, and mutilated in a variety of gruesome ways by drug-crazed rioters.

The Santa Fe penitentiary was typical of most maximum-security facilities, with prisoners subject to overcrowding, filthy conditions, and routine violence. It also housed first-time, non-violent offenders, like check forgers and drug dealers, with murderers serving life sentences. In a recent lawsuit, the American Civil Liberties Union called the prison "totally unfit for human habitation." But the ACLU says New Mexico's penitentiary is far from the nation's worst. 6

That American prisons are a disgrace is taken for granted by experts of every ideological stripe. Conservative James Q. Wilson has criticized our "[c]rowded, antiquated prisons that require men and women to live in fear of one another and to suffer not only deprivation of liberty but a brutalizing regimen." Leftist Jessica Mitford has called our prisons "the ultimate expression of injustice and inhumanity." In 1973 a national commission concluded that "the American correctional system today appears to offer minimum protection to the public and maximum harm to the offender." Federal courts have ruled that confinement in prisons in 16 different states violates the constitutional ban on "cruel and unusual punishment." 7

What are the advantages of being a convicted criminal in an advanced culture? First there is the overcrowding in prisons. One Tennessee prison, for example, has a capacity of 806, according to accepted space standards, but it houses 2300 inmates. One Louisiana facility has confined four and five prisoners in a single six-by-six-foot cell. Then there is the disease caused by overcrowding, unsanitary conditions, 8 and poor or inadequate medical care. A federal appeals court noted that the Tennessee prison had suffered frequent outbreaks of infectious diseases like hepatitis and tuberculosis. But the most distinctive element of American prison life is its constant violence. In his book *Criminal Violence, Criminal Justice,* Charles Silberman noted that in one Louisiana prison, there were 211 stabbings in only three years, 11 of them fatal. There were 15 slayings in a prison in Massachusetts between 1972 and 1975. According to a federal court, in Alabama's penitentiaries (as in many others), "robbery, rape, extortion, theft and assault are everyday occurrences."

At least in regard to cruelty, it's not at all clear that the system of punishment that has evolved in the West is less barbaric than the grotesque practices of Islam. Skeptical? Ask yourself: would you rather be subjected to a few minutes of intense pain and considerable public humiliation, or to be locked away for two or three years in a prison cell crowded with ill-tempered sociopaths? Would you rather lose a hand or spend 10 years or more in a typical state prison? I have taken my own survey on this matter. I have found no one who does not find the Islamic system hideous. And I have found no one who, given the choices mentioned above, would not prefer its penalties to our own. 9

The great divergence between Western and Islamic fashions in punishment is relatively recent. Until roughly the end of the 18th century, criminals in Western countries rarely were sent to prison. Instead they were subjected to an ingenious assortment of penalties. Many perpetrators of a variety of crimes simply were executed, usually by some imaginative and extremely unpleasant method involving prolonged torture, such as breaking on the wheel, burning at the stake, or drawing and quartering. Michel Foucault's book, *Discipline and Punish: The Birth of the Prison* notes one form of capital punishment in which the condemned man's "belly was opened up, his entrails quickly ripped out, so that he had time to see them, with his own eyes, being thrown on the fire; in which he was finally decapitated and his body quartered." Some criminals were forced to serve on slave 10 galleys. But in most cases various corporal measures such as pillorying, flogging, and branding sufficed.

In time, however, public sentiment recoiled against these measures. They were replaced by imprisonment, which was thought to have two advantages. First, it was considered to be more humane. Second, and more important, prison was supposed to hold out the possibility of rehabilitation—purging the criminal of his criminality—something that less civilized punishments did not even aspire to. An 1854 report by inspectors of the Pennsylvania prison system illustrates the hopes nurtured by humanitarian reformers: 11

> *Depraved tendencies, characteristic of the convict, have been restrained by the absence of vicious association, and in the mild teaching of Christianity, the unhappy criminal finds a solace for an involuntary exile from the comforts of social life. If hungry, he is fed; if naked, he is clothed; if destitute of the first rudiments of education, he is taught to read and write; and if he has never been blessed with a means of livelihood, he is schooled in a mechanical art, which in after life may be to him the source of profit and respectability. Employment is not his toil nor labor, weariness. He embraces them with alacrity, as contributing to his moral and mental elevation.*

Imprisonment is now the universal method of punishing criminals in the United States. It is thought to perform five functions, each of which has been given a label by criminologists. First, there is simple *retribution:* punishing the lawbreaker to serve society's sense of justice and to satisfy the victims' desire for revenge. Second, there is *specific deterrence:* discouraging the offender from misbehaving in the future. Third, *general deterrence:* using the offender as an example to discourage others from turning to crime. Fourth, *prevention:* at least during the time he is kept off the streets, the criminal cannot victimize other members of society. Finally, and most important, there is *rehabilitation:* reforming the criminal so that when he returns to society he will be inclined to obey the laws and able to make an honest living. 12

How satisfactorily do American prisons perform by these criteria? Well, of course, they do punish. But on the other scores they don't do so well. Their effect in discouraging future criminality by the prisoner or others is the subject of much debate, but the soaring rates of the last 20 years suggest that prisons are not a dramatically effective deterrent to criminal behavior. Prisons do isolate convicted criminals, but only to divert crime from ordinary citizens to prison guards and fellow inmates. Almost no one contends anymore that prisons rehabilitate their inmates. If anything, they probably impede rehabilitation by forcing inmates into prolonged and almost exclusive association with other criminals. And prisons cost a lot of money. Housing a typical prisoner in a typical prison costs far more than a stint at a top university. This cost would be justified if prisons did the job they were intended for. But it is clear to all that prisons fail on the very grounds—humanity and hope of rehabilitation—that caused them to replace earlier, cheaper forms of punishment. 13

The universal acknowledgment that prisons do not rehabilitate criminals has produced two responses. The first is to retain the hope of rehabilitation but do away with imprisonment as much as possible and replace it with various forms of "alternative treatment," such as psychotherapy, supervised probation, and vocational training. Psychiatrist Karl Menninger, one of the principal critics of American penology, has suggested even more unconventional approaches, such as "a new job opportunity or a vacation trip, a course of reducing exercises, a cosmetic surgical operation or a herniotomy, some night school courses, a wedding in the family (even one for the patient!), an inspiring sermon." This starry-eyed approach naturally has produced a backlash from critics on the right, who think that it's time to abandon the goal of rehabilitation. They argue that prisons perform an important service just by keeping criminals off the streets, and thus should be used with that purpose alone in mind. 14

So the debate continues to rage in all the same old ruts. No one, of course, would think of copying the medieval practices of Islamic nations and experimenting with punish- 15

ments such as flogging and amputation. But let us consider them anyway. How do they compare with our American prison system in achieving the ostensible objectives of punishment? First, do they punish? Obviously they do, and in a uniquely painful and memorable way. Of course any sensible person, given the choice, would prefer suffering these punishments to years of incarceration in a typical American prison. But presumably no Western penologist would criticize Islamic punishments on the grounds that they are not barbaric enough. Do they deter crime? Yes, and probably more effectively than sending convicts off to prison. Now we read about a prison sentence in the newspaper, then think no more about the criminal's payment for his crimes until, perhaps, years later we read a small item reporting his release. By contrast, one can easily imagine the vivid impression it would leave to be wandering through a local shopping center and to stumble onto the scene of some poor wretch being lustily flogged. And the occasional sight of an habitual offender walking around with a bloody stump at the end of his arm no doubt also would serve as a forceful reminder that crime does not pay.

Do flogging and amputation discourage recidivism? No one knows whether the scars on his back would dissuade a criminal from risking another crime, but it is hard to imagine that corporal measures could stimulate a higher rate of recidivism than already exists. Islamic forms of punishment do not serve the favorite new right goal of simply isolating criminals from the rest of society, but they may achieve the same purpose of making further crimes impossible. In the movie *Bonnie and Clyde,* Warren Beatty successfully robs a bank with his arm in a sling, but this must be dismissed as artistic license. It must be extraordinarily difficult, at the very least, to perform much violent crime with only one hand. 16

Do these medieval forms of punishment rehabilitate the criminal? Plainly not. But long prison terms do not rehabilitate either. And it is just as plain that typical Islamic punishments are no crueler to the convict than incarceration in the typical American state prison. 17

Of course that are other reasons besides its bizarre forms 18
of punishment that the Islamic system of justice seems uncivilized to the Western mind. One is the absence of due process. Another is the long list of offenses—such as drinking, adultery, blasphemy, "profiteering," and so on—that can bring on conviction and punishment. A third is all the ritualistic mumbo jumbo in pronouncements of Islamic law (like that talk about puberty and amnesia in the ayatollah's quotation at the beginning of this article). Even in these matters, however, a little cultural modesty is called for. The vast majority of American criminals are convicted and sentenced as a result of plea bargaining, in which due process plays almost no role. It has been only half a century since a wave of religious fundamentalism stirred this country to outlaw the consumption of alcoholic beverages. Most states also still have laws imposing austere constraints on sexual conduct. Only two weeks ago the *Washington Post* reported that the FBI had spent two and a half years and untold amounts of money to break up a nationwide pornography ring. Flogging the clients of prostitutes, as the Pakistanis did, does seem silly. But only a few months ago Mayor Koch of New York was proposing that clients caught in his own city have their names broadcast by radio stations. We are not so far advanced on such matters as we often like to think. Finally, my lawyer friends assure me that the rules of jurisdiction for American courts contain plenty of petty requirements and bizarre distinctions that would sound silly enough to foreign ears.

Perhaps it sounds barbaric to talk of flogging and ampu- 19
tation, and perhaps it is. But our system of punishment also is barbaric, and probably more so. Only cultural smugness about their system and willful ignorance about our own make it easy to regard the one as cruel and the other as civilized. We inflict our cruelties away from public view, while nations like Pakistan stage them in front of 10,000 onlookers. Their outrages are visible; ours are not. Most Americans can live their lives for years without having their peace of mind

disturbed by the knowledge of what goes on in our prisons. To choose imprisonment over flogging and amputation is not to choose human kindness over cruelty, but merely to prefer that our cruelties be kept out of sight, and out of mind.

Public flogging and amputation may be more barbaric 20
forms of punishment than imprisonment, even if they are not more cruel. Society may pay a higher price for them, even if the particular criminal does not. Revulsion against officially sanctioned violence and infliction of pain derives from something deeply ingrained in the Western conscience, and clearly it is something admirable. Grotesque displays of the sort that occur in Islamic countries probably breed a greater tolerance for physical cruelty, for example, which prisons do not do precisely because they conceal their cruelties. In fact it is our admirable intolerance for calculated violence that makes it necessary for us to conceal what we have not been able to do away with. In a way this is a good thing, since it holds out the hope that we may eventually find a way to do away with it. But in another way it is a bad thing, since it permits us to congratulate ourselves on our civilized humanitarianism while violating its norms in this one area of our national life.

Topics for Writing

1. *Respond.* Consider your childhood experiences with crime and punishment. When you misbehaved, how were you punished? Compare an occasion where the punishment seemed appropriate for your "crime" with an occasion where the punishment seemed excessive or inconsequential. What did these two experiences teach you about the consequences of wrongdoing? Draft your comparison for the advice section in a magazine such as *Parade* or *Family Circle*. (*Resources for comparison:* Anna Quindlen, "Execution"; John Holt, "Types of Discipline.")
2. *Analyze.* Examine the "cultural smugness" that may be embedded in Chapman's description of Islamic and Western forms of punishment. In particular, examine the language (the assertions and asides) he uses to comment on public floggings and prison violence and to compare the five functions of Western imprisonment with the effects of Islamic torture. Present your conclusions to a class comparing cultural customs. (*Resources for comparison:* Le Ly Hayslip, "Playing Stupid"; Edward T. Hall, "The Arab World.")
3. *Argue.* Evaluate Chapman's conclusions about the success of rehabilitation. Read studies by professional criminologists and columns by political critics that present the two responses Chapman mentions. Then write a proposal for an alternative to the "prisoner's dilemma," together with a procedure for studying its effectiveness. (*Resources for comparison:* Brigid Brophy, "The Rights of Animals"; Vicki Hearne, "What's Wrong with Animal Rights?")

DAVID HAGE et al.

The magazine *U.S. News and World Report* assigned a staff of writers to research and write the article that follows. David Hage was born in 1955 in Minneapolis, Minnesota; was educated at Yale University and the University of York; and has worked at the Minneapolis *Star Tribune*. Don L. Burroughs was born in 1963 in Lansing, Michigan, and was educated at Syracuse University. Robert Black was born in 1948 in New York City; attended the University of Wisconsin, Columbia University, and the University of California, Berkeley; and has worked at the Urban Institute and the Congressional Budget Office. Richard J. Newman was born in 1965 in St. Louis, Missouri, and was educated at Boston College. Sara Collins was born in Joliet, Illinois, and was educated at Washington University in St. Louis. In "Hidden Monopolies," this team of writers classifies various industries by the way they have conspired to fleece the American consumer.

Hidden Monopolies

(Division and Classification)

People of the same trade seldom meet together, even for merriment and diversion, but the conversation ends in a conspiracy against the public, or in some contrivance to raise prices. 1
—Adam Smith, 1776

Peanut butter is a staple in the Connecticut household of Emily Kerr, a laid-off factory worker who struggles to feed three children on an unemployment check and a part-time 2 job. But it's also surprisingly expensive, and that sticks in Kerr's craw. Like millions of hard-pressed consumers, she should blame the nation's peanut growers and the federal government, which together orchestrate an elaborate quota system that limits the number of peanut farmers in this country as well as their crop production. The resulting shortage keeps peanut prices unnecessarily high, up to 100 percent above the cost of growing them. "You hate to make children go without something they love," says Kerr. "But how can I keep paying so much?"

With recession raging and inflation all but extinguished, 3
it's hard to believe that Americans still have to pay excessive prices for many key products. But it's true. Over the past decade, deregulation, growing world trade and smashing technological advances have compelled most businesses to compete ferociously and freely to maintain profits. Yet these pressures have also forced a number of players to find crafty new ways of crushing rivals and exploiting markets.

The ingenious manipulations of the marketplace are un- 4
folding in the shadowy recesses of the economy and are often hidden from unsuspecting consumers and unsophisticated regulators. Large cable television operators, for example, are preying on fledgling competitors that offer lower-cost service by quietly blocking the smaller operators' efforts to buy popular programming. Dominant airlines are using state-of-the-art computers to solidify their control of ticket sales. And the nation's doctors have subtly expanded their business by referring patients to X-ray labs and physical-therapy clinics in which they hold ownership stakes.

Hurting customers. Sometimes, as Emily Kerr knows 5
well, Washington works in concert with private interests, and the consumer ends up getting hurt. Mindful of the new threats ravaging other industries, for example, the farm lobby redoubled its efforts to hold on to and expand government programs that shelter it from competition. This lobbying has greatly increased the prices the public pays for milk, sugar, peanut butter and a host of other supermarket products.

Laissez-faire. Ironically, during the Reagan administra- 6 tion, Washington was meddling with farm prices at the same time that it was backing away from traditional antitrust enforcement. The number of antitrust suits filed by the federal government dwindled from more than 142 in 1981 to 19 in 1989, partly because regulators felt the market was best left to itself and partly because a more conservative judiciary consistently threw out such lawsuits. "With a judiciary that was half appointed by Reagan, it became harder and harder for plaintiffs to win," says law Prof. Bob Lande of the University of Baltimore. "There were people in the business world who believed they could get away with anything they wanted."

Free-market ideology remains dominant in Washington, but there is a growing move toward reregulation. David Kessler, head of the Food and Drug Administration, has led the charge with crackdowns on food labeling and silicone breast implants. And Congress, which is considering the reregulation of cable TV and airline reservation systems, isn't far behind. 7

Last month, in a step that vindicated Adam Smith's faith in free markets, Boris Yeltsin liberated Russian food prices from government regulation. But Smith's more cynical insights were vindicated as well when Moscow's bakers promptly conspired to set prices. The new round of price fixing on this side of the Atlantic may be cloaked in technology or concealed by red tape, but the lesson is the same: There are many ways to fleece the consumer. 8

Milk. Silvia Smith-Torres, executive director of the Cari-anne Center in Dade County, Fla., spends about a third of her tight $2,000-a-month food budget buying milk for 10 recovering addicts and their 15 children. On the lucky day when she can find it for less than the regular $2.88 a gallon, the mothers and children get more eggs and fresh fruit and vegetables. When she can't, they don't. Milk prices in Florida—and throughout the nation—could be lower. But the dairy industry's precious federal milk program restricts competition, preventing low-cost reconstituted milk from reach- 9 ing Florida store shelves, mandating inflated milk prices far from the dairy heartland and keeping prices from falling to their natural levels throughout the nation. The U.S. Department of Agriculture estimated in the mid-1980s that total deregulation of the dairy industry would save consumers nearly $2 billion and taxpayers hundreds of millions more. The dairy lobby counters that the milk program benefits consumers, as well as farmers, by moderating erratic price swings. But most consumers would probably swap a little stability for a lot of savings.

The federal government adds to shoppers' grocery bills by 10
simply outshopping them. Last year, the Department of Agriculture bought up the equivalent of 837 million gallons of milk—or 5 percent of the nation's total—in the form of cheese, butter and nonfat dry milk. That shopping spree, not extravagant compared with those in recent years, cost taxpayers $785 million and may have kept the price of milk some 8 percent above its natural levels. Because government price supports swell the deficit by encouraging farmers to produce excess milk that Uncle Sam must buy, Washington started to reduce the price support level during the late 1980s. But Congress basically froze the price floor in 1990, an act that will cost consumers nearly $9 billion by 1995, according to a study by economic consultants at Sparks Commodities in Virginia.

Even on a day when the price of milk is floating above 11
the government support price, the free-market system is not allowed to determine milk prices. Under the byzantine rules of federal milk-marketing orders, virtually the only people buying milk at the market price are cheese makers in Wisconsin. The USDA takes the price Wisconsin manufacturers are offering at any given time and jacks it up according to where and for what purpose the milk is being sold. A yogurt factory in Oregon, for instance, must pay at least 42 cents more than the Wisconsin cheese makers; and a Boston milk wholesaler has to pay $3.64 extra. The system especially punishes East Coast consumers, who spend 11 to 24 percent more than they would in a freer market.

Local school districts on the lookout for price gouging have to beware of more than just government regulations. The U.S. Justice Department has uncovered a pattern of bid rigging for school milk contracts by collusive dairies from Florida to Utah. The conspiracies have already sent 18 people to jail, with convictions or plea bargains from 39 companies. Judy Whalley, deputy assistant attorney general, believes the ongoing investigation will bring to light hundreds of millions of dollars in overcharges to schools. Says Whalley: "It's shocking that people would steal milk out of the mouths of children." 12

Sugar. Gregory McCormack is proud to be the third generation of McCormacks making candy in Albany, Ga. The president of Bobs Candies generally swallows the high cost of doing business in the United States, saying it would be "un-American" to move his $30 million company. But when the exorbitant price of American sugar was hurting his firm's competitiveness, McCormack instead swallowed his pride, transplanting a small part of his operations and some 30 jobs to an offshore factory in Jamaica. Because the federal sugar program grants a near monopoly to U.S. producers by excluding most imports, McCormack spends almost 30 cents for a pound of refined sugar in Georgia, 50 percent more than the free-market price he pays beyond U.S. borders. Ironically, while America preaches the virtues of the free market to the Third World, McCormack had to go to the Third World to find one. 13

For consumers confined to shopping at their local supermarkets, that long-distance option is not available. Americans pay an annual food bill that is some $2 billion more than it would be if they could buy sugar at world prices. The government protects the U.S. sweetener industry by blocking the entry of most foreign sugar, forcing up prices. Unlike U.S. grain programs, funded by the Treasury, the sugar program rewards producers—$235,000 for the average sugar cane plantation and $50,500 for each sugar beet farm—entirely at consumers' expense. 14

Few Americans can measure the hidden costs they pay to support the sweetener industry, in part because they pay in so many ways. Only a quarter of the nation's sugar budget actually goes for the white crystals themselves. The U.S. Department of Agriculture estimates that in the late 1980s, consumers paid a $573 million premium for table sugar but an additional $1.3 billion for baked goods, sweets and drinks containing sugar. 15

Inflated prices. The USDA says the sugar program forced consumers to pay yet an additional $1.3 billion for corn syrup, largely used in soft drinks. In the 1980s, beverage makers switched from expensive sugar to corn syrup, whose prices—though lower than sugar—remain inflated as long as there is protection from world markets. The architects of U.S. sugar policy never intended to boost the profits of corn farmers and processors every time shoppers bought a six-pack of Pepsi. But now that money flows that way, Corn Belt senators have become big backers of high sugar prices. 16

With prices protected in Congress, consumers' best hope for relief may lie not in Washington but in Geneva. At the talks on the General Agreement on Tariffs and Trade, America supports a proposal to reduce quotas and subsidies for commodities like sugar by 20 percent. The Europeans, who protect their own sugar producers with even higher prices, have thus far resisted. 17

John Roney of the Hawaiian Sugar Planters' Association warns that in an unsubsidized global market, raw sugar prices would rise from the current world level of 9 cents because Europe would no longer dump excess supplies at below cost. The most efficient world producers spend some 12 cents a pound to make raw sugar. But even that would undercut current U.S. prices—a disconcerting thought for sugar planters but a sweet dream for consumers. 18

Health care. Dr. Laurent Lehmann thought science had delivered a minor miracle in 1990 when Sandoz Pharmaceuticals Corp. began marketing Clozaril, a schizophrenia drug that represented a breakthrough for 3,600 hard-to-treat pa- 19 tients under his jurisdiction at the U.S. Department of Veterans Affairs. But the miracle vanished when Lehmann learned that because Clozaril can have dangerous side effects on a patient's white blood cells, Sandoz required customers to buy an extra package of blood-monitoring services. That tripled the treatment cost to $9,000 a year per patient and hit taxpayers with an extra $24.5 million in medical costs. Lehmann said the VA could monitor its own patients and insisted that Sandoz "unbundle" Clozaril from the monitoring package. Sandoz eventually agreed, but not before the Federal Trade Commission had accused the company of an antitrust violation known as tying behavior.

Tying arrangements, which occur when a company ex- 20
ploits its control over one product to force the purchase of additional products or services, are an arcane but growing form of market manipulation. And they are costing consumers billions of dollars. Taken together, tying arrangements and other anticompetitive practices probably add 10 percent to the nation's health-care bill, according to H. E. Frech, a health economist at the University of California at Santa Barbara. That amounted to a whopping $74 billion last year, or $790 in the health bill of the typical household.

Self-serving. The most explosive example of tying behav- 21
ior in medicine has emerged in physician "self-referrals." A recent study of 23 home-nursing agencies by the Florida Health Care Cost Containment Board, for example, found that nearly one quarter had financial ties to doctors who steered patients to them. These agencies billed customers 40 percent more than nursing agencies without ties to referring doctors. In another FTC case, the government asserted that Gerald Friedman, a Pomona, Calif., doctor, had achieved a virtual monopoly in the local market for outpatient dialysis and that he was using this control to funnel patients to his inpatient dialysis service, where he could charge higher fees. An attorney for Friedman said the arrangement was designed to protect patients from hepatitis infections from competitors' machinery, but the doctor agreed to halt the practice.

The U.S. Department of Health and Human Services 22

estimates that 1 in 4 medical-testing laboratories—or at least 80,000 facilities—is now owned wholly or in part by doctors who refer their own patients. Unfortunately, surveys show that few consumers will defy their doctors' advice or shop for lower lab prices. The Florida study found that, last year, the average patient paid $46.22 at doctor-owned labs, compared with $27.85 at independent labs.

The Health and Human Services Department issued new rules in July that can cut off Medicare or Medicaid payments to a clinic that gets more than 40 percent of its business from doctor-owners. But 60 percent of the nation's health-care bill is paid privately and remains beyond direct federal regulation. And because so many consumers place themselves at the mercy of doctors and hospitals, it appears that tying behavior will remain a prescription for higher prices. 23

Cable TV. When Valley Wireless Cable Television opened shop in Bakersfield, Calif., last year, it offered consumers many reasons to switch from the incumbent cable TV franchise. Valley carries ESPN, Showtime and Home Box Office, just like its more established competitor. And because it beams its signals via microwave to tiny rooftop receiving dishes instead of using costly underground coaxial cable, it sells for $24.95 a month, not the $39 charged by its rival. But Valley can't offer Turner Network Television, which carries Sunday-night football games, or Prime Ticket, a local sports service. The incumbent cable franchise has those programming services locked up with exclusive contracts. So Valley has landed just 1,200 subscribers in a market of 150,000 television homes. 24

Valley's struggle shows how barriers to entry keep competition low and prices high as new technologies like "wireless" cable try to find a niche in the $19 billion cable business. Cable operators now have monopolies in 99.5 percent of cable-wired cities. And since 1986, when Congress deregulated rates for most franchises, prices have shot up at three times the rate of inflation. The National Cable Television Association insists that consumers have lots of alternatives, including network television, local independent stations and 25 home video. But the Consumer Federation of America estimates that true cable competition would cut cable rates by 50 percent, saving consumers $6 billion a year.

As if to cement their market control, the big cable franchisers and the companies that sell them programming have bought huge ownership stakes in each other. The nation's biggest cable operator, Tele-Communications Inc., owns 24 percent of TNT and 48 percent of the Discovery Channel. Time Warner, which owns HBO and Cinemax, has expanded into cable franchising and is now the nation's No. 2 operator. 26

Time Warner says consumers benefit from cross-ownership: It has poured $500 million, for example, into new HBO programming. Robert Thomson, senior vice president at TCI, says that without exclusive rights to certain programs, local cable franchises would never invest in risky new programming ventures such as Turner Broadcasting's TNT, into which his company poured some $240 million. 27

Still, many in Congress feel that wireless cable and other upstart technologies need a helping hand. The Senate takes up debate this week on a bill to reregulate cable, but until Washington acts, consumers will continue to receive a monthly zapping from the cable industry. 28

Airline reservations. In 1938, the U.S. Justice Department sued five big Hollywood studios to force divestiture of their movie theater chains. The government said a studio that controlled theaters could steer consumers to its own movies, and the ensuing "Paramount" decrees struck a blow against vertical integration. Yet today, 54 years later, this practice still riddles the American airline industry. Eighty percent of airline tickets—accounting for more than 400 million flights a year—are booked through travel agents using computerized reservation systems that are owned by the seven biggest airlines. Some 70 percent of those tickets are booked through two reservation systems, Sabre and Apollo, which are owned or co-owned by the nation's two largest airlines, American and United, respectively. 29

What riles regulators and smaller carriers is that studies show that travel agents steer customers to the airline that 30 owns their computer reservation system. Overt bias was banned from the computers in 1984, but the U.S. Department of Transportation estimates that remaining biases, together with volume commissions to travel agents, shift $2 billion to $3 billion in ticket sales to the big carriers that own the computers. This tidal wave of business could add to the airline industry's growing market concentration—and to the price of tickets. In 1990, for example, the U.S. General Accounting Office found that fares were 27 percent higher at airports dominated by one carrier than at airports with competition.

In addition, smaller airlines pay millions of dollars in "booking fees" to have their tickets sold on systems owned by big carriers. In 1988, Sabre and Apollo collected $430 million—or 15 percent of the industry's total profits—in booking fees. Without booking fees, says Con Hitchcock of the Aviation Consumer Action Project, "you would see some savings for consumers and you would not see so many small carriers endangered." 31

Expensive entry. Most economists agree that the threat of start-up airlines is essential to keeping airfares down. But to truly compete today, small airlines must have their own reservation systems. This, according to a GAO report, has become increasingly difficult: "The costs of establishing a new [reservation system] are so high that establishing a new [system] is impractical for an entrant." 32

Reservation systems help travelers by sifting among hundreds of flights and fares. And the big carriers argue that booking fees are a return on their investment in the systems. "I don't know of any other industry where a start-up firm could instantly have their product in front of every retailer in the country," says Greg Conley of Covia, corporate parent of Apollo. 33

But the GAO has launched a fresh study of reservation bias, and Congress may soon entertain a bill that would further level the playing field between small carriers and big computers. Though the bill's passage is uncertain, consumer advocates say it's time to crack down on this high-tech competition crusher. 34

Topics for Writing

1. *Respond.* Make a list of the goods and services you purchased this month whose cost may be inflated by the type of conspiratorial practices described by David Hage et al. Some possibilities to research include car repair, video rentals, concert tickets, and prescription drugs. Write an essay for the campus newspaper classifying these "monopolies" and alerting students to alternatives. (*Resources for comparison:* Tom and Ray Magliozzi, "Inside the Engine"; Russell Baker, "The Plot Against People.")
2. *Analyze.* Explain why Hage et al. consider the following practices "criminal": price supports, import restrictions, self-referrals, cross-ownership, and vertical integration. Read some studies of the antitrust movement. Then write an essay for your political science class in which you demonstrate how the research of Hage et al. supports the conclusion that corporate crime continues to "fleece the consumer." (*Resources for comparison:* Robert Sherrill, "Murder, Inc."; Robert Reich, "Secession of the Successful.")
3. *Argue.* David Hage et al. argue that corporate crime began when deregulation pressured companies "to find crafty new ways of crushing rivals and exploiting markets." They also argue that Boris Yeltsin's deregulation of the Russian economy produced the same results. Research a reregulation issue—such as fuel emissions—that has an effect on the environment. Then write a letter to your congressional representative arguing for (or against) such reregulation. (*Resources for comparison:* N. Scott Momaday, "The Way to Rainy Mountain"; Marjorie Kelly, "Revolution in the Market Place.")

BARBARA EHRENREICH

Barbara Ehrenreich was born in 1941 in Butte, Montana, and was educated at Reed College and Rockefeller University. She has worked as an editor for the Health Policy Advisory Center, a columnist for *Mother Jones* magazine, and a contributing editor to *Ms.* An outspoken feminist and socialist, she has contributed essays to magazines such as *Radical America, Nation, Esquire, Vogue,* and the *New York Times Magazine.* Her books include *The American Health Empire: Power, Profits, and Politics* (1970), *Witches, Midwives and Nurses* (1972), *The Mean Season: The Attack on the Welfare State* (1987), *Fear of Falling: The Inner Life of the Middle Class* (1989), and *The Worst Years of Our Lives: Irreverent Notes from an Age of Greed* (1990). In "Marginal Men," reprinted from *The Worst Years of Our Lives,* Ehrenreich defines "marginal men" as those who live in the suburbs, are unemployed, and commit crimes.

Marginal Men

(Definition)

1 Crime seems to change character when it crosses a bridge or a tunnel. In the city, crime is taken as emblematic of the vast injustices of class and race. In the suburbs, though, it's intimate and psychological—resistant to generalization, a mystery of the individual soul. Recall the roar of commentary that followed the murderous assault on a twenty-eight-year-old woman jogging in Central Park. Every detail of the assailants' lives was sifted for sociological significance: Were they poor? How poor? Students or dropouts? From families with two parents or one? And so on, until the awful singu-

larity of the event was lost behind the impersonal grid of Class, Race, and Sex.

Now take the Midtown Tunnel east to the Long Island Expressway, out past the clutter of Queens to deepest suburbia, where almost every neighborhood is "good" and "social pathology" is something you learn about in school. Weeks before the East Harlem youths attacked a jogger, Long Islanders were shaken by two murders which were, if anything, even more inexplicably vicious than the assault in Central Park. In early March, the body of thirteen-year-old Kelly Tinyes was found in the basement of a house just down the block from her own. She had been stabbed, strangled, and hit with a blunt instrument before being mutilated with a bayonet. A few weeks later, fourteen-year-old Jessica Manners was discovered along the side of a road in East Setauket, strangled to death, apparently with her own bra, and raped. 2

Suspects have been apprehended. Their high-school friends, parents, and relatives have been interviewed. Their homes and cars have been searched; their photos published. We know who they hung out with and what they did in their spare time. But on the scale of large social meanings, these crimes don't rate. No one is demanding that we understand—or condemn—the white communities that nourished the killers. No one is debating the roots of violence in the land of malls and tract homes. Only in the city, apparently, is crime construed as something "socioeconomic." Out here it's merely "sick." 3

But East Setauket is not really all that far from East Harlem. If something is festering in the ghetto, something very similar is gnawing away at Levittown and East Meadow. A "way of life," as the cliché goes, is coming to an end, and in its place a mean streak is opening up and swallowing everything in its path. Economists talk about "deindustrialization" and "class polarization." I think of it as the problem of *marginal men:* they are black and white, Catholic and Pentecostal, rap fans and admirers of technopop. What they have in common is that they are going nowhere—nowhere legal, that is. 4

Consider the suspects in the Long Island murders. 5

Twenty-one-year-old Robert Golub, in whose basement Kelly Tinyes was killed, is described in *Newsday* as an "unemployed body-builder." When his high-school friends went off to college, he stayed behind in his parents' home in Valley Stream. For a while, he drove a truck for a cosmetics firm, but he lost that job, in part because of his driving record: his license has been suspended twelve times since 1985. At the time of the murder, he had been out of work for several months, constructing a life around his weight-lifting routine and his dream of becoming an entrepreneur.

Christopher Loliscio, the suspect in the Manners case, is 6
nineteen, and, like Golub, lives with his parents. He has been in trouble before, and is charged with third-degree assault and "menacing" in an altercation that took place on the campus of the State University at Stony Brook last December. Loliscio does not attend college himself. He is employed as a landscaper.

The suburbs are full of young white men like Golub and 7
Loliscio. If they had been born twenty years earlier, they might have found steady work in decent-paying union jobs, married early, joined the volunteer fire department, and devoted their leisure to lawn maintenance. But the good blue-collar jobs are getting sparser, thanks to "deindustrialization"—which takes the form, in Long Island, of cutbacks in the defense and aerospace industries. Much of what's left is likely to be marginal, low-paid work. Nationwide, the earnings of young white men dropped 18 percent between 1973 and 1986, according to the Census Bureau, and the earnings of male high-school dropouts plunged 42 percent.

Landscaping, for example—a glamorous term for raking 8
and mowing—pays four to five dollars an hour; truck driving for a small firm is in the same range: not enough to pay for a house, a college education, or even a mid-size wedding reception at the VFW hall.

And even those modest perquisites of life in the subyuppie 9
class have become, in some sense, "not enough." On Long Island, the culture that once sustained men in blue-collar occupations is crumbling as more affluent settlers move in,

filling the vacant lots with their new, schooner-shaped, $750,000 homes. In my town, for example, the last five years saw the bowling alley close and the blue-collar bar turn into a pricey dining spot. Even the volunteer fire department is having trouble recruiting. The prestigious thing to join is a $500-a-year racquetball club; there's just not much respect anymore for putting out fires.

So the marginal man lives between two worlds—one that he aspires to and one that is dying, and neither of which he can afford. Take "Rick," the twenty-two-year-old son of family friends. His father is a machinist in an aerospace plant which hasn't been hiring anyone above the floor-sweeping level for years now. Not that Rick has ever shown any interest in his father's trade. For one thing, he takes too much pride in his appearance to put on the dark green company-supplied work clothes his father has worn for the past twenty years. Rick has his kind of uniform: pleated slacks, high-tops, Italian knit cardigans, and a $300 leather jacket, accessorized with a gold chain and earring stud. 10

To his parents, Rick is a hard-working boy for whom things just don't seem to work out. For almost a year after high school, he worked behind a counter at Crazy Eddie's, where the pay is low but at least you can listen to rock and roll all day. Now he has a gig doing valet parking at a country club. The tips are good and he loves racing around the lot in the Porsches and Lamborghinis of the stockbroker class. But the linchpin of his economic strategy is living at home, with his parents and sisters, in the same room he's occupied since third grade. Rick is a long way from being able to afford even a cramped, three-bedroom house like his family home; and, given the choice, he'd rather have a new Camaro anyway. 11

If this were the seventies, Rick might have taken up marijuana, the Grateful Dead, and vague visions of a better world. But like so many of his contemporaries in the eighties, Rick has no problem with "the system," which, in his mind, embraces every conceivable hustle, legal or illegal. Two years ago, he made a tidy bundle dealing coke in a local dance 12 club, bought a $20,000 car, and smashed it up. Now he spends his evenings as a bouncer in an illegal gambling joint—his parents still think he's out "dancing"—and is proud of the handgun he's got stowed in his glove compartment.

Someday Rick will use that gun, and I'll probably be the 13
first to say—like Robert Golub's friends—"but he isn't the kind of person who would hurt *anyone*." Except that even now I can sense the danger in him. He's smart enough to know he's only a cut-rate copy of the upscale young men in *GQ* ads and MTV commercials. Viewed from Wall Street or Southampton, he's a peon, a member of the invisible underclass that parks cars, waits on tables, and is satisfied with a five-dollar tip and a remark about the weather.

He's also proud. And there's nowhere for him to put that 14
pride except into the politics of gesture: the macho stance, the seventy-five-mile-per-hour takeoff down the expressway, and eventually maybe, the drawn gun. Jobs are the liberal solution; conservatives would throw in "traditional values." But what the marginal men—from Valley Stream to Bedford-Stuyvesant—need most of all is *respect*. If they can't find that in work, or in a working-class life-style that is no longer honored, they'll extract it from someone weaker—a girlfriend, a random jogger, a neighbor, perhaps just any girl. They'll find a victim.

Topics for Writing

1. *Respond.* Catalog the changes in your town—job cutbacks, nonresidential landlords, community-center closings. Make a list of friends, relatives, or neighbors who live with their parents, work at marginal jobs, and have had some difficulty with the law. Use this information to write a letter to your local paper defining how socioeconomic factors may explain the crime patterns in your town. (*Resources for comparison:* W. D. Wetherell, "The Bass, the River, and Sheila Mant"; Brent Staples, "Black Men and Public Space.")
2. *Analyze.* Ehrenreich mentions three related terms to define "marginal men": *deindustrialization, class polarization,* and *underclass.* What sort of definitions—direct or indirect—does she provide for these terms in her essay? Look them up in a current dictionary. Then write an essay that might be submitted to an economics class in which you analyze how such terms define a change in our social structure. (*Resources for comparison:* Lars Eighner, "My Daily Dives in the Dumpster"; Joseph Epstein, "They Told Me You Was High Class.")
3. *Argue.* Ehrenreich suggests that neither the liberal solution (jobs) nor the conservative solution (traditional values) is sufficient to change the situation of "marginal men." Draft your own solution that will provide the respect these individuals need in a letter to those establishing educational policies or administering job-training programs in your area. (*Resources for comparison:* Charles Johnson, "The Sorcerer's Apprentice"; Shelby Steele, "White Guilt.")

LUCY KAVALER

Lucy Kavaler was born in New York City in 1930 and was educated at Oberlin College. She has worked as the senior editor of medical publications for a publishing company and as the executive editor of the *Female Patient.* She has contributed articles to periodicals such as *National History, Smithsonian,* and *Redbook.* Her other publications include books on science for children—*The Wonder of Algae* (1961), *Dangerous Air* (1967), *The Dangers of Noise* (1978); books on social history—*The Private World of High Society* (1960) and *The Astors: A Family Chronicle* (1966); and several books on public issues—*Noise: The New Menace* (1975) and *A Matter of Degree: Heat, Life, and Death* (1981). In "Of Riot, Murder, and the Heat of Passion," reprinted from *A Matter of Degree,* Kavaler demonstrates how temperature, especially excessive heat, affects human behavior.

Of Riot, Murder, and the Heat of Passion

(Cause and Effect)

1 On a June Sunday in 1967, three young men broke into a photographic supply warehouse in Tampa, Florida. The temperature was in the mid-90s and the humidity was high; nonetheless, both citizens and police gave chase. One of the robbers, stripped to the waist to better endure the heat, was stopped in his run by a high cyclone fence, and there he was shot by a policeman. As the bullet struck, the young man reached up, grabbed at the fence, and hung on. He was in this position, with his hands over his head, when other

pursuers rushed up. The scene was prolonged, because the ambulance called by a bystander was lost on its way. The young man was black and the policeman was white. All the criteria for a riot were present. And by nightfall, despite police guarantees of an investigation of the shooting, crowds had gathered and police cars were being stoned, stores looted, and power lines knocked down.

Similar scenes of violence took place that year in Newark, 2
Cincinnati, Atlanta, and many other cities. By the end of September, 164 riots had broken out in 128 cities, five of them in New York and four in Chicago. The largest number took place in July, the National Advisory Commission on Civil Disorders learned, after studying the records month by month. There had been just one minor disorder in January, none in February.

The temperature records of the cities in which riots oc- 3
curred gave high readings for the day preceding the incident that precipitated the violence. It was 90 degrees Fahrenheit or higher in Atlanta, Newark, Cincinnati, Phoenix, Tucson, Dayton, Paterson, Cambridge, and Tampa and was in the 80s before riots in Rockford, Illinois; Detroit and Grand Rapids, Michigan; and Elizabeth, Englewood, New Brunswick, and Jersey City, New Jersey. And so it has become customary to blame the long hot summer for riots.

Heat alone, to be sure, does not bring on a riot; poverty, 4
unemployment, economic and social injustices, and real or fancied antagonisms are basic causes. But summertime temperatures make the lives of the city poor increasingly miserable. Brick and concrete retain much more heat than do soil and grass; even after sundown the buildings and streets remain hotter than the air, while grass by then is cooler. Winds that might bring relief are blocked by buildings. At night the inner city is an island of heat.

The discomfort of their crowded airless rooms drives city 5
residents out onto the streets in the evenings in numbers sufficient to be dangerous should a provocative incident occur. Most riots begin between 7 P.M. and 1:30 A.M., before exhaustion sends people back inside to bed.

New York City has had two major power blackouts, one 6

on a November night and the other in July. There was little looting in November. During the July blackout, stores were emptied to the bare walls, and furniture, television sets, large appliances and small, clothing, and anything else that could be carried away was taken. Estimated losses of storekeepers ranged from $150 to $300 million, and 3,076 people were arrested.

When the lights came on again, the November blackout 7
was recalled. A comparison between the two is not truly valid, because the July blackout lasted much longer; however, it seems logical to attribute some of the lawlessness to the high summer temperatures. Many New Yorkers, weary after a day of readings over 90 degrees, were out on the streets. A city plunged in darkness was provocation for plunder, and it was warm enough for looters to stay outside and go from one store to another, taking more each time.

Tempers explode when it is hot. In cool weather, discon- 8
tent may be expressed with less violence. Astronomers of an earlier day used to say that inhabitants of Mercury had to be very hot-tempered, because that is the planet closest to the sun. At the end of a ten-day heat wave, a newspaper reported that a knife fight broke out when one man asked another, "Hot enough for you?"

On the night of August 4, 1892, murder took place in 9
the town of Fall River, Massachusetts, and Lizzie Borden was accused of having hacked her father and stepmother to death with an ax. Although she was acquitted after a sensational trial, many went on believing in her guilt.

Few of the hundreds of thousands of words that have 10
been written about the murder mentioned the great heat wave in Fall River that August. But all those living in the Borden house must have been at a high level of irritability because of the heat. Was Lizzie the most affected, or might it have been the maid in her stifling attic room? Some witnesses did later claim to have seen the maid commit the act, but their words were discounted.

What really happened in Fall River long ago may never 11
be known, but deaths by violence are indeed a feature of

heat waves. Both New York and St. Louis sweltered in July 1966. Thirty-one homicides and 23 suicides took place that month, compared to 13 homicides and 38 suicides during a period of moderate temperatures.

The New York City Police Department Crime Comparison Reports reveal that 157 murders and non-negligent manslaughters occurred in July of 1977, compared to 117 in May. The total of felonies known to have been committed in July of the previous year amounted to 42,734, against 38,516 that May. August is a bad month too. In the summers of 1979 and 1980, the New York police department transferred men from headquarters duty and ordered overtime to increase the number of officers patrolling the streets. During the prolonged 1980 heat wave, the Texas Department of Human Resources found the number of cases of child abuse to be markedly higher than in previous summers, when heat was less intense. 12

To study the effects of heat on human behavior, a test was carried out at the Kansas Institute for Environmental Research in which high school dropouts, juvenile delinquents, and parolee volunteers were packed in a small, hot room. Arguments and fistfights broke out, and one young man threatened another with a knife. When the same volunteers were placed in less crowded conditions in a cooler room, nobody became aggressive. 13

Even normally calm people tend to become tense, irritable, and unreasonable, given to snapping over trivia at spouses, children, lovers, relatives, friends, and colleagues, when it is hot. Students crowded in a 90-degree room were hostile to a speaker, while those in a cooler room were prepared to give him a chance. The discomfort of heat could affect a personnel manager deciding whether to hire an applicant, a couple deciding whether to separate. 14

When heat is accompanied by humidity, irritability reaches a peak. In a study, "The Child and the Weather," reported in the *Pedagogical Seminary* in 1898, Edwin G. Dexter, a Denver teacher, related the frequency of corporal punishment in the schools to the weather. After analyzing 606 instances 15 occurring from 1883 to 1897, he claimed that humidities of 80 to 90 percent, rare in Denver, were linked to an increase of 100 percent in disciplinary problems, compared to the days of low humidity. (Little attention was paid to the fact that the decision as to whether behavior deserved punishment was made by adults, equally irritable in the humidity.)

When heat is accompanied by hot winds, the effect is even 16
more unsettling, particularly to the emotionally unstable. And some winds, like the chinook from the Rockies, can raise the temperature 40 degrees within hours. It has often been said that Italian judges are lenient about crimes of passion committed when the hot, dust-bearing sirocco blows up from the Sahara. "A society's treatment of crime may also be indicative of its emotional attitude—in Latin countries, for example, the law of murder differs considerably from that prevailing among the Teutonic people, and more allowance is made for the state of mind of the murderer." This statement from the *Encyclopaedia Britannica* (1957 edition) presents a stereotype that probably does not stand careful scrutiny. But many Americans share the implied view that a person who commits a crime of passion in certain foreign countries will be acquitted or given a mild sentence. And it happens often enough to keep the stereotype alive.

Such a case began on a March day in 1972 when Ginette 17
Vidal, a forty-one-year-old French medical secretary, and her handsome twenty-nine-year-old lover, Gerard Osselin, drew up a contract swearing to be faithful for life and stating that if either of them broke the contract, the other could kill the faithless one. Both lovers were married, but even sexual relations with spouses was considered breaking the contract. The lovers lived together, but Gerard, lonely for his wife, slipped away to see her every so often. One day Ginette came home when her lover was sleeping, went through his pockets, and found a shopping list in his wife's handwriting. Considering this sufficient proof of infidelity, she shot him where he lay.

At her trial, she cited the contract, surprised to learn it 18
was not legal. Her defense attorney pleaded, "It is hard at

this woman's age when you have heard the bells of perfect love ringing, suddenly to see all this taken away from you." The jury found her guilty, but the sentence was for only ten years. The emotion that had caused her to kill was taken as an extenuating circumstance. Although many criminals motivated by jealousy do not get off as lightly as Mme. Vidal, some sympathy is felt for them, and the "crime of passion" is seen as quite different from a murder in cold blood.

Our vocabulary reveals how, misery, riot, and murder notwithstanding, we are prejudiced in favor of heat and against cold. To be hot-blooded is to be human. Our deepest feelings are linked with heat, and even negative emotions are viewed as better than none at all. We burn with passion, or with rage or lust. We are consumed in the flame of love or, less happily, in the green flame of envy. Being human means being able to catch fire with excitement. Hot-tempered, we take action in the heat of anger, carry on heated arguments, and get hot under the collar. We may send a scorching letter without waiting to cool off. We glow, simmer, seethe, and boil. And when the passion of love or anger is spent, it leaves us burned out. We breathe fire when aroused and see fire in the eye of an angry opponent. Burned up, worked up to a white heat, we may be incited by the inflammatory words of a fiery speaker or firebrand, even a hothead. We may go into a red-hot or white-hot rage. Wishing to succeed, we become fired with ambition. We fall into a hotbed of iniquity, never a cold one. Many of us have a low boiling point. Those who are likable are warmhearted and warm in their manner. 19

Dogs, cats, and other animals who are given human attributes are warm-blooded. In contrast, cold-blooded creatures such as snakes or lizards are commonly viewed as emotionless. 20

To be a lukewarm lover is not good enough. We do not like the cold person, the cold-blooded, or the one whose heart is like ice while planning things coolly. A lack of sexual and/or emotional response is known as being frigid. We are repelled by anyone who is icy, glacial, chilly, chilling, frosty, frostbitten, or wintry in manner; who freezes us out or gives 21 us the cold shoulder. The old slang expression for jail was the "cooler," where those who were hot-tempered were sent to cool off.

The practice of combining words involving heat with words connoting deep feeling has a kind of logic, based on the fact that the body's reactions to the sudden onset of rage, fear, lust, or intense anxiety are remarkably similar to those induced by sudden exposure to extreme heat. The heart beats faster in response both to emotion and to external heat, and breathing quickens. The blood vessels in the skin dilate, and there is an increase in blood flow, making the skin flush. If the blood vessels remain dilated for long, some liquid leaks into the tissues and the face looks swollen. This is the face we associate both with sexual passion and with rage. There is not much difference between the facial expressions for each of these very different emotions. The endocrine glands are activated by heat and hormone secretion is increased. There is a heightened feeling of excitement. Sweating is not only a response to heat but also to nervousness; it begins instantly when one is trapped in an elevator, threatened by a menacing person, or interviewed for a job. 22

While excessive heat produces many unpleasant results, warmth is the state that humans prefer to all others. Cold is dreaded and the feeling of being chilled detested. Despair is associated with low temperatures, and the negativism of coldness adds a nuance to F. Scott Fitzgerald's "In a real dark night of the soul, it is always three o'clock in the morning" ("The Crackup" [1936], *Esquire*). Three o'clock in the morning, standing for the low point of the day and of life, happens to be the time when body temperature drops to its lowest level, some 3 degrees below its daytime peak. Metabolism is slowed, and it is harder to take action. 23

When we remember childhood, it is always high noon in summer, the sun is shining with a golden light, and one clear beautiful warm day follows another. The Arctic and Antarctic are described as unfriendly and hostile, while the tropics are viewed as having a friendly warmth. 24

It is only when pleasing warmth turns into unpleasant 25

hotness that negative emotional and physical characteristics appear. Some people are stimulated by the heat to perform at their peak. Well-motivated individuals compensate for their discomfort by trying harder and keep the quality of their endeavors high by more intense concentration. However, a drop in efficiency, accuracy, and judgment is so common that before air conditioning came into general use, many offices closed early on hot days.

The extent of the decline was investigated by the U.S. 26
Army Research Institute of Environmental Medicine in order to determine how soldiers would perform in hot climates, but the results apply to civilians as well. Soldiers were required to exercise in heat of 103 degrees at high humidity, which caused a rise in body temperature. They were allowed to rest for a while and then, still overheated, were asked to detect light signals flashed in a random manner. A second group of men exercised at 75 degrees. More light flashes were reported by the men who were hotter, which at first seemed to indicate that this state increased their alertness and competence. But when their detection reports were compared with the true number of signals, it was found that the increase was in false reports. Their judgment was not as sound as that of cooler men. They had become more willing to take a risk and insist that they saw a signal when in fact there was none.

Purdue University students participating in a psycholog- 27
ical test carried out in an oppressively hot room gave what they believed were electric shocks to a stranger who had written nasty things about them. However, another group of students, deliberately made angry *before* entering the overheated room, gave fewer shocks. When questioned by psychologists Robert A. Baron and Paul A. Bell, one spoke for all: "The only thing I thought about was getting the hell out of there." The less they reacted to the stranger and the fewer shocks they gave, the sooner they could leave the room. Similarly, outside of the psychology laboratory on many occasions a hot, angry person decides not to stay and argue or commit violence but simply to go home.

Have these reactions anything to do with riot behavior? Dwellers in the crowded, foul-smelling, noisy slums face the heat after having in all probability been angered by employers, shopkeepers, bus drivers, policemen, and members of their families. On very hot days, says Baron, they, like the college students, would probably prefer to escape, but they have no place to go, so they commit violent acts. While riot control depends in the long run on amelioration of basic economic and social problems, Baron sees the establishment of small neighborhood parks, swimming pools, baseball fields, basketball and handball courts, and air-conditioned community centers as a way of helping people cool off physically and emotionally. 28

The temperature that induces excitement, argument, riots, and aggression is very high, but there is an upper limit. Once heat goes beyond that, it is less rather than more stimulating. Studying mice so as to better understand human aggression, Kansas State University researcher Gary Greenberg conducted temperature experiments. To a point, the hotter it got, the more the mice bit one another. But when the temperature reached 95 degrees, the biting declined and the animals became placid, moved about slowly, trying to keep cool, and were indifferent to the other mice. 29

Animal bites of humans occur much more frequently in summer than the rest of the year, notes the New York City Department of Health, but this biting cannot just be blamed on heat-induced irritability. It is rather more in line with Noel Coward's old song about mad dogs and Englishmen going out in the midday sun. Pleasant summer weather brings dogs (mad and otherwise) and children out of doors in great numbers. Children between the ages of five and nine are the most often bitten. Once it gets really hot, stray dogs become less and less active and do less and less biting. 30

For people, too, when high temperatures are prolonged, no effort, no emotional upset, no physical activity is undertaken that will add to the burden of heat the body is enduring. A great indifference to other people and to situations that would normally be exciting or troublesome takes over. 31

"Some loss in initiative is probably the most important single direct result of exposure to a hot environment," states Douglas H. K. Lee, formerly Associate Director of the National Institute of Environmental Health Sciences and an expert on adaptations to desert conditions.

"Who cares about the troop withdrawal? It's too hot to care about anything" was the frequent comment by inhabitants of Seoul, South Korea, when American troop cutbacks were being discussed in August of 1977. In temperatures of 95 to 100 degrees, the air over Seoul was a thick, brown smaze. 32

Similarly, the French Foreign Legionnaires, waiting to go home in 1977 from newly independent Djibouti in Africa, became lethargic. Until then they had recognized the importance of carrying out their duties in the strategic Red Sea port, even though they considered it a desolate hotbox. Motivation must be high if individuals are to overcome their inclination to heat-induced lassitude. Once that motivation was lost, groups of Legionnaires spent the afternoons in the stifling Café de Paris beneath ceiling fans circulating hot air. The ice in the whiskey melted so fast that the drinks were warm before they could be swallowed. Hour after hour the men sat without speaking. They were too enervated to do more than swat the flies. And so passed one long hot afternoon after another. 33

Whenever, as in cases like these, northerners in hot regions become inactive or are unable to function effectively in their jobs, it is taken as confirmation of a popular belief, nurtured by fiction: Americans and Europeans transported to the tropics, it is said, go to seed, failing in their efforts to run the rubber plantation or hold the job in the foreign department of the bank or export-import firm, often drinking too much. As alcohol makes the body hotter, they become even more uncomfortable and incapable of effective action. Scorpions run through their houses, wives return home or take lovers, servants cheat them, meals are inedible, and sleep impossible. In fact, however, far from going to seed, most immigrants do become acclimatized and manage to run the plantation 34 and do their work in the office. But this does not make so good a story.

The stereotype of the native of Africa and the Far East is 35
also that of a lazy person, lying in the shade and refusing to do a good day's work. The custom of the siesta seems to provide additional proof of local lassitude; surely only children and old people take naps in the daytime. Northern tourists are frustrated at finding themselves with no place to go during what they view as the peak hours of the day. The hours from 12 to 3 P.M., even in a capital city such as Asunción, Paraguay, are quiet, with shops and business offices closed and everyone gone home.

It is often suggested that civilizations in the tropics have 36
lagged behind those of temperate zones in terms of scientific, industrial, literary, and artistic development, because the high temperatures make people lethargic. There is some truth in this, but not in the way it is commonly meant. Heat of itself does not prevent a high level of intellectual achievement. The great early civilizations arose in tropical and subtropical regions. High temperatures did not impede the ancient Egyptians and Babylonians. The massive temples and pyramids of Luxor, the great palace of Ashurbanipal in Assyria, are clearly the creations of highly civilized and striving peoples, not savages relaxing all day under a tree. Complex philosophies and sophisticated art forms have been developed by the hot-climate Indians and Chinese. The magnificent temple cities of Chichén Itzá and Uxmal in the torrid Yucatán survive as evidence of an extremely advanced culture in the American tropics.

Even today, with these great civilizations long gone, many 37
people, both native and foreign, are active and successful in tropical regions. The natives are physiologically well-adapted to their environment, and a good number vigorously exploit their opportunities in agriculture, industry, and government. They behave in ways that seem slow to northerners but that are appropriate to the tropics. The high-powered individual who works at top speed is the most likely to fall victim to heat exhaustion. Those who do best in the heat yield to it

to some degree. The scorned siesta is not childlike or lazy; it is advisable to work early and late in the day and avoid exertion during the hottest hours.

Still, there is no denying that progress toward industrial development is exceedingly slow in many countries of the tropics, especially where there seems little reason to achieve complex agricultural and manufacturing systems. To take the most extreme example, in some remote tropical jungles people can live off the land well enough to remain at a Stone Age stage of development to this day. The Tasadays discovered only recently in the Philippines were so primitive as to be ignorant of the fact that any humans other than their small tribe existed in the world; exploration was not necessary when sufficient food was available in the area they inhabited. 38

But tribes able to survive in this way are increasingly rare. Gradually, population pressures in hot regions have been becoming so great as to demand a real effort to fulfill basic needs. But even this has not led to rapid industrialization. The failure can be attributed largely to indirect, rather than direct, effects of heat. The natives of the tropics and deserts of the world are often weakened by famines resulting from drought, flood, or civil war and, even in better times, by a low-protein diet. Illness is rampant, causing millions upon millions to drag out their days. Thus heat contributes to a low standard of living among those best equipped by nature to endure it. 39

One might think that heat could not both quench ambition and stimulate passion, but it is so. Excitement and anger, lassitude and indolence are but a few of the many human responses to excessive heat. 40

Topics for Writing

1. *Respond.* Speculate on why you lose your temper. What factors contribute to your outbursts? If you don't lose your temper, how do you respond to someone who does? Compose a case study (of yourself or another) that analyzes a cause (such as temperature) that is often overlooked when trying to explain explosive behavior. (*Resources for comparison:* Richard Selzer, "The Knife"; Alice Stewart Trillin, "Of Dragons and Garden Peas.")
2. *Analyze.* Examine the evidence Kavaler cites to demonstrate the connection between temperature and crime. What claims do these studies make about the difference between direct and complex causes? Study one of these experiments in greater detail. Then evaluate its procedures and conclusions for a class studying research design. (*Resources for comparison:* Gerald Weissmann, "The Chart of the Novel"; Lewis Thomas, "The Technology of Medicine.")
3. *Argue.* Kavaler devotes a considerable portion of her analysis to the effects of cultural stereotyping on our attitudes toward criminal behavior. Select a crime from the news or the movies where cultural stereotyping is an issue. Then, for a class studying media analysis, demonstrate how the language of cultural stereotyping misrepresents the characters involved in the crime. (*Resources for comparison:* William Stafford, "Writing"; Alison Lurie, "Folktale Liberation.")

DIANE JOHNSON

Diane Johnson was born in Moline, Illinois, in 1934 and was educated at Stephens College in Missouri, the University of Utah, and the University of California, Los Angeles. She has taught fiction writing and nineteenth-century British literature at the University of California, Davis. Her novels include *Fair Game* (1965), *Loving Hands at Home* (1968), *Burning* (1971), *Lying Low* (1978), and *Persian Nights* (1987). In addition, she has contributed critical essays to the *New York Review of Books* and the *New York Times Book Review,* written biographies of Dashiell Hammett and Mrs. George Meredith, and collaborated with Stanley Kubrick on the film script for *The Shining* (1980). In "Rape," reprinted from her collection of essays, *Terrorists and Novelists* (1982), Johnson reviews three studies of rape to demonstrate how cultural and personal history have conditioned women to see the subject differently than men do.

Rape

(Persuasion and Argument)

No other subject, it seems, is regarded so differently by men and women as rape. Women deeply dread and resent it to an extent that men apparently cannot recognize; it is perhaps the ultimate and essential complaint that women have to make against men. Of course men may recognize that it is wrong to use physical force against another person, and that rape laws are not prosecuted fairly, and so on, but at a certain point they are apt to say, "But what was she doing there at that hour anyway?" or "Luckily he didn't really hurt her," and serious discussion ceases. 1

Women sense—indeed, are carefully taught to feel—that the institution of rape is mysteriously protected by an armor of folklore, Bible tales, legal precedents, specious psychological theories. Most of all it seems protected by a rooted and implacable male belief that women want to be raped—which most women, conscientiously examining their motives, maintain they do not—or deserve to be raped, for violation of certain customs governing dress or behavior, a strange proposition to which women are more likely to accede. 2

While women can all imagine themselves as rape victims, most men know they are not rapists. So incidents that would be resented on personal grounds if happening to their "own" women do not have even the intrinsic interest for them of arguments on principle against military intervention in the political destiny of foreign nations, as in Vietnam, where the "rape" of that country was referred to in the peace movement and meant defoliation of crops. But unlike the interest in the political destiny of Vietnam, which greatly diminished when the danger to American males, via the draft, was eliminated, rape is an abiding concern to women. 3

Even if they don't think about it very much, most have incorporated into their lives routine precautions along lines prescribed by the general culture. From a woman's earliest days she is attended by injunctions about strangers, and warnings about dark streets, locks, escorts, and provocative behavior. She internalizes the lessons contained therein, that to break certain rules is to invite or deserve rape. Her fears, if not entirely conscious, are at least readily accessible, and are continually activated by a vast body of exemplary literature, both traditional and in the daily paper. To test this, ask yourself, if you are a woman, or ask any woman what she knows about Richard Speck, the Boston Strangler, and "that thing that happened over on —— Street last week," and you will find that she has considerable rape literature by heart. 4

It seems important, in attempting to assess the value or seriousness of Susan Brownmiller's polemic on rape (*Against Our Will*), to understand that there are really two audiences for it, one that will know much of what she has to say already, 5 and another that is ill equipped by training or sympathy to understand it at all. This likely accounts for a certain unevenness of tone, veering from indignation to the composed deployment of statistics in the manner of a public debater. It is not surprising that women began in the past few years by addressing their complaints about rape to one another, not to men, and one infers that the subject is still thought to be of concern only to women. It remains to be seen what if any rhetorical strategies will prove to be of value in enlisting the concern of men.

That rape is aggressive, hostile, and intended to exact female submission, and that it is the extreme expression of underlying shared masculine attitudes, is, I think, most women's intuition of the subject, even women who have not been raped but who have tacitly accepted that this is how men are. Women who have in fact been raped (more than 255,000 each year) are certain of it after the indifference, disbelief, and brutality of police, doctors, judges, jurors, and their own families. That the actual rapists, making examples of a few women, in effect frighten and control all women seems obvious, even inarguable. 6

What is left to be explained, though neither Brownmiller nor Jean MacKellar, in another recent book on rape *(Rape: The Bait and the Trap)*, can satisfactorily explain it, is what this primal drama of domination and punishment is about, exactly. Both books communicate an impression of an escalating conflict, with the increasing collective force of female anger and indignation about rape not only effecting some changes in judiciary and police procedures and even, perhaps, in popular attitudes, but also effecting an increase in anxiety about the subject, exemplified by the obligatory rape scenes in current movies and best sellers. Perhaps it is even female anger that is effecting an increase in rape itself, as if, whatever is at stake in this ancient hostility, it is now the rapist who has his back to the wall. 7

It is not too extreme to say that Brownmiller's book is exceedingly distressing, partly because it is exceedingly discouraging; it is a history of the failure of legal schemes and 8 social sciences to improve society, at least society as viewed from a female perspective; it is the history of the failure of the social sciences even to address themselves to the peculiar mystery of male aggression toward those weaker than themselves. This failure seems in turn to demonstrate the powerlessness of human institutions before the force of patently untrue and sinister myths, whose ability to reflect, but also to determine, human behavior seems invincible. The disobedient Eve, the compliant Leda, the lying wife of Potiphar are still the keys to popular assumptions about women.

But Brownmiller's book is also distressing in another way 9
that wicked myths and scary stories are distressing, that is, because they are meant to be. Here in one handy volume is every admonitory rape story you were ever told, horrifying in the way that propaganda is horrifying and also titillating just in the way that publishers hope a book will be titillating. Brownmiller is trapped in the fallacy of imitative form, and by the duplicitous powers of literature itself to contain within it its own contradictions, so that the exemplary anecdotes from Red Riding Hood to Kitty Genovese to the Tralala scene in *Last Exit to Brooklyn* must appeal at some level to the instincts they illustrate and deprecate. The book may be criticized for an emotional tone that is apparently impossible to exclude from an effective work on a subject so inaccessible to rational analysis. Because rape is an important topic of a potentially sensational and prurient nature, it is too bad that the book is not a model of surpassing tact and delicacy, unassailable learning and scientific methodology. Instead it is probably the book that was needed on this subject at this time, and may in fact succeed where reticence has failed to legitimate the fundamental grievance of women against men.

Much of the book is devoted to an attempt to locate in 10
history the reasons for rape, but inquiry here is fruitless because though history turns up evidence, it offers little explanation. One learns merely that rape has been with us from earliest times, that it is associated variously with military policy, with ideas of property and possession (to rape someone's wife was interpreted as the theft of something from him), with interracial struggles and complicated tribal and

class polarities of all kinds (masters and slaves, cowboys and Indians), with intrasexual power struggles, as in the rape of young or weak men in prison by gangs of stronger ones, and within families, by male relatives of young girls or children.

None of these patterns is, except in one respect, wholly consistent with the others, but viewed together they induce a kind of dispirited resignation to natural law, from which are derived the supposed constants of human nature, maybe including rape. The respect in which violations of conquered women in Bangladesh and of Indian (or white) women in pioneer America, or of men in prison, are alike is that they all dramatize some authority conflict. In war between groups of males, women are incidental victims and prizes, but in the back of the car the dispute arises between a man and a woman on her own behalf. The point at issue seems to be "maistrye," as the Wife of Bath knew; and the deepest lessons of our culture have inculcated in both sexes the idea that he is going to prevail. This in turn ensures that he usually does, but the central question of why it is necessary to have male mastery remains unanswered, and perhaps unasked. Meantime, the lesson of history seems to elevate the right of the male to exact obedience and inflict punishment to the status of immutable law. 11

Anthropology seems to support this, too, despite Brownmiller's attempts to find a primitive tribe (the obligingly rape-free Arapesh) to prove otherwise. Rather inconsistently, she conjectures that the origin of monogamy lies in the female's primordial fear of rape and consequent willingness to attach herself to some male as his exclusive property. If this is so, it would be the only instance in which the female will has succeeded in dictating social arrangements. In any case, alternate and better hypotheses exist for the origin of the family, generally that it developed for the protection of the young. The insouciance of Brownmiller's generalizations invites cavil and risks discrediting her book, and with it her subject. Granting that a primitive tribe can be found to illustrate any social model whatever, one would like to know just what all the anthropological evidence about rape is. If 12 rape is the primordial norm; if, as Lévi-Strauss says, women were the first currency; if male humans in a state of nature run mad raping, unlike chimpanzees, who we are told do not, is rape in fact aberrant? Perhaps it is only abhorrent.

It seems evident that whatever the facts of our nature, it 13 is our culture that leads women in some degree to collaborate in their own rape, an aspect of the matter that men seem determined to claim absolves *them* from responsibility. Perhaps this is implicit in the assumptions about male power they are heir to. But every woman also inherits assumptions about female submission. In even the simplest fairy tale, the vaguely sexual content of the punishment needs no elaboration: every woman darkly knows what really happened to Red Riding Hood in the woods—and to Grandmother, too, for that matter. Most women do not go into the woods alone, but the main point is that the form of the prohibition as it is expressed in most stories is not "Do not go into the woods lest you be raped," but "Obey me by not going into the woods or you *will* be raped."

Thus the idea of sexual punishment for disobedience is 14 learned very early, and is accepted. Who has done this to you, Desdemona? "Nobody; I myself, farewell," says Desdemona meekly as she dies. Everyone feels that Carmen, that prick-tease, is "getting what she deserves," poor Lucrece's suicide is felt to be both noble and tactful, maybe Anna Karenina's too. So if a woman is raped, she feels, besides outrage, deep guilt and a need to find out what she has done "wrong" to account for it, even if her sin is only one of omission; for example, concerned citizens in Palo Alto were told a few days ago that "Sometimes women are raped because of carelessness."

To the extent that a woman can convince a jury that she 15 was neither careless nor seductive, her attacker may be found guilty and she may be absolved from guilt, but more often in rape trials something is found in her behavior to "account" for her fate. The point is that whatever the circumstances of a rape, social attitudes and legal processes at the present time make the victim guilty of her own rape. Even the most innocent victim is likely to be told by her mother, "I told you never to walk home alone," and this is sometimes the attitude of an entire population, as in Bangladesh, where thousands of raped wives were repudiated by their husbands.

The unfortunate rape victim is in some ways worse off the more "feminine," the better socialized, she is, for she will have accepted normal social strictures: do not play rough, do not make noise or hit. Then she will be judged at the trial of her attacker on the extent to which she has struggled, hit, bitten (though she would not be expected to resist an armed robber). Not to struggle is to appear to want to be raped. In the courtroom men pretend not to understand the extent to which cultural inhibitions prevent women from resisting male force, even moral force, though in the parking lot they seem to understand it very well. 16

In the practical world, who are the rapists, who are the raped, what is to be done? It is here that Brownmiller's account is most interesting and most disturbing. Both Brownmiller and MacKellar agree on the statistical particulars: the rape victim is most likely a teen-aged black girl but she may be a woman of any age, and she will know her attacker to some extent in about half of the cases. The rapist is the same sort of person as other violent offenders: young, uneducated, unemployed, likely black or from another deprived subculture; the rapist is *not* the shy, hard-up loner living with his mother, victim of odd obsessions; a quarter of all rapes are done in gangs or pairs. 17

The sociology of rapists has some difficult political implications, as Brownmiller, to judge from the care with which she approaches it, is well aware. She traces the complicated history of American liberalism and Southern racism which has led to the present pass, in which people who have traditionally fought for human freedom seem committed to obstructing freedom for women. Historically, she reminds us, the old left, and the Communist Party in particular 18

> *understood rape as a political act of subjugation only when the victim was black and the offender was white. White-on-white rape was merely "criminal" and had no part in their Marxist canon. Black-on-black rape was ignored. And black-on-white rape, about which*

> *the rest of the country was phobic, was discussed in the oddly reversed world of the Jefferson School as if it never existed except as a spurious charge that "the state" employed to persecute black men.*

Meantime, circumstances have changed; folk bigotry, like folk wisdom, turns out to contain a half-truth, or grain of prescience; and the black man has taken to raping. Now

> *the incidence of actual rape combined with the looming spectre of the black man as rapist to which the black man in the name of his manhood now contributes, must be understood as a control mechanism against the freedom, mobility, and aspirations of all women, white and black. The crossroads of racism and sexism had to be a violent meeting place. There is no use pretending it doesn't exist.*

It is at this crossroads that the problem appears most 19
complex and most insoluble. Not only rapists, but also people more suavely disguised as right-thinking, like the ACLU and others associated with the civil-rights movement, still feel that protection of black men's rights is more important than injustice to women, whether white or black. Black men and white women are in effect pitted against one another in such a way as to impede the progress of both groups, and in particular to conceal and perpetuate the specific victimization of black women. Various studies report that blacks do up to 90 percent of rapes, and their victims are 80 to 90 percent black women, who now must endure from men of their own race what they historically had to endure from whites. A black girl from the ages of ten to fifteen is twelve times more likely than others to be a victim of this crime.

In this situation, which will win in the long run, sexism 20
or racism? Who are the natural antagonists? It seems likely, on the evidence, that sexism, being older, will prevail.

The MacKellar/Amir book, a short, practical manual about 21
rape, something to be used perhaps by jurors or counselors, gives a picture of the crime and of the rapist which is essentially the same as Brownmiller's. But MacKellar's advice,

when compared with Brownmiller's, is seen to be overlaid by a kind of naive social optimism. What can women do? They can avoid hitchhiking; they can be better in bed: "if women were less inhibited with their men the sense of depravity that their prudishness inspires might be reduced," as if it were frustrated middle-class husbands who were out raping; authorities can search out those "many youngsters warped by a brutish home life [who] can still be recuperated for a reasonably good adult life if given therapy in time"; "Education. Education helps to reduce rape."

Maybe. But does any evidence exist to suggest that any of this would really help? Brownmiller has found none, but I suppose she would agree with MacKellar that for America's violent subcultures we must employ "the classical remedies of assimilating the people in these subcultures, economically and socially, in opportunities for education, jobs, and decent housing," and change the fundamental values of American society. "As long as aggressive, exploitive behavior remains the norm, it can be expected that individuals will make these errors and that the weaker members of society will be the victim." 22

Until aggressive, exploitive behavior is not the norm, a few practical measures are being suggested. The LEAA study, MacKellar, and Brownmiller are all in favor of prosecuting rape cases and of punishing rapists. Brownmiller feels the punishment should suit the crime, that it should be made similar to penalties for aggravated assault, which it resembles. MacKellar feels that the penalty should fit the criminal: "a nineteen-year-old unemployed black with a fourth-grade education and no father, whose uptight, superreligious mother has, after a quarrel, kicked him out of the home, should not be judged by the same standard nor receive the same kind of sentence as a white middle-aged used-car salesman, twice divorced, who rapes a girl he picks up at a newsstand during an out-of-town convention." She does not, by the way, say who should get the stiffer sentence, and I can think of arguments either way. 23

Both agree that corroboration requirements and court- 24

room questions about a victim's prior sexual history should be eliminated, and in this the government-sponsored study for the Law Enforcement Assistance Administration *(Rape and Its Victim)* also agrees. At present the established view holds that whether or not a raped girl is a virgin or is promiscuous is germane to the issue of whether a forced act of sexual intercourse has occurred in a given case. This reflects the ancient idea that by violating male standards of female chastity, a woman forfeits her right to say no.

The LEAA study found that prosecutors' offices in general were doing little to urge the revision of outdated legal codes, and that the legal system is in fact impeding reform. It observes (in a nice trenchant style that makes better reading than most government reports) that 25

> *since rapists have no lobby, the major opposition to reform measures can be expected from public defenders, the defense bar in general, and groups, such as the American Civil Liberties Union, that are vigilant with respect to the rights of criminal defendants.*

The conclusion one cannot help coming to is that whatever is to be done about rape will have to be done by women primarily. Brownmiller feels that law enforcement must include 50 percent women. She finds it significant that whereas male law-enforcement authorities report 15 or 20 percent of rape complaints to be "unfounded," among the ones they actually bother to write down, women investigators find only 2 percent of such reports to be unfounded, exactly the number of unfounded reports of other violent crimes. Apparently the goal of male-female law enforcement is not without its difficulties; women police officers in Washington, D.C., recently have complained that their male patrol-car partners are attempting to force them to have sexual intercourse. Since these women are armed with service revolvers, we may soon see an escalation of what appears to be the Oldest Conflict. 26

MacKellar and the LEAA report both favor some sort of rape sentencing by degree, as in murder, with rape by a stranger constituting first-degree rape, and third degree tak- 27 ing cognizance of situations in which the victim may be judged to have shared responsibility for initiating the situation that led to the rape—for instance, hitchhiking. This is a compromise that would be unacceptable to feminist groups who feel that a woman is no more responsible for a rape under those circumstances than a man would be thought to be who was assaulted in the same situation.

It is likely that the concept of penalty by degree, with its concession to history, will prevail here, but one sees the objection on principle. While men continue to believe that men have a right to assert their authority over women by sexual and other means, rape will continue, and this in turn suggests two more measures. One is control of pornography, which Brownmiller argues is the means by which the rape ethic is promulagated. In spite of objections about censorship and about the lack of evidence that pornography and violence are related, Brownmiller's argument here is a serious one. She also feels that women should learn self-defense, if only to give them increased self-confidence and awareness of their bodies. But it is easy to see that this is yet another way in which the female might be made to take responsibility for being raped. If a woman learns karate and is raped anyway, the question will become, why hadn't she learned it better? 28

Surely the definition of civilization is a state of things where the strong refrain from exercising their advantages over the weak. If men can be made to see that the abolition of sexual force is necessary in the long-term interest of making a civilization, then they may cooperate in implementing whatever measures turn out to be of any use. For the short term, one imagines, the general effect of female activism about rape will be to polarize men and women even more than nature has required. The cooperation of state authorities, if any, may ensue from their perception of rape, especially black-on-white rape, as a challenge to white male authority (as in the South). This in turn may produce an unlikely and ominous coalition of cops and feminists, and the generally severer prosecution and sentencing which we see as the current response to other forms of violent crime. 29

But do we know that rapists will emerge from the prisons—themselves centers of homosexual rape—any less inclined to do it again?

Meantime, one feels a certain distaste for the congratula- 30
tory mood surrounding proposed law-enforcement reforms
devoted entirely to making the crime less miserable for the
victim while denying or concealing the complicity of so many
men in its perpetuation. This implies a state of things worthy
of a society described by Swift.

Topics for Writing

1. *Respond.* Conduct an informal poll among your male and female friends about the issue of date rape on your campus. Keep track of those who react as Johnson predicts and those who seem to contradict the expected reaction. Then write an opinion column for your campus newspaper commenting on your findings. (*Resources for comparison:* Gloria Steinem, "Why Young Women Are More Conservative"; Sam Keen, "The High Price of Success.")
2. *Analyze.* Johnson seems to believe that male readers are "ill equipped by training or sympathy to understand [the problem of rape] at all." Analyze the strategies Johnson uses to reach and inform her male readers. For example, what does she accomplish by avoiding vivid descriptions of rape? Present your findings in an essay that could be discussed in a writing class concerned with the relationship of gender and writing style. (*Resources for comparison:* Gretel Ehrlich, "Rules of the Game: Rodeo"; Verlyn Klinkenborg, "The Western Saddle.")
3. *Argue.* Johnson cites the recommendation of the Law Enforcement Assistance Administration that a rape victim's prior sexual history should be eliminated as a subject for courtroom interrogration. Read the relevant sections of the LEAA study, *Rape and Its Victim,* and then argue for or against this recommendation. Or, consider the merits of making a related argument with respect to the prior sexual history of the accused. (*Resources for comparison:* Raymond Carver, "What We Talk About When We Talk About Love"; Gail Godwin, "Dream Children.")

FRANK O'CONNOR

Frank O'Connor (1903–1966), the pen name for Michael John O'Donovan, was born in Cork, Ireland. Although he briefly attended the Christian Brothers School in Cork, his family's poverty forced him to forgo more education. While still in his teens, O'Connor joined the Irish Republican Army (IRA) and fought in the civil war from 1922 to 1923. Arrested and imprisoned, O'Connor served as the prison librarian until he was released in 1923. His stories, which attempt to record the distinctive vernacular of the Irish people and which appear in more than twenty volumes, are most accessible in *Collected Stories* (1981). O'Connor also wrote novels, such as *Dutch Interior* (1940); travel literature, *Irish Miles* (1947); literary criticism, *The Lonely Voice* (1963); and two volumes of an autobiography, *An Only Child* (1961) and *My Father's Son* (1969). "Guests of the Nation," reprinted from *Collected Stories,* recounts the experiences of several Irishmen who must choose between loyalty to their guests and duty to their nation.

Guests of the Nation

At dusk the big Englishman Belcher would shift his long legs out of the ashes and ask, "Well, chums, what about it?" and Noble or me would say, "As you please, chum" (for we had picked up some of their curious expressions), and the little Englishman 'Awkins would light the lamp and produce the cards. Sometimes Jeremiah Donovan would come up of an evening and supervise the play, and grow excited over 'Awkins's cards (which he always played badly), and shout at him as if he was one of our own, "Ach, you divil you, 1 why didn't you play the tray?" But, ordinarily, Jeremiah was a sober and contented poor devil like the big Englishman Belcher, and was looked up to at all only because he was a fair hand at documents, though slow enough at these, I vow. He wore a small cloth hat and big gaiters over his long pants. He reddened when you talked to him, tilting from toe to heel and back and looking down all the while at his big farmer's feet. His uncommon broad accent was a great source of jest to me, I being from the town as you may recognize.

I couldn't at the time see the point of me and Noble being 2
with Belcher and 'Awkins at all, for it was and is my fixed belief you could have planted that pair in any untended spot from this to Claregalway and they'd have stayed put and flourished like a native weed. I never seen in my short experience two men that took to the country as they did.

They were handed on to us by the Second Battalion to 3
keep when the search for them became too hot, and Noble and myself, being young, took charge with a natural feeling of responsibility. But little 'Awkins made us look right fools when he displayed he knew the countryside as well as we did and something more, "You're the bloke they calls Bonaparte?" he said to me. "Well, Bonaparte, Mary Brigid Ho'Connell was arskin abaout you and said 'ow you'd a pair of socks belonging to 'er young brother." For it seemed, as they explained it, that the Second used to have little evenings of their own, and some of the girls of the neighborhood would turn in, and seeing they were such decent fellows, our lads couldn't well ignore the two Englishmen, but invited them in and were hail-fellow-well-met with them. 'Awkins told me he learned to dance "The Walls of Limerick" and "The Siege of Ennis" and "The Waves of Tory" in a night or two, though naturally he could not return the compliment, because our lads at that time did not dance foreign dances on principle.

So whatever privileges and favors Belcher and 'Awkins 4
had with the Second they duly took with us, and after the first evening we gave up all pretense of keeping a close eye on their behavior. Not that they could have got far, for they

had a notable accent and wore khaki tunics and overcoats with civilian pants and boots. But it's my belief they never had an idea of escaping and were quite contented with their lot.

Now, it was a treat to see how Belcher got off with the 5
old woman of the house we were staying in. She was a great warrant to scold, and crotchety even with us, but before ever she had a chance of giving our guests, as I may call them, a lick of her tongue, Belcher had made her his friend for life. She was breaking sticks at the time, and Belcher, who hadn't been in the house for more than ten minutes, jumped up out of his seat and went across to her.

"Allow me, madam," he says, smiling his queer little smile; 6
"please allow me," and takes the hatchet from her hand. She was struck too parlatic to speak, and ever after Belcher would be at her heels carrying a bucket, or basket, or load of turf, as the case might be. As Noble wittily remarked, he got into looking before she leapt, and hot water or any little thing she wanted Belcher would have it ready for her. For such a huge man (and though I am five foot ten myself I had to look up to him) he had an uncommon shortness—or should I say lack—of speech. It took us some time to get used to him walking in and out like a ghost, without a syllable out of him. Especially because 'Awkins talked enough for a platoon, it was strange to hear big Belcher with his toes in the ashes come out with a solitary "Excuse me, chum," or "That's right, chum." His one and only abiding passion was cards, and I will say for him he was a good card-player. He could have fleeced me and Noble many a time; only if we lost to him, 'Awkins lost to us, and 'Awkins played with the money Belcher gave him.

'Awkins lost to us because he talked too much, and I think 7
now we lost to Belcher for the same reason. 'Awkins and Noble would spit at one another about religion into the early hours of the morning; the little Englishman as you could see worrying the soul out of young Noble (whose brother was a priest) with a string of questions that would puzzle a cardinal. And to make it worse, even in treating of these holy

subjects, 'Awkins had a deplorable tongue; I never in all my career struck across a man who could mix such a variety of cursing and bad language into the simplest topic. Oh, a terrible man was little 'Awkins, and a fright to argue! He never did a stroke of work, and when he had no one else to talk to he fixed his claws into the old woman.

I am glad to say that in her he met his match, for one day when he tried to get her to complain profanely of the drought she gave him a great comedown by blaming the drought upon Jupiter Pluvius (a deity neither 'Awkins nor I had ever even heard of, though Noble said among the pagans he was held to have something to do with rain). And another day the same 'Awkins was swearing at the capitalists for starting the German war, when the old dame laid down her iron, puckered up her little crab's mouth and said, "Mr. 'Awkins, you can say what you please about the war, thinking to deceive me because I'm an ignorant old woman, but I know well what started the war. It was that Italian count that stole the heathen divinity out of the temple in Japan, for believe mr, Mr 'Awkins, nothing but sorrow and want follows them that disturbs the hidden powers!" Oh, a queer old dame, as you remark! 8

So one evening we had our tea together, and 'Awkins lit the lamp and we all sat in to cards. Jeremiah Donovan came in too, and sat down and watched us for a while. Though he was a shy man and didn't speak much, it was easy to see he had no great love for the two Englishmen, and I was surprised it hadn't struck me so clearly before. Well, like that in the story, a terrible dispute blew up late in the evening between 'Awkins and Noble, about capitalists and priests and love for your own country. 9

"The capitalists," says 'Awkins, with an angry gulp, "the capitalists pays the priests to tell you all about the next world, so's you won't notice what they do in this!" 10

"Nonsense, man," says Noble, losing his temper, "before ever a capitalist was thought of people believed in the next world." 11

'Awkins stood up as if he was preaching a sermon. "Oh, they did, did they?" he says with a sneer. "They believed all the things you believe, that's what you mean? And you believe that God created Hadam and Hadam created Shem and Shem created Jehoshophat? You believe all the silly hold fairy-tale about Heve and Heden and the happle? Well, listen to me, chum. If you're entitled to 'old to a silly belief like that, I'm entitled to 'old to my own silly belief—which is, that the fust thing your God created was a bleedin' capitalist with mirality and Rolls Royce complete. Am I right, chum? he says then to Belcher. 12

"You're right, chum," says Belcher, with his queer smile, and gets up from the table to stretch his long legs into the fire and stroke his mustache. So, seeing that Jeremiah Donovan was going, and there was no knowing when the conversation about religion would be over, I took my hat and went out with him. We strolled down towards the village together, and then he suddenly stopped, and blushing and mumbling, and shifting, as his way was, from toe to heel, he said I ought to be behind keeping guard on the prisoners. And I, having it put to me so suddenly, asked him what the hell he wanted a guard on the prisoners at all for, and said that so far as Noble and me were concerned we had talked it over and would rather be out with a column. "What use is that pair to us?" I asked him. 13

He looked at me for a spell and said, "I thought you knew we were keeping them as hostages." "Hostages—?" says I, not quite understanding. "The enemy," he says in his heavy way, "have prisoners belong' to us, and now they talk of shooting them. If they shoot our prisoners we'll shoot theirs, and serve them right." "Shoot them?" siad I, the possibility just beginning to dawn on me. "Shoot them exactly," said he. "Now," said I, "wasn't it very unforeseen of you not to tell me and Noble that?" "How so?" he asks. "Seeing that we were acting as guards upon them, of course." "And hadn't you reason enough to guess that much?" "We had not, Jeremiah Donovan, we had not. How were we to know when the men were on our hands so long?" "And what difference 14 does it make? The enemy have our prisoners as long or longer, haven't they?" "It makes a great difference," said I. "How so?" said he sharply; but I couldn't tell him the difference it made, for I was struck too silly to speak. "And when may we expect to be released from this anyway?" said I. "You may expect it tonight," says he. "Or tomorrow or the next day at latest. So if it's hanging round here that worries you, you'll be free soon enough."

I cannot explain it even now, how sad I felt, but I went 15
back to the cottage, a miserable man. When I arrived the discussion was still on, 'Awkins holding forth to all and sundry that there was no next world at all and Noble answering in his best canonical style that there was. But I saw 'Awkins was after having the best of it. "Do you know what, chum?" he was saying, with his saucy smile. "I think you're jest as big a bleedin' hunbeliever as I am. You say you believe in the next world and you know jest as much abaout the next world as I do, which is sweet damn-all. What's 'Eaven? You dunno. Where'e 'Eaven? You dunno. Who's in 'Eaven? You dunno. You know sweet damn-all! I arsk you again, do they wear wings?"

"Very well then," says Noble, "they do; is that enough 16
for you? They do wear wings." "Where do they get them then? Who makes them? 'Ave they a fact'ry for wings? 'Ave they a sort of store where you 'ands in your chit and tikes your bleedin' wings? Answer me that?

"Oh, you're an impossible man to argue with," says Noble. 17
"Now listen to me—" And off the pair of them went again.

It was long after midnight when we locked up the En- 18
glishmen and went to bed ourselves. As I blew out the candle I told Noble what Jeremiah Donovan had told me. Noble took it very quietly. After we had been in bed about an hour he asked me did I think we ought to tell the Englishmen. I having thought of the same thing myself (among many others) said no, because it was more than likely the English wouldn't shoot our men, and anyhow it wasn't to be supposed the Brigade who were always up and down with the Second Battalion and knew the Englishmen well would be

likely to want them bumped off. "I think so," says Noble. "It would be sort of cruelty to put the win up them now." "It was very unforeseen of Jeremiah Donovan how," says I, and by Noble's silence I realized he took my mean

19 So I lay there half the night, and thought and thought, and pict myself and young Noble trying to prevent the Brigade from sh 'Awkins and Belcher sent a cold sweat out through me. Because were men on the Brigade you daren't let nor hinder without your hand, and at any rate, in those days disunion between seemed to me an awful crime. I knew better after.

20 It was next morning we found it so hard to face Belcher with a smile. We went about the house all day scarcely saying Belcher didn't mind us much; he was stretched into the ashes as usual with his usual look of waiting in quietness for something unforeseen to happen, but little 'Awkins gave us a bad time with his audacious gibbing and questioning. He was disgusted at Noble's not answering him back. "Why can't you tike your beating like a man, chum?" he says. "You with your Hadam and Heve! I'm a Communist—or an Anarchist. An Anarchist, that's what I am." And for hours after he went round the house, mumbling when the fit took him "Hadam and Heve! Hadam and Heve!"

21 I don't know clearly how we got over that day, but get over it we did, and a great relief it was when the tea things were cleared away and Belcher said in his peaceable manner, "Well, chums, what about it?" So we all sat round the table and 'Awkins produced the cards, and at that moment I heard Jeremiah Donovan's footsteps up the path, and a dark presentiment crossed my mind. I rose quietly from the table and laid my hand on him before he reached the door. "What do you want?" I asked him. "I want those two soldier friends of yours," he says reddening. "Is that the way it is, Jeremiah Donovan?" I ask. "That's the way. There were four of our lads went west this morning, one of them a boy of sixteen." "That's bad, Jeremiah," says I.

22 At that moment Noble came out, and we walked down

the path together talking in whispers. Feeney, the local intelligence officer, was standing by the gate. "What are you going to do about it?" I asked Jeremiah Donovan. "I want you and Noble to bring them out: you can tell them they're being shifted again; that'll be the quietest way." "Leave me out of that," says Noble suddenly. Jeremiah Donovan looked at him hard for a minute or two. "All right so," he said peaceably. "You and Feeney collect a few tools from the shed and dig a hole by the far end of the booking. Bonaparte and I'll be after you in about twenty minutes. But whatever else you do, don't let anyone see you with the tools. No one must know but the four of ourselves."

We saw Feeney and Noble go round to the houseen where the tools were kept, and sidled in. Everything if I can so express myself was tottering before my eyes, and I left Jeremiah Donovan to do the explaining as best he could, while I took a seat and said nothing. He told them they were to go back to the Second. 'Awkins let a mouthful of curses out of him at that, and it was plain that Belcher, though he said nothing, was duly perturbed. The old woman was for having them stay in spite of us, and she did not shut her mouth until Jeremiah Donovan lost his temper and said some nasty things to her. Within the house by this time it was pitch dark, but no one thought of lighting the lamp, and in the darkness the two Englishmen fetched their khaki top-coats and said good-bye to the woman of the house. "Just as a man mikes a 'ome of a bleedin' place, "mumbles 'Awkins, shaking her by the hand, "some bastard at Headquarters thinks you're too cushy and shunts you off." Belcher shakes her hand very hearty. "A thousand thanks, madam," he says, "a thousand thanks for everything . . ." as though he'd made it all up. 23

We go round to the back of the house and down towards the fatal booking. Then Jeremiah Donovan comes out with what is in his mind. "There were four of our lads shot by your fellows this morning so now you're to be bumped off." "Cut that stuff out," says 'Awkins, flaring up. "It's bad enough to be mucked about such as we are without you 24 plying at soldiers." "It's true," says Jeremiah Donovan, "I'm sorry, 'Awkins, but 'tis true," and comes out with the usual rigmarole about doing our duty and obeying our superiors. "Cut it out," says 'Awkins irritably. "Cut it out!"

Then, when Donovan sees he is not being believed he 25
turns to me, "Ask Bonaparte here," he says. "I don't need to arsk Bonaparte. Me and Bonaparte are chums." "Isn't it true, Bonaparte?" says Jeremiah Donovan solemnly to me. "It is," I say sadly, "it is." 'Awkins stops. "Now, for Christ's sike. . . ." "I mean it, chum," I say. "You daon't saound as if you mean it. You knaow well you don't mean it." "Well, if he don't I do," says Jeremiah Donovan. "Why the 'ell sh'd you want to shoot me, Jeremiah Donovan?" "Why the hell should your people take out four prisoners and shoot them in cold blood upon a barrack square?" I perceive Jeremiah Donovan is trying to encourage himself with hot words.

Anyway, he took little 'Awkins by the arm and dragged 26
him on, but it was impossible to make him understand that we were in earnest. From which you will perceive how difficult it was for me, as I kept feeing my Smith and Wesson and thinking what I would do if they happened to put up a fight or ran for it, and wishing in my heart they would. I knew if only they ran I would never fire on them. "Was Noble in this?" 'Awkins wanted to know, and we said yes. He laughed. But why should Noble want to shoot him? Why should we want to shoot him? What had he done to us? Weren't we chums (the word lingers painfully in my memory)? Weren't we? Didn't we understand him and didn't he understand us? Did either of us imagine for an instant that he'd shoot us for all the so-and-so brigadiers in the so-and-so British Army? By this time I began to perceive in the dusk the desolate edges of the bog that was to be their last earthly bed, and, so great a sadness overtook my mind, I could not answer him. We walked along the edge of it in the darkness, and every now and then 'Awkins would call a halt and begin again, just as if he was wound up, about us being chums, and I was in despair that nothing but the cold and open grave made ready for his presence would convince him that

we meant it all. But all the same, if you can understand, I didn't want him to be bumped off.

At last we saw the unsteady glint of a lantern in the distance and made towards it. Noble was carrying it, and Feeney stood somewhere in the darkness behind, and somehow the picture of the two of them so silent in the boglands was like the pain of death in my heart. Belcher, on recognizing Noble, said "'Allo, chum" in his usual peaceable way, but 'Awkins flew at the poor boy immediately, and the dispute began all over again, only that Noble hadn't a word to say for himself, and stood there with the swaying lantern between his gaitered legs. 27

It was Jeremiah Donovan who did the answering. 'Awkins asked for the twentieth time (for it seemed to haunt his mind) if anybody thought he'd shoot Noble. "You would," says Jeremiah Donovan shortly. "I wouldn't, damn you!" "You would if you knew you'd be shot for not doing it." "I wouldn't, not if I was to be shot twenty times over; he's my chum. And Belcher wouldn't—isn't that right, Belcher?" "That's right, chum," says Belcher peaceably. "Damned if I would. Anyway, who says Noble'd be shot if I wasn't bumped off? What d'you think I'd do if I was in Noble's place and we were out in the middle of a blasted bog?" "What would you do?" "I'd go with him wherever he was going. I'd share my last bob with him and stick by 'im through thick and thin." 28

"We've had enough of this," says Jeremiah Donovan, cocking his revolver. "Is there any message you want to send before I fire?" "No, there isn't, but . . ." "Do you want to say your prayers?" 'Awkins came out with a cold-blooded remark that shocked even me and turned to Noble again. "Listen to me, Noble," he said. "You and me are chums. You won't come over to my side, so I'll come over to your side. Is that fair? Just you give me a rifle and I'll go with you wherever you want." 29

Nobody answered him. 30

"Do you understand?" he said. "I'm through with it all. 31

I'm a deserter or anything else you like, but from this on I'm one of you. Does that prove to you that I mean what I say?" Noble raised his head, but as Donovan began to speak he lowered it again without answering. "For the last time have you any messages to send?" says Donovan in a cold and excited voice.

"Ah, shut up, you, Donovan; you don't understand me, but these fellows do. They're my chums; they stand by me and I stand by them. We're not the capitalist tools you seem to think us." 32

I alone of the crowd saw Donovan raise his Webley to the back of 'Awkins's neck, and as he did so I shut my eyes and tried to say a prayer. 'Awkins had begun to say something else when Donovan let fly, and, as I opened my eyes at the bang, I saw him stagger at the knees and lie out flat at Noble's feet, slowly, and as quiet as a child, with the lantern light falling sadly upon his lean legs and bright farmer's boots. We all stood very still for a while watching him settle out in the last agony. 33

Then Belcher quietly takes out a handkerchief, and begins about his own eyes (for in our excitement we had forgotten to same to 'Awkins), and, seeing it is not big enough, turns and asks for a loan of mine. I give it to him and as he knots the two together he points with his foot at 'Awkins. "'E's not quite dead," he says, "better give 'im another." Sure enough 'Awkins's left knee as we see it under the lantern is rising again. I bend down and put my gun to his ear; then, recollecting myself and the company of Belcher, I stand up again with a few hasty words. Belcher understands what is in my mind. "Give 'im 'is first," he says. "I don't mind. Poor bastard, we dunno what's 'appening to 'im now." As by this time I am beyond all feeling I kneel down and skilfully give 'Awkins the last shot so as to put him forever out of pain. 34

Belcher who is fumbling a bit awkwardly with the handkerchiefs comes out with a laugh when he hears the shot. It is the first time I have heard him laugh, and it sends a shiver down my spine, coming as it does so inappropriately upon the tragic death of his old friend. "Poor blighter," he says 35 quietly, "and last night he was so curious abaout it all. It's very queer, chums, I always think. Naow, 'e knows as much abaout it as they'll ever let 'im know, and last night 'e was all in the dark."

Donovan helps him tie the handkerchiefs about his eyes. "Thanks, chum," he says. Donovan asks him if thare any messages he would like to send. "Naow, chum," he says, "none for me. If any of you likes to write to 'Awkins's mother you'll find a letter from 'er in 'is pocket. But my missus left me eight years ago. Went away with another fellow and took the kid with her. I likes the feelin' of a 'ome (as you may 'ave noticed) but I couldn't start again after that." 36

We stand around like fools now that he can no longer see us. Donovan looks at Noble and Noble shakes his head. Then Donovan raises his Webley again and just at that moment Belcher laughs his queer nervous laugh again. He must think we are talking of him; anyway, Donovan lowers his gun. "'Scuse me, chums," says Belcher, "I feel I'm talking the 'ell of a lot . . . and so silly . . . abaout me being so 'andy abaout a 'ouse. But this thing come on me so sudden. You'll forgive me, I'm sure." "You don't want to say a prayer?" asks Jeremiah Donovan. "No, chum," he replies, "I don't think that'd 'elp. I'm ready if you want to get it over." "You understand," says Jeremiah Donovan, "it's not so much our doing. It's our duty, so to speak." Belcher's head is raised like a real blind man's, so that you can only see his nose and chin in the lamplight. "I never could make out what duty was myself," he said, "but I think you're all good lads, if that's what you mean. I'm not complaining." Noble, with a look of desperation, signals to Donovan, and in a flash Donovan raises his gun and fires. The big man goes over like a sack of meal, and this time there is no need of a second shot. 37

I don't remember much about the burying, but that it was worse than all the rest, because we had to carry the warm corpses a few yards before we sunk them in the windy bog. It was all mad lonely, with only a bit of lantern between ourselves and the pitch blackness, and birds hooting and screeching all round disturbed by the guns. Noble had to 38 search 'Awkins first to get the letter from his mother. Then having smoothed all signs of the grave away, Noble and I collected our tools, said good-bye to the others, and went back along the desolate edge of the treacherous bog without a word. We put the tools in the houseen and went into the house. The kitchen was pitch black and cold, just as we left it, and the old woman was sitting over the hearth telling her beads. We walked past her into the room, and Noble struck a match to light the lamp. Just then she rose quietly and came to the doorway, being not at all so bold or crabbed as usual.

"What did ye do with them?" she says in a sort of whisper, 39
and Noble took such a mortal start the match quenched in his trembling hand. "What's that?" he asks without turning round. "I heard ye," she said. "What did you hear?" asks Noble, but sure he wouldn't deceive a child the way he said it. "I heard ye. Do you think I wasn't listening to ye putting the things back in the houseen?" Noble struck another match and this time the lamp lit for him. "Was that what ye did with them?" she said, and Noble said nothing—after all what could he say?

So then, by God, she fell on her two knees by the door, 40
and began telling her beads, and after a minute or two Noble went on his knees by the fireplace, so I pushed my way out past her, and stood at the door, watching the stars and listening to the damned shrieking of the birds. It is so strange what you feel at such moments, and not to be written afterwards. Noble says he felt he seen everything ten times as big, perceiving nothing around him but the little patch of black bog with the two Englishmen stiffening into it; but with me it was the other way, as though the patch of bog where the two Englishmen were was a thousand miles away from me, and even Noble mumbling just behind me and the old woman and the birds and the bloody stars were all far away, and I was somehow very small and very lonely. And anything that ever happened me after I never felt the same about again.

Topics for Writing

1. *Respond.* Recount an occasion in your life when you were "forced" to commit an academic crime—for example, misrepresent a source, cheat on a quiz. Describe the people/events that forced you into the situation and the motives/rationalizations you created for violating the law. In a column composed for the campus newspaper, use this narrative to speculate on what you learned as a result of your actions. (*Resources for comparison:* Mike Rose, "I Just Wanna Be Average"; Mark Twain, "Two Views of the River.")
2. *Analyze.* Consider how O'Connor's title comments on the drama of his story. In what sense are the two Englishmen "guests"? In what sense does the Irish Republican Army (IRA) represent the "nation"? In an essay that you might submit to a literature class, analyze what the narrator of the story learns about his guests, his nation, and himself as a result of his actions. (*Resources for comparison:* Paule Marshall, "To Da-duh, in Memoriam"; Francine du Plessix Gray, "On Friendship.")
3. *Argue.* In "Politics and the English Language," George Orwell states that "political speech and writing are largely the defense of the indefensible." Similarly, the discussion of "duty" in O'Connor's story is used to defend the indefensible—the murder of two "chums." Select a speech by a famous politician that persuaded people to go to war. Research the historical circumstances of the war. Then, in a speech that might be given in a history or political science class, demonstrate how the politician has used glorious language to defend gory crimes. (*Resources for comparison:* George Orwell, "Shooting an Elephant"; Loren Eiseley, "Man the Firemaker.")

ACKNOWLEDGMENTS

LIVES by Barbara Ehrenreich. Copyright © 1990 by Barbara Ehrenreich. Reprinted by permission of Pantheon Books, a division of Random House, Inc.

LARS EIGHNER "My Daily Dives in the Dumpster." THE THREEPENNY REVIEW. (Fall: 1988): 19–22. Reprinted by permission of the author.

LOREN EISELEY From "Man the Firemaker," by Loren C. Eiseley. Copyright © 1954 by Scientific American, Inc. All rights reserved.

JOSEPH EPSTEIN "They Said You Was High Class." Reprinted from THE AMERICAN SCHOLAR, Volume 55, Number 2, Spring 1986. Copyright © 1986 by the author.

DAVID GATES "Who Was Columbus?" from NEWSWEEK Special Edition Fall/Winter 1991, Newsweek, Inc. All rights reserved. Reprinted by permission.

GAIL GODWIN "Dream Children," copyright © 1976 by Gail Godwin. Reprinted from DREAM CHILDREN, by Gail Godwin, by permission of Alfred A. Knopf, Inc.

STEPHEN JAY GOULD "Carrie Buck's Daughter" is reprinted from THE FLAMINGO'S SMILE: REFLECTIONS IN NATURAL HISTORY, by Stephen Jay Gould, with the permission of W.W. Norton & Company, Inc. Copyright 1985 by Stephen Jay Gould.

ROSE del CASTILLO GUILBAULT "Americanization Is Tough on 'Macho'." THIS WORLD. (1989): 34–36. Reprinted by permission of the author.

DAVID HAGE et al. "Hidden Monopolies." Copyright February 3, 1992, U.S. NEW AND WORLD REPORT. Reprinted by permission.

EDWARD T. HALL "The Arab World," from THE HIDDEN DIMENSION by Edward T. Hall, copyright © 1966, 1982 by Edward T. Hall. Used by permission of Doubleday, a division of Bantam, Doubleday, Dell Publishing Group, Inc.

LE LY HAYSLIP "Playing Stupid," from WHEN HEAVEN AND EARTH CHANGED PLACES by Le Ly Hayslip. Copyright © 1989 by Le Ly Hayslip and Charles Jay Wurts. Used by permission of Doubleday, a division of Bantam, Doublelday, Dell Publishing Group, Inc.

VICKI HEARNE "What's Wrong with Animal Rights?" Copyright © 1991 by HARPER'S MAGAZINE. All rights reserved. Reprinted from the September issue by special permission.

EDWARD HOAGLAND "In the Toils of the Law," from WALKING THE DEAD DIAMOND RIVER, by Edward Hoagland. Copyright © 1973 by Edward Hoagland. Reprinted by permission of Random House, Inc.

JOHN HOLT "Different Types of Discipline." From FREEDOM AND BEYOND. Copyright © 1972 by John Holt; copyright © 1992 by Holt Associates Inc. Reprinted with permission.

CHARLES JOHNSON "The Sorceror's Apprentice," reprinted with the permission of Atheneum Publishers, an imprint of Macmillan Publishing Company from THE SORCEROR'S APPRENTICE by Charles Johnson. Copyright © 1983 by Charles Johnson.

DIANE JOHNSON "Rape," from TERRORISTS AND NOVELISTS. Copyright © 1982 by Diane Johnson. Reprinted by permission of The Helen Brann Agency, Inc.

LUCY KAVALER "Of Riot, Murder and the Heat of Passion" from A MATTER OF DEGREE by Lucy Kavaler. Copyright © 1981 by Lucy Estrin Kavaler. Reprinted by permission of HarperCollins Publishers.

SAM KEEN "The High Price of Success," from FIRE IN THE BELLY by Sam Keen. Copyright © 1991. Used by permission of Bantam Books, a division of Bantam Doubleday Dell Publishing Group, Inc.

MARJORIE KELLY "Revolution in the Marketplace." Marjorie Kelly is editor and publisher of *Business Ethics Magazine,* 1107 Hazeltine Blvd., Ste. 530, Minneapolis, MN 55318. Reprinted by permission of the author.

MARTIN LUTHER KING, JR. "I Have a Dream" reprinted by permission of Joan Daves. Copyright © 1963 by Martin Luther King, Jr.

VERLYN KLINKENBORG "The Western Saddle." Reprinted by permission of Sterling Lord Literistic, Inc. Copyright © 1992 by Verlyn Klinkenborg.

LEWIS LAPHAM "A Political Opiate." Copyright © 1989 by HARPER'S MAGAZINE. All rights reserved. Reprinted from the December issue by special permission.

ALISON LURIE "Folktale Liberation," from DON'T TELL THE GROWN-UPS by Alison Lurie. Copyright © 1990 by Alison Lurie. By permission of Little, Brown and Company.

TOM and RAY MAGLIOZZI "Inside the Engine," from CAR TALK by Tom and Ray Magliozzi. Used by permission of Dell Books, a division of Bantam Doubleday Dell Publishing Group, Inc.

PAULE MARSHALL "To Da-duh, In Memoriam," copyright © 1967, 1983 by Paule Marshall. From the book REENA AND OTHER STORIES. Published by The Feminist Press at The City University of New York. All rights reserved.

N. SCOTT MOMADAY "The Way to Rainy Mountain," reprinted from THE WAY TO RAINY MOUNTAIN by permission of The University of New Mexico Press.

FLANNERY O'CONNOR "Revelation," from THE COMPLETE STORIES by Flannery O'Connor. Copyright © 1964, 1965 by the estate of Mary Flannery O'Connor. Reprinted by permission of Farrar, Straus & Giroux, Inc.

FRANK O'CONNOR "Guests of the Nation," from COLLECTED STORIES by Frank O'Connor. Copyright © 1981 by Harriet O'Donovan Sheehy, Executrix of the Estate of Frank O'Connor. Reprinted by permission of Alfred A. Knopf, Inc. and Joan Daves Agency.

GEORGE ORWELL "Shooting an Elephant," from SHOOTING AN ELEPHANT AND OTHER ESSAYS by George Orwell, copyright © 1950 by Sonia Brownell Orwell and renewed 1978 by Sonia Pitt-Rivers, reprinted by permission of Harcourt Brace Jovanovich Inc., A. M. Heath, the estate of Sonia Brownell Orwell and Martin Secker & Warburg.

ANNA QUINDLEN "Execution," from LIVING OUT LOUD by Anna Quindlen. Copyright © 1987 by Anna Quindlen. Reprinted by permission of Random House, Inc.

ROBERT REICH "Secession of the Successful," copyright © 1991 The New York Times Company. Reprinted by permission.

MIKE ROSE "I Just Wanna Be Average," reprinted with the permission of The Free Press, a Division of Macmillan, Inc. from LIVES ON THE BOUNDARY: THE STRUGGLES AND ACHIEVEMENTS OF AMERICA'S UNDER-PREPARED by Mike Rose. Copyright © 1989 by Mike Rose.

LYNNE SHARON SCHWARTZ "Beggaring Our Better Selves." Copyright © 1991 by Lynne Sharon Schwartz. First appeared in HARPER'S. Reprinted by permission of the author.

RICHARD SELZER From "The Knife," MORTAL LESSONS. Copyright © 1974, 1975, 1976 by Richard Selzer. Reprinted by permission of SIMON & SCHUSTER, Inc.

GAIL SHEEHY "Predictable Crises of Adulthood," from PASSAGES by Gail Sheehy. Copyright © 1974, 1976 by Gail Sheehy. Used by permission of the publisher, Dutton, an imprint of New American Library, a division of Penguin Books USA, Inc.

ROBERT SHERRILL "Murder, Inc." by Robert Sherrill was first published in GRAND STREET in Spring 1986. Reprinted with permission.

WILLIAM STAFFORD "A Way of Writing," reprinted from FIELD, Spring 1970, by permission.

BRENT STAPLES "Black Men and Public Space," reprinted from *Harper's*, December 1986 by permission of the author.

SHELBY STEELE "White Guilt," by Shelby Steele. Copyright © 1990 by Shelby Steele. From the book THE CONTENT OF OUR CHARACTER and reprinted with permission from St. Martin's Press, Inc., New York, NY.

GLORIA STEINEM "Why Young Women Are More Conservative," from OUTRAGEOUS ACTS AND EVERYDAY REBELLIONS by Gloria Steinem. Copyright © 1983 by Gloria Steinem. Copyright © 1984 by East Toledo Productions, Inc. Reprinted by permission of Henry Holt and Company, Inc.

DEBORAH TANNEN "Rapport-talk and Report-talk," from YOU JUST DON'T UNDERSTAND by Deborah Tannen, Ph.D. Copyright 1990 by Deborah Tannen Ph.D. Reprinted by permission of William Morrow & Company, Inc.

LEWIS THOMAS "The Technology of Medicine," copyright © 1971 by The Massachusetts Medical Society, from THE LIVES OF A CELL by Lewis Thomas. Used by permission of Viking Penguin, a division of Penguin Books USA, Inc.

ALICE STEWART TRILLIN "Of Dragons and Garden Peas." NEW ENGLAND JOURNAL OF MEDICINE. 304:(March 19, 1981): 699–701. Reprinted with permission of the publisher.

CALVIN TRILLIN "A Stranger with a Camera," copyright © 1969 by Calvin Trillin. Originally appeared in *The New Yorker.*

GERALD WEISSMAN "The Chart of the Novel" reprinted by permission of the author and the Watkins/Loomis Agency.

W. D. WETHERELL "The Bass, the River, and Sheila Mant," reprinted from THE MAN WHO LOVED LEVITTOWN, by W. D. Wetherell, by permission of the University of Pittsburgh Press. © 1985 by W. D. Wetherell.

INDEX